About the Author

Alan F. Alford, B Com., FCA, MBA, is an independent researcher and author, who is now widely recognised as one of the world's leading authorities on ancient mythology, comparative religion and mysticism. His interests also encompass ancient wisdom, archaeological anomalies, the origins of *Homo sapiens*, and the nature of consciousness.

Born in 1961, he made his first visit to the Pyramids of Egypt as a fourteen year old, and this inspired him to travel extensively around the world in a quest to solve the riddles of mankind's past.

In 1996, he self-published his first book *Gods of the New Millennium*, which went on to become a number eleven bestseller upon relaunch by Hodder & Stoughton.

Since turning full-time researcher in 1996, he has been steadily peeling back the layers of the ancient mysteries.

In 1998, he stunned readers of his first book by issuing a partial retraction of his theory of 'ancient astronaut' visitation in his sequel *The Phoenix Solution*, in which he argued that ancient Egyptian religion was an 'exploded planet cult'. Acclaimed by the few, but castigated by the majority, this book was laying the groundwork for a radical shift in our understanding of modern religion.

In April 2000, Alford revealed the full extent of his conversion in *When The Gods Came Down – The Catastrophic Roots of Religion Revealed*, in which he argued that ancient Mesopotamian religion was an 'exploded planet cult' too, and that Judaism and Christianity are occulted forms of the same idea.

Now, in *The Atlantis Secret*, Alan Alford demonstrates that the religion, myths and mysticism of the ancient Greeks were also founded upon the principle of an exploded planet, and, with Plato as his guide, he reveals the full spiritual dimension of the phenomenon. Atlantis, he argues, is a cipher for a lost religion, which he now brings to life in all of its physical and metaphysical glory.

THE
ATLANTIS SECRET

A Complete Decoding of
Plato's Lost Continent

Alan F. Alford

Eridu Books
http://www.eridu.co.uk

British Library Cataloguing in Publication Data: a CIP catalogue
record of this title is available from the British Library

ISBN 0 9527994 1 3

Printed and bound in Great Britain by Bookcraft Limited.

Eridu Books
P.O. Box 107
Walsall
WS9 9YR
England
http://www.eridu.co.uk

To Sumu, my wife,
for her love, trust and endurance
through challenging times.

CONTENTS

FOREWORD

By CHRISTOPHER GILL

Ever since Plato made up the story of Atlantis in the fourth century BC, it has fascinated and puzzled its readers. Is it, as Plato claims, a 'true story', and if so in what sense: a historically accurate account or 'true' in some allegorical or mythical sense? In recent years, classical scholars have tended to assume that the story is, essentially, a political allegory, which uses primeval Athens and Atlantis to symbolise the ideal city and its opposite. It is 'true' only in the sense that it conveys a philosophically 'true' message.

However, far more popular, especially among non-specialists in ancient philosophy, is the idea that the story is 'true' in a factual or historical sense, and that Atlantis is somewhere waiting to be found. Plato, quite plainly, said that the island of Atlantis sunk in the Atlantic Ocean, and this is one place that people have looked for it – without any success. But different writers have claimed to 'find' Atlantis all over the world (including parts of the world quite unknown to Plato), latching on to one or other feature of Plato's account, but never explaining the story in its entirety. These attempts, in my judgement, are quite unconvincing and are a testimony to the power and vividness of Plato's story – and to the human capacity for self-deception.

Alan Alford's book, on the other hand, has the considerable merit that, while offering a widely accessible account of the Atlantis story, it strongly rejects the popular view that the story has a historical basis. The book takes as its starting point a fact often ignored in non-specialist treatments of Atlantis: that Plato is the original and only primary source for the story, and that we must begin by locating the story within Plato's philosophical and conceptual world-view. Alford, like recent Platonic scholarship, takes the story to be, in part at least, political allegory, based on Plato's critical view of Athens' emergence as a rich and powerful maritime empire in the fifth century BC.

But the main focus of Alford's book lies in exploring the status of the Atlantis story as a myth. Although he accepts that the story is shaped by certain distinctively Platonic concerns, he also stresses that it reflects the larger background of Greek myth, which Plato drew on and reworked for his own purposes. Also, in a move that is quite new in studies of Atlantis, Alford relates the story to the yet larger background of Near Eastern myth, particularly that of Mesopotamia. As he points out, some of the most important scholarly work on antiquity in the last twenty years has centred on bringing out the pervasive influence of earlier Near Eastern culture on archaic and classical Greece. Alford argues that, if we take account of the Near Eastern themes underlying Greek myths, we can make much better sense of Plato's version of Greek myth in the Atlantis story.

In particular, Alford claims that a specific myth-pattern plays a key role in shaping the Atlantis story. In two previous books, *The Phoenix Solution* (1998) and *When The Gods Came Down* (2000), he explored the role in Near Eastern myth of the motif of the 'exploded planet'. In essence, the hypothesis is that a whole range of myth-types are best explained by the idea that a living planet exploded and that this had dramatic and massive effects on the Earth. This idea was itself a response to human observation, over thousands of years, of cosmic disturbances such as comets and meteors in the sky and meteorites plunging to Earth. Alford claims that the influence of this particular myth-pattern can be found not only in Near Eastern and Greek myth but also in the early Greek scientific cosmologies that rationalised, and aimed to replace, this body of myth.

Alford also argues that the 'exploded planet' idea underlies crucial features of the Atlantis story – features often ignored or played down by historicising treatments. The most obvious of these is the cataclysmic convulsion in the Earth's surface in which the island of Atlantis was sunk under the Atlantic Ocean. But he sees this pattern as underlying, more indirectly, other points in the story including the quasi-cosmic 'eruption' of Atlantis into the rest of the known world. More generally, Alford uses this myth-pattern to explain a whole series of salient linkages in the Atlantis story: between Heaven and the Underworld, between the Underworld and the far West, and between 'earth-born' or divine origins and the fall of the sky. He also explains in this way the puzzling combination of Plato's claims to factual 'truth' and his vagueness and apparent inaccuracy of detail as regards chronology and topography. The story is 'true', he says, in that it expresses a profound ancient myth-type, which was seen as having immense significance for the understanding of the past. But this 'truth' attaches to a mythic pattern of thinking about time, space and human affairs, and not to history or geography in the ordinary sense.

How convincing are Alford's claims? To test his hypothesis fully, one would need not simply expertise in ancient philosophy and the Atlantis story, which I could claim to have, but also in Greek and Near Eastern myth, on which I make no such claim. The 'exploded planet' is also, I take it, a new and innovative hypothesis, which, like all new hypotheses, will take time and careful scrutiny to assess. What I can say is that Alford presents his case in a clear, effective and systematic way, which will enable readers from a wide range of backgrounds to follow his argument, to see what it is based on, and to form their own conclusions about its validity. I am not sure whether or not the 'exploded planet' hypothesis has the great explanatory power that Alford attributes to it. But I am very glad to have encountered such a lucid and wide-ranging statement of this hypothesis, and to see it applied so suggestively to the Atlantis story.

Also, quite apart from this hypothesis, there are a number of features of this book that I warmly welcome. One is the refreshing scepticism, in a work aimed at a wide readership, about attempts to 'find' Atlantis in a literal sense. Another is the way that the book points the reader firmly back to the Platonic sources and ideas, to the Greek myths that Plato certainly knew, and to the Near Eastern myth-patterns that may underlie these myths. Above all, I applaud the lucidity of Alford's argument and the transparency with which his claims are based on either quoted or fully documented sources. Whether *The Atlantis Secret* does, or does not, finally 'decode' the riddle of Atlantis, as it aims to, it certainly provides some fascinating new insights and an admirably clear point of access to this perennially powerful story.

CHRISTOPHER GILL, Exeter, September 2001.

Christopher Gill is Professor of Ancient Thought and Head of the Department of Classics & Ancient History at the University of Exeter in England. His book *Plato: The Atlantis Story* (Duckworth, 1980) presents the Greek sources of Plato's story with introduction and commentary, and an essay in *Lies and Fiction in the Ancient World*, edited by C. Gill and T.P. Wiseman (University of Exeter Press, 1993), explores the truth-status of the story. His other writings on Plato include *Form and Argument in Late Plato*, edited by C. Gill and M.M. McCabe (Oxford University Press, 1996) and *Plato: The Symposium*, a new translation with introduction and notes (Penguin Classics, 1999). In addition, he is currently the editor of an internet journal entitled *Plato*.*

* http://www.ex.ac.uk/plato/

ATLANTIS RECONSIDERED

Further back, beyond the Pillars of Heracles, extremely violent earthquakes and floods occurred and, in an unbearable day and night, your entire army sank beneath the earth all at once, and the Isle of Atlantis likewise sank beneath the sea and disappeared.

(The Egyptian priest in Plato's *Timaeus*, mid-4th century BC)

Nearly twenty-four hundred years ago, the Athenian philosopher Plato penned one of the most controversial and tantalising stories ever written. Once upon a time, he said, there had existed a magnificent seafaring civilisation which had attempted to take over the world, but had perished when its island sank into the sea – the result of an unbearable cataclysm of earthquakes and floods. This civilisation had been called Atlantis, and it had heralded from the Atlantic Ocean, taking its name from the god Atlas who presided over the depths of the sea. Its main island had sunk some nine thousand years before the time of Solon, *circa* 9600 BC by our modern-day system of reckoning.

The puzzle of Atlantis is this. On the one hand, Plato was adamant that the island had sunk in the Atlantic Ocean, and equally adamant that the story was absolutely true. And yet, on the other hand, modern scientists have mapped the floor of the Atlantic Ocean, using echo sounders, 'Geosat' radar and multibeam sonar, and found no trace whatsoever of any sunken island. The result is a deadlock on how to decipher the story. Some argue that it is a myth, of uncertain meaning. Others argue that it is a moral and political fable. And others, still, continue to argue that it is pure history, and that Plato simply got his geographical facts wrong.

Is the Atlantis story a myth? In the modern language, the word 'myth' is synonymous with a fiction or a lie. In the ancient Greek, language, however, a 'myth' (*muthos*) meant simply an 'utterance' or a 'traditional tale', and the tales of the gods and heroes were generally held to be true stories. It is no insult to Plato, then, to suggest that his story of Atlantis was a myth, and there are good reasons for thinking that it was. Firstly, the subject matter touches on traditional themes, such as the myth of the golden age, the myths of the wars of the gods, and the myths of fabulous islands lying at 'the ends of the Earth'. Secondly, he compared his story explicitly to the poems of Homer and Hesiod (in which the tales of the gods and heroes were recited). And thirdly, he declared that his story was 'true'. Nevertheless, the concept of 'true myths' belongs to the past, and modern scholars have generally dismissed Plato's story as a fiction and a fairy tale, in accordance with the modern (but not the ancient) definition of 'myth'. As a result, the theory of Atlantis-as-myth has had a bad press, and has not found favour with a populace who are generally sympathetic towards the idea of a true story.

This brings us to the more popular theory that the Atlantis story is pure history. Here, the negative evidence from the Atlantic Ocean floor has been brushed aside by the convenient assumption that the geography of the story was garbled at some point. Accordingly, the historicists – a colourful association of academics, psychics, pseudo-mystics, amateur archaeologists, catastrophists, and new age truth-seekers – have searched worldwide for the source of the tale. Atlantis is in the Caribbean Sea, the Mediterranean Sea, the Tyrrhenian Sea, the Ionian Sea, the Aegean Sea, the Red Sea, the Black Sea, the English Channel, the North Sea, and even the Arctic Ocean. The list goes on. Moreover, not satisfied with bending Plato's geography, Atlantis-hunters have bent an even more fundamental point – his claim that the island sank. Bizarrely, Atlantis has become Crete, Cuba, the Americas, even Antarctica. Plato's account of sunken Atlantis seems to count for nothing.

What's more, even if we suspend disbelief concerning the location of Atlantis and the tale of its sinking, none of the aforementioned islands or continents comes even close to matching what Plato described. What we are looking for is an island of circular shape, larger than Libya and Asia Minor combined (!), fringed by mountains, with a rectangular plain and a six-ringed, circular city within. But what we get is the mountains alone, or the plain alone – and always of the wrong dimensions – with the other features conveniently ignored. And all the time, the suggested island or continent stands proudly out of the sea – not sunk, and often not in the Atlantic Ocean – in stark contradiction to what Plato actually wrote.

The historicists are accustomed to such discrepancies, having long ago been forced, by necessity, to reject the legitimacy of Plato's account. To an outsider, however, the situation appears ridiculous, to say the least, for

Plato is the sole authority on the ancient story of Atlantis, and to ignore what he said is to invent a new myth of one's own. When viewed thus, the mystery of Atlantis cannot be solved until someone has explained *all* of Plato's words – an apparently impossible task.

In this book, however, I am going to present a theory that *will* explain *every detail* of Plato's story. It will allow that Atlantis sank in the Atlantic Ocean, as Plato alleged. It will allow that the island was 'larger than Libya and Asia Minor combined'. It will explain all of the island's features – its circular shape, its ring of mountains, its rectangular plain, and its six-ringed, circular city. It will explain the significance of the date of the cataclysm, 'nine thousand years ago'. It will explain all the other manifold features of Atlantis that were recounted in Plato's story. And, most remarkable of all, it will vindicate Plato's claim that the story was 'true', in a most unexpected way.

An impossible task? Yes, if one continues with the historicist strategy of sticking pins in a map. But the approach that I am about to adopt is going to take us off the map entirely.

My approach in this book is to go back to basics, and examine the Atlantis story in its full and proper context. What kind of person was its author, Plato? Where did he get his ideas from? What was going on in the minds of the Greeks? Why did they believe in a golden age? Why did they believe in fabulous islands lying at 'the ends of the Earth'? Why did they worship a race of invisible gods, the Olympians? Who, or what, were these gods? How did their myths and cults begin? Did the Greek culture emerge in splendid isolation, as the 'old school' scholars would have us believe, or did it absorb the ideas of earlier civilisations? These, surely, are the right questions to be asked and answered if we ever wish to solve the mystery of Atlantis, and yet, to the best of my knowledge, a study of this ilk has never been undertaken before, not even in academia. Why not? Simply because of the sheer magnitude of the task.

Take Plato. Scholars acknowledge that he was a mystic, but they are perplexed by the peculiar form of his mysticism. A key concept, for example, is the so-called Theory of Forms (or Ideas), in which all things on Earth are regarded as eroded copies of their original archetypes in Heaven. When Plato writes that the home of the archetypes is an eternal and invisible sphere, which is simultaneously 'the true Heaven' and 'the true Earth', scholars are truly baffled. They cannot comprehend what Plato is talking about. And yet this Theory of Forms is not only pivotal to Platonic philosophy but also provides the crucial backdrop to the telling of the Atlantis story.

The Greek myths, too, present a problem. It is all well and good that scholars should identify parallels and precedents for mythical themes in the Atlantis story – as cited earlier – but what do all these myths actually mean? Here, scholars have given up the chase, relying on the conclusions of earlier authorities rather than reconsidering the myths for themselves. And what do these earlier authorities say? Amazingly, they admit that the myths are incomprehensible; no theory has ever explained them and, almost certainly, no theory ever will.

From these two points, it can be seen why the mystery of Atlantis has never been studied adequately in its full and proper context, not even by academics. To succeed in such a task would require revolutionary breakthroughs in the studies of Platonic mysticism *and* the Greek myths. Only by achieving this doubly impossible task might it be possible to get inside Plato's mind and reconsider the import of his Atlantis story.

This book, then, is an attempt to sail beyond the Pillars of Knowledge, which have been set up in stone by the frustrated pioneers of academic orthodoxy. But far from sailing at random into the deep blue yonder, I have at my disposal a kind of route map in the form of two controversial but common-sense theories, whose far-reaching conclusions have yet to be fully apprehended in the world of academia.

The first of these two theories is the 'exploded planet cult' theory of ancient Egyptian and Mesopotamian religions, which I set out in my books *The Phoenix Solution* (1998) and *When The Gods Came Down* (2000). In a nutshell, the theory runs as follows. Over thousands of years, ancient man witnessed an extraordinary array of cosmic activity: comets and meteors lighting up the skies, fireballs exploding in the atmosphere, and meteorites plunging to the ground. Inevitably, man, in awe of these events, tried to rationalise their cause, at the same time as pondering on his role in the Universe. In time, an astonishing theory emerged. Long ago, the ancient sages decided, a living planet had exploded and, in the process, conveyed the seeds and waters of life to the Earth. All forms of life had thereupon emerged from the Earth, including man himself. In the meantime, the exploded planet had pulled together its aethereal substance and transformed itself into an invisible body known as God or Heaven – an immortal and intelligent soul-being. It was man's duty to worship this invisible creator-God either directly, by mystical intuition, or indirectly, by means of visible symbols (e.g. meteorites, or the dying-and-rising Sun disc). In time, however, the masses began to worship the symbols per se, and the knowledge of the true God went underground, into the mystery schools. There, the ancient scribes encoded the exploded planet myth in manifold forms – the myths of the gods coming down from the sky, the myths of the Deluge and the creation of man, the myths of wars between the gods of Heaven and Earth, and the myths of the sacred marriage of the god and the goddess. All of these myths, and many others besides, concealed a 'Secret of secrets' that was accepted, unquestioningly, as a true account of the origins of the cosmos and man.

If the 'exploded planet cult' theory is the linchpin of this study, then the theory that follows becomes the grease to the axle. This second bold theory comes from mainstream academia, where heavyweight scholars such as Walter Burkert, Martin West and Charles Penglase have argued persuasively for Greek borrowings from the religion and myths of the ancient Near East. In *The Orientalising Revolution* (1984), *The East Face of Helicon* (1997), and *Greek Myths and Mesopotamia* (1994), these three scholars, respectively, have put forward a cast-iron case for Eastern influence during the 8th-7th centuries BC – the very time when Homer and Hesiod were laying the poetic foundations for the Olympian religion. The conclusion, in Martin West's words, is that 'Greece is part of Asia; Greek literature is a Near Eastern literature.'

Until now, this mainstream breakthrough in comparative religion has found limited application, for, if truth be told, the literature of the Near East is as much of a puzzle to scholars as the literature of the Greeks. Now, however, in the light of my recent deciphering of the Egyptian and Mesopotamian myths, the full import of these parallels may be felt. For the first time ever, it becomes possible to understand the Greek myths by literally standing under them. For the first time ever, we can get inside Plato's mind and reconsider the story of Atlantis from an ancient, rather than a modern, perspective.

The result is nothing short of a sensation. In this book, I present not only a complete decoding of the lost continent of Atlantis, but also a complete decoding of ancient Greek religion in its entirety. I am able to decode the myths of the Olympian gods and their associated mystery cults; I am able to decode the myth of the golden age and the fall of man; I am able to decode the scientific cosmogonies of Thales, Anaximander, Heraclitus, Anaxagoras, Empedocles and Philolaos; I am able to decode the 'soul religion' of Orpheus, Pythagoras, Parmenides, Socrates and Plato; and I am able to decode Plato's Theory of Forms, his account of the creation by the *Demiourgos*, and his story of Atlantis. Behind all of these ideas there lies a single secret of stunning simplicity – the age-old myth of the exploded planet.

So, what exactly is my theory of Atlantis? How can this sunken island possibly be connected to an exploded planet cosmogony? The answer is not immediately obvious, and I will not spoil the reader's enjoyment by giving the game away at this point. In fact, the reader might like to have a go at solving the puzzle himself, once he has completed chapters one to fourteen of this book. But let me just say this. Plato was no historian or geographer as many Atlantologists would have us believe. Rather, as noted earlier, he was a mystic. Therefore, when Plato described Atlantis as an island, he was speaking metaphorically; and when he described Atlantis going to war, he was speaking allegorically. Furthermore, when he declared that his story was 'true', he was speaking mystically. To Plato, truth lay in Heaven, in the invisible and eternal world of God and the gods. Alas! To search for Atlantis here on Earth, in the form of a lost civilisation, is the very antithesis of Plato's philosophy. The great man would have been grieved to witness such folly. Atlantis was no ordinary island; its people were no ordinary people; its treasure was no ordinary treasure. On the contrary, the loss of Atlantis was meant to signify a totally profound event – a 'Cataclysm of all cataclysms' that disrupted the Universe at the beginning of time (equivalent to the modern concept of the Big Bang). Innocence lost, the first time.

Inevitably, this book must conclude by posing the ultimate question: is the Atlantis myth a true story? To the sceptic, the exploded planet myth is outmoded, since it found its relevance in a now discarded theory of the geocentric Universe (as opposed to the heliocentric Universe). Even if a planet did explode and seed life on Earth – an intriguing question in itself – it would now appear to be a sideshow in the much larger cosmological picture. It was Plato's genius, however, to focus not on astronomy but on metaphysics, and to couch his ideas in the language of eternity. Thus his ideas have withstood the test of time, and are as relevant today as they ever were; it is only required that they be re-expressed in the modern language of astronomy and astrophysics (as I indeed do in the postscript to this book). In summary, then, Plato's story of Atlantis prompts us to contemplate the greatest truths imaginable – the beginning of Time, the role of cataclysms in the flux of the Universe, and the fate of man's soul in the 'other world'. For it is that 'other world', in the aether, which truly deserves to be called Atlantis.

Will *The Atlantis Secret* turn out to be a true secret? Time, perhaps, will tell.

But first the tale of Time must be told.

Reading Note 1

I have written this book in twenty-one 'bite size' chapters, grouped into four parts, with the aim of introducing the reader to the Greek myths and mysteries at a fairly basic level, and then guiding him through a series of new ideas and a new theory of ancient mythology, prior to tackling the mystery of Atlantis which appears in the final part of the book. This is, in effect, a kind of initiation process, which requires a certain amount of patience, self-disclipine and thought from the reader. If the reader tries to short-cut the process by speed-reading, skipping sections, or reading chapters out of sequence, then he will assuredly struggle to see the merits of my arguments and my theory, and the initiation will have failed. You have been warned! Ideally, the reader should digest one chapter at a sitting and take time for reflection, jotting down any questions that arise and reviewing them at the end. If any points still remain unclear, then I am happy to take questions by e-mail directed to alford@eridu.co.uk.

Reading Note 2

I have used male pronouns throughout this book, and I apologise to anyone who finds this practice offensive; I have done so purely to avoid the constant clumsiness of 'he or she', 'himself or herself', 'his or her', et cetera. In addition, I have used the words 'man', 'men' and 'mankind' to refer, on occasions, to the entire human race. Absolutely no offence is intended towards women, and I certainly do not wish to suggest any inequality between the sexes. Ask my wife if you don't believe me.

Reading Note 3

An ancient Greek proverb: "The beginning and end of a matter are not always seen at once."

PART ONE

THE GREEK MYTHS

CHAPTER ONE

MYSTERIES OF THE GODS

**For those who wish to find answers, it is a real
step forward even to ask the right questions.**
(Aristotle, 4th century BC)

According to an age-old Greek myth, the Earth had once been populated by a race of gods alone, in a time before mankind had been created. But then, for reasons that were somewhat obscure, the gods had decided to create a race of people, and this they proceeded to do by sowing seeds in the earth, causing the first men and women to spring up miraculously out of the ground, just like plants.

This is the myth that forms the backdrop to Plato's story of the war between Athens and Atlantis, in which it serves to explain how those two cities had been founded by the gods and how its respective peoples had been created. In the beginning, we are told, the gods had 'received their due portions over the entire Earth region by region', with the Isle of Atlantis falling to the god Poseidon and the city of Athens (and its surrounding land Attica) falling to the gods Athene and Hephaestus.[1] These gods had then created the first peoples in the aforesaid, miraculous manner. In respect of Atlantis, Plato states only that the original people of the island 'had originally sprung up from the earth', but in respect of Athens he describes, in mysterious terms, how the goddess Athene had 'received from Earth and Hephaestus' the 'seed' from which the Athenians would come, and how she had used this seed to 'fashion good men, sprung from the land itself'.[2] The names of the first Athenian kings – Cecrops, Erechtheus, Erichthonios and Erysichthon – contain in two instances the element *chthon* ('land'), confirming the belief that they had been 'born from the land'.[3]

In Atlantis, the birth of the earth-born people was followed by another curious incident. The god Poseidon, it was said, had taken a fancy to an earth-born female – a second generation princess named Clito – and had

had sexual intercourse with her, whereupon she had given birth to the race of Atlantian kings.[4] The first of these kings, after whom the island would be named, was Atlas – namesake of the famous Titan god who supported the Heaven upon his head and shoulders.

Who, or what, were these gods? Were they real individuals, or were they purely imaginary beings? How exactly did they create mankind from the earth, and how should their sexual relationships with the earth-born race be understood? As Aristotle once said: 'For those who wish to find answers, it is a real step forward even to ask the right questions.' And this question, concerning the nature of the gods, must surely be the number one question to be asked if we are at all serious about decoding the Greek myths in general and Plato's story of Athens and Atlantis in particular. For just as Plato intimated that every word of *his* story was true, so did the majority of Greeks believe that every word of *the myths of the gods* was true.

My plan, then, in this chapter and the next, is to take a preliminary look at the Greek gods and make an initial assessment of their nature. We will begin by looking at our present perceptions of the Greek gods as human beings (or human-*like*) beings, based on the poems of Homer and Hesiod and the theory of the Sicilian writer Euhemerus. Then we will discuss some of the problems with that perception and reconsider the Greek gods in all of their aspects. We will look at the various myths that describe how the gods were born, how they fought battles against each other to establish the present order of the Universe, how they divided the Universe between them, and how they then created man to populate the Earth. And then we will consider all of the attributes of the gods – where they lived, how they travelled about, what they looked like, and how they behaved towards one another. As we shall see, the underlying theme running through these myths of the gods is the idea of cataclysmic events, in some cases the fall of the sky and in other cases the eruption of the Earth. I will therefore close our discussion by asking whether the gods truly were human-like beings, pure and simple, or whether the gods might have been personifications of the exceptional and cataclysmic forces of nature.

Did the gods create man, or did man create the gods?

Anthropomorphic Gods

Today, our common perception of the Greek gods comes largely from Homer's epic works the *Iliad* and the *Odyssey*. In these famous poems, Homer portrays the gods as a society of human-like individuals. Some are male, some are female. They form married couples and have sons and daughters. They have fathers, mothers, brothers, sisters, aunts and uncles. And their behaviour is akin to that of human kings and queens. Homer's gods live in golden palaces, sit on golden thrones and drink from golden goblets. The chief god Zeus calls assemblies to debate the issues of the day and to approve decisions. The gods argue, plot and fight against one another, exhibiting the full range of human emotions, e.g. anger, jealousy and cunning.

The physical form of Homer's gods is almost perfectly human-like. In the *Iliad*, Zeus, king of the gods, takes a decision by nodding his 'dark brows', causing his 'hair' to fall forward from his 'head'.[5] Hera, his wife, is portrayed as being 'white-armed' and 'gold-sandalled'.[6] Meanwhile, the god Apollo, the famous 'Far-shooter', is described as coming down from Mount Olympus 'with anger in his heart' and with 'his bow on his shoulders'.[7] All in all, Homer's gods are 'human almost to the last detail', as one eminent scholar has said, or, as another has put it, quite poetically, the gods 'enshrined a religious belief which was completely anthropomorphic and anthropomorphically complete'.[8]

Elsewhere in the ancient Greek literature, we read how the gods granted man the gifts of civilisation. They clothed him, gave him fire, provided him with the seeds of agriculture and taught him all of the crafts which would improve his lot on the Earth.[9] All of the myths of this ilk give the impression that man was once assisted in his development by a superior race of human-like beings.

Certain Greek philosophers gave this scenario a subtle twist. In the 5th century BC, Prodicus asserted that the gods had been an ancient group of men and women who had wandered around the world as a race of philosophers, teaching wisdom to mankind.[10] In time, he said, these characters had been elevated in status and worshipped as gods; thus the human inventor of wine had become deified as the god Dionysus, whilst the human bringer of grain had become deified as the goddess Demeter.

Prodicus may not have been fully serious with his suggestion, but the idea never went away. In the 3rd century BC, there stepped forward the Sicilian writer Euhemerus who argued forcefully that the gods had been kings, queens and heroes of an earlier age, who had been deified owing to their magnificent achievements.[11] Euhemerus was destined to lend his name to this particular theory.

Following Euhemerus, many prominent historians, philosophers and mythologists rewrote the myths of the past as if the gods had indeed been human kings and queens. Among these writers were Diodorus Siculus (1st century BC), Philo of Byblos (2nd century AD) and, to a certain extent, Plutarch (1st century AD). A common motif was the idea of an ancient king acting as a benevolent shepherd of mankind, travelling all over the inhabited world and putting barbaric races of men on the upward path to civilisation.[12]

The influence of these ancient Euhemerists on the modern perception of Greek religion cannot be overstated. During the formative stages of Hellenist studies, in the 18th and 19th centuries, many scholars assumed without question that the Greek tales contained the earliest records of the history of mankind. Even as recently as 1955, a powerful advocacy of the Euhemerist theory was made by Robert Graves in *The Greek Myths*. In this book, Graves maintained that 'the historical and anthropological approach [to myth] is the only reasonable one' and he insisted that 'a large part of Greek myth is politico-religious history'.[13] 'Early Greek mythology', he wrote, 'is concerned, above all else, with the changing relations between the queen and her lovers.'[14] Whilst acknowledging that the name Zeus meant 'Bright Sky', Graves pointed out that the name had been taken as a title by human kings and thus the role of the sky-god in myth had been largely eclipsed by human affairs.[15] According to Graves, Zeus' defeat of Kronos had been a human battle, as had the earlier struggle between Kronos and Ouranos (the castration of Ouranos had been just that – a real human castration!).[16] Thereafter, Zeus' swallowing of the goddess Metis had been an allegory for the Greeks' suppression of the cults of Metis and Athene.[17] Similarly, the various myths of Zeus' sexual conquests had been allegories for the new patrilineal society subjugating the shrines of the old matrilineal system.[18] And as for the myth of the gods rebelling against Zeus, this had been a critical moment in the struggle between the matrilineal and patrilineal systems: the queen, Hera, had attempted to overthrow the rule of the king, Zeus, but the king had survived the rebellion and avenged himself by placing Hera in bondage.[19] Hence the tradition that Zeus had suspended Hera in the sky, tying a golden rope round her hands and two anvils to her feet, was merely a case of exaggerated poetic metaphor.

In due course, we will be able to examine these various myths and draw our own conclusions. But for now, it should be noted that things have moved on somewhat since Graves wrote his epic tome *The Greek Myths*. In fact, during the last fifty years, mainstream scholars have been backing away from each and every kind of all-encompassing model, in recognition of the fact that the Greek myths are far too diverse and complex to be explained by monolithic theories of the kind advocated by Graves (see the discussion in chapter six of this book). Today, the Euhemerist/historicist theory of myths constitutes just one weapon in a whole armoury of theories, each of which is selected and brought to bear as the circumstances demand. There are no longer any simplistic dogmas in academia.

Atlantis, however, is another matter entirely. In 1882, when Ignatius Donnelly wrote his bestselling book *Atlantis: The Antediluvian World*, he relied heavily on the Euhemerist theory which was popular in his day. Toward the end of his provocative study, Donnelly made a calculated attack on the only serious alternative theory – that the gods had been meteorological phenomena – and labelled it 'absurd'. Instead, he wrote:

> There can be no question that these gods of Greece were human beings... when we read that Jove [Zeus] whipped his wife, and threw her son out of the window, the inference is that Jove was a man... The history of Atlantis could be in part reconstructed out of the mythology of Greece; it is a history of kings, queens, and princes; of love-making, adulteries, rebellions, wars, murders, sea-voyages and colonisations... Who can doubt that it represents the history of a real people?[20]

To Donnelly, then, the main gods of the Atlantis story – Zeus, Poseidon, Atlas, Athene and Hephaestus – had all been human beings. Each had been a historic individual, the member of a prestigious family. And each had performed pioneering deeds in establishing human civilisation at the sites of Atlantis and Athens respectively. This was the same story told countless times in antiquity by the likes of Diodorus Siculus and Philo of Byblos. Now here was a popular writer, nearly two thousand years later, saying basically the same thing. Donnelly's bold attempt to rewrite the 'history' of Atlantis was nothing new.

Such was the influence of Donnelly's book, however, that 'nothing new' has been the name of the game in Atlantis studies since 1882. Post-Donnelly, 'alternative' writers such as David Rohl, Andrew Collins, Colin Wilson and Rand Flem-Ath, have all been perpetuating the same Euhemerist dogma, with the gods of Atlantis and Athens being regarded as a mysterious race of ancestor beings.[21] Sadly, the field of Atlantology does not feature the kind of rational back-pedalling that has occurred in academia's study of the Greek myths. No. As far as the study of Atlantis is concerned, it is as if time has stood still, somewhere around the date 1882.

This would be fine if the Euhemerist theory really was the solution to the mystery of the Greek gods. But is it? Was this really what Homer had in mind when he portrayed the gods as human-like entities?

In fact, when we look at the tales of the gods in Homer's epic poems, we discover a rather shocking anomaly. Here, we read that the gods, far from being ordinary mortals, were immortal. Here, we read that the gods, far from being Earthly kings and queens, resided in the heavens. And here, in Homer's poems, we read of the gods travelling back and forth between Heaven and Earth in their supernatural chariots.

One is thus tempted to suggest that, if the gods were humans – as the Euhemerists maintain – then they were humans of an extraterrestrial mould! Thus the true explanation of the gods would lie in the direction of the so-called 'ancient astronaut' theory, which Erich von Daniken has been advocating so passionately since the late 1960s.[22] But this is an over-simplistic approach and the truth is more complex, involving, at some level, the personification of the cataclysmic fall of the sky.

But let us not jump ahead of ourselves, for now is the time to clear our minds of any preconceptions we might have and examine the story of the gods as it was related by the ancient Greeks themselves during the first half of the 1st millennium BC.

And where else to start but with the origin of the gods.

The Origin of the Gods

The most intelligible account of the origin of the gods comes from the poet Hesiod in his famous work *Theogony*, and this will form the basis of the story in this chapter. But before turning to Hesiod, we should look briefly at some lesser known cosmogonies, each of which sets the scene for the birth of the gods in a slightly different way. Incidentally, the word 'cosmogony' (from the Greek *kosmogonia*), meant literally 'birth, or generation, of the cosmos', where 'cosmos' (from the Greek *kosmos*), referred to 'the ordered state of the world (or Universe)'.

The simplest cosmogony, on which little comment can be offered for now, is that of Oceanus and Tethys, as recorded by Homer in the *Iliad*. In a few lines, which are frustratingly brief and opaque, Homer makes reference to Oceanus being the father of the gods, and Tethys being their mother.[23] Who or what was this original primeval couple? Not a man and woman – that much seems certain. On the contrary, the Greeks described Oceanus as a personified ocean which encircled the world (see chapter eighteen). Tethys, meanwhile, was a mysterious and elusive figure, but was surely an *alter ego* of Gaia – the mother-goddess who personified the Earth; it was probably in this sense that Tethys had become 'mother of the gods' (see chapter eight).

Another cosmogony of the short and sweet variety is the creation myth of the Pelasgian Greeks. In this account, the first being was the goddess Eurynome, whose name meant 'wide rule' or 'wide wandering'.[24] She arose naked from *Khaos* ('the yawning gap') and separated the sea from Heaven in order that she might dance on its waves. Having established herself down in the south, she was followed there by Ophion, alias Boreas – the god of the north wind – and she coupled with him until she became pregnant. When the due process of labour came to its end, Eurynome laid the Egg of the Universe, and invited Ophion to coil himself (in the form of a serpent) around the Egg until it hatched and split into two. Thereupon, everything that was to exist in the Universe was born from the Egg – Sun, Moon, planets, stars, all life on Earth and, most importantly for the gods, the heavenly mountain of Olympus.[25] One presumes that somehow, in the midst of this creative act, the various Olympian gods were born.

According to a third cosmogony – that of the Orphics – Earth, Heaven and sea had once been 'confounded in common mass together' but had then been separated from one another 'by grievous strife'.[26] Thereupon Heaven had gone to dwell far away from the Earth. But later, Heaven had returned, married the Earth and caused her to bear all living things.

In a separate account, the Orphics stated that the first god was Time, who had given birth to 'the yawning gap' (*Khaos*) and an aethereal image of Heaven (*Aither*).[27] Almost immediately, there was a 'covering over' (*erebos*) in the subterranean interior of the Earth, at which time 'all things were in confusion, throughout the misty darkness'.[28] The god Time then fashioned a silvery egg in this Underworld, and the egg 'began to move in a wondrous circle'.[29] Suddenly, the egg split into two and Phanes, the First-born god, emerged from it, gleaming amidst a supernatural light.[30] Simultaneously, the *Aither* was separated from the misty darkness of the Underworld and was lifted up to become Heaven.[31] And Phanes, the First-born, now emerged from the darkness, roaring like a bull, moving upon golden wings and looking around with his two pairs of eyes.[32] He rose up to Heaven, where he built an imperishable house and became ruler of the Universe, but he then set his mind on love.[33] In his name of Eros, he descended to the Earth at least once and impregnated the goddess Night with the seed of the gods.[34] In due course, Night gave birth to Gaia and Ouranos, and this couple, in turn, gave birth to the entire race of the gods.[35] Night also gave birth to the Sun and the Moon.[36]

A curious addendum to this Orphic theogony, paralleling Hesiod's *Theogony* (see below), states that all things in the created Universe were subsequently swallowed by Zeus and then created anew from 'the hollow of his own belly'. The passage reads:

All things were created anew in Zeus – the shining height of the broad
Aither and the heavens, the seat of the unharvested sea and the noble
earth, great Ocean and the lowest depths beneath the Earth, rivers and
the boundless sea, and all else, all immortal and blessed gods and
goddesses, all that was then in being and all that was to come to pass.
All was there, and mingled like streams in the belly of Zeus.[37]

Hesiod's Theogony

We turn now to the only detailed and completely connected narrative of
the origin of the gods – the account of Hesiod. In his poem *Theogony*
(late-8th or early-7th century BC), Hesiod confirms that the mother of the
first generation of gods was Gaia – a personification of the Earth. As for
their father, it was not Oceanus (a personified ocean) or Phanes/Eros
(personified love) but Ouranos – a personified mountain of Heaven (his
name meant 'Heaven' or 'heavens' but stemmed from the Greek word
ouros, meaning 'mountain').[38] The marriage of Ouranos and Gaia –
Heaven and Earth – is implied at the beginning of Hesiod's account, but
is reported later as if it were a repeating theme:

> Great Ouranos came, bringing on Night, and desirous of love, he
> spread himself over Gaia (Earth), stretched out in every direction.[39]

From this celestial union, Earth gave birth to mountains and sea, and to
the heavenly abode of Mount Olympus – 'a secure seat for ever for the
blessed gods'.[40] From this union, more to the point, was born the first
generation of gods, including Kronos, the three Cyclopes, and the three
giants known as the Hundred-handers. All of these gods developed inside
the Earth – in the womb of Gaia – whence they would soon be born into
the light of the world above.

Ouranos, however, was terrified lest his fearsome children depose him
from the rulership of Mount Olympus. Therefore, as soon as each child
was born, he consigned it back to the darkness of the Underworld.[41] Gaia
(the Earth) was furious. She groaned as a result of the forces that were
'tight-pressed' inside her and urged her children (the Titans) to wreak
revenge for their father's outrageous behaviour.

All of the gods were seized with fear except for young Kronos, who
bravely accepted the task. The next time his father Ouranos came down
from Heaven to force himself upon Gaia, Kronos attacked him from
within the Underworld with a sharp-toothed sickle. With one swift blow,
he castrated his father and threw the offending genitals over his shoulder.
Ouranos became a fallen god – the first in a sequence.

The victorious Kronos now re-emerged from Gaia's womb, ascended into the heavens, and established a new reign upon Mount Olympus.[42] In his service he had the fierce Titans – gods of an unknown origin.[43]

The scene was now set for a second round of divine births. Kronos, the new king of Heaven, came down from above and slept with Gaia (in her name of Rhea), causing her to bear six further, glorious children. This second generation of gods comprised three females – Hestia, Demeter and Hera – and three males – Hades, Poseidon 'the Earth-shaker' (later to become the god of Atlantis) and Zeus.[44]

But as Kronos watched these children developing in Rhea's womb, he received a prophecy that he would share the fate of his father: one of his own children would depose him from the throne of Olympus. Kronos therefore hatched a cruel plan. When each of his children came forth from Rhea's womb into the light of the world above, he would swallow them. Such, then, was the fate of Hestia, Demeter, Hera, Hades and Poseidon. Each of these five gods Kronos swallowed, in turn.

Rhea (Gaia) was desperate in her grief, but she had one remaining child, Zeus, who had yet to be handed over to the heartless Kronos. It was at this time that Rhea devised a cunning plan to save her youngest child. First, she concealed Zeus in an inaccessible Cretan cave, deep down in the secret places of the Earth. Then, she took a large stone, which she wrapped in baby-cloth and delivered to Kronos. And the cruel king of Olympus gulped the stone down, unaware that the true contender for his throne was still at large, deep down in the bowels of the Earth.[45]

The stage was now set for the battle of the Titans.

The Battle of the Titans

It may be useful, before recounting the battle of the Titans, to confirm the order of the Universe, as it existed during the latter stages of Kronos' rule. According to Hesiod, the cosmic realms were inhabited as follows:

In Heaven, on Mt Olympus: Kronos and the Titans.

In the Earth, awaiting birth: Zeus.

Confined in the Underworld   Ouranos, the Cyclopes, and the Hundred
(i.e. in the Earth's interior):   -handers.

Confined inside Kronos: Hestia, Demeter, Hera, Hades, Poseidon.

These gods were the key players in the cosmic drama about to unfold, but mention must be made of other gods who were residing quietly in the Underworld, keeping a low profile. Among these gods were the Erinyes, the Giants and the Meliai nymphs, all of whom had been propagated by the blood spilt from the genitals of Ouranos.[46] Also among these gods were the Hesperides, the Fates and the Furies, who had been borne by Night (this goddess personified the Underworld).[47] And mention must be made, too, of Aphrodite – the goddess of love – who had been formed from the genitals of Ouranos and was now drifting on the ocean waves amidst a white foam.[48] (Clearly, Ouranos was no ordinary being and his testicles no ordinary testicles!)

Meanwhile, beneath the ocean waves, another theogony had begun. The personified ocean, Sea, had had union with Gaia and fathered Nereus ('the Old Man of the Sea'), Thaumas, Phorcys and numerous sea-goddesses, and these divinities had begun to produce further generations of nymphs and subterranean monsters.[49]

As for mankind, it did not exist during this formative stage of the Universe, at least not in the form that we know it today. But according to Hesiod's *Works and Days*, there did exist, during the reign of Kronos, a pre-human form of man known as the golden race. Its origin was unknown and its whereabouts only vaguely alluded to by Hesiod.[50]

This, then, was the state of affairs during the reign of cruel-hearted Kronos. Hundreds of other divinities were yet to be born; likewise the race of demi-gods or heroes. The birth of all these beings awaited the new world order which would soon be established by Zeus. With this in mind, let us pick up the story of Zeus' vengeance against the Titans.

The young god Zeus, we are told, grew in courage and strength until he was ready to confront his wicked father. According to the popular myth, which was passed over by Hesiod, Zeus was appointed cupbearer to king Kronos and took up service in the palace of Kronos on Mount Olympus.[51] Needless to say, Kronos was unaware of his new cupbearer's real identity.

Zeus now put his plans into action, beginning with the release of his brothers and sisters from Kronos' stomach. To this end, he carefully slipped a vomiting potion into the king's goblet and waited for nature to take its course. Sure enough, Kronos brought forth the five swallowed children and, no doubt to his great surprise, the stone which Gaia had substituted for Zeus. Next, Zeus sought support for his coming battle against Kronos and his Titans. Firstly, he went down to the Underworld and released the three giant Cyclopes (sons of Ouranos) from their bondage; the Cyclopes, in return, pledged their allegiance to Zeus and gifted him three powerful weapons – 'the thunder, the lightning and the smoking bolt'.[52] Next, Zeus released from the Underworld the three sons of Ouranos known as the Hundred-handers. Each of these was a giant – an ugly, misshapen hulk, with fifty heads, a hundred arms, and unlimited strength.[53] Their names were Kottos, Briareos and Gyges.

Zeus now united his allies – the long-suffering children of Ouranos on the one hand, and his siblings, the children of Kronos, on the other hand. He called upon the two groups to fight together against Kronos and his Titans and drive them out of Heaven. And, without further ado, the battle of the Titans commenced. In the words of Hesiod:

> The Hundred-handers then engaged the Titans in grim slaughter, with sheer cliffs in their stalwart hands... the boundless sea roared terribly round about, the Earth crashed loudly, and the broad Heaven quaked and groaned. Tall Olympus was shaken to its foundations by the onrush of the immortals; the heavy tremors from their feet reached misty Tartarus [a region of the subterranean Underworld], as did the shrill din of the indescribable onset and the powerful bombardment. So it was when the two sides discharged their woe-laden missiles at each other.[54]

The battle raged on and remained finely poised until Zeus himself decided to enter the affray. He plunged down from heavenly Olympus and threw his whole might against the Titans:

> ... with continuous lightning flashes Zeus went, and the bolts flew thick and fast amid thunder and lightning from his stalwart hand, trailing holy flames. All around, the life-bearing Earth rumbled as it burned... The whole land was seething, and the streams of Oceanus, and the undraining sea. The hot blast enveloped the chthonic Titans; the indescribable flames reached the divine heavens... it was just as if Earth and the broad Heaven above were coming together...[55]

As the two generations of gods clashed amidst this cosmic conflagration, the heavenly Titans were overwhelmed, and Zeus and his allies emerged triumphant. They imprisoned Kronos and his cronies in the depths of the Underworld (in Tartarus), and set the three Hundred-handers over them as a guard.[56] Zeus was now destined to be the new king in Heaven.

Establishing the Cosmic Order

To establish the new world order, after the fall of Kronos and the Titans, it was first necessary to agree the territorial rights and privileges of the victorious gods. In *Theogony*, Hesiod tells us that the gods beseeched Zeus to be their king 'and he allotted them privileges satisfactorily'.[57] In the *Iliad*, however, Homer tells us that the gods divided up the Universe by throwing lots. The moment was recollected by Poseidon, the god of the deep ocean, who declared:

"There are three of us brothers, borne to Kronos by Rhea: Zeus,
myself, and the third is Hades, lord over the dead. The whole Universe
was divided into three lots, and each of us took his appointed domain.
When we shook the lots, to me fell the hoary sea, that I should dwell
therein for ever; and Hades drew the misty darkness (below), and Zeus
drew the broad Heaven (above), among the clouds and the aether; but
the Earth and high Olympus are yet common to us all."[58]

This, then, was the division of the Universe during the reign of Zeus, and
it was destined to remain in force for all eternity. It was a threefold
division between Heaven, the deep ocean and the Underworld (the latter
region is best understood as a sphere which filled the spherical interior of
the Earth; it represented, in effect, the womb of Gaia, and encompassed
the realms known as *Erebos*, Tartarus, and the house of Hades).

But Hesiod informs us that things might have been different if Zeus
had not been alert to the threats of potential rivals. The first of these
rivals was born in the immediate aftermath of the battle of the Titans.
Gaia, we are told, conceived once more and, in anguish of labour,
brought forth a horrible monster named Typhoeus:

Out of his shoulders came a hundred fearsome snake-heads with black
tongues flickering, and the eyes in his strange heads flashed fire under
the brows; and there were voices in all his fearsome heads, giving out
every kind of indescribable sound.[59]

Zeus, enthroned on Mount Olympus, had to amass all of his powers once
more. He plunged into mid-air combat with Typhoeus, causing Heaven
to shake, the Earth to quake, and fire to break out over sky, land and
sea.[60] But Zeus was invincible thanks to his three supernatural weapons,
the thunder, the lightning and the smoking bolt. With these, he struck
Typhoeus with crippling blows and scorched his hundred heads. The
young pretender, overcome by superior force, crashed to the ground,
causing the Earth to burn and melt from an 'unbelievable heat'.

And, vexed at heart, Zeus flung Typhoeus into broad Tartarus.[61]

Would the world now find peace and stability? Unfortunately not; for it
was a law of the Universe that Heaven would come down periodically
for bouts of cosmic love-making with Earth. And Zeus, as the incumbent
god of Heaven, would be no exception to the rule. Thus there would be
further love-making, titanic conceptions, and monstrous offspring. (One
account had it that the Giants, *Gigantes*, had sprung up from the Earth
and assaulted Olympus).[62] How long would it be before Zeus, like his

father Kronos and his grandfather Ouranos, was deposed from Olympus by a rebellious son?

This cosmic dilemma called for a cunning plan. Sure enough, the time came when Zeus, in his role as Heaven, descended in time-honoured fashion to embrace Earth. And from this embrace, Earth (in her name of Metis) began to bear a female child – the bright-eyed goddess Athene. But Zeus knew that, in due course, there would be a male child, who would be capable of usurping his throne and becoming king of the gods. And for this reason Zeus implemented his cunning plan. He swallowed Metis, including her unborn daughter Athene, and, at one fell swoop, eliminated all future threats to his kingship.[63]

In this way – in this astonishing way – Zeus established the eternal stability of the cosmic order.

More Births of the Gods

To account for the origins of all the gods in Hesiod's *Theogony* would be an arduous task. According to one authority, there are three hundred divine names in *Theogony* if one includes the mountains, the rivers and the personified abstractions such as Fate, Death, Sleep and Dreams.[64] Nevertheless, there are certain gods who merit a mention on account of their importance in Zeus' new world order and certain gods who merit special attention on account of their intriguing birth myths.

In the first category I would place Atlas, Prometheus, Epimetheus and Menoitios, who were all sons of the Titan Iapetos. Atlas, we are told, was confined at the ends of the Earth, in the remote west, where Zeus forced him 'to hold up the broad Heaven with his head and tireless hands'.[65] His task was to prevent Heaven from falling – an event that would threaten to destabilise Zeus' world order. As for Prometheus, legend had it that he was the creator and benefactor of man (the giver of fire), and for this reason he was punished by being nailed to a pillar, or by another account to a mountain which was plunged into the Underworld for eternity.[66] And as for Menoitios, Hesiod states that Zeus struck him with a smoking bolt and sent him down into the darkness of the Underworld 'because of his wickedness and overbearing strength'.[67] One gets the impression that all four sons of Iapetos were among the Titans of Kronos – the accursed enemies of Zeus; hence their fate of confinement in the Underworld, along with their father Iapetos.[68]

Also in our first category of important gods are the twins Apollo and Artemis (born to Zeus and Leto), Ares the god of war (born to Zeus and Hera), Persephone the goddess of the Underworld (born to Zeus and

Demeter), Hermes the messenger of the gods (born to Zeus and Maia), and Heracles the greatest of the heroes (born to Zeus and Alcmene). Significantly, each and every one of these gods had the archetypal divine parentage comprising father Heaven and mother Earth.

Of these divine births, the birth of Apollo, the Far-shooter, was the most famous. The myth of his birth, which was recounted in considerable detail, provides useful insights into the mystery of the gods.

In the Homeric *Hymn to Apollo*, a pregnant Leto – the mother of Apollo – searches for an island that will become the foster mother of her son, but the islands all tremble at the prospect of bearing such a mighty child.[69] Only the island of Delos is prepared to take on the responsibility, but she confesses embarrassment at her barren landscape and expresses concern at what Apollo might think of her. In recognition of her concerns, Leto promises Delos that Apollo will build a beautiful temple on the island. Leto then endures nine days and nine nights of painful labour, before finally laying back against Mount Cynthus and giving birth to Apollo in a remarkable manner:

> Leto threw her arms around the palm tree, and pressed her knees on
> the soft meadow. The Earth smiled beneath her and the child [Apollo]
> leapt forth into the light. And all the goddesses shrieked in triumph.[70]

This astonishing birth of Apollo occurred from the womb of the Earth, i.e. from the Underworld (as the scholar Charles Penglase has recently noted), hence the idea that the god sprang forth from darkness to light.[71] In another passage of the hymn, Apollo's birth coincides with shrill winds and a mysterious dark wave that surrounds the island.[72]

The newborn Apollo is fed with the nectar and ambrosia of the gods, whereupon he breaks free from his golden cords and makes a prophetic speech. Immediately thereafter, the far-shooting god begins to walk upon the Earth 'causing astonishment to all the goddesses'.[73] As he steps upon Delos, the island covers herself with gold and blossoms like a meadow of flowers on a mountain top. Apollo then goes off to wander the world.

In the second category of gods – those whose origins call for special attention – there falls the famous pairing of Athene and Hephaestus, who both figure prominently in Plato's foundation myth of ancient Athens. Both of these divine births appear to defy the normal Greek conventions.

In the case of Athene, I have already mentioned that her mother Metis (probably an *alter ego* of Earth) was swallowed by Zeus in order to prevent the birth of a future son. (This strange swallowing motif will be examined in a later chapter.) But Zeus nevertheless thought it wise to release Athene, and this he did, according to Hesiod, by giving birth to the bright-eyed goddess 'by himself, out of his head'. The Homeric *Hymn to Athene* provides the details:

> Pallas Athene, bright-eyed... powerful Tritogeneia, whom crafty Zeus
> produced himself out of his sacred head – bedecked in her spangly
> gold war armour. What awe enthralled all those immortals who saw
> her jump suddenly out of his sacred head, shaking her sharp spear –
> right out of Zeus who holds the aegis! Great Olympus shook terribly at
> the might of the bright-eyed goddess; the Earth groaned awfully; and
> the Ocean was moved... Then Helios [the Sun], the radiant son of
> Hyperion, halted his swift-footed horses and they stood still for a long
> time, until the maiden [Pallas Athene] took the god-like armour from
> her immortal shoulders; and wise Zeus rejoiced.[74]

This myth of Athene's birth is problematic to decode, but the intention seems to be that Zeus, the god of Heaven, had taken over the Earth (as was his prerogative) and hence he was able to give birth to Athene from the womb of the Earth. (This scenario gains support from the myth that Hephaestus split open Zeus' head with an axe so that Athene could emerge).[75] It follows that the passage cited above describes an ascent of Athene into the company of the gods on heavenly Mount Olympus.

Athene's birth, then, is typical of the immortals who were generally born from the womb of the Earth, i.e. from the Underworld, but it is unusual in that the deity is born, ostensibly, from a male parent.

As for the god Hephaestus, his birth from Hera seems to belong to an entirely separate tradition. Hesiod says little about the incident, revealing only that Hera (the wife of Zeus) gave birth to Hephaestus while 'furious and quarrelling with her husband'.[76] But the Homeric *Hymn to Apollo* informs us that Hephaestus was born not in the Earth but in Heaven; so said Hera in her address to the assembly of the gods:

> "Hephaestus – the one I gave birth to myself – he was weak among all
> the gods, and his foot was shrivelled. Why, it was a disgrace to me,
> and a shame in Heaven. So I took him in my hands and threw him out
> [of Olympus] and he fell into the depths of the sea."[77]

This incident is described also in the *Iliad*, where Hephaestus refers to his 'great fall' and describes how he was cared for by the goddesses Thetis and Eurynome in their hidden cave beneath the sea.[78]

This completes our rundown of the births of the gods. With the notable exception of Hephaestus, the gods were generally borne by the Earth who delivered them forth from her womb (the Underworld) into the light of the world above. Significantly, the usual method of conception was an impregnation of the Earth by Heaven – after the model laid down by the original pairing of Gaia and Ouranos.

The Settlement of the World

After the battle of the Titans, the gods established a new cosmic order, with Zeus in charge of Heaven, Poseidon in charge of the sea and Hades in charge of the Underworld (where the olden gods had been confined for ever). The rest of the gods, meanwhile, built residences in appropriate locations. Some, such as Atlas and the Hesperides, took up their stations in the Underworld; some took up their stations beneath the sea or in subterranean rivers and springs; and some took up their stations on heavenly Mount Olympus. In the latter group were the royal couple Zeus and Hera, the bright-eyed goddess Athene, the far-shooting Apollo, the huntress Artemis, the war-god Ares, the goddess of love Aphrodite, and the swift messenger of the gods Hermes. Curiously, the blacksmith-god Hephaestus was able to inhabit workshops not only on Olympus but also in the Underworld.[79] All of these gods were known as Olympians.

These were the various stations of the gods but, as a general rule, the gods were mobile between Heaven and Earth, for Olympus and Earth were regarded as a common heritage for them all. For example, we read in the *Iliad* of Zeus and Hera going down from Olympus to the Earth, either to the peaks of mountains or, in Hera's case, to the Underworld. Similarly, we read of Athene, Ares, Aphrodite and Hermes descending from Olympus to the Trojan Plain. But ascents were equally possible, hence one myth records how all the gods (with just one exception) were summoned from Earth to heavenly Olympus in order to attend the formal assembly of Zeus and Hera.[80]

This, then, was the order of the Universe as it was established by the generation of Zeus. But, in addition, the gods set about dividing the Earth itself into regions, seemingly as a prelude for the creation of mankind who was required to work the land and provide offerings to the gods.

How was mankind created? Here, the Greeks preserved a fascinating variety of traditions. By some accounts, people had been created from stones, by another account from trees, by yet another account from the ashes of the Titans, and by the most popular account from fire, water and clay. It was generally agreed, however, that the gods had created man from these materials inside the womb of Gaia (i.e. in the Underworld), and that Earth had then delivered these first people into the world above, by having them emerge from her womb, like plants from the soil.

Of the many accounts of this astonishing creation, I will cite that of the famous sophist Protagoras, as recorded in Plato:

"There once was a time when gods existed but mortal races did not. When the time came for their appointed genesis, the gods moulded them inside the Earth, blending together earth and fire and various compounds of earth and fire. When they were ready to bring them to light, the gods put Prometheus and Epimetheus in charge of decking them out and assigning to each its appropriate powers and abilities."[81]

In this myth, Protagoras' earth-born people are created at the beginning of the golden age, when men were allowed to enjoy care-free lives. But it was nevertheless necessary for the gods to endow this primeval and pre-human race of man with the necessary arts of survival. Prometheus, for example, was said to have given man the fire of the gods, having stolen it either from Olympus or from the Underworld.[82] Likewise, it was said that Athene and Hephaestus (or alternatively Prometheus) had given the first Athenians the various crafts which afforded them a comfortable living.[83]

According to Protagoras, the earth-born race had eventually been overcome by a cataclysm which caused it to sink back into the earth.[84] It was after this that the gods had created the true human race and assigned to it the childbearing responsibility which had belonged previously to the Earth herself.

A slightly different version of events was recounted by Hesiod. In his scheme, the human race had been preceded by a whole series of earlier pre-human peoples, which had comprised a 'golden race', a 'silver race' and a 'bronze race'. Each of these races, in turn, had been created by the gods but had then been destroyed (apparently by means of cataclysmic events).[85] Eventually, the gods had created the human race which, in line with the pattern of progressive decline, represented 'the iron race'.

But alongside these traditions there ran a slightly different version of events, according to which the gods had had intercourse with the race of man and produced a race of half-gods (the *hemitheoi*). These half-gods, otherwise known as the heroes, belonged to a kind of golden or twilight age that had existed aeons before the historical era of the Greeks. Among the earliest of these heroes were Theseus (a son of Poseidon), Heracles (a son of Zeus) and Perseus (a son of Zeus). A later generation of heroes included the warriors of the Trojan War – 'god-like' men such as Nestor, Menelaus, Agamemnon, Achilles, Patroclus, Odysseus, Diomedes, the two Aiantes, Priam, Hector and Paris. All were said to have met their fate on the battlefield, in an age long ago.

The race of heroes was given special attention by the gods all the way from the cradle to the grave. One immediately thinks of the battle scenes in the *Iliad*, where the gods, enthroned on heavenly Olympus, look down on the raging battles between Greeks and Trojans, sometimes lending assistance to their favourites, sometimes hindering their opponents, and all the time considering the strategies and tactics which might bring the great war to its desired conclusion (by some accounts, the decimation of man).[86] In keeping with their semi-divine bloodline, the heroes were portrayed by Homer as huge, bronze-clad giants, who were able to throw boulders that could not even be picked up by 'the folk that live now'.[87]

Chapter One Summary

* Greek theogony (the birth of the gods) seems to be closely tied in with cosmogony (the birth of the cosmos or Universe).

* The gods were usually born from the Earth, following an impregnation by Heaven – apparently a cataclysmic event.

* The gods' establishment and maintenance of the present cosmic order was achieved via a series of cataclysmic battles involving Heaven and Earth.

* The creation of man, formed inside the womb of the Earth, ranks as one of the gods' most astonishing achievements.

* Most of the gods resided in Heaven upon the mysterious mountain of Olympus. They were able to travel back and forth between Heaven and Earth by supernatural means.

* Some gods resided in the Underworld (under earth or sea), but these gods, too, had a share in heavenly Mount Olympus, and they were generally able to participate in the assembly of the gods there. It would be fair to say that the entire family of gods (with minimal exceptions) belonged in Heaven.

CHAPTER TWO

CATACLYSMS AND THE GODS

**Veiled in thick mist, the Muses walk by night,
uttering beautiful voice, singing of Zeus
who bears the aegis.**
(Hesiod, *Theogony*, 8th-7th century BC)

We now have an overview of the story of the gods. We have learned of
their origins, ultimately from Ouranos and Gaia. We have learned of
their battles, in which Kronos and then Zeus rose, in turn, to supremacy.
We have learned of their establishment of the world order and their
division of the world into regions. We have learned of the gods' creation
of mankind, apparently preceded by at least one pre-human race of earth-
born people. And we have learned of the mingling that allegedly took
place between the gods and the earth-born people, which resulted in the
race of half-gods, or god-like heroes, and their mighty descendants.

But it is now time to focus in more detail on the various attributes of
the gods. Were they really as human-like as Homer and the Euhemerists
(such as Ignatius Donnelly) have led us to believe?

We will begin with the physical appearance of the gods, and as good a
starting point as any is the hair by which so many were distinguished.
There is the 'dark' hair of Poseidon, for example, the 'long, flowing' hair
of Apollo, the 'braided' hair of Calypso, and the 'beautiful' hair of Leto
and Demeter.[1] But what should we make of the hair of Zeus, which is
described in the *Iliad* thus:

> So the son of Kronos [i.e. Zeus] spoke, and he nodded his dark brows.
> The lord god's immortal hair streamed forward from his deathless
> head and he shook the heights of Olympus.[2]

What kind of hair, might we ask, is 'immortal'? What kind of hair is
attached to a head that can shake the Heaven when it is nodded? The
unavoidable answer, surely, is the hair of a head of a supernatural body.

And, as if to confirm this supposition, the *Iliad* informs us that when the mighty Zeus sat down upon his throne the Heaven was shaken:

> Zeus took his seat on the golden throne and great Olympus was shaken under his feet.[3]

Similarly, the Heaven was shaken by the movements of Zeus' wife Hera. Again in the *Iliad*, we read:

> Queen Hera was angry. She tossed on her throne and shook the heights of Olympus...[4]

Were Zeus and Hera literally human-like giants, or are we simply dealing with exaggerated poetic metaphors? Or might there be more to it? Whatever the answer, these descriptions fit into a much wider theme of the gods' supernatural attributes.

Take the way the gods moved around, for example. Poseidon, the god of Atlantis, could descend from the highest mountain of Samos into the depths of the sea in four giant strides.[5] Hera could move from Olympus to Lemnos by hopping from one mountain peak to another.[6] Apollo, the Far-shooter, could move from Delphi to Thessaly in one stride and his footsteps could cause an entire island to shake.[7] The aforementioned descent of Poseidon is described in the *Iliad* as follows:

> Immediately the Earth-shaker [Poseidon] came down from the rocky mountain with fast strides, and the high mountains and the forests trembled under the immortal feet of Poseidon in motion. He took three strides and with the fourth reached his goal, Aigai, where his glorious palace was built in the depths of the water in gleaming gold, imperishable for ever.

Quite apart from Poseidon's supernatural footwork, we might well ask what kind of god had need of such a palace beneath the sea.

Supernatural motion went hand in hand with supernatural body-size and supernatural strength. Although the gods could and did take on the standard human form at will (see later), the true forms of the gods seem to have been literally superhuman. Thus, when the goddess Demeter took on human form in order to search for her missing daughter Persephone, she entered the palace at Eleusis and her head touched the ceiling.[8] Thus, similarly, when Aphrodite visited the hero Anchises, she stood as tall as the roof.[9] And thus, when the war-god Ares was felled by bright-eyed Athene, his body was said to have covered seven whole acres.[10]

Superhuman size and strength feature particularly in those gods who fought the battle of the Titans. In *Theogony*, for example, Hesiod tells us that the Hundred-handers had 'boundless strength'; when they went into battle, they wielded 'sheer cliffs' in their hands and when they launched their missiles they 'darkened the Titans' sky'.[11] Later, when Zeus went into mid-air battle against the monstrous god Typhoeus, Heaven and Earth were shaken, and when Typhoeus' body plunged to the ground, the Earth 'burned far and wide'.[12] And, in the aftermath of this battle, the superhuman god *par excellence* is encountered in the form of Atlas – the giant who was forced to bear the Heaven on his head and shoulders.

Men, too, were said to have had supernatural size and strength. In the *Odyssey*, Homer describes the god-like Otus and Ephialtes as follows:

> ... those short-lived twins, the god-like Otus and Ephialtes, famed in story, the largest men Earth ever nourished and finer by far than all but the glorious Orion. In their ninth year they were nine cubits across the shoulders and nine fathoms tall. It was this pair that threatened to go to war with the very gods on Olympus in the din and turmoil of battle. It was their ambition to pile Mount Ossa on Olympus and wooded Pelion on Ossa, to make a stairway up to Heaven.[13]

The case of Otus and Ephialtes may be exceptional, but it is nevertheless consistent with the general idea that the half-gods – the heroes – could throw huge rocks which could not even be picked up by 'the folk that live now'.

Cataclysmic Motifs

Supernatural size and strength might well be a case of exaggerated poetic metaphor, as I suggested earlier. But there are other aspects of the Greek gods which cannot be explained so easily, in particular their association with bright light, fire and loud noise. In the examples that follow, it will become increasingly evident that we must be dealing with something much more significant than a mere exaggeration of human attributes.

Let us begin with the bright light which features prominently in myths dealing (a) with the gods' births, (b) with their entrances into sacred shrines, temples or palaces and (c) with their ascents into Olympus.

A good example of the bright light motif occurs in the myths of Apollo, the god of the 'far-shot arrows'. After his miraculous birth on the barren island of Delos, Apollo went to Delphi, where he slew the resident dragon and constructed a beautiful temple as an oracular site. He then went looking for priests and found them in a crew of sailors aboard a Cretan ship. Accosting the sailors in the form of a huge dolphin, Apollo guided them and their ship to his temple. And then:

> The lord Apollo – the far-distant worker – jumped from the ship like a
> star in broad daylight. Sparks flew off him from all sides and their
> light reached the heavens. He entered his shrine... and he made a fire,
> revealing his [far-shooting] arrows. The brightness filled all of Crisa.[14]

These fiery arrows were the trademark of Apollo. As for the brightness,
the same motif re-occurs when Apollo ascends into heavenly Olympus:

> [Apollo], the glorious son of Leto, goes to steep Pytho [Delphi],
> playing his hollow lyre, wearing divine and perfumed clothes... And
> then, like a thought, he goes to Olympus from Earth, to the house of
> Zeus where the other gods are gathered... And Phoibos Apollo plays
> his lyre, taking big steps, and oh so beautifully! And a brightness
> swirls about him, his flashing feet and his carefully-woven gown.[15]

Another god associated with bright light was Demeter, and here the motif
occurs once again when a building is entered. The Homeric *Hymn to
Demeter* describes what happened when the goddess entered the king's
palace at Eleusis:

> The goddess [Demeter] put her foot on the threshold and touched her
> head on the ceiling and filled the doorway with a divine light.[16]

This was Demeter in the guise of an old woman, who was unable to
conceal fully her true divinity. But later in the story, the goddess did cast
her guise aside to reveal her true identity, and once again we find the
bright light motif:

> The goddess [Demeter]... changed her size and shape, throwing away
> her (guise of) old age, and beauty exuded from her on all sides, and a
> lovely fragrance wafted from her perfumed veils, and a bright light
> shone far from the goddess' immortal flesh... and the house was filled
> with a brilliance as of lightning.[17]

Why did the gods exude such a dazzling light? A likely explanation lies
in the myths of their births from the womb of the Earth, as noted in the
previous chapter. Take, for example, Zeus, the king of the gods. We have
already discussed how Gaia protected Zeus by concealing him deep in
the Underworld, 'in a cave hard of access', supposedly beneath the island
of Crete. And we have also discussed how Zeus came forth from Gaia's
womb (the Underworld) to challenge heavenly Kronos and his Titans.
But what has not yet been revealed is the manner of Zeus' birth. Hesiod
tells us only that Zeus began to grow rapidly and that his limbs were
'shining'.[18] But other sources describe Zeus as springing forth from the
Cretan mountain to the accompaniment of a tremendous noise.[19] This

myth incidentally, went hand in hand with a ritual: every year the Cretans would celebrate the mysteries of Zeus by building a great fire to commemorate his birth from the subterranean cave.[20]

Was this fiery, noisy birth of Zeus typical of all the gods? Although we are lacking a full account of all the gods' origins, it certainly does strike a chord with the birth of Apollo at Delos and with the birth of Athene who sprang from the 'head' of Zeus 'bedecked in her spangly gold war armour'.[21] Furthermore, it strikes a chord with the birth of the Giants who emerged from Gaia's womb 'in gleaming armour with long spears in their hands'.[22] And further, it strikes a chord with the Mysteries of Demeter at Eleusis, where the initiates used to celebrate the birth of a divine child, Brimos, who had appeared in the Underworld 'in the midst of a brilliant fire'.[23]

Another major feature of these divine births, in addition to the bright light (or brilliant fire) motif, was loud noise. We have already noted this motif in the birth of Zeus which, according to the writer Apollodorus, was marked by the loud shouts of his divine attendants. Similarly, Typhoeus, when he was born from Gaia, emerged from the earth 'giving out every kind of indescribable sound', causing the mountains to echo below.[24] Loud noise is a major feature, too, in Apollo's birth myth. Thus, in a passage cited earlier, it was said that the goddesses had 'shrieked in triumph' at the moment of the god's birth. This incident was paraphrased by the poet Pindar, who sang of the joint birth of Apollo and his twin sister Artemis, as follows:

> Gentle-hearted Leto was released from her sweet labour;
> The Sun blazed in full splendour,
> As the twin children entered the bright light of day,
> And Eleithyia and Lachesis poured from their mouths a great cry.[25]

This idea of loud noise at the birth of the gods must surely be connected to the idea that the Earth had to open herself up to bring forth the god from her womb-like Underworld (as at least one modern scholar has noted).[26] In this regard, a notable theme of the birth myths is the quaking of the Earth. In the Homeric *Hymn to Apollo*, for example, the birth of the monster Typhaon is preceded by Hera striking the ground with her 'thick hand' and causing the Earth to be moved.[27] Similarly, in the *Hymn to Athene*, cited earlier, the birth of the goddess caused both the Earth and heavenly Olympus to quake.

Many other gods, too, were linked to the loud noise motif. Examples include 'noisy Artemis', 'ear-splitting Dionysus', Hecate 'the Roarer', and the war-cries of Ares and Poseidon which Homer compared to 'the shout of nine thousand or ten thousand men'.²⁸ Often the loud noise originated in Heaven; hence we read of Hera darting out of Heaven with such a fearful cry that 'the vast vault of Heaven reverberated'.²⁹

Shape-shifting Immortals

There remain two aspects of the gods which we have not yet considered: firstly their alleged immortality and secondly their supernatural ability to metamorphose, i.e. to change the form of their appearance. Both of these aspects have a fundamental bearing on the Euhemerist theory that the gods might have been human or human-like beings.

Firstly, the immortality of the gods. During the course of this and the previous chapter, readers may have observed the Greeks' tendency to refer to their gods as 'the immortals' and to use the word 'immortal' as an adjective describing the gods' appearances. Thus it was supposed that Athene had 'immortal shoulders', that Zeus had 'immortal hair', that Poseidon had 'immortal feet' and that Demeter had 'immortal flesh'. The implication is that the bodies of the gods – if we are to understand them as having bodies at all – could literally not be killed. Hence the idea that the gods were, as the Greek language puts it, *aien eontes*, i.e. 'eternal beings'.³⁰ One of the earliest references to this idea is found in *Theogony* where Hesiod sings:

> Farewell, Muses, and grant me delightful singing. Celebrate the holy family of immortals, who are for ever – those who were born of Earth and Heaven and of black Night...³¹

How could the gods live for ever as the Greeks maintained? Was this just a symbolic metaphor to express the power of human or human-like beings? Or might there have been more to it? A possible clue is to be found in the popular idea that the Greek gods were shape-shifters, i.e. creatures capable of changing their shape and form at will.

Here are some examples of this supernatural shape-shifting ability: Kronos, king of the gods, was once caught in the bed of his mistress, but instantly he turned himself into a horse and fled the scene at full gallop;³² Zeus, the son of Kronos, took the form of a bull to seduce Europa, the form of a swan to mate with Leda, the form of a shower of gold to impregnate Danae, and the form of a thunderbolt to incinerate Semele;³³ The goddess Demeter, meanwhile, changed herself into a mare to escape the advances of Poseidon, but the sea-god swiftly followed suit and ravished her in the form of a stallion.³⁴

And then there were the Hesperides nymphs, who lived with Atlas in the remote west. These nymphs, it was said, could transform themselves into dust and earth at the drop of a hat.[35] Or, alternatively, they could turn themselves into tall trees.[36] The Hesperides were among the most famous shape-shifters of the Greek world.

The shape-shifter *par excellence*, however, was 'the Old Man of the Sea', variously named Nereus, Phorcys or Proteus. According to the folkloric tale contained in the *Odyssey*, Proteus, when approached, would 'try all kinds of transformations, and change himself into every sort of beast on Earth, and into water and blazing fire.'[37] In his encounter with Odysseus, Proteus turned himself into 'a bearded lion and then into a snake, and after that a panther and a giant bear', followed by a more radical change into running water and a giant leafy tree.[38] Proteus was the very personification of divine metamorphosis.

Many other examples of shape-shifting gods could be cited, such as Athene who sometimes departed from the world of men in the form of a bird, or Apollo who abducted the Cretan sailors to Delphi in the form of a dolphin.[39] In addition, there are several intriguing traditions of gods having the magical ability to transform men into animals or stones.[40]

But most intriguing of all is the gods' ability to metamorphose into specifically human forms, i.e. to assume the identities of certain known individuals (this is commonplace in the *Iliad* and the *Odyssey*, as the gods sought to influence the outcome of the heroes' affairs). And it is here that we find a weakness in the Euhemerist argument.

Consider. If the gods were human beings, as the Euhemerists maintain, then we should expect the human-human transformation to be the easiest for them to accomplish. Their disguises should be perfect. The Greeks, however, were insistent that this was *not* the case. For example, when Demeter took the form of an old woman to search for her abducted daughter Persephone, she still possessed a certain beauty that caused the daughter of the king to remark: "You look like a god."[41] Similarly, when Aphrodite, the goddess of love, took the form of a young virgin to seduce Anchises, the hero immediately saw through her disguise, saying: "Great lady, you must be one of the gods."[42] Apparently, the divine radiance of these goddesses could not be concealed.

An even better example of this 'failed disguise' motif is Poseidon. In the midst of the Trojan War, the great sea-god decided to intervene on the side of the Greeks by assuming the form of the hero Kalchas (i.e. he became a double of Kalchas). He then spoke to the two Aiantes brothers, filled them with strength from his magical staff, and urged them into the battle. Then Poseidon departed in an instant and the double of Kalchas was gone. Aias then announced to his brother:

"Aias, this was one of the gods who hold Olympus... it was not

> Kalchas... I could tell it well from the form of his feet and legs from
> the back as he left us – it is easy to recognise the gods."[43]

Was there something fishy about Poseidon's appearance? Certainly there
is something fishy about the Euhemerist theory; for why should it be that
Poseidon, Aphrodite and Demeter – among the greatest of all gods –
experienced problems in assuming the human form, when humble old
Proteus could transform himself into the shape of a tree, running water,
blazing fire or animals, without any problems? Why should this be if the
gods were truly human, or indeed human-like?

The answer, it would seem, is that the Greek poets were making a
point. And that point is summed up perfectly by the warning given by
Apollo to one of the heroes of the Trojan War:

> "Never think yourself the equal of the gods – since there can be no
> likeness ever between the make of immortal gods and of men who
> walk on the ground."[44]

This distinction between gods and men (or in this case the race of heroes)
was not just a matter of the gods possessing greater strength. No, the
difference was much more profound, as is apparent from the following
incident recorded in Homer's *Iliad*:

> The hero Diomedes sprang at Aphrodite and, lunging with his sharp
> spear, stabbed at the wrist of her soft hand. And the spear pierced
> straight through the skin... and immortal's blood dripped from her –
> *ichor*, which runs in the blessed gods' veins. They do not eat food,
> they do not drink gleaming wine, and so they are without (normal)
> blood and are called immortals.[45]

This is a perplexing statement. Homer supposes that the gods have
bodies, and they are clearly modelled on the human form – for example,
we have references to Aphrodite's hand, wrist, skin, veins and blood –
and yet, at the same time, Homer makes it clear that the gods were *not*
human; their veins were not filled with blood but with a mysterious
liquid called *ichor*; and nor did the gods eat and drink as normal flesh-
and-blood beings do. The gods, in short, did not belong to the realms of
terrestrial biology, but were something literally supernatural. Hence their
claim to be immortal beings.

Cataclysmic Gods

It is time to summarise what we have learned. In this and the previous
chapter, we have noted the following key attributes of the Greek gods:

* Often described and depicted in human-like form; but:

* Born from the womb of Mother Earth (in almost all instances).

* Originated from a primal union of Heaven and Earth – apparently a cataclysmic event.

* Fought cataclysmic battles spanning Heaven and Earth.

* Resided upon the heavenly mountain of Olympus, or in the Underworld (under earth or sea).

* Able to travel back and forth between Heaven and Earth.

* Created man in the womb of the Earth.

* Frequently associated with bright light, fire and loud noise.

* Possessed supernatural size and strength.

* Able to travel vast distances in a blink of the eye.

* Able to metamorphose into numerous different forms.

* Possessed immortality.

What to make of all this? One possibility, which the reader might have spotted, is the idea that the gods personified earthquakes and/or volcanic eruptions. This theory has a lot of mileage in it. For one thing, it is possible to argue that the Greek myths recalled the volcanic explosion of Thera in the 17th century BC. In addition, it is a fact that the gods of the Underworld (the subterranean interior of the Earth) were of considerable importance in Greece; Poseidon, for example, was a god of earthquakes, hence his nickname 'the Earth-shaker'. Furthermore, it is a fact that volcanic eruptions can eject ash to great heights, where it can be carried in the upper atmosphere for hundreds of miles, blocking out much of the sunlight. Could this perhaps explain some of the miraculous journeys of the gods, as when Aphrodite 'cut a path through the high-up clouds' in travelling from Cyprus to Troy, or as when Hermes used his magical sandals to fly vast distances over earth and sea 'as fast as the wind', or as when the Argonauts saw Apollo 'dwindle airborne into the distance, out over the sea'?[46] All of this certainly seems to be plausible.

There is one problem, however, with the earthquake/volcano theory, and it is this: throughout the ancient Greek literature, the journeys of the gods began, as often as not, in Heaven, and it was their descents from Olympus – the mountain of Heaven – that unleashed the cataclysmic forces upon the Earth. In *Theogony*, for example, Zeus came down from Heaven to fight Typhoeus and his supernatural lightning caused the whole Earth to be set afire.[47] In the *Iliad*, Hera rode out of Heaven in a 'fiery chariot',[48] whilst bright-eyed Athene came down from Heaven to Earth in a rapid and fiery movement 'like a bright star with sparks of light streaming thick from it.'[49] Then there is Prometheus, the god who brought fire from Heaven to Earth and, for his troubles, was chained to a pillar or mountain and plunged cataclysmically into the Underworld.[50] And then there is Hephaestus, the god of fire, who was cast down from Heaven into the depths of the sea; the fact that he was the blacksmith of the gods must surely make him the Greek meteorite-god *par excellence* (it is an archaeological fact that meteorites, black in colour, were the primary source of iron in the earliest civilisations).[51]

Figure 1.
THE WORLD'S LARGEST KNOWN METEORITE (60 TONS), LYING WHERE IT FELL AT HOBA, NAMIBIA.

Such is the importance of these myths among the Greeks that one is led to the irresistible conclusion that the cataclysmic forces of the gods originated in Heaven, where the vast majority of gods belonged. And it should be recalled, at this juncture, that the birth of the gods began only after Mother Earth had been impregnated by a falling Heaven – the god Ouranos whose name signified 'the Mountain of Heaven'.[52] The cycle of the gods thus began, as far as we can tell, from some kind of cosmic impact that stirred up the chthonic forces in the Earth.

It is clearly the case, then, that the myths of the Greek gods involve a catastrophism beyond that of simple tectonic or volcanic phenomena. On the contrary, the gods are 'of Heaven and Earth', and the cataclysms, too, are 'of Heaven and Earth'. Tectonic and volcanic phenomena are not excluded from the overall picture; rather, they constitute a secondary but integral factor.

What kind of 'Heaven and Earth' cataclysms are we talking about? The answer, in short, is bolides (i.e. fireballs), and meteoritic impacts resulting from stray comets or asteroids. Intriguingly, in view of the myths already discussed, these meteoritic impacts can not only trigger tectonic and volcanic activity, but can also create impact ejecta which are flung up into the atmosphere only to fall back to the ground in the form of extraordinary cosmic showers (these ejecta comprise small, molten, glass-like bodies which scientists call 'tektites').

So, did the Greek gods personify these various cataclysmic forces of nature? Is this the great secret of the Greek myths? Or is there some way that all of this cataclysmic imagery can be reconciled to the Euhemerist theory that the gods were human beings, or the von Danikenite theory that the gods were human-like astronauts from another planet?

To begin with the Euhemerist case, it is indeed possible to square the circle by arguing, quite plausibly, that human kings were glorified *by association with* cataclysmic events. This argument would acknowledge that the dazzling light, blazing fire and deafening noise of the gods was essentially cataclysmic in nature, but it would regard such things as being of secondary importance to the human kings (or indeed tribes of people) whose achievements they were intended to glorify. The upshot of this argument is that the various divine attributes, listed above, should be regarded as 'symbols of power'.

Turning to Erich von Daniken's theory of 'ancient astronauts', this has traditionally relied on a slightly different approach. Here, some of the gods' supernatural attributes are usually explained as recollections of extraterrestrial technology; hence the light, fire and noise of the gods would recall the emissions of aeronautical craft or the blast of nuclear weapons, whilst the myth of the gods creating mankind would recall a lost science of genetic engineering. It must be said, however, that these interpretations of the ancient myths have been thoroughly refuted in recent years by none other than myself (see my book *When The Gods Came Down*, 2000), and it is now evident that this particular brand of ancient astronaut theory (based on the myths) is a non-starter.[53] Not that this rules out von Daniken's theory per se, but what it does do is force its adherents to fall back on the 'symbols of power' argument, as outlined earlier. Thus, it would be argued that the Earth *was* visited by human-like beings from another planet, but that these visitors were later glorified by association with cataclysmic events.

Where does this leave us? The issue, crucially, is one of interpreting the cataclysmic imagery. Either the gods personified the cataclysmic forces of Heaven and Earth period, and the myths of the gods were about mythical cataclysmic events, pure and simple. Or the gods were human or human-like beings, and the cataclysmic motifs were used as 'symbols of power' to elevate and glorify their status.

Which is the likeliest solution? In order to decide, I have in mind a dual challenge.

Firstly, in regard to the idea that the gods personified cataclysms, the challenge for myself is to demonstrate that cataclysm theory is an end in itself, i.e. that the cataclysmic model explains adequately the profundity of the ancient Greek religion.

Secondly, in regard to the Euhemerist (or ancient astronaut) theory, the challenge is to demonstrate that there *is* a meaningful human (or alien) story behind the cataclysmic imagery, i.e. it must be explained how the cataclysmic model falls short of explaining all of the relevant literary and other data.

Of these two challenges, the second falls to the Euhemerists and von Danikenites; it is they, not I, who must advocate their case. I will say only that, from my experience of all the data, their challenge is a mighty one indeed. My aim, though, is to address the first challenge and explore, in the course of this book, whether the cataclysmic model *alone* can explain the profundity of ancient Greek religion. If I can succeed in this task (and it, too, is a mighty challenge), then I will finally put the lie to Ignatius Donnelly's statement that 'the history of Atlantis' was 'the history of a real people', and I will, instead, be in a position to reassess Plato's Atlantis story in the context of what was primarily a cataclysmic religion.

Chapter Two Summary

* The Greek gods were often depicted in human-like form, but on closer inspection it appears that they were not human at all. In fact, the poets maintained that there could be no comparison at all between the races of gods and men.

* The birth of the gods from the Earth is a probable explanation for their supernatural attributes: bright light, blazing fire, loud noise, swift movement, shape-shifting ability and eternal life.

* The myths of the gods fit a generally consistent pattern, which is essentially a cataclysmic model. This model is undeniably celestial, and is based on the archetypal idea of Heaven falling cataclysmically

to the Earth; the tectonic and volcanic aspects of some Greek myths are a natural corollary of this celestial model. The bottom line is that the gods appear to be personifications of these cataclysmic forces.

* As regards Plato's story of Athens and Atlantis, popular studies have generally assumed that the gods were human beings or extraterrestrial visitors. But this approach – based on the theory of Euhemerus – is highly questionable. What would the story of Atlantis become if gods such as Poseidon, Atlas and Athene turn out to be personifications of cataclysmic forces, period?

CHAPTER THREE

THE GREEK PERSPECTIVE

**Concerning gods I cannot say whether they exist
or not, or what they are like in form; for there are
many hindrances to knowledge – the obscurity
of the subject and the brevity of human life.**
(Protagoras, 5th century BC)

The underlying theme running through the previous two chapters was
one of cataclysms. It was an original primal union of Heaven and Earth
(Ouranos and Gaia) – apparently a cataclysmic event – which caused the
birth of the Olympian gods. Consistent with that surmise, the birth myths
of the Olympian gods were steeped in cataclysmic imagery, notably
bright light, blazing fire, and loud noise. Furthermore, we saw how these
gods engaged in a series of cataclysmic battles with the Titans as a
prelude to establishing the world order. And then, as if to underline the
cataclysmic nature of all these myths, we encountered the Titan god
Atlas, who was forced to support the Heaven on his shoulders – a potent
symbol of the idea that the sky might fall to the Earth once again. In all
of these respects, and many more, the Greek myths speak for themselves
in attesting to the importance of cataclysmic ideas. Not, it must be said,
in the form of *historical* cataclysms (as has been proposed by Immanuel
Velikovsky and his supporters),[1] but rather in the form of *mythical*
cataclysms. That is to say that the cataclysmic falls of Ouranos, Kronos
and Zeus were understood to have happened at the beginning of time,
aeons before man had been created on the Earth. (In this respect, the
Greek beliefs parallel our modern-day theories concerning the Big Bang
or the Chicxulub asteroid impact that killed off the dinosaurs, neither of
which was witnessed by man, for obvious reasons.)

    Now, it must be emphasised that virtually all the textual references in
the previous two chapters were drawn from the poems of Homer and

Hesiod, who laid the literary foundations of Greek religion during the 8th century BC. Accordingly, if Homer and Hesiod's words are not to be gainsaid, then our cataclysmic interpretation of the Greek myths should be on solid ground. Nevertheless, it is important to seek corroboration of our findings so far, and this we shall now do, firstly by considering the opinions of the ancient Greeks themselves (in the centuries that followed the 8th century BC), and secondly by considering the opinions of modern scholars.

To begin, in this chapter, we will look at the Greeks' own thoughts about the nature of the gods and the origins of the cosmos, from the 7th-5th centuries BC. As we shall see, this was a period of significant introspection, as one Greek thinker after another lined up to contribute to the great debates of the day. Who or what were the gods? Did they truly exist? How did the Universe begin? What was the nature and fate of man? Intriguingly, we shall find that the Greeks were so uncertain and confused about the meaning of their traditional religion that they turned to new cosmogonies in which the roles of the old Olympian gods were largely eclipsed. Here, in these new and non-mainstream cosmogonies, we shall discover some further astonishing examples of cataclysmic ideas.

Anthropomorphic Gods

As noted earlier, Greek religion, in the form that we know it, began with the poems of Homer and Hesiod during the 8th century BC. As Herodotus, the 'father of history', wrote: 'It was Homer and Hesiod who composed a divine genealogy for the Greeks, and who gave the gods their titles, allocated to them their powers and fields of expertise, and made clear their forms.'[2]

What were these 'forms' of the gods which Homer and Hesiod made clear? Despite the cataclysmic imagery, the underlying forms of the gods were human-like, to such an extent that, as one modern scholar has commented, the Homeric myths 'enshrined a religious belief which was completely anthropomorphic and anthropomorphically complete'.[3]

From the 8th century BC onwards, this anthropomorphic portrayal of the gods formed the mainstay of the Greeks' religious education; all schoolchildren were made to learn the works of Homer and Hesiod (Homer in particular). In time, however, the poets attracted a great deal of criticism for their portrayal of the gods, who had a marked tendency to engage in violent and immoral acts, such as raping, torturing and fighting one another, stealing one another's possessions, engaging in illicit love affairs and even committing patricide. (It should be noted that this divine propensity toward violence is exactly what one would expect to find if the gods had been conceived, originally, within a cataclysmic model.)

One of the first traces of concern about the traditional gods may be found in the saying 'much the poets lie', attributed to the statesman and poet Solon (7th-6th century BC).[4] Later, towards the end of the 6th century, the works of Homer and Hesiod were savaged by the Ionian philosopher Xenophanes for their lack of moral values:

> Homer and Hesiod have attributed to the gods everything that is held discreditable among men – stealing, adultery and mutual deception.[5]

Xenophanes went on to pen the the most damning criticism of Homeric anthropomorphism that had ever been written:

> If horses or cattle had hands, and could draw or make statues, horses would represent the forms of the gods like horses, and cattle would represent the forms of the gods like cattle.[6]

The implication was that the human-like gods described by Homer and, to a lesser degree, Hesiod did not exist. Man had created the gods in his own image.

Many other eminent Greek of the 6th-5th century shared Xenophanes' concerns. Did the gods eat mortal flesh, as the story of Tantalus and his son Pelops suggested? 'Nonsense' wrote the poet Pindar, 'I spurn the thought'.[7] Did Kronos castrate Ouranos and then swallow the gods who were his own sons and daughters? "I find it hard to accept" said Socrates, "that things like that may be said about the gods".[8] Did Zeus and the gods engage in licentious love affairs and place one another in bondage? No they did not, said the dramatist Euripides, who expressed his doubts within a play, using the voice of the hero Heracles:

> "I do not believe that the gods sought forbidden sexual relations, nor that they put one another in chains; and I will never believe it, nor that one is master over the others... (it) is the wretched words of singers."[9]

So dismayed was Euripides with the Homeric concept of the gods that when Hera persecuted Heracles later in his play, he penned the line: 'Who would pray to such a god?'.[10]

Not that any of these Greeks denied the existence of the gods. On the contrary, they had no doubts that the gods did exist in some mysterious, aethereal, sense. Rather, their complaint was with Homer and Hesiod's portrayal of the gods. By depicting them as human-like beings, engaged in violent, immoral acts, the poets had implied that unsociable behaviour was somehow acceptable. Hence Socrates, in the famous work *Republic*, would pronounce a ban on the teaching of such myths in his imaginary, ideal city-state.[11]

Scepticism

The Greek gods were, by definition, a mystery. When Herodotus wrote that 'all men know equally much about the gods', he meant that no-one knew anything about them for certain.[12] The gods, moreover, were fickle and unpredictable. They did not always respond to prayer; they did not always prevent atrocities taking place in Greek homes, streets, cities and countryside; and nor did they always bring punishment upon the wicked. The dramatist Euripides undoubtedly reflected popular concern when, in one of his plays, he had the character Bellerophontes renounce his belief in the gods on account of the fact that evil-doers were thriving at the expense of the pious.[13]

It was in a play of Euripides, or possibly of Critias, that the idea was first mooted that religion had been a contrivance, designed with the sole purpose of frightening men into civilised behaviour.[14] It was supposed that, long ago, a clever ruler had invented the kind of gods who would see and hear all things, and bring judgement accordingly upon the heads of evildoers. Religion, it was suggested, had been created as a purposeful lie, in order that an élite of men could exercise control over their fellow men.[15] The same idea was also hinted at by Isocrates (5th-4th century BC), when he wrote:

> Those who planted this fear of the gods in us brought it about that we do not behave like wild beasts towards one another.[16]

The philosopher Democritus was equally sceptical, but adopted a more generous attitude. There was no conspiracy, he said. Rather, the gods had been invented by men who were fearful of things they had seen in the sky. It was only natural that men had been terrified by the eclipses of the Sun and the Moon, and by the power of 'thunder and lightning'; and it was thus perfectly logical that men had invented the concept of gods to personify the powers of nature.[17] Democritus also offered an explanation for the so-called 'miracles' whereby gods appeared to men in dreams and visions. These apparitions were not gods at all, he said, but phantoms (*eidola*) – a curiosity, to be sure, but nothing that transcended day to day reality.[18]

A similar sceptical approach was taken by Prodicus, the pioneer of historical allegory (5th century BC). He began his account of religion by crediting primitive men with personifying and worshipping the forces of nature. But he then suggested that the gods had been very wise people (sophists), who had travelled around the land teaching on a wide range of sciences, from agriculture to horticulture, and had later been deified in honour of these marvellous achievements.[19] According to Prodicus, the goddess Demeter had been a human teacher of agriculture, whilst the god Dionysus had been a human teacher of horticulture.

Another sceptic was the poet Diagoras (5th century BC), who used a mixture of humour and outrageous behaviour to mock the existence of the gods. He once quipped, in respect of the many votive gifts set up at Samothrace in honour of sailors whom the gods had saved, miraculously, from the swelling sea, that the gifts would be more numerous still if the drowned sailors, too, had been able to present gifts![20] Diagoras was later indicted for revealing the mysteries of Eleusis to the ordinary man in the street.

All of these sceptics were playing with fire, for the Greek populace of those days were, by and large, extremely pious. Euripides, as a dramatist, could get away with just about anything. In addition, poetry and humour were useful tools for comment. But some Greeks went too far with their sceptical comments and thus incurred the wrath of the people. Here, one thinks in particular of the philosophers Protagoras and Anaxagoras (both 5th century BC).

Protagoras' crime, apparently, was to express his agnosticism in a book. In the opening section of *On Gods*, he explained his rationale:

Concerning gods I cannot say whether they exist or not, or what they are like in form; for there are many hindrances to knowledge – the obscurity of the subject and the brevity of human life.[21]

Some years later, Protagoras suffered the ignominy of having his book *On Gods* burned in public in the streets of Athens, whilst he himself was put on trial accused of not believing in the city's gods.[22] He survived by fleeing the city, but was promptly drowned at sea during the course of his flight.

Anaxagoras, meanwhile, directed his scepticism towards a different kind of god. In 5th century Athens, it was the practice of the city to worship not only the supernatural gods of Olympus but also the Sun and the Moon. These latter gods, as odd as it might seem, were regarded as aethereal entities. But Anaxagoras turned this dogma upside down with his theory that the Sun and the Moon were glowing balls of metal (based on his experience of an iron meteorite which had fallen from the sky and landed at Aegospotami in 467 BC).[23] Consequently, in 438 BC or thereabouts, the influential seer Diopeithes urged the city to 'denounce those who do not believe in the divine beings or those who teach doctrines about things in the sky.'[24] In response, the Athenian authorities made a law which indeed forbade the public teaching of 'unconventional doctrines' about 'things in the sky'. Anaxagoras, the leading rationalist of that era, was forced to leave Athens after thirty years' teaching there.[25]

Ridiculous Tales

Such was the uncertainty and scepticism about the gods, compounded by the problem of Homer's anthropomorphic portrayal of them, that many Greeks began to have serious doubts about the ancient myths that had been recited by the poets. Had Kronos really swallowed his children? Had Zeus really suspended his wife Hera in the clouds, with a golden rope round her hands and two anvils hanging from her feet? Had Hera really thrown the deformed blacksmith-god Hephaestus out of Heaven? All of these tales, and a thousand others like them, began to sound absurd to those Greeks who took the time to think about such matters.

The geographer Hecataeus of Miletus (6th-5th century BC) spoke for many when he wrote:

> What I write is as I believe it to be true; for the tales which the Greeks tell are many and ridiculous in my opinion.[26]

What, then, did these tales mean, and how had they arisen? One theory was that the myths had come about as exaggerated accounts of mundane natural or human events. Hecataeus was one of the first to take this approach, in respect of the three-headed dog Cerberus who was known as 'the hound of Hades'; it stood to reason, he said, that if the bite of Cerberus had been instantly fatal (as it was alleged to be) then Cerberus had not been a dog but a venomous snake (clearly a case of its bite being worse than its bark).[27]

Hecataeus was followed by the writer Palaiphatos, who postulated some of the most memorable allegorical ideas. Although his five-volume sceptical treatise *On Incredible Matters* has not survived, other sources relate numerous examples of his far-fetched theories, which were rooted in the most imaginative etymologies.

One of Palaiphatos' theories, for example, supposed that the story of the abduction of Europa by Zeus (in the form of a bull) recalled the abduction of a woman by a Cretan general named Tauros – the Greek word for 'bull'.[28] His ingenious interpretation might well represent a disguised form of 'bull' in the modern sense of the word. Another of his theories explained the tale of the great 'mountain-beasts' known as the Centaurs. According to the popular version of this tale, the Centaurs had been born when Ixion (a god-like man) had raped and impregnated a Hera-like cloud.[29] Ixion had ended up being confined in the Underworld (bound to a revolving wheel) whilst the cloud gave birth to the first Centaur. The name Centaur thus derived from *Kent-auros*, meaning 'prick-air'.[30] But Palaiphatos substituted the etymology *Ken-tauros* and was able thus to argue that the Centaurs were actually cowboys who had 'pricked' some troublesome 'bulls' with their hunting javelins and thus earned the nickname 'bull-prickers'![31] By a similar trick of etymology, Palaiphatos explained that Scylla, the sea-monster who had attacked the sailors on Odysseus' ship, was not a monster at all but rather the name of a pirate ship.[32]

Less far-fetched, perhaps, was Palaiphatos' theory of the monster Chimera, which was described by Homer as having the foreparts of a lion, the midriff of a goat, and the rear of a serpent, and with breath like 'a blast of blazing fire'.[33] According to Palaiphatos, this fiery Chimera had been a volcanic mountain in Anatolia.[34] (Unfortunately, his theory begged the question of how this monster came to be in the Underworld belching out fire and smoke.)

Another writer who favoured allegories of the etymological kind was Dionysios Skytobrachion (3rd century BC), who went to town on the myth of Jason and the Argonauts. In his book *Argonautai*, he made a determined effort to explain away all of the story's supernatural features. The fire-breathing, brass-footed bulls (*tauroi*) of king Aietes, which had supposedly been created by the god Hephaestus, became the guards of king Tauros ('The Bull'), equipped with bronze armour (and presumably with a fiery temper).[35] The never-sleeping serpent (*drakon*) that guarded the Golden Fleece was likewise identified as a guard named Drakon.[36] Simplicity itself. And as for the magical flying ram, from which Helle had fallen into the sea and drowned, Skytobrachion suggested that this had actually been a ship, of which the figurehead had been a ram; thus Helle had not fallen into the sea from the sky, but had rather fallen overboard during a nasty bout of *mal de mer*.[37]

The effect of all these commentaries was to gradually undermine the supernatural foundation of the Greek myths, thus setting the stage for historicisers such as Prodicus (see earlier) and, in due course, the Sicilian writer Euhemerus (early-3rd century BC). It was the latter who asserted that the gods had been kings, queens and heroes of an earlier age, deified by the people in honour of their magnificent achievements. Euhemerus, in turn, then set the stage for further writers who rewrote the myths of the past as if the gods had indeed been human kings and queens. These writers, as noted in chapter one, included Diodorus Siculus (1st century

BC), Philo of Byblos (2nd century AD) and, to a certain extent, Plutarch (1st century AD). We must also add Strabo (1st century BC) who, influenced perhaps by Skytobrachion, held steadfast to the view that the voyage of Jason and the Argonauts had simply been an exaggerated account of a colonisers' quest for gold.[38] The supernatural elements of this and other Greek myths were being marginalised by the historicist movement.

The Rational Age

A more positive product of this rational Greek age was the formulation of new theories about how the cosmos began. Traditional religion was about to give way to philosophy, at least among the intellegentsia.

From the late-7th century onwards, one philosopher after another began to abandon the old stories of the Olympian gods and substitute in their place new scientific statements about the beginning of the world. To some, it was evident that nothing had been brought into existence by any kind of god; rather, everything had appeared spontaneously by a process of 'nature and chance'.[39] To others, however, the world had obviously been created by an intelligence that is best described by the modern term 'God'. This supreme being was conceived sometimes as a 'sacred Mind' (*Nous* or *Pronoia*), sometimes as an 'unlimited Sphere' (*Sphairos*), sometimes as a 'divine craftsman' (*Demiourgos*), and sometimes simply as 'the One' or 'the God'. According to some, he or it had set things in motion and then retired; according to others, he or it had continued to steer all things by way of intelligent thought.

One of the earliest of these alternative theorists was Alcman, a Spartan poet of the 7th century BC. Little of Alcman's work has survived, but it would seem that he penned an unusual cosmogony in which Thetis – a goddess of the deep sea – was the creator of the world order.[40] Equally intriguing is Alcman's idea that the original state of the world had been 'a confused, unformed mass', presumably a confusion of waters (since Thetis was a sea-goddess).[41] Significantly, the underlying idea seems to have drawn upon the non-mainstream religion of the Orphics, whose mythical leader Orpheus had once sung of 'how, in the beginning, Earth, Heaven and sea were confounded in a common mass together'.[42]

Other philosophers had no place at all for Olympian deities such as Thetis. In the works of the Milesians (from the Ionian town of Miletus), the focus fell instead on resolving one vital scientific question: what was the ultimate nature of things? In other words, from what single elemental material was the world derived? Was it perhaps earth, air, fire or water?[43]

The first of this Milesian trio was Thales (*c.* 624-546 BC), who is widely regarded as the founder of Greek scientific reasoning. According to Thales, the primary substance and the first cause of all things had been water, which possessed the two critical attributes of life and motion.[44] In addition, he spoke about a soul-substance, saying 'the All has soul in it and is full of *daimones* [i.e. gods or spirits]'.[45] Quite what Thales meant is unclear and nowhere did he provide a connected account of how water, or soul-substance, had given rise to the All. One possibility, according to modern scholars, is that Thales was influenced by the cosmogonies of Egypt and Babylonia, in which the first god personified a primordial cosmic ocean.[46] Another possibility is that he drew his ideas from certain strains of thought within the Orphic religion.[47] Some of the Orphics, too, believed that the first principle had been water, from which there had formed a slime or mud that hardened into earth.[48] And the Orphics, too, believed that there was a vital relationship between water and the soul-substance. One Orphic reference reads cryptically: 'Water is death to soul and soul to water. From water comes earth, and from earth water again, and from that soul, quitting the vastness of *aither.*'[49]

The second great Milesian philosopher was Anaximander (*c.* 611-547 BC). He differed from Thales in believing that water was secondary and that the first principle and the first cause of all things had been a fifth element (i.e. something beyond earth, air, fire or water). Anaximander christened this fifth element *physis*, which he understood to be 'the nature of things' and the animating principle of the world.[50] It seemed an appropriate name for the elusive soul-substance.

But Anaximander went further and built a basic cosmogony around his first principle. In the beginning, he suggested, the elements of earth, air, fire and water had not had actual existence but potential existence, all being contained within a primeval undifferentiated mass which was the fifth element. He called this mass 'the Unlimited' (*Apeiron*), implying that it had had no beginning, middle, nor end.[51] But there had begun in this Unlimited a kind of nuclear reaction which caused the four elements of earth, air, fire and water to come into existence as independent elements. This reaction had begun in a nucleus or seed (*gonimon*), in which heat and cold had become antagonistic towards one another.[52] Consequently, the mass of the Unlimited had been differentiated. The cold had become a watery mass of earth, enveloped in vapour; the heat had become a sphere of flame enclosing the whole, as bark surrounds a tree. The mass of the Unlimited had then been torn apart, as the sphere of flame burst and threw off rings of fire.[53] Eventually, the fire had dried out the Earth, causing the seas to shrink back. Life had then begun in the muddy water and, in due course, it had evolved into land animals such as man.

The third of the Milesian philosophers, after Thales and Anaximander, was Anaximenes (6th century BC). He adapted Anaximander's scheme, suggesting that the primary substance *physis* took the form of air.[54] On this little needs to be said, other than to point out, as modern scholars have done, that this air was not simply the mundane air (*aer*) that exists on the Earth but rather a higher form of cosmic air (*aither*) that was no different in concept from the soul-substance.

A different theory altogether was proposed by Heraclitus, 'the dark philosopher' (*c.* 535-475 BC). Heraclitus despised conventional religion in all its forms and was sceptical, too, about non-mainstream religions, i.e. the various mystery cults. He was fascinated, however, by the search for the ultimate nature of things, and thus he proposed his own highly individual theory. Rejecting the Milesian theories about *physis*, water, and air, Heraclitus suggested that the first cause of all things had been fire. In one of his most famous lines, he wrote: 'This world order, the same for all, no-one among gods or men has made, but it always was, and is, and it always shall be. (It is) an everlasting fire, kindling in measures and going out in measures.'[55] But Heraclitus envisaged this ever-living fire in an aethereal sense (just as Anaximenes envisaged his air). For him, fire was the essence of the soul-substance itself.[56]

It should also be mentioned, in passing, that Heraclitus recognised the importance of fire in a cataclysmic context, hence his suggestion that the world was always being renewed by huge conflagrations that occurred every 10,800 years.[57]

After Heraclitus came Anaxagoras and Empedocles, who provide yet further astonishing examples of cataclysmic cosmogonies.

Anaxagoras (*c.* 500-428 BC) was another philosopher who had no place for the old Olympian gods, asserting instead that the Universe had been set in motion by Mind (*Nous*). Echoing Anaximander's concept of the Unlimited, Anaxagoras declared that originally, the four elements of earth, air, fire and water had been thoroughly commingled together in the form of tiny homogeneous particles, such that no individual element could be distinguished. Thus the first words of his book were: 'All things were together'.[58]

In the beginning, said Anaxagoras, the Universe had tilted towards the south 'in order that some parts might become uninhabitable and others habitable'.[59] It was the task of Mind (*Nous*) to transform the commingled homogeneous particles into separate elements, which might then recombine in ways suitable for the development of life on Earth. Mind had brought about this transformation, he said, by setting things moving 'in a whirling motion'.[60]

What did Anaxagoras mean when he said that the Universe had 'tilted towards the south'? To the modern eye, this might seem like a reference to the Earth tilting upon its axis. But in the context of the ancient world, it is far more likely that Anaxagoras was referring to the archetypal idea of Heaven having fallen to the Earth – according to the convention that Heaven was in the north and Earth in the south.[61] The implication is that 'All things were together', originally, in Heaven, and that the whirling motion had caused the primordial commingled elements to become separated in their fall from Heaven to Earth.

This cataclysmic cosmogony inspired one particular commentator to suggest that the Greek gods personified cataclysmic events, exactly as I am proposing in this book. The unnamed philosopher, writing *c.* 400 BC, aimed his comments at the human-like gods of the Orphic myths (i.e. Time, Phanes and Night), and asserted (in the words of Walter Burkert) that 'the mythical persons and their sexual and violent actions are in reality names describing an Anaxagorean cosmogony'.[62]

Empedocles (*c.* 490-430 BC) provides further indisputable evidence of cataclysmic cosmogony in his astonishing account of a primeval Sphere (*Sphairos*) which he called God (*Theos*). Originally, this Sphere had been bonded together in perfect harmony by Love. But then, as Empedocles put it: 'in the fullness of the alternate time, set by the broad oath, Strife leapt up to claim his prerogatives, and Strife waxed mightily in the members of the Sphere – they all trembled in turn.'[63] As a result of this discord, the primeval Sphere had given birth to the elements of earth, air, fire and water, which began to separate and then recombine.[64] Thus were created all material things on the Earth.

At the same time, said Empedocles, the soul-substance had been cast down from the heavenly region of light into 'the roofed-in cave', i.e. the Underworld, and in due course of time began to dwell in all living things, including man.[65] Empedocles thus regarded himself – his soul or true self – as an exile from God and a restless wanderer on the Earth. 'From what honour and from what a height of bliss have I fallen', he wrote. 'I left *there* to wander *here* among mortals... I wept and wailed when I saw this unfamiliar country, where there dwells murder, and wrath, and hosts of other misfortunes.'[66]

This disaster, said Empedocles, had happened because of the turning wheels of time and fate (*moira*), along with a mysterious 'broad oath' (presumably of the gods of Heaven and Earth).[67] But that which Strife had divided, he declared, Love would draw together. Thus, in the end,

Love would conquer Strife and cause the four elements of earth, air, fire and water to be reunited in a reconstructed Sphere.[68]

To a modern reader, this Empedoclean theory of the torn-apart Sphere sounds remarkably like the explosion of a celestial body, albeit expressed in mystical terms. Did the Greeks, too, understand their cosmogonies in cataclysmic terms?

As regards Anaxagoras, we can state this was indeed so. Anaxagoras, we should recall, was the man indicted in Athens for saying that the Sun and the Moon were glowing lumps of metallic stone. In 467 BC, he had predicted, in advance, the fall of meteorites (one of which landed at Aegospotami) based on a hypothetical association with a comet that had appeared in the sky. Intriguingly, certain ancient authorities inform us that Anaxagoras' knowledge of astronomy, and meteorites in particular, came from Egypt, where a meteorite cult had been practised for more than two thousand years (see chapter ten).[69] Accordingly, Anaxagoras is on record as saying that meteoritic stones fell from a whirling mass of such materials in the heavens, and that the fall of these stones had seeded the beginning of all life on Earth.[70] These ideas are thoroughly Egyptian.

The upshot of all this is that when Anaxagoras described the Universe tilting towards the south and the elements falling to Earth in a whirling motion, he was surely equating the two elements of earth and fire with the form of meteorites (although this admittedly begs the question of what the elements air and water would have symbolised).

By the same token, under the Anaxagorean perspective, the tearing apart of the God-Sphere (in Empedocles' scheme) and the breaking apart of the Unlimited (in Anaximander's scheme) would certainly have been understood in physical terms, i.e. representing a real cataclysm in the heavens (albeit one that had occurred in far-distant, mythical times).

In summary, the Greeks' non-mainstream cosmogonies offer abundant evidence of a belief in a cataclysmic event that occurred at the beginning of time (i.e. a cataclysm of the mythical variety), and this sits well with my suggestion that cataclysms could be the key to the mainstream Greek religion (based on the poetry of Homer and Hesiod). The only real puzzle is why so many sceptics of the 7th-5th centuries BC failed to guess that the violence-loving gods might have personified the cataclysmic forces of nature (the only exception being an unnamed writer *c.* 400 BC, in respect of the Orphic gods and Anaxagorean cosmogony – see earlier). How could so many eminent minds have overlooked such an obvious solution? To this question we will assuredly return. But, firstly, let us edge forward in time and see what Socrates and Plato had to say about cataclysms and the Greek gods.

Chapter Three Summary

* It is not being suggested that the Greeks actually witnessed any large-scale cataclysms. Rather, they believed in theoretical cataclysms that had occurred aeons ago, during the mythical age of the gods.

* Between the 7th and 5th centuries BC, the Greek intellegentsia began to grow increasingly uncomfortable with Homer and Hesiod's portrayal of the gods as human-like beings engaged in violent and immoral actions. The ensuing debate in Greek society demonstrates that the meaning of the Olympian religion was no longer understood in the public domain.

* Many Greek intellectuals rejected the Olympian religion and proposed alternative, non-mainstream cosmogonies in its place. These theories, of how the cosmos began, were saturated with cataclysmic imagery.

* Anaximander described how the cosmos began when a primeval mass, the Unlimited, was torn apart, producing a sphere of flame and rings of fire.

* Anaxagoras described how the Universe had tilted towards the south 'in order that some parts might become uninhabitable and others habitable'. This is a classic portrayal of Heaven falling to Earth.

* Anaxagoras believed that meteorites had fallen from the heavens and seeded the beginning of all life on Earth. He thus declared that the Sun and Moon were glowing balls of metal.

* Empedocles described how the cosmos began when a primeval God-Sphere had been torn apart, giving birth to the elements of earth, air, fire and water, and a fifth element soul, which had all been cast down into the Underworld.

CHAPTER FOUR

SOCRATES AND PLATO

**The one aim of those who practise philosophy in the proper
manner is to practise for dying and death.**
(Socrates, in Plato's *Phaedo*, mid-4th century BC)

It was against a background of a failing Olympian religion and a growing
interest in non-mainstream cosmogonies that the great philosopher
Socrates set out on his own personal quest for the truth about the nature
of reality. Born in Athens in 469 BC, Socrates grew up to become well
acquainted with orthodox Greek customs and traditions, including the
literature of Homer and Hesiod in which the tales of the human-like gods
were recited. As a young man, however, Socrates became exposed to a
brave new world of enlightened philosophy in which the old ways of
thinking were being questioned, on the authority of men such as Thales,
Anaximander, Pythagoras and Heraclitus.

Socrates was fascinated by these nascent sciences, in particular with
the theories which attempted to explain the beginning of all things and
the nature of matter. But he eventually came to realise that all these
grand theories were merely speculations which sometimes contradicted
each other and, for the most part, were beyond proof. Moreover, Socrates
began to perceive that scientific knowledge of this ilk was of limited use,
for it could not be used for the betterment of mankind.

Disenchanted with scientific cosmogony, Socrates shifted his attention
to the nature of man's being. Taking his lead from the famous inscription
at Delphi, 'Know Thyself', Socrates began to study the human condition,
both in himself and others, and eventually came to the conclusion that
man's true self was not the body (as most Greeks believed) but the soul
(*psyche*).[1] This meant, in effect, that man was an immortal being, for his
soul could survive the extinction of the body and continue to live, either
by reincarnation or by a disembodied existence in the 'other world'.

This, it must be said, was not a new idea. In fact, the theory of the immortal soul and its destiny in the afterlife had long been propounded by the followers of Orpheus and Pythagoras and, in more recent times, had been promoted by Heraclitus, Empedocles and Parmenides. In the Orphic religion, for example, it was believed that the soul of man had originated in Heaven but had fallen to Earth where it became trapped in the body (hence the saying that the body was a tomb, *soma sema*).[2] In due course of time, when the body died, the soul would go down to the house of Hades (in the Underworld), where it would be judged by the gods. The most evil souls would then be cast down deeper, into the pit of Tartarus (i.e. Hell), whilst the less culpable would be assigned to less torturous regions. But as for those souls who had lived an extremely pious life on Earth, they would be released from the Underworld and would ascend to a pure and eternal dwelling place in Heaven.

But such ideas about the soul and the afterlife were restricted largely to the intellectual fringes of society during the 5th century BC, and most Greeks continued to believe that *the body* was the self, and that the grave held nothing but darkness and gloom.[3] In Athens, the upwardly mobile classes were obsessed by materialism and the pleasures of the senses, and gave little thought to punishments or rewards in a life yet to come.

Socrates' great achievement was to bring the debate about body versus soul to the streets of Athens. In public forums, he would engage the leading citizens of his day in philosophical discussion, and make them think deeply about what they believed and why they believed it.[4] This was an approach that antagonised many people, but others were attracted to Socrates' characteristic charm, modesty, and razor-sharp wit, and were moved by his exhortations to nurture their souls as well as their bodies. Among these latter men was Plato, who would become Socrates' greatest supporter and one of the greatest philosophers who ever lived.

Plato

Born in Athens in 428 BC,[5] Plato enjoyed an education that was afforded by an aristocratic background and, on coming of age, he began to take a profound interest in politics and philosophy. At that time, Socrates was an old man in his sixties, and enjoyed a formidable reputation as a master of verbal dialectics. Plato had no hesitation in joining the entourage of Socrates, whom he would later describe as 'the wisest and justest man of that time'.[6] He could never have guessed that his prestigious mentor would soon be sentenced to death by a jury of his own citizens.

In 399 BC, at the age of seventy, Socrates was arrested and put on trial in Athens. The charge against him read: 'Socrates does wrong because he does not believe in the gods in whom the city believes, but introduces other divine powers (*daimonia*); he also does wrong by corrupting the young'.[7] Despite an eloquent personal defence to these trumped-up charges, the jury pronounced Socrates guilty and sentenced him to death. After a month's delay in prison, the noble philosopher drank the hemlock and breathed no more.[8]

In shock and disgust, Plato left Athens and went travelling, possibly as far afield as Egypt and Libya.[9] In 388 BC, at the age of forty, he visited southern Italy and Sicily where he forged an important contact with the Pythagorean community.[10] The following year, 387 BC, Plato returned to Athens and founded a new school of philosophy, the Academy, which quickly became a leading centre of Greek thought and would remain so for nearly a thousand years.

Figure 2.
PLATO

On the face of it, Plato was a prodigious writer. A modern compilation of his works (the Hackett edition, published in 1997), extends to 1,745 pages and contains no less than forty-two books, plus three additional compilations of letters, definitions and epigrams respectively, all of which were attributed to Plato in ancient times.[11] The vast majority of these forty-two books take the form of dialogues, in which most of the conversation is directed not by Plato but by Socrates. These dialogues, in the absence of any written work by Socrates himself, provide nearly all that is known about Plato's mysterious mentor.[12]

Herein lies a problem for, as modern scholars are at pains to point out, it is virtually impossible to tell if a certain idea belonged to Socrates or to Plato (as the author of the dialogues).[13] Where does Socrates' philosophy end and Plato's begin? Or, alternately, what overlap exists between the two mens' ideas?

In fact, the picture is more complicated, for modern scholars recognise that many of 'Plato's works' were not actually written by Plato himself, but by other Socratic and Platonic writers. In fact, of the forty-two books mentioned above, modern scholars believe that between thirteen and sixteen should be attributed to 'the school of Plato' rather than Plato per se.[14] One thus has to distinguish between the ideas of Plato and the ideas of *the school of* Plato, and then distinguish these ideas from the ideas of Socrates himself. This would be all very well if there were a reliable method by which scholars could judge the authorship of individual books, but there is not.

For what it's worth, my own feeling is that Plato personally authored just three books: *Timaeus*, *Critias* and *Laws* (the latter being unpublished at the time of his death in 347 BC). In my opinion, all of the other books, including the famous treatise *Republic* which acts as a direct prelude to *Timaeus*, *Critias* and *Laws*, were authored by other Socratic writers, with the credit later being given to Plato as the founder of the Academy for philosophical studies of this kind.[15]

In this scenario, *Republic* becomes a linchpin work. This book – a ten volume exposition on a theoretical form of future government known as 'the ideal state' – was probably written by one or more Socratic writers (senior to Plato) based on their many years of discussions with Socrates himself (Plato, it should be emphasised, was a relatively young man, not quite thirty years of age, when Socrates died). The ideal state would thus have been Socrates' big idea, and in time, via *Republic*, it would have provided the inspiration and impetus for Plato's own writings.

Thus, in my view, Plato would have begun his writing career with the linked pair of books *Timaeus* and *Critias* in which he told the story of Athens and Atlantis in order to illustrate Socrates' ideal state in action. Later, towards the end of his life, and after many years of failed political machinations, he would have written his final work, the twelve-volume exposition entitled *Laws*. In this huge book, unfinished at his death, Plato reformulated the legal improvements that had been urged by Socrates in *Republic*, in order to facilitate the implementation of the ideal state in the real world.

Whilst this might strike some people as an extremely sceptical theory of Plato's authorship, it nevertheless underlines the point that we do not truly know who wrote what, but what we do know is that Socrates, Plato and the school of Plato were all involved, in various ways, in what is today known as 'the Platonic corpus'. Bearing this in mind, we shall now

take a look at the ideas that were attributed to Socrates and Plato in four
key areas: cosmogony; the Theory of Forms; cataclysms; and the gods.

On Cosmogony

According to Plato, everything in the Universe had to have sprung from
some initial principle, which must, by definition, have been something
capable of springing into motion by itself.[16] This principle, he said, had
been an aethereal fifth element called 'soul' (*psyche*), which could be
defined as 'motion capable of moving itself'.[17] It had been 'born long
before all physical things' and was therefore 'the first cause to which
everything owes its birth'.[18] Accordingly, soul-substance was the original
cause of all movement in the Universe, and had stirred into motion
everything in the heavens and all life on Earth, including mankind.[19]

This, in itself, was not a new theory, for similar schemes had been
proposed earlier by the Orphics and by the Milesian philosophers Thales,
Anaximander and Anaximenes (see chapter three). But more to the point,
Plato's theory was rooted in the mystical beliefs of the Pythagoreans.

In *Timaeus*, Plato had Timaeus (a Pythagorean character) elaborate on
the theory of the soul-substance and build a whole cosmogony around it.
The Universe, said Timaeus, had been designed in the form of a sphere
by a unique God whom he called the *Demiourgos* (literally 'the divine
craftsman').[20] God had then filled this sphere with soul, which he created
in the centre and settled outwards in seven layers.[21] At the same time,
God had used earth, air, fire and water to create the celestial gods within
the sphere of the Universe.[22] The Earth was the eldest of these physical
gods by virtue of its position at the centre of the Universe (note here the
Greek concept of the geocentric Universe).[23] Around it, God had created
the Sun, the Moon and the five other planets (i.e. those known to the
Greeks), which he had set orbiting within the sphere of the Universe, one
in each of the seven layers, to act as instruments of time.[24] At the same
moment, God had created the stars, mostly out of fire, and had fixed
them on the outermost surface of the universal sphere 'to be a true
adornment for it'.[25]

Finally, God had completed his creation of the living Universe by
joining souls to bodies and setting the whole thing in motion:

> "The soul was woven together with the body, from the centre on out in
> every direction to the outermost limit of the Universe, and covered it
> all around on the outside. And, revolving within itself, it initiated a
> divine beginning of unceasing, intelligent life for all time."[26]

It should be noted that, under this scheme, the Sun, the Moon and the planets were not just 'earth and stones', as certain sceptics maintained (based on the theory of Anaxagoras), but were driven by souls, which were either contained inside the celestial bodies or attached to them invisibly.[27] All of the celestial bodies were thus living beings, all of them contained in a Universe which was itself defined as 'the Living Thing'.[28] This Universe was filled and surrounded by the soul-substance.

Intriguingly, Plato had Timaeus declare that God (*Demiourgos*) had fashioned this Universe, and everything in it, in accordance with a pre-existent model which he called 'the *real* Living Thing'.[29] The visible Universe might seem to be an eternal living thing, but it had in fact been created in the image of the pre-existent model – the one and only truly eternal and changeless 'real Living Thing', which he also called 'That which *is*'.[30]

As for God (*Demiourgos*), whilst his name meant literally 'the divine craftsman', this did not necessarily mean that God had taken physical form in order to create the Universe. Rather, according to Timaeus, God had been the first principle and had thus been 'motion capable of moving itself'. God was thus Soul with a capital 'S', in its purest and most original sense; but he was also Intelligence, in its original and most pure sense, for it was evident to the Pythagoreans that the Universe had been devised by an intelligent mind.[31]

Let us recall, at this juncture, the first principle of all Socratic and Platonic philosophy, that man's true self was an immortal soul, trapped inside a mortal body. How did this come to be? Where did man's soul come from? In *Timaeus*, Plato had the Pythagorean character Timaeus provide the answer:

> The spirit raises us up away from the Earth and toward what is akin to us in Heaven, as though we are plants grown not from the Earth but from Heaven. In saying this, we speak absolutely correctly. For Heaven is the place from which our souls were originally born...[32]

Man's soul had thus had a heavenly origin (in line with the cosmogony cited above), whereas his body had been born from the Earth.

A similar theory had been advocated by Socrates in *Phaedrus* (a book attributed to Plato but originating in all likelihood from earlier Socratic writers). In the beginning, said Socrates, all human souls had been circulating in the company of the heavenly gods. But then had come the moment of the fall from Heaven to Earth. Just before that moment, the souls had been shown a 'spectacular vision' and had been able to gaze for a moment at 'sacred revealed objects that were perfect, and simple, and unshakeable and blissful'.[33] But this heavenly glory had been lost.

Upon their fall from Heaven, the souls had become imprisoned inside
Earth-born bodies and many, in time, had forgotten their celestial origins,
remaining only dimly aware of the perfect objects which they had once
glimpsed there.[34]

Once again, it should be stressed that this theory of man's soul was
nothing new, and nor was it exclusive to Socrates and Plato. Empedocles,
for example, had already put forward a very similar scheme, in which he
imagined his soul to have been cast down from the heavenly region of
light into 'the roofed-in cave', whereupon he had become a restless
wanderer on the Earth. 'From what honour and from what a height of
bliss have I fallen', he wrote, 'I left *there* to wander *here* among
mortals'.

In fact, Empedocles, like Socrates and Plato, was drawing upon a
theory of the soul that had long been a tradition among the Orphics and
the Pythagoreans. And these brotherhoods, in turn, had almost certainly
acquired the idea from the Egyptians.[35]

The Theory of Forms

We turn now to the Theory of Forms – an off-putting appellation if ever
there was one – which is, without a doubt, the most difficult concept to
face the reader of Plato. Not only is it poorly understood by the modern
experts, but also it is awkwardly devoid of any explanation in layman's
terms. The casual reader of Plato may, at a first pass, wonder what on
earth Socrates and Plato were talking about.

In fact, the Theory of Forms (also known as the Theory of Ideas) is
perfectly straightforward. It is essentially the belief that everything on
Earth is an inferior copy of an original, supreme and heavenly master-
copy. In effect, it amounts to a philosophical counterpart of the popular
religious concept of the fallen paradise.

The classic example of this is the concept of justice. On Earth, there is
no single definition of justice, but rather a proliferation of systems which
reflect differing human conceptions of what justice should be. Thus the
typical Western idea of justice might differ considerably from that of the
the Muslims. What then *is* 'Justice' with a capital 'J'? Did it even exist?
According to Socrates and Plato, Justice *did* exist, but not among the
manifold copies of justice which had been invented by races of men here
on Earth. Instead, true Justice was to be found in Heaven. It was literally
an *arche*-type – a first type or original form. Hence the name given to
this kind of Socratic and Platonic thinking – the Theory of Forms.

The Theory of Forms concept finds its best illustration in Socrates' story of the Upper Earth which is told in one of Plato's works, *Phaedo*. The setting is Socrates' final hours in an Athenian jail cell, where he entertains a group of visitors which includes two prominent members of the Pythagorean community. As he faces death by drinking hemlock, Socrates shares his vision of what happens to man upon death. The soul, he says, is evidently immortal and experiences a variety of fates on the other side. Whilst the majority of souls go to dwell in the Underworld (either for a while or permanently), a privileged few are allowed to ascend to an upper realm which is called 'the true Heaven, the true Light and the true Earth'.[36] This Upper Earth, says Socrates, stands in stark contrast to the familiar Earth down here. Everything in it is brighter and purer. The trees are greener, the plants are more beautiful, and the stones and minerals are absolutely perfect. In contrast, the Earth down here is a spoiled and corroded world of ugliness and disease, where even our most precious stones are but crude fragments of the heavenly originals.[37]

In this myth, the Upper Earth (Heaven) symbolises what Platonic scholars like to call 'the world of Forms'. It literally *is* a world, albeit a perfect one – the prototype of the world that we know. Hence the idea that it was 'the true Earth' which contained the archetypes (the Forms) for everything that existed down here on our own imperfect Earth. And hence the idea that the Upper Earth had the shape of 'a spherical ball', in accordance with the Pythagorean belief that Earth, Heaven, planets and stars were spherical bodies.[38]

Socrates envisaged the 'world of Forms' as the sole *un*changing thing in an ever-changing Universe. In a nutshell, it was 'the realm of what *is*' and 'that which *is*'.[39] But intriguingly, Socrates declared that "that which *is* is invisible."[40] Thus the 'world of Forms' signified an invisible Heaven raised above a visible Earth.

Yet more intriguingly, Plato had his Pythagorean character Timaeus elevate the status of the 'world of Forms' from a living prototype planet to a living prototype Universe. Hence, in *Timaeus*, it was suggested that God (*Demiourgos*) had fashioned the visible Universe, and everything in it, in the image of a pre-existent model which was the one and only truly eternal and changeless living thing, 'the real Living Thing', and 'That which is' (see earlier).

All of this tied in with Plato's theory of the body and the soul, and the destiny of the soul in the afterlife. The body, said Plato, 'participated' in the ideal of its heavenly Form, but its share of the ideal fell short of the original, as did the share of all material things on Earth. The body was thus prone to corruption, decay and death. The soul, however, consisting of an aethereal substance, had received a full share of the heavenly

Forms, and was thus pure and immortal by birthright. Moreover, since the soul had originated in Heaven, it belonged in Heaven.

Plato's philosophy was not philosophy as we know it today, but rather a much higher kind of art, which he called 'true philosophy' or 'divine philosophy'.[41] The life of a man on Earth, he said, was no life at all because the Earth was an inferior, ever-changing copy of the heavenly 'world of Forms'; it was a snare for mankind. True life, and true reality, said Plato, existed only in Heaven. Thus the aim of true philosophy was not to gain knowledge of changeable things on Earth but rather to gain knowledge of 'That which always exists'.[42] And to do this, the true philosopher had to recognise that the whole Universe was an allegorical riddle, where everything visible was a coded allegory of 'That which *is*', which was invisible.

In line with Pythagorean thinking, Plato suggested that man should seek knowledge of 'That which *is*' by studying the principle of constancy wherever it occurred (or nearly occurred) in nature, notably in number, geometry, solids, astronomy and harmonic motions.[43] But to see the truth beyond the cosmic allegory, one had to look with the soul or the mind, not with the eye, and this required remembrance of the fact that one's true self was the soul.

In *Republic*, Socrates suggested that the true philosopher might indeed obtain knowledge of 'That which *is*' during his lifetime by means of an arduous series of initiations in Pythagorean doctrines. In his vision of the ideal state, Socrates proposed that true philosophy should be a necessary qualification for rulership. The aspirant to kingship would become fully initiated in his fiftieth year, and would then use his skills to govern the city in accordance with the perfect heavenly archetypes of the 'world of Forms':

> "Then, at the age of fifty, those who have survived the tests... must be led to the goal and compelled to lift up the radiant light of their souls to what itself provides Light for everything. And once they have seen the Good itself, they must each in turn put the city, its citizens, and themselves in order, using it [the Good] as their model."[44]

True philosophers were thus regarded as a series of messiah-like figures who would deliver an ideal era of peace and prosperity on Earth, but all the time preparing their own personal souls for an ultimate elevation to Heaven.[45]

Such, then, is the Theory of Forms which is generally regarded today as Plato's big idea. And yet it must be stressed that, in most respects, it was hardly an original concept. In fact, a similar theory had been taught a century earlier by Pythagoras (580-500 BC) and elements of it had been expounded quite recently by Parmenides of Elea, who is today regarded as one of the founding fathers of metaphysics. Parmenides, for his part, had dismissed the world of senses in favour of a primary metaphysical 'world of Truth' which could not be perceived by the eyes but by reason alone.[46] In a famous poem, he described how his soul had been taken into the Underworld where 'the Goddess' had revealed to him the true nature of reality. The world of the senses, he was told, was an illusion. The real world – or world of truth – was a metaphysical Sphere, which was single, stationary and unchanging. This heavenly world was 'the Thing which *is*', and it was apparent to reason alone.[47] All of this terminology should sound strikingly familiar, for it constitutes one of the central planks of Plato's Theory of Forms.

Interestingly, Parmenides described the 'world of Truth' as a Sphere, just as Socrates described his 'world of Forms' as a 'true Earth' which had the shape of 'a spherical ball'. In both cases, the philosophers were drawing on older ideas, notably Pythagorean cosmology in which the Earth and the Universe were conceived to be spheres.

As for the idea that archetypal Forms had been copied from Heaven to Earth, this, too, was not original to Socrates or Plato. Empedocles, for example (born just a few decades before Socrates), described how the four elements of earth, air, fire and water had been born on Earth as the result of a crisis in Heaven, when the Sphere of God had been torn apart by the forces of Strife (see chapter three). Once again, the Sphere makes an appearance, but this time not as an invisible world. Rather, it seems to have signified a physical object which was blown apart by a cataclysm. The scenario finds an echo in the Orphic myth in which Orpheus sings of a time when earth, sky and sea had been joined together in one mass, but had then been separated 'as the result of deadly disruption'. One is reminded, too, of Anaxagoras' cosmogony in which all things had been together until the Universe (by definition a sphere) had tilted towards the south (downwards) 'in order that some parts might become uninhabitable and others habitable' (see chapter three). Did this myth signify a physical cataclysm and a transmission of the elements from Heaven to Earth? If so, Anaxagoras' cosmogony would bear a striking similarity to Plato's Theory of Forms, in which Heaven had provided the archetypes for all life on Earth.

On which note, we turn to the subject of cataclysms per se. To what extent did Socrates and Plato recognise the importance of cataclysms in the Greek myths?

On Cataclysms

There are several important references to cataclysms in Plato's works, notably in the books *Statesman*, *Timaeus*, *Critias* and *Laws*.

To begin with *Statesman* (sometimes known as *Politicus*), one of the main features of the book is an elaborate myth concerning the beginning of the Universe, when great cataclysms occurred on the Earth. The story is told by an unnamed philosopher from Elea (the city of the leading metaphysician Parmenides). He describes a great turning point in the history of the Universe, when its direction of rotation was reversed and there occurred destruction of all living creatures on a tremendous scale:

> "Necessarily, then, there occur at that time cases of destruction of other living creatures on a very large scale, and mankind itself survives only in small numbers. Many new and astonishing things happen to them, but the greatest is the one I shall describe, one that is in accordance with the retrogradation of the Universe, at the time when its turning becomes the opposite of the one that now obtains."[48]

This cataclysm, apparently, marked the end of the golden age.[49]

Incidentally, the reference here to the Universe changing its direction of rotation is consistent with a reference given by Herodotus (5th century BC) who, in his discussion of Egyptian prehistory, spoke of the Sun moving from its wonted course on four occasions 'twice rising where he now sets, and twice setting where he now rises'.[50] In *Statesman*, the philosopher from Elea says something remarkably similar in respect of the myth of the quarrel between Atreus and Thyestes:

> "It is said that the Sun and the other stars actually began setting in the region from which they now rise, and rising from the opposite region, and that then, after having given witness in favour of Atreus, the god changed everything to its present configuration."[51]

Such was the cataclysm described in *Statesman*, and it conforms with the model which I outlined at the beginning of chapter three. That is to say, it does not sound like a historical cataclysm, but rather bears mythical and archetypal characteristics. It is essentially a mythical cataclysm – one that preceded the creation of the present race of man.

Moving on, it must be said that it is hard to find further cataclysmic references in the Socratic dialogues, until, that is, we come to the books *Timaeus*, *Critias*, and *Laws*, which just happen to be the three books most likely to have been authored by Plato (in my opinion). At this point, we hit the cataclysmic jackpot.

In *Timaeus* and *Critias*, cataclysms form the vital backdrop to the telling of the story of Athens and Atlantis. The first reference appears close to the beginning of *Timaeus*, where Critias recites the tale of how Solon went to Egypt and received the story of Athens and Atlantis from the priests at Sais. One priest in particular finds it necessary to explain to Solon why Egyptian traditions go back such a long way. The oft-quoted speech of the old priest runs as follows:

> "Ah Solon, Solon, you Greeks are ever children... Your souls are devoid of beliefs about antiquity handed down by ancient tradition... The reason for that is this: there have been, and there will continue to be, numerous disasters that have destroyed human life in many kinds of ways. The most serious of these involve fire and water, while the lesser ones have numerous other causes. And so also among your people the tale is told that Phaethon, child of the Sun, once harnessed his father's chariot, but was unable to drive it along his father's course. He ended up burning everything on the Earth's surface and was destroyed himself when a lightning bolt struck him. This tale is told as a myth, but the truth behind it is that there is a deviation in the heavenly bodies that travel around the Earth, which causes huge fires that destroy what is on the Earth across vast stretches of time... after the usual number of years, there comes the heavenly flood..."[52]

This is a remarkable passage in many ways, not least because Plato is hinting that a myth – here the myth of Phaethon crashing the chariot of the Sun-god – can contain a truth, notably a cataclysmic truth. More to the point, Plato is suggesting that a cataclysm can be portrayed poetically by means of human-like imagery (the anthropomorphic god and his chariot). This is the very idea that I have been advocating in this book.

Returning to *Timaeus*, the Egyptian priest goes on to mock the Greeks who remembered only one flood (Deucalion's flood), whereas in fact there had been many earlier ones.[53] This idea of sequential cataclysms then forms the basis for the story that follows. The first to be mentioned is the cataclysm that destroyed Atlantis:

> "... excessively violent earthquakes and floods occurred, and after the onset of an unbearable day and a night, your entire warrior force sank below the earth all at once, and the Isle of Atlantis likewise sank below the sea and disappeared."[54]

After this, there had been two further cataclysms, and then a third, much greater cataclysm – 'the greatest of these devastating floods' – namely the flood of Deucalion.[55] All of these cataclysms Plato referred to without batting an eye lid.

The books *Timaeus* and *Critias* contain several other cataclysmic allusions, too, but such is their subtlety that it needs a trained eye to spot them.[56] These will be discussed later, in due course.

We turn, then, to *Laws*, where Plato develops further the theme which he introduced in *Timaeus*, namely that the Athenians had forgotten the exploits of their remote ancestors owing to the cataclysms which had decimated the intervening populations.[57] In *Laws*, book III, Plato asks his friend Clinias whether he thinks there is any truth in the old tradition 'that the human race has been repeatedly annihilated by floods and plagues and many other causes, so that only a small fraction of it survived.' The answer from Clinias is affirmative: "Yes... all that sort of thing strikes everyone as entirely credible."[58]

Such, then, are the references to cataclysms in Plato's works, and they demonstrate the interest that Plato had in the cataclysmic prehistory of the Greeks. But before we leave this subject, a few words should be said about two particular cataclysm myths with which Plato would have been very familiar: firstly, the myth of Deucalion's flood, and, secondly, the myth of the torture of Prometheus.

As noted earlier, Plato refers to the flood of Deucalion as the last in a sequence of four cataclysms that had devastated the world. He does not go into detail about this great flood, for the story was well known among the Greeks of his day. For the modern reader, however, an elaboration of this myth is required.

The myth of Deucalion's flood was one of the most widely known flood stories in ancient Greece and it bears some remarkable parallels to the Hebrew myth of Noah's Ark. It was well known as early as the 5th century BC (as will become evident in a moment), but most of the story as we know it derives from late sources such as Apollodorus and Pausanias.[59] The versions of the myth differ in some details, but the following account gives the broad picture.

In days of yore, it was said, the chief god Zeus had become angry with the race of men and decided to destroy them by unleashing a great flood upon the face of the Earth. But a man named Deucalion had learned of the impending flood and he therefore built an ark, into which he and his consort Pyrrha embarked. The rain then began to fall and Deucalion's ark was carried away by the floodwaters as they rose up to cover the surface of the whole world. Eventually, after nine days, the waters subsided and the ark became grounded atop a sacred mountain. Thereupon, the hero and the heroine disembarked, offered the obligatory sacrifice to the gods, and prayed for the re-creation of mankind. At this point, something very strange happened. The myth runs that Themis – a Mother Earth-goddess

– appeared to Deucalion and Pyrrha and advised them: "Shroud your heads and throw the bones of your mother behind you!". Immediately, the heroic couple did as they were told. They picked up stones from the river bank and, while covering their heads, threw these stones over their shoulders. The stones thrown by Deucalion became men; the stones thrown by Pyrrha became women. And thus the human race was re-created. One of the oldest references to the event appears in the odes of Pindar (5th century BC, almost a century before Plato's time) where the poet sings briefly, in passing, of the flood and the creation as follows:

... by decree of Zeus...
there came Deucalion and Pyrrha,
Down from (Mount) Parnassus' height,
And first they made their home,
Then without wedlock founded a people of one origin,
A race made out of stone;
And from a stone they took their name...
... now the tale runs
That Earth's dark soil was flooded by the waters,
But by the arts of Zeus, their strength suddenly ebbed again,
And of that race were sprung your ancestors...
And they have ruled ever since those days,
Kings of this their native land.[60]

Here, Pindar cites the same curious tradition referred to earlier, namely that Deucalion and Pyrrha had created men and women from stones.[61] Why, we might ask, did they not populate the world by means of sexual intercourse? Did Deucalion and Pyrrha not fancy each other? Amusing quips aside, this is surely an anomaly, and an important one to boot.

Plato would have known the Deucalion flood myth very well, and he would also have been quite familiar with the myth of the torture of the god Prometheus. In the 5th century BC, Aeschylus – the so-called 'creator of tragedy' – had lent a cataclysmic setting to this age-old tale in his play *Prometheus Bound*.[62] The play focuses on the torture of Prometheus, who had been chained by Zeus to 'the Caucasus Mountain', and it climaxes with an awesome cataclysm in which Prometheus, still attached to his mountain, is plunged down into the Underworld amidst earthquakes, thunderbolts and violent storms, which shake the foundations of Heaven and Earth.[63] Prometheus' fate is to be tortured in the Underworld for an eternity, or at least until the end of the age when a further cataclysm might elevate him from the murky depths.[64]

What these myths demonstrate – the myth of Deucalion and the myth of Prometheus – is the importance of cataclysms in marking the endings and beginnings of world ages. We have already seen, in chapter one, how this idea underpins the succession myths of the gods in Hesiod's *Theogony*. But further to that, it now becomes clear that the myth of the destruction and re-creation of man forms part of the same cataclysmic equation. Consider. In the myth of Deucalion's flood, the human race is re-created from stones in the aftermath of a cataclysm. And yet Plato tells us, on the good authority of the Egyptians, that Deucalion's flood was preceded by three earlier cataclysmic events. Moreover, Plato tells us that people were already in existence, fighting the war between Athens and Atlantis, even before the first of these cataclysms. How can this be? A clue, perhaps, lies in the striking parallel between Plato's story of destructive cataclysms and the myth told by Hesiod four centuries earlier, in which the human race had been preceded by four mythical races known as the golden, silver and bronze races respectively, each of whom had been destroyed, apparently by a series of cataclysmic events, and then renewed by the will of Zeus. Whether these peoples were real or mythical is a moot point. If they were real people, then the cataclysms would, in theory, represent historical events. But if they were mythical people, then the cataclysms, too, would be mythical, and would belong to a pre-human era, as I have argued in other examples earlier.

In summary, Plato affirms that cataclysms were extremely important to the Greeks in determining the endings and beginnings of their world ages. Nevertheless, his stories beg the question concerning the nature of the peoples who populated the Earth during the earlier ages. Who, or what, were these ancient peoples? And who, or what, were the gods?

Let us turn now to the subject of the myths of the gods, and see what Socrates and Plato had to say about them.

On the Myths of the Gods

To begin with Socrates, it should be emphasised, firstly, that he did not subscribe to the view that the gods had been human or human-like beings, as had been intimated by Homer and Hesiod. In fact, he declared that these stories were essentially false, since it was impossible, in his view, that the gods could have engaged in violence and illicit sex, as the poets had maintained.[65] Nevertheless, Socrates did recognise that the poets' accounts contained some truth; hence, for example, in *Republic* (his treatise on the ideal state), he said of the stories told to children that: 'They are false on the whole, although they have some truth in them'.[66]

What truth did Socrates see in these myths? Unfortunately, Socrates never drew a firm conclusion on this matter, or at least he did not express it publicly. Furthermore, he mocked those who were in the business of making extensive allegorical critiques of Homer and Hesiod, and simply stated that: "I have no time for such things."[67] Recognising that such an investigation would prove a laborious but fruitless task, he decided to accept instead 'what was generally believed'.[68] It is therefore intriguing to read what Socrates said at his trial in 399 BC: "I do believe in the gods as none of my accusers do."[69] Unfortunately, this statement was never elaborated upon by Socrates.

Plato, like Socrates, was a devout believer in the gods, and he did not tolerate atheists gladly (as is made evident in his book *Laws*). But he was very careful in what he said about the gods. For example, in *Timaeus*, Plato uses the Pythagorean character Timaeus to broach the subject thus:

> "As for the gods [*daimones*], it is beyond our task to know and speak of how they came to be. We should accept on faith the assertions of those figures of the past who claimed to be the offspring of gods... even though their accounts lack plausible or compelling proofs... we should follow custom and believe them... Accordingly, let us accept their account of how these gods came to be and state what it is."[70]

Plato then goes on to narrate, in the briefest terms, the traditional myth of how the generations of gods had been born, beginning with the primal union of Gaia and Ouranos (Earth and Heaven). And he then attempts to reconcile this traditional myth to his own theory of a single and unique God, whom he calls the *Demiourgos* (literally 'the divine craftsman'). It is this *Demiourgos*, says Plato, who was the true 'maker and father' of the gods. Moreover, this *Demiourgos* had created the celestial gods, too, i.e. the Sun, the Moon, the planets and the stars.

How exactly did *Demiourgos* bring these daemonic and celestial gods into being? Plato does not offer any kind of layman's explanation, but rather sets out one of the most cryptic cosmogonical treatises of all time. The uninitiated reader is left baffled and confused.

And yet Plato, in his aforementioned discussion of the gods, did offer one vital insight into their divine nature by confirming something that was never made explicit by Homer or Hesiod. The Olympian gods, he said, were invisible, aethereal beings.[71]

Such is the importance of this statement to solving the mystery of the gods that the exact words of Plato should be cited.

Firstly, Plato has Timaeus describe how *Demiourgos* created the Sun, the Moon, the planets and the stars, concluding as follows:

"Let this be the conclusion of our discussion of *the visible and generated gods.*"[72]

Next, Plato has Timaeus turn his attention from this 'heavenly race of gods' (Sun, Moon, planets and stars)[73] to the pantheon of Olympian gods, saying:

"As for the other gods [*daimones*], it is beyond our task to know and speak of how they came to be... Earth and Heaven gave birth to Oceanus and Tethys, who in turn gave birth to Phorcys, Kronos and Rhea and all the gods in that generation. Kronos and Rhea gave birth to Zeus and Hera, as well as all their siblings... These in turn gave birth to yet another generation."[74]

Note the distinction in these passages between the celestial gods (Earth, Sun, Moon, planets and stars) and the Olympian gods (*daimones*). The former group Timaeus treats separately, calling them 'the visible and generated gods (*theoi*)', 'who make their rounds conspicuously'.[75] The latter group he differentiates, calling them spiritual gods (*daimones*) 'who present themselves only to the extent that they are willing'.[76] The implication is that the Olympians, by nature and for the most part, were invisible.

In what sense were the Olympian gods invisible? In Plato's appendix to *Laws*, the distinction is repeated and here, thankfully, the nature of the *daimones* is clarified:

But as to the first gods, those that are visible, greatest, most honoured, and most sharply seeing, we must declare that these are the stars, together with all the celestial phenomena we perceive. After them, second, come *daimones* (gods made of *aither*). And third come those beings made of air, whose task is to mediate between gods and humans... Both these kinds of living beings – those made of *aither* and those made of air – are wholly imperceptible. Even when they are close by we cannot see them.[77]

In other words, the gods of Olympus were made of an indeterminate fifth element called *aither*; they were invisible in an aethereal sense.

Nor do we have to rely totally on Plato for confirmation of this vitally important detail. Further confirmation comes from an Orphic fragment in which the Olympian gods are born to an Earth-goddess called Night (an *alter ego* of Gaia):

She [Night], in her turn, bore Gaia and broad Ouranos, and brought to light *those that were invisible* and the race to whom they belonged.[78]

There we have it. The Olympian gods were born from the Earth, and yet they were invisible, aethereal beings. But why? What does this mean? In the absence of any layman's explanation, the reader of the Greek myths is seemingly invited to put two and two together, and draw for himself the logical conclusion. And as far as this reader is concerned, the clues all point towards a cataclysmic explanation. After all, the gods were born from the Earth; the Earth was impregnated by Heaven (i.e. by a fall of the sky); and thus the gods came forth amidst bright light, blazing fire and loud noise to become invisible, aethereal entities. It thus seems to me that the original god of Heaven, Ouranos, personified a cataclysmic fall of the sky, in much the same way as Phaethon and the chariot of the Sun-god did. And this fact we have on Plato's authority:

> "And so also among your people the tale is told that Phaethon, child of the Sun, once harnessed his father's chariot, but was unable to drive it along his father's course. He ended up burning everything on the Earth's surface and was destroyed himself when a lightning bolt struck him. This tale is told as a myth, but the truth behind it is that there is a deviation in the heavenly bodies that travel around the Earth, which causes huge fires that destroy what is on the Earth across vast stretches of time..."

Is this the secret behind the genesis of the gods?

Chapter Four Summary

* Plato's 'true philosophy' owed a great deal to earlier, non-mainstream ideas, particularly those of the Pythagoreans and the Orphics.

* A common theme underlying much of Plato's philosophy is that of a fall from Heaven to Earth, whether it be the fall of the soul, or the fall of the archetypes from the 'world of Forms'. These ideas echo the idea of a lost paradise, which is found in many ancient cultures around the world.

* Socrates portrayed the 'world of Forms' as a perfect Earth-like planet; Plato portrayed it as a pre-existent model for the entire Universe; in both cases, the 'world of Forms' had the form of an invisible sphere. There is a parallel here to Parmenides' 'world of Truth', which also took the form of an invisible sphere. But an even more intriguing parallel is the Sphere of Empedocles, which was apparently torn apart by a physical cataclysm.

* Plato gave several prominent mentions to cataclysms in *Timaeus*, *Critias* and *Laws*, underlining their importance in marking the endings and beginnings of world ages. In addition, he referred to the myth of Deucalion's flood in which a cataclysm marked the creation of human beings (from stones thrown by Deucalion and Pyrrha).

* According to Plato, the myth of Phaethon crashing the chariot of the Sun-god into the Earth stood as a cipher for a cataclysmic event. Might this be the key to understanding other Greek myths, e.g. the impregnation of Gaia by Ouranos?

* Plato stated that the Olympian gods (*daimones*) were invisible, aethereal entities. Were these ghost-like beings born from the Earth as the result of cataclysms?

CHAPTER FIVE

THE SECRET SOCIETY

Holy things are shown to holy men. Such things are not permitted for the profane until they are initiated through the rites of knowledge.
(Hippocrates, 5th century BC)

So far, so good. Our review of alternative Greek cosmogonies during the 7th-4th centuries BC has yielded further evidence of the importance of cataclysms (albeit conceived in a mythical rather than a historical way). Nevertheless, the spotlight now falls back onto the mainstream religion, which was based upon the poetry of Homer and Hesiod. We have already seen, in chapter one, how cataclysms were fundamental to Hesiod's *Theogony* and implicit in his idea of the world ages. And yet we have seen in the previous two chapters that, with the exception of a passage in Plato's *Timaeus*, and one fragmentary comment on the Orphic myths, the Greeks *failed* to rationalise their gods as personifications of cataclysmic powers. An explanation is thus called for. If I am right that the gods personified the cataclysmic forces of nature, why is there such a paucity of thinking along these lines in the Greek writings? In this short chapter, I will argue that there is a very good reason for this apparent oversight in the shape of five important factors that were at work in Greek society – ignorance, piety, conservatism, taboos and secrets. If the reader will bear with me, I will demonstrate how these factors, together, could explain the Greeks' failure to disclose publicly the true meaning of the myths.

Piety and Ignorance

If the disposition of the Greek populace in the matter of religion had to be encapsulated in just two words, those words would have to be 'piety' and 'ignorance'. Almost without exception, the Greeks practised their religious rites and rituals with devout and heartfelt piety, worshipping the gods whom their ancestors had always worshipped – the Sun, the Moon, and the invisible *daimones*, the Olympians, whom they envisaged as human-like beings. But the Greeks also practised these rites and rituals in utter ignorance of what their gods truly were. No-one understood why they worshipped an invisible race of gods, and few ever bothered to ask. To the spiritually minded, on the one hand, belief in the gods was a matter of faith; to them it was evident that the world was controlled by greater, invisible powers, and it was equally evident that such powers were beyond the comprehension of man. To the rationally minded, on the other hand, it was clear that some important phenomenon must lie behind the myths; for, otherwise, why had so many great temples and cults been established in the gods' honour? Surely the gods *had* to exist. Other folk, meanwhile, believed in the gods as a matter of familial duty. It was enough for them that their parents and grandparents had worshipped the Olympians, and enough for them that their most ancient ancestors – the legendary heroes of the Trojan War – had attested to the gods' existence.

In this sea of ignorance, education was no life raft. Those who had studied Homer and Hesiod at first-hand were no more enlightened than the rest of the populace. In fact, if anything, they were more confused. How could the gods, supposedly paragons of virtue, have engaged in illicit love affairs and committed such despicable crimes as rape, torture, theft, violent assault, and even patricide? Traditional Greek religion was no thinking man's religion. Indeed, if one thought too hard about it, one became an agnostic or an atheist (see chapter three).

But let us assume that a small élite of people – an intellegentsia of priests, philosophers and politicians perhaps – *did* know the truth about the Olympian gods. Let us assume that a few people had been told this truth (e.g. by initiation into the greater Mysteries) or had worked it out for themselves. Assuming that this was the case, why did such persons not broadcast this important truth to their fellow citizens or indeed preserve it in writing for posterity?

A plausible explanation, as we shall now see, lies in the phenomenon of religious taboo.

Taboo

In his book *From Solon to Socrates*, the Hellenist Victor Ehrenberg writes that: 'In matters of traditional beliefs, the ordinary (Greek) people were most conservative'.[1] In other words, they were not well-disposed towards new ideas about the gods.

This conservatism was often enshrined in law, but it manifested itself mostly in the form of established social conventions which dictated how people ought to behave towards the gods. In this respect, the number one dictum was to 'honour the gods' by means of the requisite sacrifices, offerings and prayers.[2] In Greek cities, all such activities were performed with the greatest care so as not to offend the protecting deities.

Proper respect towards the gods was deemed necessary not just at formal occasions, but *at all times*. As Pindar once sang: 'It becomes man to speak fair words about the gods'.[3] One of the strongest taboos in Greek society forbade people to insult or criticise the gods, or to question the gods' existence.

This taboo worked in a complex way. Dramatists, for example, were a law unto themselves, and could say just about anything. For example, a notable scene in Euripides' play *Helena* features the chorus singing of men who had explored the farthermost reaches of the world and yet still could not decide 'what is god, or not god, or something in between'.[4] The lines verged on atheism, but Euripides could argue that he was merely parodying the confusion of the masses and/or reflecting their subliminal doubts about religion. Thus he got away with it.

However, when the sophist Protagoras aired much the same doubts about the gods in the form of prose – 'I cannot say whether the gods exist or not, or what they are like in form' – his book was burned in the streets of Athens and he was put on trial, accused of not believing in the city's gods. The taboo of proper speaking about the gods clearly affected prose writers differently from dramatists.

The dangers of discussing the gods in the form of prose are nowhere more evident than in Plato's works, where the author expresses his thoughts about the gods in the most guarded of terms. In *Cratylus*, for example, Socrates is made to say: "let us leave the subject of the gods, because it frightens me to talk about them", whilst in *Minos* he states: "there cannot be anything more impious, nor anything over which one should take more precautions, than this – being mistaken in word and deed with regard to gods and, in second place, with regard to demi-gods."[5] Similarly, in *Laws*, the Athenian (Plato) deals most carefully with the myth of Dionysus being driven mad by Hera, saying: "this sort of story I leave to those who see no danger in speaking of the gods in such terms",[6] and he goes on to note the widespread view that "so far as the supreme deity and the Universe are concerned, we ought not to bother our heads hunting up explanations, because that is an act of impiety."[7]

As far as the prose writer was concerned, to disrespect the gods was to risk social exclusion, banishment from the city or worse. The indictment of Protagoras has already been mentioned. In addition, at around the same time, there was the celebrated case of Anaxagoras, who declared that the Sun and the Moon were nothing but glowing balls of metal. Such was the conservatism, piety, and power of the people that Anaxagoras was forced to flee Athens after thirty years' teaching there.

In such circumstances, it would have taken a brave or foolish man to rationalise the identity of the Olympian gods, especially with a theory that bore the hallmarks of truth. If we were to assume, then, that a Greek élite did possess knowledge of such a truth, e.g. that the gods personified violent, cataclysmic forces, it is hardly likely that they would have aired that knowledge in public. For to do so would only have succeeded in antagonising an ultra-conservative and ignorant public.

The upshot of this is that rationalists, for the most part, spoke of the gods with extreme caution, and were ever reluctant to disclose their best ideas in writing. As Plato wrote in a letter towards the end of his life:

> Whenever we see a book... we can be sure that if the author is really serious, the book does not contain his best thoughts; they are stored away with the fairest of his possessions. And if he has committed these serious thoughts to writing, it is because men, not the gods, 'have taken his wits away'.[8]

Why, then, did Plato suggest that the myth of Phaethon crashing the Sun-god's chariot was an allegory for a cataclysmic deluge from Heaven? Was this rationalisation not a dangerous idea, in view of the taboo which we have discussed? Perhaps so. But Plato was careful to use an Egyptian priest as his mouthpiece and Phaethon, moreover, was a fairly minor deity. Thus did Plato minimise the risk of ostracism.

Secrets

Did Plato know more? Did he know the truth about the gods and yet hold back from declaring it, in the context of public hostility towards new and unconventional ways of thinking?

There are indeed many indications that certain secrets about the gods were maintained in ancient Greek society. In Hesiod's *Theogony*, for example, the Muses make an intriguing claim in the opening lines:

> "We know how to tell many lies that sound like truth, but we know how to sing reality, when we will."[9]

Could this perhaps mean that the Muses would speak to the *uninitiated* with mischievous lies ('lies that sound like truth') but to the *initiated* with truth ('reality')?

A few Greek philosophers indeed suggested that the myths of the gods contained some deeper, secret meaning. In Plato's work *Protagoras*, for example, we find an interesting reference to the fifth century philosopher Protagoras – a man who was renowned as the master of the sophists (in those days, *sophistes* meant simply 'wise man' and lacked the negative connotations which it was given later in the writings of Plato).[10] The wise old sophist boasted to Socrates of the secrets of his forebears, which had been concealed in the words of the poets:

> "I maintain that the art of the sophist is an ancient one, but that the men who practised it in ancient times, fearing the odium attached to it, disguised it, masking it sometimes as poetry, as Homer, Hesiod and Simonides did, or as mystery religions and prophecy, witness Orpheus and Musaeus... All of them, as I say, used these various arts as screens out of fear of ill will... But I believe they failed, in fact, to conceal from the powerful men in the cities the true purpose of their disguises. Meanwhile, the masses, needless to say, perceive nothing, but merely sing the tune their leaders announce."[11]

After uttering these astonishing lines, Protagoras then went on to suggest that religious secrets had been concealed in the works of the ancient poets – secrets which were still being encoded into various contemporary works of Greek music.[12] And he made an explicit link between Homer and Hesiod and the mystery religions, as if to suggest that both shared a common bond with his own art of sophism (i.e. the art of being wise).

Socrates, too, dropped a hint that a secret truth stood behind the myths. In *Republic*, he explained to his friend Adeimantus that this secret truth had no place among the populace of his ideal state, and yet it might need to be divulged to a small circle of initiates:

> "Telling the greatest falsehood about the most important things does *not* make a fine story. I mean Hesiod telling us how Ouranos behaved, how Kronos punished him for it, and how he was in turn punished by his own son [Zeus]. But even if it were true, it should be passed over in silence, not told to foolish young people. And if, for some reason, it *has* to be told, only a very few people should hear it – pledged to secrecy... – so that their number is kept as small as possible."[13]

The allusion here, and in the earlier statement by Protagoras, was to the mystery schools which were situated throughout the ancient world. In Greece, those we know of comprise: the Mysteries of Demeter and Persephone (which included the famous mystery school of Eleusis, near Athens), the Mysteries of the Kabeiroi (also known as the Samothracian Mysteries), the Mysteries of Orpheus, the Mysteries of Apollo, the

Mysteries of Dionysus, the Mysteries of Hecate and the Mysteries of Pythagoras. All of these mystery schools affirmed by their very existence that secrets of a religious nature were being maintained in Greek society.

What was the big secret? According to an Orphic hymn, the final level of initiation into the Mysteries comprised a 'Secret of secrets' which was 'a knowledge of the true God'.[14] Such was the nature of this 'Secret of secrets' that it came as a total surprise, even to the initiate who was fully prepared. The revelation, we are told, 'startled their ears' and 'overturned their preconceived opinions'.[15] But what exactly was this revelation? What was the 'knowledge of the true God'? Unfortunately, neither the Orphics nor any of the other mystery cults saw fit to record their secrets in writing – something which was expressly forbidden (perhaps for the reasons cited earlier). Thus, we can only guess at the truth from the few scattered clues that we have: for example, the Eleusinian tradition of the divine child whom the goddess of the Dead bore in the middle of the night in the midst of a brilliant fire.[16] But here, as in other Mysteries, the secret of the gods was concealed behind symbols and code-words which made no sense to the uninitiated. Thus was the mystery preserved.

In practice, the vast majority of candidates were initiated only into the 'outer mysteries', and only a few candidates were permitted to learn the 'inner mysteries' and the 'Secret of secrets'. Hence the saying in respect of the Mysteries of Dionysus and of Demeter at Eleusis: 'Many are the wand-bearers but few are the Bakchoi'.[17] These privileged few were the ones who had passed all the tests and who could be trusted not to 'spill the beans' in public.

The Problem

Clearly, it was of paramount importance that the 'Secret of secrets' should not be divulged to the common populace. But why was this such a serious matter? The answer, I believe, lies in the ignorance, piety and conservatism of the populace who were fervent in their support of the Olympian religion and hostile toward those who would rationalise it. The psychological state of the masses is summed up perfectly by Isaac Newton's famous comment on the history of religion:

> It is the temper of the hot and superstitious part of mankind in matters of religion ever to be fond of mysteries, and for that reason to like best what they understand least.

In short, the taboos of society required that the truth of religion, i.e. the *rationalisation* of religion, be kept as a secret. To speak of the gods as personifications of cataclysms – or whatever else the secret might be –

would have been disrespectful in the eyes of the masses, who believed passionately that the gods were invisible, immortal, human-like beings. To explain what the Olympians were in any kind of rational terms would have been to break the taboos of Greek society and incur the wrath of an ignorant and fanatical populace. A mystery school would have ended up proscribed; a philosopher indicted and banished.

The Greek government of the day was surely aware of this situation. Take, for example, Pericles, who ruled the city of Athens between 461 and 429 BC. He did not share the superstitious faith of the masses, but was rather a rationalist, who counted among his friends Anaxagoras and Protagoras – two of the leading rationalists of his day.[18] Pericles accepted Anaxagoras' idea that the Sun and Moon were simply glowing balls of metal, and he might well have been privy to the secret of the Olympian gods. And yet it was totally out of the question that Pericles would have enlightened the ignorant populace by forcing his intellectual ideas upon them. Indeed, if he had attempted such a folly, the people would surely have forced him from his post. Much better, as the saying goes, to let sleeping dogs lie.

This, we must surmise, was the situation in ancient Greece. Ignorance prevailed in society at large, whilst secrecy prevailed among the mystery school illuminati. It was not a case of the public being deceived by an élite. Rather, it was a case of the political and religious illuminati giving the public exactly what they wanted – a wonderful mystery in which it could credulously believe (see Isaac Newton's quote earlier). Everyone thus could live happily in peaceful co-existence – government, mystery schools and ignorant populace alike – just as long as no-one revealed the secrets of the gods in public.

Deductions

Such, then, I believe, was the Greek world of Socrates, Plato and their forebears, and, if the reader will accept it, he will wish to reflect on two important deductions that follow. The first deduction is that any Greek in the fortunate position of knowing the secret of the gods would have been quite mad to declare it publicly. This would explain why no-one among the Greek intellegentsia ever stated openly, in writing, that the gods were personifications of cataclysmic forces (although Plato came close to so doing).

The second deduction stems from the ignorance of the masses. If the situation was indeed as I have outlined, then the implication is that the early Greeks (say at the time of Homer and Hesiod, around the 8th and

7th centuries BC) did not themselves witness any large-scale cataclysms of the falling sky variety. On the contrary, in order that the Olympian religion should remain as mysterious as it evidently was, it is necessary to presume that any such cataclysms predated the beginning of Greek civilisation by some considerable time.

This, it turns out, is a plausible scenario. In the following chapters, we will see how the Greek myths of the gods and the cosmos were, in fact, borrowed and adapted from earlier civilisations of the Near East. To all intents and purposes, then, Greek religion originated outside Greece and long before the 8th century BC.

Chapter Five Summary

* The Greek populace, with the possible exception of a small élite, was entirely ignorant about the nature of the gods and the meaning of their religion.

* In Greek society, the number one dictum was to honour the gods, and it was considered taboo to insult them, criticise them, question their existence, or rationalise who or what they were. To break this taboo was to incur the wrath of an ignorant and ultra-conservative populace, risking indictment or ostracism, as in the famous cases of Protagoras and Anaxagoras.

* It is possible that a genuine secret, concerning the meaning of the gods, was preserved in the Greek mystery schools and that a small number of men were initiated into it. But in the face of ignorance, conservatism and fundamentalism in society at large, these illuminati would have been quite mad to pronounce the secret publicly. This would explain why no-one declared openly that the gods were personifications of cataclysmic forces.

* All the evidence would suggest the early Greeks did not themselves witness any large-scale cataclysms of the falling sky variety. Rather, it seems likely that the cataclysmic myths of the gods and the cosmos were borrowed and adapted from earlier civilisations.

CHAPTER SIX

IN SEARCH OF THE GRAIL

It seems incredible now that many of the best minds in 19th century Europe could envisage myths only as encoded descriptions of clouds passing over the Sun or torrents sweeping down hill-sides.
(G.S. Kirk, *The Nature of Greek Myths*, 1974)

An overall picture of the Olympian gods is beginning to emerge. Some, such as Ouranos, seem to have personified a falling sky, whilst others seem to have been invisible, immortal, aethereal entities, who were born from the Earth in cataclysmic circumstances. Significantly, perhaps, the Olympian gods came to reside upon an equally invisible, immortal and aethereal Mount Olympus in the heavens. If my hypothesis is right, the key to understanding these myths of the gods is the primeval cataclysm in which the original Heaven fell to Earth.

However, before we take this idea further, we should take into account the views of modern scholars (Hellenists). What conclusions have they drawn about the Greek myths of the gods and the cosmos?

The surprising answer, in view of the corpus of myths which I have outlined so far, is that modern scholars do *not* consider cataclysms to have been important in Greek religion and are generally hostile to cataclysmic theories of the Greek myths. Let the reader bear in mind, then, that I have broached a very contentious theory, which will – if it is validated – overturn a long-established field of academia. Nevertheless, the opinion of modern scholars is not to be gainsaid lightly, and it is important to understand what theories they hold and how they arrived at them.

Accordingly, we shall see, in this chapter, how numerous scholars, over the last three hundred years, have gone in search of a grand solution to the mystery of the Greek myths, much in the manner of an Arthurian quest for the holy grail. We will consider the various holy grails that have been proposed and examine the reasons why each, in turn, has been declared false. We will discuss the reasons why cataclysm theories have never been seriously considered as a solution to the mystery. And we shall take note of the fact that scholars have long abandoned their quest for the holy grail, and are nowadays without a single satisfactory theory for the phenomenon of the Greek gods.

Nevertheless, modern scholars, in adopting alternative, more patient approaches to the mystery of the Greek myths, have alighted upon one particular approach that has borne considerable fruit over the last fifty years, and that approach goes by the name of comparative mythology. At the end of this chapter, we will see that extensive and fundamental parallels have been discovered between the Greek myths and those of the ancient Near East (Mesopotamia, Anatolia and Egypt), and we will see how this discovery promises to revolutionise our understanding of the Greek myths. It is through an understanding of ancient Near Eastern religions, I will argue, that we can resolve the mystery of the Greek gods and thereby pave the way for a new understanding of Plato's story of Athens and Atlantis.

But first we must review three hundred years of scholarly confusion.

Monolithic Theories

For reasons that shall be discussed in due course, modern studies of ancient Greece have tended to avoid gazing directly at the Greek gods per se, but have rather focused on what scholars call 'mythology', i.e. the study of myths. One of the clearest definitions of the term 'myth' is that supplied by Professor Lowell Edmunds:

A Greek myth is a set of multiforms or variants of the same story...
The story concerns the divine or the supernatural or the heroic or
animals or paradigmatic humans living in a time undefinable by
human chronology.[1]

As Edmunds observes, myths relate to 'a time undefinable by human chronology', when gods and semi-divine heroes controlled the Earth. It is in this chronological sense that 'true myths' can be distinguished from other types of traditional tale which are commonly classified as 'legends' or 'folk tales'.

Modern research into ancient myths (in their entirety) began during the 18th century, at which time the field was dominated by the study of Greek myths in particular. At that time, and onwards throughout the 18th and 19th centuries, a constant in myth research was the belief that all myths were explainable by a single universal or 'monolithic' theory. In particular, two theories were dominant: firstly, that all myths were based on real human history;[2] and secondly, that all myths were allegories of mundane natural events.

Advocates of the real human history approach have often been called Euhemerists after the Greek historiciser Euhemerus. The ideas of these scholars received a considerable boost in the late-19th century from Heinrich Schliemann's archaeological discoveries at Troy and Mycenae, followed in the early-20th century by Sir Arthur Evans' discoveries at Knossos in Crete. Euhemerists were quick to jump on the bandwagon by asserting that the tales of the Trojan War were recollections of actual historical events pertaining to the Dark Ages of the 2nd millennium BC.

Alongside the Euhemerist theory there ran the entirely different idea that all myths involved allegories of meteorological and atmospheric phenomena. The most famous exponent of this theory was the German Orientalist Friedrich Max Müller who, in the 19th century, claimed that all myths alluded to the movements of the Sun and the stars. In support of his theory, Müller suggested that many myths had suffered, over the course of time, from 'a disease of language' and hence the original meaning of many myths had become unintelligible.[3] It was an ingenious idea, but unfortunately it did not address the vitally important fact that the solar and astral deities of the Greeks ranked second to the Olympian category of gods.[4]

As the 19th century drew towards a close, the tide of academic opinion began to turn against the historicists and nature allegorisers. In 1884, Andrew Lang published the first of several books in which he criticised the theory of nature allegories and put forward a radical new theory in its place.[5] According to Lang, all myths were to be regarded as a kind of primitive science, i.e. the myths represented ancient explanations of the processes of nature. This, yet again, was a monolithic theory, which could stand up only by flooring all of its opponents.

Meanwhile, scholars were busily founding a new approach to ancient myths which would culminate in yet another monolithic theory. Wilhelm Mannhardt in Germany and E.B. Tylor in England were advocating the idea that ancient religion had its roots in animism – a primitive belief in supernatural spirits and demons.[6] Moreover, they argued, animism itself had its roots in ancient agrarian rituals in which primitive peoples used to call upon 'the vegetation spirit' to bring about a successful harvest.

This approach brought about a revolution in the study of myth. The key to myth, it was said, was ritual, and the key to ritual was agriculture. Hence the myths of the dying-and-rising gods – widespread throughout the ancient world – could be explained as allegories of the annual death and rebirth of the crops.[7]

In England, these ideas were advocated by the so-called Cambridge School of scholars, among whom the most prominent were W. Robertson Smith, Jane Harrison and James G. Frazer. In the space of a year (1889-90), all three of these heavyweight scholars published studies urging that agricultural ritual was the key to ancient myths.[8]

James G. Frazer was destined to become the most famous scholar of the Cambridge School. In his epic work *The Golden Bough* (first edition 1890), Frazer advanced a new monolithic theory of ancient myths in which agricultural rituals were reconciled with the principle of kingship. In the beginning, he said, there had been a superstitious belief in the vegetation spirit, whom he called 'the Year Daimon'. Then there had come organised society, at which point the king became responsible for influencing the spirits or gods of vegetation in order to ensure a good harvest. This was accomplished by sympathetic magic, which was at the heart of ancient agricultural rituals. But beyond this Frazer argued that the king himself had to be reinvigorated every year by being killed off and replaced, at least in a symbolic sense. Only in this way could the ageing king maintain the strength of his magical powers, in order to continue influencing the Year Daimon. According to Frazer, this dual theory – of fertility magic and sacral kingship – could be used to explain all ancient myths. Over the course of the next twenty-five years, Frazer accumulated more and more support for his theories, and *The Golden Bough* expanded into no less than twelve volumes.[9] Frazer's ideas took the academic world by storm, and his ideas of fertility magic and sacral kingship became widely accepted as a monolithic explanation of myths during the first half of the 20th century. For a while, Frazer enjoyed the stature of a giant among scholars, and it seemed that the holy grail had finally been won.

Abandoning the Grail

Frazer's theory, however, had a fundamental weakness. In common with all those theories which had preceded it, it was monolithic and thus pretended to explain *all* ancient myths. Consequently, it was mutually incompatible with every other monolithic theory of myths, e.g. that they were historical events, or that they were allegories of meteorological/ atmospheric phenomena, or that they represented primitive science. If one theory was right, then the others had to be wrong (and vice versa). And yet the reality was that each theory had something going for it.

Eventually, after two and a half centuries of searching for the holy grail, scholars began to think that the grail probably did not exist.

In an influential study in 1974, the British scholar G.S. Kirk voiced the opinion of many:

> One could marshal scores of generalisations... each inconsistent with most of the rest, each purporting to offer a definition of the underlying essence of all myths everywhere. What is wrong with such attempts is not merely their arbitrary quality and lack of supporting evidence, but also, and even more serious, their unspoken assumption that myths are all of one kind, that there can and must be some universal explanation of the nature and purpose of all myths whatsoever.[10]

Kirk then went on to criticise his forebears, who seemed blind to the fact that ancient myths covered 'an enormous spectrum of subject, style and feeling'. It was an *a priori* probability, he stated, that myths would vary in 'their essential nature, their function, their purpose and their origin'.[11] But mythologists, in their ill-fated search for a monolithic theory, had been selective with the evidence, and had thus caused the entire field of mythological study to become badly distorted.[12] 'My own conviction', Kirk wrote, 'is that there can be no single and comprehensive theory of myths – except, perhaps, the theory that all such theories are necessarily wrong.'[13]

To make matters worse, such was the number of monolithic theories and the volume of words written about them that, by the early 1930s, scholars had become 'sated with mythical theory', as Kirk put it.[14] To paraphrase his comments, scholars were struggling desperately to keep their heads above a sea of existing data and, accordingly, they had little appetite for seeking out new data or new interpretations.

Kirk's view was to prevail. In the last decades of the 20th century, a consensus began to emerge that monolithic theories of Greek myth were not only wrong, in each and every case, but had collectively held back progress in the field.[15] After three hundred years of study, the only significant progress, said Kirk, had been a cutting back of the more outrageous speculations.[16] These 'negative gains' aside, 20th century scholars were in much the same predicament as their 18th and 19th century forebears; they could explain *some* of the myths, but their theories fell woefully short of explaining *the whole* phenomenon.

Current Theories

What, then, is the position today? What theories are Hellenists using to explain some, though not all, of the myths of the gods? The answer, not surprisingly, is that few of the old theories have been completely killed off. It would be fair to say that, in the graveyard of myth theories, many bones remain improperly buried and the ghosts of the old favourites are still dancing merrily upon their tombs.

The Euhemerist theory, for example, is still supported by many academics who continue to argue that real history lies behind many of the myths. A case in point is the tales of the Trojan War, as recounted in Homer's *Iliad*. Despite the supernatural setting of these events, hardly a voice is heard in academia today against the presumption that this war was a historical event, with the deeds of the heroes being but exaggerated accounts of human activities (on this point, contrast my approach to the Athens and Atlantis story in Part Four of this book). Furthermore, among the general public, the Euhemerist theory is as popular as ever, thanks largely to the widespread availability of Robert Graves' book *The Greek Myths* (1955), which remains the only thorough survey of the subject. Graves, who died in 1985, was an extreme Euhemerist, as the following examples will demonstrate. The tale of Ouranos impregnating Mother Earth, said Graves, was an allegory for a Hellenic invasion of northern Greece.[17] Kronos had been a Greek king, whilst the weapon-furnishing Cyclopes had been bronze-smiths and the Hundred-handers had simply been bands of fifty or a hundred men.[18] The tale of Perseus beheading Medusa had been an allegory for the Hellenes overrunning the shrines of the goddess.[19] The tale of Apollo vanquishing the monster at Delphi had been an allegory for the Greeks' capture of the Cretan shrine.[20] And the voyage of the Argonauts had described Greek trading ventures.[21] These examples could be extended ad nauseam in much the same vein. Whilst few scholars today would endorse such a dogmatic approach to all of the Greek myths, the ghost-like tentacles of Euhemerus and Robert Graves continue to spread their influence far and wide.

What about the theory of nature allegories? Here, again, the old monolithic theories have not been buried completely, although they have been down-rated significantly. Take Müller's theory about the Sun and the stars. Scholars recognise that the Greeks did worship the Sun, Moon and stars, and therefore they acknowledge that *some* of the myths *ought to be* allusions to the movements of these celestial bodies.[22] In a similar vein, James G. Frazer is nowadays regarded as 'a fallen giant', but his ghost still lives on. Scholars argue that *some* myths, though by no means all, are undoubtedly concerned with fertility magic and sacral kingship.[23]

Turning to specifics, there are two myths, in particular, that are widely agreed to be nature allegories. The first is the myth of Demeter and Persephone (it comes stamped with the authoritative approval of the

Encyclopaedia Britannica, no less).[24] The second is Hesiod's account of Ouranos impregnating Gaia. Both of these myths are worth examining in a little detail, in order to illustrate how the minds of modern scholars are working (or not, as the case may be!).

The story of Demeter and Persephone, briefly told, begins with Hades, ruler of the Underworld, abducting Persephone into his subterranean kingdom to become his wife. At this, the goddess Demeter (Persephone's mother) was outraged, and came down from heavenly Mount Olympus, causing a terrible drought to cover the face of the Earth. Immediately, Demeter began to search for her daughter, threatening to maintain the drought until Persephone was returned. Eventually, Hades was persuaded to release Persephone, the deal being that she would spend one third of each year in the Underworld and two thirds of it on Mount Olympus with her mother and the gods. Thus was Persephone released, at which event 'the whole Earth became weighted with leaves and flowers'.[25]

According to scholars, the interpretation of the myth of Demeter and Persephone is not controversial. As Walter Burkert writes: 'this myth has been understood, since antiquity, as a piece of transparent nature allegory: Persephone is the corn which must descend into the earth so that from seeming death new fruit may germinate; her ascent is the seasonal return of the corn.'[26] In support of this theory, scholars have cited certain details of the Eleusinian Mysteries, which were founded upon the myth of Demeter and Persephone ('the two goddesses'); firstly, there is the tradition that an ear of grain was shown to initiates as the symbol *par excellence* of the Mysteries;[27] secondly, there is a report that initiates were told to look to the sky shouting "Rain!" and down to the ground shouting "Conceive!".[28] (Nevertheless, we must ask ourselves why the Eleusinian Mysteries required oaths of secrecy if the initiatory acts symbolised nothing more than the simple act of rain fertilising the earth.)

The second example of a surviving nature allegory is the myth of Ouranos (Heaven) impregnating Gaia (the Earth). G.S. Kirk, who was generally ill-disposed towards nature allegories, had no doubts about this one, writing: 'the myth can be seen as a symbolic representation of the interplay between rain and soil that makes plants come to life and grow.'[29] In other words, Kirk felt certain that Ouranos had been the god of the clouds and that Gaia had been impregnated by rainwater. (It must be said, though, that the theory begs some important questions, such as the resultant tectonic stress in Gaia's womb and the ensuing cataclysmic battles between the gods of Heaven and Earth.)[30]

In addition to these fertility dramas involving water and earth, scholars also believe, on a more general note, that the Olympian gods personified the forces of nature or the institutions of society. To quote *Encyclopaedia Britannica*: 'They [the gods] were thought to control various natural or social forces: Zeus the weather, Poseidon the sea, Demeter the harvest, Hera marriage, and so on.'[31]

Further to the foregoing theories, which we might loosely term 'nature theories', there are three other kinds of theory that find some support among scholars today. Firstly, scholars accept that *some* myths are aetiological, i.e. they explain 'how things came to be', e.g. the founding of temples or cults.[32] To this category of 'just so' stories belongs the unburied bones of Andrew Lang's theory that myths were a kind of primitive science. Secondly, scholars accept that *some* myths are 'charter stories', i.e. they seek to legitimise political or social institutions, such as kingship or priesthood.[33] And thirdly, scholars accept that *some* myths are re-enacting the primordial moment of creation, as suggested by Mircea Eliade (although their concept of what this primordial creation actually entails remains extremely vague).[34]

The crucial point, however, is this: even if we add together all of these theories of myths (assuming for the moment that they have the validity ascribed to them), and even if we accept *some* of the less outrageous theories of the Euhemerists and add these in too, we still end up a long way short of explaining the whole phenomenon. Although no-one has put a figure on it, I would guess that explanations are probably wanting for at least fifty per cent of Greek mythical ideas. More seriously, one of the most crucial categories of myths – the cosmogonic tales – remains completely undeciphered, as Kirk admitted in 1974:

> These cosmogonical myths... remain uneven in detail and rather mysterious.[35]

And here is Kirk again on the overall, lamentable state of play:

> In short, it would not be unfair to say that the nature of myths is still, in spite of the millions of printed words devoted to it, a confused topic.[36]

And still the subject of myths remains a confused topic today, with progress being limited to some further pruning back of the outrageous monolithic theories that have held back our understanding during the last three hundred years.

Today, Hellenists no longer believe that the solution to the Greek myths is to be found in a single universal theory; the search for the holy grail has been abandoned. Instead, they focus on objectives that are more modest and achievable; they no longer talk of solving the puzzle but of the best way *to approach* the puzzle. Accordingly, scholars have fanned out, like an army of ants, to explore a variety of distinct but complementary approaches. Some choose to scrutinise myths for their historical content,[37] others for their links to ritual practices.[38] Some emphasise the connections between myths and iconography,[39] others the links between myths and popular folklore.[40] Some stress the importance of structuralism in myths (after the theories of Ferdinand de Saussure),[41] others the importance of psychoanalysis (after the theories of Sigmund Freud and Carl Jung).[42] Some explore the cosmic aspect of myths (after Mircea Eliade's concept of the primordial creative moment),[43] others the parallels to myths of older civilisations.[44]

On top of all this, scholars continue to argue about exactly how the word 'myth' should be defined, and how it should be differentiated from 'legend' or 'folk tale'.[45] Opinions differ, for example, on whether the tales of the heroes should be counted as myths or legends.

All in all, it would be fair to say that Greek mythology has become a subject of bewildering complexity. Gone are the days when a Frazer or a Müller presented a unified argument with a semblance of logic, albeit erroneous. Today, scholars are paranoid about the excesses of the past and have become reluctant to venture any new bold ideas. Accordingly, the academic literature abounds in carefully crafted statements in which scholars hedge their bets and avoid drawing firm conclusions about anything of substance.

It is no exaggeration to say that the most up to date textbooks on the subject of the Greek myths are a dreadful letdown. They either describe and paraphrase the myths and do little else, or they offer arbitrary and intuitive interpretations of a selected sample of myths, or they get absorbed in intricate discussions of how myths generally should be categorised.[46] If a student of Greek mythology hopes to make sense of this subject by reading from a 'recommended book list', then he will be terribly disappointed. Firstly, the myths themselves exist in a huge and varied corpus which remains inadequately classified and poorly collated. Secondly, the main academic works from the 18th to early-20th centuries present highly biased treatments of the myths and are thus misleading to a dangerous degree. And thirdly, the corrective works of the late-20th century are so preoccupied with detail that they lose the plot overall and, despite their verbosity (or perhaps because of it), they fail to explain what on earth the myths, individually and collectively, actually meant to the Greeks.

The situation is summed up by the analogy of the wood and the trees.

The Hellenist student is faced with numerous paths into the wood but, whichever path he chooses, he sees only the confusion of different types of tree. The wood itself, and the nature of the wood, remain totally imperceptible.

A Catastrophic Oversight

In a moment, we will look at one approach – comparative mythology – which does promise an overview of the Hellenist's 'wood', but first we must discuss why cataclysmic theories of the Greek myths have so far been notable only by their absence. Why did such theories not make it to the ranks of the holy grail theories that were discussed by scholars of the 18th-20th centuries? Why did cataclysm theory not even get listed as an outside contender? These are questions that apply not only to Hellenism but also to other fields of mythological studies, for cataclysmic theories are strangely absent in Egyptology, Sumerology, Assyriology, and Old Testament studies (despite, in the latter case, Yahweh's tendency to rain down fiery destruction from the heavens!). Why should this be?

As I see it, there are essentially five reasons why modern scholars have neglected cataclysmic theories of myth:

1   The Greeks themselves were ambivalent about the importance of cataclysms in the myths of the gods.

2   Scholars of the 18th-20th centuries were, for the most part, ignorant about meteorites and the importance of catastrophism.

3   Ancient myths rely heavily on metaphors and allusions which make no sense to the modern reader.

4   Many prominent scholars have missed the plot as a result of their Judaeo-Christian prejudices and taboos.

5   Modern scholars have failed to appreciate the difference between theorised, mythical cataclysms, and actual, historical cataclysms.

I will now take each of these points, briefly, in turn.

To begin with the Greeks, it has been demonstrated in the preceding chapters that they were ambivalent about the importance of cataclysms. On the one hand, cataclysms were obviously important in the myths of the gods establishing the world order, in the myths of the world ages, and in the myth of mankind's creation (in the aftermath of Deucalion's flood). And yet, on the other hand, Greek commentators of the 7th-4th centuries BC barely mentioned cataclysms in their attempted explanations for the violent and immoral behaviour of the gods. Whilst there may well be a plausible explanation for the Greeks' silence on this matter (see the previous chapter), it has weighed heavily on the minds of Hellenists, who have apparently taken the view that if the ancient Greeks scholars did not identify cataclysms as a theory of myths, then modern scholars should not have to second-guess them.

A second factor, equally important, is the ignorance that prevailed during the 18th, 19th and early-20th centuries concerning meteorites and the catastrophic effects of meteoritic impacts. During this era, when the foundations were laid for the study of myths, scholars were educated under a paradigm of uniformitarianism, and regarded catastrophism as a highly controversial idea. As astonishing as it might seem today, the majority of scientists regarded comets as harmless objects and disputed the idea that stones could fall from the sky. For example, the American president Thomas Jefferson (1743-1826), when he heard reports about meteorites, allegedly said: "I would sooner believe that two Yankee professors lied than that stones fell from the sky."[47] Similarly, at around the same time, the French Academy of Sciences stated dismissively that 'in our enlightened age there can still be people so superstitious as to believe stones fall from the sky.'[48] In that 'enlightened age', the physical evidence of the meteorites themselves was debunked by the assertion that they were terrestrial stones which had been struck by lightning. This, then, was the backdrop of scientific ignorance against which Hellenists (not to mention Egyptologists, Sumerologists and Assyriologists) formed their opinions of ancient myths. No wonder, then, that all these scholars avoided cataclysmic theories like the plague. After all, to suggest that ancient myths might recall the 'fall of the sky' in a literal sense would have been to join the ranks of the cranks and the crackpots.

The third important factor is the obscurity of the ancient myths. This, it must be stressed, is not a problem of translations – the ancient Greek language has been well understood for centuries. Rather, it is a problem of abbreviated references, metaphors and symbolism. Such devices were often used innocuously, but at other times they were used deliberately to conceal the secrets behind the myths, for the reasons which I suggested in the previous chapter. The problem here is well illustrated by the myth of Apollo's birth from the Earth and ascent to Heaven, on which the Hellenist Charles Penglase makes the following perceptive comment:

> While this ascent sequence is portrayed symbolically, indeed in such a fashion that it is hidden from anyone who does not understand the significance of the motifs, it was probably immediately obvious to the ancient audience for whom the hymn was composed... these few brief allusions were capable of conjuring up a whole complex mythological

scenario of which the full glory still remains concealed from the modern reader. There is also the possibility that the picture may have contained deep religious significance and was presented in such a fashion because it was not meant for all hearers...[49]

Indeed. It is no wonder, then, that scholars struggle to interpret the Greek myths against seemingly invincible odds (Charles Penglase happens to provide a ray of light in what is generally a most gloomy cavern).

This brings us to the fourth important factor, which may well be the most significant of all – the taboos and prejudices which have been brought to bear by scholars in their interpretations of the Greek myths. It is a subject on which I have written before – in the context of Egyptian and Mesopotamian myths – and much the same comments apply here.

The problem, in a nutshell, is that the typical scholar of the 18th, 19th and early-20th centuries was a gentleman who had been brought up to believe in the Bible and the Judaeo-Christian concept of God. Therefore, right from the beginning, he was prejudiced against the pagan religion of the Greeks, with its numerous warring, human-like gods, and its worship of the Sun and the Moon. To him, these gods were false gods, and the myths of the Greeks were false tales. There were no sacred secrets to be found there. Thus the scholar sought not, and he found not.[50]

Hand-in-hand with prejudice went taboo. The typical scholar had been brought up to believe that no-one should pry into the mysteries of God; He was a mystery not to be fathomed. Instinctively – subconsciously perhaps – the scholar feared that the Olympian gods might shed light on things which were 'not to be known', and, accordingly, he did not study them too closely. This, I believe, is the reason why modern academic works focus either on Greek *religion* or on Greek *mythology* but hardly ever on the Greek *gods*.

Intriguingly, this oversight by scholars (whatever its cause) has led to a spectacular failure to comprehend a fundamentally important element of the myths, namely the journeys of the gods. Consider, for example, the dreadful misunderstanding surrounding the location of Mount Olympus, on which subject *Encyclopaedia Britannica* (1999) pontificates thus:

> According to the Greek poet Homer, Heaven was located on the summit of Olympus, the highest mountain in Greece and the logical home for a weather god.

In other words, it is generally held that the Greek gods dwelt in a Heaven which lay no higher than the clouds in the Earth's troposphere.

But this assertion is completely misleading. In fact, the summit of the physical Mount Olympus in Greece was merely a symbol for the true and metaphysical Mount Olympus which was imagined to exist in a higher, aethereal realm. Many passages in the Greek literature allude to this idea, a notable example being Homer's story of the giants Otus and Ephialtes, who used the real world Mount Olympus as part of their 'stairway to Heaven' to scale the heights of the true Mount Olympus in the heavens. In this myth, clearly, two Mount Olympuses were involved – the one which existed visibly in Thessaly and the one which existed invisibly in or above the heavens. Whilst the first was confined to the humble *aer* of the Earth's troposphere, the second existed in the pure *aither* of the upper heavens.[51] (Lest there be any doubt about this matter, I have set out the evidence in an attached note.[52])

The Greeks themselves were well aware of the distinction between the *aither* of the true heavens and the *aer* of the troposphere. In the 4th century BC, for example, the dramatist Aristophanes wrote a play *The Clouds* in which he playfully reversed the *aither* with the *aer* to paint a satirical picture of the gods inhabiting the clouds.[53] The intention was that his audience would crack their sides with laughter at the profanity. But the funniest thing is how modern scholars have missed the joke.

The seriousness of this misunderstanding cannot be overstated. By making the journeys of the gods begin, or end, in the clouds, modern scholars have dismissed, at a stroke, the idea that the myths involved cataclysms from the heavens. Instead, scholars have invented a new myth of their own in which the gods descend to Earth in the form of thunder, lightning or hailstones, and in which Zeus, accordingly, becomes a mere weather-god. (Incidentally, this perception of the pagan Heaven differs substantially from that of the Judaeo-Christian Heaven, as if scholars have collectively resolved, consciously or subconsciously, to distance the one realm from the other. It almost goes without saying that the pagan religions have traditionally been regarded as simple-minded, primitive and deficient.)

The reader should now begin to understand that Hellenist orthodoxy is overdue for a re-evaluation and perhaps a complete upheaval. Consider, for example, the myth of Demeter and Persephone, which was discussed earlier. It has long been regarded by scholars as a transparent nature allegory, but, as we shall now see, it actually contains several allusions to cataclysmic imagery. Firstly, the Earth notably gapes open as Hades charges out to seize Persephone. Secondly, Demeter exhibits a bright, supernatural light when she comes down from Heaven into the Underworld. Thirdly, Demeter's descent into the Underworld causes a drought to afflict the Earth. And fourthly, the Eleusinian Mysteries of Demeter re-enact the arrival (*eleusis*) of a divine child at the time of a mysterious and brilliant fire.[54] Whilst the myth *is* an agrarian fertility drama, up to a point, its primary meaning is not the annual renewal of agriculture on Earth, but rather the original and sacred creation of agriculture on Earth (on this point, I am sure that Mircea Eliade would agree). Moreover, a cataclysmic interpretation of the myth would explain the remarkable secrecy that surrounded the Mysteries of Demeter; as the Homeric poet put it: 'Demeter revealed her beautiful mysteries, which are impossible to transgress, or to pry into, or to divulge, for so great is one's awe of the gods that it stops the tongue.'[55] This, surely, was no ordinary fertility myth.

The same misconception of a cloud-level Mount Olympus and its resident weather-gods also afflicts the myth of Ouranos and Gaia, which likewise has been identified by scholars as a mundane nature allegory (see earlier). Here, the problem is more serious for Ouranos' descent upon Gaia instigates the birth cycle of the Olympian gods, and it is thus absolutely fundamental to our understanding of the myths. Does Ouranos really fall from the clouds and fertilise Gaia with rainwater as G.S. Kirk and other scholars infer? In fact, Hesiod says nothing about rainwater, but rather speaks of tectonic stresses in Gaia's womb and then goes on to describe cataclysmic battles between the gods of Heaven and Earth. On the balance of evidence, Ouranos' descent upon Gaia – personifying the original fall of the sky – must be understood as a cataclysm myth, in which Heaven fertilised Earth with meteorites and cometary floodwaters (on this point, I am sure that Anaxagoras would have agreed).

The fifth important factor is that scholars have never appreciated the difference between theorised cataclysms (i.e. mythical cataclysms) and historical cataclysms (i.e. actual, eye-witnessed cataclysms). During the editing stages of this book, I contacted a number of Hellenists in order to assess their reactions to my ideas. But as soon as I mentioned the word 'cataclysms', these scholars would immediately become suspicious and defensive, mutter some dismissive remark about Immanuel Velikovsky, and politely bring the conversation to a halt. (Velikovsky caused an uproar in the 1950s with his theory that myths were records of actual, historical events in our solar system.)[56] After a few conversations of this kind, I began to realise that these men were fixated by the Velikovskian kind of cataclysm – the actual, historical, eye-witnessed variety. They had never considered the possibility that cataclysms might be important in other, more subtle and complex ways. One Hellenist kindly summed up the problem for me as follows:

Regarding the scarcity of cataclysmic theories of myth, I think it takes a fair amount of courage to stick one's neck out in such a way.

> In the academic world, of course, such theories are usually avoided because of their extremely hypothetical nature.[57]

The insinuation here is that cataclysms are 'extremely hypothetical' *in the context of ancient Greek history (or immediate prehistory)*, and that therefore any cataclysmic theory of Greek myths must be speculative in the extreme. But, as I have hinted in earlier chapters, this is not what the Greek myths are about. On the contrary, if we take the stories literally, then it becomes obvious that the series of cataclysms involving Ouranos, Kronos and Zeus all took place *in a time long before mankind had been created on the Earth*. In other words, the myth-makers never did claim that these cataclysms had occurred during their recent past. Rather, they envisaged them as primordial events which had created and shaped the Universe as they knew it. We are thus dealing with mythical cataclysms, which are no different in status to the theoretical cataclysms of modern times such as the Big Bang or the asteroid impact that supposedly killed off the dinosaurs (neither of which was witnessed by human beings).

How, then, did the myth-makers manage to describe the fall of the sky in such colourful and convincing language? Surely they must have seen something? Yes, indeed, it must be so, but it is not necessarily the case that a cataclysm from the skies was witnessed during the time of the ancient Greeks. On the contrary, it seems likely that the Greeks simply borrowed and adapted their myths from earlier civilisations in the Near East, in which case, our time frame must be extended backwards from the 1st millennium BC to the 2nd, 3rd and 4th millennia BC. And when we do this, something very significant happens. The sought-for cataclysm, which Hellenists regard as 'extremely hypothetical', becomes much less hypothetical. In fact, it becomes a probable certainty.

All of which brings us back to the one idea which has been paying dividends to Hellenist scholars during the last fifty years – comparative mythology.

Comparative Mythology

What is comparative mythology? In the Greek context, it is the process by which Hellenists compare the Greek myths to the myths of other ancient civilisations – usually older ones – in the hope that parallels will emerge. In an ideal scenario, the parallel myth in the alien culture will be expressed in sufficient detail that its broad meaning can be discerned, thereby improving scholars' reading of the parallel myth in the Greek.

It should be said, at the outset, that Hellenists have explored three different theories in the field of comparative mythology, of which two ended in failure long ago. Of the failures, the first was the Indo-European theory which proposed that the roots of Greek religion were to be found in a lost Indo-European culture, and the second was the Minoan theory, which proposed that the roots of Greek religion lay in the Minoan culture (newly discovered at the time) on the island of Crete. Little more needs to be said on these two theories for, in both cases, they are now defunct.[58] It is the third theory, rather, that we must concentrate on, for it has developed into a formidable force. It proposes that the roots of Greek religion are to be found somewhere in the East: either in the Middle East (Western Asia) or in the Near East (defined as Mesopotamia and Egypt).

Initially, scholars focused on the religion of the Hebrews. One of the earliest studies – a comparison between the Homeric myths and the Old Testament – was published as long ago as 1658 by the English scholar Zachary Bogan.[59] Much later, in 1898, another English scholar Robert Brown published a landmark work entitled *Semitic Influence in Hellenic Mythology*.[60] And between 1890-1915, James G. Frazer added grist to the mill by establishing a significant number of parallels between the myths and rituals of Greece, Western Asia and Egypt in his epic thesis *The Golden Bough*.

Archaeological support for these comparative studies was not long in coming. In 1912, the German scholar Fredrik Poulsen published a study entitled *Der Orient und die Frühgriechische Kunst*, in which he cited numerous examples of artifacts, art motifs and techniques imported into Greece from the East.[61] In addition, scholars were soon able to confirm that the Greeks had borrowed and adapted a Phoenician writing system (as the Greeks themselves claimed).[62] The parallels in the mythological literature could no longer be ignored.

The early-20th century saw revolutionary developments on the back of crucial decipherments of hieroglyphic and cuneiform writing systems in Egypt and Mesopotamia. Many parallels to the Greek myths were not spotted immediately, but everything changed in the 1930s and 1940s, when scholars began to translate the writings of the Hittites of Western Asia. When the first Hittite text was translated and published in 1922, scholars were amazed to find a description of a battle between a storm-god and a dragon named Illuyankas, which anticipated the Greek myth of the battle between Zeus and Typhoeus. The text, entitled *The Myth of Illuyankas*, hardly took the Hellenic world by storm, but eventually some scholars, such as Franz Dornseiff, were moved to pass comment.[63]

The big breakthrough came in 1945/46, with the publication of two further Hittite texts entitled *The Song of Ullikummis* and *Kingship in Heaven*.[64] In these texts, scholars found the most astonishing parallels to the myths of the Greeks: in the one, an account of a giant assaulting Heaven, along with tales of castration and one god swallowing another;[65] in the other, a succession myth similar to that told by Hesiod. Crucially, it was realised that the Hittite texts predated those of the Greeks, and thus Hellenists were forced to admit that Greece had not flowered in splendid isolation, as they had previously thought.[66] In the words of one modern scholar:

> The discovery in the thirties and forties of the Hurro-Hittite Kumarbi mythology, with its undeniable anticipations of Hesiod's *Theogony*, finally forced Hellenists to accept the reality of Near Eastern influence on early Greek literature.[67]

Scholars now began to realise that the Hittites had themselves borrowed their gods and myths from an earlier people, the Sumerians, who, along with their successors the Akkadians, had inhabited Mesopotamia (the modern-day land of Iraq) from *c*. 3800 BC. Slowly but surely, Hellenists began to plough through the recently translated Sumerian and Akkadian texts, looking for further parallels to the Greek myths. They were not to be disappointed. In 1964, the German scholar H. Petriconi drew a fascinating comparison between Homer's *Iliad* and the famous Akkadian text *The Epic of Gilgamesh* and concluded that the parallels had far-reaching implications. 'The days of an exclusively classical scholarship are over', he wrote: 'To write about Greek literature without knowing something of the West Asiatic has become as impossible as studying Roman literature without knowledge of the Greek.'[68]

But it was the scale of the eastern influence that was to really shake the world of Hellenism. In the 1950s and 1960s, archaeologists began to uncover clear evidence that the Greeks had established trading posts in Western Asia and imported numerous oriental objects into Greece. Some of the most substantial finds were made at the most sacred Greek sites – Delos, Delphi and Olympia.[69] It was now becoming evident that the Greeks had not only borrowed their alphabet and mythology from the East, but also much wider elements of their developing culture. In 1950, the German scholar H.E. Stier set down a long list of the oriental motifs that had been adopted by the Greek culture and concluded that:

> In view of this state of affairs, it would not be out of the way to ask what there was in archaic Greece that did *not* come from the Orient.[70]

A revolution was in the making. As the second half of the 20th century progressed, two heavyweight scholars stepped forward to champion the case for Near Eastern influence on the Greek religion: Martin L. West of

Oxford University in England and Walter Burkert of the University of Zurich in Switzerland.

As a student, Martin West had been exposed to the Greek-Hittite parallels, which had been published by Albin Lesky in several works from 1950-55. From an early age, West had realised that these parallels had revolutionary implications for a field of scholarship that had long been dominated by a paradigm of isolationism. But West was not one for sparing the blushes of his elders; in 1966, barely thirty years old, he published a commentary on Hesiod's *Theogony* in which he asserted confidently that 'Greece is part of Asia; Greek literature is a Near Eastern literature.'[71]

West followed this up with an equally painstaking study of Hesiod's *Works and Days* in which he cited further evidence in support of oriental borrowings. In a combined study of the two Hesiod poems, published in 1988, West wrote:

> It is becoming increasingly apparent, with the advance of archaeolog-
> ical discovery and of the study of oriental texts in cuneiform, that
> Greece received more far-reaching cultural influences from the East at
> this period [8th century BC] than anyone imagined fifty years ago...
> All this is very remarkable, and classical scholars have not yet fully
> adjusted to it. It is surprising – as we were not brought up to expect it
> – to find so much reflection of oriental literature, mythology and
> culture in a Greek poet... But as I have said, it was a time when Greece
> was open to eastern influences of many kinds.[72]

Meanwhile, Walter Burkert, professor of classics at the University of Zurich (and West's elder by six years) had also been waking up to the full significance of the eastern influences on Greece. In his authoritative study *Greek Religion* (1977), Burkert observed that the Olympian gods were no longer a unique phenomenon following the rediscovery of Near Eastern literature. The parallels were 'astonishing', he said, whilst the evidence for Near Eastern influence was 'undeniable'.[73] Furthermore, there were certain iconographical motifs (such as the god wielding the thunderbolt) which could be traced directly to Near Eastern models.[74]

In the 1980s, it began to dawn on Burkert that the oriental influences on Greece were more widespread and more fundamental than either he or other scholars had realised. Thus, in 1984, he published one of the definitive texts on Greek comparative mythology: *Die Orientalisierende Epoche in der Griechischen Religion und Literatur*. In the introduction to this book, Burkert set out his hypothesis that 'the Greeks did not merely receive a few manual skills and fetishes along with new crafts and images... but were influenced in their religion and literature by the eastern models to a significant degree.'[75] He then proceeded to cite the overwhelming archaeological evidence for cultural transfer from the East to Greece during the 8th-7th centuries BC. During this period, itinerant workers – poets, craftsmen, merchants and healers – had transferred a whole world of cultural ideas from the East to the West. It was in this so-called 'orientalising period' that the poets Homer and Hesiod had laid the foundations of Greek religion. Burkert demonstrated just how detailed and extensive were the parallels between Homer's epics, the *Iliad* and the *Odyssey*, and the Mesopotamian *Epic of Gilgamesh*, which had enjoyed a wide distribution throughout the Near East.

Such was the scale of this challenge made by Burkert and West to the isolationist orthodoxy of modern Hellenism that the phrase 'orientalising revolution' was coined in 1990 by the scholar John Boardman, and then picked up in 1992 by Burkert himself when he allowed the English edition of his 1984 book to be titled *The Orientalising Revolution: Near Eastern Influence on Greek Culture in the Early Archaic Age.*[76]

The cultural revolution of the ancient Greek epoch was now being rediscovered by a cultural revolution in modern scholarship. In 1992, eight years after the first publication of *The Orientalising Revolution*, Burkert was able to write:

> My thesis about the indebtedness of Greek civilisation to eastern
> stimuli may appear less provocative today than it did eight years ago.
> This change may be partly an effect of the original publication [*Die*
> *Orientalisierende Epoche in der Griechischen Religion und Literatur*],
> but mainly it reflects the fact that classics has been losing more and
> more its status of a solitary model in our modern world.[77]

Five years later, Martin West returned to the fray with the most definitive study ever of oriental influence on Greek culture. In *The East Face of Helicon: West Asiatic Elements in Greek Poetry and Myth* (1997), West produced a 630-page tome that was literally bursting with parallels. There was substantial evidence, he said, for oriental influence in Greek language, arts and crafts, music, song and dance, science, social customs, state institutions (e.g. kingship) and, most outstandingly, in all elements of religion – myths, gods, temples and holy places, sacrifices, rituals and attitudes of prayer.[78] Furthermore, building on earlier studies, West demonstrated profound eastern influence in the epics of Homer and in Hesiod, even down to detailed similarities in literary structures, styles and motifs, idioms, similes and forms of words. Homer's *Iliad*, he said, was 'pervaded by themes and motifs of Near Eastern character', whilst the *Odyssey* showed, in parts, 'an especially strong and clear relationship with *The Epic of Gilgamesh*.'[79] As for Hesiod, West commented that 'he displays a truly extraordinary accumulation of oriental materials'.[80] But moving beyond the usual suspects, West also found significant eastern influence in the works of the Greek lyric poets (such as Pindar), and in the plays of the dramatist Aeschylus (it was he who had described the cataclysmic punishment of Prometheus).[81]

Moreover, it appeared to West that the time scales of influence had been more complex than could be explained simply by the 'orientalising period' (8th-7th centuries BC). In addition, he suggested, Greece had been open to outside influences during the high Mycenaean period (1450-1200 BC), the final phase of the Bronze Age (1200-1050 BC), and continuously throughout the 8th-5th centuries BC.[82] Chronologically, West had beaten a path all the way to the threshold of the philosopher Socrates and his student, Plato.

To which eastern cultures should we look for the origins of the Greek myths?

Some scholars have identified close parallels to the Greek myths in the literatures of the Hebrews and Canaanites, dating back to the second millennium BC.[83] Other scholars have identified the clearest parallels in the literary traditions of the Hurrians and Hittites of Anatolia, whose civilisations date from the 17th century BC.[84] And yet there is a general recognition by scholars that all of these rich mythological traditions have their roots in older civilisations, notably those of the Egyptians and the Sumerians which both emerged *c.* 4000 BC. Here, the Egyptians are less important, for their influence would seem to lie in Greek philosophy and metaphysics, and not so much in the myths. Rather, it is the Sumerians, via their successors the Akkadians, the Babylonians and the Assyrians, who appear to hold the key to the Greek myths.

In this respect, a work of outstanding merit is Charles Penglase's *Greek Myths and Mesopotamia*, which was published in 1994. In this book, Penglase demonstrated extensive and profound Mesopotamian influences in Homer's hymns to Apollo, Demeter, Athene and Aphrodite and in Hesiod's myth of Prometheus and Pandora.[85] Most importantly, Penglase put comparative mythology into action by using the Mesopotamian parallels to decode certain crucial motifs in the Greek myths. Thus, in connection with the myth of Athene's birth, he wrote: 'the purpose of the motifs and the underlying ideas can be seen only with a thorough acquaintance with the way in which the Mesopotamian ideas seem to be applied in Greek mythology'.[86] And, as regards the myth of Apollo's birth and ascension to Mount Olympus, he wrote: 'the profound significance and purpose of these motifs and ideas in the hymn become clear only in the light of the mythology of Mesopotamia'.[87] Penglase's conclusion was that the Greek myths relied on fundamental concepts and motifs from the Mesopotamian myths and that an understanding of the latter was a vital key to an understanding of the former.[88]

The truth of the matter, however, as Penglase would acknowledge, is that there is no single source of Greek religion and mythology but rather, as Martin West put it, 'a broad stream of international tradition'.[89] This was a many-branched stream, not unlike Hesiod's fabled Oceanus. It wound across all of the Near East, from Egypt in the south-west to Mesopotamia in the south-east to Anatolia in the north-east, finally regurgitating its mixed-up waters in Phoenicia, which West called 'the grand junction where all roads met'.[90] 'When we contemplate the whole panorama, from Hesiod to Aeschylus', wrote West, 'it is obvious that we can no more count and describe the sources of all the eastern motifs and procedures than plot the flow of waters beneath the surface of a marsh.'[91] In addition to which, the Greeks must surely have mingled all these eastern waters with their own streams of millennia-old native traditions.[92]

But enough of generalities. It is now time to get down to specifics. In the next few chapters, we will take a closer look at the Greek myths, paying particular attention to the Hittite and Mesopotamian parallels. My intention is to build on the work of Burkert, West and Penglase and take it further, by demonstrating just how deep are the Greek/Near Eastern parallels in the subjects of cosmogony, theogony and cataclysm theory. In addition, I plan to put comparative mythology into action, by using my understanding of the Near Eastern myths to decode the meaning of the Greek myths, including ultimately Plato's story of Athens and Atlantis. Will the literature of the Near East support my cataclysmic interpretation of the Greek gods?

Let's take a look and see.

Chapter Six Summary

* Three hundred years of study have left Hellenists back where they started – without a single satisfactory theory for the phenomenon of the Greek gods. Scholars can explain some of the myths of the gods, but their theories fall a long way short of explaining the whole phenomenon, especially the cosmogonic myths.

* Hellenists have given up the search for a monolithic theory of myths. To their credit, they openly admit that a yawning gap exists in their understanding.

* Cataclysm theory is notable by its absence from scholars' theories of myth, but this can be explained by various factors, such as modern ignorance of catastrophism and the Greeks' own ambivalence on this matter owing to the ignorance and powerful taboos which prevailed in their day.

* Modern scholars have misconceived the nature of Mount Olympus, the home of the gods. By placing Olympus and Heaven at cloud level, they have turned the Olympians into weather-gods and precluded a cataclysmic interpretation of the myths. This is an extremely serious and fundamental error, which, in itself, justifies a complete and utter re-evaluation of the Greek myths.

* Of all the approaches attempted by Hellenists to shed light on the Greek myths, comparative mythology – based on the literature of the Near East – is the only one to make significant progress. It is now accepted that the Greeks did not invent a new religion, but adapted existing religious ideas from older Near Eastern civilisations.

* It is logical that ancient man would have created myths of the gods as a result of his experiences with the most exceptional forces of nature, i.e. cataclysms. But there is no need to suppose that such an event occurred in Greek times. On the contrary, the evidence suggests that the Greeks inherited their myths from older civilisations.

* It would seem that Greek culture was influenced by the Near East for centuries after 'the orientalising revolution', right up to the days of Socrates and Plato. Might it be possible that the Atlantis story was based on oriental ideas?

PART TWO

NEAR EASTERN PARALLELS
AND PRECEDENTS

CHAPTER SEVEN

LIGHT IN THE EAST

As I glanced round, the land had disappeared, and
upon the wide sea my eyes could not feast.
My friend, I will not ascend to Heaven!
(*The Epic of Etana*, Assyrian version, 7th century BC)

In the previous chapter, I explained how Hellenism has been undergoing
something of a revolution, with the realisation among scholars that the
myths of the Greeks were influenced significantly by the religious ideas
of Near Eastern civilisations. These oriental ideas seem to have filtered
across into the Greek culture during several key phases – the high
Mycenaean period (1450-1200 BC), the final phase of the Bronze Age
(1200-1050 BC), and the 'orientalising period' (8th-7th centuries BC).
During these periods, a rich mythological literature was circulating in the
East in the civilisations of the Egyptians, the Babylonians, the Assyrians
and (prior to 1180 BC) the Hittites. This ancient geographical region in its
entirety is known as the Near East, with the region of the Babylonians
and the Assyrians being known as Mesopotamia (equivalent to the
modern-day land of Iraq).

So profound was the influence of the Near East on Greece during the
8th-7th centuries BC in particular that modern scholars have coined the
phrase 'orientalising revolution'. It was during this period that the poets
Homer and Hesiod laid the foundations, literature-wise, of the Greek
religion. Scholars such as Burkert, West and Penglase have demonstrated
conclusively that the works of these two poets were based substantially
on the religious and mythical ideas of the Near East. Furthermore, West
in particular has argued for continuing oriental influence on Greece right
up to the time horizon of Socrates and Plato.

In this and the following two chapters, we are going to be looking at
the myths of the ancient Near East in further detail, with an emphasis on

the themes which were most fundamental to the religions of the East and the West – the origin of the Universe, the origin and nature of the gods, and the various acts of the gods, both destructive and creative. We will see for ourselves that the parallels between Greek and Near Eastern literature are indeed extensive and fundamental, as Burkert, West and Penglase have all claimed. We will also see for ourselves that cataclysm theory (of cataclysms during mythical times) is the absolute key to the myths of the Near East, just as it is to the myths of the Greeks. And thus we will begin to realise what the ancients had in mind when they spoke, as if with one voice, about the cataclysmic fall of the ancient sky.

The Same Cosmos

I would like to begin, in this chapter, by examining the broad parallels between the Greek and Near Eastern myths, firstly concerning the arrangement of the cosmos, and secondly concerning the nature of the gods who dwelt within it.

Firstly, an overview of the cosmos. In both the Greek and the Near Eastern systems, we find that the first Universe comprised solely Heaven and Earth. Then, owing to a mysterious incident or accident, Heaven fell to the Earth, the Earth conceived, and the Earth duly gave birth to a new Heaven (*inter alia*). In this way, there was born the cosmos which the ancients knew, consisting of a new Earth (re-shaped by the cataclysm) and a new, metaphysical Heaven. The original Heaven, however, had been physical, and the original Universe had comprised a bipolar system of two celestial bodies, each physically in opposition to the other.

In keeping with these ideas, the Greeks and Near Easterners both regarded Heaven as a mountain. In the Greek system, it was Mount Olympus (also known as 'the hill of Kronos'),[1] which was personified by Ouranos, whose name meant literally 'The Mountain of Heaven' (after the Greek *ouros* meaning 'mountain').[2] In Western Asia, the Canaanites knew Heaven as Mount Ll or Mount Zaphon.[3] In Egypt, it was known as *Neter-Khert*, 'the Mountain of God', Mount Bakhu or the 'Primeval Hill' of the sky-goddess Nut.[4] And in Mesopotamia, Heaven was known as E.KUR, 'the Mountain-House', alias 'the Mount of Rulership' or 'the Mount of Wisdom';[5] here, too, Heaven was personified by gods, most notably AN, whose name meant 'Heaven', and EN.LIL, whose common nickname was 'The Great Mountain'.[6]

In both the Greek and the Near Eastern systems, this dual cosmos of Heaven and Earth was joined, or linked, by a third domain known as the Underworld. My own studies of the Near Eastern myths have highlighted the belief that this Underworld was created, mythically speaking, by the aforementioned fall of Heaven to the Earth or, to be more precise, the fall of Heaven *into* the Earth. It was for this reason that the Mesopotamians knew the Underworld as a fallen mountain, calling it KUR, 'mountain', or KUR.NU.GI, 'the Mountain of No Return'; this region was, in effect, regarded as a sequence of seven concentric subterranean spheres.[7] The Canaanites, much in the same vein, believed that El, the fallen father of the gods, resided in an Underworld which was a seven-chambered mountain (the so-called 'Shad of El').[8] And the Egyptians, similarly, believed that their fallen sky-god Osiris resided in an Underworld called *Ament Set*, meaning 'the Hidden Mountain', which was envisaged, in one text, as containing seven sequential caverns.[9] The idea, in all cases, is that the Mountain of Heaven had fallen from above, entered the Earth, and *become* the Mountain of the Underworld – literally a mountain-within-a-mountain or a world-within-a-world.

In the Greek system, one of the clearest examples of the heavenly mountain falling into the Earth is the story of Ouranos (literally 'The Mountain of Heaven') coming down from the sky to impregnate Gaia. Unfortunately, it is not clear from the Greek texts whether Ouranos then *became* the Mountain of the Underworld, nor do the texts designate the Underworld specifically as a mountain. Nevertheless, as we shall see, the Greek Underworld was so similar to the Underworld of the Near Eastern myths that it is indeed plausible that Ouranos *was* synonymous with the hidden, subterranean mountain. The following broad similarities should be considered.

Firstly, the Greek Underworld comprised two realms, the subterranean and the submarine, ruled by the gods Hades and Poseidon respectively. The Mesopotamian Underworld comprised exactly the same two realms, ruled by the gods Nergal and Enki respectively. Both the Greek god Poseidon and the Mesopotamian god Enki presided over a subterranean sea.[10]

Secondly, the Greeks and Near Easterners used the same terminology in referring to the subterranean Underworld. The Greeks called it 'the house of Hades', meaning 'the house of the Unseen'.[11] The Egyptians called it 'the house of Osiris' or *Amentet*, 'the Hidden Place'.[12] And the Mesopotamians called it 'the house of the KUR', 'the house of Dumuzi', 'the house of darkness' or 'the house of dust'.[13]

Thirdly, there was a common idea in the East and the West that the god of the subterranean Underworld lived with a consort who had been abducted from the heavens. In the Greek system, Hades ruled with the goddess Persephone, whom he had abducted from her home in the upper world.[14] Similarly, in the Mesopotamian system, Nergal ruled with the goddess Ereshkigal, who had been 'carried off' from her heavenly home.[15] Both of these divine couples ruled the Underworld from iron-gated palaces, inspiring fear and terror in the hearts of mortals in the world above.[16]

Fourthly, there was a shared vision in the East and the West of the Underworld as a place of darkness and death. Mesopotamians and Greeks alike bewailed their ultimate fate, which was to return, in death, to this murky, dusty subterranean world, where they would experience a grim, depressing existence as mere shadows of their former selves. Both peoples, moreover, believed that men might be judged for their sins in the land of the dead by judges who had formerly been kings or heroes upon Earth.[17] And yet, despite this shared pessimistic philosophy, Mesopotamians and Greeks both believed that a few privileged folk might be translated to a paradisiacal land of plenty, which was situated, in both cases, in the furthermost west, at 'the ends of the Earth'.

Fifthly, despite all this imagery of darkness and gloom, the Greeks and Mesopotamians shared a remarkable vision of an infernal geography. In the Greek system, the Underworld featured mysterious meadows, groves, orchards, rivers and lakes; it also featured subterranean animals, such as cattle, sheep and unnamed beasts which roamed 'on the meadow of Asphodel'.[18] The Mesopotamian Underworld, in similar fashion, featured mountains, plains, forests, rivers and a subterranean sea, and it was occupied *inter alia* by mysterious cattle and 'creatures of the plain'.[19] The idea, in both cases, was that the Underworld was remarkably Earth-like, as if it were a world-within-a-world.

Sixthly and most significantly, in the light of my earlier comments about Heaven falling into the Earth, the Greeks and Near Easterners both believed that the Underworld contained the roots of Heaven. In the Greek system, the clearest record of this idea is found in Hesiod's *Theogony*:

> And there [in the Underworld] are the sources and extremities of dark Earth and misty Tartarus, of the undraining sea *and the starry Heaven [Ouranos]*, all in order, dismal and dank...[20]

In the Near East, the idea was the same. In Egypt, the priests and kings believed that the route to Heaven was via the Underworld, hence the souls of the pharaohs would begin their journey to the afterlife by going downwards to the Underworld, to a 'lower sky' or 'sky-in-the-middle'.[21] In Mesopotamia, similarly, tales were told of how kings of old had entered the Underworld and journeyed across seven mountains in order to reach a special mountain that allowed access to Heaven. This special, magical mountain – known variously as Mount Hurrum or Mount Mashu – remained hidden in the subterranean world.[22]

This was primarily a mythical idea, but it was incorporated from the earliest times into real world geography, specifically in respect of the highest mountains. Thus the Greeks regarded the mountains of Athos, Olympus, Ida and Atlas (in Libya) as spanning the celestial realms of Heaven, Earth and the Underworld.[23] To take Mount Ida as an example, the cave beneath it, in which Zeus was born, symbolised the Underworld, or womb of the Earth;[24] the peak of the mountain, like that of Olympus, symbolised the Mountain of Heaven; and the mountain as a whole, like the other mountains, symbolised 'the Mountain of Heaven and Earth' or, to use Mircea Eliade's term, 'the cosmic mountain'.[25]

Furthermore, this mythical, celestial symbolism was enshrined in man-made mountains, most notably pyramids, temples and ziggurats. Thus, in Mesopotamia, temples were known as 'mountain-houses' and were thought to reach into the sky, at one extreme, and into the Underworld, at the other.[26] The temple thus established the sacred *axis mundi*, which the Mesopotamians knew as *dimgal*, 'the great binding post', or DUR.AN.KI, 'the Bond of Heaven and Earth'.[27] The best known of these temples was Enlil's ziggurat at Nippur:

> Enlil, when you marked off holy settlements on the Earth,
> You built Nippur as your very own city,
> The KI.UR, the mountain, your pure place, whose water is sweet,
> You founded it in the DUR.AN.KI, in the centre of the four corners of
>   the Universe.[28]

In the last line of this Mesopotamian verse, we see the idea that the ziggurat-temple, or cosmic mountain, had to be situated at the centre of the axis between Heaven and Earth, thus representing 'the navel of the Earth'. Amazingly, the same idea was adopted by the Greeks more than a thousand years later when they made Delphi the *omphalos* or 'navel' of the world.[29] It was here that Apollo and Dionysus were allegedly buried; it was from here that Apollo ascended to Heaven 'like a thought'; and it was here that the Greeks communicated, by oracle, with the gods of Heaven and the Underworld.[30] Intriguingly, Homer took the *omphalos* idea even further, applying it to the mythical island Ogygia, which he called *omphalos thalasses*, 'the navel of the sea'.[31]

In summary, it can be seen from this overview that Greek cosmology conformed exactly to the Near Eastern model of a triple axis comprising the Mountain of Heaven, the Earth and the Mountain of the Underworld. In each case, the Underworld existed beneath the Earth, i.e. inside it, and contained the seeds, or roots, of the fallen Heaven.

The Same Gods

Turning now to the subject of the gods, we find that the broad parallels between Greece and the Near East are, once again, remarkable.

Firstly, we find the shared belief in one large family or pantheon of gods, headed by a chief god. In Greece, the chief god was Zeus, whose titles included: 'king in Heaven', 'king of the gods', 'father of men and gods', 'lord of the dark clouds' and 'thunderer on high'. In the Near East, similarly, the pantheon of gods was ruled by a chief god who was 'king in Heaven', 'father of gods and men' and, in certain circumstances, a cataclysmic storm-god.[32]

This chief god ruled, invariably, with a goddess who was his sister but also his wife. In the Mesopotamian system, this divine couple was Anu and Antu, whose names both meant 'Heaven' in masculine and feminine declensions respectively. They were effectively 'Mr and Mrs Heaven'. Amazingly, the same scheme is found in Greece. In the *Iliad*, Homer refers to Zeus' consort not as Hera but as Dione – a feminine form of the name Zeus.[33] The divine couple Zeus and Dione were thus literally 'Mr and Mrs Heaven', exactly as in the Mesopotamian system.[34]

Furthermore, we find that the gods in the Near Eastern pantheon were identified by their spheres of activity, just as in the Greek system. There was a god of war, a storm-god or weather-god, a messenger-god, a blacksmith-god, a Sun-god, a Moon-god, an Earth-goddess or mother-goddess, a goddess of love (who was also a goddess of war) and a goddess of childbearing. Conceptually, and in detail, the organisations of the gods in the East and the West are strikingly similar.[35]

Most importantly, the gods of the Near East, just like the gods of the Greeks, were depicted in human form and described in anthropomorphic terms. They walked, talked, loved and fought and stood in familial relationships to one another as fathers and mothers, husbands and wives, sons and daughters, brothers and sisters. On occasions, it is alleged, the gods came down to Earth and intervened in the affairs of man, begetting kings, founding temples and leading armies into battle. Indeed so human-like were the activities and social arrangements of these gods that they have commonly been regarded as human or human-like beings.

And yet it becomes evident, on closer inspection, that the Near Eastern gods were a distinct race of beings, who were capable of supernatural feats and who generally kept themselves apart from the race of men.

This distinction between gods and men begins with chronology. In the

Near East, as in Greece, the gods were said to have inhabited the Earth long before man was created. The Mesopotamian and Egyptian myths, in particular, make it clear that the gods had come down from Heaven at the beginning of time, whereupon they had established subterranean cities which they inhabited for a long time by themselves. It was at this time that the gods had divided the world and the Universe between them, just as the Greek gods had done. The moment is recorded in a Mesopotamian myth known as the *Atra-Hasis Epic*:

> The gods threw the lots, made the division;
> Anu went up to the Heaven,
> (Enlil) took the Earth for his realm,
> Enki-the-wise was assigned the sea [the Apsu], barred with a bolt.[36]

These lines find an amazing echo in the division of the Greek Universe, as recorded in the *Iliad*. The outcome, it should be recalled from chapter one, was that Zeus won Heaven, Hades the Underworld, and Poseidon the subterranean sea (although Earth and Mount Olympus were held, in common, by them all). As Walter Burkert has noted, the parallel is so close here that the *Iliad* passage amounts almost to a direct translation of the older Mesopotamian text.[37]

It is evident, from the passage just cited, that the Near Eastern gods had something to do with the celestial realms (Heaven and Earth), and this is indeed borne out by the supernatural size of the gods. In this respect, a classic example is the Sumerian god Ningirsu who, it was said, had appeared in a dream to Gudea, the king of Lagash. Gudea described the god thus:

> In the heart of the dream, there was a man [the god Ningirsu]:
>   his height equalled the Sky, his weight equalled the Earth...[38]

This god was of celestial proportions, as were numerous other gods of the Near East, who were likened to huge mountains of rock and ice, which fell from the sky to impregnate the Earth with the seeds of life (see the next chapter). It was often suggested that the bodies of the gods had been composed of precious minerals, such as gold, silver and lapis lazuli (hence the use of these minerals in making statues of the gods).[39]

The interesting thing about these descending gods is that they gave birth to further progeny when they entered the Earth. Thus in the Near East, as in Greece, we find numerous myths of Mother Earth giving birth to gods, demons and monsters, following receipt of the celestial seed. A good example of this idea is the birth of the evil god Azag. An Akkadian text describes his origin from a union of Heaven (Anu) and Earth (Ki):

Anu impregnated the verdant Earth and she bore him Azag.[40]

A Babylonian text, in similar fashion, describes how seven Sebitti-gods had been born following Anu's impregnation of Earth:

When Anu, king of the gods, impregnated Earth,
She bore the seven gods for him, and he named them 'Sebitti'.[41]

In both of these examples, the gods born from the Earth were possessed with supernatural powers, just like the Earth-born gods of the Greeks. In the case of Azag (alias Zu), he was said to have ascended into the skies, whereupon he took up residence on a heavenly mountain (more on this in the next chapter). In the case of the Sebitti-gods, it was said that 'their birth was strange and full of terrible portents', and they were compared to weapons which, when released from the Underworld, would wreak terrible destruction upon Heaven and Earth.[42] There is a close parallel here with Hesiod's story of the Cyclopes, sons of Ouranos and Gaia, who personified the three weapons of the Underworld – 'the thunder, the lightning and the smoking bolt'.

Amazingly, the Near Eastern myths of the gods contain the same variations of the divine birth mechanism as appear in the Greek myths. In the Hittite and Egyptian texts, for example, we find the strange idea that gods could sometimes be born from the body of a male god – something notably contrary to human nature.[43] However we choose to interpret these myths, they represent an astonishing parallel to the Greek tales of Athene being born from the head of Zeus, and Dionysus being born from the thigh of Zeus. More on the Hittite parallel in due course.

This supernatural nature of the Near Eastern gods – as evidenced so far from their celestial proportions and strange modes of birth – is further underlined by other defining characteristics – their immortality, their association with loud noise and their manifestation amidst bright and dazzling lights – all characteristics which were routinely exhibited by the Greek gods also.

Immortality is perhaps the most fundamental characteristic of the Near Eastern gods. Indeed, it is so much taken for granted in the ancient texts that there is little more to be said about it beyond stating the bald fact of the matter. It should be mentioned, however, that the Near Eastern gods did differ from their Greek brethren in one important respect: they could be killed physically, only to return to life metaphysically; and it was only at this point of resurrection that they took on their immortal forms. This difference turns out to be of crucial importance, hinting, as it does, that the Greek gods, like their Near Eastern counterparts, originally possessed physical bodies when they came down from the skies. Such ideas are preserved in the Greek traditions, most notably in the myth of Ouranos, and in the myths which describe Hephaestus (the blacksmith-god) and other gods being thrown out of Heaven.[44] For the most part, however, the Greeks chose to focus on the gods who were born from the Earth, i.e. the invisible, metaphysical gods.

The loud noise of the Near Eastern gods is exemplified by their 'Word', which, when uttered, caused Heaven and Earth to quake. The following passage, from a Sumerian text, describes the Word of Anu, the king of the gods:

> The Word of Anu, a storm crouching on the horizon [of Heaven],
>   its heart inscrutable...
> His Word which up above makes the heavens tremble,
> His Word which down below rocks the Earth,
> His Word wherewith the Anunnaki-gods destroy...
> His Word – a risen flood-storm, none can oppose it.[45]

A third fundamental characteristic of the Near Eastern gods was their association with bright and dazzling light. In Sumer, the gods were called DINGIR ('the Shining Ones') and emitted a brightness called *melammu*, 'the divine splendour', whilst in the land of the Hittites the gods similarly emitted a 'terrifying and luminous force'.[46] An interesting example of the bright light motif occurs in the myth of the 'Imdugud-bird' which was associated with the evil god Azag/Zu. The Sumerian king Gudea, it was said, had built a temple and named it after this bird: *E-ninnu-Imdugud-bar-bar*, i.e. 'Eninnu the Flashing Thunderbird'.[47] Whilst Erich von Daniken would no doubt argue that this temple was a launch pad for a spacecraft, the truth is that this bright, flashing Imdugud-bird was the centrepiece of a myth about war in Heaven and a resulting cataclysm. More on this in the next chapter.

So much for the gods' supernatural characteristics, but we should not overlook their supernatural accomplishments. Foremost among these was the creation of man, which the Near Eastern gods achieved by sacrificing one of their own (a god of junior rank) and utilising his blood, mixed with clay, to mould the first men.[48] This was but one of several creation of man myths in the East, all of which varied along similar lines. Whilst there are some differences in the Greek myths of man's creation, the fact nevertheless remains that this remarkable act is credited to the gods in Greek and Near Eastern traditions alike – a remarkable parallel in itself. Moreover, it is important to appreciate that the Near Eastern gods, just like their Greek counterparts, created the race of man in the Underworld (see chapter seventeen). In the Near Eastern myths, though not in the

Greek, the newly created men were then handed over to the Underworld gods to act as slaves in their subterranean cities.

What happened next? According to the myths of the Near East, men and gods became separated, in due course of time, owing to a rebellion or dispute.[49] The gods continued to reside in Heaven and the Underworld, much as before, but man, for his sins, was expelled from the Underworld and made to fend for himself on the surface of the Earth.[50] At this time, it would seem, the gods established the institution of kingship on Earth to facilitate mediation between men and gods, and they instigated the beginning of religious practices, most notably the rites of sacrifice in their own honour.

In the Greek myths, echoes are found of man's expulsion from the Underworld (see chapter seventeen), whilst in Greek religion generally the idea of men communicating with the gods through kingship and sacrifice is fundamental (in this regard the Near Eastern practices were virtually identical to those of the Greeks).[51] The sacrificial rites of the Greeks were, of course, established by the settlement between men and gods at Mekone, when Prometheus attempted to deceive Zeus with the sacrificial portions.[52]

This brings us to the subject of temples, where we should note that the earliest Greek temples, dating to the 8th century BC, were constructed according to a Near Eastern prototype.[53] The purpose of these temples, per the Near Eastern myths, was to re-establish man's contact with the gods. Hence, as we noted earlier, the Mesopotamian temples of the 3rd millennium BC symbolised the *axis mundi*, running vertically through 'the navel of the Earth'. The idea, to be replicated in Greece more than a thousand years later, was that the temple touched Heaven at one extreme, and the Underworld at the other. As a result of this axial reconnection, men and gods, whilst being for ever separated, were nevertheless bound together in a kind of celestial partnership, in which mortal man paid tribute to his distant, immortal and all-powerful creators. This, of course, was the very essence of Greek religion, too.

Meanwhile, it is important to realise that the gods – those of Heaven and those of the Underworld – were likewise bound together in an intimate celestial partnership. This idea is pervasive in the Near Eastern myths where, at the first sign of trouble, the chief god (usually Anu or Enlil) would call for an assembly of the gods to agree a course of action. This is evident, to cite but two examples, in the *Atra-Hasis Epic*, where the gods hold an assembly to debate the destruction of mankind, and in the myth *Nergal and Ereshkigal*, where a messenger is sent up from the Underworld to address a complaint to the assembly of the gods in

Heaven. As the scholar Martin West has observed: 'The assembly of the gods is a thoroughly Near Eastern motif... equally at home in Sumero-Akkadian, Hurro-Hittite and Canaanite literature...'.[54] The same idea pervades the Greek myths. One thinks immediately of the *Iliad*, where Zeus instructs the gods of the Underworld to ascend to Mount Olympus for an assembly, at which Poseidon abandons his submarine world and, together with all the nymph-goddesses of the rivers and springs, ascends to Olympus in an instant (almost as if these deities and their waters belonged in Heaven).[55] One thinks also of the scene in Plato's *Critias*, when Zeus calls all of the gods to an assembly, seemingly to hear his pronouncement upon the fate of Atlantis.[56]

Other gods, however, were imprisoned deep in the Underworld, in the subterranean region, and were thus excluded from the assembly. And here, once again, the idea is found both in the East and the West. In Sumer, these gods of the Underworld were called the A.NUN.NA.NUN.KI or Anunnaki, 'the seed of Enki';[57] in Babylonia they were *dingiruggu*, 'the dead gods', *ilani kamuti*, 'the fettered gods', or *ilani darsuti* 'the banished gods';[58] and in the land of the Hurrians and Hittites, they were *enna durenna*, 'the gods of down under' or *karuilies siunes*, 'the former gods'.[59] All of these groups find an echo in the Greek tradition of the Titans, who were despatched by Zeus to the misty depths of Tartarus; Hesiod actually refers to these fallen Titans as 'the former gods' – a very Near Eastern epithet.[60]

In addition to these anonymous groups of gods, many Near Eastern myths identified the former gods specifically by name. In Babylonia, the creation myth *Enuma Elish* alluded to the fall of the god Apsu, who had been cast down from Heaven at the beginning of time, thereupon to form a subterranean sea; the myth then related the fall of Apsu's heavenly consort Tiamat, who had been cataclysmically destroyed and interred in the Underworld beneath a mountain.[61] In the Ugaritic myths, it was said that the olden god El, 'creator of the Earth', resided in the Underworld 'at the source of the rivers, in the hollow of the abysses', having been deposed from Heaven by the young god Baal.[62] In the Hurro-Hittite myths, it was reported that an olden god named Alalus had been driven out of Heaven by a rival Anus, whereupon he had taken refuge in the subterranean world;[63] the same myths spoke of a subterranean giant named Ubelluris, upon whose fallen body Heaven and Earth had been built.[64] Finally, the Egyptian Pyramid Texts described the confinement of Osiris in the Underworld and alluded to his fall from Heaven during the mythical era of *Zep Tepi*, 'the First Time'.[65] The Greek parallel to these olden gods is, of course, Kronos, who was deposed from Heaven, along with the Titan gods, and confined in the Underworld by his youngest son Zeus. Incidentally, one wonders whether Ouranos shared the same fate when he was deposed, earlier, by Kronos.

In summary, it can be seen from this brief overview that the Near Eastern gods were supernatural and 'other worldly'. They were born in Heaven or from a conjunction of Heaven and Earth; they were immortal; they lived in Heaven or in the subterranean Underworld; they were of celestial proportions; their 'Word', uttered from above, caused Heaven and Earth to quake; their battles and love-making were performed on a celestial plane; and their accomplishments – such as the creation of man – were truly miraculous.

All of these things could be written about the gods of the Greeks.

Moreover, it should be evident, from this overview, that all important divine activity in the Near East occurred in a bipolar Universe, consisting of Heaven and Earth (and the Underworld inside the Earth), connected together for all time by the *axis mundi*.

This could be written equally about the cosmos of the Greek gods.

And so we have reached the point where the reader should be willing to accept that fundamental similarities exist between the myths of the East and the myths of the West (just as proposed by the eminent modern scholars Burkert, West and Penglase). Accordingly, we will now turn our attention to some of the most important ideas behind these myths – the fall and replacement of the elder god (the so-called 'succession myth'), the fall of the Mountain of Heaven (the 'deluge myth'), and the sacred marriage of Heaven and Earth.

Chapter Seven Summary

* The Greek cosmos was virtually identical to the Near Eastern cosmos. Both comprised the Mountain of Heaven, the Earth and the Mountain of the Underworld.

* The basic idea behind the cosmos was that the Mountain of Heaven had fallen into the Earth and *become* the Underworld. This would suggest that a cataclysm of a mythical ilk is the key to the ancient cosmogonies.

* The Greek gods were virtually identical, conceptually, with the gods of the Near East. But whereas the Greek myths focused on the Earth-born gods and spoke cryptically about their origins, the Near Eastern myths described in explicit terms how these gods had been propagated by descending sky-gods, who had been physical in nature.

CHAPTER EIGHT

BATTLES OF THE GODS

Go and cut off Tiamat's life; and let the winds convey her blood to secret places!

(*Enuma Elish*, early-1st millennium BC)

One of the most important Greek myths is the so-called 'succession myth' in which Zeus established the present world order. As we have seen (in chapter one), the present world order was preceded by a world order in which Kronos had been king of the gods. Moreover, prior to the birth and rule of Kronos, there had been an earlier universal order under the aegis of Ouranos, who reigned, one presumes, as the personification of the Mountain of Heaven. The transfers of power, in the first instance from Ouranos to Kronos, and in the second instance from Kronos to Zeus, had been violent in nature, involving the castration of the sky-god and, later, an all-out war between the gods of Heaven and the gods of the Underworld. The story, on the face of it, describes cataclysmic events from a mythical, primordial era, long before the days when mankind had been created on the Earth at the behest of the gods.

Now, this Greek succession myth did not suddenly appear out of a cultural vacuum, but rather stemmed from an older, Near Eastern model, traces of which can be found in the traditions of the Hurrians, Hittites, Canaanites, Assyrians, Babylonians and Sumerians. And the evidence, in fact, points to the Sumerians as the original purveyors of the myth. So, let us begin with the Sumerians and see what further information we can glean about the battles of the gods for the kingship of Heaven and Earth.

The Succession Myth

According to Sumerian texts, the world order began with the rulership of the god AN ('Heaven') together with a spouse who would later be called Antu. But various Mesopotamian 'god lists' inform us that Anu and Antu (to use their Akkadian names) were preceded by twenty-one earlier divine couples.[1] The names of these couples are notable for their repeated juxtapositions of Heaven and Earth; hence one list named the parents of Anu as AN.SHAR.GAL and KI.SHAR.GAL meaning 'Great Prince of Heaven' and 'Great Princess of Earth'. Had there been twenty-one successive marriages of Heaven and Earth? Had the world order been overthrown, mythically speaking, by twenty-one battles of the gods? To date, the Sumerian tablets have not yet yielded any evidence for twenty-one succession myths. What we do have, however, is a series of Hurro-Hittite myths which were evidently drawn from the Sumerian model; and one of these provides the kind of 'fill-in' details that we are looking for.

In the Hurro-Hittite myth *Kingship in Heaven*, we discover that Anu – here called Anus – was preceded on the throne 'in the olden days' by a king named Alalus. In an astonishing parallel to the myth of Zeus and Kronos, the text describes how Anus plotted the downfall of Alalus whilst acting as his cupbearer. Then came the battle:

> Nine in number were the years that Alalus was king in Heaven. In the ninth year, Anus gave battle to Alalus and he vanquished him. He fled before him and went down to the dark Earth. Down he went to the dark Earth, but Anus took his seat upon the throne.[2]

Following this battle, Anus ruled for nine years, served by a cupbearer Kumarbis. But then, history repeated itself: the cupbearer Kumarbis went into battle against the king Anus. The Hurro-Hittite myth informs us that Kumarbis chased Anus across the heavens and then 'dragged him down from Heaven', at the same time 'biting his knees' – a euphemism for castration.[3] Kumarbis, we are told, then swallowed the phallus of Anus, which impregnated him with the seed of three gods: the storm-god, his attendant Tasmisus, and a god who personified the river Tigris. At this point, the vengeful Anus declared: "Three dreadful gods have I planted in thy belly as seed: thou shalt go and end by striking the rocks of thine own mountain with thy head!"[4] These lines, taken together, suggest that Kumarbis would return to the 'mountain' of Earth, from which he had earlier risen up to assault Anus. In any event, following this bizarre impregnation, Kumarbis spat out some of the divine seed on to a Mount Kanzuras, whereupon it caused the birth of an awesome god. The remainder of the seed, meanwhile, germinated in Kumarbis' belly, where it eventually caused the birth of Tessub, the storm-god, who exited Kumarbis' body in an abnormal and supernatural fashion.[5]

The end of the *Kingship in Heaven* text is badly fragmented, but it would appear that Kumarbis demanded to eat his own son (presumably

Tessub) but was given, instead, a basalt stone. Having swallowed this stone, Kumarbis later ejected it and set it down on the Earth, where it became a cult object.[6] Meanwhile, as regards the divine succession, it would appear that the storm-god Tessub rose up to Heaven, defeated Anus, and became king of the gods.

What we have, in this Hurro-Hittite myth, are some truly remarkable parallels to the Greek succession myth as reported by Hesiod.

Firstly, it should be noted that *Kingship in Heaven* refers to a sequence of two battles and thus the trio of Alalus, Anus and Kumarbis parallels the Greek trio of Ouranos, Kronos and Zeus.

Secondly, we find the idea that the sky-god Anus was castrated by the young pretender Kumarbis, just as the Greek god Ouranos was castrated by his son Kronos.[7]

Thirdly, we find the idea that the young pretenders in the Hurro-Hittite myth plotted the overthrow of the rulers while acting as their cupbearers, just as Zeus overthrew Kronos while acting as his cupbearer.

Fourthly, we find the idea that Kumarbis wanted to swallow his son, just as Kronos wanted to swallow Zeus (having already swallowed his other children by Gaia). And we also find the related idea that Kumarbis swallowed a stone in lieu of the son, just as Kronos swallowed a stone in lieu of Zeus.

Fifthly, we find the idea that Kumarbis placed the ejected stone in the Earth to be a cult object, just as Zeus placed the stone ejected by Kronos in the Earth to become a cult object (i.e. the stone at Delphi).

And sixthly, the manner of the storm-god's birth from Kumarbis' body provides an extraordinary parallel to Hesiod's tale of Athene's birth from the 'head' of Zeus.

What can we learn from these parallels? For one thing, the stories can be seen to revolve around Heaven and Earth, with the gods rising up or falling down along the *axis mundi*. For another thing, we can see that the swallowing of the stone and its placement in the Earth was of paramount importance to the succession myth.

But what was this stone? Whilst we know nothing about the stone of Kumarbis, we do know a little about the stone of Zeus, of which Hesiod writes:

> Zeus fixed it in the wide-pathed Earth at Delphi, in the glens of Parnassus, to be a monument thereafter and a thing of wonder for mortal men.[8]

This sacred stone of Delphi was referred to by the Greeks as a *baetylus* and *omphalos*.[9] It was described by the poet Pindar (5th century BC) as 'the deep navel stone', 'the centre-stone of Earth' and 'the great centre-stone of Earth's broad breast'.[10] This original *baetylus* (as opposed to its later replacement) was said to have been a rough stone of ovoid shape, the size of a cannonball.[11] Modern scholars are reasonably certain that this stone was a meteorite (in support of this, the word *baetylus* generally signified a meteorite).[12] And such an identification certainly would make sense in the context of the myth of Kronos and Zeus, where the latter god cast the former god down from his heavenly throne.

Was the stone of Kumarbis a meteorite, too? On the face of it, the Hittite stone was indeed a stone of Heaven and Earth – which is exactly what a meteorite is.

As an interesting addendum, the stone of Heaven and Earth appears in a somewhat different, but no less intriguing, scenario in a related Hurro-Hittite myth: *The Song of Ullikummis*.[13]

The Song of Ullikummis tells how Kumarbis fathered a stone giant Ullikummis, who threatened to depose the storm-god from Heaven. The method of the giant's birth was curious, to say the least. Kumarbis, we are told, struck a rock and ravished it as a man would ravish a woman, whereupon the rock (seemingly symbolising the Earth) became pregnant and, in due course of time, gave birth to Ullikummis.[14] This giant grew by standing on the body of an older giant named Ubelluris, who had been confined to the depths of the Underworld at the beginning of time.[15] With this solid foundation beneath his feet, Ullikummis began to grow larger and larger, breaking out of the Underworld and rising up from the ocean towards Heaven like a pillar or tower made of *kunkunuzzi* stone.[16] Eventually, Ullikummis became so large that he made the Earth shake and the Heaven tremble, and the gods in the heavenly Kuntarra-house were seized with fear. The storm-god thereupon went into battle against Ullikummis, but the attack was indecisive and he lost seventy gods who fell into the sea. In desperation, the storm-god consulted Ea (Enki), who lived in the Apsu – the subterranean sea. Ea then saved the gods of Heaven by suggesting that the gods cut through Ullikummis' feet using the metal knife with which Heaven had been separated from the Earth in the olden days.[17] Thus weakened, the great stone giant was no match for the renewed onslaught of the storm-god and he toppled back down to the Earth. The storm-god remained king in Heaven.

We have in *The Song of Ullikummis* several fascinating parallels to the Greek myths. Consider, first of all, the metal knife or cleaver which had once been used to separate Heaven from Earth. Readers might recall that Kronos used a sharp-toothed sickle to castrate his father Ouranos after he had descended upon Gaia. Furthermore, if we visualise this conjunction of Heaven and Earth in anthropomorphic terms, with the celestial phallus of Ouranos inserted inside Gaia, then the castration by Kronos indeed amounted to a separation of Heaven (Ouranos) from Earth.[18] The idea of the personified Heaven being separated from the Earth with a knife thus appears to have its roots in *The Song of Ullikummis* or perhaps in some even earlier but unknown Near Eastern myth.

Secondly, there is the image of the giant Ullikummis who, with his head approaching Heaven and his feet in the Underworld, presents an irresistible parallel to the Greek image of Atlas, the fallen Titan god who supported the Heaven on his head and shoulders. And Atlas, too, stood in the Underworld, at the 'ends of the Earth'. The parallel, in broad terms, is exact.[19]

What can we learn from these parallels? Once again, we can see how the myths of the gods revolved around the *axis mundi*, which connected together Heaven, Earth and the Underworld. But what about the image of Ullikummis as a pillar of *kunkunuzzi* stone? Why would this pillar be founded in the Underworld and why would it rise all the way from the sea to Heaven? The explanation is that this *kunkunuzzi* stone was no ordinary stone. On the contrary, it was – in the opinion of one modern researcher – an 'iron meteorite' stone.[20] Symbolically, then, the meteorite stone of Ullikummis was scaling the heavens in an attempt to return to the place whence it came.

Once again, our investigation of the parallel myths of the East and the West has brought us back to the meteorite. Might the meteorite be the key to the myths of the gods who came down from Heaven to Earth?

In search of an answer to this question, let us follow in the footsteps of modern scholars, who have identified two further sets of Near Eastern parallels running alongside the Hurro-Hittite succession myth: firstly, the myth of the battle between Ninurta and the evil god Azag/Zu contained in the Babylonian/Assyrian *Myths of Zu* and the *Lugal-e* tablets; and secondly, the myth of the battle between Marduk and Tiamat contained in the Babylonian Epic of Creation, *Enuma Elish*.

What further light can these tales shed on the mystery of the gods and the cosmos?

Stones from the Sky

To begin with Ninurta and Azag/Zu, the story is set in the days when Enlil controlled Heaven and Earth, seemingly having taken over from his ageing father Anu. Enlil thus sat enthroned on the Mountain of Heaven and oversaw the cosmic axis, which had been established by means of the DUR.AN.KI, 'the Bond of Heaven and Earth'. The key to this axial bond was the so-called 'Tablets of Destiny' which had been stowed away securely in the Underworld.[21]

Enlil had, by this time, fathered a principal son named Ninurta (alias Ningirsu), whom the texts describe as 'foremost among the Anunnaki' and 'the offspring of E.KUR', i.e. of 'the world mountain'.[22] Ninurta was imagined to be a fierce warrior-god with the appearance of a dragon, but with the 'paws of a lion' and 'the claws of an eagle'.[23]

But the olden god of Heaven, Anu, had earlier impregnated the Earth, which had given birth to the evil Azag/Zu, and this god now fixed his sights on 'the Enlilship' – the supreme command of Heaven and Earth:

> Zu seized the Tablets of Destiny in his hands,
> Taking away the Enlilship; suspended were the norms.
> When Zu had flown away and repaired to his mountain,
> Stillness spread abroad, silence prevailed.[24]

This distant mountain of Zu was called HAR.SAG.MU, meaning 'MU of the Mountain Range'. Since the MU was a means of travelling through the heavens, Zu's mountain was apparently a 'flying mountain' or a mountain of the heavens. In other words, Zu had risen up to a heavenly throne and had established a new kingship in competition with Enlil.

Who would restore the Bond of Heaven and Earth? The challenge was accepted by Ninurta, who immediately proceeded to engage Zu in battle:

> (Ninurta) the hero hitched the seven ill winds,
> The seven whirlwinds which cause the dust to dance.
> He launched a terrifying war, a fierce conflict.
> While the gale at his side shrieked for strife,
> Zu and Ninurta met at the mountainside...
> In the midst of the mountain Zu let loose a piercing shriek.
> There was darkness, the face of the mountain was covered.[25]

Zu personified this heavenly mountain (as is clear from these and other lines) and thus he and the mountain were both destroyed by Ninurta's deadly weapons. Thereupon, HAR.SAG.MU literally did become 'a flying mountain', as a flood of rocks and ice swept down from Heaven to Earth:

> Ninurta, the son of Enlil, wrought magnificently.
> He made a heap of stones in the mountain – like drifting rain clouds
>   they came floating on outstretched wings,
> Set bar before the country as with a great wall...
> The mighty waters followed along (with) the stone.[26]

This 'heap of stones' did not comprise mundane hailstones, as modern scholars commonly suppose, for they did not melt as hailstones are prone to do. Instead, the ex-heavenly stones formed a permanent 'wall' or 'heaped-up mound' upon the Earth. Hence, in *Lugal-e*, the victorious god Ninurta is described as sitting in judgement of the 'stones' which had been piled up as a result of the battle. Some of them he blessed for being his allies, whilst other he cursed because they had formed 'the army of Azag'.[27] In addition, *Lugal-e* makes great play of the fact that Ninurta had created a 'heaped-up hill' or HAR.SAG, i.e. a 'mountain'.[28] It was no ordinary mountain, but rather a metaphor for the newly fecundated Earth, which Ninurta handed over for safe-keeping to the new Earth-goddess, whose name, most aptly, was NIN.HAR.SAG, 'Lady of the Mountain'.[29]

This same cataclysmic event was reported in anthropomorphic form, too. Ninurta, we are told, cut the throat of Azag/Zu and dispatched his 'wings' on the 'winds', all the way back to the E.KUR, i.e. to the 'world mountain' of the Earth.[30] At the same time, the Tablets of Destiny were returned as if by magic to the AB.ZU (or Apsu), i.e. to the Underworld inside the Earth.

The more popular account, however, states that Ninurta captured Zu, and flew him – in the form of the Imdugud-bird – all the way from Heaven to the AB.ZU, i.e. to the Underworld.[31] This was the reason why the city of Lagash possessed a temple, dedicated to Ninurta/Ningirsu, named *E-ninnu-Imdugud-bar-bar*, meaning 'Eninnu, Flashing Imdugud-bird'. The flashing bird had nothing to do with aeronautical technology, as von Daniken would have it, but everything to do with the cataclysmic destruction of the heavenly mountain of Azag/Zu. Here, we find that heavenly stones, once again, are the key to interpreting the myth. The name Imdugud meant 'Sling-stone' as indeed did the name Azag.[32] The implication here is that the stones of the vanquished god had been 'slung' down from his heavenly mountain to the Earth below. Were these stones really hailstones as scholars have suggested?[33] Was the disintegration of Azag/Zu's mountain nothing more than a cloudburst originating from the troposphere? Or have modern scholars totally missed the point of this story?

Three further examples of the heavenly stones should help to clarify this point.

The first example occurs in the Sumerian creation myth entitled *Enki and the World Order*.[34] In this story, we read how Enki (a son of Anu and brother of Enlil) came down from the 'Mountain-House' of Heaven (the E.KUR) to the AB.ZU of Eridu (i.e. to the Apsu, or subterranean ocean of the Earth).[35] At the same time, Enki brought down with him a great flood, comprising not just waters but also other material, which he 'piled up' in 'heaps and mounds'. Further details are lacking but the impression is given that these piled-up heaps and mounds represented permanent enhancements to the face of the Earth, much in the same manner as the stones heaped up in *Lugal-e* by Ninurta.

The second example occurs in another Enki creation myth, entitled *Gilgamesh, Enkidu and the Underworld*.[36] In this text, we read how Enki 'set sail for the Underworld' in a boat. However, as he descended from Heaven to Earth, this boat was surrounded by a confused mass of 'small stones', 'large stones' and floodwaters. This confused mass raged all around Enki's boat 'like an attacking storm', and the text gives the impression that the stones accompanied the god all the way down into the Underworld.[37]

The third example is a brief anecdote from Egypt, where it was said that the ex-sky-god Geb had let out a loud shriek and then 'entered into' the Earth (his name came from the verb *gebgeb*, meaning 'to fall headlong').[38] One particular Egyptian text seems to give the game away: it says of Geb that he carried out construction and renovation work to the Earth in 'thousands of foundations and millions of places'.[39] This lends support to the idea that the Mesopotamian gods Ninurta and Enki made permanent changes to the Earth's surface when they descended from Heaven with their celestial stones.

I must emphasise again that these heavenly stones were certainly not hailstones. Hailstones do not have the power or mass to alter the face of the Earth, nor to split open the Earth and enter the Underworld as the Near Eastern deities were in the habit of doing. Meteorites do.

The classic example of the god splitting open the Earth is Osiris, the Egyptian god of the Underworld. According to the Pyramid Texts, Osiris had been born in the sky but had 'split open the Earth... on the day when he wished to come thence'.[40] The body-parts of Osiris, interred in the Underworld, were said to be made of iron, as was his imagined throne in the sky.[41] In short, Osiris was the meteorite-god *par excellence* and the archetype of the 'vanishing god'.[42]

Another classic example of a god splitting open the Earth comes from Mesopotamia. In *The Myth of the Pickaxe*, we read how Enlil, whose popular nickname was 'The Great Mountain', used a 'pickaxe' to split open the Earth at Nippur (the 'navel of the world').[43] Thereupon, the Earth became impregnated with the seeds of vegetation and all living creatures, including a primitive, subterranean form of mankind.

What was this 'pickaxe'? In other Mesopotamian sources, such as the Sumerian *Lamentation Texts* and *The Epic of Gilgamesh*, the pickaxe is associated with fire and destruction, and with a strangely shaped, heavy object that fell from the sky.[44] Clearly this was no ordinary pickaxe. On the contrary, it would seem that the word 'pickaxe' was a metaphor for a meteorite.

It is but a short step from here to recognise similar profound imagery in the ancient myths of sacred marriages between Heaven and Earth. A particularly fine example is the Sumerian tale entitled *Dispute between Summer and Winter*, where the sky-god Enlil impregnates the Earth-mountain (the HAR.SAG) with the seasons of summer and winter:

> Enlil, the king of all the lands, set his mind.
> He thrust his penis into the Great Mountain (HAR.SAG)...
> Summer and Winter, the fecundating overflow of the land, he poured
>   into the womb.
> Wheresoever Enlil would thrust his penis, he roared like a wild bull.
> There, HAR.SAG spent the day, rested happily at night,
> Delivered herself of Summer and Winter like rich cream...[45]

This insertion of Enlil's metaphorical 'penis' into the Earth-mountain was no different from his insertion of the metaphorical 'pickaxe'. The result was the same: Earth became impregnated by the seeds of Enlil's 'Great Mountain', i.e. by its heavenly stones or meteorites.

This brings us back to the Greek myth of Ouranos, whose name meant 'Mountain of Heaven'. Just like the 'Great Mountain' Enlil, Ouranos inserted his penis into the Earth and impregnated her. The celestial event is alluded to by Hesiod in *Theogony*:

> Great Ouranos came, bringing on Night, and desirous of love, he
> spread himself over Gaia (Earth), stretched out in every direction.[46]

It is not to be doubted that Ouranos did insert his metaphorical penis into Gaia (witness the Hurro-Hittite castration myth that parallels Kronos' castration of Ouranos). Indeed, the Greek dramatist Aeschylus virtually said as much when he wrote that Ouranos came down 'drunken, to penetrate the body of Earth'.[47] The unavoidable conclusion, if we are to learn the lessons of comparative mythology, is that Ouranos impregnated Gaia with a flood of meteorites. (And thus the Earth gave birth to the gods.)

But there is much more to this story than meteorites. In the myths cited earlier, as well as in numerous other similar tales, the gods fertilised the Earth not just with stones, but also with heavenly floodwaters. It is to these heavenly floodwaters that we must now turn our attention.

Enuma Elish

As promised earlier, we turn now to the Babylonian Epic of Creation, known from its opening line as *Enuma Elish* (*'When on High...'*). This myth has long been a favourite among those Hellenists who work in the field of comparative mythology. Recently, in the 1980-1990s, Burkert and West have scored notable successes in identifying profound parallels between *Enuma Elish* and the Greek succession myth of Ouranos, Kronos and Zeus.

Enuma Elish begins by confirming the bipolar nature of the Universe of Heaven and Earth. The first line reads: 'When on high the Heaven had not been named and below the Earth had not been called by a name'.[48] With the scene having been set thus, at the beginning of time, the text goes on to describe a sexual union taking place in the heavenly abode between Apsu, the father of the gods, and Tiamat, their mother. The waters of Apsu and Tiamat, we are told, were 'commingled as a single body', as a result of which 'the gods were created within them'.[49] These gods then began to run amok inside the heavenly body of Apsu-Tiamat:

> The divine brothers [the gods] gathered together.
> They disturbed Tiamat and assaulted (her), their keeper.
> Yea, they troubled the inner parts of Tiamat,
> Moving and running about within the divine abode.
> Apsu could not quell their noise.[50]

Eventually, the noise of the gods drove Apsu to plot their destruction. Turning to Tiamat, he said: "I will destroy them, and put an end to their ways, so that silence may be restored; and then let us sleep!". At first, Tiamat was aghast, but then she concurred with Apsu's plan, saying: "Yes, O father, do destroy their mutinous ways." But Ea-the-wise – one of the gods who had been born inside Apsu-Tiamat – heard of his parents' murderous scheme, and decided to take precipitative action:

> Ea [Enki] poured sleep upon Apsu. Sound asleep he lay.
> When he had made Apsu prone, drenched with sleep...
> He fettered Apsu and slew him...[51]

Apsu's fate – shared by all gods who were slaughtered in Heaven – was to be cast down to the Earth, into the Underworld. *Enuma Elish* thus explains how it came to be that the subterranean ocean of the world was named Apsu (or, in Sumerian, AB.ZU).

At this point, the first-born gods of Apsu and Tiamat descended from Heaven to Earth, led by Ea:

He [Ea/Enki] established his dwelling on top of Apsu...
After Ea had vanquished and trodden down his foes...
He rested in his sacred chamber in profound peace.
He named it Apsu, assigned it for shrines,
(And) founded his cult hut in that same place.[52]

In due course, Ea proceeded to have sexual union with Damkina (this goddess probably personified the Earth) and together, they brought about the birth of Marduk, who was destined to become the king of the gods. *Enuma Elish* describes the newly born god in supernatural terms:

In the heart of holy Apsu, Marduk was born...
Alluring was his figure, sparkling the look of his eyes...
Perfect were his members beyond comprehension...
Four were his eyes, four were his ears;
When he moved his lips, fire blazed forth...
His members were gigantic, he was surpassing in height.[53]

Meanwhile, Tiamat was in the heavens, and she still possessed a brood of gods inside her. These gods urged Tiamat to gain revenge on the gods who had slain her husband Apsu. Taking their advice, Tiamat brought forth a new brood of dreadful monsters and crowned them with shining god-like haloes. Tiamat – now referred to as Mother Hubur, 'Mother of Noise' – raged in the heavens, while the newly born gods marched at her side, eager for battle. The text implies that they were about to go down into the Underworld and prevail over Ea and the Anunnaki.[54]

Down below, in the Underworld, Ea caught wind of Tiamat's plan, and began a series of urgent meetings with his fellow, subterranean gods. But not one was brave enough to face the raging Tiamat. Eventually, it was Marduk who stepped forward and offered to save the gods if, in return, they would make him their king after the battle. All of the gods concurred with this plan, whereupon Marduk filled himself with 'an ever-blazing flame', armed himself with a bow and arrow, a mace, a net, lightning, a flooding storm and various cataclysmic winds, mounted his 'storm-chariot', and roared up into the heavens, adorned with a 'terrible radiance'. Thus he took the fight to Tiamat, and vanquished her:

The Lord [Marduk] spread out his net to enfold her [Tiamat];
The Evil Wind, which followed behind, he let loose in her face.
When Tiamat opened her mouth to devour him,
He drove in the Evil Wind so that she closed not her lips.
The raging winds filled her belly;
Her belly became distended, and her mouth opened wide.

He shot off an arrow, and it tore her insides;
It cut through her interior, splitting her heart.
Having thus subdued her, he extinguished her life.[55]

Having thus destroyed Tiamat, Marduk cast her lifeless body into the Underworld and made the two great rivers of Mesopotamia – the Tigris and the Euphrates – flow upwards from her 'eyes'.[56] Other parts of her body he used to create the stars and constellations (see next chapter).

Figure 3.
MARDUK STANDS
VICTORIOUS OVER
THE SEA-GODDESS
TIAMAT

As for Tiamat's brood of gods, *Enuma Elish* states that Marduk put their leader, Kingu, to death and created man from his blood. The other monsters he trapped in his net and imprisoned them for eternity in the Underworld.[57]

Finally, Marduk measured the fallen Apsu and created, in its image, a metaphysical Heaven (Esharra) which would be an abode for ever for himself and the other immortal gods.[58] The text ends with Marduk being crowned king of the gods.

In *Enuma Elish*, we see several major parallels to the succession myth of the Greeks. The most useful, perhaps, is the explicit description of the god Marduk's origin, revealing how he was born from the Earth as the offspring of a sacred marriage of Heaven and Earth.[59] This is the origin of the Greek gods to a tee, in all their invisible and metaphysical glory, although it forces us, once again, to consider the implied existence of physical gods, born in the sky, who must have split open the Earth to propagate their metaphysical counterparts.

The most astonishing parallel, however, relates to the identification of the primeval Babylonian couple Apsu and Tiamat with the first Greek couple Oceanus and Tethys (named by Homer in the *Iliad*). Just as Apsu was father of all the gods, so, too, was Oceanus. And just as Tiamat was mother of all the gods, so, too, was Tethys.[60]

But the parallels run much deeper. In respect of Oceanus, modern scholars have pointed out that Homer referred to him with the epithet *apsorrhoos*, which is almost certainly derived from the Akkadian name Apsu.[61] And as for Tethys, the same scholars have virtually proven that her name, in Greek, is an exact transcription of *tawtu*, meaning 'sea', which appears in *Enuma Elish* as a variant spelling of the name Tiamat.[62]

The upshot of this is that scholars regard Apsu and Tiamat as a one hundred per cent match with Oceanus and Tethys, and are in no doubt at all that the Homeric tradition derives from the Babylonian epic *Enuma Elish*.

What can we learn from this extraordinary parallel? Firstly, *Enuma Elish* illustrates a quite remarkable Mesopotamian idea, namely that a great ocean of waters, namely Apsu-Tiamat, fell from Heaven to Earth. This is an indisputable interpretation. Firstly, it is stated in the opening lines of *Enuma Elish* that Apsu and Tiamat were in the heavens and that 'their waters commingled as a single body'. Secondly, it is stated that Ea (Enki) cast Apsu down into the Underworld and that, later, Marduk cast Tiamat down into the Underworld. Every scholar indeed recognises that Apsu was the name of the subterranean ocean – the freshwater or sweet water ocean – and that Tiamat was the saltwater counterpart (her own name is known to derive from a root word meaning 'ocean').[63]

What does this tell us about the *Greek* myths? Well, if we accept the self-evident facts concerning the fallen heavenly ocean, together with the identification of Apsu/Tiamat with Oceanus/Tethys, then we arrive at a spectacular conclusion: Oceanus and Tethys, and all the rivers of the Greek Underworld (such as the River Styx), originated in the heavens. Because that is where Apsu and Tiamat started out. This was certainly the case with the River Styx, for Hesiod asserts that the submarine palace of the river-goddess Styx was 'on every side fastened to the sky with silver columns'.[64] Further to this, Euripides gives the game away in his play *Medea*, when he has the chorus sing of a day when 'the sacred river-founts flow upwards to their source, and *Dike* [Order] and all the world are turned backwards'.[65] What else could this mean but that the waters of the rivers and springs would return to Heaven where they belonged?

And from this straightforward conclusion, there flows an even more staggering thought: that if Oceanus fell from Heaven, then he entered the Underworld (as falling gods were wont to do) and became a subterranean sea, just like Apsu. Oceanus would thus personify the mythical ocean of the Underworld.

This idea, that Oceanus was a fallen ocean of Heaven (and thus a subterranean ocean), may be a difficult concept for some people to swallow. But the fact is that I am not the first to suggest that Oceanus was an ex-heavenly god. In 1912, the eminent Hellenist Francis Cornford described Oceanus as 'the Heaven-stream'.[66] And in 1969, Giorgio de Santillana and Hertha von Dechend commented as follows in their book *Hamlet's Mill*:

> He [Oceanus] is the Father of Rivers; he dimly appears in tradition, indeed, as the original god of Heaven in the past. He stands in an Orphic hymn as 'beloved end of the Earth, ruler of the *polos* ['axis', i.e. of Heaven and Earth]', and in that famous ancient lexicon, the *Etymologicum magnum*, his name is seen to derive from 'Heaven'.[67]

This interpretation is indeed supported by two famous passages in the *Iliad*. Firstly, there is the 'golden rope' speech, in which Zeus proclaims his powers over all the other gods:

> "I [Zeus] could haul you [gods] up, earth, sea and everything; then I could hitch the rope on the peak of Olympus, so that everything, once more, should hang in mid-air."[68]

If this is not to be dismissed as mere poetic allegory, then the Earth's sea really did belong in the heavens, on the original mountain of Olympus.

Secondly, there is the passage describing the shield of Achilles, which was fabricated by Hephaestus, the blacksmith-god. The *Iliad* tells us that: 'on it he made the Earth, and Heaven and Sea, the weariless Sun and the Moon waxing full, and all the constellations...'.[69] In the words of one modern scholar: 'the fabrication of the shield is in essence a microcosmic account of the creation, with the craftsman Hephaestus cast in the role of creator'.[70] But the *Iliad* then continues: 'and on it he made the mighty river of Oceanus, running on the rim round the edge of the strong-built shield.' In other words, the creator-god Hephaestus elevated Oceanus from his station on Earth to the outermost sphere of the Universe – the highest of all the cosmic regions.[71]

In the light of these passages, there can be no doubt that Oceanus belonged in the heavens and that he fell from Heaven to Earth, just as the Babylonian god Apsu did. And if Oceanus did thus fall from Heaven to

Earth, there can be no doubt, either, that his primary identity would have been a god of the Underworld, i.e. a subterranean ocean, just like Apsu. What is more, the *Iliad* seems to affirm this very idea with its reference to 'the great strength of the deep stream of Oceanus, from which all rivers and all the sea and all springs and deep wells take their flow'.[72]

So much for Oceanus, but what about his consort Tethys? We know about her primarily from the *Iliad*, in which Homer sings of 'Oceanus, origin of the gods, and their mother Tethys'.[73] Having thus identified Tethys as the mother of the gods, Homer goes on to explain that she and Oceanus had withheld their conjugal rights from each other for a long time, having been separated by strife.[74] A further snippet of information comes from the Orphics, who stated that: 'Fair flowing Ocean was the first to marry... he wedded his sister, the daughter of his mother'.[75] These lines it must be said, are one hundred per cent evocative of the sacred marriage of Heaven and Earth, which required the union of the divine couple followed by their separation. The implication is that Tethys came down from Heaven, in the manner of Tiamat, and took over the mantle of Mother Earth-goddess, whereupon Oceanus came down from Heaven, in the manner of Apsu, and fathered the gods upon her.[76]

Chapter Eight Summary

* The battle of the gods involved the destruction of the mountain of Heaven, which unleashed a deluge of stones and floodwaters upon the Earth below. These stones and floodwaters were regarded as the seeds of creation.

* Near Eastern texts confirm that the heavenly stones were meteorites, whilst the floodwaters were of oceanic proportions.

* The myth of Ouranos and Gaia has close parallels in Near Eastern traditions of sacred marriages between the mountains of Heaven and Earth. We can thus conclude that Ouranos impregnated Gaia with a storm of meteorites and celestial floodwaters.

* The myth of Oceanus and Tethys is virtually an exact match with the Babylonian myth of Apsu and Tiamat. Thus Oceanus, like Apsu, personified the ocean of Heaven which, as a result of a cataclysm, fell into the Earth's Underworld and became a subterranean sea.

CHAPTER NINE

WHEN THE SKY FELL

**In the beginning, Earth, Heaven and sea were
confounded in common mass together; then –
as the result of grievous strife – they
were separated one from the other...**

(Orpheus, in Apollonios Rhodios' *Argonautika*, 3rd century BC)

The Greek myths, I have argued, are due for a reappraisal. The Heaven in
which the Olympian gods dwelt was not the peak of a terrestrial Mount
Olympus, but rather a metaphorical 'mountain' which existed far above
the clouds in the pure *aither* of the heavens. Hence, when Ouranos came
down to impregnate Gaia (and thus generate the gods), he did so not in
the form of thunder, lightning, rainwater or hailstones (as implied by the
modern-day myth of weather-gods), but rather in the form of meteorites
and floodwaters from a physical 'Mountain of Heaven', which had been
torn apart, at the beginning of time, by a tremendous cataclysm. This
cataclysm, it must be emphasised, was not a historical, eye-witnessed
event – for human beings had not yet been created. Rather, the cataclysm
was theorised (theorised by the ancients) and it may, or may not, have
actually occurred in reality. In short, it was a mythical cataclysm.

So far, so good. But the story is only half told, and the reappraisal of
the Greek myths is only half complete. In this chapter, I will again use
the parallels between Greek and Near Eastern myths to shed light on how
the Universe was created in the aftermath of Heaven's fall, at the same
time offering further corroboration of the cataclysmic interpretation of
the myths. Firstly, I will set out a synopsis of the act of creation, and then
I will demonstrate how the Greek and Near Eastern myths, respectively,
support the interpretation which I shall give.

First, the synopsis. In the beginning, said the myth-makers, Heaven
had been a physical body – a mountain, metaphorically speaking, that

had consisted of earth, stone and water (the latter sometimes visualised in the form of ice). Thus the original Universe had comprised two physical bodies, Heaven and Earth, arranged in opposition to each other along a celestial, bipolar axis. Next, there had been a tremendous cataclysm in which Heaven had been torn apart, unleashing upon the Earth a deluge of stones and floodwaters. These stones, I have argued, were meteorites, which split open the Earth's womb and impregnated her with the seeds of life.

This fall of Heaven to Earth (or *into* the Earth) was portrayed by the myth-makers as a sacred marriage of god and goddess, who conjoined in the Underworld for the purpose of procreation. From this sexual union of Heaven and Earth, the Earth conceived and gave birth to wonderful and miraculous things. A new, invisible and immortal Mountain of Heaven: Mount Olympus. A race of invisible and immortal gods, who ascended to dwell on Olympus. A visible canopy of the heavens (the Sun, Moon, planets and stars), which surrounded the Earth. And the first forms of primitive life, which emerged onto the Earth's surface.

All things in the present Universe were thus created as the result of a cataclysm – a mythical cataclysm, which marked the beginning of time.

That completes the synopsis. Now, I shall lay bare the full details of this astonishing story, drawing firstly on the cosmogonies of the Greeks and, secondly, on the older cosmogonies of the Near East.

Greek Cosmogonies

To begin, let us look again at the non-mainstream cosmogonies of the Greeks, which were outlined in chapter three of this book.

Firstly, Anaximander. In his scheme, the four elements of the Universe had at first been contained within a primeval, undifferentiated mass which he called 'the Unlimited'. For some unknown reason, this mass had begun to differentiate, its cold portion becoming a watery mass of earth that was enveloped in vapour, and its hot portion becoming a sphere of flame that surrounded the whole. Then the Unlimited had been torn apart. Its sphere of flame had burst into rings of fire, and these rings of fire had become 'enclosed and hidden in dark mist'.[1] Anaximander thus encapsulates perfectly the idea of a cataclysm in Heaven, followed by a fall of fire into the Underworld, the latter signified by the 'dark mist'.

Secondly, Anaxagoras. In the beginning, he said, 'all things were together'; in other words, the elements of the Universe had not yet been created separately, but were together in the form of tiny homogeneous particles. Then, Mind (*Nous*) had transformed the homogeneous particles into separate elements by setting everything moving 'in a whirling motion'. In what seems to have been a parallel account, Anaxagoras declared that the Universe had tilted towards the south 'in order that some parts of the Universe might become uninhabitable and other parts habitable'. What this means, to paraphrase, is that Heaven (the celestial 'north') had fallen to the Earth (the celestial 'south'); and thus life on Earth had begun.

Thirdly, Empedocles. According to his cosmogony, all things had originally been bonded together by Love in a harmonious Sphere, which he called *Theos* (God). But then, 'Strife waxed mightily in the members of the Sphere – they all trembled in turn'. As a result of this discord, the God-Sphere had been torn apart, the four elements of the Universe had been born, and all material things on the Earth had been generated.

The reader should note that there is a recognisable common theme in all three of these cosmogonies, namely that Heaven disintegrated and fell to the Earth. But we can also identify a second theme, too, namely the idea that the fall of Heaven caused all things to become *physically mixed together* in the southernmost, or bottom, end of the bipolar axis, i.e. in the Earth.

Consider Anaximander once again. After his Unlimited mass was torn apart, it produced 'rings of fire' which became 'enclosed and hidden in dark mist'. As those familiar with the Greek writings will appreciate, the term 'dark mist' is usually associated with the Underworld, and it would indeed make a great deal of sense here, in this context, that the rings of fire had fallen into the Underworld, whence in due course they would give birth to the Sun, Moon and stars (in accordance with the Orphic belief that these things had been created from the Underworld – see later).

Now consider the words of the poet Alcman. In the beginning, he said, the world had been 'a confused, unformed mass'. Why had the world's mass been 'confused'? Had Heaven become confused with the Earth? The words of Orpheus, as recorded in the *Argonautika* of Apollonios Rhodios, confirm that it was indeed so:

He sang how, in the beginning, Earth, Heaven and sea were
confounded in common mass together...[2]

Let us ask ourselves a natural question: how could Heaven have been mixed together with Earth and sea? The most obvious explanation, when we stop to think about it, is that Heaven had fallen physically upon the Earth.

This interpretation is indeed confirmed in the more detailed Orphic cosmogony in which Time was said to have given birth to *Khaos*, the *Aither* and *Erebos*. This *Erebos* (literally 'Darkness') was synonymous with the Underworld and thus, when the Orphics said that 'all things were in confusion, throughout the misty darkness', they were referring to a confusion of all things in the Underworld. It was from this confusion that the god Phanes had emerged to create all things in the Universe.

The theme here, clearly, is that Heaven fell into the Earth – into the Underworld – and that there was thus a confusion, or mixing together, of Heaven with Earth in the Underworld. The implication is that, as the ancients understood it, all things in the current Universe had originated in a cataclysm.[3]

Sceptics of the cataclysm theory might well wish to argue, in response to this, that all of these references to torn-apart bodies, rings of fire and subterranean confusion are cases of exaggerated poetic metaphor rather than reflections of a mythical cataclysm. But, leaving to one side the fact that Anaximander, Anaxagoras *et al* were cosmogonists rather than poets (i.e. they were the ancient equivalent of today's astrophysicists), we can lay to rest all such criticisms by examining the parallel, but older accounts of the Near East.

Near Eastern Cosmogonies

Let us turn, first of all, to what the Mesopotamians had to say. Here, it is important to appreciate that the word for Universe was the old Sumerian word AN.KI, which meant literally 'Heaven and Earth'.[4] In this scheme, Heaven (AN) was regarded as a metaphorical mountain and the Earth (KI) was regarded as a mountain, too (HAR.SAG). Crucially, however, the Universe consisted of a third domain, the Underworld, and this, yet again, was known as a mountain – hence its names KUR, 'mountain', and KUR.NU.GI, 'the Mountain of No Return'. In effect, the Underworld was a mountain-within-a-mountain.

Why was the Underworld regarded as a mountain? The explanation surely lies in the Mesopotamian myths of the Mountain of Heaven falling to the Earth, along with the mythical idea that all things descending from Heaven always entered into the Underworld. The Mountain of Heaven had thus *become* the Mountain of the Underworld.

Remarkably, the Sumerian name for Earth, KI, reflects this mythical fact, for its meaning, as a verb, was 'to cut off, to sever, to hollow out or to excavate'.[5] The Earth was thus regarded as a 'hollowed out' body, in the sense that it had been forced to accommodate, or swallow up, the fallen Mountain of Heaven.

It was from this conjoined Mountain of Heaven-and-Earth that the Mesopotamian gods were born. Thus, in the creation myth *Enki and the World Order*, Enki declared that: "My father, the king of Heaven and Earth, brought me into existence in Heaven-and-Earth (AN.KI)."[6] More explicitly, we read in *The Dispute between Cattle and Grain* how AN caused the Anunnaki-gods to be born in the Mountain of Heaven-and-Earth:

> In the Mountain of Heaven-and-Earth, AN [Heaven] caused the
>   Anunnaki to be born...[7]

The meaning here is quite unambiguous, because the Anunnaki-gods were understood to be mythical denizens of the Underworld. It follows that the Mountain of Heaven-and-Earth in which the Anunnaki were born could only have been the Earth. *QED*: Heaven must have fallen and merged with the Earth to become a new, singular mountain.

So basic was this presumption that Heaven had fallen and become the Underworld that the Mesopotamian poets rarely felt it necessary to state the fact explicitly. But, fortunately, there are some notable exceptions, such as the following passage in the Sumerian text *Lamentations over the Destruction of Sumer and Ur*:

> (It was) a day when the weapon sent forth from above wrecked the
>   city as if with a pickaxe.
> On that day, Heaven was crushed, Earth was smitten...
> Heaven was darkened, was overcast with shadow, was turned into the
>   Underworld.[8]

There we have it: 'Heaven was crushed... Heaven was turned into the Underworld.' Not only that, but the poet was kind enough to describe the cataclysm in terms of a 'pickaxe' falling from the skies like a weapon – hence our decoding of Enlil's 'pickaxe' as a meteorite, or, more likely, a whole storm of meteorites (see previous chapter).

We turn now to the accounts of the Egyptians, where we find exactly the same beliefs about a Mountain of Heaven-and-Earth, albeit expressed in the form of metaphors and cryptic allusions. Consider, for example, the following statement made by the creator-god Re:

> "I am he who made Heaven and Earth, who knotted together the
>   mountains, and created everything which exists thereon."[9]

This would mean nothing were it not for the fact that the Egyptians used the word 'mountain' as a metaphor for Heaven and Earth respectively.[10]

Thus Re's claim meant that he had made Heaven and Earth by 'knotting together' the two mountains of Heaven and Earth.

Consider, too, the Egyptian myth of 'the Union of the Two Lands'. Egyptologists assume that this signified a political joining together of Upper and Lower Egypt. But the Coffin Texts state otherwise:

> As for the Union of the Two Lands, it means that the shroud of Osiris was ordered by his father Re.[11]

Who was Osiris? He was Re's physical counterpart, who had fallen from Heaven to become the god of the Underworld. As noted in the previous chapter, Osiris was the meteorite-god *par excellence* and the archetype of the 'vanishing god' (hence the fundamental myth of his dismemberment and interment in the Earth).[12]

It follows that the Union of the Two Lands referred to the joining together of Heaven and Earth.[13]

The same idea is referred to in a text entitled *The Mysteries of the Resurrection of Osiris*, which records some of the lesser secrets of the Osirian Mystery rites. In this text, the Senior Lector Priest recounts the arrival of the meteorite-god Osiris in the Earth by reciting the words: "Heaven and Earth join... Heaven and Earth join." Four times he utters these words. Then, after further recitations of "Rising up of Heaven upon Earth", it is declared that: "our lord (Osiris) is in his house', i.e. Osiris had arrived safely in the Underworld.[14]

This fall of Osiris from Heaven to Earth was also regarded as a union between him and Isis, the goddess of the Underworld, resulting in the birth of life symbolised by the divine child Horus. Hence the strange myth reported by Plutarch in which Isis had given birth to Horus 'having had union with Osiris after his death'.[15] Older texts referred to this union in equally cryptic terms, for example: 'The lightning flash strikes... Isis wakes pregnant with the seed of her brother Osiris.'[16] It was a union of Heaven and Earth.

Much more could be said about the Egyptian myths, but the point has been made and, for the sake of brevity, we must move on to consider what happened in the immediate aftermath of Heaven and Earth being joined together.

The Separation of Heaven from Earth

After the fall of Heaven – after Heaven had become joined together with the Earth in a single confused mass – the Earth was, for a while, alone in the Universe. But then came the final, dramatic act of cosmic creation – the separation of Heaven from the Earth, the birth of metaphysical gods from the Earth, and the birth of the visible Universe, comprising Sun, Moon, planets and stars.

We will look first at the idea of the separation of Heaven from Earth, and the corresponding idea of the gods being elevated into the heavenly domain. It is an astonishing fact that, despite the prevalence of this separation myth throughout ancient literatures – it is found, for example, in the Bible, the Koran and the Rig-Veda, to name but a few – modern scholars have not the faintest clue what this separation of Heaven from Earth was all about.[17]

This time, we will begin with the Near Eastern myths, and then use them to illuminate the meaning of the Greek myths.

Let us begin with Egypt. In the Pyramid Texts – the oldest sacred writings of Egypt, dating to *c.* 2300 BC – we find an intriguing reference to a time 'when the Heaven was separated from the Earth, when the gods ascended to the Heaven.'[18] This double statement is important, for it corroborates the Greek idea that the gods went up to Heaven – to an imperishable abode – at the same time as Heaven was lifted up. Another important statement is found in Spell 334 of the Egyptian Coffin Texts, where the god-king Horus states:

> "I am that first seed of Re, he begot me in the womb of my mother
> Isis [the Earth]... My mother Isis conceived me, and she swooned
> under the fingers of the Lord-of-the-gods when he broke into her
> therewith on that Day of Lifting... on that Day of Tumult..."[19]

It can be seen from this declaration that the 'Day of Lifting' was also a 'Day of Tumult', which was elsewhere referred to as 'that day of slaying the Oldest Ones', 'that day when the rivals fought', 'that day of the great reckoning', 'that day of the storm over the Two Lands', and 'that day of the great slaughter'.[20] Thus did the Egyptians juxtapose the separation of Heaven and Earth with a war of Heaven and Earth – surely a cataclysmic event, whether real or imagined.

One of the most popular Egyptian myths of the separation of Heaven from Earth involved the sky-goddess Nut. Nut, however, was not simply the starry sky as Egyptologists so fondly imagine. On the contrary. In the Pyramid Texts, Nut made clear her original identity as 'the Primeval Hill of Land in the midst of the Sea', i.e. a 'Hill' that floated in the celestial sea.[21] This Hill had met a cataclysmic fate, remembered in myth as the cracking open of Nut's head or the bursting open of her womb. In the latter myth, Nut gave birth to five children – Osiris, Isis, Seth, Nephthys and Horus – who became known, rather appropriately, as 'the Children of Chaos'.[22] Nut was thus no different in nature from any of the heavenly mountains which we have encountered thus far.

In keeping with this interpretation, the Egyptian texts pictured Nut as a fallen sky which had to be lifted back up to the heavens. The tradition runs that she had been 'shut in' with her consort Geb on 'the day of the great slaughter' and had been performing the sacred marriage rite (in the Underworld one presumes) whereupon the god Shu became jealous and separated the two lovers by lifting up Nut to become the Heaven (or heavens).[23] Figure 4 shows Shu standing as a pillar of Heaven and Earth (like the Greek god Atlas), separating Nut above from Geb below.

Figure 4.
THE SEPARATION OF
HEAVEN FROM EARTH

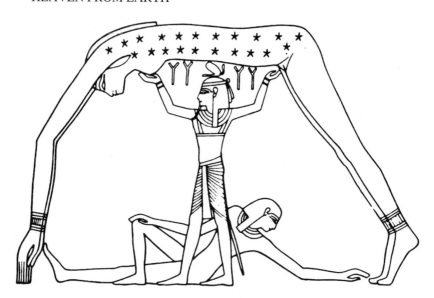

Turning to Mesopotamia, we find that the separation of Heaven from Earth was a major cosmological theme, just as in Egypt. And once again, it becomes apparent that we are dealing with a cataclysmic event. Thus in the Sumerian text *The Myth of the Pickaxe*, the separation of Heaven from Earth by Enlil coincided with his cataclysmic creation of life on Earth, when he split open the Earth with his metaphorical pickaxe.

But there is only one Mesopotamian myth that goes into detail on this subject and that is *Enuma Elish*. Picking up the Babylonian story where we left it earlier, Marduk had won his promotion to king of the gods, having vanquished the sky-goddess Tiamat, who now resided in the Underworld alongside her consort Apsu. What Marduk did next was to separate Heaven from Earth, and this he did in an intriguing fashion:

He [Marduk] crossed the heavens and surveyed the regions.

He placed himself opposite the Apsu [the Underworld], the dwelling
of Ea-the-wise [Enki].

The lord measured the dimensions of the Apsu,

And he established Esharra, 'the Great Abode', as its likeness.[24]

What this means is that Marduk measured the physical, fallen Mountain of Heaven (the Apsu) and created a new Heaven, Esharra, as an exact likeness of it, but in an invisible and metaphysical form. The Esharra thus became the heavenly abode for the invisible, metaphysical gods – an exact parallel with the Greek concept of Mount Olympus.

Significantly, we find in *Enuma Elish* a confirmation of the idea that the gods went up to Heaven at the same time as Heaven was separated from the Earth. Tablet VI of *Enuma Elish* explains that Marduk divided the gods, who had previously been bound together 'like a ball', making three hundred reside in Heaven – these became known as the Igigi-gods – whilst three hundred remained behind in the Earth – these were the Anunnaki-gods.[25] The Anunnaki were the physical gods, who had fallen from Heaven (the offspring of Anu). The Igigi were the metaphysical gods, who were equivalent, as a broad category, to the Olympian gods of the Greeks: they were 'the pure gods', who dwelt in the heavens with a 'brilliance like fire'.[26]

We turn now to the Greek myths of the separation of Heaven from the Earth. According to Hesiod's *Theogony*, the separation of Heaven from the Earth occurred after *Khaos* had given birth to *Erebos* and Night (this, it should be noted, is the same scheme as the Orphics). The relevant lines read:

Earth bore, first of all, one equal to herself, starry Ouranos, so that he should cover her all about, to be a secure seat for ever for the blessed gods.[27]

This birth of Ouranos was almost certainly his rebirth, in the guise of the invisible and metaphysical Mount Olympus which was indeed to be 'a secure seat for ever for the blessed gods'.[28] The true stars were created later in *Theogony*, as we shall see in a moment.

Having been separated thus, the idea, somewhat confusingly, was that Heaven and Earth would rejoin in marriage, but would thereafter be separated for ever. This permanent separation occurs a little later in *Theogony*, when Ouranos descends from Heaven and is castrated by his son Kronos. At this point, the last vestiges of Ouranos (his phallus and testicles) are interred permanently in the Earth, presumably joining the rest of his body there.[29] Meanwhile, the soul of Ouranos lives on, albeit passively, by becoming the aether that fills and surrounds the sphere of the Universe (hence the name Ouranos had multiple meanings: Heaven, heavens and Universe).

This exact same sequence, of conjunction and separation, followed by reunion and permanent separation, is corroborated in the works of the dramatist Euripides, who had Melanippe-the-wise state:

> "It is not my word, but my mother's word,
> How Heaven and Earth were once one form; but stirred
> And strove, and dwelt asunder far away;
> And then, re-wedding, bore unto the day
> And light of life all things that are: the trees,
> Flowers, birds and beasts, and those that breathe the seas,
> And mortal man, each in his kind and law."[30]

The mention here of strife is interesting, for it appears also in the words of Orpheus, per the *Argonautika* of Apollonios Rhodios:

> He sang how, in the beginning, Earth, Heaven and sea were confounded in common mass together and then, as the result of grievous strife, were separated one from the other...[31]

Perhaps this strife is to be understood in the context of the separation of Heaven from Earth (i.e. signifying tectonic and volcanic forces). But it nevertheless evokes the heavenly strife which caused the confused mass to arise in the first place.

A further account of the separation of Heaven from Earth occurs in the Orphic hymns to the First-born god Phanes/Eros. In the beginning, said the Orphics, Time had given birth to *Khaos*, the *Aither* and *Erebos* and 'all things were in confusion, throughout the misty darkness'. Next, Time had fashioned a silvery egg in the *Aither* (i.e. in the Underworld), and the egg had begun 'to move in a wondrous circle'. Suddenly, this egg split in two and Phanes emerged, gleaming with a supernatural light. At that moment, Heaven had been separated from the Earth:

> And at the birth of Phanes, the misty gulf below and the windless *Aither* were rent.[32]

In other words, the *Aither* had been separated from the dark, misty gulf of the Underworld and lifted up to become the invisible, metaphysical Heaven. This *Aither*, one presumes, was equivalent to Mount Olympus, for the text states, as if it were a parallel development, that Phanes 'built an imperishable house for the immortals'.[33]

In summary, the Greek myths of the separation of Heaven from Earth fit perfectly with the idea that Heaven had fallen and become conjoined with the Earth. Without the physical fall of Heaven and its union with the Earth, the separation makes no sense.

The Geocentric Universe

We turn now to the final, climactic act in the ancient cosmogonies of Greece and the Near East – the creation of the visible heavens: the Sun, the Moon and the stars.

In both the Greek and Near Eastern systems, the Sun, Moon and stars were latecomers to the cosmological scene. This may seem astonishing to modern minds, but it is important to remember that, in the ancients' view, the original cosmos comprised just two celestial bodies, Heaven and Earth, and nothing beyond that apart from an infinite ocean of cosmic waters. Nevertheless, the existence of the Sun, Moon and stars (including planets – the 'wandering stars') still had to be accounted for, and thus the ancients concluded that these lights in the sky had been created *after* the Mountain of Heaven had fallen, cataclysmically, into the mountain of Earth.

This, in effect, was a geocentric view *par excellence*, where the Earth was regarded as the mother of everything. She had given birth to plants, trees, animals and humans; she had given birth to miraculous invisible and immortal things – a replacement Mountain of Heaven and the race of gods who dwelt there; and now, to cap the performance, she gave birth to the visible heavens: the Sun, the Moon and the stars.

In Greece, the story appears in the Pelasgian myth of Eurynome and Ophion, in which Eurynome descended from Heaven to Earth and laid the Egg of the Universe. Ophion then coiled himself around the egg and caused it to split in two, whereupon the Sun, Moon, planets and stars were born.[34]

The same idea features in the Orphic myth of Phanes – the god who was born from a silvery egg in the Underworld. We may recall that Phanes separated the *Aither* from the 'misty gulf', lifting the *Aither* up to become Heaven. And we may recall that he built an 'imperishable house' for the immortal gods. It was only then, after the fall of Heaven and its separation from Earth, that Phanes created the Sun and the Moon.[35] Crucially, the Orphic text adds: 'All these things the Father made (while) in the misty darkness of the cave'.[36] The implication is that Phanes created the Sun and Moon while he was situated in the darkness of the Underworld.[37] In the Orphic scheme, then, the creation of the present

Universe was entirely geocentric.[38]

Yet again, the idea appears in Hesiod's *Theogony*. Oddly enough, it appears not at the beginning of *Theogony*, where Gaia gives birth to Ouranos as Olympus, but in a later, seemingly contrived, passage in which a new Earth-goddess Thea surrenders herself in marriage to a new god of Heaven, Hyperion.[39] The result of their union was that Thea gave birth to 'the mighty Sun and shining Moon, and to Dawn'; in other words, the Sun and Moon were born from the womb, or Underworld, of the Earth. Following this, Thea's daughter Dawn, 'the Mist-born One', surrendered herself to another god of Heaven, Astraeus (his name, significantly, meant 'the father of the stars').[40] And from this union 'the Mist-born One gave birth to the Morning Star and the shining stars that are the garland of the heavens.'[41] The explanation is that Astraeus fell from Heaven and joined with Dawn in the misty Underworld, causing the stars to be born from the womb of the Earth (all this long after the original Heaven and Earth had been joined and separated).

The fourth and final example of this Greek geocentrism appears in the cosmogony of Anaximander, albeit not very explicitly. It occurs in the aftermath of the explosion of the Unlimited, when the sphere of flame had burst and thrown off rings of fire. These rings of fire, we are told, were somehow responsible for the appearance of lights in the sky: the lights of the Sun, Moon and stars. How did this happen? The giveaway clue is that the rings of fire had first become 'enclosed and hidden in dark mist', i.e. in the Underworld.[42] Anaximander thus seems to have had in mind a fall of fire from Heaven to Earth, followed by a geocentric spinning off of the subterranean fire to generate the lights in the heavens – the Sun, Moon and stars respectively.

In the Near East, similarly, cosmogony focused on the origins of Heaven and Earth, with the creation of the Sun, Moon and stars being regarded as a subject of secondary importance. Accordingly, few texts explained how the Sun, Moon and stars had come into existence, but those that did seem to confirm the idea that these celestial bodies had been born from the sacred marriage of Heaven and Earth.

Take, for example, the Sumerian text entitled *Enlil and Ninlil*, which describes the creation of the Moon-god Sin. In this text, Enlil, the god of Heaven and the Great Mountain, impregnates his wife Ninlil with a river of semen-like water. Ninlil (a personification of the Earth) then becomes pregnant with the Moon-god Sin.[43] But there is a problem with releasing Sin from her womb and Enlil thus undertakes a secret mission into the Underworld, where he metamorphoses into three Underworld deities and impregnates Ninlil with three further children. These children then act as a ransom for Sin, who is allowed to emerge from the Underworld and shine in the heavens.[44] The idea in this myth is that the Moon was born of the Earth, and did not exist at the time when Heaven and Earth first got their act together.

As regards the stars, a Ugaritic myth confirms that they, too, were born from a celestial marriage. The myth, which is badly fragmented, states that El, the father of the gods, impregnated his two wives Asherah and Anath with the seed for the Morning Star and the Evening Star. With Asherah being known as 'Mother of the gods', it seems reasonable to presume that she and Anath represented dual Earth-goddesses.[45]

Although we do not possess such an explicit statement concerning the birth of the Sun,[46] *Enuma Elish* does provide corroborative evidence on several fronts. According to this text, Marduk created the Sun, Moon and stars using half of Tiamat's body, whilst another passage states that the slain body of Tiamat had been buried beneath a mountain, i.e. in the Underworld.[47] It can thus be surmised that the Sun, Moon and stars were born from the womb of the Earth. Whether or not this was the intention, the Sun, Moon and stars were certainly latecomers in *Enuma Elish*. In the beginning there had been only Heaven and Earth; then Heaven had fallen for the first time; then Marduk had been born; then Marduk had gone into battle against Tiamat; then Heaven had fallen again, for the second time; and only then, eventually, did Marduk create the Sun, Moon and stars.

Further to these examples, there are several other texts which give the impression that the Sun, Moon and stars were created specifically for man – to act as signs of day and night.[48] But man himself had only been created after a fall of Heaven to Earth. So, once again, it is evident that the Sun, Moon and stars were latecomers on the cosmological scene.

In closing, I should perhaps explain why modern scholars have failed to comprehend these ancient myths of the separation of Heaven from Earth. The answer is simple: scholars have not appreciated the difference between *Heaven*, which was created as an invisible mountain, and *the heavens*, which were created as the visible skies. By way of illustration, consider the following comment by the Hellenist Francis Cornford:

... it is not a simple and obvious belief... Why suppose that it [the dome of the sky, with its apparently unchanging stars] was ever 'joined in one form with the earth', and then lifted up to its present place?... The question is not commonly raised, and I do not know how it would generally be answered.[49]

This frank admission of puzzlement, dating to 1912, would not be out of place in 'authoritative' academic books today, whether the subject be Sumerology, Assyriology, Egyptology, Hinduism, Hellenic studies, Old Testament studies or Islamic studies. And yet Cornford goes astray in pondering why 'the dome of the sky, with its apparently unchanging stars', had once been 'joined in one form with the earth'. It was never like that. It was not the starry heavens that had joined physically with the Earth; it was the Mountain of Heaven. And it was this Heaven that had been separated from the Earth, in order to create an invisible, aethereal form of itself. As for the starry heavens, they were simply a by-product of this cataclysm.

No wonder modern scholars are so confused. Their equations take no account of that which is now invisible.

But what exactly was this Mountain of Heaven, whose cataclysmic fall sparked the creation of life and of all things visible and invisible?

Bear with me in Part Three, and I will unveil the secret meaning of this 'Cataclysm of all cataclysms'.

Chapter Nine Summary

* The myth of the separation of Heaven from Earth is testament to the idea that Heaven had fallen and become joined physically with the Earth in a confused mass – the Mountain of Heaven-and-Earth. In other words, a profound cataclysm lies at the heart of ancient cosmogony.

* The separation of Heaven from Earth amounted to a rebirth, from the Earth, of the Mountain of Heaven, but in invisible, immortal and aethereal form. This was the true Mount Olympus of the Greeks.

* It was also believed that the Sun, Moon and stars had been born from the Earth's womb following her impregnation by the fallen Mountain of Heaven.

* It follows from the foregoing that Mother Earth gave birth to all things in the new Universe – the geocentric view *par excellence*. In other words, all things in the new Universe were born as the result of a cataclysm.

PART THREE

THE EXPLODED PLANET HYPOTHESIS

CHAPTER TEN

THE MYSTERY REVEALED

**Friends I know indeed that truth is in the words
I shall utter; but it is hard for men, and jealous
are they of the assault of belief in their souls.**
(Empedocles, 5th century BC)

"The sky's a-going to fall!" All over the ancient world, and even today in
nursery rhymes and fairy tales, we encounter the idea that the sky has
fallen to the Earth, either once or on several occasions, and might fall
again in the future. In addition, right across the world, numerous peoples
have spoken, and continue to speak, of the sky having been separated
from the Earth – as if to suggest that the fallen sky had once been lifted
back up to its former place in the heavens.

In parallel with these tales of a fallen sky, ancient cultures right across
the world have spoken of gods coming down from the sky, sometimes in
anthropomorphic form but often accompanied by a deluge of water and
stones. They have described how these sky-gods entered the Underworld,
where they impregnated the Earth with the seeds of life. And they have
used this story to explain the creation of everything: the birth of all living
things, including mankind; the birth of giants, demons and monsters; and
the birth of a new race of invisible, immortal gods, who ascended back
up into the sky where they belonged.

All of these stories are called 'myths' – not because they are fictitious
but because they relate to 'a time undefinable by human chronology'
(Edmunds 1990). What this means, as regards the fall of the sky, is that
no human beings were around to witness the alleged event, for humans
had not at that time been created (by definition).

What was the sky that fell, and who, or what, were the gods that came
down? In answer to these questions, modern scholars have looked up to
their own contemporary skies and seen the Sun, Moon, planets, stars and

clouds. This visible sky of the present age, they have presumed, is the mythical sky that fell; and hence, they have concluded, the only gods who could possibly have come down from it were rain-gods, hailstone-gods, thunder-gods and lightning-gods.

The mystery is solved. Or is it? Well, for one thing, there is a horrible 'catch 22' in the proposed solution. Mother Earth, the ancients said, had given birth to the sky. But if Mother Earth gave birth to the sky, how could the sky have existed before she conceived? And how, then, could Mother Earth have been impregnated by the alleged rain-gods, hailstone-gods, thunder-gods and lightning-gods? It makes no sense.

The only way around this catch 22 is to redefine the sky. We must allow the troposphere to be an integral part of the Earth, and identify the sky with the starry heavens. This allows the Earth to impregnate herself, in a manner of speaking, and would explain how she gave birth to plants and trees, animals, mankind *et cetera*. But it nevertheless begs the question of why the Earth would ever have given birth to the starry heavens, as the ancient storytellers maintained. What was the seed for that birth? Moreover, if the sky is to be redefined in this way, it raises the crucial question anew: who were the gods who came down from the sky if the sky was the starry heavens?

But nor does it make sense that the gods could have come down from the starry heavens. After all, according to the myths, these heavens did not exist at the beginning – they had been born from the womb of the Earth. There was no starry heavens for gods to come down from.

And what about the fall of the sky? If the sky was the starry heavens, the implication is that the heavens in its entirety – Sun, Moon and stars – fell to the Earth. The idea seems preposterous.

Such are the contradictions facing modern scholars. It is almost as if they have taken a fatal wrong turn, leading them up a blind alley, into a cul de sac of endless confusion.

In the preceding chapter, however, I revealed a very simple way out of this confusion, by paying careful attention to what the ancients actually said. Heaven and the heavens, they said, were two different things. When the sky fell, it was Heaven, not the heavens. When the gods came down, they came from Heaven, not the heavens. When the seeds of life were sown in the womb of the Earth, they were sown by a god, or gods, who personified Heaven, not the heavens.

So, what was Heaven? As if with one voice, the ancients declared that Heaven had been a 'mountain'. It was the cataclysmic breaking apart of this mountain that had caused the sky to fall, the gods to come down, and the seeds of life to be sown in the Earth. And it was this fallen Mountain of Heaven that had subsequently been separated from the Earth, thus becoming an invisible, metaphysical world in the sky – 'a secure seat for ever for the blessed gods'.

Moreover, it was this fallen Mountain of Heaven that had provided the elusive seeds from which Earth bore the heavens – the Sun, Moon and stars – all as visible signs and tokens commemorating the death and rebirth of the true Heaven which was now an invisible mountain.

It remains only to explain exactly what this mountain was.

The Mountain of Heaven

In the beginning, said the ancient scribes, the Universe had consisted of just two celestial bodies, Heaven and Earth, situated opposite one another at either end of a bipolar axis. Each was described metaphorically as a mountain. Then, as the result of a mysterious incident, the Mountain of Heaven had fallen into the Earth, thereby becoming the Mountain of the Underworld. In the process, the Earth had been seeded with life.

The story of the gods is the same. In the beginning, they had resided on, or in, the Mountain of Heaven. Then, as the result of a mysterious incident, the gods decided to abandon Heaven and descend directly into the Underworld of the Earth, ostensibly for the purpose of the creation.

Why are these two stories – of cosmogony on one hand, and theogony on the other – so similar as to be identical? The explanation is that the god of Heaven *personified* the Mountain of Heaven. This was evident in the previous chapter, where gods such as Anu, Enlil, Enki, Azag/Zu and Ouranos personified the Mountain of Heaven by name and/or by deed. Accordingly, the fall and disappearance of the heavenly mountain was exactly the same thing as the fall and disappearance of the god; and the dismemberment of the heavenly mountain was exactly the same thing as the dismemberment of the god.[1] If, therefore, we wish to ask the question "what was the Mountain of Heaven?", we must, at the same time, ask the question "what was the god?".

What can we adduce about the identity of this mysterious mountain or god of Heaven?

Firstly, to state the obvious, the mountain or god had a supremely high status in the ancient cosmogonies. In the beginning, it alone existed in opposition to the Earth.[2]

Secondly, again to state the obvious, the mountain or god was located upwards relative to the Earth.

Thirdly, the mountain or god disintegrated and unleashed a deluge of stones and floodwaters upon the Earth.

Fourthly, the mountain or god fell to Earth with sufficient momentum that it split it open and entered into it, thus effectively becoming the mountain or god of the Underworld.

Fifthly, the mountain or god was, by some accounts, spherical.

Sixthly, the mountain or god was huge.

Seventhly, finally, the mountain or god was amazingly fertile.

So, what was this mountain or god? We will round out this picture as our discussion continues, but we already have sufficient clues to begin to draw some conclusions.

Firstly, what should we make of the long-held orthodox theory that the gods were merely storm-gods and weather-gods? Is it possible that their heavenly mountain was located in the Earth's troposphere? For this theory to work, we would have to suppose that the ancients spoke of a storm cloud in mountain-like terms. Possible, perhaps. But the theory, in any case, fails to satisfy two of the seven statements listed above. Firstly, it is difficult to see how a 'mountainous' storm cloud could have been endowed with the supremely high status which the mountain or god of Heaven possessed; storm clouds are simply much too commonplace and lack the necessary level of profundity. Secondly, storm clouds do not produce stones with the kind of momentum that would split open the Earth; hailstones have a tendency to melt, whereas ancient texts stated that the heavenly stones caused permanent and profound effects on the Earth's surface. Furthermore, if one looks up at a storm cloud, it seems remarkably close to the Earth; but ancient texts painted a very different picture. In the Akkadian *Epic of Etana*, for example, when king Etana soared up into Heaven on the back of an eagle, the land and the sea appeared to recede, becoming smaller and smaller until, eventually, both disappeared from his sight.[3] This does not sound like a trip to the clouds (and I feel sure that Aristophanes would have agreed). Accordingly, we must dispatch the idea of a storm cloud and a cloudburst into the depths of the abyss.

We must now look above the troposphere, upwards and outwards into the depths of space. By a simple process of elimination, the mountain or god of Heaven must have been something celestial and its break-up must have been a true cataclysm. When we take this approach, the stones of the mountain, or the body-parts of the god, are immediately identifiable as meteorites (and I am sure that Anaxagoras would have agreed).

This was indeed one of our conclusions in the previous chapter, where I demonstrated that the stones of the mountain, or the body-parts of the god, not only sounded like meteorites, but actually *were* meteorites in several instances. The prime example was the Egyptian god Osiris – the meteorite-god *par excellence*; his body-parts were made of iron and were concealed in the Underworld. Another good example was the Sumerian god Enlil, 'The Great Mountain', whose 'pickaxe' split open the Earth; related texts identified this pickaxe (a) with a weapon-like object that brought destruction from Heaven; and (b) with a strangely shaped, heavy object that fell from the sky. A meteorite for sure. And a third example was the myth of a god who swallowed and then ejected a stone; in the case of Kronos, the ejected stone became the original *baetylus* and *omphalos* stone of Delphi – almost certainly a meteorite.

This, I suspect, is not the place to go into a long digression about meteorites, but it is worth citing a few brief examples of how they were venerated in the ancient world.

In Egypt, the most sacred object in the land was the famous Benben Stone – a conically shaped meteorite which was worshipped at the Temple of the Benben in the city of *Annu* (Heliopolis).[4] An artist's impression of this temple appears in Figure 5, showing the meteorite atop a pillar, pointing up towards the sky whence it had come. The name Benben Stone meant 'Stone that Flowed Out', and inscriptions confirmed that it had flowed out from the body of God, in the primeval ocean, at the beginning of time.[5] The Egyptians regarded the Benben as the solidified seed of God, which had created life in the womb of the Earth – hence one of their names for the Underworld was *Het-Benben*, the 'House of the Benben'.[6]

Figure 5.
THE TEMPLE OF
THE BENBEN

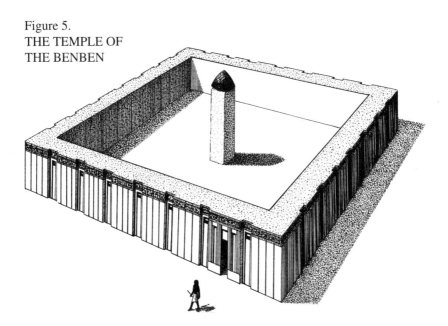

In Mesopotamia, it would seem that a temple almost identical to that of Heliopolis in Egypt existed at the city of Sippar, one of the holiest of all Sumerian cities.[7] Here, in the inner courtyard of the temple of Utu, there stood a venerated object known as 'the mighty APIN' which was said to be 'erected upwards' towards the sky.[8] The term APIN is translated by scholars as 'Object that Ploughs Through', and it is associated, in other inscriptions, with a 'piling up' of materials on the Earth by Enlil.[9] It was a meteorite for sure.[10]

Hand in hand with these archaeologically attested facts, there comes mythical information which speaks unequivocally of a great cataclysm enveloping Heaven and Earth. 'On that day, Heaven was crushed, Earth was smitten' wrote the Sumerians: 'Heaven was darkened... was turned into the Underworld.' In Egypt, similarly, 'war broke out in the entire Sky and Earth' on 'that day of the storm over the Two Lands'. And in Greece, the poet Hesiod sang of a day when the gods of Heaven and the gods of the Underworld had clashed in a stupendous cataclysm:

> All around, the life-bearing Earth rumbled as it burned... The whole land was seething, and the streams of Oceanus, and the undraining sea. The hot blast enveloped the chthonic Titans; the indescribable flames reached the divine heavens... it was just as if Earth and the broad Heaven above were coming together...[11]

All of the ancient sources agreed that the cataclysm originated in Heaven with the explosion or dismemberment of a mountain or body of a god. In the latter case, it was said that the One God had emanated from himself a multitude of lesser gods. The result was a cataclysmic deluge of lesser gods, who rained down from Heaven upon the Earth.

An Akkadian text describes the moment of the cataclysm. From the foundation of Heaven, the gods thundered forth in a black cloud, causing the posts and dykes of Heaven's ocean to be torn out. Immediately, the gods exploded outwards into the heavens, lighting up the sky with their fiery torches.[12] The wide land was 'shattered like a pot', unleashing an unprecedented deluge of fiery stones and floodwaters. For six days and six nights, this deluge swept across the celestial abyss, raging like an army in battle; and then, on the seventh day, it slammed into the mountain known as Earth.[13]

The impact was profound and widespread. According to one Egyptian text, when Geb entered into the Earth, he reconstructed it in 'thousands of foundations and millions of places'.[14] Similarly, in the Mesopotamian texts, when the gods Enki and Ninurta travelled down from Heaven, they caused huge 'heaps and mounds' of debris to be piled up on the Earth, to such an extent that the whole Earth (the HAR.SAG) was described as 'the heaped-up hill'.[15]

The effect of the gods' arrival in the Earth was destructive in the first instance. Several ancient texts described a great fire and a crisis in the world's fertility. For a while, the Earth was a wasteland. But the seeds of life had been sown in the Earth, and the crisis was soon to be reversed. The key to this turnaround was often said to be a second great cataclysm, in which a mountain or god of complementary gender fell from Heaven to Earth, joining the fallen partner in the Underworld in order to perform the sacred marriage rite.[16] The Earth was then moved as the two deities 'got their rocks off' and, as a result, the planet was revitalised.

According to another tradition, however, the gods brought about the transformation by releasing the waters of the Underworld (previously fallen from Heaven) and channelling them to the surface of the Earth. A prime example of this occurs in the Sumerian tale *Enki and Ninharsag: A Paradise Myth*, where the god Utu miraculously splits open the Earth, allowing the abundant waters to flow up from 'the mouth whence issues the waters of the Earth'.[17] In another text, it is the Anunnaki-gods who dig subterranean canals and thus cause the Tigris and Euphrates rivers to emerge into the world above.[18]

It is significant to note that both the Egyptians and Mesopotamians believed that the great life-giving rivers of their lands had had a heavenly origin. In Egypt, various hymns to the Nile-god describe how the river Nile descended from the heavens and entered the Underworld, whence it came forth subsequently into the world above.[19] In Mesopotamia, the myth *Enlil and Ninlil* tells how Enlil descended from Heaven and impregnated Ninlil (a personification of Earth) with 'a shining river';[20] similarly, the myth of *Enki and the World Order* tells how Enki filled up the Tigris and Euphrates rivers with a great flood of waters, which he ejaculated from his 'penis'.[21] Ancient cylinder seals show Enki with these two great life-giving rivers flowing into his shoulders as he steps onto the world mountain.[22] In these myths, Enlil and Enki clearly personify the great flood of Heaven.

The flood of waters unleashed from Heaven was immense – sufficient to fill the great rivers and oceans of the world. In the Egyptian Pyramid Texts, the fallen sky-god Osiris was compared to a great world ocean:

> O Osiris... you are healthy and great in your name of 'Sea'; behold, you are great and round in your name of 'Ocean'; behold you are circular and round as the circle which surrounds the *Hw-nbwt*.[23]

In Mesopotamia, similarly, Apsu and Tiamat began their existence as a watery body in the heavens, before falling to the Earth and becoming the ocean of the Underworld, which then supplied sweet and bitter waters to all of the rivers, springs and seas of the world.

In summary, if these mythical traditions are to be taken literally, then the mountain or god of Heaven must have contained an entire world ocean, thus implying an exploded celestial body of unprecedented size.

A Comet or a Planet?

It is now time to 'bite the bullet' and identify what was meant by the mountain or god of Heaven. What kind of mountain could explode in space, penetrate physically the crust of the Earth, and seed the beginning of life on our planet? As I see it, there are two, and only two, possible answers to this question: firstly, a disintegrating comet; or secondly, an exploding planet. The question to be asked is which of these two is the closest match to what the ancients described?

To take the comet theory first, there can be no doubt that the ancients did have close encounters with comets, and it seems highly likely that at least some ancient texts do describe the appearances of comets and the effects which they had on the world's environment. Furthermore, the comet theory would explain very neatly the ancient belief that the *entire* Mountain of Heaven had fallen into the Earth (this would be literally true for a comet which entered the Earth's atmosphere prior to exploding).

As regards the seven criteria which we listed earlier, the comet theory would fulfil perhaps six of them: yes, the comet nucleus is spherical; yes, it is huge; yes, it can disintegrate into meteorites and floodwaters; yes, it can split open the Earth's surface; and yes, according to the modern panspermia theorists, the comet is arguably fertile.

There is a problem, however, and it boils down to a matter of size, for even the largest comet is tiny relative to the Earth. Consider. In the first of our seven criteria, we noted that the heavenly mountain or god enjoyed a supremely high status in ancient religions. But if we imagine the original bipolar axis of the Universe with Heaven, above, as a comet, and Earth, below, as a planet, then what we see is a very small object suspended above a much larger object. Is this really the kind of heavenly mountain that the ancients had in mind? Is it really plausible that the supreme god could have been such a relatively tiny object?

By the same token, even the largest comet could not possibly have delivered the volume of floodwaters that was mentioned repeatedly in the ancient texts. To fill the oceans of the world would require not one comet but perhaps thousands of comets, all acting in unison. But such a delivery mechanism would not be a disintegrating comet at all; rather, it would be an exploding 'Father of the comets' – which brings us, rather neatly, to the exploded planet theory.

In an earlier book, *When The Gods Came Down* (2000), I advanced the argument, at some length, that the Egyptians and Mesopotamians had worshipped an exploded planet, which they referred to as the mountain or god of Heaven.[24] It now behoves me to restate and update that argument. But firstly, let me state at the outset that the 'exploded planet hypothesis' (EPH) consists of two separate fields of study: one scientific, one mythical. The scientific EPH, on the one hand, supposes that comets, asteroids and most meteorites originated in one or more planetary explosions in our solar system. This theory, advocated by the American astronomer Dr Tom Van Flandern, is well supported by observational evidence, has an excellent predictive track record, and has survived all the theoretical challenges posed by sceptical astronomers.[25] Nevertheless, it remains anathema to the vast majority of mainstream scientists.

The mythical EPH, as advocated by myself, is a completely different beast. It supposes that our ancient ancestors believed in an exploded planet, based on their experiences with comets, bolides and meteorites, and worshipped this exploded planet as their God (and/or Goddess). This form of the EPH deals not with the scientific verification of an exploded planet, but only with the existence of a religious belief system. Its significance lies only in what ancient peoples *believed* to be true. Consequently, the scientific arguments about exploded planets are neither here nor there. My theory deals with myth, not with actuality; I do not need a real exploded planet in order to argue that people *believed* in an exploded planet.

It is vitally important, therefore, that readers now put to one side any scientific preconceptions they might have about the origin of comets, asteroids and meteorites. Our modern beliefs are entirely irrelevant to determining what our ancient ancestors believed.

Now to the evidence. What follows is basically an adaptation of my argument in *When The Gods Came Down*, based on the evidence from ancient Egyptian and Mesopotamian religions (the evidence from Greek religion will be held back until the next three chapters).

The first point to be made is that the ancients, in referring to Heaven as a mountain, were using exactly the same metaphor as they applied to the Earth.[26] In Egypt, for example, the Earth was known as Mount Manu or the Mountain of the West, whilst in Mesopotamia the Earth was known as 'the Mountain of Heaven-and-Earth', 'the Mountain-House' (E.KUR), and 'The Mountain' (HAR.SAG). The implication of this is that

Heaven and Earth were the same kind of celestial body, i.e. that both were planets. If it was otherwise, then the ancients would surely have qualified the term 'mountain' as they applied it to Heaven, by calling it, for example, a *small* mountain. But such a distinction was never made.

On the contrary, the ancients were insistent that Heaven was the 'spitting image' of the Earth, both in size and weight. For example, in a Sumerian hymn to Inanna, the sky-goddess was praised as follows:

> You are known by your Heaven-like height,
> You are known by your Earth-like breadth.[27]

In a similar vein, the Sumerian king Gudea described the thunderbird-god Ningirsu:

> In the heart of the dream, there was a man [the god Ningirsu]:
>   his height equalled the Sky, his weight equalled the Earth...[28]

Putting these two citations together, the god of Heaven appears to have had a breadth equal to the Earth and a weight equal to the Earth. In other words, Heaven was a virtual double of the Earth.

Lest the above citations be dismissed as mere poetic epithets, consider the Akkadian tablet entitled by Alexander Heidel *Another Account of the Creation of Man*. Here, the scribe begins by setting the scene at the beginning of time; in the opening line, he writes nonchalantly:

> When Heaven had been separated from the Earth – its distant trusty
>   twin.[29]

This text could not be more clear – it states categorically that Heaven and Earth were 'twins'. In other words, Heaven must have been a planet, just like the Earth.

My impression is that the ancients took it for granted that Heaven and Earth were twin planets; hence the casual use of identical metaphors such as 'mountain'. In fact, the Egyptians referred to Heaven and Earth using no less than three additional metaphors which were common to both: 'island', 'throne', and 'horizon' (the last term referring to the Egyptian *Akhet* – a shining island of light).[30] Each of these three metaphors, along with the term 'mountain', was applied consistently to Heaven and Earth respectively, with no qualifiers attached. The case for a literal acceptance of these mirror image metaphor-pairs is absolutely compelling.

The next line of evidence comes from the ancients' descriptions of the Earth-like environment on the Mountain of Heaven. It has already been stated that the Mountain of Heaven had once possessed oceans of water and that its meteorites and floodwaters had seeded the beginning of life on Earth. But the ancients hardly envisaged this transfer of life in terms of invisible micro-organisms on a barren comet. On the contrary, they described Heaven as a place that had been full of plants, trees, and living creatures, and they intimated that all of these forms of life had been reincarnated from Heaven to Earth as a result of the great Deluge.

Several Mesopotamian texts confirm this idea, notably those dealing with the 'distant land' of Aratta (a city in Heaven)[31] and those dealing with Utnapishtim's ark and the transfer of life thereon from Heaven to Earth. The latter is not a standard interpretation, but it is an irresistible one following my thorough decoding of the Utnapishtim story in *When The Gods Came Down* (2000).[32] The upshot of it is that the Flood-hero set sail from a heavenly city and loaded his ark with the seeds of life in Heaven (a common-sense interpretation when one stops to think about it). Thus, when Utnapishtim describes his loading of the ark, he reveals the Earth-like environment which was attributed to the former Mountain of Heaven:

> Whatever I had of silver I laded upon her,
> Whatever I had of gold I laded upon her,
> Whatever I had of all the living beings I laded upon her,
> All my family and kin I made go aboard the ship.
> The beasts of the field, the wild creatures of the field,
> All the craftsmen I made go aboard.[33]

Nowhere is this Earth-like environment more clearly described than in the ancient Egyptian prayers for the afterlife. The Egyptians, like many ancient peoples, believed unswervingly in the heavenly origins of their race, but more than that, they believed in their absolute God-given right to return, in the afterlife, to their celestial homeland. Accordingly, they provided, for posterity, a detailed description of the environment on the heavenly mountain *Neter-Khert*, 'the Mountain-Land of God', as for example in the following citation from the Book of the Dead, in which the deceased pharaoh aims to control everything in Heaven that he has tried to control on the Earth:

> I have gained the mastery over the waters, I have gained the mastery over the canal, I have gained the mastery over the river, I have gained the mastery over the furrows, I have gained the mastery over the men who work for me, I have gained the mastery over the women who work for me in *Neter-Khert*, I have gained the mastery in *Neter-Khert* over all the things which were decreed to me on Earth.[34]

This idyllic land was known also as 'the Field of Reeds', or 'Field of

Offerings', which existed not only on Earth but also in the metaphysical sky (the so-called *Duat*). Depictions of the afterlife in Egyptian tombs and papyruses routinely showed humans ploughing and reaping in this heavenly Field, having apparently reincarnated into their body doubles.[35] The following passage, from the Book of the Dead, gives the general picture:

> Here begin the spells... of being provided for in the Field of Reeds which is in the Field of Offerings... having strength thereby, ploughing therein, reaping and eating therein, drinking therein, copulating therein, and doing everything that used to be done on Earth... I live in the Field of Offerings... This great magic of mine is powerful in this body of mine... I plough and I reap, and I am content in the City of God. I know the names of the districts, towns and waterways which are in the Field of Offerings and of those who are in them... I arrive at its towns, I row on its waterways, I traverse the Field of Offerings as Re who is in the sky.[36]

So Earth-like was this heavenly existence that the Egyptians made sure that their bodies were buried with all the necessary provisions, such as plates, water pots, drinking bowls, chairs, beds, and so on and so forth, according to the wealth of the deceased. The archaeological evidence is not to be gainsaid. Plain common sense dictates that we are dealing with an imagined ascension to an Earth-like planet.

This Earth-like Heaven is evident, too, from the manifold texts dealing with the fate and adventures of mankind in the Underworld. As explained in the previous chapter, the Mountain of the Underworld was the fallen Mountain of Heaven. As the Sumerians put it: 'On that day, Heaven was crushed... was darkened, was overcast with shadow, was turned into the Underworld.'[37] The Underworld was thus an image of Heaven, interred inside the sphere of the Earth-mountain.

But the Underworld was not just a mountain-within-a-mountain – it was also a world-within-a-world. It featured mountains, plains, forests, rivers, even a subterranean sea; moreover, it was occupied *inter alia* by mysterious cattle, 'creatures of the plain', and, in the beginning of days, by a pre-human, subterranean type of man (the so-called 'Lullu') who was created by the gods to undertake the following duties:

> To maintain the boundary,
> To fill the granary...
> To make the field of the Anunnaki produce plentifully,
> To increase abundance in the land...
> Let them increase ox, sheep, cattle, fish and fowl –

The abundance in the land.[38]

All of this in the Underworld. But why? Why was the Underworld such an Earth-like world? The simple answer is that the Underworld was the fallen Mountain of Heaven (hence the mythical ideas of the 'sky-in-the-middle' and the 'cosmic mountain'). Consequently, all of the Earth-like features of the Underworld were derived from Heaven. In short, it is evident, once again, that Heaven had been an Earth-like world.

In summary, the words of the ancients are not be gainsaid, and we must recognise their belief that Heaven had originally been an Earth-like planet. The lines of evidence are as follows:

1 Use of common metaphors to describe Heaven and Earth: mountain, island, throne, and horizon (no qualifying statements attached).

2 Heaven and Earth described explicitly as 'twins'.

3 God of Heaven described as equal to the Earth in breadth and weight.

4 Heaven described as an Earth-like domain; and the Underworld described as an Earth-like world-within-a-world.

5 Oceans of water consigned to the Earth by the explosion of Heaven.

6 Mountain and god of Heaven given a supremely high status – more befitting of a planet than a comet.

In view of all this evidence, which points consistently in one direction, it is, quite frankly, ludicrous to suggest that the Mountain of Heaven was a comet. Indeed, to suggest that Heaven was a comet (according to our modern concept of what a comet actually is) would be a complete travesty of what the ancients actually believed.

Of course, there will always be people who try to interpret ancient writings in terms of contemporary science, by drawing upon ideas that are currently fashionable (e.g. comets and the cometary panspermia theory).[39] But these people miss the point that, in dealing with ancient myths, we are dealing with ancient beliefs, and there is no law requiring such beliefs to be scientifically true. On the contrary, we are dealing with beliefs about cosmogonic events that supposedly preceded the creation of man on the Earth. Accordingly, we are dealing with events that could not have been witnessed or recorded by human beings, for the simple reason that human beings did not exist at the time. In short, we are dealing with myth.

This conclusion will strike some readers as being so logical, common-sensical and obviously correct than nothing more needs to be said. After all, the exploded planet myth is, in its barest essentials, the story that we have been told, over and over again, since we were children (if we only but realised it). Of course Heaven is a planet, what else could it be? Of course God is an exploded planet, what else could He be? It seems as if we have always known it, but refrained from speaking its name.

If only it were that obvious. My experience since 2000 has taught me that many people feel shocked and disturbed when they are confronted by the exploded planet hypothesis (EPH). Some are unable to distinguish between the scientific EPH and the mythical EPH, and reject out of hand any talk of exploded planets (because the idea is *scientific* anathema). Others feel discomfort owing to the religious taboos which have been programmed into them since childhood, for it is forbidden for some of us to rationalise the identity of the Almighty.

In view of these difficulties, it behoves me to restate some of the basic pillars of my argument:

1 The primary myth in most ancient cultures is that of a falling sky and/or gods coming down from the sky.

2 It is an incontestable fact that meteorites were worshipped in ancient times; it is a fact that, in Egypt, meteorites were revered as the seeds of life.

3 Modern scholars have affirmed, time and time again, that the ancients knew what iron meteorites were, i.e. they knew that the iron had fallen from the sky. Several ancient inscriptions actually described the iron falling down from the sky.[44] Other texts referred to meteorites as the 'efflux of God' or the 'flesh of the gods'.[45]

4 It makes perfect sense that the ancients would have associated meteorites with an Earth-like parent body, and would have speculated about the cataclysmic breaking apart of that body.[46]

5 It is imperative that we listen to what the ancients said about their religion, rather than imposing our modern preconceptions upon them. What they actually said about the mountain/god of Heaven was that it was the mirror image or 'twin' of the Earth, i.e. a planet.

6 There is no law that requires ancient beliefs to be scientifically true. We do not require scientific proof of an exploded planet to be able to accept that Near Eastern religions were 'exploded planet cults'.

Having said this, it is only fair to point out that modern astronomers and astrophysicists still lack a comprehensive explanation for the origin of comets, asteroids and meteorites. It therefore remains absolutely possible that the scientific EPH, despite being anathema to mainstream scientists, will yet emerge as the favoured model (one of the lessons of history is that the scientific consensus, at any one time, will often be hopelessly wrong!). As noted earlier, Tom Van Flandern's EPH is well supported by observational evidence, has an excellent predictive track record, and has survived the strongest of challenges. Who knows, then, whether the myth of the exploded planet might actually turn out to be a true story?

I would now like to demonstrate, again by a 'bullet point' summary, just how powerful the mythical EPH is, in terms of explaining ancient religion and myths. As I see it, the following list summarises the major strengths of the mythical EPH:

1   It explains the widespread myth of the falling sky.

2   It explains the myth of the creation of all life on Earth (an exploded *planet* neatly provides the archetypes or seeds for life on Earth).

3   It explains why Heaven had to be separated from the Earth.

4   It explains the widespread myth of the Deluge from Heaven, along with the myths of oceans and rivers falling from heavenly sources.

5   It explains the widespread myths of gods coming down from Heaven and entering the Underworld.

6   It explains the widespread myths of supernatural gods being born from the Earth.

7   It explains why Heaven/God was conceived to be invisible, immortal and aethereal.

8   It explains why Hell was a fiery pit beneath the Earth's surface (the Egyptians called the Underworld 'the Island of Fire').

9   It explains why the Underworld was conceived to be a world-within-a-world (the origin of numerous modern fairy tales).

10   It explains the ancient concept of the geocentric Universe.

11   It explains mankind's obsession with an afterlife and a return to a golden age.

12   It explains the total profundity of ancient religion.

13   It explains why the ancient Mysteries existed and were guarded so jealously.

This is a significant list. Indeed, it is noteworthy for the fact that several key strengths of the EPH lie in areas which are conveniently overlooked by mainstream scholarship or cloaked in a mist of confusion. As for the possible weaknesses of the EPH, not a single one has been identified at the time of writing.

Furthermore, the EPH can be reconciled very easily with all known forms of religious behaviour in the ancient world: the worship of nature spirits (animism), the worship of fertility-gods and the Year Daimon, the worship of weather-gods, and the worship of the Sun, Moon and stars.

There are two keys to this reconciliation.

The first key is the ancient belief that the exploded planet had sown the seeds of life in the Earth. Consequently, the death and rebirth of the crops every year was thought to echo the original death and rebirth of the planet of Heaven, when it died only to see its seeds of life reborn in the Earth.[47] A good illustration of this principle is found in Babylonia, where the beginning of the New Year was marked by the Akitu festival which celebrated Marduk's victory over the sea-goddess Tiamat; the name Akitu, from the Sumerian A.KI.TIL, meant 'power making the world live again'.[48] The purpose of such celebrations was to re-enact the original creative moment in order to ensure a healthy harvest in the year ahead (this ties in with the theory of Mircea Eliade, though he was unaware of the EPH).[49] Thus the worship of nature spirits, fertility-gods and the Year Daimon were linked inextricably to the worship of the exploded planet.

The second key is the belief that the exploded planet was invisible, which it was by definition (because it had exploded). Consequently, man sought to worship the exploded planet by means of visible symbols. One of these visible forms was thunder and lightning, hence the worship of weather-gods. Another was meteorites, hence the worship of meteorites. And another still was the celestial body, hence the worship of the Sun, the Moon and the stars. Significantly, the apparent deaths and rebirths of the Sun and Moon (at the setting of the Sun, at the winter solstice, at the end of the lunation cycle and at the time of eclipses) were thought to commemorate the real death and rebirth (as it was theorised) of the exploded planet.

With these two simple keys, the EPH can be reconciled to everything that we already know about the religions of the ancient Near East, and yet offer a deeper level of meaning to it. Readers wishing to know more about this are directed to my earlier books *The Phoenix Solution* (1998) and *When The Gods Came Down* (2000), in which I set out a detailed exposition on the subject of solar and stellar symbolism in Egypt and Mesopotamia.[50] In the interests of brevity, I will resist the temptation to repeat myself here.

Nevertheless, there is one further reconciliation that does need to be addressed in some detail, namely the connection between the EPH and the worship of gods in anthropomorphic forms. In view of the prevalence of anthropomorphic imagery in the Greek myths, this subject merits our very close attention.

Anthropomorphism

In almost all cultures, stories are told of the gods arriving in human form, teaching the arts and crafts of civilisation to mankind, and then departing with a promise to return. Many researchers have attempted to find some historicity in these stories, but in essence they seem to be repeats of the old EPH myth of the gods who came down from the sky and then went back up to the sky with a promise to return. In these EPH myths, we find exactly the same kind of anthropomorphic imagery at work, with the exploded planet gods being depicted frequently as great teachers of mankind. Are we thus to believe in ancient astronauts? Or is this rather a case of the exploded planet myth being told using familiar, human-like imagery? And, if the latter, why did the idea take root that the gods had been the teachers of mankind?

It is a good idea to begin with an example. In the writings of Plutarch (1st-century AD), we find a typical account of the travelling god-teacher. In *De Iside et Osiride*, Plutarch recounts an old Egyptian folk tale that the god Osiris had been a great king and teacher of mankind:

> Osiris, having become king of Egypt, applied himself to civilising his countrymen by turning them from their former indulgent and barbarous course of life. He taught them how to cultivate and improve the fruits of the earth, and he gave them a body of laws whereby to regulate their conduct, and instructed them in the reverence and worship which they were to pay to the gods. With the same good disposition, he afterwards travelled over the rest of the world, inducing the people everywhere to submit to his discipline, not compelling them by force of arms, but persuading them to yield to the strength of his reasons, which were conveyed to them in the most agreeable manner, in hymns and songs, accompanied with instruments of music.[51]

So said Plutarch, albeit with a note of warning that the legend should not be taken at face value. And he was right to express caution, for with the deciphering of hieroglyphics in the 19th century, a very different story emerged from the Egyptian texts. In particular, the Pyramid Texts (*c.* 2300 BC) revealed that Osiris had been a god of iron and floodwaters, and that he had fallen down from the sky and entered the Underworld. In other words, Osiris had been no human king, but rather a meteorite-god and flood-god – the personification of an exploded planet.

This brief example is an excellent illustration of how a myth can be 'dumbed down' over the course of time. In the case of the Pyramid Texts, we are dealing with the writings of highly educated priests, whose task, in all seriousness, was to get the pharaoh's soul resurrected to Heaven. But in the case of Plutarch's account, we are dealing with the popular story, composed by poets, or such like, with the less serious aim of entertaining and titillating the masses. We thus have a profound myth on the one hand, as against popular folklore on the other, and there is no contest as to which should be given the greater credence.

And yet it seems to be the case that we, in the Western world today, have absorbed far too many of these popular, folkloric ideas, and far too few of the serious myths. Why? The finger of blame must be pointed, in part, at the anthropomorphic myths of ancient Greece, by which Homer, and to a lesser degree Hesiod, inspired men such as Prodicus (5th century BC) and Euhemerus (3rd century BC) to suggest that the gods had been wandering teachers or kings and queens of an earlier age. These theories then inspired a new generation of writers, including Diodorus Siculus (1st century BC), Plutarch (1st century AD), and Philo of Byblos (2nd century AD), all of whom added fuel to the idea that the gods had been mere human beings. It would seem that, around two thousand years ago, this ill-conceived idea became accepted as an orthodoxy.

However, if I am right that the ancient religions of the Near East were exploded planet cults, why was it that their exploded planet deities were anthropomorphised in the first place? I am no psychologist so I will spare my readers an amateurish psychological explanation, but I will, instead, offer a logical and practical explanation.

Let us take as our starting point the basic premise of ancient religion – that Heaven had fallen to the Earth and that the Earth had thus conceived and given birth to life. From here, it seems quite logical that the ancients would have chosen to describe this celestial union symbolically in terms of a sexual union between two animals or two human beings. The Earth would naturally have been the female partner, for she had given birth to life, whilst the falling Heaven would have been the male partner. In this way, we can see how the act of creation would have been expressed by an analogy, in which the phallus of a male being was inserted into the womb of the female. Furthermore, given the choice of sexual union between bull and cow, stallion and mare, or man and woman, it is understandable that most societies opted for the human analogy.

This, then, is our starting point. From very first principles, we can see how the union of Heaven and Earth would have been described in terms of a marriage between a man and a woman. And thus, right from the very beginning, the two main deities of the exploded planet cult would have been conceived in human-like terms.

The next step is to recognise that ancient societies wished to do two things: (a) to worship their gods in visible form (after all, the exploded planet was, by definition, invisible); and (b) to re-enact the story of the creation. We will deal with each of these points separately.

To worship the exploded planet gods in visible form, the ancients had a number of choices: they could have worshipped meteorites (which they did); they could have worshipped the Sun, the Moon and the stars as visible symbols of the creation (which they did); or they could have worshipped the gods in the form of artefacts, notably statues. In practice, all three of these modes of worship were used, but the most popular mode, by far, was the worship of statues. (The reason for this being that meteorites were impersonal and rare, whilst the Sun, the Moon and the stars were impersonal and remote).

How could statues be made that would symbolise the exploded planet or, indeed, Mother Earth? The obvious answer – in line with the sacred marriage idea related above – was to produce statues in the likeness of human beings, or of human beings with certain animal attributes (e.g. of the bull or the ram which symbolised fertility). This was indeed what happened and thus, from the 3rd millennium BC onwards, the lands of the Near East witnessed the founding of a veritable industry in which myriads of statues and trinkets of the gods were produced in human or human-like forms.

And thus, over the millennia, the popular consciousness was flooded with images of gods in the form of human beings.

The second thing that ancient societies wished to do was to re-enact the story of the creation. Here, the statue effectively *became* the god, as it was conducted on journeys between cities, commemorating the meeting of Heaven and Earth. At other times, however, human beings took the roles of the gods. In Egypt, for example, a man re-enacted the Passion of Osiris (his death and resurrection), whilst in Mesopotamia the king took the role of the god Dumuzi in order to re-enact, with queen or priestess, the sexual union of Heaven and Earth. Numerous further examples could be cited. In virtually all cases, the rituals marked the beginning of the New Year, with creation being re-enacted in order to ensure the fertility of the land in the year ahead.

In summary, then, it was expedient to re-enact the cosmic drama using either human-like statues of the gods or human actors and actresses, and thus it was inevitable that the popular consciousness would become flooded even more deeply with anthropomorphic imagery.

But there was another important factor at work, too. In performing these re-enactments of the marriage between Heaven and Earth, it was inevitable that the action took place on the surface of the Earth, in the human dimension, rather than between Heaven and Earth in the original celestial dimension. In order to do this, the ancients designated some of their cities as 'cities of Heaven', and others as 'cities of Earth' or 'cities of the Underworld'. In Egypt, for example, the city of *Annu* (Heliopolis) symbolised Heaven, whilst *Abu* (Elephantine) or *Ab-djw* (Abydos) stood for the Earth.[52] In Mesopotamia, many cities symbolised Heaven, Nippur being the foremost, whilst Eridu (the AB.ZU of Enki) stood for the Earth and the Underworld.[53] Having thus designated their cities, the ancients would convey the human actor or human-like statue of their god on a ritual journey from one city to the other, performing various ceremonies at either end to commemorate the original journey of the god between Heaven and Earth.[54]

The upshot of this is that, all over the Near East, the celestial journeys of the gods were brought literally down to earth, thereby reinforcing the impression that the gods had been human-like beings. In time, it would seem that people forgot the symbolism of the celestial cities and the celestial nature of the gods' journeys, especially where westerners such as the Greeks borrowed and adapted the eastern traditions. As a result, later writers began to believe, quite erroneously, that the gods had been nothing but human travellers and teachers.

Doubtless there were other significant factors, too, that contributed to the anthropomorphism of the gods (such as the old myth that the gods had created mankind in their own likeness),[55] but the above discussion surely covers the gist of it.

Even so, there is one point that has been put to me again and again by correspondents, and it is this: why did the ancients claim that human-like gods had gifted them all the arts, crafts and sciences of civilisation? The question is an intriguing one, and so, perhaps, is the answer.

Consider the traditions of the Mesopotamians. In my study of 2000, I noted the myth that man had been created in the Underworld. But I also spotted the idea, in *The Epic of Etana*, that man's release from the Underworld, into the world above, had coincided with the lowering of kingship from Heaven.[56] According to my reading of this myth, the gods had established a city in the Underworld, sought a king, made him the shepherd of the people, and then raised the city and its people into the light of the world above. The implication of this myth is that all the good things associated with civilisation had been created instantly, as if by a magic wand, via the decision of the gods to grant kingship to man.

This was a bold insight on my part, and I was not totally sure of it until I studied Greek religion and found the same myth recorded in the works of Plato. It is told by Socrates in *Republic*, where he contemplates telling a 'noble falsehood' to set up his ideal city. Socrates speaks thus:

> "I'll first try to persuade the rulers and the soldiers and then the rest of the city that the upbringing and the education we gave them, and the experiences that went with them, were a sort of dream, that in fact they themselves, their weapons, and the other craftsmens' tools were at that time really being fashioned and nurtured inside the Earth, and that when the work was completed, the Earth, who is their mother, delivered all of them up into the world."[57]

Where did Socrates (or Plato) get such a strange idea from? The answer, according to the text, is that it was a Phoenician story. If so, it would stem from the East, most probably as a rendition of the Mesopotamian myth that I described earlier. Obviously, more work needs to be done on this question, but it nevertheless seems to me that the Mesopotamian tradition of civilisation being a 'gift of the gods' is merely a reflection of the elaborate 'birth from the Earth' myths that were so popular in ancient days. The idea that the gods had given man the arts, crafts and sciences of civilisation would thus be myth pure and simple – an add-on to the popular myth of the gods creating man in the Underworld. Moreover, as preposterous as it might sound, many people in ancient times really did believe that this myth was true.[58]

In summary, the depiction of the Greek and Near Eastern gods in human-like form, and the anthropomorphic imagery in the associated myths, can be explained simply from first principles as an offshoot of the exploded planet cult.

A Challenge Won

In concluding this chapter, I would remind the reader of the challenges which I laid down in chapter two. There, I juxtaposed two opposing theories: (a) that the gods personified the cataclysmic forces of Heaven and Earth period, and that Greek religion was about cataclysm theory, pure and simple; and (b) that cataclysmic images were used as 'symbols of power' in order to glorify the status of humans or human-like beings. I then outlined two challenges. For the Euhemerist (or ancient astronaut) theory, I put the onus on its supporters to demonstrate that there *was* a meaningful human (or alien) story behind the cataclysmic imagery, i.e. they would need to explain how the cataclysmic model falls short of explaining all of the relevant literary and other data. For the cataclysm theory, on the other hand, I set the challenge that it must be demonstrated to be an end in itself, i.e. the cataclysmic model would need to explain the essential profundity of ancient religion.

I now declare the second challenge won. In this and earlier chapters, we have seen that the cataclysm at the heart of ancient religions was not just any old cometary impact event – not even one that had decimated humanity. No, it was more profound than that. The event in question was a hypothesised (i.e. mythical) explosion of an entire living planet that had been thriving with life. It was the death of a world. But more than that, the cataclysm amounted to a reincarnation of life from the planet of Heaven to the planet of Earth. It thus signified the saving of the seeds of life, the beginning of life on Earth and, in due course, the creation of mankind. This is about as profound as profound gets.

Consequently, there is simply no need to suppose that the myths of the gods and the cosmos might contain any deeper, hidden imagery about historical kings and heroes, lost civilisations or ancient astronauts. On the contrary, all of the anthropomorphic imagery can be explained, and *has* been explained, as a predictable offshoot of man's belief in one or more exploded planets.

What about Greece?

What does this imply for the Greek myths? Given what has been said about the links between Greece and the Near East, it now becomes an *a priori* probability that many, perhaps most, of the Greek tales of the cosmos and the gods may have something to do with the exploded planet mythos. Some caution, however, is in order, for it does *not* necessarily follow that *all* Greek myths were about exploded planets. Some myths, for example, contain aetiological aspects – they served to explain things such as the condition of man, the origins of kingship, or the foundation of certain sites, temples, cults and mysteries (such myths might reflect exploded planet *cults*, but exploded planets *per se* do not feature in their contents or raisons d'etre). Other myths, meanwhile, contain folkloric aspects, designed for the purpose of popular entertainment. Yet others were designed to instil moral behaviour in the listener. And others still, perhaps, were intended to immortalise human achievements (although these would hardly qualify as true 'myths').

This caveat notwithstanding, there remains a large and central corpus of Greek tales that are true myths in the sense that they deal primarily with pre-human, mythical time scales. These myths – the most puzzling of all to Hellenists – are prime contenders for reinterpretation under the exploded planet hypothesis. And included among them, I would argue, is Plato's story of Athens and Atlantis.

But before we jump in at the deep end, we must first evaluate the context in which Plato's story was told. Did the Greeks follow the same kind of exploded planet cult as their Near Eastern neighbours? Did they import exploded planet imagery, knowingly or unknowingly, from the East? How extensive was the exploded planet mythos in Greek religion?

These are the questions which we must now resolve.

Chapter Ten Summary

* The god of Heaven personified the Mountain of Heaven. The story of the gods and the story of the cosmos are one and the same story.

* The Mountain of Heaven could not possibly have been a storm cloud.

* To suggest that the Mountain of Heaven was a comet (according to our modern concept of what a comet actually is) is ludicrous, and a complete travesty of what the ancients believed.

* The Mountain of Heaven was described as the Earth's twin, and it was said to have had an Earth-like environment. The ancients envisaged it, beyond any doubt, as a planet.

* The religions of the ancient Near East are best described as 'exploded planet cults'.

* The exploded planet was invisible by nature, thus explaining the ancients' worship of visible substitutes – meteorites, statues, fertility-gods, weather-gods, Sun, Moon and stars.

* The worship of the gods in anthropomorphic form was an entirely predictable offshoot of the exploded planet cult.

* The exploded planet cult was as profound as profound gets, involving the death of a living planet and the rebirth of life on another planet – the Earth. There is no need to suppose any deeper, hidden meaning to the ancient myths.

* The mythical EPH is entirely separate from the scientific EPH and does not require the actual explosion of a planet. There is no law that requires ancient religious beliefs to be scientifically true. Our modern scientific scepticism about exploding planets is thus entirely irrelevant

to determining what our ancient ancestors believed.

* Nevertheless, the origin of comets, asteroids and meteorites is still far
  from clear, and it is possible that the scientific scepticism about
  exploded planets is misplaced. Ancient myths about exploded planets
  may, or may not, be true.

CHAPTER ELEVEN

SECRET COSMOS

**To find the maker and father of this Universe is a
wearisome task; to communicate him to all
when one has found him is impossible.**
(Plato, *Timaeus*, mid-4th century BC)

Was Greek religion an exploded planet cult? Did the Greeks, knowingly
or unknowingly, follow the religion of their Near Eastern neighbours?
Before we attempt to answer this vital question, we must review what we
have learned so far about the importance of cataclysms and cataclysm
theory in Greek religion.

To begin with Homer (7th century BC), we find in the *Iliad* the earliest
confirmation that Heaven was a mountain – Mount Olympus – and we
find the first allusions to the sacred marriage of Heaven and Earth, and to
the separation of Heaven and Earth, albeit expressed in the most cryptic
of terms.[1] Homer was not particularly interested in cosmogony but the
clues to the cataclysm are there. In his descriptions of the gods, Homer
complemented his anthropomorphic imagery with an abundance of
supernatural imagery – the gods were immortal, they journeyed back and
forth between Heaven and Earth, they changed their shapes at will, and
they manifested themselves amidst bright light, blazing fire and loud
noise. Homer also cited examples of gods being flung out of Heaven,
such as Hephaestus, the blacksmith-god, whose associations with iron
surely make him the Greek meteorite-god *par excellence*. Furthermore,
in the *Odyssey*, Homer named the rivers of the Underworld: the Styx 'the
river of hatred or gloom', the Acheron 'the river of woe', the Cocytus
'the river of wailing' and the Pyriphlegethon 'the river of fire'.[2] All of
these names hint at the rivers' cataclysmic origins.

Turning to Hesiod (7th century BC), we find the cataclysmic nature of
Greek religion spelled out in more explicit terms. In *Theogony*, Hesiod

described the sacred marriage of Heaven and Earth, and identified the original god of Heaven as Ouranos, 'The Mountain of Heaven'. Hesiod also described the separation of Heaven from Earth and, crucially, stated that the roots of Heaven lay in the Underworld. In relating the battle between Zeus and the Titans, Hesiod used 'in your face' cataclysmic imagery to describe the coming together of Heaven and Earth. One of the upshots of this battle was that Zeus planted in the Earth (at Delphi) the stone that had been swallowed and ejected by Kronos.

A few words must be said about this sacred stone. As noted in chapter eight, the stone of Delphi was known by the Greeks as a *baetylus* and an *omphalos*. The poet Pindar (5th century BC) described it as 'the deep navel stone', 'the centre-stone of Earth' and 'the great centre-stone of Earth's broad breast'.[3] Scholars are as certain as they can possibly be that this sacred *baetylus* stone of Delphi was, in the olden days, a meteorite (in the ancient world, the name *baetylus* generally signified a meteorite). That a meteorite should play a central role in Greek religion, not just in the Delphic cult but also in the myth of Zeus founding the world order, underlines the importance of cataclysm theory in ancient Greece. It is no coincidence, surely, that Hesiod began his *Theogony* with a 'mountain' and ended it with a stone cult.

Still on the subject of Hesiod, he described in his other poem *Works and Days* the sequence of the world ages – gold, silver, bronze and iron – and alluded to the cataclysms, such as the flood of Deucalion, which had brought each world age to an end and consigned each of the pre-human races of mankind to oblivion in the Underworld.

Turning to Anaximander (6th century BC), he described a cosmogony in which all things had begun with the tearing apart of a mysterious mass called 'the Unlimited'. A nuclear reaction inside the Unlimited had caused it to produce a sphere of flame which first surrounded it and then exploded into rings of fire. These rings of fire ended up buried in the Underworld, but the Earth recycled the fire to the heavens in creating the lights of the Sun, Moon and stars.

Empedocles (5th century BC) described a cosmogony in which all things had begun with a God-Sphere, which was torn apart by the forces of Strife. 'Strife waxed mightily in the members of the Sphere', he said: 'they all trembled in turn.' As a result of this discord, the elements of earth, air, fire and water had been born, culminating in all material things on the Earth.

Turning to Aeschylus, he described in *Prometheus Bound* (5th century BC) the torture of Prometheus, who had been chained to 'the Caucasus Mountain' by Zeus. The climax of the play was an awesome cataclysm in which Prometheus, still attached to his mountain, was plunged into the Underworld amidst earthquakes, thunderbolts and violent storms, which shook the very foundations of Heaven and Earth. Prometheus would be punished in the Underworld for an eternity, but might be set free by another great cataclysm at the end of the age.

Turning to Euripides, he described in *Melanippe-the-Wise* (5th century BC) how Heaven and Earth had once been joined together, but had been separated by strife, whereupon they had been forced to dwell far apart from each other. But eventually Heaven and Earth had been rejoined in marriage, at which time the Earth bore all living things.

Anaxagoras (5th century BC) described a cosmogony in which the Universe had tilted towards the south 'in order that some parts might become uninhabitable and others habitable'. Thus his famous line: 'All things were together'. After a visit to Egypt, he returned to Greece with the idea that meteorites had seeded the beginning of all life on Earth, and he caused an uproar in Athens with his claim that the Sun and the Moon were nothing more than glowing balls of metallic stone.

This brings us to Plato (5th-4th centuries BC). In *Statesman*, he had an Eleatic philosopher describe an elaborate cosmogonical myth, based on the idea that the Universe rotated around the Earth in an alternating cycle of forward and retrograde motions. If the direction of this rotation were changed, a terrible cataclysm would wipe out the vast majority of all living creatures. Such a tragedy had happened long ago, said the Eleatic philosopher, when Atreus had quarrelled with Thyestes, and the Sun and the stars had set for the last time in the East, thereafter setting in the West instead.[4]

And then there are Plato's cataclysmic references in *Timaeus*. As a lead-in to his story of Athens and Atlantis, Plato had an Egyptian priest state that the Earth had been devastated on many occasions in the past by floods of fire and water that had rained down from the heavens. These cataclysms were caused, said the priest, by deviations in the courses of the celestial bodies. Significantly, Plato suggested that this kind of cataclysmic event lay behind the myth of Phaethon, the son of Helios, who had crashed his father's chariot into the Earth, setting the whole world on fire. Plato then went on to describe how the island of Atlantis had been destroyed by a cataclysm of 'extremely violent earthquakes and floods'.

All of these citations illustrate the importance of cataclysm theory to the ancient Greeks. From Homer to Hesiod, from Anaximander to Empedocles, from Aeschylus to Euripides, and from Anaxagoras to Plato, the story is basically the same. To paraphrase: in the beginning, there had been a terrible cataclysm, which caused Heaven to explode and fall; Heaven had thus joined together in marriage with the Earth; and the Earth, seeded by meteorites and floodwaters, had given birth to all things in the Universe, both visible and invisible. The implication, as discussed in earlier chapters, is that no human being had been around to witness the cataclysm. Rather, the cataclysm was a theological construct or theory, not so different in status from the modern concept of the Big Bang (which astrophysicists speak of, and believe in, even though they were not around billions of years ago to witness it).

An Exploded Planet Cult?

Did the Greeks, knowingly or unknowingly, follow an exploded planet cult like that of their Near Eastern neighbours? It must be said, based on the well-documented evidence of cataclysm theory (summarised above) and on the well-attested parallels between Greek and Near Eastern myths (see chapters seven, eight and nine), that it is an *a priori* probability that the Greek cosmogonies *do* describe an exploded planet scenario and that the Greek myths *do* describe exploded planet deities. Nevertheless, we should not jump to conclusions but rather proceed with caution and pick our way through the evidence with care.

The first crucial point to be made is that the Greeks traced the origins of all their gods to marriages of Heaven and Earth in which the original Heaven was personified as Oceanus or Ouranos. In the case of Oceanus, scholars have established a one hundred per cent identity between him and the Babylonian god Apsu, whom we identified earlier as an ocean-like mountain in Heaven. This sounds very much like a watery planet. As for Ouranos, the meaning of his name, 'The Mountain of Heaven', when combined with the manner in which he impregnated Gaia, makes him an unmistakeable cognate with the Near Eastern exploded planet gods. This is a promising start.

Also very promising is the fact that the Greeks referred to Heaven and Earth using identical epithets. Hence Gaia was 'the broad Earth', whilst Ouranos was 'the broad Heaven' and the subterranean realm of Tartarus (presumably a fallen Heaven) was 'broad Tartarus'.[5] Meanwhile, the sea – a fallen heavenly sea we should recall – was 'the broad sea', the *Aither* was 'the broad *Aither*', and all decisions of the gods were modelled on an original, mysterious 'broad oath'.[6] Inevitably, we are reminded of the common metaphors applied to Heaven, Earth and Underworld in the myths of Egypt and Mesopotamia. Should we take the word 'broad' literally? Is it telling us that the Greek Heaven was the image or twin of the Earth, as in Near Eastern traditions? Such indeed is the impression given by Hesiod in *Theogony*, when he sings that:

> Earth bore first of all one equal to herself, Ouranos, so that he should cover her all about, to be a secure seat for ever for the blessed gods.[7]

This passage, it should be stressed, relates to the birth from the Earth of the heavenly, aethereal Mount Olympus (which was, in fact, synonymous with Ouranos).[8] Note Hesiod's precise words: Heaven was 'one equal to' Gaia, who could 'cover her all about' the next time he descended to the Earth (which he did – at the time of his castration by Kronos). The implication, if we dare to take Hesiod at face value, is that Mount Olympus signified an Earth-sized planet (or, to be more accurate, the aethereal reproduction of an exploded planet).

Further evidence that Mount Olympus was indeed planetary in nature comes from the famous 'golden rope' speech of Zeus in the *Iliad*. Here, Homer has Zeus, the chief god of Olympus, boast that he is 'much the strongest of all the gods':

> "Or come on, try it, gods... Hang a golden rope down from Heaven, and all you gods and goddesses take hold of it: but you could not pull Zeus, the counsellor most high, down from Heaven to the ground, however long and hard you laboured. But whenever I had a mind to pull in earnest, I could haul you up, earth and sea and everything; then I could hitch the rope on the peak of Olympus, so that everything, once more, should hang in mid-air."[9]

It must be said that this image of Mount Olympus hanging in mid-air, complete with earth, sea and all the fallen, ex-heavenly gods, sounds remarkably like a planet – a planet that Zeus would reconstitute from its previously disintegrated elements. Mount Olympus thus appears as the vital source of all elements on Earth, just like Anaximander's Unlimited and Empedocles' God-Sphere. Moreover, Zeus' golden rope speech is entirely consistent with what we have learned about the oceans, seas, rivers and springs according to the Greek world view, namely that they had originated in Heaven (see discussion in chapter eight).

Did the heavenly Mount Olympus have an Earth-like environment? In the *Iliad*, Homer makes fleeting references to 'valleyed Olympus' and 'snowy Olympus', which might well be interpreted as an Earth-like environment.[10] On the other hand, it could be argued that Homer was merely drawing an analogy with the peaks of Mount Olympus in Greece. Unfortunately, the mainstream Greek view (pre-Plato) was not in favour of a heavenly afterlife and hence the early texts do not contain explicit descriptions of the heavenly environment.

The Underworld, however, is another matter. Here, Homer describes some amazing scenes, such as the hunter-god Orion 'rounding up the game on the meadow of Asphodel', and Tantalus being tantalised by rich fruit-trees bearing pears, pomegranates, apples, figs and olives.[11] The Orphics, similarly, described the Underworld in Earth-like terms, making reference to 'the fair meadow beside the deep-flowing Acheron river' and 'the holy meadows and groves of Persephone'.[12]

In the Underworld, too, belonged the idyllic Elysian Plain before it was transported notionally and symbolically to the remote west; ditto the fabled garden of the Hesperides, with its famous trees bearing the golden apples; ditto the island of Thrinacie, with its cattle of the Sun-god; and ditto the island of Erytheia, with its cattle of Geryon (on all of these points, see chapter eighteen).[13]

Time and time again, the Greeks described their Underworld as a world-within-a-world, as if to inform us that this Earth-like world down below had once been an Earth-like world up above.

Plato and the Upper Earth

So far, I have listed some intriguing clues to the Greek Heaven having originally been a planet in the image of the Earth (Gaia), but the evidence has been fragmentary and inconclusive. Now, we shall step up a gear by seeing what Socrates and Plato had to say about the matter.

Phaedo is a book generally attributed to Plato (5th-4th centuries BC). It purports to describe Socrates' last hours in the jail at Athens before he drank the hemlock and died. There, in his cell, he entertained a group of visitors including Phaedo, Crito, and two Pythagoreans named Simmias and Cebes. The discussion, not surprisingly, turned to the nature of death and the fate of the soul in the afterlife. In this context, Socrates delivered an extraordinary speech in which he identified Heaven as an Earth-like world, but perfect in every sense in contrast to the corroded Earth down here. Such is the importance of this report, in the context of the exploded planet hypothesis, that I will now cite it at length, and allow readers the opportunity to judge the words of Socrates/Plato for themselves:

> "The first thing of which I am convinced is that if the Earth is a sphere in the middle of the Universe, it has no need of air or any other force to prevent it from falling... The Earth itself is pure and lies in the pure heavens where the stars are situated, i.e. in the *aither*. The water and mist and air are the sediment of the *aither* and they always flow into the hollows of the Earth. We, who dwell in the hollows of it, are

unaware of this and we think that we live above, on the surface of the Earth. It is as if someone who lived deep down in the middle of the ocean thought he was living on its surface. Seeing the Sun and the other celestial bodies through the water, he would think the sea to be the heavens...

Our experience is the same: living in a certain hollow of the Earth, we believe that we live upon its surface; the air we call the heavens, as if the stars made their way through it... we are not able to make our way to the upper limit of the air; if anyone got to this upper limit, if anyone came to it or reached it on wings and his head rose above it, then just as fish on rising from the sea see things in our region, he would see things there and, if his nature could endure to contemplate them, he would know that there is the true Heaven, the true Light and the true Earth, for the Earth here – these stones and the whole region – are spoiled and eaten away, just as things in the sea are eroded by the salt water.

Nothing worth mentioning grows in the sea... there are caves, sand and endless slime and mud... not comparable in any way with the beauties of our region. In the same way, those things above are, in their turn, far superior to the things we know...

In the first place, it is said that the Earth, looked at from above, looks like one of those spherical balls made up of twelve pieces of leather; it is multi-coloured... up there, on the other hand, the whole Earth [i.e. the Upper Earth] has these colours, but much brighter and purer: one part is sea-green and of marvellous beauty, another is golden, another is white, whiter than chalk or snow; the [Upper] Earth is composed of the other colours, too, but more numerous and beautiful than any we have ever seen. The very hollows of the [Upper] Earth, full of water and air, gleaming among the variety of other colours, present a colour of their own, so that the whole is seen as a continuum of variegated colours. On the surface of the [Upper] Earth, the plants grow with corresponding beauty, the trees, flowers and fruits, and so, too, with the hills and the stones, more beautiful in their smoothness and transparency and colour. Our precious stones here are, in comparison, but fragments – our cornelians, jaspers, emeralds and the rest. All stones there [in the Upper Earth] are of that kind, but are even more beautiful. The reason is that they are pure, not eaten away or spoiled by decay and brine, or corroded by the water and air which have flowed into the hollows here...

The [Upper] Earth is adorned with all these things and also with gold, silver and other metals. These stand out, being numerous, massive and occurring everywhere, so that the [Upper] Earth is a sight for the blessed. There are many other living creatures upon the [Upper] Earth and also men, some living inland, others at the edge of the air, as we live on the edge of the sea, others again live on islands surrounded by air close to the mainland. In a word, what water and the sea are to us, the air is to them and the *aither* is to them what the air is to us. The climate is such that they are without disease, and they live much longer than people do here; their eyesight, hearing and intelligence and all such things are as superior to ours as air is superior to water and *aither* to air in purity; they have groves and temples dedicated to the gods, in which the gods *really* dwell, and they communicate with them by speech, by prophecy and by sight...

Those who are deemed to have lived an extremely pious life are freed and released from the [subterranean] regions of the Earth as if from a prison; they make their way up to a pure dwelling place and live on the surface of the [Upper] Earth. Those who have purified themselves sufficiently by philosophy live in the future altogether without a body; they make their way to even more beautiful dwelling places..."[14]

In this astonishing speech by Socrates, the Upper Earth (i.e. Heaven) symbolises what Platonic scholars call 'the world of Forms'. It is literally a world, and it resembles the Earth in every respect, except for the fact that it is perfect. The basic premise behind Plato's Theory of Forms (or Theory of Ideas, as it is sometimes called) is that the Upper Earth (or Heaven) contains the archetypes (the Forms) for all things, animate or inanimate, that exist down here on Earth. Thus, as Socrates puts it, the 'true Heaven' is equivalent to 'the true Earth' (see the second of the six paragraphs set out above).

As I noted in chapter four, the 'world of Forms' concept finds its religious echo in the widespread idea of a fallen paradise. But now, armed with what we know about the exploded planet cults of the ancient Near East, the Theory of Forms and the account of the perfect Upper Earth in *Phaedo* take on an explosive significance.

In the Near Eastern tradition, we should recall, Heaven had been the twin of the Earth and its explosion had seeded the Earth with all forms of life; afterwards, Heaven had been reborn, but in invisible, aethereal form. Socrates' and Plato's Theory of Forms is essentially the same. They present Heaven as a twin of the Earth, i.e. as an Upper Earth, and they vary the story only by having Heaven seed the Earth *with the archetypes* for all things (*arkhetupos* meant literally 'first-moulded'). Moreover, following the ideas of Parmenides, Socrates and Plato make their Heaven an ever-unchanging sphere that transcends space and time. It is 'that which *is*', and to quote Socrates: "that which *is* is invisible."[15] In other words, Heaven – the world of Forms – is an invisible Earth-like world, accessible only by metaphysical means, such as the journey of the soul in the afterlife.

The Theory of Forms, it must be said, is the Near Eastern exploded planet cult to a tee. Indeed, so close is the conceptual similarity that the scheme must surely have been rooted in a knowledge of exploded planet cosmogony, perhaps that of the ancient Egyptians.

And yet knowledge can sometimes be subliminal. What I mean to say is that the human mind is able to absorb ideas and reproduce those ideas without ever being consciously aware of what those ideas mean. Today, for example, we routinely speak of Heaven as if it were an aethereal, Earth-like paradise, and yet few of us consciously make the connection between this Earth-like Heaven and a planet that exploded. Therefore, it is quite possible for people to give the semblance of knowing something when, in fact, they truly know nothing at all. Was this the case with the Theory of Forms? Might it be possible that Socrates and Plato were simply reproducing a millennia-old theme in a poetic context without fully realising what it meant?

It is possible, yes. However, as we shall now see, there was a group of people in Greece, with whom Socrates and Plato were well acquainted, who almost certainly did know what it all meant.

That group was the Pythagoreans.

Pythagoras

Pythagoras was a philosopher and mathematician who must surely rank among the most original geniuses of all time. Born on the island of Samos *c*. 580 BC, Pythagoras became a student of philosophy, astronomy, geometry, music and science, and these interests he blended together in a distinctive philosophy that became known as Pythagoreanism. One of his most important teachings was that the Universe was a harmony in which the motions of the celestial spheres were determined by mathematical relationships. But many of his teachings were religious and mystical. He taught, by means of various forms of mathematical 'proofs', that all things in existence had originated from the One. Furthermore, he taught, in common with the Orphics, that the soul was immortal and experienced reincarnations according to a vast cycle of cosmic motions.

According to Pythagoras, the Universe had been created in the image of God, and the aim of man should be to seek knowledge of the Universe and thus return to a unity with God.[16] This could be done by studying all things in nature, but it could be done most effectively by (a) studying things which were most like God itself, i.e. which approximated to the eternal, ever-unchanging nature of God; and (b) by looking for an overall pattern or unity behind the creation. To this end, the Pythagoreans became adepts in numbers, geometry, music and astronomy.[17] Numbers and geometry were considered to be important because they seemingly embodied a constant, perfect and universal truth,[18] whilst astronomy was deemed important because the celestial bodies seemed to be eternal, with their motions ever-unchanging.[19] According to Pythagoras, the entire Universe was a *harmonia*, i.e. 'a being in tune',[20] and the aim of the true philosopher was to tune in to this harmony and learn to sing the 'song' of the Universe.[21]

After the death of Pythagoras *c.* 500 BC, his teachings were continued by the Pythagorean school of philosophy, which was based in southern Italy and Sicily. There, one of the most famous teachers was Philolaos (active *c.* 475 BC), who allegedly inspired the philosophy of Plato.[22]

The Counter-Earth and the Central Fire

The Pythagorean Philolaos is credited with a most remarkable picture of the Universe, which is reconstructed in Figure 6. Instead of placing the Earth at the centre of the Universe – as was the norm in ancient Greek astronomy – Philolaos placed there a Central Fire (*Hestia*); it must be emphasised, however, that this Fire was *not* the Sun. Then, in the next position outwards from the Central Fire, Philolaos placed a Counter-Earth. Thereafter, the rest of the Universe followed the standard pattern, with the Earth being surrounded by the orbits of the Sun, the Moon, the five known planets and finally the stars.[23] The stars are to be visualised as forming the shell of the Universe but spherical rather than circular, for the whole Universe was conceived as being a sphere.

What was the Central Fire? As already noted, it was not the Sun. In fact, Philolaos stated that the Sun was *not* an original source of heat and light, but rather *reflected* light and heat *from another source* towards the Earth.[24] Exactly how this happened is not entirely clear, owing to the ambiguities of the Greek language and the differing opinions of the later philosophers who studied Philolaos. Either the primary source was the Central Fire, which fed its fire to the Sun, which then reflected it towards the Earth. Or the primary source was an aethereal 'body of Fire' outside the visible Universe, which fed its fire to the Sun, which then refracted it towards the Earth. Whichever way we look at it, the Philolaon scheme is very puzzling indeed.

Figure 6.
THE COSMOS OF
PHILOLAOS

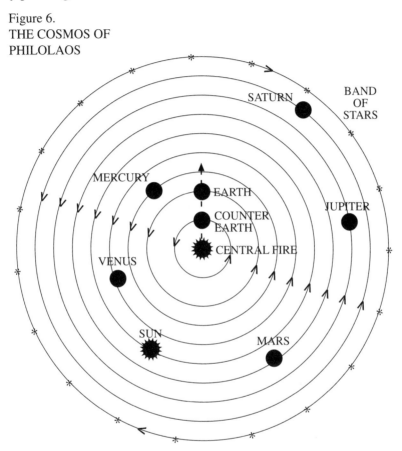

So puzzling indeed that modern scholars have been scratching their heads in confusion for hundreds of years. Why on earth would Philolaos have developed such an obscure explanation for the fiery orb of the Sun? And why would he have invented two celestial bodies that did not visibly exist, namely the Central Fire and the Counter-Earth? It would be fair to say that Philolaos' portrayal of the cosmos presents as great a mystery as Plato's story of Athens and Atlantis.

But let us scratch our heads no longer. If we look at Figure 6 again, through the eyes of the ancient Egyptians and Sumerians, we recognise instantly a cosmos that was at the heart of ancient religions for thousands of years. At the centre of Philolaos' scheme is the triple vertical axis of the Universe, comprising the three world mountains – the Mountain of

Heaven, the Mountain of Earth and the Mountain of the Underworld. Indeed, the positioning and the nomenclature is perfect. Firstly, the Earth and the Counter-Earth imply a pair of twin Earth-like planets, which is exactly how the mountains of Heaven and Earth were always conceived. And secondly, the Central Fire, situated below the Earth, implies the fallen Mountain of Heaven. Indeed, the Central Fire (*Hestia*) is a dead ringer for the Egyptian Underworld, which was called 'the Island of Fire' to commemorate the fallen Heaven that had been buried cataclysmically within it.[25]

Philolaos' mysterious cosmos can also be explained using the Greek nomenclature: the 'Earth' turns out to be Mount Olympus, the 'Counter-Earth' turns out to be our Earth, and the 'Central Fire' turns out to be Tartarus. The respective positioning of these three bodies is confirmed by Hesiod who sang: 'as far below the Earth as Heaven is from the Earth... so far it is from Earth to misty Tartarus... for nine nights and days a bronze anvil might fall from Heaven, and on the tenth reach the Earth; and for nine nights and days a bronze anvil might fall from Earth, and on the tenth reach Tartarus.'[26] Figure 7, below, encapsulates this idea, although it should be noted that the Underworld's position is portrayed symbolically; it was normally conceived to be *inside* the Earth.

Figure 7.
THE TRIPLE AXIS OF THE UNIVERSE
(Copyright Alan F. Alford)

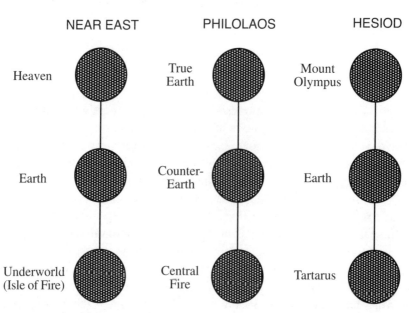

NEAR EAST

Heaven

Earth

Underworld
(Isle of Fire)

PHILOLAOS

True
Earth

Counter-
Earth

Central
Fire

HESIOD

Mount
Olympus

Earth

Tartarus

The game is up and the mystery is revealed. In the Pythagorean scheme of Philolaos, a celestial body *called the Earth* was suspended above a second Earth (the Counter-Earth). But thanks to our knowledge of the Near Eastern triple axis of Heaven, Earth and the Underworld, we can understand that: (a) the upper Earth, which Philolaos called 'Earth', was actually the Mountain of Heaven, i.e. the now invisible and aethereal exploded planet; (b) the lower Earth, which Philolaos called 'Counter-Earth', was actually our real Earth; and (c) the Central Fire signified the fallen Mountain of Heaven, i.e. the Underworld.[27]

As regards the supply of heat and light to Earth via the Sun – the other puzzling aspect of Philolaon cosmology – this can now be understood either as the Sun reflecting the energy of the physical Central Fire, or as the Sun reflecting the energy of the metaphysical exploded planet (the upper Earth in the Philolaon scheme). Or perhaps it was even conceived as a combination of both.

But Philolaos' placement of the planet of Heaven near the centre of the Universe was not the typical Pythagorean perspective. Rather, it was believed that this archetypal planet had been resurrected to an invisible orbit *outside and above* the visible Universe (the Universe which it had created in its own spherical image). From this position, the exploded planet was thought to provide heat and light to the Earth by a process of refraction (rather than reflection) through the Sun.

Such was the scheme of Parmenides, who referred to the exploded planet as 'the Fire of Heaven, a gentle thing, very light, in every direction the same as itself' (i.e. spherical),[28] and called it 'the world of Truth' and 'the Thing which *is*' (see discussion in chapter four). In contrast to this aethereal body, he spoke of the physical aspect of the exploded planet as 'Night', the Underworld, which was 'a dense and heavy body'.[29]

Such, too, was the scheme of Socrates, as recorded in the mystical vision of Plato's *Phaedo* (cited earlier). Here, Socrates declares that we who dwell on the Earth cannot see the 'true Heaven' because we are trapped in a layer of air which is the sediment of the *aither* (the air was envisaged as extending no further than the Moon whereas the *aither* stretched from the Moon to the stars and surrounded the shell of the Universe). If a person could penetrate the upper limit of the air, he would see things that were not normally visible: "and, if his nature could endure to contemplate them, he would know that there is the true Heaven, the true Light and the true Earth".[30] As discussed earlier in this chapter, this is, prima facie, a description of an Earth-like planet, albeit one that is invisible to the naked eye, and it matches perfectly with Philolaos' invisible 'Earth', and Parmenides' invisible, spherical 'world of Truth'

It is of this mystical world that Socrates speaks in *Phaedrus*, where he describes the gods ascending in their chariots to the highest tier of the heavens to join with Zeus at a divine banquet. The same journey, he said, could be made by human souls who, when perfectly initiated, could grow wings and ascend to the highest ridge of the heavens (i.e. the outermost band of stars). There, they would be carried round by the circular motion of the Universe while gazing in awe at the place outside and above the heavens:

> "The place above the heavens – none of our Earthly poets has ever sung or ever will sing its praises enough! Still, this is the way it is: risky as it may be, I must attempt to speak the truth... What is in this place is without colour and without shape and without solidity – a being that really is what it is, the subject of all true knowledge, visible only to Intelligence, the steersman of the soul."[31]

This 'place above the heavens' was the sphere of God, the true Heaven, the true Earth, the true Light, the 'world of Forms' and 'that which *is*'. And "that which *is*", said Socrates, "is invisible", i.e. it could not be seen by the eye but only by the mind or the soul. This mystical scheme – a well-kept secret to this day – is depicted in Figure 8, opposite, where the invisible exploded planet is notionally suspended above the visible sphere of the Universe.

This astonishing scheme (Figure 8), I would suggest, is the key to the Pythagorean idea that even the most perfect initiate had only observed 'seven of the eight orbits' (i.e. those of the Sun, Moon and five planets).[32] Why only seven of the eight? Simply because one of the orbits – the eighth – was invisible. This secret 'eighth orbit' was pictured sometimes as existing *inside* the heavens (as in Philolaos' invisible 'Upper Earth' scheme, see Figure 6, and as in a cryptic section of Plato's *Timaeus*),[33] and sometimes as existing *outside and above* the heavens (as in Figure 8 opposite). As regards the latter scenario, the idea seems to have been that the soul, having studied seven of the eight orbits, would ascend from the Earth to its companion star at the highest tier of the visible Universe,[34] whereupon, from this vantage point, it would witness the secret 'eighth orbit' of the invisible sphere of God. This orb, according to Socrates, was 'that which provides light for everything'.[35]

We see here the very essence of Platonic and Pythagorean mysticism. What matters is not what is visible and unreal but what is invisible and 'truly real'.[36] Hence Socrates' famous dictum to 'leave the (visible) things in the sky alone'.[37] As Francis Cornford observed in 1912: 'To the mysticism of all ages, the visible world is a myth, a tale half true and half

Figure 8.
THE CREATOR
AND HIS UNIVERSE
(Copyright Alan F. Alford)

THE SPHERE
OF GOD
(not to scale)

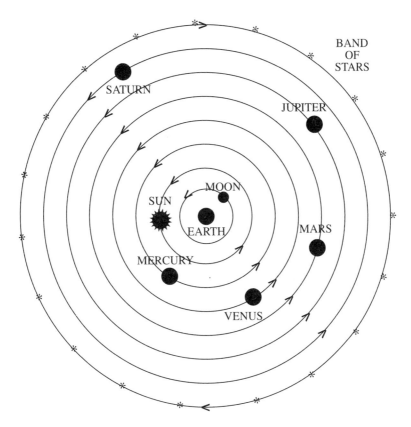

false, embodying a *logos*, the truth which is one.'[38]

Did Philolaos, Parmenides and Socrates truly understand what all this meant, i.e. that the God-Sphere was an exploded planet?

As far as Philolaos is concerned, it is difficult to believe that anyone could have produced the scheme in Figure 6 without being consciously aware of the exploded planet hypothesis. Philolaos and the Pythagoreans must not only have known the EPH, but also believed implicitly in its truth. As for Parmenides, he certainly spoke in cryptic terms, as if he had just been initiated into the secret. And as for Socrates, it is interesting to note that two members of the Pythagorean brotherhood were allegedly present when he delivered his extraordinary death-bed speech about the

Upper Earth (according to Plato in *Phaedo*); he even referred to the leader of their group as Philolaos![39] In summary, whilst it is possible that Socrates was producing his mystical accounts subconsciously, we can at least say that his vision of the heavenly world of Forms as an Earth-like planet was rooted in a profound mystical belief system, which was itself rooted in the millennia-old exploded planet cults of the Near East.

Much evidence has now been amassed to support an identification of ancient Greek religion as an exploded planet cult. Firstly, we have noted the importance of meteorites and cataclysm theory. Secondly, we have identified Heaven as having had an Earth-like size and environment. Thirdly, we have identified the Underworld (i.e. the fallen Heaven) as having had an Earth-like size and environment. Fourthly, we have marvelled at Socrates' description of Heaven as an Upper Earth and 'world of Forms'. And fifthly, we have discovered an exact transcription of the exploded planet cult in the Earth, Counter-Earth and Central Fire cosmology of the Pythagorean philosopher Philolaos.

Just two mysteries now remain to be solved, if we are to place these matters beyond dispute. One is Plato's cosmogony of the *Demiourgos*, as recorded in *Timaeus*. The other is the enigma of the Orphic cosmogony. As regards the *Demiourgos*, I shall deal with this mystery in appendix a, for the subject is of labyrinthine complexity. In the meantime, let us move directly to a discussion of the Orphic mystery of the creation.

The Mystery of Khaos

In the beginning, said the Orphics, the first god, Time, had given birth to *Khaos*, the *Aither* and *Erebos*. As a consequence of this primal act, 'all things were in confusion, throughout the misty darkness'. The god Time had then fashioned a silvery egg in the divine *Aither*, and the egg 'began to move in a wondrous circle'. Suddenly, the egg split in two and Phanes, the First-born god, emerged, gleaming amidst a supernatural light. At this moment, Heaven was separated from the Earth:

> And at the birth of Phanes, the misty gulf below and the windless
> *Aither* were rent.

What is the meaning of all this? A good place to start is the term *Erebos*, which meant literally 'covered' or 'darkness', implying something that was concealed in the Underworld. In addition, the terms 'misty darkness' and 'misty gulf' signified the Underworld. And so it should be evident, in the passage cited above, that the *Aither* is being separated *from the Underworld* (the misty gulf) as it is lifted up magically to the heavens.

What is the *Aither*? Normally, this would be an aethereal, heavenly substance.[40] But in this Orphic cosmogony, it is implied that the *Aither* had fallen from Heaven to Earth, into the Underworld. Hence the idea that Phanes had been born in the *Aither* and had caused it to be separated from the Underworld. The *Aither* thus seems to represent the spiritual essence of the exploded planet.[41]

What, then, of *Khaos*, which had been born from Time alongside the *Aither* and *Erebos*? This is where things get really interesting. According to the *Collins English Dictionary*, the Greek word *khaos* is the origin of the modern word 'chaos'. Hellenists, however, stress that *khaos* did *not* have any chaotic connotations in Greek;[42] rather it came from the verbs *khaino/khasko*, meaning 'to gape/yawn'.[43] The noun *Khaos* thus meant literally 'the yawning gap'.[44]

In what sense did Time create a yawning gap? Some scholars think that *Khaos* might be related to the gap that was created by the separation of Heaven from Earth.[45] Other scholars think that *Khaos* was a yawning gap in the sense of a vast expanse of undifferentiated darkness.[46] But it is Martin West who has surely come closest to the mark with his suggestion that *Khaos* might have related to the Earth gaping open and swallowing something (hence the modern word 'chasm' from *khasko*).[47] But what was it that the Earth had swallowed?

We will now take a brief detour to examine the 'swallowing motif' and its cosmic significance in the Greek myths.

Our first stop is the Orphic cosmogony and the climax to the account that I have just related. In order to reconcile the myth of Phanes, the First-born god, with the rival myth of Ouranos, Gaia, Kronos and Zeus, the Orphics had Phanes impregnate the goddess Night, who gave birth to Ouranos and Gaia, who, in turn, gave birth to Kronos and the Titans and, later, to almighty Zeus. The latter then established the present world order by swallowing Phanes. The Orphic account of this latter re-creation reads as follows:

> Thus, by swallowing the might of Erikepaios [Phanes], the First-born, he [Zeus] held the body of all things in the hollow of his own belly; and he mingled with his own limbs the power and strength of the god [Phanes]. Thus, together with him, all things were created anew in Zeus – the shining height of the broad *Aither* and the heavens, the seat of the unharvested sea and the noble earth, great Ocean and the lowest depths beneath the Earth, rivers and the boundless sea, and all else, all immortal and blessed gods and goddesses, all that was then in being and all that was to come to pass. All was there, and mingled like streams in the belly of Zeus.[48]

How exactly did Zeus come to 'swallow' Phanes? Although the textual fragments remain unclear, the Orphic account provides an astonishing parallel to other Greek myths in which the Universe was born from the Underworld – from the womb of the Earth. Significantly, for this to be the case – for Zeus to hold *all things* 'in the hollow of his own belly' – Zeus must have become one with the planet Earth.

For our second stop, we turn to the strange story of Zeus swallowing Metis and then giving birth to Athene. The tale is recorded by Hesiod in *Theogony*:

> Zeus as king of the gods made Metis his first wife... But when she was about to give birth to the pale-eyed goddess Athene, he tricked her deceitfully with cunning words and put her away in his belly... For from Metis it was destined that clever children should be born: first, a pale-eyed daughter Tritogeneia [Athene]... and then a son she was to bear (who would be) king of gods and men... But Zeus put her away in his belly first...[49]

What is the meaning of this? To decode the story, one must realise that Zeus is Heaven and Metis is Earth. We then perceive a classic case of Heaven and Earth joining in sexual union and giving rise to children, one of whom is destined to depose Zeus and become 'king of gods and men'. Zeus, hearing a prophecy of this event, protects himself by swallowing the goddess Metis (Earth), thereby taking control of her birth-giving powers. Lest there be any doubt about this, Hesiod goes on to inform us that Zeus eventually gave birth to Athene 'by himself – out of his head'.[50] Significantly, the word translated 'head' also meant literally 'mountain peak'.[51] Thus Athene was born, according to this myth, from the Earth-mountain. Once again, we encounter the idea that Zeus could swallow a god, or goddess, of the Earth, and thereby become one with the planet Earth.[52]

For our third and final stop, we turn to the account of how Kronos swallowed his own children. In *Theogony*, Hesiod records the myth as follows:

> Rhea, surrendering to Kronos, bore resplendent children – Hestia, Demeter, gold-sandalled Hera, mighty Hades who lives beneath the Earth... [Poseidon] the booming Earth-shaker, and Zeus-the-wise... Those other gods [apart from Zeus] great Kronos swallowed, as each of them reached their mother's knees from her holy womb. His aim was that none but he of the lordly celestials should have the royal station among the immortals.[53]

Readers will probably recall the rest of the story. Rhea, furious at this treatment of her children, concealed her youngest child Zeus in a remote cave, deep inside the Earth, and delivered to Kronos a stone in his stead. This was duly swallowed, allowing Zeus to remain safe and orchestrate his father's downfall. To this end, Zeus became Kronos' cupbearer on Olympus, whereupon he slipped a vomiting potion into the Titan's drink. The plan worked and Kronos spewed out the swallowed gods, along with the stone which Rhea had substituted for Zeus:

> The first he spewed out was the stone – the last he had swallowed. Zeus fixed it in the wide-pathed Earth at holy Delphi, in the glens of Parnassus, to be a monument thereafter and a thing of wonder for mortal men.[54]

This marvellous stone, as discussed at the beginning of this chapter, was an *omphalos* and *baetylus*, i.e. it was originally a meteorite.

How did Kronos manage to swallow the gods, his children? Hesiod's tale is obscure and impenetrable, but nevertheless the context of the tale (eliminating the threat of a potential successor) parallels the myth cited earlier in which Zeus swallowed Metis to prevent the birth of her prophesied son. And this parallel allows us to surmise that Kronos, like Zeus, may have swallowed his children by becoming one with the Earth.

Does this make sense? Well, under the exploded planet hypothesis, it does. To visualise what is happening, we must understand that when a god fell from Heaven, his body entered the Underworld whilst his soul – separated from his body – rose up to Heaven. This was seemingly the case with Ouranos, the fallen 'Mountain of Heaven'. When he rose up to personify the visible heavens and the invisible Heaven, he would have left behind his physical body, which filled the interior of the Earth. Thus his fallen body was able to perform an act of swallowing.[55]

The story of Kronos is a replay of the same saga of Heaven and Earth. In order to impregnate Rhea, Kronos must, by definition, have fallen from Heaven. Therefore, at the time when Hestia, Demeter, Hera, Hades, Poseidon and Zeus were born, *the physical body* of Kronos was filling the interior of the Earth. Thus Kronos was able to swallow his children at the very moment they were born to Rhea (the Earth).

Much more could be said about the 'swallowing motif', but the point has been made and we have seen enough to conclude that Martin West was close to the truth when he suggested that the Orphic principle of *Khaos* might have related to the Earth gaping open and swallowing something. But what an appetite! First the Earth swallowed Ouranos. Then the body of Earth/Ouranos swallowed their offspring. Then the body of Earth/Ouranos/Kronos swallowed their offspring. Then the body of Earth/Ouranos/Kronos/Zeus swallowed their offspring. And then Zeus put a stop to the process by keeping his own future successor confined inside his belly or head.

As for the nature of these swallowed 'mountain' gods, it should hardly be necessary any longer to underline the fact that they were meteoritic in nature. The *baetylus* swallowed by Kronos underlines the point, as does the parallel cult-stone of Kumarbis in the Hittite tradition. It is also worth noting that in Philo's adaptation of Sanchuniathon's *Phoenician History* (2nd century AD), one of the sons of Ouranos and Gaia is actually named Baetyl, i.e. 'Meteorite';[56] furthermore, in this work, it is said that Ouranos 'created *baetuli*, contriving stones that moved as if having life, which were supposed to fall from Heaven.'[57] Surely the clues to the 'swallowing motif' have been staring us in the face for centuries.

So, back to *Khaos*, 'the yawning gap', and the meaning of the Orphic cosmogony. In the beginning, said the Orphics, the first god, Time, had given birth to *Khaos*, the *Aither* and *Erebos*. The meaning of this can now be determined. *Khaos* is surely 'the yawning gap' inside the Earth (compare my comments on KI in chapter nine); the *Aither* is some kind of aethereal image of the fallen Heaven; and *Erebos* is surely an ex-heavenly mountain that has been interred in the Earth, thus becoming the Underworld or mountain of misty darkness. In each and every case, the fall of Heaven – the exploded planet – is implied, hence the Orphic idea that 'all things were in confusion, throughout the misty darkness'.

Two passages in *Theogony* support this interpretation of *Khaos* being in the Underworld. In one, Hesiod refers to a vast, gloomy *Khasma* (a cognate of the word *Khaos* according to scholars) specifically in the Underworld.[58] In the second, cited below, Hesiod describes how, during the battle between Zeus and the Titans, a terrible cataclysm broke out in the place known as *Khaos*:

> All around, the life-bearing Earth rumbled as it burned... An amazing conflagration prevailed over *Khaos*: to see it directly with the eyes and to hear the sound with the ears, it seemed just as if Earth and the broad Heaven above were coming together...[59]

Taking these references together, and bearing in mind the context of the story, it makes a great deal of sense that *Khaos* was a 'yawning gap' in the Underworld. But it nevertheless seems a strange idea to say that Time gave birth to a 'yawning gap' in the Underworld and, indeed, it turns out that our deciphering of *Khaos* is not quite complete. If we now turn to the beginning of *Theogony*, we find Hesiod making what appears to be a contradictory two-part statement about *Khaos*:

> First came *Khaos*; and then broad-breasted Earth, secure seat for ever of all the immortals...; and the misty Tartarus in a remote recess of the broad-pathed Earth; and Eros...

> Out of *Khaos* came *Erebos* and dark Night; and from Night, in turn, came *Aither* and Day, whom she bore in shared intimacy with *Erebos*. Earth bore first of all, one equal to herself, Ouranos...[60]

The reader will no doubt agree that this is a confused statement – hence the fact that no-one has ever understood it. It would appear to be a hybrid of three cosmogonies – the traditional account of Ouranos and Gaia; the Orphic account of *Khaos*, *Erebos*, Night and Eros; and a third account involving misty Tartarus.

But, confusion aside, Hesiod's account contains a striking anomaly. Instead of giving *Khaos* equal status with the *Aither* and *Erebos*, as the Orphics did, Hesiod asserts that 'out of *Khaos* came *Erebos* and dark Night... and... *Aither*'. Note the words 'out of' (Night, by the way, was a goddess who personified the Earth's Underworld). Moreover, Hesiod gives *Khaos* precedence even to Earth, saying 'first came *Khaos*', as if *Khaos* had been the first principle of all cosmogony. And, furthermore, a Pelasgian creation myth lends a similar priority to *Khaos* by suggesting that the goddess Eurynome arose naked from *Khaos* as a prelude to descending from Heaven to Earth (see chapter one).

This can mean only one thing: *Khaos* was not just the yawning gap of the Underworld, but was also the original mountain or god of Heaven, who gave rise to the fallen *Erebos* and the fallen goddess Night. Thus the name *Khaos* surely signified the yawning gap in the place above the Earth, where the physical Heaven no longer existed. In other words, the god had vacated his post, the gap had yawned in the midst of space, and *Khaos* had come down to the Earth, thus becoming the yawning gap of the Underworld. It is somewhat comforting to find that the Greek word *Khaos* did, after all, contain an element of true chaos.

In conclusion, it must be said that this Orphic cosmogony – which has always remained obscure and impenetrable to scholars – makes perfect sense under an exploded planet scenario. Moreover, it is evident that obscure metaphors such as Time, *Khaos*, *Erebos*, *Aither* and Night were used deliberately by the Orphics to conceal the secret of their cosmogony (i.e. the exploded planet) from the eyes of the uninitiated. It was the Orphics, we may recall, who spoke of a 'Secret of secrets' which was revealed only to the highest initiates and which amounted to a knowledge of 'the true God' (see chapter five). This Secret, it was said, would 'startle the ears' and 'overturn the preconceived opinions' even of the fully-prepared initiand. The reader has now been initiated into a secret that would fit the bill very well indeed: the secret of the exploded planet.

Chapter Eleven Summary

* The Greek Heaven was personified by Ouranos, 'The Mountain of Heaven', who is a dead ringer for the Near Eastern exploded planet deities. In addition, Heaven was personified by Oceanus, whose fallen ocean is difficult to reconcile with anything but a water-bearing planet.

* The Greeks referred to 'the broad Heaven', 'the broad Earth' and 'the broad Underworld', as if to imply (in line with the Near Eastern model) that Heaven was a planet of Earth-like dimensions.

* Hesiod described Ouranos (Mount Olympus) as one 'equal to' Gaia, who would 'cover her all about'. This implies that Heaven was a planet, of equal size to the Earth.

* Homer described how earth, sea, gods and everything could be reconstituted on Mount Olympus 'so that all once more should hang in mid-air'. This is the exploded planet to a tee.

* Although the Greeks were averse to describing the environment of Heaven, they did describe the Underworld (the fallen Heaven) as if it were an Earth-like world-within-a-world.

* Socrates/Plato described Heaven as an Earth-like planet, but perfect in every respect, containing the archetypes for everything on Earth. This idea of Heaven as the world of Forms – 'the true Earth' – was no innocent metaphor; it was the exploded planet to a tee.

* Philolaos, a leading Pythagorean, reproduced the exploded planet cult perfectly with the inclusion in his cosmos of two invisible bodies – 'the true Earth' and 'the Central Fire'. The former was the aethereal reproduction of the exploded planet, alias Heaven; the latter was its physical, fallen counterpart, alias the Underworld.

* Parmenides reproduced the exploded planet cult perfectly in his initiate's vision of the paired opposites 'the Fire of Heaven' (an aethereal sphere) and Night, the Underworld ('a dense and heavy body').

* In the Orphic cosmogony, the first god Time and the first principle *Khaos* ('the yawning gap') represented secret ciphers for the exploded planet.

* All of the mysteries of Greek cosmogony, cosmology and philosophy can be explained perfectly by the exploded planet hypothesis (EPH). No other theory has ever come close to deciphering Socrates' 'world of Forms', or Philolaos' weird cosmology of the Earth, Counter-Earth and Central Fire (in addition, see appendix a on Plato's cosmogony of the *Demiourgos*). To solve any one of these millennia-old mysteries would be an amazing achievement; the EPH explains all of them and reconciles them perfectly.

* Whilst it is tempting to conclude that Greek religion was an exploded planet cult, it must be conceded that only a few people consciously knew it as such, notably those who were initiated into the inner circle of the Pythagoreans and other bona fide mystery schools (on this, see the discussion in chapter five). Intriguingly, it would seem that the meaning of the religion was concealed from the earliest times by use of obscure metaphors such as Time, *Khaos*, *Erebos*, *Aither* and Night. It may therefore be best to say that Greek religion was an *occulted* exploded planet cult.

CHAPTER TWELVE

GENESIS OF THE GODS

Everything is full of gods.
(Thales, 6th century BC)

In the previous chapter, we looked at Greek cosmogony and cosmology and discovered some extraordinary connections with the exploded planet cults of the ancient Near East. We also discovered that many of the olden Greek gods – Time, *Khaos*, *Erebos*, *Aither*, Night, Tartarus, Oceanus, Ouranos, Kronos, Zeus – were encoded personifications of an exploded planet. Many questions, however, remain unanswered. In particular, it is not quite clear to what degree the exploded planet cults permeated into the cults of the Olympian gods.

In this chapter, my aim is to round out our picture of ancient Greek religion by looking in more detail at the Olympian gods, but now in the context of what we have learned about exploded planets. Can it be argued, without fear of contradiction, that Zeus and his associates were exploded planet gods?

Recapitulation

To begin, it is worth summarising what we have learned so far about the Olympian gods:

1 The Greeks distinguished between the visible, celestial gods (Sun, Moon and stars) and the invisible Olympian gods (*daimones*). One of the greatest mysteries of Greek religion is why the latter gods – invisible by nature – were accorded the greatest importance.

2 The *daimones* (see definition in 1 above) were born from the Earth, ultimately from a primal union of Heaven (Ouranos) and Earth (Gaia). Since the name Ouranos meant literally 'The Mountain of Heaven', it would seem, prima facie, that the gods had their origin

in a cataclysmic event. And the present world order was indeed established via a series of cataclysmic battles involving the gods of Heaven and Earth.

3   The *daimones* were often depicted in human-like form, but on closer inspection it appears that they were not human at all. In fact, Homer maintained that there could be no comparison at all between the races of gods and men.

4   The *daimones* were supernatural beings, associated with bright light, blazing fire, loud noise, swift movement, shape-shifting ability and eternal life.

5   The *daimones* were invisible and immortal gods, i.e. they were aethereal, metaphysical entities. Only on rare occasions did they manifest themselves visibly.

6   Just as the *daimones* were invisible and aethereal by nature, so too was their heavenly dwelling place, Mount Olympus, an invisible and aethereal sphere.

7   Whilst some *daimones* resided in Heaven (Mount Olympus), others resided in the Underworld (under earth or sea), ostensibly as the result of a cataclysmic insertion from Heaven. Hence the overlap between cataclysmic celestial phenomena and volcanic and tectonic phenomena.

8   Overall, the *daimones* were virtually identical, conceptually, with the gods of the Near East.

Based on the foregoing points, together with the parallels that have been drawn between the cosmogonies of the Greeks and the exploded planet cosmogonies of Near Eastern civilisations (see the previous chapter), it is extremely likely that the Olympian gods (the *daimones*) *were* exploded planet gods, just like their Near Eastern counterparts. However, to rely upon a likelihood would be to rest upon our laurels. Instead, we should explore other ways of sustaining and strengthening the argument.

Accordingly, my plan, in this and the next chapter, is to build a case from first principles in three mutually supportive ways: firstly, by demonstrating an extremely good conceptual fit between the category of Olympian gods (*daimones*) and the idea of an exploded planet; secondly, by illustrating how the pantheon of Greek gods could have evolved under an exploded planet scenario; and thirdly, by highlighting some intriguing clues to the exploded planet personae of the most popular deities: Zeus, Hades, Hera, Demeter, Leto, Apollo, Artemis, Ares, Hermes, Dionysus,

Poseidon, Athene and Hephaestus.

Invisible Gods

As we shall see in a moment, the conceptual fit between the Olympian gods (*daimones*) and the exploded planet hypothesis is profound and astonishing in its simplicity, and yet it is elusive in the sense that it cannot be grasped until we recognise and accept the fundamental point that the *daimones* were, by nature, invisible and aethereal beings.

This point may be difficult for some people to accept, for a number of reasons. Firstly, the Greeks identified the gods (*daimones*) with a variety of visible phenomena – the Sun and the Moon, certain planets and stars, comets, lightning bolts, meteorites and other cult objects. Secondly, the Greeks worshipped the *daimones* in the shape of human-like statues. Thirdly, the Greeks had a literary tradition in which the *daimones* were pictured in human-like and animal-like forms (albeit as shape-shifters). And fourthly, the Greeks would refer to the *daimones* sometimes as *theoi* (singular *theos*) – a word which was normally reserved for the visible gods, such as the Sun, the Moon and the stars.[1]

Nevertheless, the reader must understand that the true nature of the Olympian gods (*daimones*) was that of invisible and aethereal beings, who were associated with visible forms (a) for symbolic purposes; and (b) for the sake of poetic convenience. For this essential fact, our main source is Plato who, in *Timaeus*, made a clear distinction between 'the visible and generated gods' and 'the other spiritual beings'. The former were the Earth, Sun, Moon, planets and stars, which he called *theoi*. The latter were the Olympian gods, which he called *daimones*.[2] The key point of distinction, said Plato, related to visibility; hence the *theoi* were said to 'make their rounds conspicuously', whilst the *daimones* were said to 'present themselves only to the extent that they are willing'.[3] The crucial implication, confirmed by a passage in Plato's appendix to *Laws*, is that the *daimones*, i.e. the Olympian gods, were fundamentally invisible by nature.[4]

It must be emphasised, however, that this idea of the *daimones* being invisible, aethereal beings was not an invention of Socrates' or Plato's. On the contrary, one of the clearest references in this regard appears in Hesiod's *Works and Days* (7th century BC), where the poet sang of the fate of the golden race:

> Since the Earth covered up that race, they have been divine *daimones* by the design of great Zeus, good *daimones* on the face of the Earth – watchers over mortal men...[5]

The meaning here is abundantly clear. The golden race of mankind had begun their existence in the form of souls trapped in bodies. Then, upon their bodily deaths, the souls of the golden race had been released to become *daimones*, i.e. free spirits or ghosts.[6] This is no different from Plato's concept of the gods as *daimones*, but it does raise an intriguing question: did the gods, like the golden race, originally possess physical bodies?

Let's Get Metaphysical

How did the gods become invisible, aethereal *daimones*? In the Greek myths, this essential point is taken for granted, and no clear explanation of it is provided. However, the question can be resolved by recourse to the parallel myths of the Near East, where we learn that the gods, in the beginning, had come down into the Earth in physical form, whereupon they had died a bodily death. It was this death-upon-impact that had led to the birth, from the Earth, of invisible, aethereal doubles of the gods, which we might describe in modern-day language as 'souls', 'spirits' or 'ghosts'.

This crucial concept is best seen in Egypt, in the resurrection myth of the god Osiris. The Book of the Dead states:

> ... the corpse of Osiris entered the [world] mountain, and his soul walked out shining... when Osiris came forth from death as a shining thing, his face white with heat.[7]

Osiris, we should recall, was the Egyptian iron-god and meteorite-god, who personified the fallen, physical aspect of the exploded planet – hence his status as chief god of the Underworld (the so-called Island of Fire). But as this passage reveals, Osiris's soul had separated from his body at the moment of impact and resurrected itself, phoenix-like, from the funeral pyre.[8] This was the archetypal moment of death and rebirth which gave hope of an afterlife to every Egyptian; hence their dictum: 'The body to Earth, the soul to Heaven'.

This idea, of the death and rebirth of the gods, was anathema to most Greeks, who had a child-like belief in the aethereal, immortal nature of their deities. But the irony is that the Olympians only acquired this status by means of their birth from the Earth in the aforementioned physical to metaphysical transformation. In other words, the Olympian gods had originally come down physically from Heaven (as meteoritic offspring of the exploding planet) and had 'died', thereby releasing their spiritual, invisible doubles, the *daimones*.

That this is so is evident from the many Greek myths that speak of gods being flung out of Heaven, the prime example being Hephaestus, the blacksmith-god and meteorite-god.[9] In addition, the succession myth by which kingship of Olympus passed from Ouranos to Kronos to Zeus only makes sense when the body-soul separation process is understood.

Consider. In the beginning, Ouranos came down physically from Heaven (perhaps, in this context, we should say 'from the yawning gap'); his body entered the Underworld; and his soul then rose up to form the invisible Mount Olympus and the aether that filled and surrounded the sphere of the Universe. Thereafter, Kronos' body fell from Heaven to become a sphere of the Underworld (hence his ability to swallow his own children), but his soul rose up to Heaven to take over the invisible Mount Olympus. Finally, Zeus' body fell from Heaven to become a sphere of the Underworld (hence his swallowing of Metis), but his soul rose up to Heaven to take over the invisible Mount Olympus from Kronos. In all of these cases, the body-soul separation is implicit in the myth.

This physical-metaphysical separation of the divinity is absolutely fundamental to our understanding of ancient Greek religion. Using the template from Egypt (and indeed Mesopotamia) we can predict that the Greek *daimones* would have dispensed with their physical *alter egos* at the moments of their cataclysmic births from the Earth.[10] Consequently, they became free spirits or ghosts, like the *daimones* of Hesiod's golden race and, in the process, they acquired immortality. They could not be killed because they had, in effect, been killed already, at the beginning of time. How does one kill a ghost?

In summary, it can be seen that the Olympian gods – the *daimones* – were indeed invisible beings, owing to their metaphysical nature. Having grasped this point, it is but a short step to appreciate how excellently this concept fits with the exploded planet hypothesis.

Consider, again, the gods who were worshipped by the Greeks. Firstly, there was the *visible* category of gods – the Sun, Moon, planets and stars (the *theoi*). Secondly, there was the race of *invisible* Olympian gods (the *daimones*), who dwelt upon (or had shares in) an invisible heavenly sphere – Mount Olympus, alias Ouranos 'The Mountain of Heaven'. In such a system, one might reasonably expect that priority would be given to the *visible* gods. But this was never the case in Greece, nor was it ever the case in the Near East. On the contrary, it was always the *invisible* race of gods, the Olympians, which was granted the higher status.

Why were the Greeks – patently an intelligent people – obsessed with a race of invisible gods, who dwelt upon an equally invisible mountain? Why were the gods of this mountain given pre-eminence over the Sun and the Moon and all the other visible orbs in the sky? These are vexing questions to which scholars have never given a satisfactory answer. But the elusive answer *can* now be given: the Olympian gods (the *daimones*) were granted supreme importance *because they personified an exploded planet*. Thus, whilst other celestial bodies remained visible and for ever separate from the Earth, the Mountain of Heaven had exploded, causing its fragments to fall and sow the seeds of life in the Earth. Only the exploded body had interacted physically with the Earth; hence the fact that the gods who personified this exploded body enjoyed a unique and supreme status among the Greeks. It is as simple as that; as profound and astonishing as that. Once again, the exploded planet hypothesis makes sense of that which otherwise is inexplicable, and which has remained inexplicable for millennia.

Manifestations of the Gods

In the next chapter, I will offer some comments on individual members of the Greek pantheon. Firstly, however, I would like to preface those comments by explaining in broad terms how the pantheon of gods evolved into the form that it did. Why do we find retired gods such as Ouranos and Kronos? Why do we find a chief god (Zeus) ruling with a divine consort (Hera)? Why do we find a sky-god (Zeus), a deep-sea-god (Poseidon) and a god of the Underworld (Hades)? Why do we find an Earth-goddess of many names? Why do we find a Sun-god (Helios), a Moon-goddess (Selene) and various associations of gods with planets and stars? Why do we find a messenger-god (Hermes), a god of war (Ares), a goddess of war (Athene), a goddess of hunting (Artemis) and a blacksmith-god (Hephaestus)? Why do we find some gods who frustrate all attempts to categorise them (e.g. Demeter/Persephone, Apollo and Dionysus)? How can this wonderfully diverse society of human-like gods be reconciled with the exploded planet hypothesis (EPH)?

Some of these questions have been answered already; others remain to be answered, and now they will be.

Firstly, as regards the fact that one god ruled the sky, another the deep sea, and another the Underworld, enough has already been said in earlier chapters; this division of the cosmos is perfectly consistent with the EPH.

Secondly, as regards the worship of a goddess personifying the Earth, it has already been explained that, under the geocentric system, she was the oldest celestial god and the mother of all things in the Universe. As for the many names of the Earth-goddess, these derive from the idea that numerous mother-goddesses had descended from the heavens, each in turn taking over the mantle of Mother Earth (after the Near Eastern model of the goddess Mami/Ninharsag). More on this in due course.

Thirdly, as regards the worship of the Sun, Moon, planets and stars, the explanation has already been proffered. The Earth had given birth to these celestial gods as *visible* tokens of the *invisible* exploded planet. It is for this reason that we read of Phaethon, the son of Helios, crashing the chariot of the Sun cataclysmically into the Earth – a myth that makes perfect sense if the Sun-god is understood to be a visible symbol for an exploded planet, but is otherwise nonsensical.[11] As for the planets, it is significant that the Platonic/Pythagorean model of the visible Universe (see Figure 8 in previous chapter) reflects the exact sequence of the exploded planet gods who fell to Earth: firstly, the outer shell of stars, Ouranos; secondly, the planet Saturn, Kronos; thirdly, the planet Jupiter, Zeus.[12] As for the other planets, these, too, were made to symbolise invisible Olympian deities: the planet Mars, Ares; the planet Venus, Aphrodite/Athene; and the planet Mercury, Hermes. More on these gods and their exploded planet connotations in due course.

Fourthly, as regards the human-like portrayal of the gods, enough has been said in chapter ten; anthropomorphosis was an entirely predictable offshoot of the exploded planet cult.

But now to a matter that requires some extended discussion, namely 'the succession myth'. Why do we find the idea of a promoted younger god and a retired olden god, coinciding with a changeover from an old cosmic order to a new cosmic order?

The Succession Myth

Over the years, scholars have ventured numerous opinions on the meaning of the Greek succession myth. According to one theory, the violent overthrow of the Titans by Zeus recalled the triumph of Greek civilised values over a previous barbarian culture at the end of the Dark Ages.[13] According to another theory, Zeus' cataclysmic overthrow of the Titanian age was simply a metaphor for the replacement of one religious system by another, perhaps caused by cultural evolution or by an immigration and conquest of the Hellenic lands.[14]

And yet there must be more to the Greek succession myth than mere local factors. The fact is that this myth was not unique to Greece, but was prevalent in the much older civilisations of the Near East, dating back to the late-3rd millennium BC at least. And scholars have proven, beyond any doubt, that the Greek succession myth was modelled on these older versions. The proper question, then, is not why the Greeks adopted the idea of an old cosmos giving way to a new cosmos, but why the idea had arisen thousands of years earlier, in the oldest civilisations.

My feeling is this. At some point in the remote past, perhaps during the early history of civilisation, or perhaps during prehistory, the Earth experienced a lethal encounter with a comet. At this time, a widespread failure of crops caused human society to be thrown into turmoil. Almost overnight, the old order of society collapsed and anarchy ensued. Later, when a semblance of normality returned, people began to regroup and impose a new order of society. Predictably, the leaders of this new group began to rebuild society as a continuation of the past, whilst seeking, in some ways, to make a clean break. Thus the old chief god was retired, and a new chief god, reflecting the values and fears of the new society, was appointed. But to establish the legitimacy of this new god, it was imperative that he be made 'the son of' the old god, in accordance with the time-honoured tradition of human society.

This most traumatic of incidents probably happened, as I said earlier, during the early history of civilisation (4th-3rd millennia BC), or during an earlier, prehistorical era. But in all likelihood, it happened not once but many times.

As noted in chapter ten, the scientists Victor Clube and Bill Napier have identified a major cause of these recurrent cataclysms in the form of Encke's Comet and the Taurid meteor stream which, they say, are the remnants of a huge comet (Proto-Encke) that broke apart in the solar system some eighty thousand years ago. According to Clube and Napier, the Earth's orbit has been intersected by that of the cometary debris on numerous occasions during the last eighty thousand years. In their 1990 book *The Cosmic Winter*, Clube and Napier plotted the most recent of these intersection points as follows: 7200-7100 BC, 3900-3600 BC, 600-500 BC and 200-100 BC.[15] The dates are not to be taken as gospel – Clube and Napier's model is complex and the intersection dates have been adjusted, in any case, since 1990. But what these dates do illustrate is the way in which one single cometary phenomenon can pose a repetitive threat to human society across the millennia. And Encke is by no means the only potential threat circulating in the heavens.

In my view, the exploded planet hypothesis is rooted in cataclysmic events of the kind postulated by Clube and Napier (see my comments in chapter ten). In such circumstances, it is natural that the ancients would have asked questions about the origin of comets and meteorites; and it is perfectly logical that they would have hypothesised the explosion, aeons earlier, of a planetary body that had seeded all life on Earth (whether or not such a planet had exploded in reality). Exactly when this belief in an

exploded planet took hold is impossible to say. But once one accepts the
evidence that it did, and that it became the foundation stone of Near
Eastern religions, it then becomes possible to visualise, in broad terms,
how that belief might have evolved over time. Significantly, in the
context of the succession myth, it becomes clear that any subsequent 'fall
of the sky' would have been interpreted as one exploded planet god
being cast into the Underworld, with a new exploded planet god being
born from the Earth as a 'son' of the 'father'. The succession myth, then,
would have been rooted in a genuine cataclysm – one in a series of such
cataclysms – that marked the end of the old cosmos and the beginning of
the new.

And yet it would be naive to suggest that *all* such upheavals in human
society coincided with full-blown cataclysmic events. On the contrary,
man has a habit of manipulating events to suit his own purposes and
religious archetypes are one of the most valuable tools at his disposal.
Inevitably, then, there would have been occasions when even a minor
meteoritic storm was used as justification for an archetypal revolution
and overthrow of the old world order.

This brings us to the subject of Zeus, the mighty son of Kronos, where
it is pertinent to note that his succession myth placed great emphasis on
the eternality of his reign. To that end, Zeus placed Atlas in charge of
supporting the sky, thus ensuring that it did not fall again, whilst he
himself went on to vanquish Typhoeus (the immediate pretender to his
throne) and then swallow Metis, thereby preventing the birth of the son
who was prophesied to depose him. In each of these myths, the reign of
Zeus symbolised a never-ending, stable society. There was no need to
worry about the sky falling again; it would not happen. There was no
point in plotting the overthrow of the government; it could not happen.
The myths of Zeus thus amounted in part to a 'comfort blanket' and in
part to political propaganda.

The Evolution of the Pantheon

So much for the myth by which Zeus came to power; the archetype is
clear enough. But how was it that Zeus became chief god historically
speaking? If the impression has been given that he was a new god, borne
by Earth to Kronos, then this idea needs to be quashed immediately. This
was *the myth* of Zeus, written *after* his appointment as 'king of the gods'.
It is hardly the historical reality. It seems much more likely that Zeus was
a long-established god, and one of many gods worshipped in Greece
prior to his elevation to supreme power. After all, Homer sang of Zeus

throwing lots with Hades and Poseidon, whilst Hesiod sang of Zeus having five elder siblings: Hestia, Demeter, Hera, Hades and Poseidon. Surely, then, Zeus did not come to power because he was borne by Earth to Kronos; rather he was promoted because, at the time of the cultural revolution (i.e. at the time of the perceived change in the cosmic order), he enjoyed the richest cult and the most widespread popularity in the Greek lands. If things had been different, we might today think of Hades or Poseidon as the chief god of Olympus.

Such a scenario raises many questions. For instance, who was Hades before he became god of the Underworld, and who was Poseidon before he was appointed god of the sea?

And indeed the questions have only just begun. If Zeus had been intent on maintaining stability in the cosmic order, why was it that he displayed such a prodigious sexual appetite? Why did he descend from Olympus to make Earth (in her many names) bear so many gods, any one of whom might have risen up to depose him? As Walter Burkert writes: 'The host of children sired by Zeus is astonishing both in quantity and quality, and the stream of goddesses and mortal women who shared his bed is no less so... Zeus is the only god who has great and powerful gods as children: Apollo and Artemis by Leto, Hermes by Maia, Persephone by Demeter, Dionysus by Semele or Persephone, and Athene by Metis; the ill-favoured Ares is the child of his legitimate spouse Hera.'[16]

Was Zeus truly able to 'have his cake and eat it' by having all of these powerful gods support him rather than oppose him? Or do we see here a mischievous rewriting of the myths? In other words, might Zeus' alleged sons and daughters have originally been independent deities, historically speaking? Did there exist cults of Apollo, Artemis, Hermes, Persephone, Dionysus, Athene and Ares *before* Zeus was elevated to chief god? Were these deities, originally, not his sons and daughters at all?

My view – and I am sure many Hellenists would support it – is that powerful deities such as Apollo, Dionysus and Athene did indeed have cults that were formerly independent of Zeus. But once Zeus had been promoted to become 'father of gods and men', such cults would have found it difficult to remain independent. It seems plausible that, wherever possible, the priests of the Zeus cult would have persuaded their rivals to accept the 'fact' that their deities were either sons or daughters of the all-powerful Zeus. Thus, it is quite possible that the myths of Apollo, Hermes, Dionysus, Athene, et cetera, were all rewritten to make these deities the offspring of Zeus.

There is an important implication here. To make a god the offspring of Zeus is to make him or her a purely invisible, aethereal god, i.e. an earth-born *daimon*. Thus, to rewrite birth myths in this way is to create an entire family of *metaphysical* gods, at the same time reducing the number of myths that might speak of a *physical* god coming down from the heavens. The result is a biased picture concerning the nature of the gods, and a source of confusion for anyone seeking to understand the ancient Greek religion.

The upshot of this is that the practice of worshipping Zeus above all other gods would have obscured the physical-metaphysical duality that is so crucial to our understanding of the Greek gods. Add to this the myth that Zeus himself was an earth-born *daimon* (as was his father Kronos) and the confusion becomes complete. (Only the falling Ouranos gives the game away for the keen-eyed investigator). Is it any wonder that the physical, cataclysmic nature of the Greek gods has remained a mystery for so long?

But what if Zeus, Hades, Poseidon, Apollo, Ares, Hermes, Dionysus, Hephaestus, along with all the manifold goddesses, had originally been independent deities? What would these deities have been in the absence of any requirements to make them a son of 'god x' or a daughter of 'god y'? Might they perhaps have embraced the full physical-metaphysical duality that was the prerogative of the exploded planet deities?

In the next chapter, I shall be examining each of the aforementioned deities, in turn, citing what I believe to be the vital clues to their ex-physical, exploded planet identities. My survey will be brief, and is not intended as a proof of any kind. Rather, I aim only to identify a recurring pattern which has hitherto never been apprehended and which is entirely consistent with the exploded planet hypothesis. The scenario that I am about to portray is one of a Greek world that was once saturated with the cults of numerous exploded planet deities, each personifying exactly the same idea, but expressed in a variety of different ways. If the reader will bear with me, he will discover an astonishingly plausible explanation for the evolution of the Greek pantheon and the confusion that has reigned for the past two and a half millennia.

Chapter Twelve Summary

* It is an *a priori* probability, based on the defining attributes of the Greek gods and the fundamental parallels between Greek and Near Eastern religions, that the Greek gods were exploded planet deities.

* The invisible, aethereal and ghost-like nature of the Olympian gods (*daimones*) makes a truly excellent fit with the exploded planet hypothesis. It explains the long-standing puzzle of why the Greeks

paid the greatest reverence (above that paid to the Sun and the Moon) to an invisible race of gods from an invisible heavenly mountain.

* The true nature of the Greek gods (as physical-metaphysical dualities) has been obscured by the father-son requirements of the succession myth and by the fact that the cult of Zeus took over the cults of the other gods. Might it be possible that all of the Greek gods were once exploded planet deities in their own right?

CHAPTER THIRTEEN

THE OLYMPIANS UNVEILED

**Though this Word is true evermore, yet men are
no better off for hearing it the first time than
never hearing it at all.**
(Heraclitus, 5th century BC)

In this chapter, I present a brief survey of the Olympian gods and argue
that all of them were exploded planet gods, who once enjoyed individual
cults in the ancient Greek world. The survey comprises the gods Zeus,
Hades, Hera, Demeter, Leto, Apollo, Artemis, Ares, Hermes, Dionysus,
Poseidon, Athene and Hephaestus. Included in this list are several gods
who are important in Plato's story of Athens and Atlantis. There is Zeus,
the king of Olympus, who made the decisions and ordained the fates;
there is Poseidon, 'the Earth-shaker', who founded the colony of Atlantis
and created the race of Atlantians; and there is Athene who, together
with Hephaestus, founded the city of Athens and created the race of
Athenians. Clearly, it is necessary to know more about these particular
deities and the divine race to whom they belonged before we can draw
firm conclusions about the story of Athens and Atlantis. This chapter,
then, will complete our study of the Greek gods and pave the way for the
decoding of Plato's story which follows in the fourth and final part of
this book.

Zeus and Hades

On the face of it, Zeus was a *daimon* (i.e. an aethereal type of god). His
birth myth speaks of him coming forth in a Cretan cave amidst great
noise, foaming blood and a tremendous conflagration – the product of a
cataclysmic union between Heaven (Kronos) and Earth (Rhea).[1] Zeus
was thus an invisible, earth-born god, destined to become chief of the
Olympian *daimones*.

But when we probe a little deeper, Zeus exhibits the full range of characteristics to be expected of an exploded planet god. Consider, first of all, how Zeus takes on the physical role of Ouranos, the exploding planet. In Hesiod's *Theogony*, we read:

> ... with continuous lightning flashes Zeus went, and the bolts flew
> thick and fast amid thunder and lightning from his stalwart hand,
> trailing holy flames. All around, the life-bearing Earth rumbled as it
> burned... The whole land was seething, and the streams of Oceanus,
> and the undraining sea. The hot blast enveloped the chthonic Titans;
> the indescribable flames reached the divine heavens... it was just as if
> Earth and the broad Heaven above were coming together...[2]

Note the closing line: 'it was just as if Earth and the broad Heaven above were coming together'. In this passage, Zeus personifies Mount Olympus in its original, physical form as Ouranos, the falling Mountain of Heaven. His onslaught against the Titans in the Underworld is appropriate not to an aethereal *daimon*, but to a physical, exploding god. Consistent with this, his name Zeus meant 'Bright Sky', as if to suggest that the Greeks long envisaged him in this way – as a physical god who could descend cataclysmically from the heavens.[3]

Secondly, Zeus takes on the role of the fallen mountain of Heaven. In the Orphic myth, he swallows Phanes and gives birth to the Universe from his stomach, whilst in *Theogony* he swallows Metis and gives birth to Athene from his head. In both myths, Zeus takes over the creative powers of the Earth by *becoming* the Underworld, i.e. the fallen mountain of Heaven. Hence the Orphic saying: 'Zeus is foundation of Earth and the starry heavens'.[4]

This same idea is evident in the early traditions surrounding Hades, the god of the Underworld, who was supposedly an elder brother of Zeus. According to several references, Hades was known as 'the other Zeus' or 'Zeus *Chthonios*', i.e. 'subterranean Zeus'.[5] It is a remarkable idea that has not passed unnoticed. Walter Burkert, for example, has observed that Hades was, in effect, 'a subterranean counterpart to the Sky father'.[6] This, it must be said, is exactly what we would predict if Zeus was originally an exploded planet god.

In summary, there was a lot more to Zeus than an invisible, aethereal *daimon*. His original cult might well have comprised a proto-Zeus, who descended into the Earth (for the purpose of the creation), and then split, Osirian fashion, into body and soul, the former becoming the mountain of the Underworld, to be called Hades (from Aides 'the Unseen'), the latter ascending to Heaven (Mount Olympus), to be called Zeus 'Bright

Sky' (bright indeed, but with a now invisible light).

Oddly enough, or perhaps not so oddly, the Minoans of Crete used to celebrate the death and rebirth of Zeus, which had supposedly occurred in the sacred cave beneath Mount Ida.[7] The mystery was the subject of the Idaean Dactyl initiation rites, and one of the men initiated here was the mystic and mathematical genius Pythagoras (6th century BC). Legend had it that Pythagoras was purified with a 'lightning stone', whereupon he was made to lie by the sea during the day, then lie on the fleece of a black ram by the river during the night; finally, Pythagoras was allowed to enter the sacred Idaean cave where he made a sacrifice of fire and witnessed the indescribable throne of Zeus.[8]

It is of particular interest to note that this celebration was anathema to most Greeks, involving as it did the death of Zeus. The poet Callimachos famously accused the Cretans of being liars because everyone knew full well that Zeus could not die.[9] We have here a perfect example of the confusion that existed owing to the widespread belief that Zeus was a *daimon* and had never been anything but a *daimon*.

This mention of the initiation of Pythagoras with the lightning stone brings us to the subject of meteorites, on which several points need to be made. Firstly, in respect of the *baetylus* stone of Delphi (by all accounts a meteorite), not only was it called 'Zeus *Baetylus*', but it had also been swallowed by Kronos as a direct substitute for the newborn Zeus.[10] The equation between Zeus and the meteorite is thus confirmed. Secondly, it is known that Zeus was worshipped at the site of Heliopolis-Baalbek (in modern-day Lebanon) in the form of black conical stones – meteorites without a doubt.[11] And thirdly, the 'thunderbolt' of Zeus was almost certainly a metaphor for 'meteorite' on account of the thunder-like sound which accompanies falling meteorites. The case for this last point was made by the scholar G.A. Wainwright who stated that: 'The *omphalos* is representative of the meteorite and, in religion, the meteorite and the thunderbolt are the same thing.'[12] This would indeed explain why Zeus' thunderbolt was forged in the Underworld by the Cyclopes.[13]

This completes our survey of Zeus and Hades. Although it has been brief, there are many clues to the effect that Zeus-Hades was originally the god of a full-blown exploded planet cult. As to when and why this original identity of Zeus-Hades was abandoned, the answer must surely lie in a major or minor cataclysm, coinciding with the elevation of the cult of Zeus-Hades to supremacy in Greece. At this time, the 'succession myth' would have required that Zeus and Hades be made 'sons of Kronos'. And this could have been achieved only by casting Zeus and Hades in the mould of earth-born *daimones* (and nothing but earth-born *daimones*). Afterwards, as the centuries passed, the populace would inevitably have forgotten about the ex-physicality of Zeus and Hades.

Goddesses of Heaven and Earth

On the face of it, Hera, the wife of Zeus, was an aethereal *daimon*, who resided upon Mount Olympus alongside her celestial husband (also a *daimon*). Her birth myth is recorded by Hesiod, who declares Hera to have been among the offspring of Kronos (Heaven) and Rhea (Earth).[14] She was thus portrayed as an earth-born *daimon* – a sister of Zeus.

And yet there must be more to it, for Hera appears in numerous other myths and traditions as a personification of the Earth. Hence in Homer's *Iliad*, she is called 'the greatest of goddesses' and unites with Zeus in a sacred marriage upon Mount Ida, veiled in a golden cloud.[15] Hence in the *Argonautika* of Apollonios Rhodios, she is called 'bed-mate of Zeus, goddess of marriage'.[16] Hence her name Hera is thought to come from the word *hora*, meaning 'season' and 'ripe for marriage'.[17] Hence she was the Earth-goddess at her temple in Plataea.[18] Hence she was a model of marital strife – this being the role of Mother Earth at the time of the conjunction with Heaven and the ensuing separation.[19] And hence in the *Homeric Hymn to Apollo*, Hera bore Typhaon – the monster who was designed to overthrow Zeus.[20]

In summary, Hera was no mere *daimon*, born of the Earth; rather she *was* Mother Earth, the very personification of our life-bearing planet.

And yet there must be more to Hera even than this, for in the *Iliad* and the *Homeric Hymn to Apollo*, we learn that Hera gave birth by herself to the meteorite-god Hephaestus, whom she flung out of Heaven. In the latter text, Hera declares:

> "Hephaestus – the one I gave birth to myself – he was weak among all
> the gods, and his foot was shrivelled. Why, it was a disgrace to me,
> and a shame in Heaven. So I took him in my hands and threw him out
> [of Olympus] and he fell into the depths of the sea."[21]

The most telling aspect of this myth is that Hera gave birth to Hephaestus *in Heaven and by herself*, as if to suggest that Hera had once been an exploded planet deity in her own right.[22]

Such a suggestion is indeed borne out by certain passages in the *Iliad* and the *Argonautika*, where Hera rides out of Heaven on a fiery chariot, making a noise so loud that 'the vast vault of Heaven resounded'.[23] And further to this, there is an intriguing passage in the *Iliad* where Zeus reminds Hera of a dispute that once arose between them concerning the god-like hero Heracles:

"Or do you not remember when you were strung up on high, and I hung two anvils from your feet and fastened a golden rope around your hands that could not be broken? You hung there in the sky and the clouds, and the gods throughout high Olympus were distraught. They stood round quite unable to help you – any one I caught I would seize and hurl from the threshold, till they fell to the Earth..."[24]

Here, the fixing of Hera in the sky tends to suggest that the goddess had once belonged there, but had fallen from Heaven to Earth. And this, incidentally, would explain why Hera's festivals always involved, in the words of Walter Burkert, 'a deep crisis in which the established order breaks down and the goddess herself threatens to disappear'.[25] Hera, surely, was no *daimon* but an exploded planet goddess in her own right.

How does this picture reconcile with Hera's role as Earth-goddess, as described earlier? The answer is provided by the myths of Mesopotamia which describe unequivocally how the mother-goddess Mami/Ninharsag came down from the heavens to assume the mantle of Mother Earth.[26] Using this model, it can be hypothesised with some confidence that Hera was originally an exploded planet deity who descended from Heaven to Earth, thereby taking over the role of Mother Earth.

This is all a long way from Hesiod's assertion in *Theogony* that Hera was an earth-born *daimon* and it raises the question of how Hera could have been *born of* the Earth when she *was* the Earth? The explanation here is basically the same as that given earlier for Zeus. Coincident with a cataclysm, we must surmise that Hera, an existing deity, was promoted alongside Zeus to become the new 'queen of Olympus'. This would have required Hera, like Zeus, to be made a successor of the previous incumbent in order to establish legitimacy to the throne. Thus Hera would have become the adopted daughter of Kronos and Rhea. And thus Hera would have been remembered, misleadingly, as a *daimon*.

In the same vein, this succession myth, by which Hera supplanted Rhea as Earth-goddess, would explain the numerous *alter egos* which were applied to Mother Earth in the Greek literature. In the beginning, it would seem, the first Earth-goddess had been Gaia or Night, or, by a separate tradition, Tethys. Then, as *Theogony* has it, Gaia had given way to Rhea, Rhea had given way to Metis, Metis had given way to Themis, Themis had given way to Eurynome, Eurynome had given way to Demeter, Demeter had given way to Memory, Memory had given way to Leto, and, finally, Leto had given way to Hera.[27]

But to some extent, Hesiod's sequence of Earth-goddesses must surely be artificial. The Orphics, for example, believed that Rhea had become

Demeter *directly*, at the time of the birth of Zeus, whilst another tradition hinted that Hera had succeeded Rhea *directly*, not seven generations later as Hesiod alleges.[28] Nevertheless, the principle is the important thing and what we find here is a deep-rooted belief that the role of Earth-mother was transferred from one goddess to another on several occasions at least, thereby marking several fallings of the ancient sky.

Is there any evidence to support the notion that these Earth-goddesses really came down from Heaven? Indeed there is. Apart from the Near Eastern parallels and the myths of Hera, already cited, we can also point to the myths of Night, Demeter and Leto.

Firstly, as regards the Earth-goddess Night, the giveaway clue occurs in *Theogony*, where Hesiod alludes to the idea that Ouranos brought her down with him from Heaven:

> Great Ouranos came, bringing on Night, and, desirous of love, spread himself over Gaia, stretched out in every direction.[29]

This idea – of the goddess Night being carried to Earth by her consort, the god of Heaven – differs from the usual Near Eastern model where the goddess came down from Heaven independently, but there is a striking precedent to it in the Sumerian myth entitled *Gilgamesh, Enkidu and the Underworld*. Here, the opening lines describe Enki setting sail from Heaven to the Underworld, adding that 'Ereshkigal was carried off into the Underworld as its prize' – as if to suggest that the goddess had been abducted from Heaven.[30] Ereshkigal, it should be noted, became the goddess of the Underworld and, in that capacity, was one of several different goddesses who personified the Earth, whilst Enki, we should recall, became the god of the subterranean ocean (the Apsu).

The second set of clues involve the Earth-goddess Demeter, who, as scholars have noted, was more than a mere Earth-goddess (although they have never been able to put their finger on what exactly she was).[31] But in the *Homeric Hymn to Demeter*, the celestial origins of this goddess are made perfectly clear. The story begins with the abduction of Persephone into the Underworld by Hades, which coincides with a terrible drought on the face of the Earth. The poet then describes Demeter, the mother of Persephone, descending from Olympus to recover her daughter:

> Wrapped in the clouds of Zeus, she [Demeter] withdrew from the company of gods, and from great Olympus, and went down to the cities of men...[32]

For nine days, the grieving Demeter sped over the Earth bearing fiery torches, searching for Persephone.[33] Then, on the tenth day, she went into the Underworld, where she encountered the subterranean goddess Hecate and the subterranean form of the Sun-god Helios. Far from searching in 'the cities of men', Demeter had entered a subterranean palace; hence it was said that her head touched the roof and that she filled the doorway with a divine light (this light was later compared to lightning).[34]

Once Demeter had learned the fate of Persephone, she decided to remain in the Underworld in mourning, vowing never again to set foot on high Olympus; and as long as she did so, the Earth remained a barren wasteland.[35] Eventually, the drought grew so serious that it threatened to destroy the race of men and end their service to the gods. Alarmed, Zeus dispatched the messenger-god Hermes into the Underworld, and he persuaded Hades to release Persephone. The happy ending involved the Earth regaining her fertility, Demeter teaching her mysteries to men and the two goddesses ascending to heavenly Olympus (though Persephone was required to return to the Underworld for one third of each year).[36]

From this myth, briefly told, it can be seen that Demeter, far from being a *daimon* borne by Rhea to Kronos, was actually a goddess of Heaven and Earth, in the mould of the exploded planet goddesses of the ancient Near East. Her name, it may be surmised, is a derivative of *Diameter*, meaning 'mother of the sky'.[37]

If Demeter was the exploding mother, then Persephone, her daughter, was her fallen *alter ego*. Hence her name, *Phersephone*, meant 'she who brings destruction',[38] and hence she ruled in the Underworld as 'the iron queen'.[39]

We have come a long way from the theory of Prodicus (5th century BC) that Demeter was a human teacher of agriculture, and we have come equally far from the modern consensus that the myth of Demeter and Persephone was a mundane nature allegory (see discussion in chapter six). But we have arrived at a point where we can understand something of the Mysteries of Demeter, which were encapsulated by an ear of corn and yet were so profound that no-one dared divulge the secret 'for so great is one's awe of the gods that it stops the tongue'.[40]

Leto

We turn now to Leto, for further evidence that the Greek mother-goddess came down from Heaven to Earth. At the same time, we will discover some interesting facts pertaining to the true nature of Leto's two children Apollo and Artemis.

According to Hesiod, the goddess Leto was the daughter of the god Koios and the goddess Phoebe, a genealogy which, one presumes, made

Leto a *daimon*.[41] These two Titans also bore Asteria as a sister to Leto.[42] Later, after the battle of the Titans, Zeus came to the bed of Leto and she conceived, afterwards bearing the famous twins Apollo and Artemis.[43] On the face of it, Apollo and Artemis belonged to the race of invisible, aethereal *daimones*.

The myths surrounding Leto and Asteria are evocative of our earlier discussion of the two goddesses Demeter and Persephone. According to the poet Pindar (5th century BC), Asteria 'of the starry sky' was cast into the Ocean by Zeus, whereupon she became a floating island known as Ortygia (alias Delos).[44] But Zeus then took a shine to the island:

> Then the powerful one [Zeus] fell in love with her,
> And had union with her,
> And she brought forth a race of archers [i.e. Apollo/Artemis].[45]

It was to this fallen island of Delos/Asteria that Leto came to give birth to Apollo and Artemis. The story is a little confusing, but we can just about unravel it. According to the *Homeric Hymn to Apollo*, Leto was already pregnant with the young god Apollo when she arrived at Delos (whence she came and how Zeus impregnated her, we are not told). Her first task was to persuade a reluctant Delos/Asteria to bear the mighty child. Eventually, Delos/Asteria agreed, but for nine days and nights Leto was seized with terrible labour pains and was unable to give birth.[46] Then, on the tenth day, Eilithyia, the midwife of the gods, arrived and, as if by magic, Leto began to deliver her child. At this time, we are told, shrill winds surrounded the island causing a mysterious 'dark wave' to encroach upon the shore.[47] Leto (or was it Delos/Asteria?) then gave birth to Apollo in a remarkable manner:

> Leto threw her arms around the palm tree, and pressed her knees on
> the soft meadow. The Earth smiled beneath her and the child [Apollo]
> leapt forth into the light. And all the goddesses shrieked in triumph.[48]

But which goddess gave birth to Apollo? On the one hand, it is stated that Leto bore him. But on the other hand, it is stated that Delos/Asteria (i.e. the Earth) bore him. To reconcile the story we must suppose either that Leto passed the child into the womb of the Earth, allowing the Earth to bear him, or that Leto took over the body of Asteria, thus becoming one with the Earth, to bear the child herself.[49]

Several things, however, are clear. Firstly, Delos symbolises the womb of the entire Earth; hence in one of Pindar's odes the gods of Olympus viewed Delos as 'the far-seen star of the dark blue Earth'.[50] Secondly, the goddess Asteria fits the classic mould of the goddess of Heaven and

Earth; she is cast down from Heaven and then takes over the mantle of the Earth (symbolised by Delos). Thirdly, the seed of Zeus is brought to the Earth not by the chief god himself but by the goddess Leto.

What does this mean? A big clue, I think, lies in the fact that Leto's name meant 'Stone', though with the special connotation 'thunderbolt' or 'meteorite' (as in the Greek-named Egyptian town of Letopolis which was famed for its connections with thunderbolt- and meteorite-gods).[51] In view of this connection, as well as the parallel to the story of Demeter and Persephone recounted earlier, my feeling is that we are seeing the traces of an archaic Leto cult, in which Leto personified the exploded planet, with her and Asteria representing two aspects of one and the same concept – the exploding planet and the fallen planet respectively. As for the idea that Zeus had impregnated Leto, this is surely another example of the Zeus cult subsuming all rival cults, in this case that of Leto's son Apollo.

This theory, however, will stand or fall according to its decoding of the deities Apollo and Artemis. Were these gods truly the offspring of Zeus and Leto, and thus of the race of aethereal *daimones*, or might there be more to it?

Apollo and Artemis

The first thing to realise with Apollo and Artemis is that they were probably not twins originally. In fact, Hellenists are of the opinion that the sacred island of Delos was originally the cult centre of Artemis alone, whilst Apollo's cult was centred on the shrine of Delphi.[52] But at some stage, Delos was annexed to the cult of Apollo and he and Artemis were paired up as twins, presumably on account of the similarity in their arrow-shooting cults. Consequently, as Walter Burkert has written: 'the historian can and must separate Apollo and Artemis.'[53] We will indeed follow Burkert's advice.

So, who was Apollo? The meaning of his name is obscure, with many possibilities to choose from. Of those I have come across, the most likely is that of Aeschylus (5th century BC), who connected the name Apollo to *apollunai*, meaning 'to destroy';[54] this would tie in neatly with Apollo's reputation as the one who brought pestilence with his deadly arrows (see further comment below).

But it seems to me that the name Apollo is rather a shortened form of the epithet *arche polou*, meaning 'ruler of the axis'. My reason for suggesting so is that Apollo's main cult at Delphi was focused on an *omphalos* (originally a *baetylus* or meteorite) which marked the centre of the world. When we consider Plato's description of Apollo as 'this god, sitting upon the stone at the centre of the Earth', we would indeed seem to be dealing with a god who was *arche polou*, or 'ruler of the axis', i.e. the axis of Heaven and Earth.[55]

As to the various myths of Apollo, the foundation myth of Delphi portrays him as anything but an aethereal *daimon*. It was here that Apollo slew with his arrows the dragon that came to be known as Python, whilst one legend said that Apollo himself was killed in this battle and buried at Delphi.[56] Furthermore, Apollo's arrival at Delphi, as recorded in the *Homeric Hymn to Apollo*, is highly evocative of a cometary or meteoritic impact; the relevant passage reads:

> The lord Apollo – the far-distant worker – jumped from the ship like a star in broad daylight. Sparks flew off him from all sides and their light reached the heavens. He entered his shrine... and he made a fire, revealing his arrows. And the brightness filled all of Crisa.[57]

Was Apollo originally an exploded planet deity in his own right? All of his epithets seem to indicate cometary imagery, at the very least. Thus he was called Phoibos Apollo 'bright Apollo', Apollo Aiglatas 'Apollo of the radiant sky', Apollo Lykeios 'wolf-like Apollo', as well as 'Apollo of the flowing hair' and 'Apollo of the golden sword'.[58] Above all, though, Apollo was known as 'the god of the far-shot arrows' and 'Far-shooter, most deadly of the gods', referring to the arrows of pestilence which he sent from Heaven, where he resided in his temple at a remote distance from the Earth.[59]

Concerning this far-shooting arrows imagery, which Apollo shared with his sister Artemis, the scholar G.A. Wainwright has highlighted an important symbolic connections to meteorites. In his article on the Egyptian meteorite town of Khem-Letopolis (named by the Greeks after Leto, the mother of Apollo and Artemis), Wainwright wrote:

> Min's thunderbolt [symbol] was developed from a double arrow, therefore the Letopolite symbol was probably derived from the same thing... The thought is continued in the deities whom the Greeks connected with Letopolis, for they were Leto and Apollo... both he and her other child, Artemis, were famous archers, and both were *omphalos* and meteorite deities.[60]

Wainwright went on to discuss, at some length, the symbolic association of arrows with thunderbolts and meteorites, highlighting *inter alia* the Syrian deity Resheph, who was called 'Resheph with the arrow' and whose name meant 'lightning, flame, heat'.[61]

In view of the well-established connection between Apollo and the *omphalos*/meteorite cult of Delphi, Wainwright's words are not to be gainsaid. The surprise, perhaps, is that he identified *Artemis* so firmly as a meteorite-deity. In his footnotes, he even suggested that Artemis – in her Roman name of Diana – had been worshipped at her famous temple of Ephesus in the form of a meteorite:

> The *omphalos* at Apollo's city of Delphi is well known, and at Perga, Pogla, and Andeda, Artemis was represented by *omphaloi*. The Stone of Kronos at Delphi must have been a meteorite, and at Ephesus the image of Diana 'which fell down from Jupiter' must have been one also.[62]

In saying this about Artemis/Diana, Wainwright was in all likelihood correct, for the name Diana (*Dia-na*) seems to have meant literally 'stone from Heaven'.[63] Perhaps this would explain Homer's obscure reference to 'noisy Artemis with her golden arrows... who likes murdering animals on the mountains'.[64]

Nor would Artemis/Diana be the only example of a Greek goddess being associated with an *omphalos* or meteorite. In addition, there is Gaia, to whom the *omphalos* at Delphi was originally dedicated;[65] there is the Phrygian goddess Cybele, who was worshipped at Pessinus in the form of a black stone which had fallen from the sky (this meteorite was conveyed to Rome in 204 BC);[66] and there is Aphrodite, the goddess of love, who was worshipped on Cyprus at the shrine of Palae Paphos in the form of a conical stone that had fallen from the sky.[67] All these examples support my contention that the Greek Earth-goddesses, like those of the ancient Near East, were originally goddesses of Heaven and Earth, who personified a 'female' exploded planet.

In summary, there are many clues to suggest that Apollo and Artemis were originally exploded planet deities in their own right. In respect of Apollo, a likely scenario would have him descending to Earth in his physical form (meteorites and floodwaters),[68] entering the Underworld, and coming forth in his aethereal form as a *daimon*. This would make him simultaneously god of Heaven, foundation of Heaven and Earth, and ruler of the axis (*arche polou* or *A-polou* for short). The story of Artemis would have been identical. Both personified the exploded planet, in male and female form respectively.

As for whether Leto was originally the mother of Apollo and Artemis, the point is debatable, for it is possible that three separate cults were long ago merged. Perhaps at this point, the meteoritic nature of the deities was still evident, but the confusion would have arisen, as usual, when the cult of Zeus subsumed the cult of Leto, thus making Apollo and Artemis the offspring of Zeus and hence *daimones* (and nothing but *daimones*).[69]

Ares

We turn now to Ares, the god of war, whom Zeus famously criticised in the *Iliad*, saying: "You are the most hateful to me of all the gods who hold Olympus; strife and wars and fighting are forever dear to you."[70] This, despite the fact that Ares was supposedly Zeus' son by his wife Hera. But was Ares really a son of Zeus, and thus an aethereal *daimon*, or might there have been something more to his original identity? Although we know relatively little about Ares (he never enjoyed great popularity in Greece), we nevertheless possess some telling clues which suggest that he was indeed more than a *daimon*.

Firstly, Ares was, above all things, a god of war. His own name meant literally 'war' or 'throng of battle', whilst the horses that pulled his chariot were named Phobos and Deimos, meaning literally 'Fear' and 'Terror'.[71] But this was no ordinary horse-driven chariot; rather it was something supernatural and celestial. In the *Homeric Hymn to Ares*, it is said that Ares' fiery horses carried him for ever 'over the third orbit' – apparently a reference to the planet Mars, whose visibly reddish colour was associated symbolically with blood and warfare.[72] But Ares was not a god of Mars but rather a god of Heaven and Earth; hence in the *Iliad*, Homer describes how Aphrodite borrowed the chariot and horses of Ares to ascend from the Trojan Plain to heavenly Olympus.[73] It would thus seem that the fiery horses of Ares were a cataclysmic motif.

Secondly, we can say that Ares had a profound association with the Underworld. One of the best examples of this idea is found in the *Iliad*, where Homer describes how Otus and Ephialtes imprisoned Ares in a bronze jar for thirteen months – the bronze jar being an unmistakeable metaphor for the Underworld.[74] Another example is found in the *Odyssey*, where Homer describes Ares' disastrous love affair with Aphrodite, which culminated in his imprisonment in a net made of bronze chains.[75] The setting for such sexual liaisons was usually the Underworld and this myth, set in the palace of Hephaestus, the husband of Aphrodite, seems to be no exception to that rule.[76] Yet a third example of subterranean Ares is found in the *Argonautika* of Apollonios Rhodios, where Jason and his Argonauts enter the Underworld in their search for the magical golden Fleece.[77] The Fleece is said to be hung from a tree in 'the grove of Ares', where it is guarded by a never-sleeping serpent, referred to elsewhere as 'the serpent of Ares'.[78]

Why such an important link between Ares and the Underworld? It makes no sense if Ares was purely a *daimon*, but it does make sense if he was originally an exploded planet god who descended from Heaven and, in time-honoured fashion, entered into the Underworld. And this does tie in well with Ares' war-loving nature, his chariot of Heaven and Earth, and the fiery disposition of his horses.

Finally, it should be mentioned that the Amazonians (a mythical race of warmongering women) used to worship Ares in the form of a sacred black stone that was fixed inside his temple (this according to Apollonios Rhodios in the *Argonautika*).[79] A meteorite was undoubtedly intended.

In view of all these factors, it would not be unreasonable for us to conclude that Ares was once the focus of an independent exploded planet cult, though one of minor importance, which was later eclipsed by the cult of Zeus. At that time, Ares would have been cast into the mould of 'son of Zeus', making him an earth-born *daimon* and nothing but an earth-born *daimon*.

Hermes

On the face of it, Hermes the messenger-god was a son of Zeus by Maia, the daughter of Atlas. Supposedly, he had been born in Maia's cave (symbolising the womb of Mother Earth), whence he sprang forth as an earth-born *daimon*.[80] And yet the story of Hermes contains many hints of the god's ex-physical nature.

The most obvious clue to Hermes' original identity is his name, which derives from *herma*, 'a heap of stones'.[81] Some modern scholars presume that Hermes obtained this name from an association with the stone herms that marked boundaries or way-points in ancient Greece. But other scholars consider this to be an 'astounding' and thoroughly implausible scenario.[82] So what is the answer? In my view, the significance of Hermes and the *herma* can be traced to the millennia-old Mesopotamian myths of the battle of the gods, in particular the myth in which Ninurta, foremost among the Anunnaki, vanquished the mountain-god Azag/Zu by turning him into a heap of stones. These stones, we might recall, were no ordinary stones but meteoritic seeds of creation, and this would go a long way towards explaining why Hermes was famous as a phallic god (the herm being symbolic of the phallus).[83]

In support of this theory, it is enlightening to find Homer referring to Hermes as 'the slayer of the keen-eyed Giant' and 'the slayer of Argos', referring to the hundred-eyed giant whom Hermes had destroyed with a sling-stone.[84] Was this giant a Greek form of the Mesopotamian demon-god Azag/Zu? Perhaps it is no coincidence that Azag/Zu, like Argos, was 'keen-eyed' in the sense that he gazed intently on Enlil's Tablets of Destiny which he coveted.[85]

All of this shows Hermes in an entirely new light. And yet we should not be surprised to discover that there was more to Hermes than meets the eye. He was, after all, famous for his mediating role between Heaven and Earth and for knowing his way through the Underworld.[86] He was thus known as 'greatest herald of those above and below' and Hermes *Chthonios*, i.e. 'subterranean Hermes'.[87]

Finally, mention should be made of another exploded planet motif in Hermes' armoury, namely his theft of Apollo's cattle.[88] The subject needs greater length than can be spared here, but suffice to say that the terms 'cattle' and 'sheep' were used as metaphors by ancient poets to personify the cloud of meteoritic debris that was swept down from Heaven into the Earth.[89]

In summary, there are numerous clues to suggest that Hermes was originally an exploded planet deity in his own right, much in the same mould as the Mesopotamian god Ninurta. As such, Hermes, personifying the exploded planet, would have 'died' and metamorphosed into an earth-born *daimon*. But as for the idea that he was a *daimon* and nothing but, this was surely the result of the cult of Hermes being subordinated to the cult of Zeus, thereby making Hermes the son of Zeus and Maia.

Dionysus

We turn now to Dionysus (alias Bakchos) who was allegedly a son of Zeus, either by the Earth-goddess Persephone or by the mortal woman Semele.[90] Unlike the other gods who were made sons of Zeus, Dionysus never yielded his ex-physical identity and never became a mere *daimon* (although he did have a metaphysical aspect). Thus, we do not have to look very hard to find evidence of a Dionysian exploded planet cult.

Let's begin with the name Dionysus. Although its origin is perplexing to scholars, it stems from a simple combination of *Dio-Nysa*, meaning literally 'Nysa of Heaven' (Nysa being the celestial mountain associated with Dionysus).[91] In addition, Nysa could mean 'lame', alluding to the fall of the god from Heaven, just as the meteorite-god Hephaestus had become lame from his fall.[92]

Speaking of meteorites, Dionysus was associated with the meteorite site of Delphi, where his body was said to have been buried beside the *omphalos*.[93] In addition, numerous temples in Greece possessed sacred Dionysian cult objects in the form of *xoana* which were alleged to have fallen from the sky.[94] Supposedly, these *xoana* were made of wood, but if this was so (and we should bear in mind that the Mesopotamians used to refer to meteorites metaphorically as '*mesu*-wood'), they would have symbolised meteorites; thus, once again, the true nature of Dionysus is revealed.[95]

In many respects, Dionysus seems to have been an *alter ego* of the Egyptian meteorite-god Osiris. This is particularly evident in the myth of his dismemberment at the hands of the Titans, followed by the gathering together of his body-parts (at Delphi), his resuscitation and his ascension into Heaven.[96] It was this myth which caused Dionysus to become the Greek mystery god *par excellence*, much in the same mould as Osiris in Egypt. Herodotus (5th century BC) seems to have made the connection,[97] as did Plutarch (1st century AD) who asserted: 'That Osiris is the same as Dionysus.'[98] Plutarch would have been well-informed on such matters for he was the high-priest of Delphi and an initiate into the Mysteries of Dionysus. He was surely close to the truth, too, when he wrote that the dismemberment of Dionysus symbolised the division of the cosmos into its constituent elements.[99] If it were not for the ambiguity of the Greek word *kosmos* (meaning 'world order' or 'Universe'), Plutarch might well have given the game away to all and sundry, namely that the true *kosmos* was the exploded planet, personified by Dionysus, the dismembered god.

When we stop to think about it, the myths of Dionysus are absolutely pervaded by exploded planet motifs – the arrival of the god by sea; his noisy advent (as 'Bromios the roaring one'); his sudden appearance and disappearance; his erect but castrated phallus; his bull symbolism; his link to wine and the harvest – his infamous 'vines of a day' were said to have flowered and produced grapes in a few hours; and the idea that he was reborn in the form of the divine child.[100] To run through all of these motifs and their meaning would be tedious, but one important principle does need to be highlighted, namely the dual personae of the god, firstly as elder Dionysus (the physical falling god) and secondly as young Dionysus (the god reborn in the womb of the Earth). Thus, as Euripides put it so succinctly in *Bacchae*, Dionysus was both 'god *and* child of a god' – a characteristic which has caused tremendous confusion for the uninitiated scholars of both ancient and modern times.[101]

To close, the reader may wish to reflect on the dramatic myth of how the babe Dionysus was rescued from his burning mother Semele (surely an Earth-goddess, not a mortal woman).[102] The lines are from Euripides' *Bacchae*:

Bearing him within her, in forced
Pangs of childbirth,

When Zeus' lightning flew
His mother thrust him premature
From the womb, and she breathed her last
At the lightning's stroke.[103]

At this cataclysmic moment, Zeus took hold of the reborn Dionysus, and concealed him in his thigh 'in chambers of birth' using golden pins. In due course, Dionysus became 'born of Zeus' in what can now be seen as another successful takeover by the cult of Zeus.

Poseidon

We turn now to the gods of the Atlantis story, beginning with Poseidon, who was said to have inherited the primeval mound of Atlantis, where he fathered the first generation of Atlantians by the 'mortal woman' Clito.

Who was Poseidon? According to Hesiod, Poseidon was the brother of Zeus and Hades (though it might now be preferable to use the combined form Zeus-Hades) and, as such, he was the son of Kronos and Rhea (i.e. of Heaven and Earth). Poseidon was thus an earth-born *daimon*.

But surely there was more to Poseidon than an aethereal *daimon*. As noted in earlier chapters, Poseidon was a subterranean god – 'the Earth-shaker' or god of earthquakes. Moreover, by the same token, Poseidon was the god of the subterranean sea, an idea underlined by the fact that his palace was said to lie *beneath* the waves.[104] In this regard, several Hellenists have suggested that Poseidon paralleled the old Mesopotamian god Enki, who ruled a subterranean sea known as the Apsu.[105] Indeed, it has been argued that the Sumerian name EN.KI, 'Lord Earth', was the etymological root of the name Poseidon via the Greek *Potei-Das*, 'Lord of the Earth'.[106] If this parallel is correct, whether in whole or in part, then Poseidon, like Enki, would have been an exploded planet god, who ruled an ocean that had fallen from Heaven.

In support of such a view, Poseidon was regarded not just as the god of the sea but also as the source of freshwater springs, just like the god Oceanus, the god of the western Ocean and the subterranean sea, whom we identified as an ex-heavenly god in chapter eight.[107] Further to this, Homer did describe Poseidon in Oceanus-like terms, calling him 'the Encircler of the Earth' (for the Greeks believed that the river of Oceanus went right around the world).[108] The suggestion is that Poseidon and Oceanus were, at one time, *alter egos* of one another.

In addition to this, it should be noted that Poseidon had a heavenly aspect, as is made clear in the *Iliad* where he staked his claim for a share of heavenly Mount Olympus in no uncertain terms, saying: "but the

had swallowed her mother Metis.[126] As decoded in chapter eleven, this meant that Zeus took over the role of the Earth-mother and gave birth to Athene from the Earth, thus making her an aethereal *daimon* and nothing but an aethereal *daimon*.

And yet there was much more to Athene than this. In the *Argonautika* of Apollonios Rhodios, it was said that Athene had been bathed by the Libyan desert-goddesses in Lake Triton on the same day, long ago, as she had sprung forth from the head of Zeus.[127] How could Athene have been bathed in the Tritonian Underworld at the same time as ascending from Earth to Olympus? The explanation, based on our understanding of Near Eastern myths, is that Athene must have descended from Heaven in physical form, entered the Underworld and given birth to a metaphysical, aethereal double. It was this double that had been resurrected following the bathing of the fallen goddess in the Tritonian Lake.

In support of this interpretation, I enter into evidence two aspects of Athene's character which appear to be contradictory and yet are fully reconcilable under the exploded planet hypothesis – her creative and destructive aspects.[128]

As regards Athene's creative aspect, we have already noted her role in the founding of Athens and the creation of the Athenians but, in addition, she also played a key role in the creation of Pandora, who signified the race of human women.[129] Further to this, Athene assisted humankind by inventing the chariot and the bridle for the horse, and by building the first ship, the Argo; it was even said that she had had a hand in constructing the Wooden Horse of Troy.[130] But more important than these things, perhaps, is the fact that Athene's birthday festival, the *Panathenaia*, celebrated the rebirth of vegetation, as if to connect Athene with the seeding of all life on Earth.[131]

On the other hand, Athene exhibited a terrifying, destructive aspect that is equally consistent with an exploded planet persona. She was, as the Orphics put it, 'the dread accomplisher of the will of Zeus' or, as Hesiod put it, 'the fearsome rouser of the fray, leader of armies, the lady whose pleasure is in war and the clamour of battle'.[132] When Homer describes Athene descending from Heaven to the Trojan Plain 'like a bright star, throwing off sparks of light', he seems to recall her physical, ex-heavenly nature.[133] Significant, too, are the lines in which Homer describes Athene coming down from Heaven in a fiery chariot, bearing the fearsome aegis of Zeus:

> She hung round her shoulders the tasselled aegis, a fearful weapon, set with Panic all round it in a circle: and on it there is Strife and Power, and chilling Rout, and set there too is the head of the fearful monster

Gorgon, a thing of fright and terror... She stepped into her flaming chariot... the gates of Heaven groaned open...[134]

This aegis exemplified the war-like aspect of Athene, but what exactly was it? In one passage of the *Iliad*, it is described as 'ageless and immortal' with 'a hundred tassels of pure gold fluttering from it';[135] in another passage, it is 'that fearful thing which not even the thunderbolt of Zeus can break';[136] and in another 'the mighty aegis, a fearful thing, shaggy-fringed and brightly seen, which the smith Hephaestus had given to Zeus to wear for the panicking of men'.[137] In addition, we find a fascinating description of the aegis when Athene lends it to Achilles: a burning flame is said to have blazed up from his head to the heavens.[138]

From these clues, not to mention others, it would appear that the aegis of Athene was associated with a comet – hence the bright tassels of gold – and with a cataclysm of Heaven and Earth – hence the burning flame from the head of Achilles – and with a meteorite – hence the equation to the thunderbolt (i.e. meteorite) of Zeus.[139] Predictably, it was Hephaestus, the blacksmith and meteorite-god, who had forged the aegis, presumably under the guidance of the original smiths, the subterranean Cyclopes, who had taught he and Athene 'all the cunning works that the Heaven contains'.[140] Overall, it seems likely that the aegis belonged originally to Athene rather than Zeus, particularly in view of the fact that Hephaestus was Athene's cult partner at Athens (see later).

We turn now to one of Athene's most prominent epithets, Pallas. Why was the goddess called Pallas Athene? According to one Greek tradition, Pallas was a giant, Athene's father, whose skin she stripped off to make her aegis.[141] But there were several Greek characters named Pallas, some male, some female, for the name meant literally both 'maiden' and 'youth'.[142] With an obscure etymology to boot, modern scholars generally regard the meaning of Athene's epithet Pallas as an insoluble mystery.[143]

Nevertheless, some scholars (such as Walter Burkert) have highlighted an intriguing connection between the name Pallas and the Palladion, the latter being the name given to small, armed statues of the goddess Pallas Athene.[144] Such palladia were important in myth as the protectors of cities; hence the idea that the city of Troy could not be sacked until Odysseus and Diomedes had entered the city covertly and stolen its precious Palladion.[145] How does this help us? Because the Greek writer Apollodorus describes the Palladion of Troy – an image of Pallas – being thrown down from Heaven to Earth. His startling account is paraphrased by Robert Graves, in his book *The Greek Myths*, as follows:

Ilus [the mythical founder of Troy] prayed to Almighty Zeus for a sign, and next morning noticed a wooden object lying in front of his tent, half buried in the earth... This was the Palladion, a legless image three cubits high, made by Athene in memory of her dead Libyan playmate Pallas... Athene had first set up the image on Olympus... but when Ilus' great-grandmother, the Pleiad Elektra, was violated by Zeus and defiled it with her touch, Athene angrily cast her, with the image, down to Earth... Accordingly he [Ilus] raised a temple on the citadel to house the image.

Some say that the temple was already rising when the image descended from Heaven as the goddess' gift... Others say that Elektra gave the Palladion to Dardanus, her son by Zeus, and that it was carried from Dardania to Troy after his death. Others, again, say that it fell from Heaven at Athens... Still others believe that there were two palladia, all similarly cast from Heaven... The College of Vestals at Rome now guards what is reputed to be the genuine Palladion.[146]

The upshot of this is that the Palladion was a wooden statue of the war-goddess, Pallas, that had been cast down from Heaven to Earth (Graves described the Trojan figure as wielding a spear, with the fearful aegis wrapped around the breast).[147] The Palladion thus belonged to the class of objects known as *palta*, meaning 'things hurled from Heaven'.[148]

But how did a wooden statue come to fall from the sky? Graves provided the only obvious explanation: the genuine *palta*, he said, were meteorites. The rest was symbolism:

Worship of meteorites was easily extended to ancient monoliths, the funerary origin of which had been forgotten; then from monolith to stone image, and from stone image to wooden or ivory image is a short step.[149]

So, according to Graves, the Palladion could have been a meteorite, or a stone substitute for a meteorite, or a wooden statue in the image of the deity (in which case the Trojans' 'legless' statue of Pallas seems highly befitting).

All of this casts a new light on the goddess named Pallas Athene. Was she so named because she had fallen down from Heaven in the form of meteorites? What we do know is that the city of Athens claimed to have captured the Trojan Palladion and made it the protectress of their city, calling it not simply Pallas, but Pallas Athene.[150] This mysterious image (known as a *xoanon* – see earlier comments) was thereafter safeguarded in the temple of the goddess and greatly revered.[151] Once a year, it would be taken in a grand procession to the sea, stripped, washed, dressed, and then returned to the temple (symbolising the baptism of fallen Athene in the Tritonian lake – see the myth recounted earlier).[152] At New Year, the Palladion (*xoanon*) would be presented with a newly woven robe (the *peplos*) in a tradition which mirrored the Egyptian cult of weaving the dress of Hathor/Isis.[153] The act symbolised the knitting back together of the dismembered goddess, i.e. the reconstitution of the exploded planet (this in line with the parallel myth of dismembered Osiris).

For another crucial piece in this puzzle of the *peplos*, we must return to the subject of Athene's dreaded weapon, the aegis. According to one of the Greek myths, mentioned briefly earlier, Athene had made the aegis from the skin of a winged, goat-like giant named Pallas and had, by donning the aegis, effectively 'clothed herself in his skin'.[154] This Pallas was, by one account, Athene's father, who had later attempted to rape her.[155] If we recall what we learned in chapter eleven about gods falling physically from Heaven, entering into the Underworld and taking over the mantle of the Earth, this myth starts to make a lot of sense. Pallas the giant would be the exploded planet (parent aspect); Athene would be the exploded planet (daughter aspect); and hence the fallen Athene could have clothed herself in her father's torn-off planetary skin and become vulnerable to planetary rape by her own father (according to the peculiar rules of the resurrecting god myth).[156]

In this case, the exploded planet hypothesis can be virtually proven by etymological means. Pallas, as we have just learned, was a goat-like giant and the Palladion was an object fallen from Heaven. Meanwhile, the aegis was literally a 'goat-skin' (from the Greek word *aigis*),[157] whilst the Greek word for meteorite, *baetylus*, stemmed from *baite*, meaning 'goat or goat-skin' (tradition had it that the *baetylus* stone swallowed by Kronos had been wrapped in a goat-skin).[158] In summary, we have a linguistic link between the goat-skin of Pallas, the Palladion, the aegis and the meteorite that surely stretches the boundaries of coincidence.[159]

In conclusion, we have come a long way from the idea that Athene was nothing but an aethereal, earth-born *daimon*. Yes, she had become a *daimon*, but only because her original, physical aspect had fallen from Heaven. Far from being born from the fallen head of Zeus, Athene had been born, more likely, from the head of a celestial Pallas, and thus personified the deluge from the exploding planet. It is this cataclysm, I suggest, which is recalled in the *Homeric Hymn to Athene* in which the poet recalls the day when the Sun stood still:

> Great Olympus shook terribly at the might of the bright-eyed goddess; the Earth groaned awfully; and the Ocean was moved... Then Helios [the Sun], the radiant son of Hyperion, halted his swift-footed horses

and they stood still for a long time, until the maiden [Pallas Athene] took the god-like armour from her immortal shoulders.[160]

Hephaestus

Finally, in connection with Plato's story of Athens and Atlantis, we must look briefly at the blacksmith-god Hephaestus, who partnered Athene in the creation of the Athenian people.

Who was Hephaestus? For once, we do not have to penetrate behind the veil of a daemonic identity. Whilst Hephaestus *did* have the nature of a *daimon*, he retained, in addition, all the trappings of his original, ex-physical identity. Thus the myths of Hephaestus' birth relate that he was born to Hera in Heaven, whence she flung him down to the Earth into the depths of the sea.[161] (Although another myth identified Zeus as the one who had flung Hephaestus out of Heaven.)[162]

As a result of this fall, Hephaestus was renowned as a lame god, a god of fire and, above all, a blacksmith-god – a master of the forge who could fabricate all kinds of marvellous things out of iron and bronze.[163] On the one hand, his foundry was said to be situated in the Underworld, either beneath the island of Lemnos or beneath the island of Sicily or beneath the mythical island of the Wandering Rocks.[164] But on the other hand, his foundry was said to be located in heavenly Olympus.[165] All in all, the message is clear: Hephaestus personified not just fire and metalwork but the fiery metals of Heaven and Earth; in short, he personified the fireball and the meteorite.[166]

As for the cult of Hephaestus, it was located primarily at two places – Lemnos and Athens. At the island of Lemnos, the priests of Hephaestus presided over the Samothracian Mysteries, otherwise known as the Mysteries of the Kabeiroi. (The Kabeiroi, literally 'the Great Gods', were said to be the sons of Hephaestus; little is known about this cult owing to the secrecy that surrounded it.)[167] At Athens, meanwhile, Hephaestus enjoyed a special and remarkable relationship with Athene.[168] According to a popular myth, it was the axe of Hephaestus that had cracked open the head of Zeus, enabling the *daimon* Athene to be born from the Earth. The poet Pindar describes it thus:

Thereupon the great king of the gods [Zeus] rained upon the city
  snowflakes of gold,
In the day when the skilled hand of Hephaestus wrought with his craft
  the axe, bronze-bladed,
Whence Athene, from the cleft summit of her father's brow, sprang
  up, and pronounced her loud war-cry to the broad sky above.

And Heaven and Mother Earth trembled to hear.[169]

Thus did Hephaestus facilitate the Athene's birth (in her metaphysical aspect) with his axe, allegedly at the site of the subterranean river Triton.[170] According to Hesiod, this mighty deed coincided with the birth of Hephaestus to Hera at the time when she was 'furying and quarrelling with her husband (Zeus)'.[171] The implication is that Hephaestus followed Athene down to the Earth, split it open with his meteoritic axe and thus effected the release and ascension of Athene's daemonic aspect. This cataclysmic event would explain Athene's nickname Tritogeneia, which meant 'born (i.e. reborn) in her third day'.[172]

Coincident with this cataclysmic release of the goddess, there came the birth of the Athenian race, stemming from the first mythical king, variously named Erichthonios or Erechtheus. According to the popular myth, it happened as follows: Hephaestus, wishing to deflower the virgin he had brought into the world, pursued Athene and managed to spill his semen on her thigh. The reaction of the goddess was to wipe off the semen and throw it to the Earth, whereupon Earth conceived and, in due course of time, gave birth to Erichthonios or Erechtheus, who came up out of the earth to become the first king of Athens and progenitor of the Athenian race.[173] According to Plato, it was this first generation of earth-born people, led by Erichthonios or Erechtheus, who had fought in battle against the people of Atlantis.[174]

In conclusion, I would emphasise that we should not take at face value the myths that *Hera or Zeus* threw Hephaestus down out of Olympus; these are understandable political accretions. Rather, it seems likely that Hephaestus was originally an exploded planet god in his own right; hence the fact that he was father of the Kabeiroi, 'the Great Gods'; and hence Homer's myth which made him the creator of the Universe.[175] When seen in this light, Hephaestus' partnership with Athene at Athens would constitute a typical archetypal pair of exploded planet deities, male and female.

Chapter Thirteen Summary

* Each of the Olympian gods possessed an ex-physical counterpart to its daemonic persona (in other words, they had originally descended physically from the sky). In most cases, the physical-metaphysical dualities of the gods were obscured following takeovers of their cults by the cult of Zeus.

* Each of the Olympian gods had once been an exploded planet god in his or her own right. Before the cult of Zeus took over, Greece had

been a land of numerous, competing exploded planet cults.[176]

* Each of the four gods in Plato's story of Athens and Atlantis – Zeus, Poseidon, Athene and Hephaestus – personified the exploded planet. What might this imply for our understanding of the story?

PART FOUR

PLATO'S LOST CONTINENT DECODED

CHAPTER FOURTEEN

THE ATLANTIS STORY

**Let me tell you this story then, Socrates.
It's a very strange one, but every word of it is true.**
(Critias in Plato's *Timaeus*, mid-4th century BC)

In the introduction to this book, I discussed the many difficulties of interpreting the Atlantis story, and spoke of the need to understand the story in its full and proper context. Who was its author, Plato? How was he influenced by the culture of the Greeks? What were the origins of the Greeks' religion and mythology? What was the meaning of the manifold myths of the gods and the golden age?

In Parts One to Three of this book, I have proposed revolutionary answers to these weighty questions. The Greek religion, I have argued, was an exploded planet cult, in which the gods personified physical and metaphysical aspects of the exploded planet. The myths of the gods, I have argued, were 'true stories' about the exploded planet cosmogony, whilst the myth of the golden age signified the demise of an entire living planet. All of these myths, I have argued, were rooted in the myths of Mesopotamia and Egypt, where exploded planet cults had been practised for thousands of years. Crucially, however, the exploded planet religion had become occulted, and its mysteries had become the preserve of the few.

Among these few, I have suggested, were Pythagoras, Philolaos, and Plato. Significantly, it is known that Plato visited the Pythagoreans in southern Italy in 388 BC at the age of forty, whereupon he returned to Athens and founded the Academy. At that time, almost certainly, he was initiated into the secret of the exploded planet, which he then made the basis of his Theory of Forms and his *Demiourgos* cosmogony in the Pythagorean treatise *Timaeus*.

Knowing all this, we are now in a position to re-evaluate Plato's story of Athens and Atlantis. To what extent might it be laced with exploded planet mythology?

There is only one logical place to begin, and that is with the story as it was told by Plato in the mid-4th century BC. In this chapter, I shall re-tell the story, sticking as closely as possible to the original text, but adding some initial insights which will pave the way for a complete decoding of the story in the chapters that follow.

It is, of course, necessary to keep any summary to a length which is suitable for its purpose, and my purpose here is to tell the essential story of Atlantis as directly as possible and with the minimum of distractions. To this end, it has been necessary for me to paraphrase a great deal of the text. In so doing, I have tried hard not to omit anything that might be of consequence in assessing the meaning of the story. Nevertheless, the reader may wish to return to this chapter at a later time with a copy of Plato's works to hand, so that he might judge for himself whether I have omitted anything important. With this *caveat* in mind, let us begin.

The Ideal State

Strictly speaking, the story of Atlantis begins not with Plato's *Timaeus*, but with an earlier book *Republic*, in which Socrates advocates his vision of the 'ideal state'. As we shall see, the story of Athens and Atlantis was told for the specific purpose of bringing Socrates' 'ideal state' to life. And so a brief synopsis of *Republic* is required.

The background to *Republic* was as follows. In the centuries leading up to the time of Socrates and Plato, the Greeks had experimented with different systems of government, namely dictatorship, oligarchy and democracy, but all had suffered from fundamental problems. Nor had foreign systems of government fared much better. As the Greeks saw it, the autocracies of Egypt and Assyria had achieved great power, but the cost in terms of strife in society had been inestimable. The author of *Republic*, surveying the state of human society in the 5th-4th centuries BC, was therefore struck by two things in particular: firstly, the tendency for tyrants to seize and abuse the reins of power; and secondly, the tendency for all nation-states to degenerate and become morally corrupt.

The challenge facing the author of *Republic* was twofold: firstly, to design a system of government that would foster a happy, harmonious and peaceful society; and, secondly, to design safeguards that would prevent this ideal society from becoming corrupted. Here lay a dilemma. This ideal state needed to be powerful, economically and militarily, to resist external threats to its status quo, and yet power of this kind led invariably to greed, expansionism and ultimately a fall from grace.[1]

The solution, advocated by Socrates and Plato, was that the ideal state should be led by philosopher-kings. Socrates expressed the idea thus:

> "Until philosophers rule as kings, or kings become conversant with philosophy... cities will have no rest from evils... and nor will the human race... And, until this happens, the [ideal] constitution we've been describing in theory will never be born to the fullest extent possible..."[2]

Similarly, Plato, in a letter written towards the end of his life, identified the crucial leadership quality which the ideal state required:

> I came to the conclusion that all existing states are badly governed and the condition of their laws practically incurable without some miraculous remedy... I was forced to say, in praise of true philosophy, that from her height alone was it possible to discern what the nature of justice is... and that the ills of the human race would never end until true philosophers come into political power, or the rulers of our cities learn true philosophy...[3]

True philosophy – as we discussed in chapter four – was not philosophy as we know it today, but rather a much higher kind of art in which a man sought knowledge of 'That which always exists' and 'That which *is*', i.e. the invisible, heavenly 'world of Forms'. The true philosopher, by means of an arduous series of initiations in Pythagorean doctrines, would learn how to access the aethereal 'world of Forms' and thereby perceive the perfect archetypes on which the ideal state should be founded. Above all, he would come to know the eternal and unchanging archetypes of Justice and 'the Good', and he would bring these archetypes down from Heaven to Earth. Socrates put it thus:

> "Then, at the age of fifty, those who have survived the tests... must be led to the goal and compelled to lift up the radiant light of their souls to what itself provides Light for everything. And once they have seen the Good itself, they must each in turn put the city, its citizens, and themselves in order, using it [the Good] as their model."[4]

By such means, true philosophers would deliver everlasting peace and prosperity on Earth – the era of the ideal state.

Could this ambitious mix of politics and mysticism ever be brought to fruition? Socrates indeed admitted that his vision of the ideal state was theoretical and utopian, and he conceded that one must imagine a state that 'most closely approximates' to his ideal requirements.[5] Then, having outlined the difficulties of bringing this kind of state into being, Socrates went on to provide a fascinating scenario as to how it might happen.[6] But that is not relevant here. At the end of *Republic*, crucial questions are left still unresolved. Has Socrates produced a workable version of the ideal state here on the Earth, or does the ideal state remain suspended up in the heavens where it belongs?

Timaeus – Setting the Scene

We turn now from *Republic* to the follow-on work *Timaeus*. Here, Plato describes a meeting between Socrates and his three friends Timaeus, Hermocrates and Critias.[7] Apparently, the group had met the previous day when the subject of conversation had been 'the kind of political structure cities should have and the kind of men that should make it up, so as to be the best possible city'.[8] In other words, Socrates had been extolling the merits of his ideal state. Significantly, the day's proceedings had concluded with Socrates inviting his friends to make a speech in reply on the following day.

The next morning, Socrates recapitulates his vision of the ideal state and then summarises his feelings about it:

> "I'd like to go on now and tell you what I've come to feel about the political structure we've described. My feelings are like those of a man who gazes upon magnificent looking animals, whether they're animals in a painting or even actually alive but standing still, and who then finds himself longing to look at them in motion or engaged in some struggle or conflict that seems to show off their distinctive physical qualities. (Well) I felt the same thing about the city we've described. I'd love to listen to someone give a speech depicting our [ideal] city in a contest with other cities, competing for those prizes that cities typically compete for. I'd love to see our city distinguish itself in the way it goes to war and in the way it pursues the war... Already yesterday I was aware of this when you asked me to discuss matters of government, and that's why I was eager to do your bidding. I knew that if you'd agree to make the follow-up speech, no-one could do a better job than you. No-one today besides you could present our [ideal] city pursuing a war that reflects her true character. Only you could give her all she requires."[9]

In the midst of this speech, Socrates' friends are referred to as experts in the subject to be discussed; Timaeus is one who 'has mastered the entire field of philosophy', whilst Critias is 'no mere layman in any of the areas we're talking about'.[10]

Hermocrates is the first to reply and he asserts enthusiastically that he,

Timaeus and Critias have spent the previous evening in deep discussion about the ideal state. Moreover, he says, Critias had brought up a story 'from ancient times' (*ek palaios*) about a war between ancient Athens and Atlantis, and it might well suit the purpose of the assignment (i.e. it describes a war).[11] Critias then relates his tale, or rather a concise version of it. It is the story of Atlantis in its original version – the story that has puzzled commentators for more than two thousand years.

The Athens and Atlantis Story in Brief

Critias is the next to speak, initially setting out a 'concise version' of the story. He begins his speech in *Timaeus* as follows:

> "Let me tell you this story then, Socrates. It's a very strange one, but even so, every word of it is true. It's a story that Solon, the wisest of 'the seven sages', once vouched for... The story is that our city had performed great and marvellous deeds in ancient times, which, owing to the passage of time and to the destruction of human life, have vanished. Of all these deeds one in particular was magnificent. It is this one that we should now do well to commemorate and present to you as our gift of thanks."[12]

In response to Critias' introduction, Socrates declares that he has never heard of this singular magnificent feat of the ancient Athenians. The onus is therefore on Critias to justify the authenticity of the story before he relates it to his host, who is one of the most wise and learned men of the day.

Critias thus explains the origins of his 'very strange' story. He assures Socrates that the story has been transmitted privately through his family across a span of four generations, beginning with his great-grandfather Dropides, who had heard the story from Solon, a famous Athenian statesman.[13] Solon, in turn, had learned the story in Egypt from some wise old priests at the town of Sais (this would be in the 6th century BC by our reckoning). Yes, it did seem odd that the present-day Athenians were unfamiliar with the magnificent feat of their ancestors, but this could be explained by the great antiquity of the event, which caused it to have been preserved only in the annals of the Egyptian Saites.

Critias himself had heard the story as a ten-year-old boy, when his ninety-year-old grandfather, Elder Critias, had recited it from memory at the Apaturia festival.[14] He now relies on his own memory to recall what his grandfather had said concerning Solon's visit to Egypt. The crucial conversation, says Critias, occurred when Solon began to speak of Greek antiquity. It was at this point that one of the Saite priests – 'a very old man' – mocked Solon and the Greeks for their inadequate understanding of the past. "Ah Solon, you Greeks are ever children" the priest said: "You are young in soul every one of you".[15] He then informed Solon that: "There have been, and there will continue to be, numerous disasters that have destroyed human life in many kinds of ways."[16] The most serious of these, said the priest, involved deluges of fire and water, which would sweep down from the heavens at regular intervals. He then explained that the Greek myth of Phaethon contained a profound truth concerning these recurrent cataclysmic events (see citation in chapter four of this book).

The Egyptian priest then mocked Solon again, comparing his account of Greek antiquity to 'a nursery tale'. Firstly, he said, the Greeks knew only one flood (the flood of Deucalion), whereas in fact there had been a great many before. Secondly, he said, there had lived in Athens 'before the greatest of these floods' a distinguished race of men who had been the progenitors of the Athenian people and its civilisation. This race of ancient Athenians had been the finest of all ancient civilisations in the natural justice of their laws and in their bravery on the battlefield, and yet their deeds had been completely forgotten by Solon and the present-day race of Athenians.[17]

Solon, astonished, then begged the Saite priest to tell him everything that he knew about the ancient Athenians, and thus it was that he learned the story of the war against Atlantis.

The priest began the story as follows:

> "Your city [Athens] the goddess [Neith/Athene] founded first, a
> thousand years before our city [Sais], when she had received from
> Earth and Hephaestus the seed from which your people were to come.
> Now our social arrangement, according to the records inscribed in our
> sacred documents, is eight thousand years old. Nine thousand years
> ago, then, did these fellow citizens of yours live, whose laws and
> finest achievement I'll briefly describe to you..."[18]

Note the implication here. The ancient Athenians, who were about to go to war against Atlantis, were *the first generation* of Athenians, whom the goddess Athene had created from the earth using the meteoritic seed of Hephaestus. As we shall see, we are dealing with a people who lived aeons before the flood of Deucalion.

The priest now continues with his story:

> "Now many great accomplishments of your city recorded here are
> awe-inspiring, but there is one that surely surpasses them all in
> magnitude and excellence. The records speak of a vast power that your
> city once brought to a halt in its insolent march against the whole of

Europe and Asia at once – a power that sprang forth from beyond, from the Atlantic Ocean. For at that time this ocean was passable, since it had an island in it, in front of the strait that you people say you call 'the Pillars of Heracles'. This island [Atlantis] was larger than Libya and Asia [Minor] combined, and it provided passage to the other islands... From those islands one could then travel to the entire continent on the other side, which surrounds that real sea beyond..."[19]

Note the clear statement here that the Isle of Atlantis lay in the Atlantic Ocean, beyond the Pillars of Heracles (i.e. the straits of Gibraltar).[20] But note also the reference to the continent that lay beyond Atlantis 'on the other side'. This has led some commentators to suggest that the continent beyond (the so-called 'opposite continent') is America. But are things really so simple? Unfortunately, the passage throws up two anomalies of supernatural proportions. Firstly, the Isle of Atlantis is said to be 'larger than Libya and Asia Minor combined' – a quite implausible notion. And secondly, the opposite continent is said to completely surround the Atlantic Ocean – a quite remarkable idea. When we stop to think about it, neither statement makes any sense in a geographical context.

The priest now relates to Solon a very brief account of the war:

"Now on this Isle of Atlantis a great and marvellous royal power established itself, and ruled not only the whole island, but many of the other islands and parts of the [opposite] continent as well... Now one day this power gathered all of itself together, and set out to enslave all of the territory inside the strait, including your region and ours, in one fell swoop. Then it was, Solon, that your city's might shone bright with excellence and strength, for all mankind to see. Pre-eminent among all others in the nobility of her spirit and in her use of all the arts of war, she first rose to the leadership of the Greek cause. Later, forced to stand alone, deserted by her allies, she reached a point of extreme peril. Nevertheless, she overcame the invaders and erected her monument of victory. She prevented the enslavement of those not yet enslaved, and generously freed all the rest of us who lived within the boundaries of Heracles."[21]

This is as much detail as we are going to get concerning the war between Athens and Atlantis. The account, it must be said, is extremely sketchy. What is clear, once again, however, is that the Atlantians invaded the Mediterranean region via the Pillars of Heracles (the straits of Gibraltar), so strictly speaking it is a mistake to seek Atlantis anywhere but in the Atlantic Ocean.

The Egyptian priest now reaches the climax of his story:

"Further back, excessively violent earthquakes and floods occurred, and after the onset of an unbearable day and a night, your entire warrior force sank below the earth all at once, and the Isle of Atlantis likewise sank below the sea and disappeared. That is how the Ocean in that region has come to be even now unnavigable and unexplorable, obstructed as it is by a layer of mud at a shallow depth, the residue of the island as it settled."[22]

This passage contains two extraordinary anomalies which must be added to the two highlighted earlier. Firstly, it is said that the entire Athenian warrior force sank into the earth at the same time as the island of Atlantis sank into the sea – a highly implausible coincidence (indeed, the fates of both sides lend a surreal and mythical note to the story). And secondly, it is suggested that the island of Atlantis turned into a shallow sea of mud – a most unlikely occurrence (even more bizarrely, it is implied that the mud caused a blockage in the Atlantic Ocean for a span of nine thousand years, right up to the time of Solon!).

True Fiction

Critias closes his report of Solon's story by emphasising the amazing correspondence between the ancient Athenians and the citizens of Socrates' ideal state.[23] Referring to his opening speech as merely 'a concise version' of Solon's story, he proposes that he and Timaeus will now take turns to provide further details. Their plan is to fulfil Socrates' wish by supposing that the citizens of his ideal state – a purely imaginary people – are identical to the ancient Athenians 'who really existed' nine thousand years ago:

"We'll translate the citizens and the city you described to us in mythical fashion yesterday to the realm of fact, and place it before us as though it is ancient Athens itself. And we'll say that the citizens you imagined are the very ones the [Egyptian] priest spoke about, our actual ancestors. The congruence will be complete and our song will be in tune if we say that your imaginary citizens are the ones who really existed at that time."[24]

There can be no clearer statement that the story of Athens and Atlantis is a literary fiction, designed for the purpose of bringing Socrates' ideal state to life. Nevertheless, whilst this fictional dimension must always be borne in mind, there is an emphasis, too, on the essential 'truth' of the story; hence the idea here that the ancient Athenians 'really existed at that time'. The question is this: are we dealing with people who 'really existed' in the sense of history, or with people who 'really existed' in the sense of myth?

Returning to the text of *Timaeus*, Critias at this point hands over to his friend Timaeus who embarks on a long and complicated exposition on the subject of the origin of the Universe, the gods and man. Quite how this connects with Socrates' ideal state or the story of the war between Athens and Atlantis remains something of a mystery. It should be noted, however, that Timaeus' subject is Pythagorean cosmogony, and that his mystical God-Sphere, *Demiourgos*, is a cipher for the exploded planet (see chapter eleven and appendix a). Might this be a hint that the Athens and Atlantis story has a cosmic dimension?

Bearing this in mind, let us continue with the story by passing over Timaeus' speech and proceeding to the next of Plato's works: that which is entitled *Critias*.

Critias – The Detailed Account

Critias is a direct follow-on to the book entitled *Timaeus*. As the latter comes to an end with Timaeus' lengthy exposition on the subject of Pythagorean cosmogony, the reader is conscious of being left hanging in the midst of an unfinished story. Critias is supposed to speak again in more detail about Athens and Atlantis, whilst Hermocrates stands in the wings as if waiting to make his own contribution.

Critias now resumes the story of Athens and Atlantis which he began earlier, with a reminder of its subject matter:

"We should recall at the very beginning that, in very rough terms, it was nine thousand years since the time when a war is recorded as having broken out between the peoples dwelling outside the Pillars of Heracles [i.e. the Atlantians] and all those dwelling within."[25]

This passage sounds, at first, like a repeat of an earlier statement, but in fact it contains an intriguing anomaly. Previously, in *Timaeus*, Critias stated that *Athens was founded* nine thousand years before the time of Solon. And yet now Critias declares that *the war between Athens and Atlantis occurred* nine thousand years before the time of Solon. If we take these chronological references at face value, then it follows that the city of Athens must have fought the war *at the same time as it was founded by the goddess Athene* – indeed at the same time as Hephaestus, the meteorite-god, planted the seed of the Athenian people in the earth. Is this passage a little sloppy with its chronology, as most scholars seem to think, or might it be a vital clue towards some other understanding of the story?[26]

Continuing with the story, Critias confirms once again the remarkable size of Atlantis – greater than both Libya and Asia [Minor] combined – and reminds his audience about the cataclysmic climax of the war, mentioning the earthquakes and the resulting sea of mud, but this time omitting to mention the 'floods' or the disappearance of the Athenian army.[27] He also makes it explicit that the sea of mud (i.e. sunken Atlantis) was located 'in the great Ocean', i.e. in the Atlantic Ocean.

Critias now promises to describe the war in detail, along with the roles of various Greek peoples and barbarian nations as they 'emerged' from place to place.[28] But first he sets about describing the condition of Athens and Atlantis in respect of their powers and constitutions before the war.

Ancient Athens

Critias begins by describing how the gods Hephaestus and Athene were assigned the region of Attica, wherein they 'fashioned good men, sprung from the land itself'.[29] The names of these first men, according to the Saite priest, were Cecrops, Erechtheus, Erichthonios, Erysichthon and other men who preceded the generation of Theseus.[30] In the beginning, says Critias, the gods raised all men as their chattel and livestock (as do shepherds their sheep) whilst, as regards the Athenians, Hephaestus and Athene granted them an ideal constitution for the government of their society.

Critias goes on to describe this ancient constitution in terms which match Socrates' vision of the ideal state (as expounded in *Republic* and summarised at the beginning of *Timaeus*). Accordingly, the Athenian warrior class comprised both men and women who lived in seclusion from the other citizens on the heights of the acropolis, around the walled sanctuary of Athene and Hephaestus, where they all lived together as a commune, maintaining no private possessions, but rather holding all their possessions jointly and asking for nothing beyond what they needed to live.[31] As regards their activities, Critias confirms that they were "all of the activities that were spoken of yesterday", i.e. when Socrates outlined the requirements for the ideal state.[32]

Critias now shifts his attention to the ancient land of Athens, which, according to the Egyptian priest, was far more expansive and more fertile than the Athenian territories of Critias' day:

"In its great fertility our land far surpassed every other... at that time our land produced not only with high quality but also in great abundance... compared to the land it once was, Attica of today is like the skeleton revealed by a wasting disease... But in that age our land was undiminished and had high hills with soil upon them."[33]

This report was quite 'plausible and true', insisted Critias, for the fertile soil of those days had been washed away by a series of cataclysms:

"Many and great were the floods that occurred in the space of nine thousand years – for this is the number of years between that time and the present..."[34]

A similar picture is drawn for the acropolis of Athens. Before the war with Atlantis, it had been much larger and covered with soil, but all of this had disappeared in a single night in a ferocious cataclysm:

"A single night of torrential rain stripped the acropolis of its soil and reduced it to bare limestone in a storm that was accompanied by earthquakes. Before the destructive flood of Deucalion, this was the third such cataclysmic storm."[35]

This cataclysm is reckoned by scholars to be the very same flood that caused Atlantis to sink (hence the simultaneous earthquakes).[36] Whilst the floods had washed away the soil from the acropolis, the earthquakes had caused the single, idyllic spring to become choked with debris. It is of great significance that this flood, in which the acropolis was ruined and Atlantis sank, was the third cataclysm before the flood of Deucalion (per the citation above).

Critias concludes his report of the ancient Athenians by praising their considerable virtues. They were renowned throughout Asia and Europe, he notes, not only for their prowess on the battlefield, but also for their system of justice, their mental and spiritual acumen, and even their beautiful bodies. All in all, Athens was the most eminent of the nations of that age, and thus the other Greek peoples followed them willingly.

Ancient Atlantis

Having established the situation of ancient *Athens* before the war, Critias now turns to the power and constitution of *Atlantis*. To begin, he recites the myth of the division of the Earth between the gods, and describes how Poseidon (the god of the deep sea, but also an exploded planet god per my decoding in chapter thirteen) was allotted the Isle of Atlantis as one of his domains. What follows next sounds like a fairy tale.

The first Atlantians, says Critias, sprung up from the earth in ancient times, as did all peoples according to the Greek myths. Foremost among them was a man, Evenor, and a woman, Leucippe, who lived together as man and wife in a low, flat hill in the centre of the island.[37] This couple produced an only child, Clito, but when Clito reached marriageable age they both died.[38] It was then that Poseidon, 'the Earth-shaker', had sexual intercourse with Clito (supposedly 'a mortal woman') and fathered the race of Atlantian kings.

Strangely, the sexual intercourse between Poseidon and Clito was marked by a supernatural restructuring of the island:

> "... Poseidon conceived a desire for her [Clito] and slept with her. To make the hill on which she lived a strong enclosure, he broke it to form a circle and he created alternating rings of sea and land around it... He made two rings of land and three of sea as round as if he had laid them out with compass and lathe..."[39]

After this, Poseidon drew up two subterranean streams to act as springs – one with warm water and one with cold water – and caused all manner of crops to grow from the earth.[40] In the due course of time, he fathered five separate pairs of twin sons upon Clito, and appointed them to be the first ten kings of the island, which he divided accordingly into ten regions.[41]

The name of the first king – the first-born of the first pair of twins – is intriguing. According to the Egyptian priest, Poseidon named him Atlas, after the famous Titan god who supported the heavens on his head and shoulders. Whilst the connection to the Titan god Atlas is not explicit, it does seem to be deliberate, as if the priest (or Plato, as the author of the story) was playing on the Greek myth of the downfall of the Titans.

Whilst on the subject of Atlas, Critias confirms once again that the island of Atlantis had been situated in the Atlantic Ocean:

> "His name was Atlas; the island is called Atlantis and the sea Atlantic after him."[42]

Having listed all the names of Poseidon's sons, Critias then relates how these ten kings, their sons, and their later descendants, all ruled the Isle of Atlantis – and 'many other islands in the Atlantic Ocean' (further confirmation, if any be needed, of where Atlantis sank) – over the course of many generations, all prior to the war with Athens. Thus, whilst the Athenians would fight the war against Atlantis with their first, earth-born generation, the Atlantians would benefit from centuries of progress in the expansion of their kingdom.[43]

The linchpin of the Atlantian kingdom was the island's vast wealth, which Critias now describes in minute detail. Firstly, there were the mines that produced an abundance of gold, silver, copper, tin, and a mysterious metal called *oreichalkos*.[44] Secondly, there were the huge stone quarries that provided three types of stone (coloured white, black and red).[45] Thirdly, there were trees 'of extraordinary beauty and height' which provided vast quantities of timber, as well as consumable drink, food and oils.[46] Fourthly, there were plants and crops which sprang up out of the earth of their own accord – 'products lovely, marvellous and of abundant bounty'.[47] And fifthly, the island swarmed with animal life, both domestic and wild, including a large herd of elephants that provided the Atlantians with ivory for the decoration of their temples.[48]

Critias goes on to explain how the Atlantian kings used this abundance of produce to improve the island, by building temples, palaces, harbours and ship-sheds. Their first project was to build a magnificent palace for themselves on the central island, along with connecting bridges that spanned the rings of sea, enabling the people to visit the sacred hill of their ancestors. The palace was said to be 'a dwelling astonishing in size and manifold beauty' and 'magnificent in its monumental architecture'.[49] Close to the palace, but in the centre of the island, they built a shrine for Clito and Poseidon, which they enclosed with a wall of gold.[50] And next to this shrine they built a huge temple of Poseidon (three times the size of the Parthenon in Athens), which they invested externally with gold and silver, and internally with gold, silver, ivory and *oreichalkos*. The temple housed a giant statue of Poseidon standing in a chariot with a team of six winged horses, which was surrounded with statues of a hundred Nereids riding dolphins.[51] Finally, outside the temple, they built a monumental altar and this was complemented, over the course of time, by numerous lavish dedications, notably statues of the former kings and their wives.[52] Such was the splendour of the central island.

In the meantime, the kings built bridges that linked the central island to the two outer land rings, and dug canals that linked together the three sea rings.[53] And, further to this, they excavated a Grand Canal that linked this entire complex of land and sea rings to the true sea (see Figure 9).[54] Consequently, ships were able to sail all the way into the city from the coast of the island, and moor in a magnificent harbour in the city's outer sea ring. In addition, the kings constructed a race course for horses, which ran right round the outer land ring.[55]

Enormous walls were built so as to enclose both the city and the whole island in every conceivable way. On the central island, the Atlantians built a wall of gold around the shrine of Clito and Poseidon, and they surrounded the central island itself with a wall of stone, invested with *oreichalkos*.[56] In the outer parts of the city, they built walls around the two land rings and even built walls along the sides of the bridges.[57] And at the coast, they built a circuit wall, invested with bronze and tin, that ran right round the circumference of the island.[58]

Figure 9a.
THE ISLAND
OF ATLANTIS

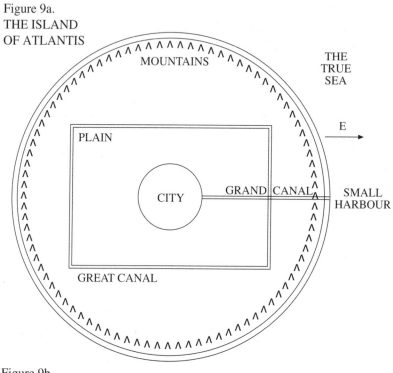

Figure 9b.
THE CITY
OF ATLANTIS

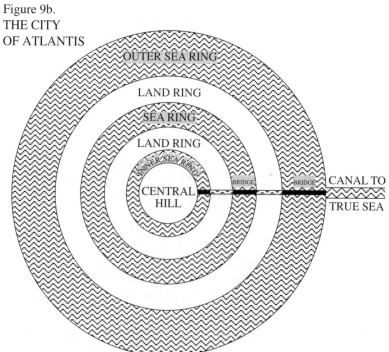

Such was the fertility of the island that it supported a vast population, most of whom lived in tightly packed houses in the outer regions of the island.[59] In addition, the city teemed with traders from all parts of the world, whose comings and goings produced 'a commotion and hubbub that could be heard day and night'.[60] The only respite from this noise was in the central island, which was occupied by the kings in their palaces and the highest rank of soldiers in their quarters nearby, and, to a lesser extent, in the first land ring (occupied by the next rank of soldiers) and in the second land ring (which featured gardens, temples, gymnasia, and the race course for horses).[61]

This, says Critias, was the description of Atlantis received by Solon from the Egyptian priests. However, he now goes on to recall a slightly different tradition.

Firstly, Critias states that the island of Atlantis was surrounded by a ring of mountains, 'legendary for their number, size and beauty', which sloped down to the true sea.[62] Moreover, he declares that the entire island was 'very high' and 'rose sheer from the sea'.[63] But this contradicts what he said earlier, for if it were so, how could ships have sailed inwards from the coast to the city's harbour?

Secondly, Critias describes a rectangular plain that stood inside the ring of mountains and enclosed the city; he gives the plain dimensions of three thousand by two thousand stades (enclosed by a Great Canal, ten thousand stades in length).[64] And yet earlier, Critias reported that this plain – 'the loveliest of all plains and quite fertile' – was smaller than the size of the island which was itself only one hundred and twenty-seven stades in diameter.[65] This anomaly has caused scholars to visualise Atlantis with the most bizarre combinations of city and plain.[66] And yet the more likely explanation is that two different traditions concerning the size of the island have been preserved in the text. Indeed, if we recall the idea of Atlantis being 'larger than Libya and Asia Minor combined', then the text actually preserves three different traditions of the size of the island. All in all, one should place these various measurements to one side, and focus instead on the broad outline of the island, city and plain, as I have sketched in Figure 9.

On the subject of the rectangular plain, Critias reports that it was organised into sixty thousand districts, from which men (but not women) would be drafted into military service. Each district was assigned to one of the ten cities (and ten kings) of Atlantis, comprising the 'royal city' in the central island and nine other cities (it is implied) in the outer parts of the plain.

Finally, Critias describes the laws and rituals by which the kings governed their lands, drawing attention to a bloody bull sacrifice which was made every fifth or sixth year in the temple of Poseidon.[67] There he concludes his account of Atlantis, and returns to the main story of its invasion of the Mediterranean and its defeat at the hands of the heroic Athenians.

The Unfinished Story

"Now, this was the power, so great and extraordinary, that existed in that distant region at that time. This was the power the god mustered and brought against these [Mediterranean] lands."[68]

With these lines, Critias returns to his main theme – the war between ancient Athens and Atlantis. The Atlantians, he says, became filled with lust for further wealth and power, and thus antagonised the gods. Zeus thereupon decided to orchestrate the downfall of the Atlantians, so that only a chastened remnant would remain.[69] The chief god called the other gods to an assembly, and, as they looked down upon the Earth, he spoke. But at this point the text ends in mid-sentence, and Zeus' words are lost. It is as if Plato, the author of the story, simply put down his pen and left the unfinished manuscript on his desk.[70]

That it is an unfinished story is beyond question. Not only was Critias due to complete his speech, but Hermocrates was ready and waiting to offer Socrates the third and final segment in which he would demonstrate the model behaviour of the Athenians, both during the war with Atlantis and in its immediate aftermath.[71] Much of the tale thus remained to be told.

No-one knows for certain what Zeus was about to say in his address to the gods, but his probable intention was to prompt the Atlantians, by some means, to embark upon an expansion into the Mediterranean, thus instigating their downfall at the hands of the Athenians. But the detailed exposition of the conflict remains far from complete. How exactly did the Athenians intervene and repulse the Atlantians? Why did Zeus cause the Athenian warriors to be swallowed up by the earth? (Was this a fate befitting of heroes?) And what happened to the many other islands in the Atlantian kingdom? Unfortunately, none of these questions are answered due to the vagueness that pervades Critias' story.

The Moral of the Story

Whatever the wider ramifications of Plato's story (which we will discuss in due course), there is a consensus among scholars on one fundamental point – that the story of Athens and Atlantis makes moral and political observations that were relevant to Plato's Athens during the 4th century BC. But before we can discuss how this worked exactly, we must first grasp the overview of the rise and fall of Atlantis.

In the beginning, the Atlantians inherited a divine constitution, based on the sacred laws of Poseidon. Accordingly, their earliest endeavours were to build marvellous temples and palaces, dedicated to Poseidon and his wife Clito. But as time passed, the Atlantians turned their minds to secular activities, building canals, bridges, ships, a magnificent harbour and a race track for horses. At this time, Atlantian ships began to ply the ocean, seeking to establish trade links with neighbouring islands, and they indeed achieved remarkable success. As a result of this international trade, the Atlantians multiplied their wealth immeasurably, becoming the richest race of kings ever to have lived in the world.[72] Over the course of many generations, they built up a huge empire which encompassed many neighbouring islands, parts of the continent that surrounded the Ocean, and even certain regions inside the straits of Gibraltar.[73]

But even this empire proved insufficient for the Atlantians, who felt inclined to take over the entire world. And thus it came to pass, as Plato tells it, that: 'one day this power gathered all of itself together and set out to enslave all of the territory inside the strait... in one fell swoop.'[74] It was then that Zeus decided to punish the greed of Atlantis by bringing Athens against it. But instead of regaling us with details of the war, Plato ends his story by driving home its moral point. In the penultimate passages of the unfinished *Critias*, he writes as follows:

"For many generations and as long as enough of their divine nature survived, they were obedient unto their laws and they were well disposed to the divinity they were kin to. They possessed conceptions that were true and entirely lofty... They bore their vast wealth of gold and other possessions without difficulty, treating them as if they were a burden. They did not become intoxicated with the luxury of the life their wealth made possible; they did not lose their self-control and slip into decline... they saw that both wealth and concord decline as possessions become pursued and honoured. And virtue perishes with them as well... But when the divine portion in them began to grow faint... at that moment, in their inability to bear their great good fortune, they became disordered. To whoever had eyes to see, they appeared hideous, since they were losing the finest of what were once their most treasured possessions. But to those who were blind to the true way of life oriented to happiness it was at this time that they gave the semblance of being supremely beauteous and blessed. Yet inwardly they were filled with an unjust lust for possessions and power. But Zeus... observed this noble race lying in this abject state and resolved to punish them and to make them more careful and harmonious..."[75]

In these passages – arguably the most pertinent in the entire work – the moral point of the story is unmistakeable. The Atlantians have become corrupted by material possessions and have lost touch with their divine constitution. Having developed a huge army and navy, they are about to indulge their imperialist ambitions by invading the lands of the East. Puffed up with pride and self-importance, they can see nothing wrong with their actions. Zeus, however, is able to see beyond their materialistic wealth to recognise their true spiritual poverty.

To a Greek reader of Plato's day, there would have been no mistaking the parallels between ancient Atlantis and the modern-day state of 4th century Athens.[76] Athens, like Atlantis, had used sea power to achieve economic success; Athens, like Atlantis, had used its riches to embark on a huge building programme (under the leadership of Pericles 461-429 BC); Athens, like Atlantis, had turned away from her divine inheritance and become obsessed with material wealth and secular activities; Athens, like Atlantis, had developed a powerful army and navy for the purpose of expanding her empire; and Athens, like Atlantis, had tried to impose herself on neighbouring peoples.[77]

However, as Plato was well aware, his city's arrogance and aggression had ended in spectacular failure: Athens had arrogantly over-reached herself in the Second Peloponnesian War and the Spartans had forced her into a humiliating surrender in 404 BC. Having briefly enjoyed the status of a superpower, Athens had fallen into ruins physically, financially and psychologically.[78] Athens, then, like Atlantis, had been thwarted in her grand designs, as if by the will of almighty Zeus.

Lest anyone have any doubts about this analogy, Plato lent Atlantis certain detailed features that were remarkably evocative of 4th century Athens. The island's huge walls and canals, for example, surely recalled the famous Long Walls of Athens, whilst its harbours and ship-sheds were surely reminiscent of the Peiraeus.[79] In addition, the lavish temple of Poseidon must have called to mind the Parthenon at Athens, whilst the huge statue of the Atlantian god, almost touching the roof with its head, must have sounded remarkably like the statue of Zeus at Olympia.[80]

All of these connections would have prompted Plato's readers to think about the moral point of the story, which applied as much to 4th century Athens as it did to Atlantis.

This moral would have been perfectly clear to an alert reader. In the beginning, all men on Earth had inherited a divine constitution that had been lowered from Heaven. However, as soon as this system of laws had taken root in the Earth, it had become corrupted, just as all terrestrial things were prone to corrosion and decay in Plato's Theory of Forms. This had been the fate of the ancient Atlantian kingdom, and it had also been the fate of Plato's city, Athens, during the 5th-4th century BC. The common problem – seemingly shared by all nations of the world – was man's insatiable lust for material wealth.[81]

What, then, was the best form of human government? In Plato's story, the hereditary kingship of Atlantis had failed to safeguard the original divine constitution and, by analogy, the democracy of 4th century Athens would not have fared any better. Meanwhile, the story was an advert for Socrates' ideal state (as advocated in *Republic*) – a theoretical system of social organisation that was designed to prevent the corruption of man by material wealth (as far as it was humanly possible to do so). Thus, it may be seen that Plato's story had a political as well as a moral point. It was advocating, ever so subtly, the rulership of the state by true philosophers such as Plato himself.[82]

So much for the moral and political points of the story. But what about the underlying myth of the war between Athens and Atlantis? Did Plato simply make this up, as some commentators have suggested, or might it, in some way, have been a 'true' myth, as Plato indeed maintained that it was?

Chapter Fourteen Summary

* The story of Atlantis is told only in the works of Plato – specifically *Timaeus* and *Critias* – and nowhere else.

* The main theme of the story is a war between Athens and Atlantis, in which the Athenians, not the Atlantians, are portrayed as the noble and victorious race. This war had a very strange climax.

* The story of the ancient Athenians attacking Atlantis was told as an analogy of Socrates' ideal state going to war.

* The ancient city of Athens was founded by the gods nine thousand years before the time of Solon (*circa* 9600 BC by our modern system of reckoning). The war against Atlantis was fought by the first generation of Athenians – an 'earth-born' race.

* Oddly, Critias seems to suggest that the war occurred in exactly the same year that Athens was founded (both the war and the founding of the city occurred nine thousand years before the time of Solon).

* The kingdom of Atlantis was founded 'many generations' before the city of Athens. It consisted of one large island and many subsidiary islands, all situated in the Atlantic Ocean, opposite the Pillars of Heracles.

* Atlantis took its name from its first king, Atlas, the first-born son of Poseidon and Clito. Atlas was the name of the god who supported the Heaven on his head and shoulders; the western Ocean was named 'Atlantic' after him.

* The island of Atlantis was circular, as was its city, the latter being laid out in concentric rings of sea and land around the central, primeval mound of Poseidon and Clito.

* According to one account, the island of Atlantis was supernaturally large – bigger than Libya and Asia Minor combined. Other accounts made it much smaller, but of inconsistent dimensions. This tends to suggest the preservation of three variant traditions in all.

* The city of Atlantis was said to possess a magnificent harbour, which was a centre for international trade. Ocean-going ships accessed this harbour by means of a fantastic canal (although this account seems to be contradicted by one tradition that the island rose steeply out of the surrounding sea).

* At around the time of the war with Athens, the island of Atlantis sank beneath the sea and disappeared, following a day and a night of 'excessively violent earthquakes and floods'. Strangely, the entire army of Athenians soldiers sank into the earth at the same time. This cataclysm was the third before the famous flood of Deucalion.

* The site of sunken Atlantis was said to be identifiable by a layer of mud at a shallow depth – the residue of the island as it settled. This sea of mud was said to still be extant nine thousand years after the cataclysm.

* Plato described Atlantis in extensive, vivid and realistic detail in order to draw an analogy with 5th-4th century Athens and thereby make important moral and political points.

* Despite all the contradictions and absurdities in the story, Critias insisted that every word of it was 'true'. While the moral and political points of the story are incontestable, the suspicion remains that the myth of the war is somehow important.

CHAPTER FIFTEEN

ONCE UPON ATLANTIS

It's too bad that Solon wrote poetry only as a diversion . . .

(Plato, *Timaeus*, mid-4th century BC)

After Plato's death, in 347 BC, the status of his story about Athens and Atlantis was disputed. Some thought the story to be historically true,[1] but others were not so convinced. In the 4th century BC, the philosopher Aristotle – who surely knew more about Plato's ideas than we do – commented that 'the man who invented Atlantis made it disappear'.[2] In other words, he believed that Plato had simply made the whole thing up. In a similar vein, Theopompus (mid-4th century BC) and Euhemerus (early-3rd century BC) incorporated the Atlantis story in their fictional works, as if to imply that Plato's story, too, was a fiction.[3] No consensus was ever reached, despite many centuries of debate in Platonist and Neo-platonist schools, and thereafter the subject of the lost continent faded into obscurity, where it would remain for many more centuries.

In 1882, however, the debate was reignited by Ignatius Donnelly in his bestselling book *Atlantis: The Antediluvian World*, in which he argued passionately that Atlantis had been a real place and that the cataclysm which destroyed it had been a genuine historical event in the Atlantic Ocean.[4] As a result, the Western world experienced a renaissance of interest in Atlantis, and a myriad of authors emerged to speculate on the whereabouts of the lost kingdom. Almost to a man, these researchers took Plato literally and asserted that Atlantis had sank nine thousand years before the time of the Greek poet Solon, i.e. approximately 9600 BC by our modern system of reckoning. This pattern has continued right up to the present day, with connections now being made to a 'proven' cometary impact during the 10th millennium BC.[5] However, the fact is that no-one has yet located the lost continent and, as we shall now see, there are fundamental problems with the historicist interpretation of

Plato's story.

Problem 1: Plato

As much as Atlantis-hunters would wish Plato to have been a historian in the mould of Herodotus or Thucydides, he was not. And nor was he a geographer in the mould of, say, Hecataeus. On the contrary, Plato was a philosopher and a part-time mythologist. Moreover, he was not even an ordinary philosopher; rather, he was a 'true philosopher', whose interests lay primarily in metaphysical, otherworldly matters. Therefore, if there is any truth behind Plato's account of Atlantis (and that's a big 'if'), it is unlikely to have anything to do with history or geography; rather, it should be rooted in myth, mysticism, esotericism and the metaphysical world.

Problem 2: Herodotus

It is highly significant that Herodotus, the so-called 'father of history', said nothing at all about any war between Athens and Atlantis. Writing almost a century before Plato, Herodotus was widely travelled (he had visited Egypt where the Atlantis story supposedly came from) and very knowledgeable about military history. But as far as he was concerned, the greatest wars of history had been those between Greeks and Persians, notably the battle of Marathon (490 BC), the battles of Thermopylae and Salamis (480 BC), and the battle of Plataea (479 BC).[6] Moreover, in regard to the battle of Plataea, Herodotus tells a highly revealing story of a bragging contest between the Athenians and the Tegeans in which each side listed their greatest military accomplishments. Here, the Athenians recited their heroism at the battle of Marathon, but spoke also of their achievements in 'ancient times' – their intervention in the war of 'the Seven against Thebes', their repulsion of the Amazonians who had invaded Attica, and their instrumental role in the Trojan War.[7] But as for the idea that their ancestors had repulsed the invasion of Atlantis, the Athenian soldiers said nothing at all – a very strange omission if Plato's account contained any historical truth.

Plato's story is also called into question by several other statements made by Herodotus. The greatest danger ever faced by the Athenians, he said, was when the Persian army had invaded Attica and instigated the battle of Marathon (490 BC).[8] The biggest armed force ever assembled, he said, was that of the Persian king Xerxes (480 BC).[9] The biggest island in the whole world, he said, was Sardinia.[10] And the earliest sea empire in the Mediterranean, he said, had been forged by king Minos of Knossos.[11]

All of these claims fly in the face of Plato's claim, nearly a century later, that Atlantis had been the biggest island in the world and had assembled the largest army ever, to forge the first sea empire of the Mediterranean.

Thus spoke the historian Herodotus who, had he lived a century later, would have been highly sceptical of the historicity of Plato's story.

Problem 3: Socrates

Socrates was one of the greatest intellectuals of his day, and yet when Critias introduced the story of Athens' heroic victory over Atlantis, he responded by saying: "Tell me though, what was that ancient deed our city performed...? I've never heard of it."[12] If the Athenian victory had been magnificent in a historical sense, or even in an orthodox mythical sense (as in their involvement in the Trojan War or the earlier epic battle 'the Seven against Thebes'), then Socrates certainly *would* have heard of it. *QED*. We must be dealing here with a myth and, moreover, with a *new* myth – perhaps a variation on a theme.

Problem 4: The Saite Calendar

That a cataclysm could have instigated the beginning of a calendar nine thousand years before the time of Solon (*c*. 9600 BC) is not implausible. Nor is it implausible that such a calendar could have been preserved for nine thousand years and handed down for posterity via the Egyptian Saites (compare the Hebrew calendar which is today nearly six thousand years old). It is therefore *possible* that Solon (or perhaps Plato himself) learned the date of the Atlantis cataclysm from the Egyptian priests at the town of Sais. But the important question is this: is it really *likely* that the date of the cataclysm originated in this way?

In fact, everything we know about ancient Egypt argues against the possibility. Archaeologists have found no evidence at all for a calendar of this ilk.[13] Nor is there any such evidence in the Egyptian texts, which generally refer to ancient events in the vaguest of terms.[14] Moreover, even when we do find numbers in these texts, they usually turn out to be sacred, symbolic or rounded, the latter suggesting some imaginative ex-post rationalisation by the priests.[15] To presume, as some researchers do, that the Saites possessed a calendar dating back nine thousand years (to a time one thousand years earlier than the foundation of their own state) is to go far beyond what can be justified.

There is more. Why is it that the Saite tradition preserved only the date of the Atlantis cataclysm? After all, Plato had the Egyptian priest claim that *several* cataclysms had occurred *after* the sinking of Atlantis,

including the famous flood of Deucalion. And yet nowhere in Egypt, nor
in Plato, nor anywhere else in the Greek writings, do we find any record
of the dates of these subsequent cataclysms. If Solon (or Plato) really did
receive the date of the Atlantis cataclysm from the Egyptian priests, why
did he not also receive the dates of the other, more recent events?

There is another problem, too. Why is it that *only the Egyptian Saites*
preserved the date of the Atlantis cataclysm? If the event was historical
and as dramatic as Plato suggests, then it would have affected much of
the world and would have been recorded in other ancient traditions. But
despite the prevalence of worldwide flood myths (generally offshoots of
the exploded planet mythos) no record has ever been found pointing to
the date 9600 BC.

In summary, it is a leap of faith to suppose that the Egyptian Saites
had access to the purported date when no-one else in the world did; it is a
further leap of faith to suppose that the Egyptian records were entirely
destroyed (from an archaeological perspective); it is a further leap of
faith to suppose that Solon had access to these records when no-one else
did; and it is a leap of faith, too, to suppose that Solon's testimony fell
into the hands of Plato and no-one else. To go with all these suppositions
is to hop, skip and jump into the land of improbability. And there still
remains the awkward problem of explaining how Plato (or the Egyptians,
if one prefers) knew the date of the Atlantis cataclysm but not the dates
of the three, more recent cataclysms that followed it, including the well-
known flood of Deucalion.

Problem 5: Lost Civilisations

The implication of the historicist argument is that *two* highly advanced
civilisations – Atlantis and Athens respectively – existed *c*. 9600 BC. And
yet, according to archaeologists, civilisation began much more recently,
c. 4000 BC (in the lands of ancient Egypt and Mesopotamia). How, then,
could the two fantastic civilisations described by Plato have existed more
than five thousand years earlier, during what archaeologists call 'the
neolithic period'? The idea is controversial, to say the least.

As regards Atlantis, it should be abundantly clear from the citations in
the previous chapter that Plato placed the former island in the Atlantic
Ocean. On this point, his language is unequivocal. Atlantis had been in
the great Ocean, in the Atlantis Ocean, in the realm of Atlas, opposite the
Pillars of Heracles (the straits of Gibraltar) and, fully consistent with this,
the Atlantians had directed their hostilities against Europe and Asia. To
look for Atlantis anywhere else but the Atlantic Ocean is to totally ignore

what Plato actually wrote. Unfortunately for Atlantis-hunters, this leads to a fundamental problem, namely that scientists have nowadays mapped the floor of the Atlantic Ocean, in outline, using echo sounders, 'Geosat' radar and multibeam sonar, without discovering any trace of the sunken island or continent as described by Plato.[16] The historicist interpretation of Plato's Atlantis is thus strongly contradicted by scientific evidence.

Moreover, there is equally strong evidence against the idea of a 10th millennium BC civilisation in Athens in Greece. The earliest temples in Athens, for example, have been dated archaeologically to only the 8th century BC; below their foundations there is only virgin soil.[17]

On the face of it, then, as we enter the 21st century AD, the notion of two highly advanced civilisations fighting a worldwide war *c.* 9600 BC would seem to be a complete fantasy.

Reasons to be Dogmatic

The reaction of Atlantis-hunters to this non-discovery of Atlantis on the floor of the Atlantic Ocean has been to suggest that the story was garbled at some point or else expressed in poetic terms, thus causing Plato to cite an incorrect geography. This assumption means that the lost island can be moved from the Atlantic to any other alternative location, preferably one that has not been mapped by sonar! The problem with this approach is that, once one presumes Plato to have made one mistake (with the location), it becomes tempting to take a little licence with the text, and then some more licence still, and thus the situation arises where Atlantis-hunters produce 'solutions' that owe little to what Plato actually said. At the extreme, some researchers have actually staked their reputations on islands that have not yet sunk.[18] To which one might well retort that if an island isn't sunk, then it aint Plato's Atlantis.

Why is it that so many researchers (often very intelligent people) have sought Atlantis in direct contradiction to Plato's words? The answer must surely be their unquestioning belief in the historicity of the story. Atlantis existed, but it is not on the floor of the Atlantic Ocean. *QED.* It must be somewhere else.

Why, then, do Atlantis-hunters hold so dogmatically to their historicist interpretation of the story?

The explanation is twofold.

Firstly, Plato describes the island of Atlantis – its sacred mound and temple, its land and sea rings, its bridges, harbour and canals, its inhabitants, and its topography – in such vivid and realistic detail that it is difficult to believe he was not recalling an account of someone's actual visit to the lost kingdom. As Geoffrey Ashe commented in 1992:

> [Plato's] description of the lost land... ranges so far beyond his
> requirements as to excuse a feeling that there is more here than meets
> the eye, that there must be something in it.[19]

Secondly, Plato insisted repeatedly that the Atlantis story was 'true'. The
first such remark comes from Critias, who assures Socrates that 'every
word of the story is true'.[20] A short while later, Critias reports how Solon
brought the tale back from Egypt, and he again refers to it as a 'true
story'.[21] Then, after Critias has finished his short version of the story, it is
Socrates himself who comments that: "the fact that it's no made-up story
but a true account is no small matter."[22] In addition, similar comments are
made about Athens and the Athenians. The Egyptian report about ancient
Athens is declared to be 'true', whilst the Athenians are said to be 'the
ones who *really* existed at that time', i.e. nine thousand years before the
time of Solon.[23] The whole point of the Athens and Atlantis story is that
Socrates' theoretical ideal state should be illustrated by a true account
from ancient history.

But do these two points really argue for a historicist interpretation of
Atlantis? To begin with the first point, it has been amply demonstrated in
the previous chapter that Plato brought Atlantis to life in order to make a
moral and political commentary on the 4th century state of Athens; this
would explain much of the vivid detail, and it might well explain all of it.
Everything, then, rests on the second point – that the story was a true
account from ancient history. However, as we shall now see, this idea
may be understood perfectly well from a non-historical point of view.

Mythical Truth

The gist of this book, so far, is that the myths of the gods, as related by
the poets Homer and Hesiod, reflected a sacred 'truth' concerning the
beginning of the Universe and of life on Earth. This 'truth', which had
been invented by earlier civilisations and maintained for millennia by
way of encoded myths and rituals, postulated the explosion of a living
planet and the conveyance of its oceanic waters and meteoritic seeds of
life to the Earth. Significantly, this myth, of the fall of Heaven to Earth,
could be told in many different ways – as an act of love, as a rape, as a
war between gods and Titans, as a monster cast into the Underworld, as a
god flung into the depths of the sea, and so on and so forth.

Whether or not this exploded planet myth fulfils the modern, scientific
criteria for 'truth' is an interesting but moot point. The important thing is
that the ancient Greeks *believed* that this myth was true (although in most

cases without actually knowing what the myth meant!).[24] Accordingly, those in the know could recite the myths of the gods from Homer's *Iliad* and *Odyssey*, and from Hesiod's *Theogony* and *Works and Days*, and maintain, in all seriousness, that they were retelling a 'true story', i.e. the encoded story of the exploded planet.

Might Plato's story of the war between Athens and Atlantis be 'true' in this mythical sense? Plato indeed asserts in *Timaeus* that his story was of exactly the same ilk as the poems of Homer and Hesiod:

> (Elder Critias:) "It's too bad that Solon wrote poetry only as a diversion... And too bad that he never finished the story he'd brought back home with him from Egypt... Otherwise not even Hesiod or Homer, or any other poet at all, would ever have become more famous than he."[25]

This point is later reiterated, when Critias refers to "Solon, when he was contemplating his own poetic version of this tale..."[26] Together, these two statements – that Solon's story was 'poetic' and that it was comparable to the poetry of Homer and Hesiod – raise intriguing questions about the status and meaning of the story. Might it somehow relate to mythical events at the beginning of time? Might it be 'true' in the sense that things had 'truly' happened when the exploded planet gods fought wars and then divided up the whole world between them?

If we view Plato's story in this way, as a myth, a new picture emerges which challenges fundamentally the historicist theory. The war between Athens and Atlantis, for example, would become an allegorical war, no different in concept from the war between Zeus and the Titans. And thus, by the same token, the ancient Athenians who fought the war might have 'really existed' in the same sense as Kronos and the Titans existed, i.e. in a mythical sense, as personifications of cosmic powers – a theme that was indeed very close to Plato's heart (see chapter four).

In the remainder of this chapter, I shall be demonstrating just how well Plato's story does fit the mould of a myth pertaining to the beginning of the world. In particular, I will explain how the Atlantis story involves:

1   Mythical Places.

2   A Mythical Time Scale; and

3   Mythical Peoples.

If the reader will indulge me, I will explain why Atlantis was no ordinary island, its people no ordinary people, and its war against Europe and Asia no ordinary war.

Mythical Places

Let us begin with ancient Athens. In the previous chapter, we saw that the city which Athene and Hephaestus founded 'nine thousand years ago' was radically different from the Athens of Plato's day. In particular, the acropolis had been much larger and covered with soil (as opposed to bare limestone), and it had boasted an idyllic spring which provided abundant waters to the twenty thousand soldiers who lived there.[27] It was the same story in the surrounding state of Attica. Not only had the territory been much greater, but also it had benefited from an extensive covering of rich and fertile soil, and an abundance of waters.[28]

This ancient land of Athens and Attica, said Critias, had surpassed all other lands in its fertility.[29] In addition, the entire region had enjoyed a perfect climate ('moderately harmonised'),[30] whilst the spring on the acropolis had boasted waters that were 'neither too cold in the winter nor too hot in the summer'.[31] All in all, Plato's language is reminiscent of that used elsewhere in the Greek myths to describe idyllic utopias and golden ages.[32] It would be fair to say that this fictional ideal state was 'ideal' in more ways than one.

Unfortunately, however, this ancient, utopian state of Athens had been eroded gradually over the space of nine thousand years as a result of a sequence of cataclysms. Ancient Athens had, in effect, become a lost paradise.

Turning to the island of Atlantis, we find a similar story. Once again, we find a highly fertile soil, waters in abundance, and a perfect climate ('a fostering Sun').[33] As a result, the 'sacred island' had produced all kinds of plants and crops in abundance ('products lovely, marvellous and of abundant bounty'), and 'trees of extraordinary beauty and height'.[34]

In addition, there were the mines of Atlantis, which had produced gold, *oreichalkos*, silver, copper and tin in such prodigious quantities that the kings had amassed more wealth than any other dynasty in the world.[35] Here, the *oreichalkos* constitutes a mystery in itself. It was recalled by Critias as 'that metal which is now only a name to us, but which was then more than a name', as if to imply that it belonged to a long-lost, fairy tale world.[36] Its name meant simply 'mountain bronze', but it was clearly no ordinary kind of bronze, for Plato ranked it above silver and second only to gold.[37]

According to Critias, everything in Atlantis had been the biggest or prettiest of its kind existing anywhere in the world. Enclosing the city, for example, there had been a highly fertile plain, 'the loveliest of all plains', whilst surrounding this plain there had been a ring of mountains, 'legendary in number, size and beauty' and beyond compare of any mountain ranges of the 5th-4th centuries BC.[38]

This is heady stuff, of a fairy tale nature, and it elicits visions of an otherworldly paradise or utopia, as in the case of Athens and the land of Attica discussed earlier. Many scholars have noted this theme; the British academic Christopher Gill, for example, commented as follows in his 1980 book *The Atlantis Story*:

> The fertility of the earth in ancient Athens and Atlantis, the profusion of its gifts, the biannual harvests in Atlantis, the relative freedom from the toils of agriculture – all this recalls the life of the golden race in Hesiod (*Works and Days*) and of Homer's Phaeacia (*Odyssey*).[39]

Gill's first reference here is to the golden race, of whom Hesiod sang:

> They lived like gods, with carefree heart, remote from toil and misery... All good things were theirs, and the grain-giving soil bore its fruits of its own accord in unstinted plenty, while they at their leisure harvested their fields in contentment amid abundance.[40]

Whilst the whereabouts of this land was not identified, Hesiod did make it perfectly clear that the golden race had lived in a primordial age, long before true men and women (the so-called 'iron race') had been created at the time of Deucalion's flood. In other words, the utopian paradise of the golden race belonged to a purely mythical time frame.

As for Phaeacia, there is indeed a remarkable parallel with Atlantis in that its king, Alcinous, dwelt in a fantastic palace built of gold, silver and bronze, whilst a walled garden nearby contained fruit trees 'whose fruit never fails nor runs short, winter and summer alike', and a vineyard and vegetable beds which were 'luxuriantly productive all the year round'.[41] Significantly, perhaps, this utopian paradise was not a real place, but a mythical location, situated on the island of Scherie in the western Ocean, in the remote west, 'at the edge of the world'.[42] It was one of many fairy tale lands which Homer had invented for his poem of the wanderings of Odysseus, whom the Phaeacians had conveyed home from the Ocean in their magical ships.[43]

The mythical status of Scherie is underlined by the mythical qualities of its people, the Phaeacians. According to Homer, they were 'famous and intrepid mariners', whose sole raison d'etre was to spend their days sailing the ocean, for no apparent purpose other than to occasionally convey a dignitary abroad or rescue a stranded sailor.[44] Moreover, the ships of the Phaeacians were magical ships – 'as swift as a bird or as thought itself' – and they had no rudders but knew intuitively what their captains and crews were thinking.[45] And, in addition to this, the origin of the Phaeacians was steeped in legend. Their first king, Nausithous, it was said, had been a son of Poseidon and was descended, on his mother's side, from the race of the Giants.[46] He had led his people on an exodus from Hypereie – their former homeland – and settled them in Scherie, 'at the edge of the world', where they would remain 'close to the gods' but separate from other peoples.[47] It was from Poseidon that the Phaeacians had received their supernatural gifts and sea-faring privileges. But the Earth-shaker had warned them that one day he would wreck one of their ships, turning it to stone and fixing it to the bottom of the sea, or, failing this, surround their capital city with a wall of mountains (the parallels here to Atlantis are intriguing).[48]

Was Atlantis, too, a utopian paradise like the island of Scherie? Did it, too, exist as a kind of never-never land in a mythical time frame?

Perhaps the answer to this question is to be found in the rectangular plain of Atlantis – 'the loveliest of all plains' – which is reminiscent of the Elysian Plain – an otherworldly location to which the blessed dead would be conveyed in the afterlife. One of the earliest literary references to this Plain appears in Homer's *Odyssey*, where the hero Menelaus is told:

> "It is not your fate to die in Argos... Instead, the immortals will send
> you to the Elysian Plain at the ends of the Earth, to join auburn-haired
> Rhadamanthus in the land where living is made easy for man, where
> no snow falls, no strong winds blow, and there is never any rain..."[49]

The idea here was that the souls of the blessed dead could be conveyed, in the afterlife, to an idyllic environment, as if travelling back in time to the golden age (as described by Hesiod, see earlier). Accordingly, the utopian paradise motif reoccurs, but this time associated with an abode in the remote west ('the ends of the Earth') – the same direction, it should be noted, as the island of Atlantis (not to mention Scherie, the island of the Phaeacians).

But there is more. In *Works and Days*, Hesiod referred to the Elysian land as a series of *islands*, the Islands of the Blessed:

> To some [of the heroes] Zeus granted a life and home apart from men,
> and settled them at the ends of the Earth. These dwell with carefree
> heart in the Islands of the Blessed, beside deep-swirling Oceanus –
> fortunate heroes indeed, for whom the grain-giving soil bears its
> honey-sweet fruits three times a year.[50]

The parallels between the Elysian islands and Atlantis are stunning and

age, the bronze age, and the age of heroes (the present age was known, poetically, as the iron age).[59] This scheme of Hesiod's was as close as the early Greeks ever came to a chronology of the past but, significantly, it involved no absolute or even relative dates. On the contrary, Hesiod used the succession of metals – gold, silver, bronze and iron – to illustrate, in the broadest of terms, the progressive decline of man, from his carefree life in the golden age to his life of 'ceaseless toil and misery' in the present age of iron.

The heroic age, too, lacked a time line. Despite all the attention paid by poets to the Trojan War and the earlier epic battle 'the Seven against Thebes', no absolute or relative dates were ever given, and there are good reasons for believing that these battles were essentially mythical, involving as they did 'god-like' heroes who were capable of superhuman and supernatural feats.[60] All things considered, the heroic age is best imagined as a twilight age which existed somewhere between the time of the gods and the time of the true human race.

So, in the absence of any absolute or even relative chronology of the past, where did Plato's date 'nine thousand years ago' spring from? The answer, it transpires, is not from any ancient Saite calendar, but from a Greek way of speaking about large numbers and long periods of time.

Consider, for example, the following citations from the books of Plato himself.

Firstly, in *Laws* book III, a Cretan named Clinias relates a simplistic version of the history of man:

> "The upshot of all this, I suppose, is that for millions of years these techniques remained unknown to primitive man. Then, a thousand or two thousand years ago, Daedalus and Orpheus and Palamedes made their various discoveries, Marsyas and Olympus pioneered the art of music, Amphion invented the lyre, and many other discoveries were made by other people."[61]

Here, we find an arbitrary reference to 'thousands of years', and a loose way of speaking about one-thousand-year intervals. Elsewhere, however, we find specific references to periods such as 'nine thousand years' or 'ten thousand years'.

For example, in Plato's discussion of the soul and its cycle of rebirth, he describes the Orphic belief in a great cycle of ten thousand years, at the culmination of which a soul could return to its former place in the heavens.[62] The following lines are spoken by Socrates in *Phaedrus*:

> "In fact, no soul returns to the place from which it came for ten thousand years, since its wings will not grow before then, except for

the soul of a true philosopher. If, after the third cycle of one thousand years, the last-mentioned souls have chosen such a life three times in a row, they grow their wings back, and they depart [for Heaven] in the three-thousandth year."[63]

As we see here, the ten-thousand-year Orphic cycle was divided into ten periods of a thousand years. Indeed, it is pertinent to note that, with a thousand years being spent in Heaven or beneath the earth, nine thousand years played a key role in the cycle. Hence Socrates went on to refer to the soul 'tossing around for nine thousand years on the Earth'.[64]

This is not to suggest that the 'nine thousand years' of the Athens and Atlantis story is linked to the Orphic cycle of the soul. Rather, the point is that the Greeks referred to one thousand years, nine thousand years or ten thousand years as convenient markers of time. Moreover, the Greeks sometimes used even higher multiples, as in the myth that Zeus had bound Prometheus to the Caucasus Mountain and consigned him to the Underworld for thirty thousand years (or, by other traditions, for one thousand years or ten thousand years).[65] The idea, in each case, was that Prometheus had been bound for an eternity. The figures, individually, should not be taken too literally.

Turning now, briefly, to the works of Homer, we find further food for thought. In the *Odyssey*, when Odysseus visits the land of the dead, the spirits come up from the world below 'in their tens of thousands'.[66] Here, the number 'ten thousand' seems to have been purely symbolic of a great multitude.

A similar idea is evident in the *Iliad*, but here with a twist:

Then Diomedes, master of the war-cry, made his attack... and Pallas Athene leaned on the spear and forced it into the base of Ares' belly... And brazen Ares screamed, loud as the shout of *nine thousand or ten thousand* men on a battlefield...[67]

This same expression reoccurs later in the *Iliad*, when Poseidon departs from Agamemnon's presence uttering a war-cry 'as loud as the shout of nine thousand or ten thousand men...'.[68]

What to make of this? Homer, one of the founding voices of ancient Greek tradition, was using 'nine thousand' and 'ten thousand' as almost interchangeable expressions for the idea of 'a vast multitude'. Surely the Greeks – brought up in their youth on a staple diet of Homer – would have known these expressions and used them in everyday conversation, in numerous different ways.

This is indeed reflected in the works of Plato. In *Republic* book VII, for example, Socrates suggests that the insight of the soul is worth more than 'ten thousand eyes'.[69] And in *Statesman*, the philosopher from Elea describes how the craftsman of the cosmos allows the Universe to 'travel backwards, for many tens of thousands of revolutions'.[70]

In view of these references, and those cited earlier, it is surely unwise to take Plato literally when he writes that certain states were founded 'nine thousand years ago' or 'ten thousand years ago'.

None of this should come as a surprise to qualified academics. In the book *Aeschylus: Prometheus Bound*, Mark Griffith, Professor of Classics at the University of California, observes the very practice which I have just identified. In his discussion of the ten thousand years' punishment of Prometheus, he translates the Greek 'ten thousand' as 'for ages' and adds the note 'ten thousand used, as often, to denote untold numbers'.[71] In a later set of notes, pertaining to the related play *Prometheus, Bearer of Fire*, Griffith adds the note 'ten thousand years long, i.e. many years long', and finally he adds the comment that 'Prometheus was apparently sentenced to 30,000 years of punishment, i.e. a virtual eternity.'[72] Clearly I am not the first to have pursued this line of thought.

So much for the significance of ten thousand years. But what about the 'nine thousand years' in the story of Athens and Atlantis? Is this figure, likewise, symbolic of an eternity? Although I am not aware of scholars commenting specifically on this point, Plato seems to provide the answer in *Laws* book III, where he records the belief that the founding of states had been happening for 'an enormously long period of time' and for 'an indefinitely long period of time'.[73] And yet it was Plato himself who said that Egypt was ten thousand years old, Athens nine thousand years old, and Sais eight thousand years old.[74] Logic would thus dictate that all of these figures symbolised 'an enormously long period of time' and 'an indefinitely long period of time', i.e. a virtual eternity.

The point is underlined still further in Plato's appendix to *Laws* (*Epinomis*), where an Athenian philosopher discusses how the science of astronomy began in Egypt and Syria, and then observes that:

> "From there, after being closely examined *for thousands of years, in fact an infinite time*, this knowledge spread everywhere including Greece."[75]

Here, the equation is made totally explicit. 'Thousands of years' amounts to 'an infinite time'. *QED*.

Plato, it must be emphasised, knew and used the popular Greek idioms involving 'thousands' and 'ten thousand' and 'thousands of years'. And, furthermore, he was perfectly aware of the Pythagorean symbolism of the numbers '9' and '10', in addition to the poetic tradition concerning these same numbers (for an explanation and examples, see the attached note).[76] Therefore, there is nothing particularly unusual in Plato's claims that Egypt was founded '*ten* thousand years ago', Athens '*nine* thousand years ago', or Sais '*eight* thousand years ago'. He was simply using the idiomatic language of his day to lend great antiquity and prestige to these lands, which had been founded by the gods ten, nine and eight *aeons* ago, respectively.

There is no contradiction, therefore, in the idea that Atlantis sank 'nine thousand years ago' and yet, at the same time, during a pre-diluvian, pre-Deucalion age. No. We are dealing, quite clearly, with a mythical time frame, when the gods were in charge of the Earth, and when a mythical, pre-human type of man was roaming our planet.

This way of thinking will come as a shock to most Atlantologists, who are committed to a historicist perspective. But the truth is that ancient peoples have always regarded the past with a different perspective from the one that we hold so sacrosanct today. Take, for example, the ancient Hebrews. They believed that the world had been created by God in just six days (perhaps symbolising six thousand years) and that the first man, Adam, had been born only 1,948 years before the birth of their ancestor Abraham. This chronology, which still finds support today among Jewish and Christian fundamentalists, makes the Earth only some thousands of years old. And yet modern scientific studies, in contrast, have estimated the Earth's age at around 4,600,000,000 years. All those zeros underline the considerable variance between the ancient and modern perspectives of time. To us modern folk, nine thousand years seems paltry and takes us back merely to a phase in human prehistory, more than four billion years *after* the Earth was formed. But to the ancient Hebrews, nine thousand years took them back to the very beginning of time, when Elohim was contemplating his creation of Heaven and Earth.

The point is brought home forcefully by the fact that the priests of the Mazdean religion of ancient Iran believed that the Universe was nine thousand years old – exactly the same age which Plato cited for sunken Atlantis.[77]

Oddly enough, I am not the first to visualise the story of Atlantis against the backdrop of a primordial age. Back in 1869, the French writer Jules Verne expressed the very same idea in his book *Twenty Thousand Leagues under the Sea*. The theme of the novel, briefly, is this: a marine biologist, Professor Aronnax, is captured by a Captain Nemo, who takes the professor aboard his revolutionary submarine the *Nautilus*. Nemo then conducts Aronnax on a tour of the ocean depths, using diving outfits to occasionally explore the sea-bed. On one of these excursions, Nemo takes his guest to the sunken ruins of Atlantis. In the following extract, the first lines spoken by Aronnax are memorable, for they are quoted often by mystery writers for the purpose of titillating their readers. But the lines which follow are barely known at all for reasons which will soon become apparent. Here, then, are Aronnax's thoughts as he stands in his diving suit in awe at the vast sunken ruins:

> Down below, before my very eyes, lay the ruins of a submerged city, swallowed by the sea... Where was I? Where could all this be? I had to know, regardless of consequences! I felt a sudden impulse to speak, to tear off the helmet I was wearing! But Captain Nemo stopped me with a gesture. He came to me, picked up a piece of chalky rock, walked to a block of black basalt, and scribbled one single word: 'ATLANTIS'. What a thrill that word gave me!... Here I was, by the strangest destiny setting foot on one of the mountains of that continent! With my hand I was touching those ruins thousands of centuries old, contemporary with geological times! I was treading the same ground where the contemporaries of the first man had trodden! My heavy boots were crushing the skeletons of animals of prehistoric times...![78]

What a revelation it is to read these lines, penned by Jules Verne in 1869. The lost continent of Atlantis, said Verne, was 'thousands of centuries old', i.e. at least two hundred thousand years old and perhaps a great deal older than that. Perhaps he was thinking of nine thousand centuries, i.e. nine hundred thousand years; although 'geological times' might suggest to us an even older figure, such as 'nine million years ago' or even 'nine hundred million years ago'. Of course, the actual figure is irrelevant. Our concept of the Earth's age and its geological eras differs from Verne's concept, just as his concept differed from Plato's. Verne was simply telling us, in the early scientific language of his day, that Atlantis had sunk at a time when some of the earliest primordial creatures had been moving on the surface of the Earth. Plato, it would seem, was telling us the same thing, but in the idiomatic language of the Greeks.

Mythical People

Was the war between ancient Athens and Atlantis fought by mythical, pre-human peoples? Was it similar in concept to the war between Zeus and the Titans, in which the gods personified the violent clash between Heaven and Earth? Was the war simply a retelling of the age-old true myth of the exploded planet? All of these points will be discussed in due course, but first the reader must grasp the concept of pre-human peoples, and understand how the Greeks visualised them.

As discussed earlier, the Greeks believed that time had begun with a golden age, when the gods themselves had been in charge of the Earth, under the leadership of Kronos. In those days, there had been people on the Earth, but they were not of our kind. Plato gives an account of this idyllic era in *Laws*, book IV:

> "Countless ages before the formation of the states described earlier, they say there existed, in the age of Kronos, a form of government and administration which was a great success, and which served as a blueprint for the best run of our present-day states... The traditional account that has come down to us tells of the wonderfully happy life people lived then, and how they were provided with everything in abundance and without any effort on their part... (Kronos) appointed kings and rulers for states; they were not men, but beings of a superior and more divine order – spirits... the result of their attentions was peace, respect for others, good laws, justice in full measure, and a state of happiness and harmony among the races of the world."[79]

A similar scenario had been portrayed by Hesiod some three centuries earlier in his poem *Works and Days*:

> The race of men that the immortals who dwell on Olympus made first of all was of gold. They were in the time of Kronos, when he was king in Heaven; and they lived like gods with carefree heart, remote from toil and misery. Wretched old age did not affect them either, but with hands and feet ever unchanged they enjoyed themselves in feasting, beyond all ills, and they died as if overcome by sleep. All good things were theirs, and the grain-giving soil bore its fruits of its own accord in unstinted plenty, while they at their leisure harvested their fields in contentment amid abundance.[80]

The idyllic imagery here is reminiscent of Plato's ancient Athens and Atlantis. But what about the golden age people? Although they were human-*like*, they were not actually human, for they were not affected by 'wretched old age'. Rather, they constituted a superhuman, mythical race of people. The message for Atlantologists should ring loud and clear.

What happened to the golden race? Hesiod reports that they were simply 'covered up by the earth'. But then, a strange thing happened. The golden race overcame death and returned to life in the form of ghost-like spirits (*daimones*) who dwelt upon the face of the Earth as 'watchers over mortal men'. This, as we shall see, was a unique distinction.

Hesiod then goes on to describes how the gods made a new people, the silver race:

Afterwards [after the demise of the golden race], the gods of Olympus made a second race, much inferior, out of silver. It resembled the golden one neither in body nor in disposition. For a hundred years a boy would stay in the care of his mother, playing childishly at home; but after reaching adolescence and the appointed span of youthful manhood, they lived but a little time, and in suffering, because of their witlessness.[81]

Evidently, this silver race was not humanity as we know it. Admittedly, it was human-*like*. But what kind of humans could have lived as infants for one hundred years? What kind of humans could have experienced natural deaths in early adulthood? Once again, we are dealing with a mythical race.

As for the fate of the silver people, Hesiod states that: 'they were put away by Zeus... angry because they did not offer honour to the blessed gods who occupy Olympus. Since the earth covered up this race in its turn, they have been called the mortal blessed below, second in rank...'[82]

After the demise of the silver race, Hesiod claims that Zeus made a new people out of bronze:

Then Zeus the father made yet a third race of men, of bronze, not like the silver in anything. Out of ash-trees [*meliai*] he made them, a terrible and fierce race, occupied with the woeful works of Ares [the god of war] and with acts of violence; they ate undomesticated crops, their stern hearts were made of adamant [an unconquerable metal], they were unshapen hulks with great strength and indescribable arms growing from their shoulders above their sturdy bodies. They had bronze armour, bronze houses, and with bronze they laboured... they were laid low by their own hands, and they went down to chill Hades' house of decay leaving no names; mighty though they were, dark death got them and they left the bright sunlight.[83]

Once again, we find a human-*like* people. But human they certainly were not. Intriguingly, the mention of 'stern hearts', 'unshapen hulks', 'great strength', 'sturdy bodies' and 'bronze armour' evokes the giants and god-like heroes who featured in the Homeric epics the *Iliad* and the *Odyssey*.[84] Were these giants and bronze-clad heroes really human beings (as scholars generally presume), or were they, in fact, a race of genuinely superhuman beings, i.e. a truly mythical race? Hesiod's description, just like Homer's, teasingly begs the question.

In any event, Hesiod makes it clear that true human beings originated with the iron race, who were created *after* the various peoples described above. The overall picture is summarised in the table below:

Hesiod's Scheme of the Five World Ages

Age	People	Fate of the people
Gold	Golden race of men (lived carefree lives)	For no apparent reason, the Earth covered them up, and they became guardian spirits.
Silver	Silver race of men (lived a prolonged childhood, and a brief, anarchic adulthood)	Refused to serve the gods; Zeus put them away; covered up by the Earth.
Bronze	Bronze race of men (terrible, fierce and violent)	Killed each other and descended to Hades.
Iron	The true human race (ceaseless toil and misery)	Destined to be destroyed by Zeus.

(Source: Hesiod's *Works and Days*, but excluding the race of heroes.)[85]

As for the transition from the bronze race to the iron race, this is covered by two Greek myths – the creation of Pandora (a prototype woman) by the gods, and the creation of men and women by Deucalion and Pyrrha. Both of these myths are now worth examining briefly, for they confirm beyond doubt that the true human race, and particularly human women (as we know them today), did not exist before the flood of Deucalion. And this would imply that the peoples of Athens and Atlantis, living as they did three aeons *before* the flood of Deucalion, could not possibly have been real human beings, but must have been mythical, pre-human beings.

The myth of Pandora begins with the god Prometheus who was, by some accounts, the creator of mankind. According to Plato's version of events, Prometheus had been responsible for providing man with all the arts and crafts that he required for survival on the day when he was due to be born from the Underworld (i.e. from the womb of the Earth).[86] But Prometheus had asked his ill-fated brother Epimetheus to oversee this task, and Epimetheus had messed up.[87] Man had therefore emerged into the world above naked and in danger of imminent extinction; and thus it came to pass that Prometheus had stolen the fire of the gods (either from the Underworld or from Heaven) and given it to man, thus saving our species and putting it on the road to civilisation.[88]

For his theft of fire, Prometheus had been punished by Zeus, who had nailed him to a pillar or, by another tradition, chained him to the Caucasus Mountain and plunged him into the Underworld.[89] Either way, Prometheus had been sentenced to an eternity of torture. In addition, Zeus had decided to punish man by creating a bane that would cause him unhappiness and trouble for all eternity. Accordingly, Zeus had specified the design for the first ever woman, Pandora, and ordered Hephaestus to mould the creature out of earth and water. In due course, Pandora had been led out of the Underworld and presented to man, who, bewitched by her great beauty, immediately accepted her. The name of the newly-created woman was Pandora, meaning 'All-gift'. Hesiod takes up the story in *Works and Days*:

> At once the renowned Hephaestus moulded from earth the likeness of a modest maiden... and the pale-eyed goddess Athene dressed and adorned her... In her breast, Hermes [the messenger of the gods] fashioned lies, and wily pretences, and a knavish nature... and he put in a voice... and he named this woman Pandora, All-gift, because all the dwellers on Olympus made her their gift – a calamity for men who live by bread...

> For formerly the tribes of men on Earth lived remote from evils, without harsh toil and the grievous sicknesses that are deadly to men. But the woman unstopped the jar and let it all out, and brought grim cares upon man. Only Hope remained there, inside in her secure dwelling, under the lip of the jar...[90]

Hesiod makes it clear that Pandora was the archetype of the present-day race of human women (of whom he obviously had no high opinion), and, moreover, he pinpoints the time scale of events by linking the myth of Pandora to the beginning of the present iron age, which he describes in much the same terms as above – an age of 'toil and misery', 'constant distress' and 'harsh troubles' for mankind.[91] The important implication is that the earlier races of bronze, silver and gold were *pre-human* peoples.

This conclusion is confirmed by the myth of the creation of men and women from stones, in the aftermath of Deucalion's flood. The tale was dealt with earlier, in chapter four, and I will not regurgitate it here, but I will cite the version by Apollodorus (2nd century BC), for he identifies most clearly the all-important time line:

> *When Zeus wanted to eliminate the race of bronze*, Deucalion, on the advice of (his father) Prometheus, built a chest, and after storing it with provisions, climbed into it with Pyrrha. (Then) Zeus poured an abundance of rain from Heaven to flood the greater part of Greece, and caused all of mankind to be destroyed... But Deucalion was carried across the sea in his chest for nine days and as many nights until he was washed ashore at (Mount) Parnassus; and there, when the rain stopped, he disembarked and offered a sacrifice to Zeus, God of

Escape. Zeus sent Hermes to him and allowed him the choice of whatever he wished; and Deucalion chose to have people. On the orders of Zeus, he picked up stones and threw them over his head; and the stones that Deucalion threw became men, and those that Pyrrha threw became women.[92]

This was the moment, in popular Greek tradition, when the true human race had been created. Moreover, the myth of Deucalion was equated by the Greeks with the myth of Pandora cited earlier (the links between Prometheus and Pandora, on the one hand, and Deucalion and Pyrrha, on the other hand, are legendary).[93] Both marked the close of the bronze age and the beginning of the present iron age (as Apollodorus puts it, 'Zeus wanted to eliminate the race of bronze'). And therefore, it follows (as it did earlier) that the earlier races of gold, silver and bronze were *pre-human* peoples.

My argument, to recap, is simple. Plato said that ancient Athens had been devastated and Atlantis destroyed by 'the third cataclysmic storm *before* the flood of Deucalion', i.e. aeons before the close of Hesiod's bronze age. And yet true humans had been created in the *aftermath* of Deucalion's flood. *QED*. True humans were not around to fight in the ancient war of Athens and Atlantis; Plato's story could not have involved real human beings. On the contrary, the ancient Athenians and Atlantians belonged to the pre-human classes of people who populated the world long before true humans were created. The Athenians 'really existed', as Plato put it, but only in the mythical sense.

This conclusion might well cause outrage among Atlantologists, but, when we stop to think about it, it is less outrageous than the notion of a historical civilisation being swallowed up, without trace, by the Atlantic Ocean. But the fact of the matter is that mythical peoples of the kind I am postulating have long been taken as read by scholars and mythologists who have studied the Greek texts. William Guthrie, for example, in his study of the Orphic cosmogony, observes that: 'There are men, too, in the (golden) age of Phanes, but they are not of our race.'[94] Professor Lowell Edmunds, in a similar vein, notes the existence of 'paradigmatic humans' who lived in a time 'undefinable by human chronology'.[95] And then there is Christopher Gill's comment about the Athens and Atlantis story:

> (Plato) sets his story in the remote past, at a time known to the Greeks only through myths, when the world was being organised by the direct intervention of gods and 'god-like' men or heroes.[96]

Here, Gill seems to imply that Plato's ancient Athenians were mythical people, but he minces his words and makes nothing of it. And Edmunds and Guthrie, it must be said, likewise skirt around the issue. But the fact is that 'god-like' men, half-god heroes, and paradigmatic races are all pre-human, superhuman and non-human by definition.

Most crucially of all, the heroes of ancient Athens were no exception to the rule; in *Critias*, Plato provides an enlightening list of their names:

> "(Solon) said that the Egyptian priests, in their account of the war of that time, gave for the most part names such as Cecrops and Erechtheus, and Erichthonios, and Erysichthon, and the names of most of the others which have come down in tradition before the generation of Theseus."[97]

Each of these names cited here is associated with a fantastic mythology. Whilst it would be labouring the point to examine them all, Cecrops and Erichthonios deserve mention, in particular, for the tradition that they were part-human, part-serpent hybrids! In Cecrops' case, this astonishing tradition is recorded in Apollodorus' *Library* as follows:

> Cecrops, who was born from the earth and had the body of a man and a serpent joined into one, was the first king of Athens...[98]

On this highly mythical note, it is time to draw this chapter towards its close.

Figure 10.
CECROPS LOOKS
ON, AS HIS SON
ERICHTHONIOS
IS PASSED BY
GAIA TO ATHENE

Fiction or True Myth?

My argumentation in this chapter has shared much common ground with the opinions of qualified academics, who rightly regard the Athens and Atlantis story as myth, not history. But the problem with the academics' approach is that they have failed to understand the significance of myth, and have hence rejected Plato's story, prematurely, as a work of fiction. Christopher Gill, for example, in his book *The Atlantis Story*, writes that:

> Despite Plato's narrator's claim of the truth of his ancient story of Atlantis, this seems unlikely. The epic allusions in his story are to the most fantastic and supernatural areas of ancient myth...

> ... this extraordinary story... seems to be a Platonic invention. But, as an invention, it may be taken as a political allegory, a pastiche of history, or an exercise in fiction.[99]

At this point, I must part company with the academics, and pursue my own line of enquiry. As explained in the introduction to this book, the modern word 'myth' derives from the Greek word *muthos*, and *muthos* meant literally 'an utterance' or 'a traditional tale'. But what were these tales about? Professor Lowell Edmunds supplies a splendid definition:

> A Greek myth is a set of multiforms or variants of the same story... The story concerns the divine or the supernatural or the heroic or animals or paradigmatic humans living in a time undefinable by human chronology.[100]

Here, Edmunds recognises that myths (a) are variants of the same story; and (b) relate to the primordial era of the gods. But what exactly was this singular story of the gods? The answer, as we have seen, is that a hard core of ancient myths pertained to an exploded planet cosmogony, to a degree which is only now becoming apparent (and, even so, remains not fully apprehended).[101] Moreover, the ancients were quite adamant that this singular story – the fall of Heaven to Earth – was an absolutely true account of the seeding of life on Earth and of the creation of the Universe as we know it. In the exploded planet, then, we have a primary 'Myth of all myths' which was not only extremely profound, but also, allegedly, true.

Significantly, this 'Myth of all myths' was told and retold, over the millennia, in numerous different ways. Father Heaven had impregnated Mother Earth; the gods had come down from the sky; a heroic god had attacked an evil god in Heaven and imprisoned him in the Underworld; an angry god had descended from Heaven to destroy mankind with a deluge; a man had saved the seeds of life by transporting them in an ark from Heaven to Earth; the story goes on and on, infinitely mutable, and yet always remaining the same story. It is indeed 'a set of multiforms or variants' as Professor Lowell Edmunds has put it.

And there's the rub. When Socrates confesses that he has never heard of the war between Athens and Atlantis, it becomes obvious to the reader that this is not an old myth but a new myth – an invention of Plato's. And this then opens the door for scholars to criticise the status of Plato's story and dismiss it as a fiction, despite Plato's insistence that 'every word of it is true'. But what if Plato was simply retelling the exploded planet myth in a new variation on the theme (for that, after all, was how ancient myth worked)? In that case, scholars would be doing Plato a great disservice in labelling his story a 'fiction', when it would rather constitute a form of 'true myth', of equal status to the 'true myths' of Homer and Hesiod, the ancient Babylonians, the Akkadians, the Sumerians and the Egyptians.

Chapter Fifteen Summary

* Historicist interpretations of the Athens and Atlantis story suffer from fundamental problems. Firstly, its author, Plato, was not a historian or a geographer but a 'true philosopher'. Secondly, the war between Athens and Atlantis was unknown to Herodotus and Socrates. Thirdly, the existence of the Saite calendar seems highly improbable. Fourthly, archaeological evidence argues against the existence of a civilisation at Athens c. 9600 BC. And fifthly, scientific evidence argues against the sinking of an island continent in the midst of the Atlantic Ocean.

* Plato never claimed that his story was historical; in fact, he said that it was a poem, comparable in status to the poems of Homer and Hesiod. These poems were generally set in the primordial past, when gods and heroes ruled the Earth.

* When Plato said that Atlantis sank 'nine thousand years ago', he was speaking idiomatically, and meant 'nine aeons ago', i.e. an infinitely long time ago. Consistent with this, the Atlantis cataclysm was the third cataclysm before the flood of Deucalion.

* Plato's story is set in a pre-diluvian era, aeons before human beings were created (at the time of Deucalion's flood). It follows that the war between Athens and Atlantis was fought by mythical, pre-human peoples, comparable to Hesiod's gold, silver and bronze races. These peoples were human-*like*, but not human; they really existed, but only in a mythical sense. Consistent with this, one of the Athenian heroes was Cecrops – a mythological being who was part-human and part-serpent.

* Plato portrayed Athens and Atlantis as idyllic lands of abundance and, in so doing, evoked the myths of the golden age and the otherworldly Elysian Plain. In addition, he credited Atlantis with an immense size

('larger than Libya and Asia Minor combined'), a perfect circular shape, and a supernatural manner of creation (from the primeval hill of Clito). All of this tends to suggest that we are dealing with a mythical, not a historical, location.

* The story of the war between Athens and Atlantis may have been 'true' in a mythical sense, for myths enshrined a sacred 'truth' about the beginning of the Universe and of life on Earth, i.e. the exploded planet cosmogony. Was Plato's story a retelling of this 'Myth of all myths'?

CHAPTER SIXTEEN

THE FALL OF ATHENS

**And I, John, saw the Holy City, the new Jerusalem,
coming down out of Heaven from God, prepared
as a bride beautifully dressed for her husband.**
(Book of Revelation, New Testament)

There is a stark contrast in Plato's story between ancient Athens, which became the city that is Athens today, and the Isle of Atlantis, which sank beneath the sea and was lost for ever. With Athens being well-known and Atlantis unknown, it was inevitable, as the centuries passed by, that Atlantis would move centre stage as readers of Plato's story began to speculate as to its whereabouts. In this respect, the watershed event was the publication in 1882 of Ignatius Donnelly's *Atlantis: The Antediluvian World*, in which the role of idyllic Athens and its heroes was edited out as Donnelly focused all his attention on solving the mystery of Atlantis.[1] Since then, countless other writers have followed in Donnelly's footsteps and fallen into the same trap. So much so that the story of ancient Athens and Atlantis has become known, misleadingly, as 'the Atlantis story'.

It behoves me, then, to put the record straight by emphasising, in the strongest possible terms, that Plato's story was primarily about *ancient Athens* and its heroes who fought the war *against* Atlantis. The story does not glorify Atlantis but Athens, as classical scholars have long been at pains to point out.[2] Indeed, the whole point of the story is to cast ancient Athens in the role of Socrates' ideal state. Thus, whilst Atlantis *is* important, it is so only in the sense that its people are the enemies whom the Athenians must defeat in battle. It is this interaction between the two peoples – in the form of a war – that is the main subject of Plato's story.

This might seem like a statement of the obvious, and indeed it is, but Atlantologists have generally ignored it, because it links their cherished lost island to a city that still exists, Athens, where the archaeological

evidence stands in stark contradiction to the notion of any war during the
10th millennium BC. Accordingly, the war is off limits for Atlantologists,
despite the fact that it is *the* subject of the story. Everything will work
out just as long as nobody mentions the war!

Such are the problems with the historicist perspective. However, if we
adopt the mythical perspective instead, then the war between Athens and
Atlantis calls to mind the manifold myths of the wars between Heaven
and Earth, in which Heaven, personified by Zeus, assaulted the chthonic
forces, personified by the Titans, the Giants, or Typhoeus. Significantly,
each of these myths represents a variant of the 'Myth of all myths' which
stood at the very heart of ancient Greek religion, namely the myth of the
exploded planet and the ensuing cataclysmic union of Heaven and Earth.

Might Plato have been retelling this same 'Myth of all myths' using
the established allegory of the war between Heaven and Earth? Might
Athens have signified Heaven and Atlantis the Earth? It is a controversial
theory, which raises a whole host of tantalising questions, and yet three
points speak immediately in its favour. Firstly, Plato was fascinated by
the twin subjects of cosmogony and cataclysms (see chapters four and
eleven). Secondly, the war *does* end in a violent cataclysm, in which the
Isle of Atlantis sinks beneath the sea, at the same time as the Athenian
heroes sink, as one body, beneath the earth. And thirdly, as I pointed out
in the previous chapter, Poseidon's breaking apart of the primeval hill of
Clito to create the circular city of Atlantis, with its six rings of land and
sea, is strongly reminiscent of the Mesopotamian and Greek myths of the
subterranean ocean contained inside the Earth, in which case the hill of
Clito and the city of Atlantis would both symbolise the Earth.

But there is more. For it is a fact, largely taken for granted by scholars,
that Plato identified ancient Athens with an original, prototype city in the
heavens.

Heavenly Athens

As noted in chapter fourteen, the story of ancient Athens and Atlantis is
told in the context of Socrates' vision of the ideal state. At the beginning
of *Timaeus*, Socrates makes it perfectly clear that he wants his friends to
deliver a speech bringing the ideal state to life. He speaks thus:

> "I talked about politics yesterday and my main point, I think, had to do
> with the kind of political structure cities should have and the kind of
> men that should make it up, so as to be the best possible city... I'd like
> to go on now and tell you what I've come to feel about the political
> structure we've described... I'd love to listen to someone give a speech

depicting our [ideal] city in a contest with other cities, competing for those prizes that cities typically compete for. I'd love to see our city distinguish itself in the way it goes to war and in the way it pursues the war..."[3]

In response to this request, Critias tells Socrates how ancient Athens had once defeated an invasion of Europe and Asia by Atlantis, and says:

"We'll translate the [ideal] citizens and the [ideal] city you described to us in mythical fashion yesterday to the realm of fact, and place it before us as though it is ancient Athens itself."[4]

Thus it is made explicit that ancient Athens will represent *the ideal state* going to war.

But how, exactly, should we understand this concept of the ideal state? In *Republic* (the prelude to *Timaeus*), Socrates expounds his vision of an ideal state *on Earth*, ruled by philosopher-kings, and yet in the same breath he admits that such a state can only be an 'approximation' of the truly ideal state which exists only in archetypal form *in Heaven*. This is stated most clearly in the following conversation between Socrates and his friend Glaucon:

Glaucon: "You mean that he [the wise person] will be willing to take part in the politics of the city we were founding and describing, the one that exists in theory, for I don't think it exists anywhere on Earth."

Socrates: "But perhaps there is a model of it in Heaven, for anyone who wants to look at it and to make himself its citizen..."[5]

Thus the concept of the ideal state is to be understood as a classic example of Plato's Theory of Forms, in which all things on Earth are but imperfect copies of perfect heavenly originals (see chapter four). As much as man might try to create the ideal city of Athens on Earth, the truly ideal city of Athens would always remain in Heaven.[6]

Returning to *Timaeus*, which kind of ideal state did Socrates have in mind when he requested a story of it going to war? Was he thinking of a conventional war, fought by an imperfect, man-made approximation of the ideal city, located somewhere on the Earth? Or was he thinking of a mythical war, fought by a perfect, original and true city, located in the heavenly and aethereal 'world of Forms'? The question may seem to be unanswerable – and modern scholars would certainly consider it so – but, as we shall now see, Plato left a stunning clue that surely puts the matter beyond any doubt.

The Founding of Athens

Scholars believe that there is a strange contradiction in Plato's story of the war between Athens and Atlantis, in respect of the chronology that he gives for the founding of ancient Athens and the outbreak of the war. The puzzle may be summarised briefly as follows.

Firstly, in *Timaeus*, Plato has the Egyptian priest state that the city of Athens was founded 'nine thousand years ago':

> "Your city the goddess [Neith/Athene] founded first, a thousand years before our city [Sais]... Now our social arrangement, according to the records inscribed in our sacred documents, is eight thousand years old. Nine thousand years ago, then, did these fellow citizens of yours live, whose laws and finest achievement I'll briefly describe to you..."[7]

But then, in *Critias*, Plato has Critias state that Athens fought the war against Atlantis nine thousand years ago, as if to suggest that the city had gone into battle on the very day of its foundation:

> "We should recall at the very beginning that, in very rough terms, it was some nine thousand years since the time when a war is recorded as having broken out between the peoples dwelling outside the Pillars of Heracles and all those dwelling within."[8]

This coincidence of dates strikes scholars as absurd – how could Athens have had the resources to fight a full scale war virtually on the day of its foundation? The idea seems so ridiculous that scholars have attributed it to a careless chronological error. Christopher Gill, for example, writes:

> The slip shows that Plato does not take the historical status of his account too seriously.[9]

And there the matter is left to rest.

However, it is no small thing to accuse Plato – one of the greatest philosophers and writers who ever lived – of being absent-minded about his dates. And, indeed, if we re-examine the first of Plato's two passages cited above, we find the so-called 'slip' appearing again: "Your city the goddess founded first, a thousand years before our city... Nine thousand years ago, then, did these fellow citizens of yours live, whose laws and whose finest achievement [i.e. the defeat of Atlantis] I'll briefly describe to you...". So, might it be the case that Plato really did imagine Athens fighting the war on the day of its foundation? Did he, perhaps, not make a slip at all?

In fact, there is a very good mythical explanation for this coincidence of dates, and it lies in the Greek myth that all things upon Earth had

t first, the Lord of Aratta resists the demands of Uruk. But the goddess
hanna then intervenes and settles the city's fate, for it is her desire to
escend from heavenly Aratta and dwell in the Earth-city of Uruk.[26] The
tory then concludes with the destruction of Aratta:

> From the city, darts poured down like rain and, from Aratta's walls,
> clay sling-stones came clattering as hailstones come in spring.[27]

This destruction – this submission to Uruk – brought the plan of the gods
to fruition. All of the minerals of Aratta – its gold, silver and lapis lazuli
– were 'heaped up' in the courtyard of the E.AN.NA temple of Uruk and
thereupon the mythical people of Aratta set about building the temple of
the gods.[28] As a result of this fall, the city of Aratta came to be described
in myth, poetically, as 'the house grown up with Heaven – its base a
felled tree, its top a sundered tree'.[29]

The upshot of this myth is that the fallen city of Aratta symbolised a
fallen celestial body, presumably the exploded planet that stood at the
heart of ancient Mesopotamian religion.

The fall of Aratta is paralleled by a similar, but in some ways very
different, tale involving the fall of the city Kish. The fall of Kish is
described in a Sumerian text entitled *Gilgamesh and Agga*. In this myth,
we again find a stand-off between two cities, with Kish representing the
falling city of Heaven, and Uruk representing the Earth (or possibly the
Underworld). This time the king of Uruk is not Enmerkar but a later king
named Gilgamesh.

The tale begins with Agga, the king of heavenly Kish, sending an
envoy to Gilgamesh at Uruk demanding that his city submit to Kish or
otherwise take the consequences. Thus threatened, Gilgamesh decides to
go before an assembly of the city elders seeking a resolution for war. But
all he achieves is a poetic stalemate:

> *Gilgamesh says*: "Let us *not* submit to the house of Kish, let us smite it
> with weapons."
> *The Elders say*: "Let us submit to the house of Kish, let us *not* smite it
> with weapons."[30]

In frustration, Gilgamesh turns to the common men of Uruk, and they
encourage him to fight, arguing that: 'Kish's army is small, it is scattered
behind Agga'.[31] Gilgamesh thus grows confident that Agga, when he
comes down from Heaven, will have his 'judgement confounded'
through fear of Uruk. But his optimism is misplaced; when Agga's army
arrives to besiege Uruk, it is Uruk's judgement that is confounded. The
cataclysmic meeting of the two armies is described in poetic terms:

originally been lowered from Heaven into the Underworld, whence they
had then been born into the light of the world above. A prime example of
this myth appears in *Republic*, where Socrates reports a Phoenician story
of something that had occurred in many places, namely that an entire
city, comprising the people and all their weapons and craftsmens' tools,
had been 'fashioned and nurtured inside the Earth' prior to being brought
into existence in the world above (see citation in chapter ten).

This, I suggest, was the myth of Athens' foundation. In the beginning,
the city had been lowered from Heaven, together with its people and its
laws, and planted in the depths of the Underworld. Thereafter, it had
undergone a gestation period inside the womb of the Earth, as all things
had done. And finally, it had been delivered – ready made – into the light
of the world above, thus becoming 'the city that is Athens today'.[10]

Did Plato have this entire, three-stage metamorphosis in mind when he
claimed that the foundation of Athens nine aeons ago had coincided with
'the most magnificent thing our city has ever done'?[11] Significantly, this
foundation myth does play a prominent role in his story. For example, in
Timaeus, the Egyptian priest informs Solon how the goddess Athene
'founded, nurtured and educated our cities' – words that are evocative of
the myths in which Prometheus (or, in the case of Athens, Athene and
Hephaestus) had taught men all the skills they needed to know on the day
when they were to be delivered up by the Earth.[12] Then, the priest goes
on to refer to Athene's founding of Athens 'when she had received from
Earth and Hephaestus the seed from which your people were to come'.[13]
And finally, it is interesting to note that Critias tells his story on the day
of Athene's festival, the Panathenaia, which celebrated her creation of
life in the Athenian earth. This point is mentioned twice – firstly by
Critias in dedicating his speech to the goddess, and secondly by Socrates
who declares: "We're in the midst of celebrating the festival of the
goddess, and this speech really fits the occasion."[14] Indeed it did fit the
occasion, for Athene's seeding of life in the Earth was a parallel idea to
the descent of Athens itself from Heaven into the Underworld.

In summary, I would argue that Plato's story, portraying the ideal state
going to war, pertained to the true kind of ideal state that existed in the
heavens, and that ancient Athens signified this mythical, heavenly city.
Hence the fact that the war coincided with the founding of Athens (in the
Earth).

Many other things now begin to make sense, too. The fact that ancient
Athens was an idyllic utopia, with far more land than present-day
Athens. The fact that the army lived on the Heaven-like acropolis.[15] The
fact that the war took place in the infinite, pre-diluvian past. The fact that

the war climaxed in a cataclysm of 'excessively violent earthquakes and floods'. The fact that the acropolis was devastated by these floods and earthquakes. And, perhaps most telling of all, the fact that, at the time of the cataclysm, the Athenian heroes 'sank below the earth all at once', just as if they had fallen, as one body, from Heaven into the Earth.

Could it be that the war between Athens and Atlantis was no ordinary war, but a war of Heaven and Earth? Could it be that ancient Athens was no ordinary city, but a metaphor for Plato's 'world of Forms', i.e. the exploded planet? Could it be that the Athenian heroes were a mythical race of heavenly men who personified the fall of Heaven?

All of these questions I shall now address by means of the proven methodology that I used in earlier chapters – comparative mythology. In the remainder of this chapter, we shall see how the myths of the ancient Near East contain amazing precedents for the myth of 'cities' descending from Heaven to Earth, whilst, in the next chapter, we shall see how the same myths contain equally amazing precedents for the myth of war-like 'peoples' falling from the sky.

Cities from Heaven

It should be said, at the outset, that it is not such an unusual idea that a city might exist in the heavens, or that Heaven itself might be a city. For example, many Christians will be familiar with the Book of Revelations passage in which the author, John, exclaims: "And I, John, saw the Holy City, the new Jerusalem, coming down out of Heaven from God, prepared as a bride beautifully dressed for her husband."[16]

But this, it transpires, is just the tip of a vast ancient iceberg, for the metaphor of the heavenly 'city' was, in fact, used widely throughout the ancient Near East. Let's take a brief look at some of the examples that I cited in my previous book *When The Gods Came Down*.

To begin with the ancient Egyptian texts, we find that Heaven was frequently referred to as 'the City of God' or 'the Great City'. However, at the same time, the Egyptians regarded Heaven as an Earth-like planet, where the soul of a good person could reincarnate into a body-double and do everything he had ever wished to do on Earth, but for eternity (see chapter ten).[17] The word for 'city' was thus used as a metaphor for an imaginary planet – a metaphor which sprang, no doubt, from the fact that certain cities along the river Nile were identified with Heaven and Earth for symbolic and ritual purposes.

Turning to the texts of the Hindus, Hittites and Mesopotamians, here we find that the city of Heaven was depicted in the context of past events

involving destruction and cataclysm. In the Hindu texts, w... tales of the gods warring in their heavenly cities. For e... *Mahabharata*, there is an incident in which three cities a... bolt of light by the god Mahadeva, whereupon they explode... In addition to this, the *Varnaparvan* contains a passag... celestial city called Hiranyapura is destroyed with a missi... Arjun, whereupon it is reduced to smithereens and all of its... the Earth.[19] And a similar destructive theme is found in the... *The Song of Ullikummis*, where Kumarbis urges his son Ul... ascend to Heaven and destroy Kummiya, the city of the s... Clearly the word for 'city' is used in all of these texts as a m... something that orbits in the heavens (but not an orbiting spac... Erich von Daniken would have it!).

It is on the Mesopotamian texts, however, that I would rea... focus our attention. Here, we find a series of fascinating refe... mythical cities or city-states existing in the heavens. There is Di... example, which was described as a 'mountain' or an 'island', a... was synonymous with the heavenly mountain of the gods, o... known as 'the great city, the place where Utu rises'.[21] Also, ... Shuruppak, the city of the great Flood, which we shall return to... For the moment, though, I would like to focus our attention on the... surrounding the city-states of Aratta and Kish, both of which app... fell from Heaven to Earth.

The fall of the city Aratta is described in a Sumerian text e... *Enmerkar and the Lord of Aratta*. In this myth, Enmerkar, ruler... Earth-city of Uruk, demands that the Lord of Aratta, a heavenly... submit to his city of Uruk. His demand is that the people of Aratta sh... come down from their high 'mountain' and bring with them 'the st... of the mountain' with which they should build in Uruk a great temp... the gods.[22] These stones, we are told, include gold, silver and pure l... lazuli.[23] The negotiations with Aratta take place through an envoy... Enmerkar, who makes the long journey to Heaven across the se... mountains of the Underworld to dictate the terms of the surrend... Significantly, the herald threatens the Lord of Aratta with the t... destruction of his heavenly city:

> "I will make the people of the city flee like the . . . bird from its tree
> I will make them flee like a bird into the neighbouring nest.
> I will make Aratta desolate like a place of . . .
> I will make it hold dust like an utterly destroyed city,
> Aratta, that habitation which Enki has cursed,
> I will surely destroy the place."[25]

> The multitude [of Kish] cast itself down, the multitude rose up,
> The multitude rolled in the dust,
> The foreigners, the lot of them, were overwhelmed,
> On the mouths of the natives [of Uruk], dust was heaped...[32]

The story then concludes with Agga giving Gilgamesh the breath of life
and setting him free, as if to suggest that Gilgamesh had been trapped in
the Underworld. This would, of course, mean that Uruk, in this particular
myth, was a city of the Underworld (in fact, a Mesopotamian name for
the Underworld was *urugal*, meaning 'great city').[33]

This myth of Kish and Uruk is important because it describes the fall
of Heaven to Earth as a war between two cities, and this provides a
strong parallel and precedent for Plato's story of Atlantis. Moreover, this
city 'succession myth' fits in to a broader picture of warring cities which
forms the backbone of the Sumerian Kings List.

In the section of the Sumerian Kings List dealing with events after the
great Flood, we read an amazing account of how kingship had been
transferred from one city to another:

> After the Flood had swept thereover, when the kingship was lowered
> from Heaven, the kingship was (first) in Kish... Twenty-three kings
> reigned its 24,510 years, 3 months and 3.5 days.
> *Kish was smitten with weapons*; its kingship was carried to E.AN.NA
> [Uruk]... Twelve kings reigned its 2,310 years.
> *Uruk was smitten with weapons*; its kingship was carried to Ur... Four
> kings reigned its 177 years.
> *Ur was smitten with weapons*; its kingship was carried to
> Awan...[34]

And so the Kings List continues, with each city, in turn, being 'smitten
with weapons'.

Where did this curious idiom spring from? As I have argued in *When
The Gods Came Down*, it almost certainly derives from the cataclysmic
model upon which the ancient Sumerian religion was based. More to the
point, the Kings List portrays Heaven in the form of a succession of
Sumerian cities and suggests that each of them captured kingship and
capital status by falling cataclysmically from Heaven to Earth, in the
process destroying and replacing the previous capital city. Thus Kish,
Uruk (E.AN.NA), Ur, Awan, et cetera, would all have been cities in
Heaven prior to becoming conventional cities on Earth (compare the
foundation myth of Athens which I recited earlier). Consistent with this,
the E.AN.NA temple of Uruk was said to be a 'temple descended from

Heaven'.[35]

It may also be deduced that the kingship data applied originally to the idea of kingship among the heavenly cities. This idea is best seen in the pre-diluvian section of the Sumerian Kings List which records what happened from the beginning of time ('When the kingship was lowered from Heaven') to the day of the great Flood:

> When the kingship was lowered from Heaven, the kingship was in
>   Eridu... two kings reigned its 64,800 years.
> *I drop Eridu*; its kingship was carried to Bad-tibira... three kings
>   reigned its 108,000 years.
> *I drop Bad-tibira*; its kingship was carried to Larak... one king reigned
>   its 28,800 years.
> *I drop Larak*; its kingship was carried to Sippar... one king reigned its
>   21,000 years.
> *I drop Sippar*; its kingship to Shuruppak was carried.
> In Shuruppak, Ubar-Tutu became king,
>   and reigned 18,600 years...
> The Flood swept thereover.[36]

Were these five cities 'dropped', quite literally, from the sky? The idea might seem outrageous, but it happens to be totally in accord with the way the Sumerians viewed their world. Their belief, in a nutshell, was that everything had fallen from Heaven to Earth – the waters of life, the seeds of life, temples, cities and kingship. To the Sumerians, each of their temples and cities symbolised 'the Bond of Heaven and Earth', i.e. the mythical conjunction of the two planets. The five pre-diluvian cities – Eridu, Bad-tibira, Larak, Sippar and Shuruppak – each claimed to be *the* city that had been lowered from Heaven and founded in the Earth, and hence *the* microcosm of the entire Universe.[37] It was not necessarily the case that the sky had fallen five times. Rather, it had fallen just once (or, as some experts maintained, twice), and hence the Kings List reflected the political rivalry between different cities that each claimed to be the capital.

The final piece in this Sumerian jigsaw is the city of Shuruppak which, according to the closing lines of the Kings List just cited above, was the last city to hold kingship (seemingly in Heaven) prior to the great Flood. Was Shuruppak, too, a heavenly city? Did it fall from Heaven at the time of the great Flood?

These questions, fortunately, can be answered by a close reading of the famous Mesopotamian text known as *The Epic of Gilgamesh*, where the fall of the city Shuruppak is related to king Gilgamesh, in cryptic terms, by king Ubar-Tutu's son Utnapishtim, the hero of the great Flood (equivalent to the biblical Flood-hero Noah).

On the face of it, Utnapishtim's story seems to involve a normal city that is populated by normal people, all of whom, bar Utnapishtim, are overwhelmed by the Flood cataclysm. But the story is deceptive, perhaps quite deliberately, and certain crucial anomalies in the story confirm, beyond any question, that the setting is celestial.[38] And so it transpires, as I explained in my book *When The Gods Came Down*, that Utnapishtim's city Shuruppak actually symbolised a heavenly planet. Furthermore, it transpires that the Flood was produced by the explosion of this celestial city, which unleashed *from itself* a deluge of floodwaters and meteoritic materials. The following passage from *The Epic of Gilgamesh* gives the general picture:

> A black cloud came up from the foundation of Heaven.
> Adad thundered within it,
> While Shullat and Hanish went in front,
> Moving as heralds over hill and plain.
> Erragal [Nergal] tore out the mooring posts,
> Ninurta came forth and caused the dykes to give way;
> The Anunnaki raised their (fiery) torches,
> Lighting up the land with their brightness.
> The confusion of Adad reached unto the (highest) heavens,
> Turning into darkness all that had been light.
> The wide land was shattered like a pot![39]

This wide land, which was 'shattered like a pot', was the city (or ex-city) of Shuruppak. It was also referred to metaphorically as a 'house', which was torn down by Utnapishtim and converted into a metaphorical 'ship', in which the Flood-hero conveyed the seeds of life to the Earth (as noted in chapter ten).[40] Just as Shuruppak citified the exploded planet, so did the Flood-hero Utnapishtim personify it. It is a classic example of how the ancient myth-makers brought the exploded planet story to life.

In summary, the myths of the Near East provide ample corroboration of the idea that Heaven could be a city, and that this metaphorical city (i.e. an exploded planet) could fall cataclysmically from Heaven to Earth, in some cases violently assaulting and succeeding a rival city on Earth or in the Underworld.

Was Plato's myth of ancient Athens and Atlantis drawing on this long-established Mesopotamian tradition? Before we jump to conclusions, we should examine the parallels and precedents for a complementary idea – that a war-like race of men could descend from the heavens. This is the task for the next chapter.

Chapter Sixteen Summary

* The subject of Plato's story is a war between ancient Athens and Atlantis. Any plausible theory of Atlantis must explain the absence of evidence for the historicity of such a war.

* Many of the most famous wars in Greek myths (e.g. Zeus versus the Titans) were encoded forms of the exploded planet myth, the basic idea being that the falling Heaven went into cataclysmic battle against the Earth (or the Underworld).

* The purpose of Critias' story was to illustrate Socrates' ideal state going to war, with the ideal state being represented by ancient Athens. And yet the truly ideal state existed not on Earth but in Heaven. Was ancient Athens thus envisaged as a heavenly city? Did its war against Atlantis signify the mythical battle between Heaven and Earth?

* The city of Athens was founded 'nine thousand years ago', and went to war against Atlantis at the very same time. If the story is historical, then Plato has committed a careless error. But if the story is mythical, then his chronology is vindicated, for Athens could have been lowered from Heaven and founded in the Underworld, whilst simultaneously assaulting Atlantis in a mythical war between Heaven and Earth (or the Underworld).

* The war indeed climaxed with a cataclysm in which the Athenian warriors sank mysteriously into the earth. This strange event is quite consistent with a mythical body of men descending from Heaven.

* The myths of the Near East provide ample parallels and precedents for the idea of Heaven falling to Earth in the form of a city, and for the idea that the falling city could violently assault and succeed a rival city on Earth or in the Underworld.

CHAPTER SEVENTEEN

THE FALL OF MAN

———————————————

I am a child of Earth and starry Heaven, but my race is of Heaven alone.
(Orphic gold plate, 4th-3rd century BC)

Were the ancient Athenians a mythical race of people, who went to war against Atlantis by descending from Heaven? In this chapter, I aim to demonstrate that this was indeed the case by citing evidence from the myths of Greece and the ancient Near East. These myths will establish, beyond question, two important principles: (a) that a race of 'men' once lived upon the planet of Heaven – this to be understood in a literal sense, relating to the myth of the golden age; and (b) that the explosion of the planet of Heaven caused these heavenly men to descend to Earth, into the Underworld, like a flood-storm or raging army – this to be understood in a metaphorical sense. Together, these two principles underpin the age-old Western myth that is popularly known as 'the fall of man'.

Our study begins with the most fundamental idea in the ancient Greek myths of the creation of man, namely that the first men had been 'born from the earth', and goes on to reveal, for the first time ever, the full, astonishing story behind this intriguing myth.

Greek Myths of the Creation of Man

Virtually every Greek people had a tradition that their original tribe had been *autochthon*, i.e. 'earth-born', in many cases born from the very land that they worked for a living. This tradition was often traced back to one particular ancestor or king, who had originally been born from the earth.

In Athens, this first king was known as Erechtheus, 'the shatterer', or Erichthonios, 'strife of the earth'.[1] A famous line in the *Iliad* refers to the city of Athens as 'the land of great-hearted Erechtheus' and describes how Athene had reared Erechtheus 'after the grain-giving ploughland had given him birth'.[2] Plato, too, referred to this myth in his account of how Athene and Hephaestus had 'fashioned in the land good men sprung from the land itself'.[3]

In other Greek cities, the tale was essentially the same. In Arcadia, which claimed to be the oldest land in Greece, the first man was known as Pelasgus, who had sprung from the soil followed by certain others of his race; his name meant 'ancient one' or 'seafarer'.[4] In Thebes, the first man was known as Kadmos, literally 'ancient one' or 'easterner', who had created his people, the *Kadmeioi*, by planting in the ground the teeth of a serpent; the Thebans or *Kadmeioi* were thus known as 'the sown men'.[5] In Sparta, it was said that the first king had been born from the local earth, and thus reigned on his mother's ground; the name Spartans (from *spartoi*) thus meant 'the sown men'.[6] Other examples could be cited, but the point has been made.[7]

Why did the Greeks maintain such a strange myth of their birth from the earth (*gegenes*)? According to the scholar G.S. Kirk, writing in 1974, the idea is a 'charter myth', i.e. of a territorial and patriotic (or rather matriarchic) nature, and should not be taken literally as a creation myth.[8] But I must beg to differ. As we shall now see, the myth of man's birth from the earth applied to the entire human race and followed the cosmic pattern that has already been well documented in this book.

A good place to start is with Hesiod. In *Theogony* we are told that Hephaestus, the god of fire, created the first woman Pandora from earth (an implied mixture of fire and earth), whilst in *Works and Days* we are told that he created her from earth and water (an implied mixture of fire, earth and water).[9] Crucially, the creation of Pandora led to the creation of all human females, so this is hardly some local charter myth.

As regards the origins of the male species, Hesiod was vague, but other writers asserted that man, too, had been born from the Earth.[10] The idea is most clearly expressed in Plato's *Protagoras*, where the sophist Protagoras informs Socrates that:

> "There once was a time when gods existed but mortal races did not. When the time came for their appointed genesis, the gods moulded them inside the Earth, blending together earth and fire and various compounds of earth and fire. When they were ready to bring them to light, the gods put Prometheus and Epimetheus in charge of decking them out and assigning to each its appropriate powers and abilities."[11]

The idea here is that mankind *in its entirety* had been born from the constituent elements of the Earth.

Such was the profundity of this earth-born myth that it applied not just to man, but to all living things. Thus in Plato's *Menexenus,* Socrates reports the teachings of a wise lady named Aspasia:

> "Our land is indeed worthy of being praised... by all of humanity... in the age when the whole Earth was causing creatures of all kinds – wild animals and domestic livestock – to spring up and thrive... out of all the animals she selected and brought forth the human..."[12]

But even this was not the limit of the earth-born myth. As discussed in chapter ten, Socrates reported a Phoenician story of something that had occurred in many places, namely that *entire cities*, comprising not just men but also their tools and weapons, had been born from the Earth. An old man's tale dreamed up by Socrates? Perhaps not. In fact, the Greeks were so obsessed with this earth-born myth that they actually claimed that entire lands had been delivered up from the womb of the Earth. A classic example is the Libyan continent, which the Greeks knew as *autochthon*, i.e. 'earth-born'.[13] In addition, many Greek islands were said to have been born from the sea, having formerly been 'floating islands' in the oceanic womb of the Earth. Examples include Ortygia/Delos, Kalliste/Thera, the Symplegades (alias the Cyanean islands), Rhodes, and possibly Cyprus and Sicily.[14] Indeed, it might well have been an unspoken belief that *all* Greek islands had once been floating islands, prior to their birth from the sea.

Why this obsession with the idea of men, women, animals, cities, islands and even the Libyan continent being born from the earth or the sea? The explanation, surely, is to be found in the cosmogonic myths, cited in earlier chapters, where the Sun, Moon, planets, stars and gods (*daimones*) were all born from the womb of the Earth, who was praised by the poets as 'mother of us all, the oldest (god) of all... the mother of all the gods, the mother of all men'.[15]

But what was the one common factor behind all of these cosmogonic birth myths? The answer, as we have seen – and will now see again – is the impregnation of the Earth by the falling Mountain of Heaven.

Heavenly Seed

Was it a falling heavenly seed that caused mankind to be born from the Earth? To begin, let us recall the myth of the Athenians' origin, which Plato alluded to in *Timaeus* as follows:

> "Your city [Athens] the goddess [Neith/Athene] founded first... when she had received from Earth and Hephaestus the seed from which your people were to come."[16]

In *Critias*, Plato went on to elaborate slightly on this statement, writing that Athene and Hephaestus had 'fashioned in Athens good men sprung from the land itself' – these first kings being named Cecrops, Erechtheus, Erichthonios, and Erysichthon.

But what exactly was this 'seed' which Athene planted in the Earth to create the Athenians? In Apollodorus' version of the story (2nd century BC), we learn that the seed was the semen of Hephaestus:

> Some say that Erichthonios was a son of Hephaestus and Atthis...
> while according to others, he was born to Hephaestus and Athene, in
> the following way. Athene visited Hephaestus, wanting to fashion
> some arms. But Hephaestus, who had been deserted by Aphrodite,
> yielded to his desire for Athene and began to chase after her, while the
> goddess for her part tried to escape. When he caught up with her at the
> expense of much effort (for he was lame), he tried to make love with
> her. But she, being chaste and a virgin, would not permit it, and he
> ejaculated over the goddess' leg. In disgust, she wiped the semen away
> with a piece of wool and threw it to the ground. As she was fleeing,
> Erichthonios came to birth from the seed that had fallen on the earth.[17]

As discussed in chapter thirteen, Hephaestus was an exploded planet god, and hence his 'seed' or 'semen' signified meteorites – the seeds of all life according to Anaxagoras and the ancient Egyptians. The meaning of the myth, then, is that Hephaestus created the first Athenians by planting meteorites in the Earth at the site of Athens.

Let us now recall and reconsider the myth in which men and women were created at the time of Deucalion's flood. The crucial scene occurs in the flood's aftermath when Deucalion and Pyrrha have disembarked from their ark and descended to the plain from the peak of Parnassus. According to the popular version of the tale, the heroic couple then made a sacrifice and beseeched Zeus to renew the race of mankind. Zeus, on hearing this plea, sent Hermes to confirm that their request would be granted, whereupon Themis – a Mother Earth-goddess – appeared and told Deucalion and Pyrrha to: "Shroud your heads and throw the bones of your mother behind you!". At this, Deucalion and Pyrrha picked up the stones that were lying on the river bank, and, covering their heads, threw the stones behind them. Incredibly, the stones thrown by Deucalion became men, whilst the stones thrown by Pyrrha became women; and thus the human race was created.

By now, it should be perfectly apparent *why* Deucalion and Pyrrha did not propagate the race of mankind by doing what comes naturally for a man and a woman. The explanation is that this couple were *not* man and woman, but metaphorical people who personified the Flood-storm just as Utnapishtim did in Mesopotamia (see previous chapter). The descent of Deucalion and Pyrrha from Mount Parnassus is thus to be understood in allegorical terms as the disintegration and fall of the Mountain of Heaven (compare Utnapishtim's descent from heavenly Shuruppak: 'The wide land was shattered like a pot!').[18] Hence their names, Deucalion's meaning 'new wine sailor' and Pyrrha's meaning 'fiery red'.[19] And hence the loose 'stones' that were lying on the 'river bank', which were surely no ordinary stones, but meteorites.[20]

For a third example of the creation of man from meteorites, let us consider the myth by which man was created not from heavenly 'seed' or 'stones' but from heavenly 'teeth'. The metaphor may be less obvious, but the story is exactly the same; indeed, it is even more explicit.

According to the Pelasgian Greeks, their earliest ancestors had been sown in the Earth in the form of teeth from a serpent named Ophion.[21] Who was Ophion? According to the Pelasgian cosmogony, the goddess Eurynome and the serpent-god Ophion had each descended, in turn, from Heaven to Earth, whereupon they had brought about the creation of the cosmos. Then, having accomplished this task, the couple had ascended to Mount Olympus (in their metaphysical forms) where they began to rule the Universe they had made. In due course of time, however, Ophion (alias Boreas, god of the north wind) had vexed Eurynome by claiming to be greater than she. In response, she had bruised his head with her heel, kicked out his teeth and dispatched him to the dark caves of the Underworld.[22] And meanwhile, the teeth of Ophion had been sown in the Earth, where they gave rise to the earth-born race of Pelasgians.

This same story features in the myth of Kadmos, who was the alleged founder of the Pelasgian race. His encounter with the serpent occurred at the spring of Ares in the Underworld, to which he had travelled on a quest for his sister Europa (her name meant 'west', whilst his meant 'east'; thus the myth recalled a journey from Heaven to Earth).[23] Kadmos crushed the head of the Arean serpent with a rock, whereupon Athene appeared and told him to sow the serpent's teeth in the earth. This Kadmos duly did, whereupon a race of armed men immediately sprang up, clashing their weapons together.[24] The story is better known for its telling in the *Argonautika*, where king Aietes, inheritor of half of the serpent's teeth, challenged Jason to sow these teeth in the earth and to slaughter the army of giants who sprang up therefrom.[25]

From these tales, it is clear that the serpent's teeth were at home in the Underworld, and yet it is equally clear that the teeth belonged originally in Heaven, where they had been kicked out of the mouth of the serpent-god Ophion. The logical implication is that the ex-heavenly 'teeth' of the serpent were meteorites, and that meteorites were the seeds for Pelasgian man.

A complementary theme in these myths that merits our attention is the role of fire and cataclysm in the creation of man.

Consider, first of all, the role of fire. According to the Athenian myth, man had been created by the seed of Hephaestus, who was renowned (alongside Prometheus) for being the Greek god of fire. According to another myth, Prometheus himself had created man from water and earth, at the same time as giving him fire in a fennel-stalk (some said that he had brought this fire down from Heaven, others that he had stolen it from Hephaestus).[26] In the Orphic myth, meanwhile, man had been created from the ashes of the Titans, who had been consigned to flames by the weapons of Zeus.[27] Hesiod, however, said that the mothers of man had been the Meliai nymphs, whose ash-trees courted the lightning flash.[28] One of these ash-nymphs, Melia, had allegedly borne the first man, Phoroneus, who was said to be the inventor and bearer of fire.[29] Although another account named the first man as Kabeiros, a son of the mysterious Kabeiroi blacksmith-gods who were themselves sons of the famous fire-god Hephaestus.[30]

As for the creation of the female species, the myth of Pandora states that Hephaestus provided fire when he made the prototype woman from earth and water, moulding her as if he were a potter, whilst the myth of Deucalion's flood states that the female race was created from the stones thrown by Pyrrha, whose name meant 'fire' or 'fiery red'.

Plato himself authenticates all of these myths, writing in *Protagoras* that man had been created from 'earth and fire, and various compounds of earth and fire'.[31]

In addition, the Greek myths make it clear that pre-human races of men had been destroyed periodically by cataclysms and then replaced by new races of men, the classic examples being the golden race who had been swallowed up by the earth at the fall of the golden age, and the bronze race who had been destroyed in the cataclysm of Deucalion's flood.[32] The poet Pindar put the idea thus, in singing of the foreboding eclipse of the Sun:

Will you overwhelm the Earth with flood and create a new race of men from the beginning?[33]

There is a broad pattern here that cannot be gainsaid, and it has nothing to do with G.S. Kirk's theory that man's 'birth from the earth' (*gegenes*) was some local charter myth. On the contrary, we are dealing, quite clearly, with mythical events on a global scale, in which successive races of man were created by cataclysmic falls of the sky. Hence the ideas that man was created from fire, or from meteorites, known metaphorically as the 'seed of Hephaestus', the 'stones' of Deucalion and Pyrrha, and the 'teeth' of the serpent Ophion. If this is a charter myth, then it must be said that the charter was being established over the cosmic realms of Heaven and Earth.

The Heavenly Race of Men

So far, so good, but we are still missing a vitally important piece of the puzzle, namely those myths which speak of a golden race of men who formerly lived upon the planet of Heaven.

Let us consider, first of all, the Orphic tradition. The race of man, they said, had been created from the ashes of the Titans after they had been vanquished by Zeus and cast down into Tartarus. Accordingly, man had inherited a partially evil nature, but he could at the same time boast of a partially celestial origin, for the Titans were believed to be 'sons of Earth and Heaven'.[34]

Nevertheless, an inscribed Orphic gold plate, dating back to the 4th or 3rd century BC, provides an interesting twist to the myth. It is a religious poem in which an Orphic initiate enters the Underworld and speaks to the guardians of the Lake of Memory as follows:

"I am a child of Earth and starry Heaven;
But my race is of Heaven alone.
This ye know yourselves.
But I am parched with thirst and I perish.
Give me quickly the cold water,
Flowing from the Lake of Memory."[35]

Why, if he was a child of Heaven and Earth, did the Orphic initiate assert so confidently that his race was 'of Heaven alone'? One possibility is that the initiate was contrasting the origin of his body with the origin of his soul. But another, more intriguing, possibility is that he was referring to an ancestral race of heavenly men. For the Greek myths hinted of a time when all men had lived together in Heaven, conversing in a single language and co-existing peacefully during an age of eternal springtime.[36] This was the true golden race of the true golden age.

The most obvious example of this golden age race may be found in Hesiod's poem *Works and Days*, in which he describes a first race of men made of gold:

The race of men that the immortals who dwell on Olympus made first of all was of gold. They were in the time of Kronos, when he was king in Heaven; and they lived like gods with carefree heart, remote from toil and misery. Wretched old age did not affect them either, but with hands and feet ever unchanged they enjoyed themselves in feasting, beyond all ills, and they died as if overcome by sleep. All good things were theirs, and the grain-giving soil bore its fruits of its own accord in unstinted plenty, while they at their leisure harvested their fields in contentment amid abundance. Since the Earth covered up that race, they have been divine spirits [*daimones*]... good spirits on the face of the Earth, watchers over mortal men...[37]

Did this golden race live in Heaven? Hesiod is ambiguous on this point, but simple logic tells us that it must have done. Consider the alternatives. If the golden race had lived on the Earth, it could not have been 'the first race' as Hesiod says it was, for it would have been preceded by a race in the Underworld. Or, if the golden race had lived in the Underworld, it could not have been swallowed up by the Earth as Hesiod implies that it was; so this possibility is negated. On the other hand, if the golden race had lived in Heaven then it *would* have been been the first race and it *would* have been swallowed up by the Earth when it fell, and so Hesiod's myth would make perfect sense.

Hesiod's myth would also make sense in several other aspects. Firstly, the fall of Heaven is implied by the fact that the golden age ended with Kronos being cast down from Olympus. Secondly, when Hesiod says that the golden race 'died suddenly, as if overcome by sleep', this is evocative of a sudden, collective death by way of falling from Heaven.[38] Thirdly, the golden race rose up in death to become divine *daimones*, like ghosts on the face of the Earth; this is highly evocative of the body-soul separation that normally occurs when mythical beings fall from Heaven into the Earth.[39] Fourthly, the ensuing silver race was known for its innocent, child-like behaviour – an idea evocative of a new-born race being nurtured in the Underworld, implying that its predecessor, the golden race, had fallen from Heaven.[40] And fifthly, the ancients used the metal gold to symbolise Heaven, and it would have been a travesty for Hesiod to use such a privileged metaphor for a mere earth-born race.[41]

Enough on Hesiod's golden race. For a much clearer example of the heavenly race, let us turn to the strange myth of the Hyperborean people.

Significantly, Pindar described the Hyperboreans as enjoying the same kind of life that was attributed by Hesiod to the golden race:

In their banquets and rich praise Apollo delights...

On all sides the feet of maidens dancing...
They throng with happy hearts to join the revel.
Illness and wasting old age visit not
This hallowed race, but far from toil and battle
They dwell secure from fate's remorseless vengeance.[42]

So, who were these happy Hyperboreans and where exactly was their perpetual party land? Unfortunately, all studies of this people, in ancient and modern times alike, have been plagued by confusion, not least by the fact that Greek tradition located the Hyperboreans in two completely different regions – one in the remote north and the other in the remote west.[43] This anomaly, however, has largely been ignored by investigators who have sought the mysterious people in the explorable regions of the north, assuming without question that they are looking for a real race of people. Such were the preconceptions of Hecataeus (the famous Greek geographer of the 6th-5th centuries BC) when he suggested that the Hyperboreans lived in Britain – an idea that has caused some experts to suggest that the circle of Stonehenge might have been the legendary 'spherical temple' of Hyperborean Apollo (as if Britain was the 'sunny enclave' in which the Hyperboreans were said to live!).[44]

The truth, however, is that the Hyperboreans were a mythical people. Hence the reports of their peaceful existence, their happiness and their apparent immortality. And as for the location of their distant land, Pindar sang that it was impossible to reach it:

Neither ship, nor marching feet, may find the wondrous way
To the gatherings of the Hyperborean people.[45]

This, it must be said, is the language of myth. And mythical, too, is the description of Hyperborea provided by Herodotus, 'the father of history', who reported in *The Histories* some interesting folklore about the place, notably the idea that it lay in the distant north beyond the land of the one-eyed Arimaspi and the gold-guarding griffins![46] But the great historian clearly took such tales with a large pinch of salt; hence his affirmation that, in his opinion, no Greek had ever set eyes on this fabled land. His conclusion, somewhat tongue in cheek, was that: 'this much is clear: if there are Hyperboreans, then there must also be Hypernotians.'[47]

Nevertheless, one tale reported by Herodotus does catch the eye, and this is the tale of the Hyperborean maidens, who brought sacred offerings to the island of Delos 'wrapped in wheat-straw' and who were buried there and paid the highest honours.[48] The tale seems innocuous enough until we read that the two maidens (known variously as Hyperoché and Laodicé or Argé and Opis) had travelled from Hyperborea to Delos by the same road once taken by the great gods Apollo and Artemis. Indeed, it was said that Argé and Opis had come to Delos *at the same time* as Apollo and Artemis, as if to equate Hyperborea with the heavenly realm of the gods.[49]

That the Hyperboreans were indeed a heavenly race is clear from their name which, by all accounts, meant 'beyond Boreas', i.e. 'beyond the North Wind'.[50] The bearing, needless to say, is celestial, and refers to the popular idea that Heaven was in the north; hence Boreas was not just the god of the North Wind, but was also Ophion, the god of Heaven.[51] The name of the Hyperboreans would thus suggest that they were a mythical race of people who lived in Heaven but, in a poetic sense, 'beyond the North Wind' – hence the idyllic nature of their land.

Further evidence, if any be needed, comes from the tradition (reported by Diodorus Siculus) that the Hyperboreans worshipped the god Apollo in a temple in the north that was spherical in shape (*sphairoeide to schemati*).[52] This spherical temple could hardly have been Stonehenge, as some modern writers have argued (not even Stonehenge with a dome!).[53] Rather, it was a celestial temple and thus a true sphere – the *Sphairos* of God, alias Mount Olympus, alias Ouranos, alias the aethereal planet of Heaven. This was the spherical temple of Hyperborean Apollo. This was Hyperborea.

Having followed the logic thus far, it becomes highly significant to note that the Hyperboreans were linked to the remote west, too, where they were said to reside close to Atlas and the garden of the Hesperides.[54] Since the West symbolised the Underworld (for reasons that will be explained in the next chapter), these Hyperboreans would fit the mould of a race who had been cast down from Heaven into the Earth.

It thus becomes possible to reconstruct the myth of the Hyperboreans as follows. In the beginning, during the golden age, the Hyperborean race had lived upon the planet of Heaven. Then, this golden age had ended with the explosion of the planet, which had caused the Hyperboreans to fall from Heaven into the Underworld. But consequently, in accordance with the laws of metaphysics, Heaven had been resurrected in aethereal form, and likewise the Hyperboreans. And thus it came to pass that the Universe contained a physical population of Hyperboreans, hidden in the Underworld, and a metaphysical population of Hyperboreans, elevated to Heaven – the western and northern Hyperboreans respectively.[55]

In summary, we now hold both ends of the chain in our hands. On the one hand, I have cited three Greek examples of golden age races who once lived upon the planet of Heaven (other possible examples could be cited, but the point has been made).[56] On the other hand, I have cited the

Greek myths of man's birth from the Earth following its impregnation by the meteoritic seed of the exploded planet of Heaven. All that remains, then, if I am to prove that Plato's ancient Athenians were a golden age race, is to draw the equation between meteorites falling from Heaven to Earth and the golden age race descending from Heaven to Earth *in the form of a metaphorical army*. For that, we must turn to the Near Eastern myths of the creation of man, which will not only complete our chain of evidence but also provide vital parallels and precedents for all of the Greek myths that I have cited thus far.

Near Eastern Myths of the Creation of Man

The similarities between the Near Eastern myths and the Greek myths of the creation of man are well known to modern scholars, some of whom feel certain that the Greeks borrowed fundamental ideas from the East, and from the Mesopotamian myths in particular. Here, the usual suspects are involved, namely the Babylonian *Enuma Elish* and the Akkadian *Atra-Hasis Epic*.

As regards *Enuma Elish*, scholars have focused their attention on the myth of man's creation from the blood of Kingu, which seems to parallel the Greek myth of man's creation from the ashes of the Titans. In both myths, there is a battle (in the sky – scholars please note), with Marduk destroying Kingu and Zeus destroying the Titans, respectively. In both cases, man is created from the remnants of the fallen god, and in both cases, the fallen god is portrayed as having an evil nature.[57]

In the *Atra-Hasis Epic*, it is the creation of man from clay that has caught the scholar's eye, for this finds a strong parallel in the Greek myth of Prometheus and Pandora. But numerous other parallels between these two myths have been identified, most notably the idea that two gods co-operated to bring about the creation of man (Enki and Mami/Ishtar in the *Atra-Hasis Epic*; Prometheus and Athene in the myth of Pandora). In all, Charles Penglase has listed twelve broad similarities between these two myths, prompting him to conclude that: 'the major underlying ideas and issues... are essentially the same... the myths surrounding Pandora and Prometheus appear to be the Greek rendition of the Mesopotamian tradition of the creation and early history of mankind.'[58]

That covers the individual myths – the detailed parallels are evidently impressive as far as they go – and yet it is the wider parallels between the East and the West that merit our attention.

Firstly, there is the common idea that man was an earth-born creature. In the Greek myths, as we have seen, the emphasis was on man's birth from the Earth, following a heavenly impregnation by meteorites. In the Mesopotamian myths, the same ideas are in evidence, albeit the focus is more on the creation of man in the Underworld and his hardships therein as a slave to the gods.[59]

The second broad parallel is the idea that man, despite being earth-born, possessed an ex-heavenly element. In the Mesopotamian myths, this idea is seen most clearly in the use of the gods' flesh and blood to create man. In *Enuma Elish*, for example, the blood comes from Kingu who is clearly a sky-god.[60] Similarly, in the *Atra-Hasis Epic*, a god named Geshtui is picked out from the heavenly assembly and cast down into the Underworld, where his sacrificed flesh and blood is mixed with clay to create man.[61] And a third example is *The Myth of Ulligarra and Zalgarra*, in which two sky-gods, Ulligarra and Zalgarra, are sacrificed in the Bond of Heaven and Earth so that man might be created from their blood.[62] In each of these myths, it is implicit that the heavenly flesh and blood of the sacrificed sky-gods is meteoritic in nature.

That this is so is stated more explicitly, albeit metaphorically, in the tale known as *The Myth of the Pickaxe*. Here, Enlil, the 'Great Mountain' of Heaven, uses his 'pickaxe' to break open the Earth at the city of Nippur, whereupon the race of man appears inside the hole and surges towards him (we should imagine Enlil to be buried in the Underworld).[63] Immediately, Enlil is besieged by the subterranean gods, the Anunnaki, who demand that the newly created beings be handed over to them to work as their slaves in the Underworld. The myth is simple enough to understand once Enlil's 'pickaxe' is recognised as a metaphor for a meteorite (on this, see chapters eight and nine). The fundamental idea is that the meteorite is the seed of mankind.

As in the Greek myths, this seeding of Mesopotamian man coincided with a cataclysmic flood from Heaven. The following passage from the Akkadian text *Lugal-e* captures this idea well:

> After the Flood had ravaged the Earth,
> After mankind had first been conceived,
> After the seed of mankind had been deposited (by Heaven in the
>   Earth),
> After the people, the black-headed ones, had risen...[64]

Here, the poet captures brilliantly the idea of the Flood impregnating the Earth with the seed of mankind, causing a new race of man – 'the black-headed ones' – to arise. And yet it must be appreciated that this was not the human race as we know it, but rather a mythical subterranean race, whose fate was to be enslaved by the gods of the Underworld. It was only aeons later that these mythical people would emerge from the Underworld to become the true human race (in which regard it should be noted that the Sumerians actually used the name 'black-headed ones' to refer to their common populace).[65]

The nickname 'black-headed ones' is intriguing. Although modern scholars assume that it related to the dark hair colour of the Sumerian people, it is much more likely that it recalled the blackened appearance of meteoritic iron (when in its natural state), in which case the Sumerian people would have been proclaiming themselves as 'the people of the meteorites'. The idea finds support in the fact that the black-headed ones were sometimes called 'the living creatures of Heaven and Earth', as if to imply that they had indeed come down from the sky in the form of meteorites.[66]

That this was indeed the origin of the black-headed ones may be seen from the myth of Shuruppak, Utnapishtim and the great Flood, which I mentioned in the previous chapter. According to my interpretation of the relevant texts (see *When The Gods Came Down*, 2000), the story may be summarised, briefly, as follows.

Before the Flood, a race of heavenly men had been living in certain 'cult-centres' upon the heavenly city of Shuruppak. Then the gods who dwelt in Shuruppak decided to bring about a cataclysm to destroy the golden race of men. Enki, however, disclosed this fact to Utnapishtim, telling him: "By our command a flood will sweep over the cult-centres to destroy the seed of mankind."[67] And he advised Utnapishtim to build a ship, thus to save the seed of all living things. No sooner had the Flood-hero prepared his 'ship' than the cataclysm occurred as foretold. A black cloud arose from the planet's interior, the dykes of the planet's ocean gave way, the Anunnaki-gods lit up the heavens with their fiery torches and 'the wide land was shattered like a pot'. It was at this moment that the mother-goddess, known variously by the names Mami/Ninharsag/Inanna/Ishtar, gave birth to her people, the black-headed ones, *in the heavens*. The Neo-Assyrian version of the *Atra-Hasis Epic* describes the event as follows:

Ninurta goes forth, bursting the dykes,
Erragal [Nergal] roots up the mooring posts.
. . . with his claws the heavens . . .
Ishtar [Inanna] like a pot went to pieces.
. . . destruction is the fate of the black-headed ones.[68]

This 'destruction' was, at the same time, a cataclysmic 'birth', as is made clear in the equivalent section of *The Epic of Gilgamesh*:

The gods were terrified by the Flood;
They shrank back, fled upwards to the highest heavens...
Ishtar [Inanna] cried out like a woman giving birth...
"Alas, the olden days are turned to clay...
How could I order battle for the destruction of my people?
Alas, I myself (now) give birth to my people!
Like the spawn of fish they (now) fill the sea!"[69]

Note how the poet visualises the black-headed ones bursting forth from
the womb of the sky-goddess to fill the celestial ocean.

At this point, the authors of *The Epic of Gilgamesh* and the *Atra-Hasis
Epic* fall all over themselves in a veritable deluge of metaphors. They
inform us that the Flood 'roared like a bull' and 'fought like an army'.[70]
Furthermore, they tell us that the people, the black-headed ones, filled up
the celestial sea 'like fish', clogged up the river of Heaven and Earth
'like dragonflies', and were scattered abroad 'like white sheep'.[71] Amidst
this total chaos, no man could see his fellow; everything turned dark as
the Flood-storm overtook and overwhelmed the black-headed ones 'like
a battle'.[72]

Eventually, after raging Earthwards for six days and six nights, the
Flood-storm, personified by the unfortunate black-headed ones, swept
into the Earth, depositing them therein as the seed of mankind. The
Flood-hero Utnapishtim, personifying the Flood-storm (just as the black-
headed ones did), looked out of his 'ship' to find that 'all of mankind had
returned to clay'.[73] However, as the Sumerian myth of Ziusudra explains,
one of the gods (probably Enki) had promised that man would be saved
from the destruction by being resettled in the cult-centres or cities of the
Underworld:

"As for my people, from its destruction will I cause it to be . . .
For Nintu I will return the . . . of my creatures,
I will return the people into their settlements,
In cities, let them build places of divine ordinances."[74]

Thus the black-headed ones were reincarnated from the planet of Heaven
to the Underworld of the Earth, where they were described poetically as
a 'beclouded people'.[75] Immediately, the Anunnaki-gods conquered this
fallen race. They enslaved them, barred the gates of their settlements and
put them to work in the farms and excavations.[76] But 'a stated time' had
been decreed for man when he would reacquire the kingship which had
been lost,[77] and eventually, aeons later, the gods lowered kingship from
Heaven (and perhaps the first king too). It was at this point that the
prototype king had led the poor black-headed ones on an exodus out of

the Underworld into the light of the world above.[78]

Such, then, is the myth of the black-headed ones ('the living creatures of Heaven and Earth'), and, on the face of it, it might strike the reader as a ridiculous tale. But the myth, in fact, conveys an extraordinary 'truth' that is concealed behind allegory and metaphors. The ancient 'city' of Shuruppak is the planet of Heaven, as is the 'house' of Utnapishtim. The conversion of Utnapishtim's 'house' into a 'ship' (the original Noah's Ark) signifies the explosion of the planet of Heaven and the transmission of its seeds of life across the celestial waters to the Earth.[79] And finally, most significantly for our investigation, the black-headed people signify the black iron meteorites which were swept across space to be imbedded in the Earth as the seeds of life. It is truly profound stuff.

Just how relevant this allegory is to the Greek myths will now become evident as I disclose two astonishing parallels that have hitherto never been spotted. The first concerns the myth of Deucalion's flood, and the second the myth of the children of Niobe.

As regards Deucalion's flood, one of the curious details of the myth is the epithet given to the stones, namely 'the bones of the mother', i.e. the mother of Deucalion and Pyrrha. Whilst it has always been presumed that these bones belonged to Mother Earth, the Mesopotamian flood myth would rather suggest that they belonged to the heavenly mother-goddess Mami/Ninharsag/Inanna who 'went to pieces like a pot'. This would make more sense, and it would also explain why the stones just happened to be lying on the river bank (the phrase 'river bank' should be understood in the Mesopotamian sense, as the resting point of the flood-river that descended from Heaven to Earth).[80]

Secondly, there is an amazing parallel between the myth of Mami and the black-headed ones and the myth of Niobe and her children as told by Homer in the 24th book of the *Iliad*. According to Homer, Niobe had borne twelve children (six sons and six daughters) who were all in the prime of their youth. But Niobe and her children came to grief when she arrogantly compared herself to the goddess Leto who had borne just two children, Apollo and Artemis. In a response that might seem somewhat heavy-handed (if we were not dealing with a myth), Apollo proceeded to strike down Niobe's six sons with his arrows, while Artemis destroyed the six daughters likewise. Homer then reports a strange scenario indeed:

> For nine days they [the children] lay in their blood, and there was no-one to bury them, as the son of Kronos had turned the people into stones: but on the tenth day the heavenly gods buried them.[81]

In addition, Niobe herself was famously turned into stone by the gods.[82]

What does this story mean? In the light of the Mesopotamian myth of the Flood, the interpretation becomes straightforward. Niobe parallels the Mesopotamian sky-goddess who gives birth to the black-headed people, and thus, in accordance with the exploded planet hypothesis, she and her people are turned into stones. As for Niobe's boast aimed at the goddess Leto, this is highly appropriate since, according to my decoding in chapter thirteen, Leto personified the exploded planet (her name, we should recall, meant 'Stone,' whilst her children, Apollo and Artemis, were famous arrow-shooting deities, i.e. meteorite-gods, according to Wainwright).

Thus did the Mesopotamian allegory of the meteorite-people find its way into the poetry of Homer. But might it also have been picked up by Plato? Could his ideal race of heroic Athenians have been modelled on the black-headed people, who descended, like a storm, from Heaven to Earth?

The War of Heaven and Earth

In the above cited myth, the poet compared the Flood from Shuruppak to a raging army fighting a battle, as the following citations from *The Epic of Gilgamesh* and the *Atra-Hasis Epic* demonstrate:

> (Ishtar:) "How could I order *battle* for the destruction of my people?"[83]

> For one day, the south-storm blew, gathering speed, overtaking the people *like a battle*.[84]

> The *kasusu*-weapon overcame the people *like an army*. No-one could see anyone else.[85]

> On the seventh day of its coming, the south-storm-Flood broke from its *battle*, which it had *fought like an army*.[86]

In addition, the poet personified the Flood either as Utnapishtim or as the black-headed ones, causing these characters likewise to be pictured as a raging army. This makes sense of a very odd reference to Utnapishtim in *The Epic of Gilgamesh*:

> (Gilgamesh to the Flood-hero Utnapishtim:) "My heart had pictured thee as one perfect for the doing of battle."[87]

The principle here is the important thing. Given the widespread myths of the cataclysmic fall of the sky, and given the tendency of ancient poets to anthropomorphise the falling fragments of the sky (e.g. the myths of the gods who came down), it is absolutely logical that the Flood-storm from

Heaven should be personified as a falling army of men who ravaged the Earth and the Underworld.

Further examples of this allegory are not hard to find. In the myth of *Enmerkar and the Lord of Aratta* (see previous chapter), the heavenly city of Aratta contains fighting-men, metal-workers, stone-workers, a council of elders, a *mashmash*-priest and apparently an entire population, all led by a king, the Lord of Aratta.[88] This heavenly city is subjected to a war of nerves by the Earth-city of Uruk, which eventually forces its surrender, whereupon Aratta is destroyed and its people rain down from Heaven in the form of gold, silver, lapis lazuli and clay.

A variant on the theme is the myth of *Gilgamesh and Agga* (again see previous chapter), where this time the heavenly city of Kish subjects the Earth-city of Uruk to a war of nerves, and then launches an invasion. Here, the falling city of Kish is personified by Agga and his army whose cataclysmic assault on the Earth is described poetically thus:

> The multitude [of Kish] cast itself down, the multitude rose up,
> The multitude rolled in the dust,
> The foreigners, the lot of them, were overwhelmed,
> On the mouths of the natives [of Uruk], dust was heaped...[89]

A further example of the allegory occurs in the Sumerian *Lamentation Texts*, where the poet personifies Enlil's Flood from Heaven in the form of the Guti 'mountain-people':

> On the land fell a calamity, one unknown to man...
> On that day, Enlil brought down the Guti from the mountain-land,
> Whose coming is the Flood of Enlil, that none can withstand...
> They overwhelmed at once the bright day with tumult.
> It was a day when mouths were drenched, heads wallowed in blood,
> A day when the weapon sent forth from above wrecked the city as if
>   with a pickaxe.
> On that day, Heaven was crushed, Earth was smitten...
> Heaven was darkened, was overcast with shadow, was turned into the
>   Underworld.[90]

In this passage, the cataclysmic imagery is perfectly explicit, and there can be no doubt that the poet intended the Guti mountain-people to personify the Flood-storm of Heaven (the 'pickaxe'/meteorite metaphor is particularly explicit here).[91]

Finally, I would refer the reader to more familiar territory, namely the Old Testament book of Isaiah, where the author warns of the heavenly army that Yahweh would bring against the Earth at the End of Days:

(There is) the noise of a multitude in the mountains, like that of a great
    people...
Yahweh-Sabaoth ['LORD of Hosts'] is mustering an army for battle.
The LORD and the weapons of his wrath – they come from a faraway
    land, from the end of Heaven, to destroy the whole Earth.
Lament, for the day of the LORD is at hand; it shall come as a
    destruction from El Shaddai.[92]

What kind of army, we might ask, can be brought down from 'the end of
Heaven' to destroy the whole Earth? The answer is not an army of
people, but a storm of meteorites and floodwaters *personified* by an army
of people. The Holy Bible thus enshrines the very same principle of
allegorical representation that we have discovered in the Mesopotamian
texts.

In summary, the Mesopotamian myths contain numerous examples of
allegorical wars being fought between peoples of Heaven and peoples of
Earth, and these mythical ideas were in circulation many centuries before
the beginning of Greek civilisation. Moreover, it is entirely reasonable to
conclude that this type of myth was transmitted to Greece along with all
the other myths, including, significantly, the allegorical wars between the
gods of Heaven and Earth. The big question, then, is not whether Plato
could have used this allegory for his war between Athens and Atlantis,
but whether he *actually did*.

An Athenian Golden Race?

Were Plato's ancient Athenians a golden race of heroes who descended
from Heaven to Earth? At first glance, the reader might doubt the idea in
view of the fact that the kings who fought the war, Cecrops, Erechtheus,
Erichthonios and Erysichthon, were all 'born from the earth'. But this, it
turns out, is only one half of the story.

Take Cecrops. Whilst he was earth-born by some accounts, one myth
reports that he fathered Erichthonios upon Gaia (Earth), implying that he
came down from Heaven, personifying the fall of the sky (see Figure 10
at the end of chapter fifteen).[93]

Or take Erechtheus. He, too, was supposedly earth-born, and yet his
cult had apparently been instigated when Poseidon rammed him into the
ground during the ancient war between Eleusis and Athens. The strange
fate of Erechtheus seems to recall a proto-myth in which the original
king descended from Heaven.[94]

A parallel situation exists with the ancient Athenian king Theseus,
whose name was mentioned by Plato in connection with the kings who

fought the Atlantian war. Theseus, too, was prima facie an earth-born king.[95] And yet some myths report that he descended into the Underworld as if descending from Heaven. In one myth, Theseus dived into the depths of the sea, at the sign of a thunderbolt, to prove that he was the son of Poseidon, whilst in another he entered the subterranean labyrinth to release the boys and girls of Athens (both acts are strongly suggestive of descents from Heaven).[96] Furthermore, a classic motif in Greek art was Theseus, drawn sword in hand, attacking the goddess Medea – symbolic, surely, of a sexual assault by Heaven on Earth.[97]

There is a pattern here which echoes the myth of the foundation of Athens. In that myth, Athens fell from Heaven, entered the Underworld, and was then reborn into the world above (see previous chapter). In these myths, similarly, the kings descend from Heaven, enter the Underworld, and are then reborn into the world above. Cecrops I thus begets a son, Cecrops II, who emerges from the Underworld to become the ruler of Athens (thus explaining the myth of his 'half-man half-serpent' identity). In parallel myths, Erechtheus I begets Erechtheus II, and Theseus I begets Theseus II. As for the other mythical kings of Athens, the song, now lost, was surely the same.[98]

Therefore, when Plato named the ancient Athenian heroes as he did, it is quite possible that he had in mind a war fought *not* by the earth-born generation, but rather by their heavenly, golden age fathers. In fact, the evidence, when it is assembled, is most compelling. Consider:

1   Plato compared ancient Athens to the ideal state, which was predicated upon a heavenly model.

2   The city of Athens fought the war against Atlantis at the same time as it was founded on Earth 'nine thousand years ago'.

3   The war ended with a cataclysm in which the Athenian heroes sank into the Earth, just as if they had descended from Heaven.

4   The names of the Athenian heroes match those of mythical kings who descended from Heaven into the Underworld.

5   Plato described Athens and its acropolis in mythical, idyllic terms, consistent with the golden age planet of Heaven.

6   The ancient Athenian army had its headquarters on the acropolis, which, as a high place, would have symbolised Heaven. Sure enough, the statue of Athene there bore arms, and the acropolis was ruined by the same cataclysm that caused Atlantis to sink.[99]

7   The war occurred in mythical times; it was the third cataclysm prior
    to the flood of Deucalion.

In addition, some important arguments of principle have been brought to
bear:

1   In ancient times, the 'Myth of all myths' was that of the falling sky.

2   The ancient myth-makers personified the fall of the sky by having
    human-like gods and golden age peoples descend from Heaven to
    Earth.

3   The fall of Heaven to Earth was portrayed in Near Eastern and
    Greek literature as a cataclysmic war between the gods of Heaven
    and the gods of the Underworld. It was also portrayed in Near
    Eastern literature as a cataclysmic war in which a race of men came
    down from Heaven like an army.

4   The Greeks borrowed extensively, through much of their history,
    from Near Eastern mythical motifs (see chapters six to nine, plus
    the examples cited in this chapter concerning the myths of the
    golden race and the creation of man from meteorites).

In the light of all these eleven points, I would argue that it is very likely
indeed that Plato's ancient race of heroic Athenians were a golden age
race who descended from Heaven to Earth (into the Underworld). They
would thus fulfil the allegorical role of a mythical army from Heaven
that came crashing down on the heads of their victims, like the proverbial
ton of bricks.

It now remains only to explain how the island of Atlantis fits in to the
picture.

Chapter Seventeen Summary

* The Greeks believed that man had been 'born from the earth', having
  been created in the Underworld. This idea stemmed from the myth that
  mankind had been created in a fiery cataclysm from meteorites, known
  metaphorically as the 'seed of Hephaestus', the 'stones' of Deucalion
  and Pyrrha, and the 'teeth' of the serpent Ophion. The origins of this
  myth seem to lie in the Mesopotamian myth of 'the black-headed
  ones' – 'the living creatures of Heaven and Earth'.

* The Greek myths allude to a golden age during which a race of ideal
  men had lived upon the planet of Heaven. But this race had then fallen
  to Earth, into the Underworld – hence the myths of the Hyperboreans

and the golden race whose spirits became 'watchers over mortal men'. Clear parallels and precedents for this idea are found in the myths of Mesopotamia.

* In the exploded planet myths of Mesopotamia, the Flood-storm from Heaven was personified as an army of men who raged, as if in battle, as they descended from Heaven to Earth, into the Underworld. The same theme is found in the Old Testament book of Isaiah, where the author warns of the heavenly army that Yahweh would bring against the Earth at the End of Days.

* Plato seems to be drawing on the Mesopotamian 'falling army of Heaven' idea when he describes the ancient Athenians going into war against Atlantis. Hence the war ends with a cataclysm in which the Athenian heroes sink into the Earth.

* Consistent with this, the names of the Athenian heroes who fought the war match those of mythical kings who descended from Heaven into the Underworld (e.g. Cecrops and Erechtheus).

* In the light of all this, Athens must surely have signified a city that fell from Heaven, as suggested in the previous chapter. This would explain why the city was founded in the Earth at roughly the same time as the war with Atlantis, 'nine thousand years ago'.

* In summary, Plato's story of the war between ancient Athens and Atlantis seems to have been a retelling of the age-old 'true story' of the exploded planet, with the city of Athens and its people, the Athenians, citifying and personifying, respectively, the falling Mountain of Heaven.

CHAPTER EIGHTEEN

MYSTERIES OF THE DEEP

Out there is a real sea, and the land that embraces it all the way around deserves most truly to be called a continent.
(Plato, *Timaeus*, mid-4th century BC)

So far, so good. The role of Athens in Plato's story has been explained. But what about Atlantis? In what sense did this island-continent exist? In what sense did its people attack the known world by sailing through the Pillars of Heracles? And in what sense did it sink beneath the waves, at the time of the cataclysm, leaving behind only a sea of mud to mark the spot? Was Atlantis a real island, destroyed by earthquakes and floods? Or did it, in fact, symbolise the entire Earth or Underworld, as I hinted in chapter fifteen? Many readers, following their predilections, will opt for the 'real island' alternative, for that, on the face of it, is how Plato described Atlantis. Nevertheless, there are several clues to suggest that Plato had a deeper meaning in mind. For example: the abnormal size of the island; its perfect circular shape; its supernatural manner of creation (from the primeval hill of Clito); its idyllic, paradisiacal nature; its similarities to the otherworldly Elysian Plain and Islands; its existence during pre-diluvian and pre-human times; and the shallow sea of mud that it left behind after it sank. All of these points argue for a mythical rather than a historical Atlantis (see chapter fifteen).

Above all, the reader must bear in mind that there is no evidence whatsoever of any sunken island or continent beneath the Atlantic Ocean (in fact, quite the opposite), and Plato was quite adamant that Atlantis did sink in this region. Here, the textual evidence is unequivocal. Critias, for example, explained that the names 'Atlantis' and 'Atlantic Ocean' shared an etymological root in 'Atlas '– a god who dwelt in the Atlantic Ocean:

> "To the son who was oldest and king he gave the name from which the entire island and its surrounding sea derive their names... His name

was Atlas; the island is called Atlantis and the sea Atlantic after him."[1]

To pretend, as Atlantis-hunters do, that Atlantis might have existed somewhere other than in the Atlantic Ocean is to stray dangerously from Plato's text. The fact is that Plato did place the sunken continent in the Atlantic and this fact must be explained, in conjunction with the lack of findings on the Atlantic Ocean's floor.

Accordingly, I now ask that the reader grants me his greatest possible indulgence while I explore a new approach to the mystery. The question I would now like to ask is this: *why* did the Greeks have a tradition of a lost island in the Atlantic Ocean, together with an 'opposite continent' beyond it, which in Plato's words 'embraced the true Ocean all around'?

The Underworld in the West

A good place to start is the Elysian Plain. As discussed in chapter fifteen, the Elysian Plain was a mythical paradise in the remote west, to which the souls of the blessed dead would be translated in the afterlife. There, man's spiritual *alter ego* would enjoy an easy life in an almost heavenly climate 'where no snow falls, no strong winds blow, and there is never any rain.'[2] Significantly, the poet Pindar referred to the Elysian land as a series of islands:

> But those who had good courage... these travel
> Along the road of Zeus to Kronos' tower.
> There, round the Islands of the Blessed, the winds
> Of Ocean play...[3]

These Elysian islands, like the Elysian Plain, were located in the remote west, at the limits of the western Ocean (the Atlantic), 'at the ends of the Earth'.

The dream of an afterlife in the Elysian Plain is, when we stop to think about it, a curious concept. The Greeks, after all, knew full well from practical experience that the land of the dead lay beneath their feet in the subterranean region, where the deceased were buried. It was for this reason that they referred idiomatically to death as 'sinking down to the House of Hades' or 'going down to the world below', where loathsome Hades and fearsome Persephone presided as king and queen in a dark and dreary Underworld.[4] But at some point, apparently, the Greeks came to the view that certain souls deserved a better fate and, with Heaven 'off limits' to man, they invented (or possibly borrowed from the Near East) the concept of an afterlife in the light and airy paradise of the Elysian

Plain in the West.[5]

But why was it supposed that the Elysian Plain lay, of all places, in the remote west? The explanation is that many ancient peoples, the Greeks included, regarded the West as symbolic of death, owing to the fact that the Sun 'dies' every night when it sets in the western horizon. The idea was particularly popular in ancient Egypt, but was equally at home in the civilisations of Mesopotamia.[6] The upshot of this was that the land of the dead could lie in two places simultaneously – beneath one's feet, in a physical sense, but also in the remote west, in a symbolic sense.

There is an important principle at stake here which could overturn everything we ever believed about the Isle of Atlantis and the 'opposite continent' beyond. The principle is this: that the Underworld could be portrayed *either* as the interior of the Earth *or* as a region of the remote west; and, accordingly, the poets of old could chop and change, as they wished, between mythical *subterranean* locations and equally mythical *western* locations. It might be argued, therefore, that the Elysian Plain, for example, belonged not in the remote west 'at the ends of the Earth', but rather in the subterranean Underworld which was the true home of the dead.

The Adventures of Odysseus

The confusion of the two Underworlds – the one, real and subterranean, the other, symbolic and western – is a major feature in the myths and folklore of Odysseus. In Homer's *Odyssey*, when the hero reached the island of Aeaea, something remarkable occurred. Even though the Sun set and rose just as normal, Odysseus gathered his men together and complained: "We are utterly lost. We do not know where east or west is; where the light-giving Sun rises or where it sets."[7] The reader might be forgiven for thinking that Odysseus had suddenly entered the twilight zone. But the straightforward explanation is that Homer was mentally shifting his scene from an island of Aeaea in the west *to an island of Aeaea underground*, where perpetual darkness would have prevented Odysseus and his men from seeing the rising and setting of the Sun.

An equally bizarre scene follows. Upon leaving the island of Aeaea, Odysseus was told by the witch Circe to travel to the land of the dead and consult with the soul of Teiresias, the blind prophet. This quest, says Homer, required Odysseus to sail his ship into 'the Halls of Hades and dread Persephone' – an unmistakeable reference to the subterranean region![8] However, instead of sinking underground, Odysseus continued sailing into ever more remote regions of the Ocean (i.e. the Atlantic) until eventually he found himself at 'the banks of Ocean'. Significantly, this was a place of darkness where the Sun never shone. The details are narrated by Odysseus as follows:

> "So our ship reached the furthest parts of the deep-flowing river of Ocean where the Cimmerians live, wrapped in mist and fog. The bright Sun cannot look down on them with his rays, either when he climbs the starry skies or when he turns back from the skies to earth once again. Dreadful Night spreads her mantle over that unhappy people. Here we beached our ship and... made our way along the banks of the river of Ocean till we reached the place that Circe had described."[9]

The place that Circe had described occurs in an earlier passage:

> "When the North Wind has brought you across the river of Ocean, you will come to a wild coast and Persephone's grove... Beach your boat there by Ocean's swirling stream and go on into Hades' kingdom of decay. There the river Pyriphlegethon and the river Cocytus (which is a branch of the Styx) meet at a rocky pinnacle, and pour their thundering streams into the Acheron."[10]

True to this instruction, Odysseus beached his ship, made his way along 'the banks of Ocean', and marched his men into Hades' Underworld, as if it were a conventional continent in the remote west. But what Homer is describing, in fact, is an entry into the subterranean Underworld, with the geographical landscape (of east and west) being merged poetically with the mythical landscape (of above and below).

This same principle is at work in the myths of the Elysian Plain and Islands. They, too, were located, for symbolic effect, in the West, at the so-called 'ends of the earth'. And yet no-one would claim that they were geographical places. On the contrary, they were mythical places intended for the dwellings of souls in the afterlife and, as such, they belonged, in truth, to the land of the dead, i.e. to the subterranean Underworld.

What might this mean for the Isle of Atlantis? It, too, was located in the West, in the midst of the western Ocean. It, too, belonged to a chain of islands (reminiscent of the Elysian Islands). And it, too, possessed an idyllic plain (reminiscent of the Elysian Plain). Did Atlantis belong, in truth, to the mythical subterranean Underworld?

In search of an answer to Atlantis, and the chain of islands under its command, it is appropriate that we now turn to the traditions of Atlas, for Plato tells us that this god was the key to the naming of Atlantis and the Atlantic Ocean in which it lay.

The Mystery of Atlas

Who was Atlas? According to Hesiod, Atlas was fathered by the Titan god Iapetos who slept with the nymph Clymene, thus making Atlas, on the face of it, an earth-born *daimon*.[11] Atlas was better known, however, as one of the Titans who had been expelled from Heaven by Zeus. Hence Pindar imagined him as a god exiled from his heavenly homeland:

> Does not even now great Atlas struggle to bear up
> The weight of Heaven, far from his father's land
> And his possessions?[12]

It was the task of Atlas, as Pindar observed, to support the Heaven and prevent it from collapsing again onto the Earth (yet another example of cataclysmic thought inherent in the ancient Greek traditions). By one tradition, Atlas did this with his head, hands and shoulders; by another tradition, he did it by supporting the pillars 'that hold Earth and Heaven together in opposition'; and by a third tradition he did it in the form of Mount Atlas.[13]

The latter tradition is illuminating. Mount Atlas, in the mythical sense, had its foundations in the Underworld and its peak, symbolically, in the heavens; it was the 'Mountain of the Universe'.[14] The geographical Mount Atlas, on the other hand, stood at the north-west corner of Libya, opposite the Rock of Gibraltar. This mountain (it is actually part of a mountain range), together with the Rock of Gibraltar, formed the Pillars of Heracles, which, during Greek times, signified the limits of the known world and the beginnings of the unknown world, i.e. the unexplored depths of the western Ocean – the very region in which Atlantis was said to lie.[15]

Significantly, though, the realm of Atlas was not confined in any way by the Pillars of Heracles, but instead extended throughout the western Ocean to its uttermost ends – hence Homer's declaration in the *Odyssey* that 'Atlas knows the depths of all the seas'.[16] Of equal significance, Hesiod, in *Theogony*, stated that Atlas stood in the furthermost west, at the 'ends of the Earth':

> Atlas, under strong constraint, holds up the broad Heaven with his
> head and tireless hands, standing at the ends of the Earth, away by the
> clear-voiced Hesperides, for Zeus-the-resourceful assigned him this
> lot.[17]

The Hesperides goddesses, mentioned here, were said to live upon the slopes of Mount Atlas, where they tended the trees of the golden apples.[18] But this Mount Atlas, it must be stressed, was not the one in Libya, but the mythical 'Mountain of the Universe' which was located in the remote west at 'the ends of the Earth' (the same location as the Elysian Plain and Islands).[19] Hence the fact that the Hesperides goddesses Hespere, Aegle and Erytheis were named after the setting Sun (as indeed was the western Ocean in its former name of the Erythraean sea).[20]

But did 'the ends of the Earth' lie in the remote west, as the poets often claimed, or did they, in fact, lie underground? Hesiod, in *Theogony*, gives us considerable food for thought:

> There [in Tartarus] the Titan gods are hidden away down in the misty gloom... at the end of the vast Earth. They have no way out... There are the sources and extremities of dark Earth and misty Tartarus, of the undraining sea and the starry Heaven, all in order, dismal and dank... And there stands the fearful house of gloomy Night... Next to that, the son of Iapetos [Atlas] stands holding the broad Heaven firmly upon his head and untiring hands...[21]

In this passage, 'the ends of the Earth' are located underground, as are the banished Titan gods. Atlas, from being a god of the deep ocean and a god of the remote west, has suddenly become a god of the subterranean Underworld.[22]

Lest there be any doubt about this, the same idea occurs earlier in *Theogony* in respect of the three Titans known as the Hundred-handers. Of their fate, Hesiod sang thus:

> When their father [Ouranos] first became hostile to Briareos, Kottos and Gyges, he bound them in powerful fetters... and settled them below the wide-pathed Earth. There they sat at the ends of the Earth, living in misery below the earth, at the great world's limits, and for a long time they were suffering there with great pain at heart.[23]

The true 'ends of the Earth', it would seem, lay not in the remote west, but underground at the deepest point in the Earth – effectively at the centre of the Earth's sphere.[24]

So, did Atlas support the Heaven by standing in the West, or did he, in fact, perform this task by standing in the Underworld? The answer to this question becomes perfectly simple once we understand how Atlas and the other Titans came to be assigned their various fates.

In this respect, Hesiod's *Theogony* provides just about everything we need to know. Here, we learn that the Titans, led by Kronos, had once ruled Mount Olympus, but had been driven out of Heaven by Zeus owing to the cruelty and deviousness of their reign.[25] Atlas had been one of four Titan brothers (sons of Iapetos and Clymene), the others being named

Menoitios, Prometheus and Epimetheus. Of Menoitios, Hesiod sang: 'he was sent down into the darkness by wide-seeing Zeus with a smoking bolt',[26] whilst of Prometheus, he sang: 'Zeus bound him in inescapable fetters... driving them through the middle of a pillar' (Aeschylus would later suggest that Zeus had bound Prometheus to the Caucasus Mountain, which he despatched into the Underworld amidst a fiery cataclysm).[27] Of Epimetheus, Hesiod tells us nothing (in Greek tradition, he was regarded as a bungling *alter ego* of Prometheus),[28] whilst of Atlas we are told that Zeus confined him to 'the ends of the Earth' to support the broad Heaven for eternity (see the passage cited earlier).

The meaning of all this should be abundantly clear. The Titans, cast down from Heaven, had ended up where fallen gods always ended up; they were denizens of the subterranean Underworld (Tartarus).[29] Atlas thus belonged truly to the chthonian realm, where he acted as the pillar or mountain of the Universe, connecting together Heaven, Earth and the Underworld. The rest, we may presume, was the work of the poets who, on the one hand, incarnated Atlas into a real world Mount Atlas, to mark one of the Pillars of Heracles, and, on the other hand, relocated chthonian Atlas to the furthermost west, purely for poetic effect.

This, I would remind the reader, is the account of Atlas, the Titan god, after whom the Atlantic Ocean, the Isle of Atlantis, and its first king, Atlas, were named.

The Pillars of Heracles

Significantly, the 'ends of the Earth' were also the destination of the hero Heracles in an adventure that inspired the tales of his famous 'twelve labours'. The poet Pindar (5th century BC) tells the original tale thus:

> No further tempt then the uneasy task,
> Beyond the Pillars of Heracles to sail the uncharted Ocean,
> Those famous marks the hero-god set up
> To bound the sailor's voyage. And he slew
> Huge monsters in the deep,
> And he traced out the shoals and eddies.
> And journeying to the farthest goal destined
> For safe return, he made plain the ends of the Earth.[30]

Here, Pindar alludes to the popular belief that Heracles had thrust apart the continents of Europe and Libya (which had previously been joined together), or cut a passage between them, to create the straits of Gibraltar and the two opposing Pillars that bore his name.[31] As Pindar observes, the Greek tradition had it that the Pillars of Heracles marked the boundary between the known world – the lands that framed the Mediterranean Sea – and the unknown world of the great western Ocean (i.e. the Atlantic). It was beyond these Pillars of Heracles – somewhere within the 'uncharted Ocean' as Pindar puts it – that the Isle of Atlantis was located by Plato.

But did the Pillars of Heracles simply mark a geographical boundary? Or did they perhaps mark a mythical boundary, distinguishing the known world of men from the unknown world of the subterranean gods, such as loathsome Hades and Persephone, the 'Earth-shaker' Poseidon, and the unswerving Atlas? In other words, did the Pillars of Heracles mark the gateway to the subterranean Underworld, once again relocated to the West for poetic effect?

The myths of Heracles would indeed suggest that the Pillars bearing his name were the gateway to the Underworld. Of his twelve labours (a fairly late tradition), three can be identified right away with subterranean domains. There is the tenth labour, in which Heracles sailed to Erytheia – a distant island beyond the Ocean – and fetched back the cattle of the three-headed monster Geryon.[32] There is the eleventh labour, in which he travelled beyond the Ocean again, to Mount Atlas, where he stole three golden apples from the garden of the Hesperides.[33] And there is the twelfth labour, in which he descended into Tartarus and brought back the dog Cerberus, the fifty-headed hound of Hades.[34] Scholars agree that each of these three labours was performed in the Underworld.[35]

In addition, a strong case can be made that the other nine labours of Heracles were also performed in the Underworld.

In his first labour – the slaying of the Nemean lion – Heracles trapped and killed the lion in a dual-mouthed cave; this cave might well have symbolised the Underworld for, according to myth, the lion had been borne by a subterranean monster (either Echidna or Hydra of Lerna), having been cast down from Heaven to Earth.[36] In his second labour – the slaying of the Hydra of Lerna – Heracles found the menacing monster living beneath a marsh at the sevenfold source of the river Amymone; this sounds remarkably like an Underworld location, which would fit with the fact that the Hydra was a sibling of Orthos, the dog of Geryon, and Cerberus, the dog of Hades.[37] In his third labour – the capturing of the Ceryneian hind – Heracles chased the golden-horned hind, which lived at Oinoe ('the land of wine'), towards the mountain of Artemis and the river Ladon, and felled it there with an arrow; this sounds very much like the mythical landscape of the Underworld.[38]

The fifth labour of Heracles was to clean out the stables of the cattle of king Augeias; but what kind of cattle were these that had filled up the valleys with dung? (Were they akin to the cattle of Geryon, or the cattle of the Sun-god, or the cattle of Atlas or of Hades – those mythical cattle that lived at 'the ends of the earth'?)[39]

The sixth labour of Heracles was to remove the supernatural birds from the Stymphalian Marsh and the banks of the Stymphalian river; but marshes and river were often said to be located in the Underworld and a good argument can be mounted that the Stymphalian Marsh and river belonged to this subterranean ilk.[40]

In his seventh labour – the capture of the Cretan bull – it would seem that Heracles dragged the fire-breathing monster from its subterranean labyrinth.[41]

In his ninth labour – the fetching of the golden girdle of Hippolyte – Heracles travelled to the land of the Amazonians, which was not only a geographical location but also a mythical land of the remote west.[42]

Finally, an argument can be made that Heracles' fourth labour (the capture of the Erymanthian boar) and his eighth labour (the capture of the man-eating mares of Diomedes) were also performed in the Underworld.[43]

All of this tends to confirm the words of Pindar: that Heracles created the straits of Gibraltar and the Pillars of Heracles, entered the uncharted Ocean, slew sea-monsters in the deep, and made plain 'the ends of the earth'; in other words, split open the Earth and circumnavigated the limits of the Underworld. And thus it was that Heracles won the gift of immortality and ascended to Olympus to dwell with the heavenly gods (for, in ancient myths, this was something that could only be achieved by conquering the dangers of the Underworld).[44]

In summary, the adventures of Heracles testify to the fact that the Pillars of Heracles marked the entrance to the subterranean Underworld. And yet, there is more. For, as we shall now discover, the Pillars of Heracles marked also the entrance to a subterranean sea.

The Subterranean Sea

The idea of a subterranean sea might seem a little bizarre to those of us who are unfamiliar with ancient myths and the ancient way of thinking. Nevertheless, it is a fact that the ancient Mesopotamians and the Greeks believed in an underground ocean that was the source for all the world's rivers and springs.

A prime example is the Greek god Oceanus. As the scholar Martin West has explained, Oceanus personified the great western Ocean, and yet he also signified a subterranean body of water:

Although Oceanus is normally mentioned only in connection with the ends of the Earth, as the stream that encircles the Earth, he also appears as the father of all the world's rivers and springs... This implies a mass of water, or at least of water channels, below the Earth, and it makes Oceanus into something not altogether unlike the Hebrew *tehom*... or the Mesopotamian Apsu.[45]

The comparison here between Oceanus and Apsu is highly significant. As noted in chapter eight, the god Apsu started his career in the heavens as a partner to Tiamat, but was later cast down into the Earth, where he became the ocean of the Underworld. The scenario is to be understood in the context of an exploded planet cult, with Apsu signifying a planetary ocean that fell from Heaven.

The story, apparently, is the same for Oceanus. He, too, was depicted as an ocean of Heaven (e.g. on the cosmic shield of Hephaestus). And yet he, too, was a subterranean body of water – 'from which all rivers and all the sea and all springs and deep wells take their flow' (*Iliad*, 21.195-97). If scholars are correct in their view that Oceanus was modelled on the Mesopotamian Apsu – and the evidence is persuasive (see chapter eight) – then Oceanus, like Apsu, would signify the ocean that fell from the planet of Heaven.

Nevertheless, the Greek and Mesopotamian perspectives of the fallen ocean differed in one crucial respect: the Greeks, as a result of their sea-faring culture and proximity to the seemingly unnavigable Ocean of the West, converted Oceanus from a god of the subterranean sea to a god of the real world ocean in the West – otherwise known as the Atlantic. For such was the mystique of this unknown and unfathomable Ocean that it encapsulated perfectly the mysterious Underworld and the subterranean sea – the true Oceanus – that lay within it.[46]

That this was so is evident from the idea that the Pillars of Heracles marked not only the entrance to the Atlantic Ocean, but also the entrance to the subterranean Underworld and, indeed, to the subterranean sea (Heracles, for example, was said to have slain huge sea-monsters in the deep during his circumnavigation of 'the ends of the earth'). Moreover, it is a fact that the Greeks knew the straits of Gibraltar by a variant name 'the Pillars of Kronos', and that they knew Oceanus and the Atlantic by a corresponding variant name 'the Sea of Kronos'.[47] This is a significant fact because Kronos was the former god of Heaven whom Zeus had banished 'beneath the earth and beneath the harvestless sea', i.e. into the Underworld.[48] The Sea of Kronos would thus have been a subterranean sea in the first instance (making Kronos a cognate of Enki/Ea, the old Mesopotamian god of the Apsu).

Indeed, when we stop to think about it, it turns out that every major god associated with the western Ocean was a chthonic power. Kronos is but one example. Another is Atlas, who was cast into the Underworld by Zeus; he was said to 'know the depths of all the seas', and the Atlantic Ocean was presumably named after him. Another is Oceanus who, like Apsu, was truly a subterranean sea (cast down from Heaven). And finally there is Poseidon, the deep-sea god who was known as 'the Earth-shaker', i.e. the god of earthquakes. All of these gods belonged primarily in the subterranean Underworld, and indeed in the subterranean sea, and yet they were associated symbolically with the real world Ocean of the West.

What, then, of the various islands that were said to lie in the western Ocean? Did these islands belong, in truth, to the mythical subterranean sea?

Consider the various islands which Homer made famous in his epic poem the *Odyssey*. Here, in the supposedly unknown western Ocean, was the floating island of Aeolia whose king presented Odysseus with the winds, imprisoned inside a leather bag;[49] here was the wooded island of Aeaea where the witch Circe preyed on men and transformed them into fawning animals;[50] here was the fateful island of the sweet-voiced Sirens who robbed so many sailors of their promised homecomings;[51] here was the splendid island of Thrinacie where the Sun-god kept his sacred cattle – the bane of hungry men;[52] here was the lonely island of Ogygia, where Odysseus was wooed for seven long years by the goddess Calypso;[53] and here, last but not least, was the isolated island of Scherie whence those supernatural sailors, the Phaeacians, conveyed Odysseus home in their magical ships.[54] By and large, all of these fabled islands were said to lie in the remote west, at the very 'edge of the world'.

Odysseus had some other strange experiences, too. Somewhere out in the depths of the great Ocean, he ran across the country of the Lotus-eaters, the land of the Cyclopes giants and the land of the Laestrygonian giants.[55] And, in addition to these dangers, he navigated his ship past the sky-high cliff of Scylla the sea-monster and the frightening whirlpool of Charybdis.[56]

This is fairy tale stuff, and it makes no sense in the context of real world geography.[57] However, if the western Ocean was symbolic of the subterranean Underworld, as I have argued, then the supernatural nature of its various lands and inhabitants would begin to make sense, for it is in the subterranean Underworld, and indeed in the subterranean sea, that magic and monsters are truly at home.

Might this mythical subterranean sea be the key to the many mythical qualities of the island of Atlantis? Before we begin to contemplate this question in earnest, we must consider another, equally intriguing puzzle from Plato's story – the mystery of the 'opposite continent'.

The Opposite Continent

In Plato's *Timaeus*, the Egyptian priest tells Solon about an expansive continent that lay beyond Atlantis and its neighbouring islands, on the other side of the Ocean:

> "From those islands one could then travel to the entire continent on
> the other side, which surrounds that real sea beyond [i.e. the Atlantic].
> Everything here inside the strait we're talking about [Gibraltar] seems
> nothing but a harbour with a narrow entrance, whereas out there is a
> real sea, and the land that embraces it all the way around deserves
> most truly to be called a continent..."[58]

The identity of this 'true continent' is a tantalising mystery – arguably as great a mystery as that of Atlantis itself. Indeed the two ideas are often confused, for example by those who have claimed that the American continent is Atlantis (an odd idea, given that the American continent has not sunk!).[59] But Plato's words are not to be gainsaid and what he actually says is that there is both a huge island *in* the true Ocean (i.e. Atlantis) and a huge continent on the other side which *surrounds* the true Ocean.[60]

In order to visualise this, it is necessary to know that the early Greeks believed that the continents of Europe, Asia and Libya were surrounded by Oceanus, which flowed all around them in the shape of an exact circle 'as if described by a pair of compasses'.[61] Hence the idea that Oceanus was *apsorrhoos*, i.e. 'back-flowing' in the sense of 'Ocean whose stream bends back in a circle' (*Iliad* 18.400) and 'the stream of Oceanus that circles back on itself' (*Odyssey* 20.65).[62] Plato is thus building on this tradition to suggest a unique idea of his own – that the circle of Oceanus was surrounded by a larger circle, namely that of the true continent (see Figure 11, overleaf).[63]

What on earth did Plato have in mind by this true continent? The idea, it must be said, seems absurd in a geographical context.[64] But might there be a non-geographical explanation?

Well indeed there is. The first key to this mystery is to recognise that the two concentric circles of the true Ocean and the true continent are, in fact, concentric *spheres* (true to the Pythagorean leanings of *Timaeus*). The second key is to recognise that Oceanus is primarily a subterranean sea that is enclosed within the Earth; hence Plato's idea of it being

Figure 11.
PLATO'S VISION
OF THE WORLD

'the true sea'. When we put these two crucial insights together, Oceanus becomes the spherical, Apsu-like sea of the Underworld and, hey presto, the true continent becomes the spherical, planet-sized crust of the Underworld (see Figure 12, opposite). Simplicity itself.

This makes sense, for, as discussed in chapters eight and ten, Oceanus was the fallen ocean of Heaven whom Homer called 'the source of the gods' creation', i.e. Oceanus was the father of the gods.[65]

In summary, Plato's continent that surrounded the true Ocean was not so much an *opposite* continent as a *nether* continent, relocated from the subterranean Underworld to the West purely for poetic effect, just as Homer had relocated the kingdom of Hades to the West, beyond the Ocean, making it accessible like an ordinary continent to Odysseus and his men. Plato, it may be confidently surmised, picked up this motif from Homer's *Odyssey* and adapted it by making the continent at the 'ends of the earth' surround the Ocean completely. What he created (Figure 11) was a total absurdity in terms of geography (was he parodying Homer or

Figure 12.
THE SPHERE OF THE EARTH AND ITS INTERIOR (IN ANCIENT MYTH)
(Copyright Alan F. Alford)

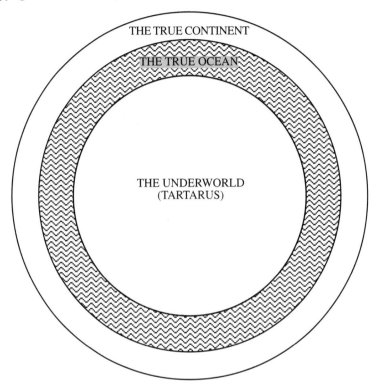

THE TRUE CONTINENT

THE TRUE OCEAN

THE UNDERWORLD
(TARTARUS)

Hecataeus?),[66] but it was quite correct in terms of myth, for the true Ocean indeed belonged inside a continent, namely the Earth's rocky mantle which contained the Underworld.[67]

This idea – of the true Ocean circulating inside the true continent in a planetary sense – is a simple concept 'once the penny drops', but the reader may struggle with it at first, unfamiliar as we are, these days, with the world of the ancient myth-makers. Nevertheless, 'the rugged road is easy to endure when you get to the top', as Hesiod once sang, and the struggle, in this case, is well worthwhile. For one thing, it enables us to understand all the manifold legends of mysterious islands and continents in the remote west (such legends flourished for centuries after Plato's day).[68] And, for another thing, it virtually proves that Plato *deliberately and knowingly* placed the Isle of Atlantis in the midst of *a subterranean sea.*

Chapter Eighteen Summary

* Plato's description of Atlantis lends the island a surreal and mythical air.

* Atlantis was situated beyond the Pillars of Heracles, in the western Ocean – the same location as numerous fairy tale islands in Greek folklore.

* To the Greeks, the West symbolised the land of the dead, owing to the fact that the Sun 'dies' every night when it sets in the western horizon. The poets were thus able to portray the Underworld either as the interior of the Earth or as a region of the remote west.

* Any god or land situated at the westernmost 'ends of the earth' was, in truth, a subterranean god or land. Prime examples are the Titan gods Atlas and Kronos, 'the banks of Ocean' and the nearby kingdom of Hades, and the Elysian Plain and Islands.

* In Greek myth, the Pillars of Heracles signified the entrance to the subterranean Underworld. Inside this Underworld, there lay a subterranean sea (identical in concept to the Mesopotamian Apsu).

* The Greeks made the actual western Ocean (the Atlantic) symbolise the mythical subterranean sea. This explains why all the major gods of the Ocean (Kronos, Atlas, Oceanus and Poseidon) were primarily gods of the subterranean Underworld.

* Plato's 'opposite continent' was, in fact, the subterranean Underworld. The same idea features in the *Odyssey*, where Homer relocated the subterranean kingdom of Hades to the far west, purely for poetic effect. The opposite continent was, in truth, a nether continent.

* Plato adapted Homer's idea of the nether continent in the West by making it surround the true Ocean completely. The idea is bizarre in a geographical context, but absolutely correct in a mythical context, for the continent of the Underworld was a sphere which enclosed the sphere of the subterranean sea.

* By adapting Homer's story thus, Plato made it clear that his story of Atlantis involved the subterranean Ocean (hence his term 'the true Ocean'). By placing Atlantis in the midst of this Ocean, beyond the Pillars of Heracles, Plato was telling his readers, in no uncertain terms, that Atlantis was a mythical island in a mythical subterranean sea.

CHAPTER NINETEEN

ATLANTIS DECODED

My good Crito, why should we care so much for what the majority think?
(Socrates in Plato's *Crito*, mid-4th century BC)

Was Atlantis a fairy tale island, situated within a mythical subterranean sea? Or did it symbolise something more? In this chapter, I will argue that the Isle of Atlantis virtually filled the Underworld, and thus signified the Underworld in its entirety. And I will go on to suggest, in accordance with the laws of ancient myth, that Atlantis the Underworld fell from the sky. Once again, I ask that the reader grants me his greatest possible indulgence while I present the case for this revolutionary, and therefore controversial, idea.

Clito's Hill – The Giveaway Clue

In Plato's *Critias*, we read a fascinating account of how Poseidon, 'the Earth-shaker', created the city of Atlantis:

> "... Poseidon conceived a desire for her [Clito] and slept with her. To make the hill on which she lived a strong enclosure, he broke it to form a circle and he created alternating rings of sea and land around it... He made two rings of land and three of sea as round as if he had laid them out with compass and lathe..."[1]

As noted in chapter fifteen, the sea water in this six-ringed city of Atlantis originated from within Clito's primeval hill, suggesting that the hill was a cipher for the Earth which, in Greek and Mesopotamian myths, contained a subterranean sea. The implication is that Poseidon descended from Heaven and, in cataclysmic fashion, broke apart the Earth (i.e. the hill), thus structuring the Underworld into six rings of alternating land and sea. The city of Atlantis, then, would be the product of a sacred marriage of Heaven and Earth, with Poseidon personifying the exploded planet and Clito personifying the Earth.[2] Accordingly, the six-ringed city would signify the Underworld in its entirety, with its rings existing three-dimensionally as spherical bands within a sphere.

What, then, of the greater island of Atlantis, with its rectangular plain and mountainous coast? How would this work, if the six-ringed city within it symbolised the entire Underworld? The explanation, I suggest, is that Plato merged several variant traditions about the lost island of the Underworld. On the one hand, he recorded the tradition that it had been structured into six rings. On the other hand, he recorded the tradition that it had been enclosed by a wall of mountains, along with the tradition that it had contained an idyllic plain.[3] The most logical way for Plato to have reconciled all these conflicting ideas would have been to notionally extend the size of the island beyond the city. And a telling clue that he did exactly this is the fact that his rectangular plain (measuring 3,000 by 2,000 stades) was far too large to fit inside his greater island (diameter of just 127 stades).

In fact, when seen as a whole, Plato's island constitutes *seven* rings (counting the hill of Clito as the innermost, and the coast of the island as the outermost) – a design which echoes the seven concentric 'mountains' of the Mesopotamian Underworld. Consider the definition provided by the eminent Sumerologist Thorkild Jacobsen:

> The Underworld was of old imagined as a city ringed securely around by seven walls, and so entered through seven successive gates.[4]

This is indeed the design shown in Figure 13, albeit Plato has enclosed the seven-ringed island of Atlantis by the eight and ninth spheres of the 'true sea' and the 'true continent' respectively.

Spherical Atlantis

The idea that Atlantis was the sphere of the Underworld is supported by two curious anomalies in Plato's description of the island's design and construction.

The first of these curious anomalies appears in Plato's description of the bridges that were made to span the land and sea rings. As the scholar Christopher Gill has observed: 'Plato has overlooked the fact that the bridge over the outer ring of water passes directly on to the canal and has no obvious means of support on the outer side.'[5] In other words, the outer bridge could not have existed as Plato described it! However, if we imagine the ringed city to have been a series of concentric spheres in the Earth's spherical Underworld, the picture changes dramatically. When

Figure 13. ATLANTIS IN THE OCEAN OF THE UNDERWORLD
(Copyright Alan F. Alford)

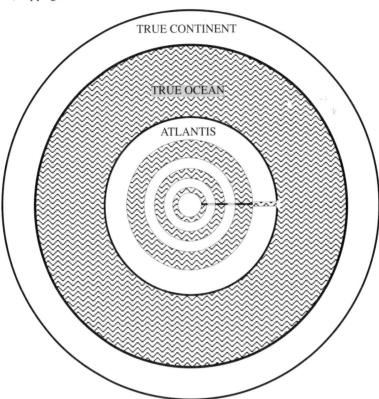

we do this, the bridges (and roofed channels) become a set of tunnels that run through the concentric spheres, connecting the small central island of Poseidon and Clito to the outside of the city (marked by the inner end point of the Grand Canal).

This brings us to the second anomaly – the Grand Canal. According to Plato, this canal stretched all the way from the city's harbour to the true sea that surrounded the island. And yet elsewhere Plato described the island as surrounded by mountains and rising 'sheer from the sea' to a great height, making a Grand Canal to the coast a physical impossibility.[6] But physical constraints of this kind evaporate if we envisage Atlantis as the spherical Isle of the Underworld. Then, in an echo of the point made earlier (about the bridges and roofed channels), the Grand Canal would become a tunnel that stretched from the surface of the Earth to its centre.

Far-fetched? Not at all. In fact, a tunnel of this very ilk is described in the ancient Egyptian books of the afterlife (specifically in 'The Book of

What is in the Duat', 'The Book of Gates', and 'The Book of Caverns'), in which Re, the exploded planet god, descends from Heaven, enters into the Earth, and journeys through a long network of tunnels in order to rendezvous with his chthonic counterpart Osiris in a chamber at the centre of the Earth.[7]

These two anomalies, then, add further grist to my mill that Atlantis was the sphere of the Earth's Underworld. And this, significantly, would have required Atlantis to be supernaturally large.

The Size of Atlantis – Another Giveaway Clue

In *Timaeus* and *Critias* respectively, Plato emphasises the idea that the Isle of Atlantis was supernaturally large:

> "This island was larger than Libya and Asia combined, and it provided passage to the other islands..."[8]

> "This island, as we were saying, was at one time greater than both Libya and Asia combined."[9]

No theory of Atlantis has ever managed to explain the remarkable size of the island as described in these two passages. As far as Atlantis-hunters are concerned, it defies belief that their lost island could have been larger than two continents combined (something of that size does not get lost easily!). Therefore, they generally turn a blind eye to Plato's statement, despite the fact that he repeats it for emphasis. Scholars, meanwhile, fare little better. By putting the remarkable size of Atlantis down to massive exaggeration and poetic licence, they do not really explain Plato's idea; rather, they explain it away.

However, whilst the size of the island seems totally implausible in a geographical context, it does make sense in a mythical context. Consider. If Atlantis was the Underworld, as I suggested earlier, then the only constraint on its size would be the dimensions of the Underworld in which it existed, i.e. the dimensions of the Earth's interior. Plato would then be absolutely correct in making Atlantis to be 'larger than Libya and Asia combined'. Indeed, by comparing Atlantis to the continents of the known world, he strikes a harmonious chord.

What, then, of Plato's alternative statement that the Isle of Atlantis had a diameter of only 127 stades (23 kilometres), with a central island of diameter 5 stades, a city of land and sea rings with diameter 27 stades, and a Grand Canal to the ocean of length 50 stades?[10] Who is to say that these figures should not be taken literally as opposed to the incredible statement that the island was 'larger than Libya and Asia combined'?

Who better than Plato himself? No sooner does he begin to outline this alternative set of measurements, than he furnishes his reader with a very curious observation. He asserts that, in the beginning, before ships had been invented, humans had not been able to reach the central island of Clito.[11] And yet this is nonsensical for, if the measurements which he provides are to be taken literally, any able-bodied person could have swum with ease the widths of the sea rings, which measured only three, two and one stade(s) respectively (i.e. 0.5, 0.4 and 0.2 kilometres).[12] Why, then, suppose the need of a ship? Was Plato hinting that the city plan was a miniaturisation of Atlantis? Was he prompting his reader to scale it up accordingly, along with the rest of the island, to make it equivalent to a size 'larger than Libya and Asia combined'? I put it to the reader that this was indeed the case, and that the supra-continental size of Atlantis is the all-important dimension. This, then, constitutes the second giveaway clue to what Plato had in mind.

Atlantis, the Daughter of Atlas

To identify Atlantis as the sphere of the Underworld is, in itself, a major breakthrough, which will enable us, in due course, to understand Plato's story of the war between Athens and Atlantis as a classic re-telling of the myth of the war between Heaven and Earth. More on this allegory in the next chapter. However, to halt our investigation at the point of 'Atlantis = Underworld' would be to miss a greater 'truth' of the ancient myths, namely that all gods, goddesses, seas, islands, and mountains of the Underworld had originated in Heaven, whence they had fallen into the interior of the Earth. This was the fate of Oceanus, 'the true Ocean', in which Atlantis was said to lie; it was the fate of Poseidon, the god of Atlantis; and it was the fate of the Titan Atlas, who lent his name to the island.

Did Atlantis, too, fall from Heaven? At this point, I would like to enter into evidence the name 'Atlantis' which, according to scholars, meant 'daughter of Atlas'.[13] (This expression, 'daughter of-', was a common designation for Greek islands.) The name immediately calls to mind the goddess Calypso, whom Homer identified as 'the child of the malevolent Atlas'.[14] According to Homer, Calypso was an 'awesome goddess with braided hair', who lived in a vaulted cavern on the island of Ogygia, where she passed the time weaving with her golden shuttle and singing out loud with her beautiful voice.[15] It was she who had wooed Odysseus for seven long years, virtually keeping him captive on her remote and lonely island, isolated from the rest of the world.[16] Might there have been a connection between Calypso's island, Ogygia, and the Isle of Atlantis?

Where was Ogygia, the island of the daughter of Atlas? On the one hand, Homer placed it in the Ocean, in the furthermost west, beyond 'the ends of the earth'. And yet, on the other hand, he lent it the epithet *omphalos thalasses*, 'the navel of the sea', as if to suggest that the island were located in the very middle of the sea.[17] At first glance, the reader might think that Homer has contradicted himself. But the contradiction disappears when we recall that the West symbolised the subterranean Underworld, and that this Underworld contained a subterranean sea. Everything is then resolved as the island of Ogygia becomes the island at the centre of the Earth – the 'navel' indeed of the subterranean sea.

This account of Ogygia, the island of the daughter of Atlas, lying in the centre of the subterranean sea, provides a remarkable precedent for Plato's account of Atlantis, literally 'the daughter of Atlas' and also lying in the centre of the subterranean sea (according to my earlier decoding of 'the true sea' that was enclosed by 'the true continent'). But how did it come about that Ogygia acquired such a station? Significantly, the name Ogygia connects the island to the ancient Ogygian flood – one of several great floods which preceded the flood of Deucalion.[18] This Ogygian flood was only dimly recalled by the Greeks. It had been caused, they said, by an ancient king named Ogygus, who had survived it by setting sail in a ship.[19] Did Ogygus, like Deucalion and the earlier Mesopotamian Flood-heroes, set sail from a heavenly land? The myth-makers indeed seem to have left the requisite clue in the tradition that the waters of the Ogygian flood had reached up to the very heavens – a most curious idea.[20] The most likely conclusion, bearing in mind the lessons of comparative mythology, is that Ogygus personified the island of Ogygia, and that this island fell from Heaven, bringing with it the Ogygian flood (compare the Mesopotamian myth of Shuruppak, Utnapishtim and the flood, cited in chapter sixteen); thereupon, Ogygus and Ogygia would have entered the Underworld, with the island becoming *omphalos thalasses*, the 'navel' of the subterranean sea.[21]

Did Atlantis, too, fall from Heaven into the Earth, thus becoming the Underworld? Did Plato knowingly play on the connection between Ogygia, the fallen island of Calypso, the daughter of Atlas, and the island of Atlantis, which meant literally 'the daughter of Atlas'?[22]

Atlas the Exploded Planet

The idea that Atlantis (and perhaps Ogygia) was the offspring of the god Atlas certainly gives one pause for thought, for Atlas was one of the four

Titan brothers whom Zeus had ejected from Heaven and imprisoned in the Underworld. But the concept of the 'daughter of Atlas' becomes even more arresting when we consider the evidence that Atlas was not just a mere Titan, but a personification of the exploded planet.

There is, for example, a telling myth in which Atlas took the role of the mountain-god who came down from Heaven and impregnated the Earth. The myth is known to us in two related forms. In the first, Atlas is said to have married the goddess Hesperis ('Sunset') and sired upon her the Hesperides – the three clear-voiced nymphs who minded the golden apples on the slopes of Mount Atlas in the Underworld.[23] In the second, Atlas is said to have married the goddess Pleione and sired upon her the seven deep-sea nymphs, the Pleiades, whom Pindar referred to as 'the mountain maids'.[24] Both myths work on the unspoken presumption that Atlas descended from Heaven in order to impregnate the goddess (this being the usual practice for the sacred marriages of the gods).

The first of these myths is admittedly disputed, for Hesiod claims that the Hesperides were conceived by the goddess Night 'bedded with none of the gods'.[25] But Hesiod does concur with the second myth, to which he alludes in his *Works and Days*:

> When the Pleiades, born of Atlas, rise before the Sun, begin the reaping; when they set (before the Sun, begin) the ploughing.[26]

The Pleiades, as I have already noted, were born to Atlas in the form of seven deep-sea nymphs, consistent with an impregnation of Pleione in the subterranean sea. And yet here Hesiod is singing of the Pleiades as seven visible stars in the heavens, who likewise had been 'born of Atlas'. What does this mean? The answer lies in the geocentric myth which I outlined in chapter nine, in which the Sun, Moon and stars were all created from the womb or Underworld of the Earth by the fallen creator-god. The crucial implication of this is that the Pleiades stars would have been 'born of Atlas' as a result of this god's fall from Heaven into the Underworld.[27] Atlas, then, would be a typical exploded planet god, with Pleione, the mother of the Pleiades, being a typical personification of Mother Earth.

This, of course, challenges the tradition that Atlas was fathered by Iapetos upon the nymph Clymene, and yet it must be said that Hesiod's genealogy of the Titans does conceal several ancient question marks about Atlas' parentage. The Phoenicians, for example, believed that Atlas was not the son of Iapetos but of Ouranos, the original 'Mountain of Heaven'.[28] The Libyans, furthermore, stated that Atlas was the first of all gods,[29] i.e. the equivalent of the great god Ouranos himself – an idea that rings true in the light of his exploits with Hesperis and Pleione, as well as his fall from Heaven in the battle of the Titans, and his identity as Mount Atlas, the fallen cosmic mountain of the Underworld.

All in all, it seems very plausible that Atlas was originally an exploded planet god in his own right. The original Atlas, it can be surmised, was the physical god or mountain of Heaven, who suffered the usual fate of cataclysmic dismemberment, and fell into the Underworld. At this point, the fallen Atlas would have separated the Heaven from Earth (in effect resurrecting a metaphysical form of his old self) and created the visible heavens (not just the Pleiades), prior to retiring to his fate as the cosmic pillar of the Universe. In summary, then, the original Atlas would have personified the exploded planet in all of its aspects – the hidden sphere of the Underworld (the so-called 'cosmic mountain'), the raised-up sphere of the invisible Heaven, and the starry sphere of the visible heavens. In this triple aspect, Atlas would have been an exact cognate for Ouranos, 'The Mountain of Heaven'.[30]

In summary, it makes sense that Atlas personified the exploded planet, and one is thus tempted to wonder whether the 'daughter of Atlas' might have been ejected physically as a land mass from his exploding body, whereupon it would have entered the Underworld and been 'born' in the subterranean sea.[31] It is quite plausible that Plato – a Pythagorean initiate and an expert in mythology – had exactly such a scenario in mind when he called his subterranean island 'Atlantis', meaning 'daughter of Atlas'.

It must be borne in mind, however, that we are dealing here with the ancient Mysteries, and we should not expect Plato to be providing any explicit statements about the true identity and origins of Atlantis. Rather, Plato composed a puzzle that would make sense only to the initiated, and to that end he used cryptic statements that would require decipherment. And, on this note, we turn to the most crucial clue of all that Atlantis did indeed fall from Heaven into the Underworld – the abundant presence on the island of a mysterious metal called *oreichalkos*.

The Island of the Meteorites

In his detailed description of Atlantis, Plato makes several references to a mysterious, highly valuable, and sacred metal called *oreichalkos*, which was available on the island in great abundance. The salient points are brought out in the following three citations from *Critias*:

"... in many regions of the island they exploited that metal which is now only a name to us, but which was then more than a name – *oreichalkos*. In that age it was valued only less than gold."[32]

"And the wall surrounding the acropolis itself they invested with *oreichalkos*, which glittered like darting fire... "[33]

"... the kings were regulated by the laws of Poseidon... according to an inscription which the first kings had cut on a stele of *oreichalkos*."[34]

What exactly was this fabled metal *oreichalkos*? Its name meant literally 'mountain bronze', but clearly it was not ordinary bronze, for Plato gives it a superior value, greater than bronze or indeed silver, and second only to the ultimate metal, gold itself. What kind of metal could it have been?

Our first clue comes from Homer, who alluded to *oreichalkos* in the *Iliad*. There, he equated it to the god Sleep (the brother of Death), whom he described perching, bird-like, on the pine-tree of Heaven and Earth:

Here Sleep sat, close-hidden by the pine branches, in the shape of a singing bird of the mountains, which the gods call *chalkos* [bronze], but men call it *kymindis*.[35]

According to Homer, then, *oreichalkos* ('bronze of the mountains') had been a bronze bird of the mountains and, more to the point, a bronze bird of Heaven and Earth.

There is more. In the same section of the *Iliad*, Sleep recounts what happened on the occasion when he put Zeus to sleep at Hera's request, so that she might scheme against Heracles. When Zeus woke up, he went crazy:

Zeus was furious when he awoke, hurling gods around his house, and looking for me [Sleep] above all. And he would have thrown me out of the sky to vanish in the sea, if I had not been saved by Night...[36]

Sleep was not actually thrown into the sea to vanish for ever; instead he ended up in the bosom of Night, the goddess of the Earth's Underworld. Nevertheless, there are remarkable parallels here to the fate of Atlantis, and also to the fate of Hephaestus, the meteorite-god, who *was* thrown from Heaven into the depths of the sea.[37]

Might the *oreichalkos* of Atlantis have been a meteoritic metal? Might this be the reason why Plato ranked *oreichalkos* above bronze and silver and second only to gold? Indeed it might.

In ancient times, gold, being the purest of metals, was regarded as the metal of Heaven.[38] Other metals, such as silver, bronze, and iron, were regarded as having a lower, terrestrial status (hence Hesiod's scheme of the degenerating races of men, made of gold, silver, bronze and iron respectively). But in between the heavenly metal, gold, and the terrestrial metals, there stood one particular metal (an alloy, in fact) that really did bridge the gap between Heaven and Earth. That metal was meteoritic iron (an unusual alloy comprised of iron and nickel), which, by virtue of the fact that it had fallen from the sky, ranked second only to the gold of Heaven itself. In effect, the meteoritic iron amounted to 'fallen gold'.[39]

I therefore put it to the reader, taking cognizance of the sanctity of meteorites in ancient times, that meteoritic iron – a metaphorical fallen gold – was the fabled *oreichalkos* of Plato's Atlantis.[40]

Lest there be any doubt about this identification, a perfect illustration of the meteorite as a metaphorical fallen gold occurs in the *Histories* of Herodotus, where the great historian describes a Scythian myth about four golden implements that fell from the sky – a plough, a yoke, a battle-axe and a drinking-cup.[41] According to Herodotus, this astonishing event had been witnessed in the most ancient of times by three brothers of the first Scythian dynasty who each attempted to pick up the fallen gold. But when the first brother approached: 'lo! the gold took fire and blazed'.[42] Then, when the second brother approached, the same thing happened again. But eventually, when the third brother stepped forward, the fire went out, so it was he who collected the golden implements and became king of all Scythia. As for the gold, Herodotus tells us that it was placed under the protection of the royal Scythian guards and that great sacrifices were held every year in its honour.[43]

Few would disagree that this is an account of a meteorite fall and the retrieval of its fragments by the brothers (poetically rendered, of course, for meteorites flare up in the sky rather than on the ground). But it is the metaphor here that catches our attention. For if the meteorite is regarded as fallen gold, then logically it is composed of metals that are second in rank to the gold of Heaven. Or, to look at it another way, the meteorite is metaphorical gold, ranking second only to true heavenly gold.

Plato's description of the *oreichalkos* as 'glittering like darting fire' provides strong support for this identification, as does his account of the stele of *oreichalkos* which stood in the centre of Atlantis in the sanctuary of Poseidon (see citations above). On the significance of the latter, a whole chapter could be written. But suffice to say that Plato's story of the bull sacrifice and the blood that was made to run down the stele over the laws of Poseidon (which were inscribed thereon), fits well with everything that is known about meteorites, *omphaloi*, the god Poseidon, bull symbolism, sacrificial ritual and the idea of the heavenly gods implanting divine law codes in the Earth.

Strong support, too, is found in Plato's assertion that the *oreichalkos* is 'now only a name to us' (first passage cited above). Whilst it is likely that certain temples in Greece (such as Delphi) did possess meteorites during the 5th-4th centuries BC, it should be noted that ordinary Greeks were hardly allowed any contact with these sacred objects. Thus it could fairly be said that the ex-heavenly metal 'is now only a name to us'.

Atlantis, however, was another matter entirely. In saying that Atlantis had an abundance of *oreichalkos* (to such a degree that it was even used in building walls!), Plato is, at the very least, connecting the island to a mythical era when an abundance of meteoritic iron had fallen from the sky; less the golden age, perhaps, than the *fallen gold* age. But more than this, Plato is surely evoking the idea that the entire island of Atlantis had fallen from the sky, bringing these meteoritic materials with it. Indeed, if the reader will accept my earlier decoding of Atlantis as the sphere of the Underworld, then there can be no doubting Plato's intention: that the Isle of Atlantis became the Isle of the Underworld by falling from Heaven. Hence its abundance of *oreichalkos*.[44]

It Fell from the Sky

It might seem controversial to suggest that Atlantis fell from the sky, based simply on the mythical metal *oreichalkos* and the island's identity as 'daughter of Atlas', but is it really so hard to believe? In fact, the Greek myths are bursting with examples of cities, islands, continents and gods that were cast down from the sky into the Underworld. Why should Atlantis be an exception? To close this chapter, I would like to highlight the crucial importance of this motif in other Greek myths.

Take the city. For an example of a city being cast down from Heaven into the Underworld, we need look no further than Athens, the ideal state which went to war against Atlantis. If my interpretation of Athens is correct (see chapter sixteen), then it stands to reason that Atlantis arrived in the Underworld by similar means. Indeed, the war between Athens and Atlantis is strikingly reminiscent of the wars in the ancient Sumerian Kings List, in which a whole sequence of cities fell cataclysmically from Heaven, each smiting the previous capital city in the Earth and assuming the kingship. Plato's story parallels this older myth, with Athens smiting Atlantis to become a new ideal city, which was destined to be born from the Earth.

Another interesting example of a 'fallen city' features in the cycle of myths pertaining to the character Tantalus. According to one source, a cataclysm overtook Mount Sipylus (presumably a heavenly mountain), causing the mount to be overturned.[45] Amidst violent earthquakes, a chasm opened up in the Earth and a city disappeared into it.[46] The chasm then filled up with water to become a lake and, in due course, the ruins of the city became covered by mud.[47] According to Strabo, the submerged city was Troy, but Pausanias and Pliny said it was Tantalis – a name remarkably similar to (in fact an anagram of) Atlantis.[48] Admittedly, this is a late myth (1st-2nd centuries AD), but it was based on an older myth, about a king Tantalus, which predated Plato by centuries. According to this older myth, a king named Tantalus had dismembered his son Pelops and fed him to the gods, thus incurring their wrath.[49] Accordingly, the gods had sentenced Tantalus to a life of eternal torture in the Underworld where a huge stone from Mount Sipylus was suspended over his head.[50] The intriguing implication is that Tantalus and Mount Sipylus and (in the later myth) the city of Tantalis all fell from Heaven into the Underworld.

Moving on from cities to islands, can we find a precedent for the idea that an island fell from the sky? The answer, again, is yes. We have already discussed the idea that Ogygia, the island of Calypso, fell from Heaven into the Underworld at the time of the Ogygian flood. But a more transparent example is the sacred island of Delos (alias Asteria/Ortygia). As Pindar explains, Zeus cast this island down from the heavens after she had spurned his advances:

> The daughter of Koios [i.e. Asteria].
> Disdaining the love of Zeus . . .
> I am afraid to say what is incredible: . . .
> Hurled into the sea, she became a shining rock,
> And the sailors of old called her Ortygia.
> She drifted hither and thither on the Aegean.[51]

In keeping with this myth, Pindar described the fallen island as 'Heaven-built Delos' and 'the body of Asteria'.[52] The name Asteria, significantly, meant 'of the starry sky'.[53] As we might expect, Delos/Ortygia initially became a floating island – an idea that might well be based on the notion of it bobbing around in a subterranean sea.[54]

Moving on from island to continents, is there any precedent for the idea of a continent fallen from the sky? Again, the answer is yes. We need look no further than *Erebos*, the covered-up mountain of misty darkness that came out of Time or *Khaos* (chapter eleven), or Tartarus which united with Gaia in the aftermath of the Titans' fall.[55] Another good example is Ouranos, the fallen 'Mountain of Heaven', who became the Underworld and was thus able to swallow his own children – a feat emulated by his successors Kronos and Zeus (in the case of Kronos, it was actually said that he dwelt on a continent, albeit relocated to the remote west).[56] That these fallen celestial bodies were visualised as being continental in size is clear from Anaxagoras' assertion that the Sun was a blazing stone 'bigger than the Peloponnese'.[57]

In summary, there are a number of powerful precedents for the idea that Plato's Atlantis was cast down from the sky as a metaphorical city, a metaphorical island and a metaphorical continent, all rolled into one.

Chapter Nineteen Summary

* Clito's primeval hill was a cipher for the Earth. And it was this very hill that Poseidon broke apart to create the city of Atlantis in the form of concentric rings of land and sea. It follows that the six-ringed city of Atlantis signified the Underworld (i.e. the interior of the Earth).

* If we allow for the merging of different traditions (for which there *is* evidence), then the entire island of Atlantis – not just the city – would represent the Underworld.

* The size of Atlantis, 'larger than Libya and Asia combined', makes no sense in a geographical context, but is perfectly consistent with a mythical Isle of the Underworld. With hindsight, this anomalous size is a dead giveaway to what Plato had in mind.

* Seen as a whole, the Isle of Atlantis took the form of seven concentric spheres, forming a spherical Isle of the Underworld, enclosed by the greater spheres of the 'true sea' and the 'true continent' respectively.

* The Grand Canal, which pierced the island of Atlantis as far as the six-ringed city, signified a tunnel into the centre of the Earth (as found in the ancient Egyptian books of the afterlife).

* It is implicit in Plato's story that Atlantis must have originally been an island or city-state in Heaven. It was indeed a law of ancient myth that all gods, goddesses, seas, islands, and mountains of the Underworld had fallen thither from Heaven.

* The name 'Atlantis', meaning 'daughter of Atlas', connects the island to the god Atlas, who was originally an exploded planet god in his own right. It may have been implied that the exploding body of Atlas ejected the Atlantian land mass, and thereby caused it to fall from Heaven into the Earth, to become the Isle of the Underworld.

* *Oreichalkos*, the mythical metal of Atlantis, was meteoritic iron. The fact that the island possessed such an abundance of this substance is a dead giveaway to Plato's intentions: the Isle of Atlantis had fallen from Heaven.

CHAPTER TWENTY

THE WORLD VOLCANO

There is no need for new continents
but there *is* need for new men.
(Captain Nemo, *The Nautilus*, 1869)

I have argued, in the preceding chapters, that Plato's story of the war between Athens and Atlantis was myth pure and simple. Ancient Athens, for its part, signified Heaven, or the 'world of Forms', which fell to the Earth. The Isle of Atlantis, on the other hand, signified the Underworld, i.e. the interior of the Earth, which acted as the receptacle for all things that fell from Heaven. Thus did Plato set the scene for a re-telling of the age-old 'true story' of the war between Heaven and Earth, in which both sides were personified by armies of men, in accordance with the custom of the ancient poets.

This, then, is the basic theme, which is clear enough. And yet there are certain aspects of Plato's story which represent an elaboration of this basic theme. Firstly, it was not the heavenly Athenians who instigated hostilities in the war, but the Atlantians, who invaded the known world through the Pillars of Heracles; it was thus the Underworld which struck first if my decoding is correct. Secondly, it seems a little strange that, at the climax of the war, the Isle of Atlantis sank into the Underworld. How could Atlantis *sink into* the Underworld if Atlantis *was* the Underworld?

In order to address these important questions, it is vital that we now study the story of the war once again, paying careful attention to what Plato actually said. To this end, I will be focusing in this chapter on the war from the Atlantian perspective in its three key stages:

1 The invasion of the known world through the Pillars of Heracles.

2 The ensuing intervention by the Athenian warriors.

3 The sinking of Atlantis into the depths of the sea.

The Atlantian Invasion

According to the Egyptian priest in Plato's *Timaeus*, the army of Atlantis instigated hostilities by sailing eastwards through the straits of Gibraltar and attacking the continents of Europe and Asia:

> "The records speak of a vast power that your city once brought to a halt in its insolent march against the whole of Europe and Asia at once – a power that sprang forth from beyond, from the Atlantic Ocean."[1]

> "Now one day this power gathered all of itself together, and set out to enslave all of the territory inside the strait [of Gibraltar], including your region and ours, in one fell swoop."[2]

Significantly, this invasion took place via the Pillars of Heracles (the straits of Gibraltar), which marked the limits of the known world and the entrance to the Underworld (as discussed in chapter eighteen). Thus the invasion symbolised an eruption of the Underworld into the world above – in effect, a volcanic eruption on a global scale.

Did the invading Atlantians personify volcanic ejecta? The idea seems reasonable on several counts. Firstly, the Greeks were quite familiar with volcanic phenomena.[3] Secondly, we have already seen how the Isle of Atlantis could have symbolised the Underworld. And thirdly, it may be no coincidence that Poseidon, the god of Atlantis, was the Greek god of earthquakes *par excellence*.[4]

Nevertheless, the 'eruption of the Underworld' is a new theme to the reader of this book and, moreover, it represents a fundamental twist on the standard myth of the war of Heaven and Earth. Accordingly, it becomes essential to corroborate this interpretation. Might there be any parallels or precedents for this 'eruption of the Underworld' theme in the earlier myths of Greece or in the myths of the ancient Near East?

The answer, as we shall now see, is an affirmative yes.

The Eruption of the Underworld

In the myths of the Near East, a popular motif was the threat from the Underworld to attack the world above. In the myths of Mesopotamia, for example, two memorable scenes involve the goddesses Ereshkigal and Inanna, respectively, threatening to send up the infernal dead to devour the living.[5] Similarly, in the myths of ancient Egypt, there is a notable scene in which Osiris, the subterranean god of the dead, threatens to send up fierce-faced demon-messengers to seize the hearts of evildoers in the human world above.[6] The key idea behind these scenes is the ancients' fear of the Underworld, pertaining not only to a revulsion of the land of the rotting dead, but also, more pertinently, to a terror of earthquakes and volcanic explosions.

Accordingly, two of the most striking themes in the myths, hymns and rituals of the Near East were the appeasement of the chthonic gods and the confinement of their powers in the great world below. In the latter case, the poets spoke of a sacred stone that held in check the waters of the Apsu, or a lid or gate that kept contained the forces of chaos.[7] In a similar vein, in Egypt, it was said that seven deadly 'words' had been locked inside a chest in the Underworld, and that these words, if ever pronounced out loud, would bring on the cataclysmic end of the world.[8] Aptly enough, these words had been spoken long ago by God, when he had ordained the beginning of the world – a cataclysmic creation.

A similar idea appears in the Babylonian myth *The Erra Epic*, in which seven Sebitti-gods play an equally cataclysmic and threatening role. The myth, dating to around the 9th century BC, describes how Anu (Heaven) had fathered the Sebitti-gods in the Underworld, giving them the power to rise up and devastate the world above:

> When Anu, king of the gods, impregnated Earth,
> She bore the Seven Gods for him and he named them Sebitti...
> He summoned the first and gave him orders: "Wherever you band
>   together and march out, you shall have no rival."
> He spoke to the second: "Ignite like Gerra and blaze like a flame!"
> He said to the third: "You must put on the face of a lion, so that
>   anyone seeing you will crumble in terror."
> He spoke to the fourth: "Let the mountain flee before the one who
>   bears your fierce weapons!"
> He ordered the fifth: "Blow like the wind, and seek out the rim of the
>   world."
> He commanded the sixth: "Go through above and below, and do not
>   spare anyone!"
> The seventh he filled with dragon's venom, (saying) "Lay low living
>   things!"[9]

The Erra Epic describes how these seven Sebitti-gods (also known as the Craftsmen or Seven Sages of the Apsu) had run amok at the time of the great Flood, but had subsequently been reconfined in the Underworld.

One day, however, the Sebitti became impatient and began to goad Erra, the god of the Underworld, into action, by mocking his recent feebleness and reminding him of his divine duties. Thus prompted, Erra came up out of the Underworld with his faithful companion Ishum and the seven Sebitti-gods, and devastated the world:

Ishum set his face towards the mountain Hehe,
The Sebitti, unrivalled warrior-force, stormed behind him.
The warrior-force arrived at the mountain Hehe,
It raised its hand and destroyed the mountain...
It finished off the cities and made of them a wilderness,
Destroyed mountains and struck down their cattle,
Stirred up the seas and destroyed their produce,
Devastated reed-beds and groves, and burnt them like Gerra,
Cursed the cattle [mankind] and turned them into clay.[10]

The plan was to destroy mankind completely, but eventually Erra and Ishum relented, and allowed a remnant of man to survive. The myth thus ends on a positive note with Erra going back into the Underworld and a new king rising up to unite the scattered people.[11]

The Erra Epic is unquestionably an allegory involving cataclysmic forces, with Erra, Ishum and the Sebitti all personifying the eruption of the Underworld. Significant, too, is the idea that all of these gods had descended from Heaven. In the case of the seven Sebitti, *The Erra Epic* reports that the falling Heaven, Anu, had placed them inside the Earth (see citation above). And, in the case of Erra (alias Nergal), a separate myth *Nergal and Ereshkigal* describes how he had 'descended the long staircase of the heavens' to become the chief god of the Underworld.[12] Thus the connection is established between the falling sky, on the one hand, and the cataclysmic activity in the heart of the Earth, on the other (Erra/Nergal, incidentally, was the Babylonian god of earthquakes).[13]

Is this the key to Plato's story of Atlantis? I have already ventured the idea that Atlantis fell from Heaven to become the Isle of the Underworld, and that its army then personified the eruption of the Underworld when it launched its attack against Europe and Asia via the Pillars of Heracles. Now, we have *The Erra Epic*, extant in Babylonia through most of the 1st millennium BC, which offers a most impressive precedent for both of these connected mythical themes.

Did Plato know of, or adapt, *The Erra Epic*? It seems unlikely, for the attack by Atlantis does not incorporate any of the specific details from the myth of Erra, Ishum and the Sebitti; and, moreover, there is no clear evidence for the Babylonian epic being imported into the Greek corpus of myths.[14] It is possible, perhaps, that Plato heard *The Erra Epic* during his travels, or from one of the itinerant, bilingual poets who used to recite the tales of the Orient in Greece. However, the most likely scenario is that Plato simply wished to have a pretext for the Athenians to go to war against Atlantis, and that an eruption of its army from its subterranean base provided the perfect story line. In this scenario, Plato would not have needed knowledge of any particular foreign myth, but would simply have drawn on what he knew about volcanic phenomena, along with the myths which linked subterranean gods to volcanic fire (prime examples being Hephaestus at the island of Lemnos, and Typhoeus or Hephaestus at Mount Etna),[15] and thus fabricated an entirely new myth of his own: it was the people of Atlantis, rather than Hephaestus or Typhoeus, who personified the volcanic eruption of the Underworld.

The War of Athens and Atlantis

So far, so good. But if the Atlantians were bursting forth, as a kind of 'world volcano', to attack the continents of Europe and Asia in the world above, how and where did the war with the Athenians take place?

The conventional view, in this respect, is that the war took place in the Mediterranean Sea and in the surrounding lands of Europe and Asia. But the simple truth is that Plato never actually said anything about Athens defending Europe and Asia *from a base within the known world*. This is just something that modern readers have assumed in accordance with their historicist interpretation of the story.

Admittedly, Plato does allude to Europe and Asia being inhabited at the time of the war; he has the Egyptian priest credit Athens for 'freeing all the rest of us who lived within the Pillars of Heracles'.[16] But it must be remembered that Plato is setting the war in the remote past, at a time when the races of man were still in the process of being born from the earth. Consequently, it becomes a matter of speculation as to which particular races had been born, which remained in the womb of the Earth, and which still lived in their heavenly cities, waiting for the final curtain call on the harmonious golden age.

Who, then, were the inhabitants of Europe and Asia at the time of the war? The impression is given that the Egyptians were there, which would make sense for it was generally supposed that their race was the oldest (it was ten thousand years old, according to Plato).[17] In addition, it might be speculated that the Arcadians were there, for they were said to be the oldest of the Greek peoples.[18] But the crucial question concerns the Athenians. Were they already in Europe, having been born from the Earth 'nine thousand years ago'? Or did they still reside in their heavenly city of Athens? The likely answer, as I have argued in chapter sixteen, is that they were in Heaven. Hence the dramatic nature of their intervention in the war.

Plato's vagueness about the inhabitants of Europe and Asia is matched by his vagueness about the course of the war. With the exception of the climactic cataclysm – a subject to which we will return in a moment – there is actually no specific account of any engagement between the two sides. Indeed, all we learn about the Athenian intervention is contained in one brief and opaque passage, where Critias quotes the Egyptian priest as follows:

> "Pre-eminent among all others in the nobility of her spirit and in her use of all the arts of war, she [Athens] first rose to the leadership of the Greek cause. Later, forced to stand alone, deserted by her allies, she reached a point of extreme peril. Nevertheless, she overcame the invaders and erected her monument of victory. She prevented the enslavement of those not yet enslaved, and generously freed all the rest of us who lived within the boundaries of Heracles."[19]

This passage has always been interpreted from a historicist perspective, and yet it makes very good sense under the mythical perspective, too. For example, if Athens had descended from Heaven, from a cluster of Greek heavenly cities, it could very well be said that she had been 'deserted by her allies' and 'forced to stand alone'. And, by the same token, if Athens had descended into the Underworld, it could very well be said that at that time 'she reached a point of extreme peril'. Indeed, to a reader of ancient myths, the words 'extreme peril' are especially evocative of subterranean danger.[20]

The idea that Athens went to war in the Underworld is not so strange to the student of ancient mythology. In the Babylonian *Enuma Elish*, for example, Tiamat, when she was the goddess of Heaven, threatened to send down her brood of monsters against Ea and his fellow gods in the Underworld.[21] Similarly, in Hesiod's *Theogony*, Zeus plunged down from Mount Olympus to create a huge conflagration, which enveloped the *Khasma* and 'the chthonic Titans' therein.[22] In my opinion, the war of Heaven and the Underworld is a far more pervasive theme in the Greek myths than scholars have yet realised.[23] But to cite further examples at this point would be to court unnecessary controversy. As Pindar once sang: 'Sometimes the ways of silence are best.'

So, did Athens go to war in the Underworld? Plato's vagueness about the war may be a telltale sign. Another clue, perhaps, is his failure to complete the story. Is it a tad too convenient that Plato put down his pen just as Hermocrates, the military expert, was preparing to describe the course of the war? What exactly would Hermocrates have had to say about this war if, as I surmise, it was an allegory involving an eruption of the Underworld and a fall of the sky? Is this why Plato stopped the story? Would Hermocrates' account of the war have been too awkward, or too revealing? One final question: did Plato intend that Hermocrates should stand *in name only* for the secret of the war? After all, the name 'Hermocrates' stemmed from *herma*, 'heap of stones', and from Hermes, the god who had slain the giant Argos with a sling-stone.[24] Might this be more than a coincidence, bearing in mind the ancient myths of the battles of the gods in which meteoritic stones were cast down from Heaven and heaped up in huge piles upon the Earth?

Speculations aside, what cannot be denied is that the war of Athens and Atlantis coincided with a great cataclysm:

> "Further back, excessively violent earthquakes and floods occurred, and after the onset of an unbearable day and a night, your entire warrior force sank below the earth all at once, and the Isle of Atlantis likewise sank below the sea and disappeared."[25]

At this juncture, I must highlight a fundamental error in the standard translation of this passage and justify the alteration that I have made.

The first word of this passage, in the standard translation, is rendered 'Afterwards', giving the impression, misleadingly as it turns out, that the cataclysm took place *after* the war and was unconnected with it.[26] Oddly enough, this standard translation has always produced a most unlikely scenario: the Athenian warriors would have died an unheroic death in a meaningless, tragic accident.

But it turns out that the Greek word translated 'Afterwards' has two possible meanings, depending on the context in which it is used. On the one hand, it can mean 'afterwards' (in relation to time), but on the other hand it can mean 'further back' (in relation to place).[27] To establish the appropriate translation, we must look at the context and decide which of the two meanings is intended. What we then find is that the preceding sentence does deal with the subject of place, namely by speaking of the freeing of peoples *inside the Pillars of Heracles*. Accordingly, a valid translation of the next line would be: "*Further back*, excessively violent earthquakes and floods occurred...", meaning further back, beyond the Pillars of Heracles, i.e. in the Underworld.

Hellenists have discounted this possible translation because it would involve the Athenians being swallowed up beyond (outside) the Pillars of Heracles – an idea that makes no sense to them.[28] However, if we view the Athenians as an ideal race who descended from Heaven, then it does make sense that they should have sunk into the Earth beyond the Pillars of Heracles, i.e. sunk into the Underworld. The 'Further back' translation would then lead in perfectly to the next line of the text which describes the sea of mud that was formed in that exact same region, beyond the

Pillars of Heracles.

By correcting the translation in this way, significant progress is made on three fronts. Firstly, it is no longer necessary to suppose that the cataclysm took place *after* the war; on the contrary, Plato's intention seems to be that the cataclysm *coincided* with the war (hence the idea that the Athenians sank into the earth, and hence the idea that the war coincided with the foundation of Athens). Secondly, it is revealed *where* the Athenian warrior force disappeared, namely in the region 'further back', beyond the Pillars of Heracles. And thirdly, it becomes apparent that the Athenians did, after all, die a heroic death, in that their plunge into the Underworld brought the invasion by Atlantis to a halt.

The upshot of this is that the Athenians never laid a hand on the Atlantians directly, but rather entered the subterranean territory that the latter had vacated (when they erupted into the world above), and thereby brought about a violent upheaval which, metaphorically speaking, caused the Isle of Atlantis to sink back into the Underworld whence it had come.

Does this make sense? Indeed it does. Plato never did suggest that the Athenians and the Atlantians had fought hand-to-hand in combat. No. What he actually said was that a war had broken out between 'all the peoples dwelling outside the Pillars of Heracles and all those peoples dwelling within', and that the Athenians had intervened in this war, overcome the invaders, erected her victory monument, and freed all the peoples whom the Atlantians had enslaved.[29] Significantly, all of these marvellous deeds could have been achieved by the Athenians in truly heroic fashion by descending from Heaven, entering the Underworld, and creating violent earthquakes therein. The Athenians could thus have won the day by the simple act of undermining the Atlantians from below, causing the insurgents and their volcanic isle to return to the Underworld whence they came. And this, I suggest, is exactly how they did it.

And so it came to pass that the Isle of Atlantis, having risen, volcano-like, against the inhabited world, was forced back beneath the sea into the Underworld, never to be seen again. Which brings us to yet another peculiar and illuminating detail of Plato's story – the transformation of the sunken island into a shallow sea of mud.

The Sea of Mud

One of the strangest aspects of the Atlantis story is the shallow sea of mud into which the island was apparently transformed. It is referred to twice by Plato, once in *Timaeus* and once in *Critias*, as follows:

"Further back [i.e. beyond the Pillars of Heracles], excessively violent earthquakes and floods occurred... your entire warrior force sank below the earth all at once, and the Isle of Atlantis likewise sank below the sea and disappeared. That is how the Ocean in that region has come to be even now unnavigable and unexplorable, obstructed as it is by a layer of mud at a shallow depth, the residue of the island as it settled."[30]

"This island [of Atlantis]... because of earthquakes, it has subsided into the great Ocean and has produced a vast sea of mud that blocks the passage of mariners who would sail into the great Ocean from Greek waters, and for this reason it is no longer navigable."[31]

According to these two passages, Atlantis was transformed, when it sank, into a sea of mud, which hindered navigation across the western Ocean for more than nine thousand years, from the time of the cataclysm right up to the time of Solon and, it would seem, to the time of Plato. The idea seems totally far-fetched, and yet in recent years it has been suggested that Plato might have been referring to the Sargasso Sea – a region of floating seaweed that drifts in the Atlantic Ocean.[32] It is an ingenious idea and yet it barely helps the cause of Atlantis-hunters, for a mountainous island does not turn magically into a region of seaweed any more than it turns magically into a sea of mud. It is a preposterous thought.

Might there be a more rational interpretation of this sea of mud? Let us put aside the geographical approach, for a moment, and consider, instead, the mythical perspective.

For starters, it is an incontestable fact that Plato's island of Atlantis sank. Accordingly, the sea of mud into which Atlantis was transformed (it is called 'the residue of the island') amounts, in effect, to a sunken sea. It belongs, strictly speaking, to the Underworld.

Secondly, I have explained that the Pillars of Heracles signified the gateway to the Underworld, and that the Atlantic Ocean was a cipher for the mythical subterranean sea, and that Atlantis itself signified the Isle of the Underworld (see chapters eighteen and nineteen). It therefore follows that the sea of mud – the sunken remnants of Atlantis – must lie in the Underworld or the region thereof known as the subterranean sea.

Thirdly, in the myths and rituals of Greece and the Orient, mud was always associated with the Underworld, and it thus makes sense that Plato's sea of mud would indeed signify a region of the Underworld.[33]

Fourthly, the Greek myths contain two plausible contenders for this mythical sea of mud: the Stymphalian Marsh and the Tritonian Marsh respectively. Here, there are some highly impressive parallels that have been consistently overlooked by students of the Atlantis story (who, for the most part, have shown more interest in geography than mythology). It is now time to put the record straight.

To begin with the Stymphalian Marsh, it features in the sixth labour of Heracles, in which the 'Hero of heroes' had to clear it of a noxious flock of Stymphalian birds. These were supernatural birds: their beaks were capable of piercing metal breast-plates, and they were renowned for attacking men with showers of brass feathers and for destroying crops with their poisonous excretions.[34] As for the marsh, Heracles found it to be a real challenge, because it was neither solid enough to support a man walking, nor liquid enough to permit the use of a boat. Intriguingly, the name of the marsh and its birds derived from the word *stymphallos*, meaning 'phallic member'.[35] Where was this Stymphalian Marsh? According to my decoding of the Heracles cycle (see chapter eighteen), this hero's adventures took place in the Underworld and in the subterranean sea. Accordingly, the Stymphalian Marsh must have been located somewhere in the great world below. (The Stymphalian birds would thus have allegorised the fall of the sky into the Underworld.)[36]

Turning to the Tritonian Marsh, its significance may be decoded largely from the associated myths of Lake Triton. The Tritonian lake, it must be emphasised, existed both geographically and mythically. In the former sense, it was a shallow inland lake in Libya that had once covered substantial tracts of lowlands.[37] In the mythical sense, however, it was part of the Tritonian Underworld, ruled by the deep-sea-god Triton, the son of Poseidon. It was here, at Lake Triton, that the goddess Athene had been bathed and reborn in days of yore, when Hephaestus had split open the head of Zeus with an axe, allowing Athene's *daimon* to ascend from the Underworld into Heaven (hence Athene's epithet 'Tritogeneia').[38] It was also here, at Lake Triton, that Jason's ship, the Argo, had become trapped, requiring him to strike a deal with Triton; in return for a tripod, the god had helped the Argonauts to escape from the inland lagoon, to continue on their quest for the Golden Fleece.[39] And it was here, in Lake Triton, on the island of Hespera, that the Amazonian 'moon-women' had lived, prior to expanding their empire into the surrounding Tritonian Marsh and beyond.

The disappearance of Lake Triton into the Underworld is alluded to in a myth recorded by Diodorus Siculus in the 1st century BC (but drawing, no doubt, on much older material). In his account of the war between the Amazonians of Lake Triton and their neighbours, the Atlantioi (both of them representing subterranean races),[40] Diodorus makes an illuminating statement:

And it is said that, as a result of earthquakes, the parts of Libya toward the Ocean engulfed Lake Tritonis, making it disappear.[41]

What does this mean? The statement cannot apply to the real world Lake Triton for this was an inland lake, which lay far from the ocean. But it does make sense in a mythical context, especially if Libya and Ocean are taken to be metaphors for the Underworld. The meaning of Diodorus' statement then shines through: it was *the Underworld* which engulfed Lake Triton, making the lake disappear; or, in other words, Lake Triton fell from Heaven and disappeared into the Underworld.

In the myths of Lake Triton and the Tritonian Marsh, we have all the attributes of Plato's sea of mud. The Lake was in the West, but was truly subterranean; the Lake was difficult to navigate and was shallow (in the *Argonautika*, it appears as the shallow 'Libyan sea');[42] and the Lake was intimately linked with a marsh. In effect, then, Lake Triton *was* a shallow sea of mud in the Underworld, virtually identical in concept to the shallow sea of mud in Plato's story of Atlantis.

Was Lake Triton the inspiration for Plato's sea of mud? With so many points of coincidence, and with the myths of the Tritonian Underworld dating back to the 5th century BC, if not earlier, the odds must indeed be high that Plato had Lake Triton in mind when he envisaged Atlantis as collapsing into a sea of mud.

In summary, the sea of mud motif completes what we might term 'the Atlantis cycle'. In the beginning, Atlantis had been an island in Heaven. Then, it fell from Heaven and became the Isle of the Underworld. Next, after a long gestation period in the Underworld, Atlantis rose up, like an erupting volcano, to attack the inhabited world of Europe and Asia. And then, finally, when the sky fell again (in the form of ancient Athens), the convulsions in the Underworld caused Atlantis to subside and return to the subterranean depths.

Atlantis – The Final Solution?

We have now assembled the complete picture of Plato's lost continent of Atlantis, and an overview of some kind is warranted. In order to do this, I have identified all of the key identifying characteristics of Atlantis, as cited in Plato's story, and I have listed these points below together with the interpretations which arise from the mytho-allegorical theory, as presented in this book.

I now invite you, the reader, to judge for yourself whether my theory hits the mark or not.

Characteristic of Atlantis	Mytho-Allegorical Explanation
1 A Greek-like city with palaces, temples, harbour, fortified walls.	It was a fictional city, modelled on 5th century cities such as Athens.[43]
2 A circular city designed around rings of land and sea water.	Poseidon originated these rings by breaking apart the primeval hill of Clito (the Earth) – a cataclysmic act.
3 A very high island, ringed by mountains, that rose sheer from the sea.	A popular myth in Greece involved a god founding a city in the Underworld and surrounding it with mountains.[44] This description echoes that theme.
4 A central city in a circular island, connected to the surrounding sea by a huge canal.	The island was a sphere, and the canal running through it was a tunnel cutting into the heart of the Earth.
5 A land containing a large and beautiful plain.	This recalls the Elysian Plain which truly belonged in the Underworld.
6 A land inhabited by huge numbers of people.	A popular idea in ancient myths was that pre-human peoples had descended from Heaven and colonised the Underworld, prior to being born from the Earth.
7 A highly fertile land, with an abundance of produce.	This evokes the paradisiacal land of the golden age, which truly belonged in Heaven or in the Underworld.
8 A land rich in minerals, most notably the precious, long lost metal *oreichalkos*.	*Oreichalkos* signified fallen gold, i.e meteoritic metal. Its abundance in Atlantis suggests that the island fell from Heaven into the Underworld.
9 An empire with international trade links.	Plato was drawing an analogy between Atlantis and 5th century Athens. This idea was essential to the moral purpose of the story.
10 An island situated in the Atlantic Ocean, the true Ocean, opposite the Pillars of Heracles.	The West signified the Underworld whilst the Atlantic Ocean symbolised the subterranean sea.
11 Beyond it was a true continent which completely surrounded the true Ocean.	This continent was the Earth's crust – a sphere that enclosed the sphere of the subterranean sea. The idea was adapted from Homer's vision of the kingdom of Hades in the West.

12	Of varying size but, according to one tradition, larger than the continents of Libya and Asia combined.	The true Underworld was immense and might indeed be envisaged as continental in size.
13	A colony founded by Poseidon.	Poseidon was the god of earthquakes and ruler of the subterranean sea. In days of yore, he had descended from Heaven into the Underworld.
14	Named after Atlas; its name meant 'daughter of Atlas'.	Atlas was a fallen god or mountain of Heaven, and a god of the subterranean sea. His daughter would logically be an island in the subterranean sea (as was Ogygia, the island of Calypso, the daughter of Atlas).
15	The largest of several islands, which all belonged to its empire.	All these islands would be 'daughters of Atlas'. Plato may have had in mind the seven Pleiades.[45]
16	Invaded Europe and Asia via the Pillars of Heracles.	The Pillars marked the gateway of the Underworld. The invasion by Atlantis signified the Underworld erupting like a volcano into the world above.
17	Earlier, it had conquered parts of the true continent, and even parts of Libya and Europe.[46]	This would signify an earlier eruption of the Atlantian Underworld. Such an eruption would, by definition, have conquered parts of the true continent (the crust of the Earth).
18	Its invasion failed owing to the intervention of the ancient Athenians.	The Athenian heroes descended from Heaven into the Underworld, causing violent floods and earthquakes.
19	It sank suddenly amidst violent earthquakes and floods.	Having risen from the subterranean, Underworld, Atlantis sank back into the depths whence it came.
20	Upon sinking, it was transformed into a shallow sea of mud.	Mud signified the Underworld. Plato probably had in mind the mythical Tritonian Marsh of the Underworld.
21	It sank nine thousand years before the time of Solon.	'Nine thousand' was Greek idiom for a great multitude. Thus Atlantis sank 'nine aeons' ago, in the mythical era, at the same time as its adversary, Athens, was founded in the Earth.

Strengths and Weaknesses

As the reader may see from the above summary, my theory provides a plausible explanation for all twenty-one key identifying characteristics of Atlantis, and it thus satisfies a kind of minimum condition that should be met by any Atlantis theory that pretends to be taken seriously (indeed, it is probably the first theory ever to meet this minimum condition). But what of the theory's strengths and weaknesses?

To deal with the weaknesses first, I have read through all of Plato's words with the greatest care, looking for any anomalies that my proposed interpretation might raise, but I can report nothing of consequence (it must be borne in mind, as one reads Plato's story, that it is an allegory, in which familiar, human-like imagery is constantly being used to express mythical concepts). Indeed, the only word that did threaten to cause a serious upset turned out to be a mistranslation ('Afterwards' makes better sense when translated 'Further back', as discussed earlier). Admittedly, this concordance owes much to Plato's brevity and vagueness about the war, but I would regard this lack of detail as a deliberate ploy on Plato's part. The reader, however, is entitled to disagree, in which case the apparent concordance might be dismissed as nothing but a fortunate accident. Nevertheless, the fact remains that nothing in Plato's *Timaeus* or *Critias*, or in any other Platonic text, contradicts the theory proposed in these pages (and that, it must be said, is something of a first in Atlantis studies).[47]

Beyond this, it might be argued that my interpretation of Near Eastern and Greek religions as exploded planet cults goes beyond what is known in the world of academia, and is therefore too controversial to be used as a basis for decoding Plato's story. That may be true as far as scholars are concerned. They are innately suspicious of new theories, especially when they herald from outside the ivory towers and challenge the reputations of those who dwell within. Nevertheless, as E.R. Dodds once said: 'the accepted truths of today are apt to become the discarded errors of tomorrow', and as Michael Rice has put it: 'this season's heterodoxy is next season's orthodoxy'.[48] How prophetic these two statements might be for a discipline that, despite two centuries of scholars' best efforts, still lacks a satisfactory theory of myths (see chapter six). As I see it, the exploded planet hypothesis is controversial only because scholars have not discovered it yet, and it *will* be next season's orthodoxy, albeit the seasons of academia turn according to Orphic time scales.

So much for weaknesses, or perceived weaknesses. But what about the theory's strengths? Here, we find some very weighty points indeed.

The first strength of my theory is that it accords with everything that Plato said about Atlantis. By proposing that Atlantis was the erupting Underworld, it allows Atlantis to be in the Atlantic Ocean – just where Plato says it was; it allows Atlantis to be sunk – just like Plato says it was; and it allows Atlantis to be larger than two continents – just like Plato says it was. These are fundamental points, and yet all other Atlantis theories reject the legitimacy of either one, two or all three of these statements and suppose, instead, that Plato somehow, like an idiot, got things cockeyed. On this basis alone, my theory ought to be ranked first among all Atlantis theories currently extant (for all that that's worth).

A second major strength of my theory is that it decodes Atlantis in the context of its invasion of the world and ensuing war with ancient Athens. The worst thing a researcher can do is to study either one of these cities in isolation from the context of the war. My theory, however, makes the inter-relationship between Athens and Atlantis a fundamental basis of the interpretation.

Thirdly, my theory accounts for all of the bizarre elements in Plato's story. It explains how the six-ringed city of Atlantis came out of Clito's primeval hill. It explains why the island was a perfect circle (code for a sphere). It explains the unknown metal *oreichalkos*. It explains how the island was transformed into a shallow sea of mud. It explains why the Athenian army sank suddenly into the Earth. And it even explains the opposite continent which, bizarrely, was said to completely surround the true Ocean.

Fourthly, my theory is able to resolve a crucial perceived anomaly in Plato's text. By proposing that Athens descended from Heaven against Atlantis, it verifies Plato's statement that the war between the two sides coincided with the foundation of Athens in the Earth 'nine thousand years ago', and it thus exonerates Plato from the accusation that he made a careless chronological error. The supposed error, in fact, turns out to be a linchpin to understanding the story.

Fifthly, my theory improves substantially the reading of the story. By proposing that the Athenian army descended from Heaven, it explains why the warriors sank, all at once, beneath the earth. The Athenians, far from suffering a tragic accident some time after the war (as the badly mistranslated text suggests), rather died a heroic death at the climactic moment of the war. This, surely, was Plato's intention, given that the story was told, ostensibly, to depict Socrates' ideal state in action ("I'd love to see our city distinguish itself in the way it goes to war and in the way it pursues the war...").

Sixthly, my theory vindicates Plato's claim that the story of Athens and Atlantis was absolutely true. By proposing that the story was a re-telling of the age-old exploded planet myth (the war between Heaven and Earth variant), it allows that the story be true in the mythical sense.

Seventhly, my theory takes into account the wider aspects of Platonic philosophy. It must be emphasised (no doubt to the great disappointment of many Atlantis-hunters) that Plato was no historian or geographer, and thus we are hardly likely to find an account of a lost civilisation at the heart of his works. On the contrary, both Plato and Socrates were 'true philosophers', who were obsessed with cosmogony and the theory of the soul. In their way of thinking, something important had indeed been lost, but it belonged to myth rather than to history, and to Heaven rather than to Earth. Here, the Theory of Forms is the key, for it presupposes a fall of the archetypes from Heaven to Earth, including, most significantly, the archetype of the ideal state, which was, after all, the subject of Plato's story. By proposing that Atlantis and Athens, each in turn, fell from Heaven to Earth (into the Underworld), my theory cuts to the very heart of Platonic philosophy.

Eighthly, my approach in this book has been to set Plato's story of Athens and Atlantis against the broader context of ancient Greek religion and mythology. Here, my theory has its roots in fundamentally important myths, such as the birth of the Universe in a cataclysm, the fall of the sky, the fall of the golden age, the wars of the gods of Heaven and the Underworld, the fall of gods, islands and continents from Heaven into the Underworld or subterranean sea, the birth of all things from the Earth or subterranean sea (impregnated by the seed of Heaven), and the idea that mythical peoples dwelt in Heaven, the Earth or the Underworld. In all of these myths, precedents are to be found for my theory that Atlantis was the Isle of the Underworld and that Athens came down from Heaven, signifying the fall of the sky. Overall, my theory fits extremely well with the most fundamental religious ideas of Plato's day.

Ninthly, my approach has been to set the Greek myths (of the 8th-4th centuries BC) against the broader context of the Near Eastern myths (3rd-1st millennia BC). Here, as we have seen, the parallels and precedents are profound and extensive, and there can be little doubt that we are dealing with the same basic theory about the cosmos and the gods. Significantly, the Near Eastern myths have yielded vital precedents for the ideas of the fallen sky, the seeded Earth, the wars of Heaven and the Underworld, the celestial city succession myth, the subterranean sea (the Apsu), and the mythical peoples of Heaven and the Underworld. Most importantly, these older myths enshrine the principle of personification, with the poets using human-like gods to personify the falling sky and the erupting

Underworld. My interpretation of Plato's story thus has its roots in a well-documented, three-thousand-year-old literary tradition. It gains strength accordingly.

In summary, I would remind the reader that there is no archaeological evidence for the historicity of the war between Athens and Atlantis (quite the opposite); that there is no evidence whatsoever for a sunken island-continent on the Atlantic Ocean floor; that Herodotus and Socrates had never heard of the Athens-Atlantis war; that Plato did insist on the poetic nature of Solon's story (comparing Solon to the great poets Homer and Hesiod); that Plato did place the war in a pre-diluvian era; and that Plato was not a historian, nor a geographer, but a true philosopher, whose interests lay primarily in metaphysical, otherworldly matters.

In all of these respects, my theory hits the mark. The island of Atlantis was no ordinary island; rather, it was the Isle of the Underworld. The invasion by Atlantis was no ordinary invasion; it was a volcanic eruption (from no ordinary volcano, but 'the world volcano'). Ancient Athens was no ordinary city; rather, it signified the ideal state which descended from Heaven. The war of Athens and Atlantis was no ordinary war; rather, it was a mythical war of Heaven and Earth.

So much for the main story line. And yet, as I pointed out in chapter nineteen, Atlantis was not always the Isle of the Underworld. Indeed, for Atlantis to be the Underworld, it was imperative that it must have fallen from Heaven to Earth at an earlier juncture. The Isle of Atlantis, then, is surely to be regarded as a cipher for the exploded planet, with all that that entails. Accordingly, to know the full and true story of lost Atlantis, we must know the full and true story of the exploded planet, not just in the physical sense but also in the metaphysical sense. This is the task of the next and final chapter.

Chapter Twenty Summary

* The invasion of Europe and Asia by Atlantis symbolised an eruption of the Underworld, with the Atlantian army personifying ejecta from 'the world volcano'. Such a myth had long been told in the Near East, inspired, no doubt, by man's experiences with volcanic phenomena.

* At the time of the Atlantian invasion, the Athenians were a mythical golden age race, residing in the heavenly city of Athens.

* The Athenians intervened in the war by descending from Heaven, thus personifying the fall of the sky. They entered the subterranean territory that the Atlantians had vacated and brought about a violent upheaval, causing the Isle of Atlantis to sink back into the Underworld whence it

had come.

* The cataclysm occurred at the moment of the war, not afterwards. The Athenian warriors sank into the Earth because they descended from Heaven. Thus they died in a manner befitting of true heroes.

* The transformation of Atlantis into a sea of mud signified the return of the island to the Underworld. Plato was almost certainly inspired by the myths of the Lake and Marsh Triton in the Tritonian Underworld.

* Plato's story is a unique combination of two separate, but connected, cataclysm myths, which had been told and retold for millennia: the fall of Heaven into the Underworld, and the eruption of the Underworld. Myth-makers in Greece and the Near East routinely used human-like gods and/or paradigmatic men to personify these cataclysmic forces. Moreover, it was implicit that these myths conveyed the 'true story' of the creation.

* For the first time ever, a theory has been put forward that explains *all* aspects of the Athens and Atlantis story, and accords with *all* of Plato's words. This does not guarantee that the theory is correct, but it does make it the *only* satisfactory theory currently available.

* The lost continent of Atlantis was a cipher for the exploded planet. But to understand the true significance of this fact, we must consider both the physical *and metaphysical* aspects of the exploded planet mystery.

CHAPTER TWENTY-ONE

THE TRUE ATLANTIS

Immortal mortals, mortal immortals, living the death of the one, dying the life of the other.
(Heraclitus, 5th century BC)

In this final chapter, I aim to take a step back from the story of Athens and Atlantis per se, and try to capture the bigger picture which Plato was trying to convey. Taking my lead from Plato himself, I will be arguing that the true Atlantis was not simply the exploded planet, which stood at the heart of the ancient Mysteries, but rather *the idea* that lay behind the exploded planet cults, namely the idea that *spirit, or soul-substance,* had created and energised the world that we live in. This idea, which is to be found not only in Plato's 'true philosophy' but also, as we shall see, in the writings of earlier sages of the 2nd and 3rd millennia BC, is, I will argue, the primary aspect of the exploded planet religion, for it amounts to a theory of what 'life' truly is. And this hypothesis – of the existence, nature and origin of the spirit or soul – sums up, I believe, what Plato would have understood as *the true* Atlantis.

This spiritual approach to the ancient Mysteries represents a marked change of emphasis from my previous books, in which I focused my thoughts on the physical and scientific aspects of the Mysteries, notably in the shape of Dr Tom Van Flandern's theory that planets have actually exploded in our solar system (for which there is a great deal of mounting evidence).[1] For the sake of clarity, let it be said that nothing I am about to say reduces the importance of the exploded planets question; it is rather that Plato would have us contemplate a deeper question concerning the origin of *all* life, in the entire galaxy and in the entire Universe; and this requires that the exploded planet be viewed as a metaphor for an even bigger bang that brought the entire Universe into being (incidentally, the modern Big Bang theory is, to my mind, just an upgraded model of the ancients' exploded planet hypothesis, and it is equally controversial).

This spiritual and metaphorical approach may not be to every reader's taste, but it is, I believe, true to Plato's philosophy, and Plato, after all, is the author of the story which is at the heart of this book. I make no apologies, therefore, for proposing in this chapter that the true Atlantis is a spiritual, mystical and metaphysical idea.

Atlantis in Perspective

Before we can discuss legitimately the spiritual side of Atlantis, we must first establish the identity of Atlantis as the exploded planet. So, let us reconsider, at the outset, my decoding of the Atlantis story.

In this book, I have argued that Plato's 'true story' of the war between Athens and Atlantis was an allegory for a war between Heaven and Earth, which was itself an allegory for the age-old myth of the creation of the cosmos by the exploded planet. In this war, Athens signified Heaven, whilst Atlantis signified the Underworld, i.e. the interior of the Earth (implying that Atlantis itself had fallen from Heaven into the Underworld at an earlier juncture). It was for this reason that Plato located Atlantis in a 'true sea', which was surrounded by a 'true continent'. His meaning – deciphered for the first time in this book – is that Atlantis lay in the subterranean sea, which was located in the interior of the Earth, making Atlantis the lost island-continent of the Underworld.

How did Atlantis end up as the lost continent of the Underworld? The crucial answer, suggested by parallel myths and by Plato's references to an abundance of *oreichalkos* (i.e. meteoritic iron) on the island, is that Atlantis originally existed in Heaven and only became the Isle of the Underworld when it fell from Heaven and entered the Earth. The upshot of this is that Atlantis should be understood as a continent that was lost from the heavens.

What was this lost continent of the heavens? Plato made the answer perfectly clear (for those who had 'ears to hear') by telling the story of Athens and Atlantis in the context of the 'ideal state' and the Theory of Forms. Consider. Both Atlantis and Athens signified the 'ideal state' that had been lowered from Heaven to Earth. The ideal state, meanwhile, signified the 'world of Forms' (the invisible sphere of Heaven). And this 'world of Forms', in turn, signified the exploded planet – hence Plato's description of the 'world of Forms' in *Phaedo* as a supernatural, Earth-like world: 'the true Heaven, the true Light and the true Earth'.[2] Thus the equation is completed, enabling both Atlantis and Athens to be identified as metaphors, or ciphers, for the exploded planet which stood at the heart of ancient religions (albeit heavily occulted in the Greek religion).

The upshot of this is that Atlantis was indeed a lost paradise, as the modern reader has always envisaged it, but not in the form of a lost city, a lost island or a lost continent, but rather, in the form of a lost planet – the planet of the former golden age. Plato's story is thus decoded in a particularly harmonious fashion.

The mystery is solved. Or is it? On the contrary, Plato would be the first to admit that the mystery is not solved at all. In fact, all that we have achieved, at this point, is a decoding of the story in so far as Atlantis signifies the exploded planet. But the crucial question is this: what does the exploded planet *itself* actually signify?

Anticipating this question, Plato provided a theory to get his readers thinking. He interrupted the story of Atlantis and inserted, in *Timaeus*, a detailed exposition of Pythagorean cosmogony, in which he pictured the exploded planet as the *Demiourgos* – a perfect sphere of soul which had created the visible Universe in its own spherical image (see appendix a). In this scheme, soul was made 'the first cause', to which everything in the Universe owed its birth. According to Plato, the primeval soul had stirred the Universe into life, firstly at the centre (the Earth) and then outwards in seven concentric bands (of the celestial bodies), until finally it had surrounded the outermost sphere of the stars. The *Demiourgos*, meanwhile, stood above and beyond the visible, created Universe in splendid isolation from it, its invisible body comprising the original, pure soul-substance, which had issued forth from the original *Demiourgos* creator-planet. Plato called this eternal, spiritual being 'That which *is*' and 'the *real* Living Thing'.[3]

Here, then, is the essence of the exploded planet mystery and, if the reader will accept my decoding of Plato's story, the essence of the Atlantis mystery too. To Plato, the exploded planet signified the idea of soul creating the Universe and bringing it to life, and then separating from it to become an invisible soul-sphere beyond the heavens, where none but the 'true philosopher' might find it. Atlantis, as a cipher for the exploded planet, signified exactly the same idea. To search for Atlantis in the physical world, or in the physical Universe, as many people do, is contrary to Plato's most fundamental belief that reality was not to be found in this world – a world of decay – but in the 'other world' – the world of Truth.[4] The true quest for Atlantis is therefore to be envisaged as a mystical quest.

This might sound, to some, like Platonic psycho-babble, but the fact is that Plato was by no means alone in thinking this way. On the contrary, in emphasising the primacy of the soul-substance and the importance of the spirit world, Plato was merely reiterating what religious philosophers had been saying for thousands of years.

The Spirit of Creation

It is implicit in the most ancient texts that the gods were immortal and supernatural entities, and that their abode was an invisible mountain. In Egypt, this mountain was known by various names such as *Neter-Khert*, 'Mountain of God', and *Akhet*, 'Mountain of Light', and it existed in an invisible realm called the *Duat*. In Sumer, the mountain was personified by the chief god Anu, whose name meant 'Heaven', and later by Enlil, whose popular epithet was 'Great Mountain'. That these mountains were conceived as being invisible is made clear by the Babylonian creation epic *Enuma Elish*, in which the mountain of Heaven, Esharra, is created in the image of the fallen Heaven, Apsu, and is populated by a race of spiritual gods, the Igigi, who are separated from their fallen, subterranean counterparts, the Anunnaki, having previously been bound together with them 'like a ball'.[5]

How did Heaven and the gods acquire spiritual forms? Where, exactly, did the divine spirit come from? The straightforward explanation is that the gods had physically come down from the sky *as a unity of body and soul* and that the soul had been released following the gods' impact with the Earth. The idea here was that the gods' bodies – meteoritic solids and floodwaters – had become trapped inside the Earth, whilst the gods' souls had separated and returned to their homeland in the sky.

Why did the falling sky-gods comprise such unities of body and soul? The explanation is that the sky-gods were conceived as offshoots of a living planet that had exploded at the beginning of time. This planet, the ancients believed, had not only harboured biological life (in contrast to a barren Earth prior to the creation), but had also itself been a living entity, comprising a single unity of body and soul (as per the modern Gaia hypothesis). When this living planet had exploded, it had produced a deluge of fragments, each of which comprised a unity of body and soul.

It was the destiny of the spirit, or soul-substance, not simply to ascend back to Heaven but also to spark the creation of life in the Earth. In my previous books, I overlooked this crucial point by focusing instead on the physical and biological aspects of the exploded planet creation myth. Nevertheless, it was implicit in the myths that the exploded planet did convey life to the Earth in a spiritual manner.

In Egypt, for example, the spiritual aspect of the creation may be seen in the myth of the Bennu-bird, or Phoenix, which flew from Heaven to Earth at the beginning of time, carrying the vital essence of life known as

Hike. In the Coffin Texts, a soul ascending to Heaven exclaims:

> "I come from the Island of Fire [the Underworld], having filled my
> body with *Hike*, like that bird who came and filled the world with that
> which it had not known."[6]

The *Hike* is almost certainly to be equated with soul or spirit.

The same idea is found also in the Egyptian kingship ritual known as
the 'Opening of the Mouth'. In this vitally important ritual, a spiritual
essence, the *Ka*, was transferred from the mummified body of the dead
king, Osiris, to the living body of the new king, Horus, in order to keep
the *Ka* alive (like an Olympian flame). The ritual was a re-enactment of
the First Time, when Osiris – the exploded planet god – had brought the
meteoritic seeds of life and oceanic waters of life to the Earth.[7] But the
transmission of the *Ka* – a purely metaphysical concept – underlines the
spiritual element that accompanied the seeds and waters of life.

Turning to Mesopotamia, here the poets described how a barren Earth
had received life from the exploded planet via a river of semen-like water
or via the flesh and blood (*ki-sir*) of sacrificed gods.[8] At first glance, the
spiritual element of the creation is hard to see. However, in the parallel
myths of the creation of man, the blood of the gods endows the prototype
man with a mysterious *napishtu* ('breath' or 'wind') or *etemmu* ('ghost'
or 'spirit').[9] Thus it is implied that the semen, flesh or blood of the gods
actually contained a spiritual essence.

The Bible tells essentially the same story. In the beginning, according
to the book of Genesis, God's 'Spirit' or 'Breath' (*ru'ach*) had hovered
over the waters of the Earth.[10] Consequently, all living creatures had been
endowed with 'the quickening breath of life' (*nishmat ru'ach hayim*).[11]
The first man, Adam, was no exception:

> And the LORD God formed man from the dust of the ground, and
> breathed into his nostrils the breath of life; and man became a living
> being.[12]

The Spirit of God then separated itself from the Earth and ascended back
to the Heaven whence it came, thereupon becoming a perfect, immortal,
and invisible being, just like Plato's *Demiourgos*.[13]

In Greece, Plato was by no means the first to emphasise the primacy
of the spirit or soul-substance. That distinction, in fact, belonged to
Homer and Hesiod, whose poems enshrined the belief in a spiritual race
of gods (the *daimones*) and a spiritual Mount Olympus, not to mention
the ghost-like heroes of the golden age who had become 'good spirits on
the face of the Earth, watchers over mortal men'.[14] There can be no doubt

that the Olympian religion was a spiritual religion.

In the realm of Greek philosophy, Thales was one of the first to talk of the spirit, saying: 'the All has soul in it and is full of *daimones* [i.e. gods or spirits]'.[15] To Thales, the first cause of all things had been water, which, in his view, contained the all-important spiritual principles of life and motion.

After Thales, Anaximander took up the spiritual cause, naming the soul-substance as *physis*, and declaring that *physis* was the true nature of things and the animating principle of the Universe. In Anaximander's cosmogony, the *physis* had originated in a mass which he called *Apeiron*, 'the Unlimited' (implying that it had no beginning, middle, nor end). The explosion of the Unlimited had caused the four elements of earth, air, fire and water to be born and despatched into the Earth's Underworld (see chapter three). Accompanying these elements, however, had been the all-important *physis*, which had energised all things with the breath of life.

Empedocles propounded similar ideas, drawing an analogy between *physis* and Love. In the beginning, he said, there had been a primeval God-Sphere (*Theos/Sphairos*) which he described as 'equal on every side and quite limitless – a rounded Sphere rejoicing in his circular solitude'.[16] This Sphere had contained the four elements of earth, air, fire and water, all bound together by a fifth element, Love. But it had been torn apart by the forces of Strife. Love had poured out of the Sphere and, along with the other four elements, had descended to the Earth, where it breathed the breath of life into all living things.[17] In a parallel account, Empedocles described how soul (*psyche*) had been cast down from Heaven into 'the roofed-in cave' or 'meadow of Ate', i.e. into the Underworld, whereupon it sparked the development of all living things (see chapter three). The soul and Love both signified the spiritual life-essence *physis*.

The Orphics, meanwhile, called the *physis* '*aither*', and deified it as *Aither*. In the beginning, they declared, Time had given birth to *Khaos*, *Erebos* and *Aither*, and all had fallen from Heaven into the Underworld. But whilst *Erebos* and *Khaos* had been trapped in the world below, the *Aither* had been separated from the Earth to become the 'pure air' or 'upper air' (*aither*) of the Universe.[18] In the Orphic creation myth, Night advises Zeus: "Surround all things with the ineffable *aither*, and in the midst of that set the heavens, and in the midst the boundless Earth, in the midst the sea, and in the midst all the stars with which the heavens are crowned."[19] It was from this invisible *aither* that the soul was drawn into the body at birth, later to return to it upon death, according to the Orphic belief.[20] Today we call this region of *aither* 'space', imagining it to be an inert medium, but to the Orphics it comprised the very essence of life.

With all this emphasis on the spiritual nature of life and reality, it is no surprise to find descriptions of a reconstructed Sphere of God, made of soul, spirit, or *aither*, lying above and beyond the visible Universe. The earliest Greek example of this idea is Mount Olympus, the home of the Olympian gods. To Parmenides, it was 'the world of Truth', 'the Thing which *is*', and 'the Fire of Heaven, a gentle thing, very light, in every direction the same as itself'.[21] To Socrates, it was 'the true Heaven, the true Light and the true Earth', and 'a being that really is what it is – the subject of all true knowledge'.[22] And to Plato, as we have seen, it was the *Demiourgos*, which he described as the only true, unchanging reality: 'That which *is*', 'the *real* Living Thing', and the home of the archetypes or Forms.

The Spiritual Atlantis

Plato's Atlantis, I have argued, is a cipher for the exploded planet and, as such, it represents everything that has just been discussed.

Atlantis *is* the Egyptian 'Mountain of God' or 'Mountain of Light'.

Atlantis *is* the Sumerian Heaven of Anu and Enlil.

Atlantis *is* the true Mount Olympus, or Ouranos, of the Greeks.

Atlantis *is* the Unlimited of Anaximander.

Atlantis *is* the God-Sphere of Empedocles.

Atlantis *is* 'the Fire of Heaven' of Parmenides.

Atlantis *is* 'the true Light' of Socrates.

Atlantis *is* the *Demiourgos*, or world of Forms, of Plato.

Atlantis *is* the Orphic god Time.

But these are all just names for one and the same principle, namely the creation of the entire Universe, both visible and invisible. The dramatist Aeschylus expressed it thus:

Zeus is *aither*, Zeus is Earth, Zeus is the heavens, Zeus is everything and what is still higher than this.[23]

But we may justifiably substitute the word 'Atlantis' for 'Zeus', and say:

Atlantis is *aither*, Atlantis is Earth, Atlantis is the heavens, Atlantis is everything and what is still higher than this.

Or, we may put it another way:

Atlantis is the spirit that breathed life into the Universe.

Whereupon we can complete the loop by saying that the spirit of Atlantis is identical to the *Hike* of the Phoenix, the *Ka* of Osiris, the Breath of God (*napishtu* or *ru'ach*), and the quintessential *physis* in its manifold names of aether (*aither*), soul (*psyche*), wind (*pneuma*), water (*hudor*), breath (*anima*), and love (*eros*).

All of these related cosmic and spiritual ideas, I believe, encapsulate what Plato would have understood by the expression 'the *true* Atlantis'. Moreover, when we view Atlantis thus, the exploded planet concept per se becomes almost secondary to *the idea* for which it stands, namely the mystery of what life actually is and how it began. The crucial question which naturally arises is this: should we be taking the exploded planet concept literally, or should we be regarding it as a metaphor?

Atlantis as a Metaphor for the Creation

As noted earlier, there is strong scientific evidence for the explosion of one or more planets in our solar system, and one is therefore compelled to wonder whether ancient religions might actually enshrine a scientific truth. Indeed, if the evidence continues to mount as it has done in the late-1990s and early-2000s, many will be tempted to regard the ancient religions as literally true. Nevertheless, there is a serious problem with such a literary, or fundamentalist, perspective, and it can be summed up in one word: geocentrism.

According to the Greeks, the Earth marked the centre of the Universe, and the Sun, Moon, planets and stars orbited around her. Furthermore, it was believed that the Earth (Gaia) had actually given birth to the Sun, Moon, planets and stars as a direct result of her impregnation by the exploded planet (see discussion in chapter nine). Plato himself followed this geocentric orthodoxy in his mystical account of the creation by the *Demiourgos* (see appendix a). It was also the orthodoxy of Pythagoras and Philolaos, and, we may surmise, of the Egyptians and other ancient civilisations.

This geocentric theory is, of course, completely unacceptable today. Even if we concede the possibility that a planet did explode in our solar neighbourhood, we now know that the Earth is not the centre of the solar system and, furthermore, we know that the solar system is not the centre of the galaxy, nor of the Universe. Accordingly, no-one today would give any credence whatsoever to the idea that the Universe had begun with just two planets (one of which was the Earth) and that all things had been born from their cataclysmic conjunction. In short, the secret of ancient cosmogony has been overtaken by modern science.

What does this imply for Plato's account of the origin of the Universe? Does geocentrism spell doom for the *Demiourgos* and apocalypse for Atlantis? On the contrary, it seems to me that Plato was not in any way committed to the geocentric paradigm and nor was he committed to any particular theory of cosmogony. Indeed, far from beginning his quest for truth with a belief in exploded planet cosmogony, Plato took his lead, as did Socrates, from the famous edict inscribed at Delphi: *gnothi seauton*, 'Know Thyself'.[24] Thus prompted, he examined the nature of himself and others, and came to the conclusion that man's true self was an immortal soul, trapped inside a mortal body. This was the starting point of Plato's philosophy; hence the saying of Proclus (5th century AD): '*Let the knowledge of ourselves* be the start of philosophy and of the teaching of Plato.'[25] It was from this all-important premise that Plato developed his theory that the soul, or spirit, was the essence of the Universe and, moreover, the basis of all true life and reality.

Now, given that this was the basis of Plato's 'true philosophy', how would he have conveyed this 'truth' to an audience of the 4th century BC? The answer, I would suggest, is by telling the story of the primacy of the soul in the context of myths which were in circulation at that time and which, by necessity, reflected the cosmological theories which were extant. In other words, Plato had no choice but to express his ideas in terms of the geocentric Universe and the exploded planet mythos, just as a modern-day Plato would be forced, by necessity, to express the same ideas in terms of the myth of the Big Bang. In no way did Plato endorse the scientific assumptions of his day. In fact quite the opposite. In *Timaeus*, he writes that: 'the accounts we give of things have the same character as the subjects they set forth', and he distinguishes between accounts of things which are ever-*un*changing (i.e. pertaining to the invisible, metaphysical realm), and accounts of things which are ever-changing (i.e. pertaining to the visible, created realm), and he observes that the former will generally be fixed and stable, whilst the latter will inevitably be inconsistent and inaccurate.[26] Plato is therefore stating, in effect, that specific theories of astronomy – such as geocentrism and the exploded planet – should not be taken as literal truth.

The scholar William Guthrie has expressed much the same thoughts, writing as follows in his book *Orpheus and Greek Religion*:

> It is a part of Plato's greatness to have confessed that there are certain ultimate truths which it is beyond the powers of human reason to demonstrate scientifically. Yet we know them to be true and have to explain them as best we can. The value of myth is that it provides a way of doing this. We take account of myth not because we believe it to be literally true, but as a means of presenting a possible account of things which we know to exist but must admit to be too mysterious for exact scientific demonstration.[27]

Guthrie's statement may not be true for the usage of myths generally, but it is right on the mark concerning Plato, whose theory of the soul clearly transcends human opinions concerning specific scientific issues such as geocentrism and exploded planets.

In summary, I contend that if Plato were alive today he would not be bothered one iota by the abandonment of the geocentric theory or by the antipathy towards the exploded planet hypothesis. On the contrary, he would happily accept the evidence for Earth's position in a heliocentric system in a minor backwater of the Milky Way, and he would truly be fascinated by the Big Bang model for the origin of the Universe. And taking these ideas on board, he would not hesitate to re-present his theory of the soul in this exciting new context (see the postscript to this book for an illustration of how such a revision might work).

A key point here is that Plato's theory concerned the origin of the entire Universe, not the evolution of our local solar system. Therefore, whilst there is good evidence for the actual explosion of planets in our solar system (threatening a revolution one day in the Earth and space sciences), such explosions must be seen in perspective as 'little bangs' relative to the singular 'Big Bang' which Plato and others had in mind for the origin of the Universe. Accordingly, it is wrong to take Plato's exploded planet myth literally as an account of the creation, and it is imperative that we instead take it to be a metaphor for *the idea* behind the myth, namely that the entire Universe had been stirred into life by a mysterious spirit, or soul-substance.

Atlantis, as a cipher for the exploded planet, must be viewed likewise.

Atlantis Rises

In conclusion, my findings vindicate the stance taken by many people in the 'new age' community, who have long felt that Atlantis should be viewed as a symbol or metaphor of spiritual perfection and a lost golden age. Until now, this approach has relied solely on intuition, but in this book I offer a complete intellectual justification for it. Indeed, if the reader will accept my argument, which in essence is straightforward and logical, he will retrieve Plato's Atlantis from its metaphorical position at the bottom of the sea, and restore it to its rightful place as the supreme symbol for the spiritual quest – the quest for knowledge of the origins of the Universe, the quest for knowledge of the origins of life, and the quest for knowledge of what life truly is. Plato – one of the world's greatest ever spiritualists and mystic visionaries – surely deserves nothing less.

Of course, not everyone will agree with Plato, Socrates, Empedocles,

Parmenides, Heraclitus, Pythagoras and Orpheus that the true nature of the self was the soul and that the true nature of reality was the invisible, spiritual world, but there are many people today who do believe this, and who seek to develop their spiritual awareness of what awaits them on the other side. To these people, I cannot recommend enough the writings of Plato – all 1,745 pages of the Hackett translation! If the reader is up to this gargantuan task, however, he should bear in mind the *caveat* that I mentioned earlier: do not take Plato's myths to be *literally* true, for they are just *illustrations* of his general belief in the immortality of the soul and its fate in the afterlife. I have in mind here Plato's tales of the soul's translation to an Earth-like planet, such as the Upper Earth described by Socrates in *Phaedo*. Did Plato really believe that the soul could return to the exploded planet, i.e. to its ultimate source of creation? Perhaps. Or, then again, perhaps not. As Plato wrote in a letter towards the end of his life:

> Whenever we see a book... we can be sure that if the author is really serious, the book does not contain his best thoughts; they are stored away with the fairest of his possessions. And if he has committed these serious thoughts to writing, it is because men, not the gods, 'have taken his wits away'.[28]

The reader has been warned! If something is written down explicitly in Plato's works, it is not necessarily to be trusted. It probably belongs to the class of tale which Plato described as 'noble falsehoods', i.e. nice stories told to fool a gullible populace.[29] Nevertheless, it is my belief that Plato's 'best thoughts' are included in his writings in the form of hints and allusions which do make sense to those who have the understanding of the myths and hence the ability to spot the subtle nuances in Plato's presentation.

Did Plato succeed in cracking the ultimate mystery? Will you be able to crack Plato's secret?

Who knows, perhaps one day I'll be seeing you in Atlantis.

Thought for the Day

Many are the wand-bearers but few are the Bakchoi.
(from the Eleusinian Mysteries)

ON THE THEORY OF THE SOUL

**We know how to tell many lies that sound like truth,
but we know how to sing reality, when we will.**
(The Muses in Hesiod's *Theogony*, 8th-7th century BC)

And so we come to the sixty-four million dollar question: is Plato's story 'true', as he claimed it to be? Did a mysterious spirit, or soul-substance, instigate the beginning of the Universe? Is man's true self an immortal soul? Is Plato's 'true philosophy' the key to a spiritual afterlife?

As I have explained in the closing chapter of this book, Plato's theory of the soul transcended human opinions concerning scientific issues such as geocentrism and exploded planets, and it would therefore be wrong to reject his ideas on the basis that geocentrism is an outmoded theory or that planets have not exploded (an arguable point). That would be to 'throw out the baby with the bath-water'. But Plato deserves better than that. His baby – his theory of the existence, origin and fate of the soul – deserves to be nurtured and acclimatised to the 21st century. It cries out for new clothes in the form of a modern scientific framework. To throw it out would be fail to contemplate Plato's 'truth' in its most fundamental regard.

In the following pages, therefore, I would like to demonstrate, by way of illustration, how Plato's theory of the soul might be updated to take account of 21st century theories of astronomy and astrophysics. It is a daunting task, but it is, without doubt, what Plato would have wanted. What follows, then, is in honour of Plato, and I hope that his spirit will forgive me if I fail to do justice to his remarkable and challenging idea.

To adapt Plato's theory, it is essential to understand the principles on which it was founded. The first of these principles is a Socratic premise: if the soul of man exists and is immortal, then the soul has always been immortal; therefore, the soul has always existed, right from the beginning of Time (if Time can be conceived as having a beginning at all). From this simple premise, Socrates and Plato developed their model of the soul's origin and destiny.

The original model, in brief, is as follows. At the moment before the creation, there existed a planet that had existed for all time in a unity of body and soul. This planet had then exploded, causing its body and soul-substance to merge with the Earth. Consequently, the fallen planet (the *Demiourgos*) had created the Universe as a sphere in the image of itself, and had resurrected itself metaphysically by spreading its soul-substance outwards from the Earth and through the entire Universe to its outermost rim. Meanwhile, the soul-substance initiated the chain of life on Earth by breathing the breath of life into every type of organism. Being immortal, it survived the death of its host bodies and departed to a mysterious region of aether, whence it was later recycled back into new host bodies. This process continued ad infinitum for all species, but in man's case his soul was at certain stages rewarded or punished according to its deeds. Accordingly, Socrates and Plato urged their fellow Greeks to purify their souls and become as God-like as possible, in order that their souls might return to unity with their creator. These are the essential principles of Plato's 'true philosophy'.

The above scenario may, on the face of it, strike the modern reader as absurd. It does not make sense, today, to speak of soul-substance having a unique point of origin in the explosion of a planet above the Earth; nor does it make sense to visualise this soul reforming itself in Heaven in the shape of a planet. No. Such a planetary explosion, if it occurred, would not have been the unique event that Plato's universal scheme demands.

Nevertheless, it is the underlying principles that are the important thing, and I would now like to demonstrate how Plato's theory of the soul *might* work in an up-to-date scientific framework. What follows is purely illustrative and I cannot emphasise enough that it is not intended to be a definitive scheme. Rather, its purpose is to demonstrate in broad terms how Plato's most fundamental idea *might* be true, in order that the reader might develop thoughts of his own. The truth, or otherwise, of this matter will be very much in the mind of the beholder.

A New Platonic Theory of the Soul

Imagine, if you will, a bubble that has existed for all time. This bubble may be of any size or colour you wish, and of any composition that you wish, but it must be a sphere – in accordance with the very reasonable doctrine of the Pythagoreans. Now visualise within this bubble a unity of five elements – earth, air, fire, water and the all-important spirit, or soul-substance. None of these elements should be understood as having an independent existence. Rather, they are proto-elements, mixed together in a singular primeval unity.

Now imagine that, owing to some latent instability, this bubble bursts in cataclysmic fashion, causing the elements to be born, and that these elements course like a storm through the new Universe which they bring into being. From the unity, there comes initially a separation into earth, air, fire, water and soul. But then there begins a recombination of these elements as they are attracted irresistibly to one another. Thus the new Universe begins to form, naturally in the shape of a sphere, containing within it superclusters of galaxies, and in these galaxies stars are formed. The evolving Universe is in a state of flux. Galaxies give birth to quasars which, in turn, give birth to new galaxies, in which further stars are destined to be born. From each of these stars, planets are born, and from some of these planets there are born moons. At each birth event, the five primeval elements are disintegrated and then reintegrated, as the cosmic genesis proceeds in a never-ending chain reaction. At the heart of this process is the spiritual fifth element which permeates the newly forming galaxies, quasars, stars, planets and moons, and energises the birth-giving process. Some of this soul-substance finds itself bonding with the material elements, but other soul-substance, attracted too late towards the mix, is destined to surround each new-born cosmic body like an aethereal protective shield, in effect like an invisible outer skin.

Eventually, our own solar system is born from a star, the Sun, whose body contains the five elements mixed together, surrounded by a layer of the disembodied soul (as discussed). The Sun, energised from within by its embodied soul, then gives birth to the planets, the material for which it spins off into a sequence of surrounding orbits. In each of the planets, the five primeval elements are reintegrated, whilst other soul-substance, drawn irresistibly towards the newly formed planet, comes to surround it like an invisible outer skin (as explained earlier). Such a planet is the Earth.

The embodied soul-substance now goes to work, seeking to propagate itself in any suitable shape or form. Its mission, quite simply, is to thrive and survive. All it knows is propagation of itself. In the case of the Earth, the soul-substance, operating from within, energises grass, shrubs and trees which rise up from the ground. Then, the first autonomous creatures begin to move independently from their planetary host. At this crucial moment, the free-floating soul that surrounds the Earth is attracted irresistibly towards material life and enters the fertilised ovum. The autonomous creatures become possessed of two kinds of soul. The first kind inhabits the DNA and directs the evolution of the body, doing all that is necessary to ensure its survival. The second kind of soul brings a new component to animal behaviour – the beginning of a consciousness that is separate from the body. At bodily death, the first kind of soul returns to the earth whence it came, whilst the second kind returns to the invisible cloud of aether that surrounds the Earth.

Life on Earth now evolves into more complex forms, doing so not through descent with modification driven by statistics and chance, but rather through descent with modification driven by intelligence. In other words, the soul-substance in the DNA senses environmental changes and reacts intelligently to ensure its survival. Eventually, by this process, there evolves *Homo sapiens*, no different conceptually from any other creature. In its DNA it has the same intelligent soul-substance that directs the evolution of the body, whilst in its head it has the other kind of soul-substance which is in its nature identical but which exists as the separate consciousness of the mind.

All creatures on Earth develop thus, energised by the twin sparks of spiritual life which must, by necessity, find a way to co-exist. The soul of the DNA, for its part, focuses on survival and propagation, and it does its job well; but the soul of the mind, in contrast, is disorientated by the fact of its bodily incarnation. As a result, the soul of the DNA takes charge, whilst the soul of the mind tags along for the ride – a veritable hostage to fortune. The creature thus lives its life like an automaton, doing what it needs to survive and no more. Just occasionally the soul of the mind gets to think the question: "Who am I, and why am I here?". The question is asked by every kind of species.

As for man, his unique evolutionary niche causes him to face moral choices at virtually every turn. Consequently, he, more than any other creature, gets to ponder his existence, origins and destiny. Furthermore, man's astonishing brain and dexterity enable him to pursue answers to these eternal questions in ever more inventive ways. First microscopes and telescopes; then submarines; then spacecraft. By these means, man witnesses more of the Universe than any other creature in the history of the Earth.

So much for the origins of man's soul, but what about its fate? Is it to be recycled endlessly, undergoing repeated reincarnations on the Earth, or is there a better existence to be had? If Plato were alive today, and took over the story at this point, he would probably say something like this. The soul of man consists of two types of soul-substance, which are each attracted, by nature, to material things. The first type is the soul of the DNA. Upon the death of its host body, this type of soul-substance returns to the earth to be recycled into new living creatures; it is bound up for ever with the material world and it has no control over its fate; it will be recycled endlessly. The second type is the soul of the mind, i.e. man's personality or true self. Upon the death of its host body, this type of soul-substance returns temporarily to the aethereal cloud surrounding the world, where it is given a choice of fate: either reincarnation on Earth or a higher, aethereal form of existence. In nearly all cases, however, the choice is a foregone conclusion. The soul of man, having become deeply attached, by way of its experiences, to the material pleasures on Earth, no longer remembers that it is, by nature, a free-floating spirit. Accordingly, it chooses bodily reincarnation. Or, as Plato might say: hell on Earth.

A few souls, however, become enlightened during their incarnation on Earth. They recognise their nature as immortal, spiritual beings, and they achieve total recall of their spiritual origins. Such a soul seeks to escape the cycle of endless reincarnation, and this it accomplishes firstly by avoiding an excess of material pleasures (abstinence and moderation are the watchwords), and secondly by fixing its gaze upon a higher, invisible reality. In this way, the enlightened soul, upon the death of its body, is able to by-pass the masses who jostle in the queue for reincarnation, and proceed upwards to the heavenly dwelling place of the spirits.

Where would this heavenly dwelling place be? Plato, if writing for a modern audience, would no doubt tell a fine story of the soul's quest to retrace the steps of its evolution. He would envisage the soul of man ascending from the Earth to the Sun; from there to the primeval proto-Milky Way; from there to a quasar or galactic supercluster; and from there to the surface of the ever-existing bubble from which the Universe had begun. For this 'bubble of beginning' would surely signify Socrates' 'true Heaven' and Plato's true Atlantis.

Is this a 'true story'? Personally, I feel that there is some truth in it, but also, perhaps, a little deception.

This is Plato's secret.

This is *The Atlantis Secret*.

But is it a true secret? Time will surely tell.

Another Thought for the Day

Who knows if life be death, and death be thought life in the other world.
(Euripides, 5th century BC)

APPENDIX A
THE DEMIOURGOS DECODED

**It follows by unquestionable necessity that
this Universe is an image of something.**
(Plato, *Timaeus*, mid-4th century BC)

In the midst of Plato's Atlantis story, the character Timaeus – a fictitious Pythagorean from southern Italy – launches into a long digression about the origins of the Universe. His account, concerning the creation by the *Demiourgos*, is generally recognised to be the most connected account that exists of Pythagorean cosmogony. As I aim to show in this appendix, it is also one of the most ingenious ciphers ever constructed for exploded planet cosmogony.

Timaeus' Account in Brief

To produce a faithful summary of Timaeus' *Demiourgos* cosmogony is a virtually impossible task. But nevertheless it must be attempted.

To begin, Timaeus declares that the Universe must have had an origin, and must have come to be by some agency or cause. This cause he then names as *Demiourgos* (literally 'the craftsman') whom he identifies as the 'father' of the Universe. Next, Timaeus declares that the *Demiourgos* must have used a model for his work, and he asserts that this model must have been something perfect, eternal and ever-unchanging: "It follows by unquestionable necessity" he states "that this Universe is an image of something."[1]

Of what was the Universe an image? The answer, says Timaeus, is the *Demiourgos* himself, who wanted everything to be as much like himself as was possible.[2] Thus the Universe was created as a living thing in the image of the real Living Thing, i.e. the *Demiourgos* himself.[3]

To create the Universe, the *Demiourgos* carried out a number of tasks, more or less simultaneously. He mixed the body of the Universe, using the four proto-elements of earth, air, fire and water, and agitated it 'like a shaking machine', thus causing the elements to become separated and purified. In this way, he formed the Sun, Moon, planets and stars, which he set in seven concentric bands around the Earth.

At the same time, the *Demiourgos* mixed the soul of the Universe, which he planted in the centre, in the Earth, and then extended outwards, thereby energising the Sun, Moon, planets and stars. Finally, he wrapped this soul-substance around the outside of the Universe so that it totally surrounded the sphere, and he set the sphere of the Universe spinning upon itself, round and round in a circular motion.

All of these things the *Demiourgos* created according to 'a symphony of proportion', employing Pythagorean mathematical relationships as the basis for cosmic order.[4]

Next, Timaeus describes the creation of mankind – a joint project between the *Demiourgos* and the Olympian gods. First, the *Demiourgos* mixed the soul of man and divided the mixture into the same number as the stars which he had created in the heavens. Then, he introduced these newborn souls to their 'companion stars'.[5] And then he sowed them in the Earth, whereupon the Olympian gods took over and, in accordance with the *Demiourgos'* instructions, wove the immortal souls to mortal bodies, thereby creating mankind.[6]

Where did the Olympian gods come from? Here, Timaeus cites the ancient Greek myth of how Gaia and Ouranos gave birth to Oceanus and Tethys, who then gave birth to Kronos and Rhea, who then gave birth to Zeus, Hera and their siblings, who then gave birth to another generation of Olympians, and he suggests that this myth should be accepted on good faith. Nevertheless, Timaeus goes on in the same breath to assert that the *Demiourgos* is the 'maker' and 'father' of the Olympian *daimones*, who, by the same token, are his 'children'. The implications of this claim will be discussed in a moment.

Now, on the face of it, the creation by the *Demiourgos* is an entirely peaceful affair; there are no obvious references to the cataclysm theory which features so strongly in other Greek accounts of the creation. It is my aim, however, to demonstrate, using our newly acquired knowledge of Greek and Near Eastern cosmogony, that the *Demiourgos* is, in fact, a secret cipher for the exploded planet.

The Mystery Decoded

Who, or what, is the *Demiourgos*? Let us run through a few salient points from *Timaeus* whilst remembering to follow the old Pythagorean maxim of 'fixing our eye on unity'.[7]

Firstly, Timaeus argues from first principles that 'this Universe is an image of something', and he then goes on to declare that the *Demiourgos* created the Universe as 'a living thing' in the image of an eternal model which he called '*The* Living Thing'. He thus implies that God himself is the pre-existent archetype on which the Universe has been modelled.

What does this tell us about the *Demiourgos*? For one thing, it tells us that he must be a sphere, for the Universe which he has created in his own image and likeness is a sphere.

Secondly, we may conclude that the *Demiourgos* is invisible, for he is described as 'that which always is', and as Socrates tells us: "That which *is* is invisible."[8]

Thirdly, Timaeus presents his *Demiourgos* as a craftsman who stands aloof and separate from that which he creates. He thus implies that the *Demiourgos* stands *outside* the Universe as he creates it.

Putting these three facts together, we can say that the *Demiourgos* is conceived to be an invisible sphere, existing outside the visible Universe, which he has created in his own image (see Figure 14 opposite).

And yet, despite Timaeus' portrayal of the *Demiourgos* as a mystical creator, it must be said that there is much in his cosmogony that evokes the more traditional cataclysmic cosmogonies.

Consider. Timaeus declares that the *Demiourgos* is the 'maker and father' of the Olympian gods.[9] But if this were so, then the *Demiourgos* would have to be an *alter ego* of the original Ouranos, 'The Mountain of Heaven', and this would make him an all too physical figure.

Secondly, when Timaeus describes the *Demiourgos* fashioning the Sun, Moon, planets and stars, he omits to mention the Earth, as if to suggest that the Earth was *already in existence*. He indeed goes on to say that the Earth ranks as 'the first and oldest' of the celestial gods, and 'the one with the greatest seniority'.[10] And he makes the curious observation that before the coming to be of the Sun, Moon, planets and stars 'the Universe had already been made to resemble in various respects the model in whose likeness the god was making it'.[11] Taken together, all of these clues point to the early Universe being synonymous with Gaia, whom the *Demiourgos* used as a birth vessel for the creation of the other celestial bodies (in accordance with the cosmogony of Hesiod and the Orphics – see chapter nine).

Thus, linking the second point to the first point, the sphere of the Universe would stand to the sphere of the *Demiourgos* as the sphere of Gaia stands to the sphere of Ouranos 'The Mountain of Heaven'.

Figure 14.
THE DEMIOURGOS
AND HIS UNIVERSE
(Copyright Alan F. Alford)

THE SPHERE
OF GOD
(not to scale)

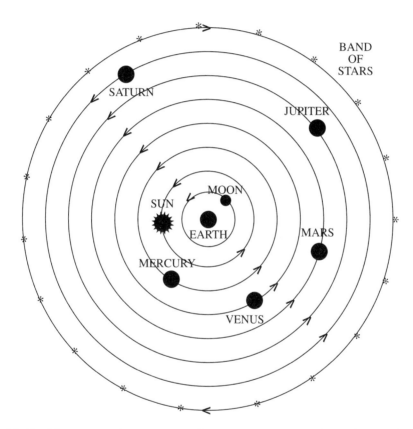

Thirdly, Timaeus makes a very curious statement about how the creation began. He says that: "The god wanted everything to be good... and so he took over all that was visible, not at rest but in discordant and disorderly motion, and brought it from a state of disorder to one of order...".[12] This is a most perplexing statement in the context of what otherwise appears to be an *ex-nihilo* creation, and it seems to suggest that something very real and chaotic was already taking place in the proto-Universe, as if something cataclysmic had already happened.

The plot thickens as we probe deeper. The *Demiourgos*, we are told, 'set the Universe turning continuously in the same place, spinning around upon itself.'[13] This would arguably make sense at the end of the creation, but it here purports to describe the proto-Universe, *before* the creation of the Sun, Moon, planets and stars. Why on earth would this proto-Universe have been set spinning? More to the point, *how could it* have been spinning? Motion, after all, exists only in a relative sense; if nothing else exists, relative motion is impossible. Thus, in the context of a singular Universe, Timaeus' statement makes no sense. And yet it would make sense if his spinning proto-Universe is a cipher for the Earth (Gaia), which indeed spins on its axis.

A similar anomaly occurs later in Timaeus' account, where he declares that he must introduce the principle of 'the Straying Cause' in order to explain the creation properly. He then recalls the traditional myth of the marriage of Ouranos and Gaia by asserting that: "this Universe (*Kosmos*) is of mixed birth: it is the offspring of a union of Necessity and Intellect."[14] And having thus attributed the origin of the Universe to the subjugation of Necessity, Timaeus goes on to describe the origin of the four elements of earth, air, fire and water. The proto-elements, he says, were placed in the Universe – 'the receptacle of all becoming' – and then shaken within it as the Universe was agitated 'like a shaking machine'.[15] This is a remarkable detail, for it echoes the older Greek cosmogonies in which the primordial elements were thrown down from Heaven and then shaken in the womb of the Earth. Once again, Timaeus seems to be drawing an analogy (perhaps deliberately) between the spheres of *Demiourgos* and his Universe, and the twin planets of Ouranos and Gaia.

And then there is the ambiguity of the language used in *Timaeus*. The Universe is a sphere; so is the Earth. The Universe is a unique sphere; so was the Earth in the aftermath of the exploded planet. The Universe spins on its axis in a fixed place; so does the Earth. The Universe is a 'visible living thing'; so is the Earth. The Universe is 'a shrine for the everlasting gods'; so is the Earth according to the first lines of Hesiod's *Theogony*.[16] The Universe is a *kosmos*, i.e. an 'ordered whole'; so is the Earth.[17] And finally, the Universe is called *Ouranos*, which happens also to be the name of the fallen Mountain of Heaven, hidden inside the Earth.

Is Timaeus' Universe a secret cipher for the Earth? The implications, as I shall explain in a moment, are astonishing. But first, let us consider something else.

If the reader will turn back to Figure 14, he will see that the visible Universe consists of seven circular bands surrounding the Earth/Moon system, namely the bands of the Sun, the five planets and the stars. This, remarkably, is the structure of the Earth's Underworld as cited in ancient Mesopotamian myths (see chapter nineteen of this book). The sphere of the Universe thus bears a most uncanny resemblance to the sphere of the

Earth!

How did the Earth's Underworld become structured in seven spheres? The explanation, undoubtedly, is to be found in the idea of seven fallen heavens. The first of these fallen heavens was, of course, Ouranos, who corresponds to the outer sphere of stars in Figure 14 (the ambiguity of the name Ouranos allows him to be the sphere of stars but also the sphere of the Universe in its entirety). The second of the fallen heavens was, of course, Kronos, who corresponds to the planet Saturn in Figure 14. And the third of the fallen heavens was, of course, Zeus, who corresponds to the planet Jupiter. Coincidence? Absolutely *not*. What we are looking at in Figure 14 is a deliberately encoded system which links the below to the above: seven celestial spheres *fall into* the Earth and, hey presto, as if by magic, seven celestial spheres are *born from* the Earth.

I therefore put it to the reader that the *kosmos*, i.e. 'ordered whole', of the Earth is a cognate for the *kosmos*, i.e. 'ordered whole', of the Universe. And, furthermore, I put it to the reader that the creation of the Universe by the *Demiourgos* is, in fact, a cipher for the creation of the Earth, which is after all literally a 'universe' (for the literal meaning of the word is 'a single thing that turns on its axis', deriving from the Latin *universum*, i.e. *uni+vertere*). This cipher, I would venture to suggest, is the brainchild of Pythagoras, who was said to have been the first Greek to describe the Universe as a sphere and to call it a *kosmos*.[18]

From this deduction, there emerges an astonishing implication. If the *Demiourgos* created the Universe in his own image and likeness, and if the Universe is a cipher for the Earth, then the *Demiourgos* created *a planet* in his own image. And for the *Demiourgos* to create a planet in his own image, the *Demiourgos* must be... a planet! *QED*. Timaeus' account of the Universe is an elegant, stunning, and beautiful cipher, in which the *Demiourgos* encodes the mystery of the exploded planet.

It is worth recalling, at this juncture, Plato's assertion that the souls of men had companion stars, to whom they could return in the afterlife. Timaeus expresses the idea thus:

> "The *Demiourgos* divided the mixture into a number of souls equal to the number of stars and assigned each soul to a star. He mounted each soul in a carriage, as it were, and showed it the nature of *Ouranos*...
> And if a person lived a good life throughout the due course of his time, he would at the end return to his dwelling place in his companion star, to live a life of happiness in accord with his character."[19]

These stars are, of course, situated in the outermost sphere, or rim, of the visible Universe, according to the Platonic scheme. But what happens if we envisage the sphere of the Universe as a cipher for the sphere of the Earth? Then, intriguingly, the 'companion stars' would signify the seeds of mankind that were planted in the Earth's surface.[20] And, by the same token, man's quest to return to his star would become analogous to his primeval ascent from the Underworld onto the surface of the Earth. Or, to put it another way, his ascent from darkness into the light.

This analogy strikes me as particularly harmonious, given Plato's view that the soul of man was living in darkness upon the Earth and needed to ascend to the rim of the heavens in order to perceive the true Light of God beyond. One is reminded especially of the account given in Plato's *Phaedrus*, where Socrates imagines the gods ascending in a procession to 'the high tier at the rim of the Universe'. He then goes on to describe what they see:

> "When the souls we call immortals reach the top, they move outward and take their stand on the high ridge of the Universe, where its circular motion carries them around as they stand while they gaze upon what is outside the Universe. The place above the heavens – none of our Earthly poets has ever sung or ever will sing its praises enough! Still, this is the way it is: risky as it may be, I must attempt to speak the truth... What is in this place is without colour and without shape and without solidity – a being that really is what it is, the subject of all true knowledge, visible only to Intelligence, the steersman of the soul. Now a god's mind... is delighted at last to be perceiving what is real and apprehending what is true, feeding on all this and feeling wonderful, until the circular motion brings it around to where it began. On the way around it has a view of Justice as it is; it has a view of Self-control; it has a view of Knowledge... the knowledge of what *really is what it is*. And when the soul has seen all the things that are as they are, and feasted upon them, it sinks back inside the Universe and goes home."[21]

But I must stop before I say too much. He who has ears, let him hear.

Another Thought for the Day

Fine things are very difficult to know.
(ancient Greek proverb)

APPENDIX B
CLARIFICATIONS

It is open to all men to know themselves and to be wise.
(Heraclitus, 5th century BC)

The problem with any book is that, no matter how carefully the author expresses his ideas, misunderstandings invariably occur in the minds of his readers. As Socrates once put it: 'Every discourse, once it has been written down, roams about everywhere, reaching indiscriminately those with understanding no less than those who have no business with it, and it doesn't know to whom it should speak and to whom it should not.'[1] It is for this reason that I set out below some brief clarification statements concerning subjects which are, to a greater or lesser degree, impinged upon by the theory in this book.

Lost Civilisations

It is an unfortunate fact of life that Atlantis has become a byword for the idea of a lost civilisation, and the reader might therefore wonder whether my decoding of Atlantis, involving as it does a refutation of the sunken island interpretation, amounts to a veiled attack on the lost civilisation theory. Such a thought would be ill-conceived, for it would stem from a confusion of two subjects which, in fact, represent separate ideas: (a) Atlantis; and (b) lost civilisations. As I see it, this book underlines the need to separate these two ideas, and there is nothing within these pages that argues against the lost civilisation theory per se. On the contrary, I am of the opinion that there is some good evidence for the existence of highly advanced, but unidentified, civilisations in the past, and it might well be the case that an undefined senior culture did bequeath a set of ideas and beliefs to all ancient civilisations around the globe. But, for Heaven's sake, let us stop calling this hypothesised culture 'Atlantis' and find a better name for it.

Ancient Astronauts

It is another unfortunate fact of life that the myths of the gods coming down from Heaven to Earth have been adopted as one of the pillars of the 'ancient astronaut' hypothesis, as it has been advocated over the years by Erich von Daniken, Zecharia Sitchin and others. Accordingly, the reader of this book might construe my forceful rejection of this interpretation of the myths to be a deliberate attack on the ancient astronaut hypothesis per se. It behoves me to emphasise that nothing could be further from the truth. Far from being a critic of the ancient astronaut theory, I am, on the contrary, sympathetic to the idea that an extraterrestrial race may have intervened on the Earth at some time in the remote past. The last thing I wish to see is this rather interesting baby being thrown out with the bath-water.

To my mind, the pursuit of the truth is the most important thing, and it is therefore essential to evaluate each line of 'evidence' for the ancient astronaut theory independently and non-dogmatically on its own merits. As I see it, myths may not be the best place to look for evidence of extraterrestrial intervention, but if they are to be seen as relevant it must surely be in directing us to the idea that a planet exploded in the Earth's vicinity, especially since the myths allege that the planet in question was formerly populated by a golden race of men! In the light of the scientific exploded planets hypothesis (see below), one may legitimately ask the question whether the ancient poets understood this golden age myth to be something more than metaphorical.

Exploded Planets

I have been careful, in this book and my previous book, to distinguish the exploded planet hypothesis of ancient religions and myths (the mythical EPH) from the exploded planet hypothesis of the origins of comets and asteroids (the scientific EPH). The reader might thus wonder whether I have cooled my enthusiasm towards Dr Tom Van Flandern's scientific EPH. It behoves me, then, to clarify my position on this question.

Firstly, I must confess that I find the modern orthodox theory for the origin of comets and asteroids totally unconvincing, both scientifically and intuitively. As I see it, the prevailing theory is constantly failing to predict new scientific data in advance, and is repeatedly being 'patched up', causing it to become ever more complicated and unwieldy. As any honest scientist will tell you, the mark of a good theory is its predictive ability, but scientists have long given up using their theory of comets and asteroids to predict new data. Instead, they wait for the new data to come in, and then they 'patch up' their model.

Secondly, the orthodox theory for the origin of comets and asteroids is rooted in sub-theories (e.g. the Oort Cloud) which are over-elaborate and implausible. I am reminded here of the incredibly elaborate models which the ancient Greeks produced to explain the 'fact' that the Sun, the Moon, the planets and the stars orbited around the Earth! These theories were all very impressive in their day, but all of them were totally wrong. The lesson of history is that scientists occasionally get caught up in a kind of collective madness, which necessitates a revolution in thinking – the Copernican revolution being a case in point.

Thirdly, regarding Van Flandern's scientific EPH, I am not qualified to say that it is correct, but I can confirm from meeting him that he is no crank and that his evidence is impressive. As Van Flandern put it to me in May 2000: 'Rest assured that the EPH part of this matter has been before the world experts in all forums, and has survived the strongest challenges anyone could muster.'[2] This statement, to the best of my knowledge, is quite correct. Admittedly, there is an outstanding problem concerning the mechanism by which a planet might explode, but, as Van Flandern has pointed out, there is as yet no adequate model for the explosion of stars, but their explosion is an observed and accepted fact.

It may seem from the foregoing that I am a Van Flandern supporter, but, to borrow a phrase that Aristotle once used of Plato, 'Van Flandern is dear to me, but dearer still is the truth'. Personally, I have no axe to grind as to whether the scientific EPH is right or wrong. As I see it, it might conceivably be the case that both the orthodox theory *and* Van Flandern's theory are wrong, and that the true explanation for the origin of comets and asteroids has yet to be conceived.

For a detailed overall assessment of the scientific EPH and for further updates to an unfolding situation, visit my website at http://www.eridu. co.uk. Or subscribe to Van Flandern's *Meta Research Bulletin* by visiting his website, http://www.metaresearch.org, or writing to Meta Research, P.O. Box 15186, Chevy Chase, MD 20825-5186, USA.

Another Thought for the Day

It is necessary to keep re-investigating whatever I say, since
self-deception is the worst thing of all.
(Socrates in Plato's *Cratylus*, early-4th century BC)

ACKNOWLEDGEMENTS

First and foremost, I would like to thank my wife Sumu for her patience, endurance and trust through some difficult and challenging times. It is no exaggeration to say that this book could not have been written without her. She is one in a million.

I would also like to thank my mother and father for their love and support; Greg Hughes for technical support and help with illustrations; Andrew Whitting for technical support; Neil Gould for another superb jacket design; Robert Bauval for his kind permission to use illustrations and for his moral support (despite the hostility of his associates towards my ideas); Lloyd Pye for moral support likewise; Charles Penglase for reading and commenting on the original typescript; and Christopher Gill for sparing the time from his very busy schedule to read the manuscript of this book and write the foreword.

In addition, I must express my appreciation to certain people who have influenced my writing career: firstly, Erich von Daniken, who captured my imagination as a young man with his myths of the gods; secondly, Tom Van Flandern, whose scientific theories provided the vital template for decoding ancient religion; thirdly, Victor Clube for shedding light on how the exploded planet religion began; and fourthly, Plato, for helping me put the spirit back into the exploded planet religion.

Finally, I must acknowledge the work of all those archaeologists and scholars who devoted their lives to the recovery of the ancient Greek and Near Eastern cultures, and thus made this book possible.

Illustration Credits

NOTES AND BIBLIOGRAPHY

CHAPTER ONE: MYSTERIES OF THE GODS

1 Plato, *Critias,* 109b-d, 113c. Unless otherwise stated, all citations from Plato are from J.M. Cooper ed., *Plato: Complete Works,* Hackett Publishing Company Inc., 1997.
2 Plato, *Critias,* 113c-d; Plato, *Timaeus* 23e; Plato, *Critias* 109d.
3 C. Gill, *Plato The Atlantis Story,* Bristol Classical Press, 1980, p. 55. In addition, Homer's *Iliad,* 2.547-48, refers to Athens as 'the land of great-hearted Erechtheus' and describes how the goddess Athene reared Erechtheus 'after the grain-giving ploughland had given him birth'.
4 Plato, *Critias,* 113d-e.
5 Homer, *Iliad,* 1.528-30. Unless otherwise stated, all citations from the *Iliad* are from *Homer The Iliad,* trans. Martin Hammond, Penguin Books, 1987.
6 Homer, *Iliad,* 1.195; Hesiod, *Theogony,* 454.
7 Homer, *Iliad,* 1.43-45.
8 W. Burkert, *Greek Religion,* Harvard University Press, 1985, p. 183; N. Hammond, *History of Greece,* Oxford, 1967, p. 170.
9 See, for example, Plato, *Statesman,* 274c-d.
10 W. Burkert, *Greek Religion,* op. cit., p. 314.
11 *Encyclopaedia Britannica,* 1999 standard edition.
12 Diodorus, for example, made the god Kronos the first king and also the benevolent culture hero who 'transformed the way of life of the men of his day from wild to civilised... and travelled all over the inhabited world, introducing justice and open-heartedness to all.' (*Library* 5.66.4); see L. Edmunds ed., *Approaches to Greek Myth,* The John Hopkins University Press, 1990, p. 176. On Philo, see M.L. West, *The East Face of Helicon,* Clarendon Press, 1999, pp. 283-86. On Plutarch, see *De Iside et Osiride* (cited in chapter ten of this book).
13 R. Graves, *The Greek Myths,* combined edition, Penguin Books, 1992, pp. 20, 17.
14 Ibid., p. 16.
15 Ibid. See Index and cf. to pp. 18, 43, 56.
16 Ibid., pp. 37-44.
17 Ibid., pp. 20-21.
18 Ibid., p. 56.
19 Ibid, pp. 53-55.
20 I. Donnelly, *Atlantis: The Antediluvian World,* Dover Publications edition, 1976, pp. 285, 293.
21 D. Rohl, *Legend,* Century, 1998; A. Collins, *Gods of Eden,* Headline, 1998; A. Collins, *Gateway to Atlantis,* Headline, 2000; C. Wilson, *From Atlantis to the Sphinx,* Virgin, 1996; R & R. Flem-Ath, *When The Sky Fell,* Stoddart, 1995; R. Flem-Ath & C. Wilson, *The Atlantis Blueprint,* Little Brown, 2000.
22 E. von Daniken, *Chariots of the Gods?,* Souvenir Press, 1969.
23 Homer, *Iliad,* 14.201. Cf Hesiod, *Theogony,* 337 ff; Plato, *Cratylus,* 402b, *Theaetetus,* 152e.
24 R. Graves, *The Greek Myths,* op. cit., Index.
25 See ibid., p. 27, for all the details of this account.

26 F.M. Cornford, *From Religion to Philosophy*, Princeton University Press, 1991, p. 67. The citations are from Apollonios Rhodios, *Argonautika*, 1.496-98 ('grievous strife' can also be translated as 'deadly disruption').

27 W.K.C. Guthrie, *Orpheus and Greek Religion*, Princeton University Press, 1993, pp. 79-80, 137 fragment 66 (it is a 'lofty Aither' per fragments 73, 74).

28 Ibid., pp. 80, 92, 137 fragment 67. On the meaning of *Erebos*, see R. Graves, *The Greek Myths,* op. cit., p. 24, and M.L. West, *The East Face of Helicon*, op. cit., p. 154.

29 Ibid., p. 137 fragments 70, 71.

30 Ibid., pp. 80, 137-38 fragment 86.

31 Ibid., pp. 80, 137 fragment 72.

32 Ibid., pp. 80, 137 fragments 76, 78, 79.

33 Ibid., pp. 80, 137-38 fragments 89, 82, 98.

34 Ibid., p. 137 fragment 85.

35 Ibid., p. 138 fragment 109.

36 Alternatively, Phanes created the Sun and the Moon whilst situated 'in the misty darkness of the cave' (ibid., p. 138 fragment 97).

37 Ibid., p. 140 fragment 167 (this passage from Proclus).

38 Hesiod, *Theogony*, 96-161. On the link between Ouranos and *ouros* 'mountain', see R. Graves, *The Greek Myths,* op. cit., pp. 32, 782.

39 Hesiod, *Theogony*, 161-91 (trans. M.L. West). All citations from Hesiod are from M.L. West, *Hesiod, Theogony & Works and Days*, Oxford University Press, Oxford World's Classics paperback edition, 1999.

40 Hesiod, *Theogony*, 128 (trans. M.L. West).

41 Hesiod, *Theogony*, 155-61. Plato, in *Euthyphro*, 6a, suggests that Ouranos swallowed his offspring. Alternatively, Hesiod may be implying that the offspring were forced back into the Underworld by means of repeated sexual unions between Ouranos and Gaia. As we shall see in chapter eleven of this book, these two explanations are not mutually exclusive under the peculiar laws of divine metamorphosis.

42 The ascent of Kronos is implied by the later statement that Kronos was to be driven from his 'high station' (Hesiod, *Theogony*, 491-92).

43 The Titans of Kronos are not to be confused with the other Titans who were sons of Ouranos. The latter, described as 'the proud Titans from high Mount Othrys', were enlisted by Zeus in the battle against the Titans of Kronos.

44 Hesiod, *Theogony*, 453-58.

45 Hesiod, *Theogony*, 459-97.

46 Hesiod, *Theogony*, 178-87.

47 Hesiod, *Theogony*, 215-22.

48 Hesiod, *Theogony*, 188-99.

49 Hesiod, *Theogony*, 226-336.

50 Hesiod, *Works and Days*, 109-24.

51 R. Graves, *The Greek Myths,* op. cit., p. 40.

52 Hesiod, *Theogony*, 502-8.

53 Hesiod, *Theogony*, 148-54, 617-42.

54 Hesiod, *Theogony*, 675-86 (trans. M.L. West, though I have rendered 'sky' as 'Heaven').

55 Hesiod, *Theogony*, 691-704 (trans. M.L. West; I have paraphrased slightly). It should be remembered that Zeus is secretly stationed on Olympus as Kronos' cupbearer. It is not clear exactly where the battle takes place. If the word translated 'chthonic' is to be taken literally, then Zeus takes the battle to the Titans of Kronos in the Underworld. Alternatively, the word translated 'chthonic' might be anticipatory (M.L. West, *Hesiod, Theogony & Works and Days*, op. cit., p. 70), in which case it should be translated 'ill-fated', and the battle would take place somewhere between Heaven and Earth.

56 Hesiod, *Theogony*, 718-45. The imprisonment of Kronos goes unmentioned by Hesiod but is recalled by Homer in *Iliad*, 14.201-2; see citation in note 29 to chapter eighteen, below.

57 Hesiod, *Theogony*, 885-86.

58 Homer, *Iliad*, 15.185-194. The translation draws on F.M. Cornford, *From Religion to Philosophy*, op. cit., p. 15.

59 Hesiod, *Theogony*, 824-29 (trans. M.L. West). Hesiod cites the father of Typhoeus as Tartarus,

a personified region of the Underworld. The episode does not fit well into the structure of the 'succession myth', and was probably originally a self-contained story; see M.L. West, *The East Face of Helicon*, op. cit., pp. 300-1.

60 Hesiod, *Theogony*, 839-68.

61 Hesiod, *Theogony*, 867 (trans. M.L. West).

62 Hesiod, *Theogony*, 185-86; Orphic fragment 63, cited in W.K.C. Guthrie, *Orpheus and Greek Religion*, op. cit., p. 137; R. Graves, *The Greek Myths,* op. cit., pp. 131-32. The Giants were borne by Gaia, who had been impregnated by the spilt blood of castrated Ouranos.

63 Hesiod, *Theogony*, 886-99. Metis meant 'Wisdom'; thus, by swallowing Metis, Zeus had carried Wisdom in himself ever since. Another myth had it that the sea-goddess Thetis would produce a son and rival to Zeus (Aeschylus, *Prometheus Bound*; Apollodorus, *Library*, 3.13.4).

64 M.L. West, *Hesiod, Theogony & Works and Days*, op. cit., Introduction, p. x.

65 Hesiod, *Theogony*, 517-18.

66 Hesiod, *Theogony*, 521-22; Aeschylus, *Prometheus Bound*; Apollodorus, *Library,* 1.7.1. The chronology of events is unclear, but one presumes that Prometheus brought the heavenly fire of the gods to a pre-human form of mankind, perhaps the 'silver race'.

67 Hesiod, *Theogony*, 514-16 (trans. M.L. West).

68 Homer, *Iliad*, 8.477-79, refers to Iapetos being confined in Tartarus. See also note 29 to chapter eighteen, below.

69 C. Boer trans., *The Homeric Hymns*, Spring Publications, 1970, pp. 149-60.

70 Ibid., p. 156. Cf G.S. Kirk, *The Nature of Greek Myths*, Penguin Books, 1990 edition, p. 124. Mount Cynthus is the hill that dominates the small island of Delos.

71 C. Penglase, *Greek Myths and Mesopotamia*, Routledge, 1994, pp. 82-85, 187.

72 C. Boer trans., *The Homeric Hymns*, op. cit., pp. 150-51.

73 Ibid., p. 158.

74 Ibid., pp. 137-38. This incident was re-enacted in ritual at Athene's festival, the Panathenaia, in the form of the war-dance known as *pyrrhiche*. See W. Burkert, *Greek Religion*, op. cit., p. 102.

75 Pindar, *Olympian 7*, 33-40; Pindar, fragment 34. The scene was depicted on the east pediment of the Parthenon.

76 Hesiod, *Theogony*, 926-28.

77 C. Boer trans., *The Homeric Hymns*, op. cit., pp. 168-69.

78 Homer, *Iliad*, 18.394 ff. Thetis was associated with the salty sea of Nereus, Eurynome with the pure streams of Oceanus.

79 The heavenly workshop of Hephaestus features in Homer, *Iliad*, 18.135 ff, 18.369 ff. On Earth, he was primarily associated with a foundry beneath an island; see Homer, *Iliad*, 1.594, and Ap. Rhodios, *Argonautika*, 3.41-43, 4.760-64, 4.925-29.

80 Homer, *Iliad*, 20.4-9. The exception was Oceanus.

81 Plato, *Protagoras*, 320d (trans. S. Lombardo/K. Bell). Cf Plato, *Statesman*, 274c-d, Plato, *Menexenus*, 237e-238b, and *Homeric Hymn to Hephaestus*, 20.3 ff.

82 Hesiod is vague about whence Prometheus stole the fire (*Theogony*, 562 ff, *Works and Days*, 50-58). Plato states that Prometheus no longer had access to high Olympus and hence stole the fire from the temple of Athene and Hephaestus (*Protagoras*, 321d-e). But elsewhere Plato alludes to Prometheus as 'fire hurled down from Heaven' (*Philebus*, 16c). A late source (Servius) suggests that Prometheus stole the fire from the Sun.

83 Plato, *Statesman*, 274c-d; Plato, *Protagoras*, 321e; Plato, *Critias*, 109c-d.

84 Plato, *Statesman*, 270d-271c, 272d-e.

85 Hesiod, *Works and Days*, 105-157.

86 See M.L. West, *The East Face of Helicon*, op. cit., pp. 480-82.

87 Homer, *Iliad*, 5.304, 12.380, 12.449, 20.286.

CHAPTER TWO: CATACLYSMS AND THE GODS

1 On Poseidon, see Homer, *Iliad*, 15.173. On Apollo, see R. Stoneman ed., *Pindar The Odes and Selected Fragments*, Everyman, 1997, p. 166. On Calypso, see Homer, *Odyssey*, 5.30, 7.245. On Leto, see C. Boer trans., *The Homeric Hymns*, op. cit., p. 155. On Demeter, see C. Boer trans., *The Homeric Hymns*, op. cit., p. 111. In addition, Phaethon had 'yellow hair'.

2 Homer, *Iliad*, 1.528-30 (trans. M. Hammond). Cf C. Boer trans., *The Homeric Hymns*, op. cit.,

p. 17 (*Third Hymn to Dionysus*).

3 Homer, *Iliad*, 8.441-43 (trans. M. Hammond).

4 Homer, *Iliad*, 8.197-98 (trans. M. Hammond).

5 Homer, *Iliad*, 13.17-23 (the translation that follows is by M. Hammond).

6 Homer, *Iliad*, 14.225-30. Cf *Iliad*, 5.770-72.

7 Pindar, *Pythian 3*, 43; Ap. Rhodios, *Argonautika*, 2.679-80.

8 See full quote in this chapter, note 16 below.

9 C. Boer trans., *The Homeric Hymns*, op. cit., p. 76 (*Hymn to Aphrodite*). See comment in C. Penglase, *Greek Myths and Mesopotamia*, op. cit., p. 175.

10 Homer, *Iliad*, 21.405-8. Cf the myth of Tityus who was stretched out over nine acres in Tartarus. Cf also the myth of Typhoeus, whose fall caused widespread fires on the Earth. Cf also the size of Prometheus' body on the rock face in Aeschylus, *Prometheus Bound*.

11 Hesiod, *Theogony*, 148-54, 671 ff. Cf the Cyclops throwing huge rocks in Homer's *Odyssey*.

12 Hesiod, *Theogony*, 861-62.

13 Homer, *Odyssey*, 11.307-16 (trans. E.V. Rieu/D.C.H. Rieu). The twins would have succeeded had Apollo not destroyed them. These twins feature also in Homer, *Iliad*, 5.384, where they imprison Ares in a bronze jar. As for the giant Orion, it is worth noting that his name derives from *ouros* 'mountain' (R. Graves, *The Greek Myths*, op. cit., p. 154).

14 C. Boer trans., *The Homeric Hymns*, op. cit., p. 175 (*Hymn to Pythian Apollo*).

15 Ibid., p. 162.

16 Ibid., p. 106 (*Hymn to Demeter*).

17 Ibid., p. 114. Cf M.L. West, *The East Face of Helicon*, op. cit., p. 113.

18 Hesiod, *Theogony*, 493-94.

19 Apollodorus, and the Palaikastro hymn. See C. Penglase, *Greek Myths and Mesopotamia*, op. cit., pp. 82-83.

20 W. Burkert, *Greek Religion*, op. cit., pp. 127, 262, 280; C. Penglase, *Greek Myths and Mesopotamia*, op. cit., pp. 187-88; R. Graves, *The Greek Myths*, op. cit., p. 165.

21 See note 74 to chapter one, above.

22 Hesiod, *Theogony*, 185-86 (trans. M.L. West)

23 A.F. Alford, *When The Gods Came Down*, Hodder & Stoughton, 2000, p. 6. See also N. Richardson, *The Homeric Hymn to Demeter,* Clarendon Press, p. 318.

24 Hesiod, *Theogony*, 820-35 (trans. M.L. West).

25 Pindar, *Paean 12*, 11-16 (trans. G.S. Conway & R. Stoneman). All Pindar translations come from R. Stoneman ed., *Pindar The Odes and Selected Fragments*, Everyman, 1997.

26 C. Penglase, *Greek Myths and Mesopotamia*, op. cit., p. 83.

27 C. Boer trans., *The Homeric Hymns*, op. cit., pp. 169-71. Elsewhere, Typhaon was linked with the fall of the sky. In Ap. Rhodios, *Argonautika*, 2.1210-15, Zeus struck Typhaon with a thunderbolt and he 'rained from his head hot death-drops', as he fell down from the sky into the Underworld. It should be noted that Typhaon was a different monster to Typhoeus.

28 On Artemis, see C. Boer trans., *The Homeric Hymns*, op. cit., p. 69. On Dionysus, see ibid., pp. 9-17. On Hecate, see Ap. Rhodios, *Argonautika*, 3.1211. On Poseidon and Ares, see Homer, *Iliad*, 5.860, 14.148-49.

29 Ap. Rhodios, *Argonautika*, 4.640-43. Cf Hera's mighty war-shout in Homer, *Iliad*, 5.784-92; cf also her fiery chariot in Homer, *Iliad*, 5.745.

30 W. Burkert, *Greek Religion*, op. cit., p. 184.

31 Hesiod, *Theogony*, 104-7 (trans. M.L. West; I have paraphrased slightly).

32 Ap. Rhodios, *Argonautika*, 2.1235-37.

33 R. Graves, *The Greek Myths*, op. cit., pp. 194, 206, 238; G.S. Kirk, *The Nature of Greek Myths*, op. cit., p. 157. Cf comment by W. Burkert in *Greek Religion*, op. cit., p. 128.

34 G.S. Kirk, *The Nature of Greek Myths*, op. cit., p. 225; W. Burkert, *Greek Religion*, op. cit., p. 138. Another example is when Poseidon disguises himself as a river to make love to Tyro in Homer, *Odyssey*, 11.230-46.

35 Ap. Rhodios, *Argonautika*, 4.1406-9.

36 Ibid., 4.1427-30.

37 Homer, *Odyssey*, 4.415-24 (trans. E.V. Rieu/D.C.H. Rieu).

38 Ibid., 4.455-59.

39 On Athene, see Homer, *Odyssey*, 1.319-20, 3.371-72, 22.239-40. On Apollo, see C. Boer trans.,

The Homeric Hymns, op. cit., p. 173 (*Hymn to Pythian Apollo*).

40 In Homer, *Iliad*, 24.610-16, it is said that Zeus turned the race of mankind into stones, and that Niobe, too, was turned to stone. In Homer, *Odyssey*, 10.235-43, Circe turns Odysseus' men into pig-like creatures.

41 C. Boer trans., *The Homeric Hymns*, op. cit., p. 103 (*Hymn to Demeter*).

42 Ibid., pp. 72-73 (*Hymn to Aphrodite*).

43 Homer, *Iliad*, 13.68-72 (trans. M. Hammond). Cf the 'true appearance' of the Triton, the son of Poseidon, as reported in Ap. Rhodios, *Argonautika*, 4.1610-13 (trans. P. Green): 'His body, from the crown of his head down his back and flanks to his belly, was in shape wondrously like those of the blessed gods; but from under his loins there stretched a great sea-beast's tail.'

44 Homer, *Iliad*, 5.440-43 (trans. M. Hammond; I have paraphrased slightly). Cf *Iliad*, 5.864 ff, where 'immortal blood' drips from Ares' wound.

45 Ibid., 5.335-42 (trans. M. Hammond; I have paraphrased slightly).

46 On Aphrodite, see C. Boer trans., *The Homeric Hymns*, op. cit., p. 72. On Hermes, see Homer, *Iliad*, 24.311-49. On Apollo, see Ap. Rhodios, *Argonautika*, 2.674-84 (trans. P. Green).

47 Hesiod, *Theogony*, 839 ff.

48 Homer, *Iliad*, 5.744 ff. Cf comment in M.L. West, *The East Face of Helicon*, op. cit., p. 363.

49 Homer, *Iliad*, 4.76-77 (trans. M. Hammond).

50 Hesiod, *Theogony*, 521-22; Aeschylus, *Prometheus Bound*.

51 See M. Eliade, *A History of Religious Ideas*, Volume 1, University of Chicago Press, 1978, pp. 52-54, and R. Graves, *The Greek Myths*, op. cit., p. 445. It is worth noting that the Greek word for iron, *sideros*, is related etymologically to the word for star, *sidus*.

52 R. Graves, *The Greek Myths*, op. cit., pp. 31-33 and Index. Graves linked Ouranos to the word *ouros* 'mountain', and suggested that his name was a masculine form of *Our-ana* 'queen of the mountains'; thus he presumed Ouranos to mean 'king of the mountains'. This would indeed make sense in the light of the discussion yet to come in later chapters of this book.

53 A.F. Alford, *When The Gods Came Down*, op. cit. See also my earlier book *The Phoenix Solution*, Hodder & Stoughton, 1998. These do not constitute a refutation of the ancient astronaut theory per se, but they do provide a far more plausible explanation of certain crucial myths, such as the gods' creation of mankind in their own image and their fiery journeys between Heaven and Earth.

CHAPTER THREE: THE GREEK PERSPECTIVE

1 I. Velikovsky, *Worlds in Collision*, Dell Publishing, 1950.

2 Herodotus, *Histories*, 2.53. Modern scholars acknowledge the truth of this statement.

3 N. Hammond, *History of Greece*, op. cit., p. 170.

4 W. Burkert, *Greek Religion*, op. cit., p. 246.

5 Ibid., p. 246; M.L. West, *Hesiod, Theogony & Works and Days*, op. cit., Introduction, p. xx.

6 F.M. Cornford, *Before and After Socrates*, Cambridge University Press, 1932, p. 16. As one scholar has commented of Xenophanes: 'his criticism of Homeric religion could not be outdone, and it was never refuted.' (W. Burkert, *Greek Religion*, op. cit., pp. 308-9.)

7 Pindar, *Olympian 1*, 51-52.

8 Plato, *Euthyphro*, 6a.

9 Euripides, *Heracles*. See W. Burkert, *Greek Religion*, op. cit., p. 318.

10 Ibid. See W. Burkert, *Greek Religion*, op. cit., p. 246.

11 Plato, *Republic II*, 377-79. Socrates says: "We must not allow *any* stories about gods warring, fighting, or plotting against one another... The battles of gods and giants, and all the various stories of the gods hating their families or friends, should neither be told nor even woven in embroideries... We will not admit stories into our city – whether allegorical or not – about Hera being chained by her son, nor about Hephaestus being hurled from Heaven by his father when he tried to help his mother, who was being beaten, nor about the battle of the gods in Homer. The youth cannot distinguish what is allegorical from what is not..." (trans. G.M.A. Grube/C.D.C. Reeve). See also *Republic III*.

12 Herodotus, *Histories*, 2.3. See W. Burkert, *Greek Religion*, op. cit., p. 313.

13 Euripides, *Bellerophontes*. See W. Burkert, *Greek Religion*, op. cit., p. 316.

14 W. Burkert, *Greek Religion*, op. cit., p. 314; V. Ehrenberg, *From Solon to Socrates*, Routledge,

1968, p. 353.

15 W. Burkert, *Greek Religion*, op. cit., p. 257: 'That religion is a means to maintain authority and domination was stated by ancient authors from the 5th century BC onwards as a self-evident state of affairs'.

16 Isocrates, *Bus.,* 25. See W. Burkert, *Greek Religion*, op. cit., p. 247.

17 W. Burkert, *Greek Religion*, op. cit., p. 314. The omission of exceptional phenomena, such as comets, bolides and meteorites, is noteworthy.

18 Ibid. See also discussion in R. Temple, *The Crystal Sun,* Century, 2000, pp. 247-50.

19 W. Burkert, *Greek Religion*, op. cit., pp. 313-14; V. Ehrenberg, *From Solon to Socrates*, op. cit., p. 346. Apparently, Prodicus was a friend of Socrates.

20 W. Burkert, *Greek Religion*, op. cit., p. 316.

21 Ibid., p. 313; F.M. Cornford, *Before and After Socrates*, op. cit., p. 31.

22 W. Burkert, *Greek Religion*, op. cit., p. 313.

23 W. Burkert, *Greek Religion*, op. cit., p. 313; R. Temple, *The Crystal Sun,* op. cit., pp. 287-88. Apparently, a comet was shining in the sky at the time; see Aristotle, *Meteorologica*, 1.7.

24 W. Burkert, *Greek Religion*, op. cit., p. 316; V. Ehrenberg, *From Solon to Socrates*, op. cit., p. 251; C. Freeman, *The Greek Achievement*, Penguin, 1999, p. 263. Cf Plato, *Apology*, 26d, Plato, *Laws X*, 886, Plato, *Laws XII*, 967.

25 W. Burkert, *Greek Religion*, op. cit., p. 316. V. Ehrenberg, *From Solon to Socrates*, op. cit., pp. 251-52 comments that: 'No doubt the action was inspired as much by the hostility to Pericles personally as to the modern spirit as represented by the great philosopher.'

26 N. Hammond, *The Classical Age of Greece*, Weidenfeld & Nicolson, 1999 edition, p. 129.

27 P. Green trans., *Argonautika*, University of California Press, 1997, Introduction, p. 31.

28 Ibid., p. 32.

29 See R. Stoneman ed., *Pindar The Odes and Selected Fragments*, op. cit., p. 111. Ixion had murdered his father-in-law by pushing him into a pit of fire, but Zeus had forgiven Ixion and raised him to Heaven. Ixion then attempted to rape Hera, but Hera sent a cloud (*nephele*) in her own image to deceive him; from this cloud was born the first Centaur. The myth seems to echo the divine succession myth and the sacred marriage of Heaven and Earth.

30 Ibid., p. 111.

31 P. Green trans., *Argonautika*, op. cit., Introduction, p. 32.

32 *Encyclopaedia Britannica,* 1999 standard edition.

33 Homer, *Iliad*, 6.180-83 ('a creature none could conquer, born of gods not men').

34 P. Green trans., *Argonautika*, op. cit., Introduction, pp. 31-32.

35 Ibid., p. 32.

36 Ibid.

37 Ibid.

38 Ibid., p. 33.

39 Plato, *Laws X*, 889b-c. See also F.M. Cornford, *From Religion to Philosophy*, op. cit., p. 242.

40 M.L. West, *The East Face of Helicon*, op. cit., pp. 524-25.

41 Ibid., p. 525.

42 Ap. Rhodios, *Argonautika*, 1.496-97 (trans. P. Green, but I have rendered 'sky' as 'Heaven').

43 The sought-for first principle was known as *arche* or *physis*. The philosophers took as read the traditional four-element system. See F.M. Cornford, *From Religion to Philosophy*, op. cit., pp. 1-12; F.M. Cornford, *Before and After Socrates*, op. cit., p. 18; G.S. Kirk, *The Nature of Greek Myths*, op. cit., p. 297; V. Ehrenberg, *From Solon to Socrates*, op. cit., pp. 106-7.

44 F.M. Cornford, *From Religion to Philosophy*, op. cit., p. 4; N. Hammond, *The Classical Age of Greece*, op. cit., pp. 45-46.

45 F.M. Cornford, *From Religion to Philosophy*, op. cit., pp. 6, 128-29.

46 In Egypt, Nun; in Babylonia, Apsu-Tiamat. See W. Burkert, *The Orientalising Revolution*, Harvard University Press, 1995 edition, p. 92; G.S. Kirk, *The Nature of Greek Myths*, op. cit., p. 295.

47 It is disputed whether there ever was an Orphic religion per se; an excellent book on this subject is W.K.C. Guthrie, *Orpheus and Greek Religion*, Princeton University Press, 1993.

48 W.K.C. Guthrie, *Orpheus and Greek Religion*, op. cit., pp. 78-79.

49 Ibid., p. 141 fragment 226.

50 F.M. Cornford, *From Religion to Philosophy*, op. cit., pp. 7, 145.

51 Ibid., p. 145. Cf the Orphic description of *Khaos* which had 'no limit, no bottom, nor foundation' (W.K.C. Guthrie, *Orpheus and Greek Religion*, op. cit., p. 137 fragment 66).

52 F.M. Cornford, *Before and After Socrates*, op. cit., p. 18.

53 Ibid., pp. 18-19. The rings of fire lent their fiery light to the Sun, Moon and stars.

54 F.M. Cornford, *From Religion to Philosophy*, op. cit., pp. 7, 129-30, 148-50.

55 W. Burkert, *Greek Religion*, op. cit., p. 309. Cf G.S. Kirk, *The Nature of Greek Myths*, op. cit., p. 298.

56 F.M. Cornford, *From Religion to Philosophy*, op. cit., pp. 132, 184-88; W.K.C. Guthrie, *Orpheus and Greek Religion*, op. cit., pp. 224-26.

57 I. Velikovsky, *Worlds in Collision*, op. cit., p. 46; M. Eliade, *The Myth of the Eternal Return*, Princeton University Press, 1954, pp. 87-88, 120. Cf Aristarchus of Samos (3rd century BC), who taught that the Earth underwent destruction by fire every 2,484 years.

58 F.M. Cornford, *From Religion to Philosophy*, op. cit., p. 153; he called the confused mass 'a mixture of all seeds'. Cf Plato, *Phaedo*, 72c, *Gorgias*, 465d: 'all things mixed together in the same place'.

59 W.K.C. Guthrie, *Orpheus and Greek Religion*, op. cit., p. 248.

60 *Encyclopaedia Britannica*, 1999 standard edition.

61 This was one of the two schemes known to the Egyptians; see A.F. Alford, *When The Gods Came Down*, op. cit., pp. 145-49. In Greece, the idea is particularly noticeable in the myth of Boreas (Ophion) and Eurynome, and in the myth of Hyperborean Apollo. See note 55 to chapter seventeen, below.

62 W. Burkert, *Greek Religion*, op. cit., p. 320. In other words, the sexual union of the gods Phanes and Night stood for a mixing of the primordial elements.

63 F.M. Cornford, *From Religion to Philosophy*, op. cit., pp. 230-40; W. Burkert, *Greek Religion*, op. cit., p. 318; W.E. Leonard, *The Fragments of Empedocles*, 1908, p. 30.

64 The scheme is very similar to Anaximander's Unlimited; see F.M. Cornford, *From Religion to Philosophy*, op. cit., pp. 231, 240-41. Empedocles stated of the *Sphairos* that: 'he was equal on every side and quite limitless, a rounded sphere rejoicing in his circular solitude' (ibid., p. 234 fragment 28). Perhaps the Sphere concept explains the Orphic idea that the first cosmic principle had 'no limits'.

65 F.M. Cornford, *From Religion to Philosophy*, op. cit., p. 229. The 'roofed-in cave' was synonymous with 'the dark meadow of Ate' (fragments 119-21).

66 W.K.C. Guthrie, *Orpheus and Greek Religion*, op. cit., p. 169.

67 F.M. Cornford, *From Religion to Philosophy*, op. cit., pp. 236-37, 241.

68 Ibid., p. 230. Later, the process would begin again; thus Empedocles' cosmogony amounted to an ever-repeating cycle. Cf Plato, *Theaetetus*, 152e.

69 Per Ammianus Marcellinus, *Roman History*, Book II, chapter 22. See R. Temple, *The Crystal Sun*, op. cit., pp. 287-88.

70 R. Temple, *The Crystal Sun*, op. cit., p. 288.

CHAPTER FOUR: SOCRATES AND PLATO

1 The saying 'Know Thyself' (*gnothi seauton*) was inscribed on a wall of Apollo's temple at Delphi. Opinions differed on how to interpret it. On the Socratic approach, see Plato, *Alcibiades*, 130e ff; *Hipparchus*, 228d-e; *Rival Lovers*, 138; *Charmides*, 164d-165b; *Protagoras*, 343b. On alternative understandings, see V. Ehrenberg, *From Solon to Socrates*, op. cit., pp. 115, 333; W. Burkert, *Greek Religion*, op. cit., p. 148; M. Griffith ed., *Aeschylus: Prometheus Bound*, Cambridge University Press, 1983, p. 144.

2 W.K.C. Guthrie, *Orpheus and Greek Religion*, op. cit., pp. 156-57.

3 The 7th century poet Alcman, for example, wrote: 'Let no man fly up to Heaven'. Similarly, when Bellerophon dared to ascend to Olympus on Pegasus, Zeus sent a gadfly to sting the horse, which then threw Bellerophon down into the Underworld, to the 'Plains of Wandering'. The 5th century poet Pindar echoed these ideas: 'A man must seek from Heaven only what is fitting for mortal minds, perceiving well the path before his feet – the lot that is our portion.'

4 See Plato, *Apology*.

5 Some authorities give a slightly later date of 427 BC.

6 Plato, *Letter VII (To the Friends and Followers of Dion)*, 324e.

7 Plato, *Apology*, 24b; W. Burkert, *Greek Religion*, op. cit., p. 317; V. Ehrenberg, *From Solon to Socrates*, op. cit., pp. 377-80. 'Other divine powers' is sometimes translated as 'new spiritual things'. The problem was not that Socrates didn't believe in the city's gods but that his beliefs took an unusual and highly individual form, and this caused many people to envy and slander him with disinformation (Plato, *Apology*, 28a-b). He was also a threat to the status quo because he taught people to make their own souls the ultimate arbiters of what was right and wrong.

8 Plato, *Phaedo*.

9 C. Freeman, *The Greek Achievement*, op. cit., pp. 268-69; Plutarch, *De Iside et Osiride*, 354d-e; Ammianus Marcellinus, *The Roman History*, 22, xvi, 22.

10 C. Freeman, *The Greek Achievement*, op. cit., pp. 268-69; F.M. Cornford, *Before and After Socrates*, op. cit., p. 62.

11 J.M. Cooper ed., *Plato: Complete Works*, Hackett Publishing Company Inc., 1997.

12 The next best source of information is Xenophon. The only contemporary reference is by Aristophanes in *Clouds*. Other than that, the sources are very fragmentary; see V. Ehrenberg, *From Solon to Socrates*, op. cit., pp. 371-72.

13 F.M. Cornford, *Before and After Socrates*, op. cit., p. 56; G.S. Kirk, *The Nature of Greek Myths*, op. cit., p. 108.

14 J.M. Cooper ed., *Plato: Complete Works*, op. cit., pp. v-vi, 1678.

15 It is not disputed in principle that Plato was not the only Socratic writer to write Socratic dialogues. See J.M. Cooper ed., *Plato: Complete Works*, op. cit., p. xviii; V. Ehrenberg, *From Solon to Socrates*, op. cit., p. 372.

16 Plato, *Laws*, 894e-895a.

17 Plato, *Laws*, 896a. *Psyche* meant literally 'breath'.

18 Plato, *Laws*, 892a, 899c.

19 Plato, *Laws*, 896a, 896e-897a.

20 *Demiourgos* is sometimes simply translated as 'maker' or 'fashioner'.

21 Plato, *Timaeus*, 36d-e; the soul-substance was also made to surround the Universe.

22 Plato, *Timaeus*, 31b-32d.

23 Plato, *Timaeus*, 40c (cf 34b).

24 Plato, *Timaeus*, 38b-d (cf 39d).

25 Plato, *Timaeus*, 40a.

26 Plato, *Timaeus*, 36e (trans. D.J. Zeyl).

27 Plato, *Laws X*, 898c-899b; *Epinomis*, 983a-c. On Anaxagoran scepticism, see Plato, *Laws X*, 886d-e, *Laws XII*, 967b-c.

28 Plato, *Timaeus*, 30c-31a.

29 Plato, *Timaeus*, 39e.

30 Plato, *Timaeus*, 29a-b, 31a, 39e; Plato, *Republic VII*, 521d, 529b.

31 Plato, *Timaeus*, 30b-c, 47e-48a, *Laws XII*, 967d-e. Cf the *Nous* of Anaxagoras and the *Pronoia* of Diogenes.

32 Plato, *Timaeus*, 90a (trans. D.J. Zeyl, though I have slightly reworded the final line). Note that 'Heaven' could be read as 'heavens'.

33 Plato, *Phaedrus*, 250c. Cf *Phaedrus*, 250a.

34 Plato, *Phaedrus*, 249c, 249e-250a, 250e. Hence Socrates' idea that learning was remembrance; see Plato, *Phaedo*, 72e, and *Meno*. Herein lies the origin of 'Platonic love'; when a man saw marvellous beauty, either in a woman or in a male youth (as was the wont of Socrates and many Greek noblemen), he would be reminded of the eternal form of Beauty which had once been revealed to him in Heaven, and he would be overcome by the madness of love (*Phaedrus*, 250d ff); here, the physical aspect of love is made secondary to a much higher cosmic 'reality'.

35 W.K.C. Guthrie, in *Orpheus and Greek Religion*, op. cit., p. 166, states that Empedocles was 'saturated with Orphic and Pythagorean notions'. In *Histories*, 2.123, Herodotus declares that the Egyptians were the first to hypothesise the immortality of the soul and its transmigration in a cycle of three thousand years. 'There are Greek writers, some of an earlier, some of a later date', he says, 'who have borrowed this doctrine from the Egyptians and put it forward as their own.' (Orpheus and Pythagoras were undoubtedly intended). See also Herodotus, *Histories*, 2.81: 'here [re: wool taboo], the Egyptian practice resembles the rites called Orphic and Bacchic, but which are in reality Egyptian and Pythagorean.' (trans. G. Rawlinson).

36 Plato, *Phaedo*, 110a. Cf Plato, *Republic VII*, 540a. Cf also the 'pure light' of the heavenly

vision in Plato, *Phaedrus*, 250c.

37   Plato, *Phaedo*, 109-114; see the citation in chapter eleven of this book. A similar idea is found in Homer, *Odyssey*, 4.77: 'no mortal can compete with Zeus... his house and all his possessions are everlasting.'

38   Plato, *Phaedo*, 110b-c.

39   Plato, *Republic VII,* 521d, 529b.

40   Plato, *Republic VII,* 529b.

41   Plato, *Republic VII,* 521c, *Phaedo*, 66 ff, *Phaedrus*, 239b.

42   The definition of *philosophia* used by Plato's Academy was: 'the desire for the knowledge of what always exists' or 'the state which contemplates the truth'. See J.M. Cooper ed., *Plato: Complete Works,* op. cit., p. 1682.

43   Plato, *Republic VII*; Plato, *Epinomis*, 990 ff.

44   Plato, *Republic VII*, 540a-b (trans. G.M.A. Grube/C.D.C. Reeve).

45   In Plato, *Phaedo*, 64a, Socrates says: "The one aim of those who practise philosophy in the proper manner is to practise for dying and death." (Cf. *Phaedo*, 67e). The qualities required of these philosopher-kings were: to love the truth and be without falsehood; to have good memory, courage and high-mindedness; to be a lover of hard work; and to serve the people (Plato, *Republic VI*, 485c, 494b, 535c).

46   N. Hammond, *History of Greece*, op. cit., p. 127.

47   Ibid. Cf F.M. Cornford, *From Religion to Philosophy*, op. cit., pp. 215-16, 234 (footnote 2).

48   Plato, *Statesman*, 270c-d (trans. C.J. Rowe).

49   Plato, *Statesman*, 271d.

50   Herodotus, *Histories*, 2.142. It is possible that the *Statesman* myth might similarly have drawn upon an Egyptian source.

51   Plato, *Statesman*, 269a (trans. C.J. Rowe). It is worth noting, in passing, the connection between the myth of Atreus and Thyestes and the 'sign of the golden lamb', i.e. the lamb with the golden fleece; see R. Graves, *The Greek Myths*, op. cit., pp. 406-7.

52   Plato, *Timaeus*, 22b-d, 23a (trans. D.J. Zeyl).

53   Plato, *Timaeus*, 23b.

54   Plato, *Timaeus*, 25d (trans. D.J. Zeyl). The beginning of the sentence is omitted at this point, for the translation is questionable; it will be discussed later, in chapter twenty of this book.

55   Plato, *Critias*, 111e-112a. The Atlantis cataclysm was 'the third such cataclysmic storm before the destructive flood of Deucalion'. There was a popular belief in ancient Greece that every third wave or storm was greater than the others; see M. Griffith ed., *Aeschylus:Prometheus Bound*, op. cit., p. 265.

56   For example, the myth of Hephaestus' seed (*Timaeus*, 23e), the myth of Poseidon creating the ringed city of Atlantis from Clito's primeval hill (*Critias* 113d), and the myth of *Demiourgos* creating the Universe (see chapter eleven and appendix a of this book).

57   Plato, *Critias*, 109d. Cf *Laws III*, 676-81, and *Laws VI*, 782a.

58   Plato, *Laws III*, 677a (trans. T.J. Saunders). Plato is 'the Athenian'.

59   Apollodorus, *Library* (2nd century BC); Pausanias (2nd century AD). For a summary of the myth, see R. Graves, *The Greek Myths*, op. cit., pp. 138-43.

60   Pindar, *Olympian 9*, 43-57 (trans. G.S. Conway & R. Stoneman).

61   The Greeks saw an etymological connection between the words for stone (*laas*) and people (*laos*), as noted here by Pindar. A similar connection exists in Hebrew between the words for stones (*abanim*) and children (*banim*), hence the idea in Matthew 3:3-9 and Luke 3:8.

62   M. Griffith ed., *Aeschylus:Prometheus Bound*, op. cit.

63   Ibid., pp. 4, 10, 30, 265, 271, 274, 276-77, 280.

64   Ibid., pp. 266-67.

65   Plato, *Euthyphro*, 6a-c; Plato, *Republic II*, 377-82.

66   Plato, *Republic II*, 377a.

67   Plato, *Phaedrus*, 229e-230a. Socrates used allegories only on rare occasions, e.g. Oceanus and Tethys; see Plato, *Theaetetus*, 152e, 180d.

68   Plato, *Phaedrus*, 230a.

69   Plato, *Apology*, 35d (trans. G.M.A. Grube). He was deadly serious, too, as his comments in *Republic* make clear.

70   Plato, *Timaeus*, 40d-e (trans. D.J. Zeyl). Cf *Philebus* 16c-d: 'The people of old, superior to us

and living in closer proximity to the gods, have bequeathed us this tale...' (trans. D. Frede).
71 This would explain the inherent contradiction that is apparent in so many myths, e.g. Ap. Rh., *Argonautika*, 2.537-40, where Athene is transported by a light cloud 'huge though she was'.
72 Plato, *Timaeus*, 40d (trans. D.J. Zeyl, emphasis added).
73 Plato, *Timaeus*, 39e-40a. Cf *Timaeus*, 38b-d.
74 Plato, *Timaeus*, 40d-41a (trans. D.J. Zeyl).
75 Plato, *Timaeus*, 40d, 41a (trans. D.J. Zeyl). Cf *Cratylus*, 397c ff, where Socrates identifies *theoi*, originally, as the visible gods whose nature was to run (*thein*) across the heavens.
76 Plato, *Timaeus*, 40d, 41a (trans. D.J. Zeyl). For an orthodox academic approach to the problem of *theoi* versus *daimones*, see F.M. Cornford, *From Religion to Philosophy*, op. cit., pp. 37-38, and W. Burkert, *Greek Religion*, op. cit., pp. 179-81, 271-72, 331-32.
77 Plato, *Epinomis*, 984d-e (trans. R.D. McKirahan, Jr.). A similar distinction is made in Plato, *Cratylus*, 408.
78 W.K.C. Guthrie, *Orpheus and Greek Religion*, op. cit., p. 138 fragment 109 (emphasis added). A further precedent for this idea is found in Hesiod, *Works and Days*, 108 ff, where the golden race, upon death, turn into invisible, ghost-like *daimones* (cf Plato, *Cratylus*, 398a).

CHAPTER FIVE: THE SECRET SOCIETY

1 V. Ehrenberg, *From Solon to Socrates*, op. cit., p. 252.
2 This was one of the so-called 'three Greek Commandments' – honour the gods, honour one's parents, and honour strangers; see V. Ehrenberg, *From Solon to Socrates*, op. cit., p. 210. On the matter of not offending the gods, see C. Freeman, *The Greek Achievement*, op. cit., p. 235. See also Plato's ideal scenario in *Laws IV*, 716d-718a.
3 Pindar, *Olympian 1*, 35.
4 V. Ehrenberg, *From Solon to Socrates*, op. cit., p. 312.
5 Plato, *Cratylus*, 407d (trans. C.D.C. Reeve); Plato, *Minos*, 318e (trans. M. Schofield, though I have rendered 'divine humans' as 'demi-gods').
6 Plato, *Laws II*, 672b (trans. T.J. Saunders).
7 Plato, *Laws VII*, 821a, 821d (trans. T.J. Saunders).
8 Plato, *Letter VII (To the Friends and Followers of Dion)*, 344c (trans. G.R. Morrow). Cf Plato, *Theaetetus*, 152c, where Socrates suggests that Protagoras did not write down his greatest wisdom in his book *Truth*, but reserved it as a secret doctrine for his personal pupils.
9 Hesiod, *Theogony*, 27-28 (trans. M.L. West). See comment in W. Burkert, *Greek Religion*, op. cit., p. 246.
10 W. Burkert, *Greek Religion*, op. cit., p. 311: 'Ever since Plato, the word sophist has been a term of abuse, designating a charlatan who deceives with pseudo-knowledge.'
11 Plato, *Protagoras*, 316d-317b (trans. S. Lombardo & K. Bell).
12 Ibid. He suggested that the secrets were encoded not only in music but also in athletics. Cf note 8 above.
13 Plato, *Republic II*, 377e-378a (trans. G.M.A. Grube/C.D.C. Reeve; I have paraphrased slightly).
14 R.H. Brown, *Stellar Theology and Masonic Astronomy*, Truth Seeker Co., 1997 ed., p. 31.
15 Ibid., pp. 31-32.
16 M. Eliade, *A History of Religious Ideas*, Volume 1, op. cit., p. 298.
17 W.K.C. Guthrie, *Orpheus and Greek Religion*, op. cit., p. 142 fragment 235.
18 V. Ehrenberg, *From Solon to Socrates*, op. cit., pp. 242-44, 251-52. Earlier rulers were also deeply interested in science and mysticism, e.g. Peisistratus; see ibid, pp. 84-85.

CHAPTER SIX: IN SEARCH OF THE GRAIL

1 L. Edmunds ed., *Approaches to Greek Myth*, op. cit., p. 15.
2 See ibid., p. 92.
3 G.S. Kirk, *The Nature of Greek Myths*, op. cit., p. 43; *Encyclopaedia Britannica*, 1999 ed.
4 W. Burkert, *Greek Religion*, op. cit., p. 174.
5 A. Lang, *Custom and Myth*, 1884; also *Myth, Ritual and Religion*, 1887, and *Modern Mythology*, 1897.

6 L. Edmunds ed., *Approaches to Greek Myth*, op. cit., pp. 28, 69.
7 The best known examples of these dying-and-rising gods are Attis, Adonis, Tammuz and Osiris. A useful discussion of myth and ritual theory appears in G.S. Kirk, *The Nature of Greek Myths*, op. cit., pp. 66-68.
8 W. Robertson Smith, *Lectures on the Religion of the Semites*, Edinburgh, 1889; J. Harrison, *Mythology and Monuments of Ancient Athens*, London, 1890; J.G. Frazer, *The Golden Bough*, 12 vols, London, 1890-1915; L. Edmunds ed., *Approaches to Greek Myth*, op. cit., pp. 28 ff.
9 J.G. Frazer, *The Golden Bough*, 12 vols, London, 1890-1915.
10 G.S. Kirk, *The Nature of Greek Myths*, op. cit., p. 18.
11 Ibid.
12 Ibid., p. 29.
13 Ibid., p. 38.
14 Ibid., p. 16.
15 L. Edmunds ed., *Approaches to Greek Myth*, op. cit., p. 17.
16 G.S. Kirk, *The Nature of Greek Myths*, op. cit., p. 17.
17 R. Graves, *The Greek Myths,* op. cit., p. 32.
18 Ibid.
19 Ibid., p. 17.
20 Ibid.
21 Ibid., p. 494.
22 G.S. Kirk, *The Nature of Greek Myths*, op. cit., p. 40.
23 L. Edmunds ed., *Approaches to Greek Myth*, op. cit., pp. 30, 44; W. Burkert, *Greek Religion*, op. cit., p. 174. Scholars would do well to reflect on the manner of the regicide: being flung off a cliff, burned alive, wrecked in a chariot, devoured by wild horses, struck by lightning etc.
24 *Encyclopaedia Britannica,* 1999 standard edition.
25 For the details of this myth, see C. Boer trans., *The Homeric Hymns*, op. cit., pp. 89-135.
26 W. Burkert, *Greek Religion*, op. cit., p. 160. Similarly, G.S. Kirk in *The Nature of Greek Myths*, op. cit., pp. 252-54, describes the Demeter and Persephone myth as 'a conversion of a Mesopotamian famine myth into a crude *aition* for seasonal agriculture.'
27 M. Eliade, *A History of Religious Ideas*, Volume 1, op. cit., p. 298.
28 Ibid., p. 297.
29 G.S. Kirk, *The Nature of Greek Myths*, op. cit., p. 46. Cf F.M. Cornford, *From Religion to Philosophy*, op. cit., p. 116.
30 Kirk was surely close to the mark with his comment that the Greeks perceived Ouranos and Gaia to be 'great world masses' (p. 46).
31 *Encyclopaedia Britannica,* 1999 standard edition.
32 G.S. Kirk, *The Nature of Greek Myths*, op. cit., pp. 53-59.
33 The most famous charter theorist was B. Malinowski. See G.S. Kirk, *The Nature of Greek Myths*, op. cit., pp. 59-63; L. Edmunds ed., *Approaches to Greek Myth*, op. cit., pp. 40, 74.
34 G.S. Kirk, *The Nature of Greek Myths*, op. cit., pp. 63-66.
35 Ibid., p. 119.
36 Ibid., p. 17.
37 For example C. Brillante, 'History and the Historical Interpretation of Myth' in L. Edmunds ed., *Approaches to Greek Myth*, op. cit., pp. 91-125.
38 For example H.S. Versnel, 'What's Sauce for the Goose Is Sauce for the Gander: Myth and Ritual, Old and New' in L. Edmunds ed., *Approaches to Greek Myth*, op. cit., pp. 24-67.
39 For example, C. Sourvinou-Inwood, 'Myths in Images: Theseus and Medusa as a Case Study' in L. Edmunds ed., *Approaches to Greek Myth*, op. cit., pp. 393-45.
40 For example, W.F. Hansen, 'Odysseus and the Oar: A Folkloric Approach' in L. Edmunds ed., *Approaches to Greek Myth*, op. cit., pp. 239-72.
41 For example, C. Calame, 'Narrating the Foundation of a City: The Symbolic Birth of Cyrene' in L. Edmunds ed., *Approaches to Greek Myth*, op. cit., pp. 275-341.
42 For example, R. Caldwell, 'The Psychoanalytic Interpretation of Greek Myth' in L. Edmunds ed., *Approaches to Greek Myth*, op. cit., pp. 342-89. A useful discussion appears in G.S. Kirk, *The Nature of Greek Myths*, op. cit., pp. 69-91.
43 G.S. Kirk, *The Nature of Greek Myths*, op. cit., pp. 63-66.
44 See discussion and references later in this chapter.

45 G.S. Kirk, *The Nature of Greek Myths*, op. cit., pp. 19-29; L. Edmunds ed., *Approaches to Greek Myth*, op. cit., p. 7.
46 Ibid., p. 13. Kirk makes the following general comment about books on Greek myths: 'If they add anything at all in the way of interpretation it tends to be arbitrary and intuitive – in other words, valueless.'
47 Cited in T. Van Flandern, *Meta Research Bulletin* 7:4 (December 1998), p. 60.
48 A. Tomas, *We Are Not The First*, Bantam Books, 1971, p. 57; I. Velikovsky, *Worlds in Collision*, op. cit., pp. 56-57; R. Schoch, *Voices of the Rocks*, Thorsons, 2000, p. 180. There were, of course, certain enlightened individuals who *did* believe in the physical reality of comets and meteorites, and who did appreciate the danger they posed. In 1822, the English poet Lord Byron actually drew on Greek mythology to suggest that comets had devastated the Earth on several occasions, with the battle of the Titans being the memory of just such a cataclysmic event. But Lord Byron was a poet, not a Hellenist, and one can safely assume that early Hellenists were unaware of his ideas or paid little attention to them.
49 C. Penglase, *Greek Myths and Mesopotamia*, op. cit., pp. 89-90 (cf pp. 77, 94, 107, 113, 118, 148-49, 243). Cf similar comments in L. Edmunds ed., *Approaches to Greek Myth*, op. cit., p. 146, and G.S. Kirk, *The Nature of Greek Myths*, op. cit., p. 14: 'the myths were so well known that formal exposition was unnecessary'.
50 W. Burkert, *Greek Religion*, op. cit., pp. 296-304, highlights the problems that 'hidden Christian or anti-Christian motivations on the part of the interpreters' has caused for the understanding of the Orphic religion.
51 W.K.C. Guthrie is one of the few scholars to appreciate the difference. In *Orpheus and Greek Religion*, op. cit., p. 185, he writes: '*Aither* was the substance which filled the pure outer reaches of Heaven, beyond the impure atmosphere (*aer*) which surrounds the Earth and extends as far as the Moon. It was in this pure region that divinity dwelt, and the *aither* itself was supposed to be divine.' (Cf. p. 186.)
52 In Homer's *Iliad*, 15.189-94, the lots are drawn and Zeus gains control of 'the broad Ouranos among the clouds and the upper air'. What does this mean? To many scholars, it is implied that Ouranos is 'the sky' and hence they envisage Zeus living among the clouds that are gathered around the peak of Mt Olympus. But the word Ouranos can also be translated 'the heavens' or 'Heaven' (literally 'the Mountain of Heaven'), and I would thus argue that Zeus, in fact, gains control of two higher regions: on the one hand, the visible heavens of the Sun, Moon and stars (in effect, the entire visible Universe), and, on the other hand, the invisible Heaven of Mt Olympus. Significantly, these domains both lay above the mundane *aer* of the troposphere in the pure *aither* (or 'upper air') of space. My argument, quite simply, is that there were two Mt Olympuses – the visible Mt Olympus of Thessaly in Greece, and the invisible Mt Olympus of the aethereal 'other world'. The former, I maintain, was merely symbolic of the latter, and hence it could fairly be said that the gods dwelt on both. (The same argument, it should be noted, applies to Mt Ida; see *Iliad*, 3.275, 3.320, 7.202, 24.308).
To prove this point, one has to pick through the evidence with care. For example, in many Greek texts, the words Ouranos and Olympus are used interchangeably, and hence we read of the gods 'descending from Heaven and Olympus', which, on the face of it, would support my argument. However, the ambiguity of the word Ouranos is such that equally valid translations would be 'descending from the sky and Olympus' or 'descending from the heavens and Olympus' or 'descending from the starry Heaven and Olympus'. Such is the confusion caused by these ambiguities that scholars have managed to get away with their weather-gods theory. Other evidence, however, offers compelling proof of my 'two Mt Olympuses' theory.
Firstly, consider *Odyssey*, 6.41-47: 'Athene withdrew to Olympus, where people say the gods have made their everlasting home. Shaken by no wind, drenched by no showers, and invaded by no snows, it is set in cloudless limpid air with a white radiance playing over all. There the blessed gods spend their days in pleasure...'. There is no way that this Olympus – devoid of cloud and snow – could possibly be the Mt Olympus of Thessaly. On the contrary, what is being described is the aethereal Mt Olympus.
Secondly, in support of the aethereal Mt Olympus, consider *Iliad*, 8.22-29, in which Zeus says he will haul up the gods, earth, sea and everything, hitch the golden cord of Heaven and Earth around the peak of Mt Olympus, and make everything hang in mid-air. There is no way that this Olympus – hanging in mid-air – could be the Mt Olympus of Thessaly.

Thirdly, consider the myth of Otus and Ephialtes in *Odyssey*, 11.305-20. When these two giants went to war against the gods, it was their aim 'to pile Mt Ossa upon Mt Olympus and Mt Pelion on Mt Ossa, to make a stairway to Ouranos'. Here, it is made perfectly clear that Mt Olympus of Thessaly was merely part of the stairway to the true Heaven of Mt Olympus, which lay somewhere high up above the Earth's troposphere.

Fourthly, consider Pindar, fragment 33c, where the island of Delos appears to the heavenly gods as 'the far-seen star of the dark blue Earth'. In other words, Earth is as far away from Heaven as the stars are as distant from the Earth. (This reminds one of the Earth becoming as small as a bread-basket to the hero Etana when he ascended to Heaven on the back of the eagle in *The Epic of Etana*).

In addition, further telling clues are found in the journeys of the gods, as recited in the *Iliad* and the Homeric hymns.

For example, in the *Homeric Hymn to Pythian Apollo*, it is said that 'Apollo, like a thought, goes to Olympus from Earth' – a choice of phrase which implies that Olympus is quite apart from our Earth. Similarly, in *Iliad*, 5.744-78, when Hera and Athene descend from Mount Olympus to the Trojan battlefield, it is said that they 'flew between Ouranos and Earth'. Once again, the choice of phrase implies that Olympus is quite apart from our Earth (cf the juxtaposition of Ouranos and Earth in *Iliad*, 21.387-88).

Consider also *Iliad*, 8.41-52, in which Zeus descends from the highest peak of Mt Olympus, flying between 'Ouranos and Earth', to alight upon the peak of Mt Ida (cf. *Iliad*, 11.184). The passage makes no sense if Zeus begins from Mt Olympus of Thessaly. He must begin from a mountain in the heavens that is separate from the Earth. This idea gains further support from *Iliad*, 8.392 ff: as Zeus sits on the peak of Mt Ida, Hera and Athene prepare to descend from Mt Olympus; Zeus then sends Iris to them, who *ascends* from the peak of Ida to Olympus (cf *Iliad*, 15.79). The journey makes sense only if Olympus lies in the true heavens.

And then there is the fall of Hephaestus from Mt Olympus to the island of Lemnos (*Iliad*, 1.589 ff). It is difficult to see how Hephaestus could have fallen to Lemnos from Mt Olympus of Thessaly. But his journey does make sense if he was thrown out of a higher, aethereal Heaven (and Hephaestus was, after all, a meteorite-god).

All in all, it makes good sense that invisible Olympian gods would have dwelt on an invisible, aethereal Mt Olympus – a mountain re-created in the image of the fallen Ouranos.

53 C. Freeman, *The Greek Achievement*, op. cit., pp. 253-55, 263.
54 M. Eliade, *A History of Religious Ideas*, Volume 1, op. cit., p. 298.
55 C. Boer trans., *The Homeric Hymns*, op. cit., p. 133 (*Hymn to Demeter*).
56 The book to read is I. Velikovsky, *Worlds in Collision*, Dell Publishing, 1950.
57 E-mail dated 15th April, 2001. The said scholar wishes to remain anonymous!
58 The connections turned out to be weak or poorly attested, and thus the research ran into dead ends. On the Indo-European theory, see J. Falaky Nagy, 'Hierarchy, Heroes and Heads: Indo-European Structures in Greek Myth' in L. Edmunds ed., *Approaches to Greek Myth*, op. cit., pp. 199-238. On the Minoan theory, see W. Burkert, *Greek Religion*, op. cit., p. 39 ff.
59 M.L. West, *The East Face of Helicon*, op. cit., Preface, p. x.
60 See L. Edmunds ed., *Approaches to Greek Myth*, op. cit., p. 141.
61 W. Burkert, *The Orientalising Revolution*, op. cit., p. 4.
62 Herodotus, *Histories*, 5.58; M.L. West, *The East Face of Helicon*, op. cit., pp. 24-25.
63 W. Burkert, *The Orientalising Revolution*, op. cit., pp. 4-5.
64 Ibid., p. 5.
65 *The Song of Ullikummis* (see chapter eight of this book). The comparison is to the myth of the Giants who fought the Olympians, also to the myth of the giant 'men' Otus and Ephialtes who piled mountain upon mountain in their attempt to conquer heavenly Olympus.
66 M.L. West, *The East Face of Helicon*, op. cit., p. 278. W. Burkert has complained bitterly about apathy, prejudice and even obstructionism by diehard and dogmatic isolationists; see W. Burkert, *The Orientalising Revolution*, op. cit., pp. ix, 1-8.
67 M.L. West, *The East Face of Helicon*, op. cit., Preface, p. x.
68 Ibid., Preface, p. xi.
69 W. Burkert, *The Orientalising Revolution*, op. cit., p. 17. All of these sites began to flourish in the 8th century BC.
70 M.L. West, *The East Face of Helicon*, op. cit., pp. 11-12.

71 See L. Edmunds ed., *Approaches to Greek Myth*, op. cit., p. 141.

72 M.L. West, *Hesiod, Theogony & Works and Days*, Oxford University Press, Oxford World's Classics paperback edition, 1999, Introduction, pp. vii-viii, xvii.

73 W. Burkert, *Greek Religion*, Harvard University Press, 1985, pp. 182, 121.

74 Ibid., pp. 124, 126. See W. Burkert, *The Orientalising Revolution*, op. cit., pp. 19-20.

75 W. Burkert, *The Orientalising Revolution*, op. cit., p. 6.

76 W. Burkert, *The Orientalising Revolution*, Harvard University Press, 1995 edition. The credit to Boardman appears on p. 156.

77 W. Burkert, *The Orientalising Revolution*, op. cit., Preface, p. ix.

78 M.L. West, *The East Face of Helicon*, Clarendon Press, 1999, pp. 10-60.

79 Ibid., pp. 401-402; West's chapter eight is a real eye-opener.

80 Ibid., p. 332.

81 Ibid., chapters ten and eleven.

82 Ibid., pp. 625-26.

83 Ibid., pp. 401, 587.

84 Ibid., pp. 3, 589; W. Burkert, *Greek Religion*, op. cit., p. 182. But note West's comment on p. ix: 'Hurrian and Hittite literature was deeply influenced by the Sumero-Babylonian.'; and similarly p. 3: 'When the Hittite kingdom grew up, starting in the 17th century, it was from the first exposed to Assyrian literacy and cultural influence.'

85 C. Penglase, *Greek Myths and Mesopotamia*, Routledge, 1994.

86 Ibid., p. 230.

87 Ibid., p. 1.

88 Ibid., pp. 8, 73-75, 237. Penglase's view gains much support from other scholars, e.g. G.S. Kirk, *The Nature of Greek Myths*, op. cit., pp. 255, 275; M.L. West, *The East Face of Helicon*, op. cit., p. 587.

89 M.L. West, *The East Face of Helicon*, op. cit., p. 401 (cf p. ix: 'such far-reaching supra-regional interrelationships that one cannot treat the countries in question in isolation.'). Cf W. Burkert, *Greek Religion*, op. cit., p. 19: 'there is no single origin of Greek religion'.

90 M.L. West, *The East Face of Helicon*, op. cit., p. 4. Cf G.S. Kirk, *The Nature of Greek Myths*, op. cit., p. 255.

91 M.L. West, *The East Face of Helicon*, op. cit., p. 629.

92 M.P. Nilsson, *The Mycenaean Origin of Greek Mythology*, Berkeley, 1931. But cf the comment in G.S. Kirk, *The Nature of Greek Myths*, op. cit., pp. 218-19.

CHAPTER SEVEN: LIGHT IN THE EAST

1 On the hill of Kronos, see Pindar, *Olympian 5*, 17: 'O saviour Zeus, high in the clouds [of Heaven], dwelling on the hill of Kronos' (trans. C. Penglase). It should be noted that the conical hill of Kronos was also a prominent feature of the site at Olympia.

2 See note 52 to chapter two, above. 'The Mountain of Heaven' is my translation, but is clearly implied by the references cited in Graves. Curiously, the Titans were sons of Ouranos but were at the same time 'the proud Titans from high Mount Othrys' (Hesiod, *Theogony*, 632).

3 M.L. West, *The East Face of Helicon*, op. cit., p. 112. Cf the Hebrew names for Heaven: Mount Paran, Mount Seir, Mount Horeb, and Mount Sinai.

4 See A.F. Alford, *The Phoenix Solution*, op. cit., and *When The Gods Came Down*, op. cit.

5 A.F. Alford, *When The Gods Came Down*, op. cit., pp. 155-56, 158.

6 Ibid., chapter two.

7 Ibid., p. 93; A. Heidel, *The Gilgamesh Epic and Old Testament Parallels*, University of Chicago Press, 1963 edition, p. 171. In the myth of Inanna's descent to the Underworld, the goddess passes through seven consecutive gates of the Underworld. Similarly, in the myths *Gilgamesh and the Land of the Living* and *Enmerkar and the Lord of Aratta*, the heroes cross the seven mountains of the Underworld. Furthermore, the city of the Underworld (*urugal*) was protected by seven walls, each pierced by a gate (see note 4 to chapter nineteen, below). It is implied, to my mind, that these seven walled regions were concentric spheres.

8 J.B. Pritchard ed., *ANET (Ancient Near Eastern Texts Relating to the Old Testament)*, Princeton University Press, 3rd edition, 1969, *Poems about Baal and Anath*, pp. 129-142, especially p. 137. See also A.F. Alford, *When The Gods Came Down*, op. cit., p. 327, and

commentary by M. Eliade, *A History of Religious Ideas*, Volume 1, op. cit., chapter six.

9 A.F. Alford, *When The Gods Came Down*, op. cit., p. 93; A.F. Alford, *The Phoenix Solution*, op. cit., chapter eight.

10 In Enki's case the AB.ZU or Apsu. See various indexed references in this and the following chapters.

11 For example, Homer, *Iliad*, 3.319-59. On the meaning 'house of the Unseen', see Plato, *Gorgias*, 493b.

12 A.F. Alford, *When The Gods Came Down*, op. cit., pp. 70-71.

13 M.L. West, *The East Face of Helicon*, op. cit., p. 158.

14 See C. Boer trans., *The Homeric Hymns*, op. cit., *Hymn to Demeter*, pp. 89-135. That Persephone was abducted from Heaven is evident from the fact that she went up to Heaven with Demeter upon release from the Underworld (p. 133). It should also be noted that the Earth did not swallow her up at a real location, but at the mythical 'ends of the Earth' in the remote west. The descent of the goddess from Heaven into the Underworld follows a well-established pattern in the myths of the ancient Near East.

15 S.N. Kramer, *The Sumerians*, University of Chicago Press, 1963, pp. 200-1, the myth of *Gilgamesh, Enkidu and the Underworld*.

16 On the palace of Hades and Persephone, see Plato, *Axiochus*, 371a-b. On the palace of Nergal and Ereshkigal, see A. Heidel, *The Gilgamesh Epic and Old Testament Parallels*, op. cit., pp. 172-73. The common pattern is noted in M.L. West, *The East Face of Helicon*, op. cit., p. 159.

17 The comparison is between Gilgamesh and Rhadamanthys; see M.L. West, *The East Face of Helicon*, op. cit., p. 420.

18 Homer, *Odyssey,* 11.574. Cf the 'dark meadow of Ate' and the 'plain of Oblivion'. The Greeks regarded the Underworld literally as a 'world below'; see Homer, *Iliad*, 6.1-30, Plato, *Laws X*, 904d, and Plato, *Letter VII*, 335b-c.

19 A.F. Alford, *When The Gods Came Down*, op. cit., pp. 123-25, 131-32, 208-9, 234. A notable parallel with the Greek Underworld is the river and boatman motif; see M.L. West, *The East Face of Helicon*, op. cit., pp. 155-56.

20 Hesiod, *Theogony,* 738, 808 (trans. M.L. West, emphasis added).

21 A.F. Alford, *When The Gods Came Down*, op. cit., pp. 94-95.

22 Ibid., pp. 124, 129-31, 150, 160.

23 The same idea is found in the biblical description of Mount Sinai.

24 Hesiod has Zeus born in a cave of Mount Aigaios on Crete (Mount Ida is probably intended). Other sources have Zeus born in a cave of Mount Dikte on Crete. On the womb of the Earth symbolism, see C. Penglase, *Greek Myths and Mesopotamia*, op. cit., pp. 82-83, 186-87.

25 M. Eliade, *The Myth of the Eternal Return*, op. cit., pp. 12-17; A.F. Alford, *When The Gods Came Down*, op. cit., p. 115.

26 M. Eliade, *The Myth of the Eternal Return*, op. cit., p. 15; A.F. Alford, *When The Gods Came Down*, op. cit., pp. 82-83, 115.

27 Ibid., and G. de Santillana & H. von Dechend, *Hamlet's Mill*, David R. Godine, 1969, p. 412.

28 J.B. Pritchard ed., *ANET,* op. cit., p. 574. Cf S.N. Kramer, *The Sumerians*, op. cit., p. 120.

29 See notes 8-12 to chapter eight, below.

30 On the burial of Dionysus and Apollo, see J.G. Frazer, *The Golden Bough*, Oxford University Press, a new abridgement 1994, p. 224, and W. Burkert, *Greek Religion*, op. cit., p. 224. On the ascent of Apollo, see C. Boer trans., *The Homeric Hymns*, op. cit., p. 161 (*Hymn to Pythian Apollo*).

31 Homer, *Odyssey*, 1.50. Cf G. de Santillana & H. von Dechend, *Hamlet's Mill*, op. cit., p. 295.

32 M.L. West, *The East Face of Helicon*, op. cit., pp. 108, 557.

33 Homer, *Iliad*, 5.370-81.

34 M.L. West, *The East Face of Helicon*, op. cit., p. 362; W. Burkert, *The Orientalising Revolution*, op. cit., p. 98.

35 M.L. West, *The East Face of Helicon*, op. cit., p. 107.

36 Ibid., pp. 109-10; S. Dalley, *Myths from Mesopotamia*, Oxford University Press, 1998 edition, p. 9. I have paraphrased the translation slightly.

37 M.L. West, *The East Face of Helicon*, op. cit., p. 110.

38 G. Roux, *Ancient Iraq*, Penguin Books, 1992 edition, p. 166.

39 See, for example, the description of the Egyptian god Re in A.F. Alford, *When The Gods Came*

Down, op. cit., pp. 98, 110.

40   *Lugal-e, c.* 2100 BC. T. Jacobsen, *The Treasures of Darkness*, Yale Univ. Press, 1976, p. 95.

41   *Erra and Ishum* (trans. S. Dalley, *Myths from Mesopotamia*, op. cit., p. 286).

42   Ibid., pp. 286, 309 (see citations in chapter twenty of this book). Cf the seven weapons used by Ninurta in *The Myth of Zu*, J.B. Pritchard ed., *ANET*, op. cit., pp. 111-12.

43   On the Hittite myth of the birth of gods from Kumarbis, see chapter eight of this book. On the Egyptian myth of the birth of Thoth from the head of Seth, see B. Watterson, *Gods of Ancient Egypt*, Sutton Publishing, 1996 ed., p. 182.

44   On Hephaestus, see Homer, *Iliad*, 1.585 ff, 18.393 ff; C. Boer trans., *The Homeric Hymns*, op. cit., pp. 168-69 (*Hymn to Pythian Apollo*); Plato, *Republic II*, 378d. On other gods being thrown out of Heaven, see Homer, *Iliad*, 14.257-60 (the god Sleep), 15.18 ff (the gods generally), and 19.124 ff (the goddess Ate). In addition, there are the various myths of gods being deposed from the throne of Heaven, e.g. Kronos and the Titans, and Ophion.

45   T. Jacobsen, *The Treasures of Darkness*, op. cit., pp. 102-3. Cf indexed references in A.F. Alford, *When The Gods Came Down*, op. cit., and see comment in M.L. West, *The East Face of Helicon*, op. cit., p. 354, comparing the nod of Zeus to the Word of Enlil.

46   E.C. Krupp, *Echoes of the Ancient Skies*, Oxford University Press, 1983, p. 64; M. Eliade, *A History of Religious Ideas*, Volume 1, op. cit., pp. 69, 140; G. Roux, *Ancient Iraq*, op. cit., p. 87; M.L. West, *The East Face of Helicon*, op. cit., pp. 69, 140. The Sumerian sign DINGIR resembled a comet or bolide; see A.F. Alford, *Gods of the New Millennium*, Eridu Books, 1996, pp. 125-26. Many gods additionally took the nickname 'shining one', e.g. Utu, Ninurta.

47   T. Jacobsen, *The Treasures of Darkness*, op. cit., p. 17.

48   A.F. Alford, *When The Gods Came Down*, op. cit., chapter eight.

49   Ibid., p. 98 (the Egyptian myth *The Destruction of Mankind*).

50   Ibid., pp. 206-8.

51   M.L. West, *The East Face of Helicon*, op. cit., chapter one.

52   Hesiod, *Theogony*, 535 ff. See W. Burkert, *Greek Religion*, op. cit., p. 57; C. Penglase, *Greek Myths and Mesopotamia*, op. cit., pp. 221-22.

53   W. Burkert, *The Orientalising Revolution*, op. cit., pp. 17, 20, 53-55, 81; M.L. West, *The East Face of Helicon*, op. cit., p. 37.

54   M.L. West, *The East Face of Helicon*, op. cit., pp. 173, 112, 177. Cf W. Burkert, *Greek Religion*, op. cit., pp. 126, 182.

55   Homer, *Iliad*, 20.1-12. Only Oceanus remained at his station, presumably to maintain the stability of the cosmos. Cf *Iliad*, 5.384-424, where Hades ascends to Olympus.

56   Plato, *Critias*, 121c. Plato's words deserve careful reading.

57   A.F. Alford, *When The Gods Came Down*, op. cit., p. 93. Cf M.L. West, *The East Face of Helicon*, op. cit., pp. 298-99.

58   M.L. West, *The East Face of Helicon*, op. cit., pp. 111, 299; W. Burkert, *The Orientalising Revolution*, op. cit., p. 94.

59   M.L. West, *The East Face of Helicon*, op. cit., pp. 111, 298.

60   Hesiod, *Theogony*, 486. See M.L. West, *The East Face of Helicon*, op. cit., p. 111.

61   See chapter eight of this book and A.F. Alford, *When The Gods Came Down*, op. cit., pp. 98 ff.

62   M. Eliade, *A History of Religious Ideas*, Volume 1, op. cit., pp. 152-53. Cf U. Oldenburg, *The Conflict Between El and Baal in Canaanite Religion*, Leiden, 1969, pp. 101-63.

63   M. Eliade, *A History of Religious Ideas*, Volume 1, op. cit., p. 145.

64   J.B. Pritchard ed., *ANET*, op. cit., p. 125. Ubelluris lay in the Underworld, whence another giant Ullikummis grew up from his shoulder. See note 19 to chapter eight, below.

65   A.F. Alford, *When The Gods Came Down*, op. cit., chapter three. See also A.F. Alford, *The Phoenix Solution*, op. cit.

CHAPTER EIGHT: BATTLES OF THE GODS

1   H. Frankfort, *Kingship and the Gods*, University of Chicago Press, 1978 ed., pp. 280-81, 284. (the 'An-Anum' list). Cf Z. Sitchin, *The Wars of Gods and Men*, Avon Books, 1985, pp. 82-83.

2   J.B. Pritchard ed., *ANET*, op. cit., p. 120 (*Kingship in Heaven*, sometimes known as *The Song of Kumarbis*). The 'dark Earth' is possibly a metaphor for the Underworld.

3   Ibid.

4 Ibid.
5 Ibid., p. 121.
6 M.L. West, *The East Face of Helicon*, op. cit., p. 279.
7 The castration motif seems to appear also in the Ugaritic myth of El and Baal. See M. Eliade, *A History of Religious Ideas*, Volume 1, op. cit., pp. 152-53.
8 Hesiod, *Theogony*, 498-501 (trans. M.L. West; 'Pytho' signifies Delphi).
9 M.L. West, *The East Face of Helicon*, op. cit., pp. 294-95.
10 Pindar, *Pythian 4*, 74 (cf *Paean 6*, 17); *Pythian 8*, 59; *Pythian 11*, 9; *Nemean 7*, 34 (trans. G.S. Conway & R. Stoneman). Cf Plato, *Republic IV*, 427c: 'this god [Delphian Apollo] sitting upon the rock at the centre of the Earth'.
11 R. Bauval & A. Gilbert, *The Orion Mystery*, William Heinemann, 1994, pp. 201-2. The original meteorite was replaced by a limestone *omphalos*, described by R. Graves in *The Greek Myths*, op. cit., p. 75, as 'inscribed with the name of Mother Earth, stands 11.25 inches high and measures 15.5 inches across'. The cult of the heavenly stone could persist long after the original meteorite had been stolen or destroyed by the ravages of time.
12 Scholars are generally coy about using the word 'meteorite' because a *baetylus* could be any type of sacred stone. However, it is very probable that meteorites were the source of baetylism and that non-meteoritic *baetuli* were meteorite substitutes; in this respect, two useful sources are: I.S. Serra, 'Gods Who Fell From the Sky' in *Meteorite*, 6:2 (May 2000), pp. 25-28, and R. Temple, *The Crystal Sun*, op. cit., chapter eight. One of the few scholars to speak his mind on this subject is R. Graves in *The Greek Myths*, op. cit., p. 43: 'The stone at Delphi... seems to have been a large meteorite'.
13 J.B. Pritchard ed., *ANET*, op. cit., pp. 121-25.
14 Ibid., pp. 121-22. Cf the Greek myth of Boreas ravishing Oreithyia 'fury of the mountain'.
15 Ibid., p. 125.
16 Ibid. pp. 122-25, translated 'diorite stone'. For a full discussion of the Hittite word *Kunkunuzzi*, see H.G. Guterbock, *The Song of Ullikummi*, New Haven, 1952.
17 J.B. Pritchard ed., *ANET*, op. cit., p. 125.
18 M.L. West, *The East Face of Helicon*, op. cit., pp. 290-91. Symbolically, the phallus and seed of the sky-god remained in the womb of the Earth. There may be a connection to the myth of the missing phallus of Osiris; see A.F. Alford, *When The Gods Came Down*, op. cit., pp. 65-67.
19 M.L. West, *The East Face of Helicon*, op. cit., pp. 295-96. The role of Ullikummis is sometimes confused, in error, with that of Ubelluris, e.g. M. Eliade, *A History of Religious Ideas*, Volume 1, op. cit., p. 146.
20 Personal correspondence with E. Grondine, January 1999.
21 The Tablets of Destiny are sometimes translated as 'the ME's'. They play a central role in several other Mesopotamian poems, e.g. *Inanna and Enki*.
22 A.F. Alford, *When The Gods Came Down*, op. cit., p. 43.
23 Ibid.
24 J.B. Pritchard ed., *ANET*, op. cit., p. 113.
25 Ibid., p. 515.
26 T. Jacobsen, *The Treasures of Darkness*, op. cit., pp. 130-31. Prior to this, the floodwaters had been locked up as 'ice, long accumulating in the mountain on the other side' (p. 130). Cf Ninurta's HAR.SAG.MU storm to that created by Inanna in ibid., p. 136: 'O destroyer of mountains, you lent the storm wings!... O beloved one of Enlil, you came flying into the land.'
27 S.N. Kramer, *The Sumerians*, op. cit., pp. 152-53; T. Jacobsen, *The Treasures of Darkness*, op. cit., p. 131.
28 S.N. Kramer, *The Sumerians*, op. cit., p. 152.
29 Ninharsag was a goddess of many aliases: e.g. Mami 'Mother', Ninti 'Lady of Life', and Nintu 'Lady Birth-hut'; also Ninmah, Ninlil, Sud, Aruru, Dingirmah, Ninmenna and Belit-ili.
30 J.B. Pritchard ed., *ANET*, op. cit., pp. 515-17. For a vivid example of the E.KUR as the 'mountain' of Earth, see the legend of Etana in *ANET*, op. cit., p. 118 and footnote 46: after the eagle had borne Etana aloft, he told Etana to peer down at the E.KUR – the 'World Mountain'.
31 T. Jacobsen, *The Treasures of Darkness*, op. cit., p. 132. Hence Ninurta had a bird-like *alter ego* named Ningirsu.
32 Ibid., p. 130.
33 Ibid., pp. 128, 130. Jacobsen erroneously equated the epithet 'Sling-stone' with hailstones and

a 'ball of clay'.

34 S.N. Kramer, *The Sumerians*, op. cit., pp. 171-83.

35 Ibid., p. 175. On Eridu, the AB.ZU and the Underworld, see comments in C. Penglase, *Greek Myths and Mesopotamia*, op. cit., pp. 22, 43-44, 108.

36 S.N. Kramer, *The Sumerians*, op. cit., pp. 197-205.

37 Ibid., and cf S.N. Kramer, *History Begins at Sumer*, University of Pennsylvania Press, 1981 ed., pp. 169-70, 294. In the latter, Kramer suggested that the Underworld (KUR) was hurling the stones against Enki's boat, and trying to devour it. In fact, it is not altogether clear where the stones were coming from; the context suggests to me that the stones were coming down from Heaven *with* Enki's boat. Cf also the little stones and big stones motif in a hymn to Shulgi; S.N. Kramer, *History Begins at Sumer*, op. cit., p. 287.

38 A. Gardiner, *Egyptian Grammar*, 3rd ed., Griffith Inst., Oxford, 1994, p. 598. Citation from Coffin Texts, Spell 829. Cf the great cry of the Bennu-bird at the time of the creation.

39 D. Meeks & C. Favard-Meeks, *Daily Life of the Egyptian Gods*, John Murray, 1997, p. 84. Both Geb and Shu were credited with organising the land and establishing the first cities.

40 Pyramid Texts, Utterance 254, para 281-2; see R.O. Faulkner, *The Ancient Egyptian Pyramid Texts*, Aris & Phillips, Oxford University Press, 1969, p. 63. On the origins of Osiris, see Pyramid Texts, Utterance 668, para 1960: 'The king [Osiris] is bound for the eastern side of the Sky, for the king was conceived there and the king was born there.'

41 A.F. Alford, *When The Gods Came Down*, op. cit., pp. 71-72.

42 See A.F. Alford, *The Phoenix Solution*, op. cit., pp. 323-24. On the vanishing god motif, see for example the Hittite myth of Telepinus. The Osiris myth was sometimes linked to a succession myth in which his son Horus ascended to Heaven; see R.T. Rundle Clark, *Myth and Symbol in Ancient Egypt*, Thames and Hudson, 1993 ed., pp. 213-17.

43 T. Jacobsen, *Toward the Image of Tammuz*, Harvard University Press, 1970, pp. 111-14; T. Jacobsen, *The Treasures of Darkness*, op. cit., p. 103; S.N. Kramer, *The Sumerians*, op. cit., p. 145.

44 On the pickaxe in the *Lamentation Texts*, see the citation in chapter seventeen of this book. On the pickaxe in *The Epic of Gilgamesh*, see J.B. Pritchard ed., *ANET*, op. cit., p. 77.

45 S.N. Kramer, *History Begins at Sumer*, op. cit., p. 304. See also T. Jacobsen, *The Treasures of Darkness*, op. cit., pp. 103-5. Cf the Sumerian poem cited in A.F. Alford, *When The Gods Came Down*, op. cit., p. 50.

46 Hesiod, *Theogony*, 176-78 (trans. M.L. West). This passage may allude to Ouranos bringing to Earth the goddess Night who signified the Underworld. If so, there is a close parallel to the Sumerian myth of *Gilgamesh, Enkidu and the Underworld*, in which Ereshkigal is carried off from Heaven to the Underworld by Enki; see S.N. Kramer, *The Sumerians*, op. cit., pp. 200-1.

47 M. Eliade, *A History of Religious Ideas*, Volume 1, op. cit., p. 248.

48 J.B. Pritchard ed., *ANET*, op. cit., pp. 60-61. This does not mean that Heaven and Earth did not exist per se. It means that the Heaven and Earth of the current Universe had not yet been created by the interaction of the Heaven (Apsu-Tiamat) and Earth of the old Universe.

49 Ibid., p. 61. The names of these gods were Lahmu, Lahamu, Anshar, Kishar, Anu and Ea.

50 The translation is a composite of J.B. Pritchard ed., *ANET*, op. cit., p. 61, S. Dalley, *Myths from Mesopotamia*, op. cit., p. 233, and A. Heidel, *The Babylonian Genesis*, op. cit., p. 19.

51 J. B. Pritchard ed., *ANET*, op. cit., p. 61.

52 Ibid. This cult-hut (*giparu*) picks up the 'reed-hut' mentioned at the beginning of *Enuma Elish*.

53 The translation is a composite of J.B. Pritchard ed., *ANET*, op. cit., p. 62, and A. Heidel, *The Babylonian Genesis*, op. cit., pp. 21-22.

54 *Enuma Elish*, Tablet I, 150-61. Anunnaki was a general term used for the gods of the Underworld; in this instance, it seems to refer to Ea, Lahmu, Lahamu, Anshar, Kishar and Anu.

55 The translation is a composite of J.B. Pritchard ed., *ANET*, op. cit., p. 67, and A. Heidel, *The Babylonian Genesis*, op. cit., p. 40.

56 *Enuma Elish*, Tablet IV, 104, 132; Tablet V, 53-60; Tablet VII, 70-71.

57 *Enuma Elish*, Tablet IV, 107-20; Tablet V, 71-80. According to one tradition, Marduk confined the monsters in the subterranean sea; see M.L. West, *The East Face of Helicon*, op. cit., p. 146.

58 *Enuma Elish*, Tablet IV, 141-46.

59 Hence Marduk's name, meaning 'son of the Duku' or 'Son of the Mountain of the Gods'; see W. Burkert, *Greek Religion*, op. cit., p. 182.

60 M.L. West, *The East Face of Helicon*, op. cit., pp. 147-48, 383; W. Burkert, *The Orientalising Revolution*, op. cit., pp. 92-93.

61 M.L. West, *The East Face of Helicon*, op. cit., p. 148.

62 W. Burkert, *The Orientalising Revolution*, op. cit., pp. 92-93: *tawtu* is a variant of *tiamtu* or *tamtu*, the Akkadian word for 'sea'. Cf M.L. West, *The East Face of Helicon*, op. cit., p. 147.

63 On the etymology of Tiamat and the link to the Hebrew *tehom*, see A.F. Alford, *The Phoenix Solution*, op. cit., p. 156, and S. H. Hooke, *Middle Eastern Mythology*, Penguin Books, 1963, p. 119. In fact, there is some overlap in the traditions of Apsu and Tiamat, for *Enuma Elish* claims that Tiamat's fall created the source of all the world's rivers and springs.

64 Hesiod, *Theogony*, 777-78 (trans. M.L. West).

65 Euripides, *Medea*, 410. See F.M. Cornford, *From Religion to Philosophy*, op. cit., p. 172.

66 F.M. Cornford, *From Religion to Philosophy*, op. cit., p. 24. Cf W. Burkert, *Greek Religion*, op. cit., p. 176: 'Oceanus, the encircling river at which Earth and Heaven meet.'

67 G. de Santillana & H. von Dechend, *Hamlet's Mill*, op. cit., p. 191.

68 Homer, *Iliad*, 8.5-30. The translation is a composite of Martin Hammond, *Homer The Iliad*, op. cit., p. 118, and Richmond Lattimore, *The Iliad of Homer*, Chicago, 1951.

69 Homer, *Iliad*, 18.483-84 (trans. M. Hammond, though I have rendered 'sky' as 'Heaven').

70 R. Mondi in L. Edmunds ed., *Approaches to Greek Myth*, op. cit., p. 187.

71 Cf the separation of the waters in Genesis 1:6-8. See comments in A.F. Alford, *When The Gods Came Down*, op. cit., pp. 225-26.

72 Homer, *Iliad*, 21.194-95 (trans. M. Hammond). Cf M.L. West, *The East Face of Helicon*, op. cit., pp. 144-45.

73 Homer, *Iliad*, 14.196 ff (trans. M. Hammond).

74 Ibid. This evokes the Orphic myth of the strife that separated Heaven from Earth. Whilst the physical Oceanus was trapped in the Underworld, his metaphysical counterpart had resurrected to Heaven (cf the earlier reference to Oceanus on the cosmic shield of Hephaestus).

75 Plato, *Cratylus*, 402b-c (trans. C.D.C. Reeve).

76 The sharp-eyed reader will notice that the Greeks adapted *Enuma Elish* by having the goddess fall to Earth before the god (rather than vice versa) and by having the sacred marriage occur in the Earth rather than in Heaven. In this latter regard, *Enuma Elish* was quite unconventional.

CHAPTER NINE: WHEN THE SKY FELL

1 F.M. Cornford, *Before and After Socrates*, op. cit., pp. 18-19.

2 Ap. Rhodios, *Argonautika*, 1.496-97 (trans. P. Green, though I have amended 'sky' to read 'Heaven'). Cf Euripides, cited later in this chapter: 'It is not my word, but my mother's word, how Heaven and Earth were once one form'.

3 It might well be the case that a cataclysm myth lies behind Thales' water-based cosmogony, too, given the close parallels between Oceanus/Tethys and Apsu/Tiamat. It is an arresting thought that this most innocuous of cosmogonies might have its roots in a cataclysmic model.

4 S.N. Kramer, *The Sumerians*, op. cit., pp. 112-13. Cf R. Mondi in L. Edmunds ed., *Approaches to Greek Myth*, op. cit., p. 163: 'the original conjunction [of earth and sky] is represented by the compounding of their names An-Ki'.

5 Z. Sitchin, *Genesis Revisited*, Avon Books, New York, 1990, chapter 5, p. 90.

6 S.N. Kramer, *The Sumerians*, op. cit., p. 175.

7 Ibid., p. 220. I have amended 'on' to read 'in'.

8 J.B. Pritchard ed., *ANET*, op. cit., p. 613. I prefer to render 'harrow' as 'weapon'. The Sumerian Lamentation Texts were composed *c.* 2000 BC – a time of great chaos in the Near East, possibly due to Earth's interaction with cometary debris. However, it would be naive to suppose that the Lamentation Texts were simply describing then-contemporary celestial events. On the contrary, the lamentations may well have been adapted from pre-existing myths, which described an imaginary destruction of mankind at the beginning of time. This would account for much of the exaggerated cataclysmic language in the Lamentation Texts.

9 *The Legend of Re and Isis*. See A.F. Alford, *When The Gods Came Down*, op. cit., p. 94.

10 A.F. Alford, *When The Gods Came Down*, op. cit., chapters three and four. The idea of Earth and the fallen Heaven being 'mountains' is evident in the very earliest Egyptian inscriptions:

certain tax receipts from tomb of king Scorpion, *c.* 3300 BC, refer to the 'Mountain of Darkness' in the West and the 'Mountain of Light' in the East.

11 Coffin Texts, Spell 335 Part II. See R.O. Faulkner, *The Ancient Egyptian Coffin Texts*, Volume I, op. cit., p. 265.

12 The dismemberment of Osiris is known in its popular form from Plutarch (1st century AD), but is alluded to frequently in the Pyramid Texts, *c.* 2300 BC.

13 See also Coffin Texts, Spell 358: 'that day of the storm over the Two Lands', and Spell 701: "My mouth speaks to me with a knife on the day of the union of the Two Lands."

14 E.A. Wallis Budge, *From Fetish to God in Ancient Egypt*, Oxford University Press, 1934, p. 505. This idea of Heaven 'rising up' upon Earth is reflected in the name of the Egyptian sky-god and creator-god Re, whose name literally meant 'Rising' and whose hieroglyphic sign was a spherical rising mound. It is apparent also in the creator-god Ptah's nickname *Ta-tenen*, which meant literally 'the Risen Land'. These creator-gods, along with others such as Atum, Neber-Djer and Aten, were each equated with the God of Heaven, who had created a multitude of lesser gods by emanation from himself.

15 Plutarch, *De Iside et Osiride*, cited in E.A. Wallis Budge, *Legends of the Egyptian Gods*, 1912, Dover edition 1994, p. 228.

16 The Coffin Texts, Spell 148. See R.O. Faulkner, *The Ancient Egyptian Coffin Texts*, Volume I, Aris & Phillips, 1973, p. 125.

17 On the Bible, see Genesis 1:4 and 1:6-7 (separation of light from darkness, and upper waters from lower waters). On the Koran, see N.J. Dawood trans., *The Koran*, Penguin Books, 1974 edition, p. 298 (traditional chapter no. 21): 'Are the disbelievers unaware that the heavens and the Earth were one solid mass which we tore asunder?'. On the Rig-Veda, see F.M. Cornford, *From Religion to Philosophy*, op. cit., p. 67. G. Roux writes in *Ancient Iraq:*, op. cit., pp. 94-95: 'The theory that... the shape of the universe had resulted from a forceful separation of Heaven from Earth by a third party was generally adopted in Sumer, Babylonia and Assyria.'

18 Pyramid Texts, Utterance 519, para 1208. See R.O. Faulkner, *The Ancient Egyptian Pyramid Texts*, op. cit., p. 192.

19 Coffin Texts, Spell 334. See R.O. Faulkner, *The Ancient Egyptian Coffin Texts*, Volume I, op. cit., pp. 257-58.

20 Pyramid Texts, Utterance 273, para 399; Coffin Texts, Spell 335; Book of the Dead, Spell 125; Coffin Texts, Spell 358; E.A. Wallis Budge, *From Fetish to God in Ancient Egypt*, op. cit., p. 150.

21 Pyramid Texts, Utterance 484, para 1022. See R.O. Faulkner, *The Ancient Egyptian Pyramid Texts*, op. cit., p. 171.

22 A.F. Alford, *The Phoenix Solution*, op. cit., pp. 126-27.

23 R.T. Rundle Clark, *Myth and Symbol in Ancient Egypt*, op. cit., p. 50, and E.A. Wallis Budge, *From Fetish to God in Ancient Egypt*, op. cit., p. 150. In the Coffin Texts, Spells 76 and 78, Shu states: "I lifted up my daughter Nut from upon myself, so that I might give her to my father Atum in his realm, and I have set Geb under my feet... and I am between them."

24 The translation is a composite of J.B. Pritchard ed., *ANET,* op. cit., p. 67, and A. Heidel, *The Babylonian Genesis*, op. cit., p. 43. Heidel confused the Esharra with the Earth, but it is clearly stated in line 145 of Tablet IV that Esharra was the Sky or firmament; see T. Jacobsen, *The Treasures of Darkness*, op. cit., p. 179. The creation of Esharra parallels the reconstruction of the destroyed 'constellation' in Tablet IV, 20 ff. See A.F. Alford, *When The Gods Came Down*, op. cit., pp. 98-101 and p. 425 note 44.

25 *Enuma Elish*, Tablet VI, 5-10, 35-44. See A.F. Alford, *When The Gods Came Down*, op. cit., pp. 318-19, and cf Plato, *Axiochus*, 371b.

26 J.B. Pritchard ed., *ANET,* op. cit., pp. 58-9, 164. Just as Zeus was chief of the Olympians, so was Marduk the chief of the Igigi.

27 Hesiod, *Theogony*, 125-29 (trans. M.L. West).

28 The Earth, too, was 'a secure seat for ever of all the immortals'. Whilst the Earth was a seat for the gods' physical bodies, heavenly Olympus was a seat for the gods' aethereal bodies.

29 See note 18 to chapter eight, above.

30 Euripides, *Melanippe-the-Wise*, fragment 484. See F.M. Cornford, *From Religion to Philosophy*, op. cit., p. 67.

31 Ap. Rhodios, *Argonautika*, 1.496-98 (trans. P. Green, but I have rendered 'deadly disruption'

as 'grievous strife, in line with F.M. Cornford, *From Religion to Philosophy*, op. cit., p. 67).

32 W.K.C. Guthrie, *Orpheus and Greek Religion*, op. cit., pp. 80, 137. A very late source states that 'the Light [Phanes], cleaving the *aither*, lightened the Earth' (ibid., p. 98). Only Night gazed directly at the birth of Phanes (ibid., p. 138).

33 Ibid., p. 138, fragment 89. Cf W. Burkert, *Greek Religion*, op. cit., p. 320, citing a Hippocratic writer: '[at the beginning of the world, when] everything was in confusion, most of it [the soul-substance] withdrew to the highest circle of the heavens and this, it seems to me, the ancients called *aither*.'

34 R. Graves, *The Greek Myths,* op. cit., p. 27.

35 W.K.C. Guthrie, *Orpheus and Greek Religion*, op. cit., p. 138.

36 Ibid., fragment 97.

37 Cf the cosmogony of Anaximander, discussed later in this chapter.

38 Witness the ensuing re-creation of the Universe from the belly of Zeus, cited in chapter one of this book.

39 Hesiod, *Theogony*, 370 ff.

40 Ibid. See M.L. West, *Hesiod, Theogony & Works and Days*, op. cit., Introduction, p. x.

41 Hesiod, *Theogony*, 382-83 (trans. M.L. West). The Morning Star, in this passage, may be a metaphor for the reborn mountain of Heaven.

42 F.M. Cornford, *Before and After Socrates*, op. cit., pp. 18-19.

43 S.N. Kramer, *The Sumerians*, op. cit., pp. 146-47. See comments in A.F. Alford, *When The Gods Came Down*, op. cit., pp. 36-39, 139-40.

44 S.N. Kramer, *The Sumerians*, op. cit., pp. 146-47.

45 M. Eliade, *A History of Religious Ideas*, Volume 1, op. cit., pp. 151, 153.

46 The Sumerian Sun-god Utu was famously born from a mountain, amidst a fiery cataclysm. I had previously assumed in *When The Gods Came Down* that this birth was from the mountain *of Heaven*. This assumption may now need to be reconsidered in the light of the Greek myths.

47 *Enuma Elish*, Tablet IV, 138; Tablet V, 1-20, 53, 59, 61; Tablet VII, 70-71.

48 See, for example, *The Creation of Moon and Sun* in A. Heidel, *The Babylonian Genesis*, op. cit., pp. 73-74.

49 F.M. Cornford, *From Religion to Philosophy*, op. cit., p. 68.

CHAPTER TEN: THE MYSTERY REVEALED

1 The most famous dismembered god, and the oldest, is the Egyptian god Osiris. In the Ugaritic myths, the gods Yam and Mot were dismembered. In the Greek myths, the god Dionysus was dismembered, as was Orpheus, as was Pelops, the son of Tantalus. An important variant of this myth was the idea of a multiplicity of gods emanating from the One God (or Goddess).

2 I follow, for the sake of simplicity, the monotheistic version of the exploded planet myth. The more elaborate version involved two exploded planets: one male, one female.

3 J.B. Pritchard ed., *ANET*, op. cit., p. 118.

4 The Greek name Heliopolis meant 'City of the Sun', but in Egypt it was known as *Annu,* the City of Heaven, or the City of the Pillar (of Heaven). See A.F. Alford, *When The Gods Came Down*, op. cit., pp. 111-12, 145-50, 154-55.

5 A.F. Alford, *When The Gods Came Down*, op. cit., pp. 63-65, 79.

6 Ibid., pp. 63, 65-68. The connection should be noted between the Benben and the Bennu-bird. This bird, better known as the Phoenix, was said to have emitted a piercing cry, instigating the beginning of time; and yet the Egyptians prophesied that it would return to the Earth in the future at periodic intervals causing huge conflagrations (ibid., pp. 111-12). It was also said that the Phoenix was an *alter ego* of Osiris (ibid., p. 112).

7 Sippar was one of the five pre-diluvian cities. In the Deluge account of Berossus, the hero was told to go and bury the writings of Heaven in Sippar, where they might afterwards be retrieved.

8 Z. Sitchin, *The Twelfth Planet*, Avon Books, 1978 (first published by Bear & Co, 1976), p. 167.

9 Ibid., pp. 167, 273-77 (I would emphasise that I do not agree with Sitchin's interpretation).

10 The Sumerians called meteoritic iron KU.AN and knew that it was extraterrestrial. See J.K. Bjorkman 'Meteors and Meteorites in the Ancient Near East' in *Meteoritics*, 8 (1973) pp. 91-132. Scholars have not yet recognised the importance of meteorite worship in Mesopotamia, partly because the translators of texts have suffered from 'meteorite blindness' and partly

because of their failure to recognise that *baetuli* were originally meteorites.

11 Hesiod, *Theogony,* 693-704 (trans. M.L. West, although I have rendered 'sky' as 'heavens').

12 *The Epic of Gilgamesh.* See J.B. Pritchard ed., *ANET,* op. cit., p. 94; cf trans. in I. Donnelly, *Atlantis: The Antediluvian World,* op. cit., p. 79. The fiery torches find parallels in Greek literature in the myth of Demeter and Persephone, and in Aeschylus' *Choephoroi,* where dangerous 'torches' or 'lamps' (*lampades*) fly between Heaven and Earth (see M.L. West, *The East Face of Helicon,* op. cit., p. 576). Cf also the use of torches in ritual. It seems very likely that all of this fiery torch imagery was inspired by man's experience with comets and bolides.

13 J.B. Pritchard ed., *ANET,* op. cit., p. 94. Cf ibid., p. 44.

14 D. Meeks & C. Favard-Meeks, *Daily Life of the Egyptian Gods,* op. cit., p. 84.

15 S.N. Kramer, *The Sumerians,* op. cit., p. 152.

16 See, for example, the Hermetic text *Virgin of the World,* cited in A.F. Alford, *When The Gods Came Down,* op. cit., p. 57 (and cf. pp. 78-80).

17 J.B. Pritchard ed., *ANET,* op. cit., p. 38. See the interpretation of this myth in A.F. Alford, *When The Gods Came Down,* op. cit., pp. 39-41, 155-56.

18 *Atra-Hasis Epic.* See S. Dalley, *Myths from Mesopotamia,* op. cit., pp. 9-10, and A.F. Alford, *When The Gods Came Down,* op. cit., pp. 193-94.

19 A.F. Alford, *When The Gods Came Down,* op. cit., pp. 150-51, 153-54.

20 Ibid., pp. 36-38 (and on celestial rivers generally, see pp. 149-52).

21 S.N. Kramer, *The Sumerians,* op. cit., p. 179.

22 See plate 9 in A.F. Alford, *When The Gods Came Down,* op. cit. (on reflection, perhaps Enki and Utu are entering the western mountain of the Earth; see note 46 to chapter nine, above).

23 Pyramid Texts, Utterance 366, para 626, 628-9. For other references to Osiris as the ocean of the world, see R.T. Rundle Clark, *Myth and Symbol,* op. cit., p. 117, H. Frankfort, *Kingship and the Gods,* op. cit., pp. 191-92, D. Meeks & C. Favard-Meeks, *Daily Life of the Egyptian Gods,* op. cit., p. 142, and A.F. Alford, *When The Gods Came Down,* op. cit., pp. 74-77.

24 A.F. Alford, *When The Gods Came Down,* Hodder & Stoughton, 2000.

25 See the assessment on the Exploded Planets section of my website (http://www.eridu.co.uk).

26 The Egyptian god Anubis, for example, was called 'Prince of the West' and 'He who is upon his mountain'. Incidentally, the metaphor still survives today, e.g. in the English words 'mound' and 'mountain' and the French word *monde* ('world'), deriving from the Latin *mundus* ('world' or 'heavens') which is closely related to the Latin *mons* ('mountain').

27 J.B. Pritchard ed., *ANET,* op. cit., p. 581; S.N. Kramer, *History Begins at Sumer,* op. cit., p. 291.

28 G. Roux, *Ancient Iraq,* op. cit., p. 166.

29 A. Heidel, *The Babylonian Genesis,* op. cit., p. 68.

30 See A.F. Alford, *When The Gods Came Down,* op. cit., and *The Phoenix Solution,* op. cit., indexed references.

31 A.F. Alford, *When The Gods Came Down,* op. cit., chapter six, and chapter sixteen of this book.

32 Ibid., chapter seven.

33 J.B. Pritchard ed., *ANET,* op. cit., p. 94.

34 E.A. Wallis Budge, *The Egyptian Heaven and Hell,* Dover Pubs., 1996 ed., Vol. III, pp. 65-66.

35 Such images can be seen in many archaeological museums. One such scene in the British Museum is captioned 'agriculture in the afterlife'.

36 Book of the Dead, Spell 110. See R.O. Faulkner, *The Ancient Egyptian Book of the Dead,* op. cit., pp. 103-8.

37 J.B. Pritchard ed., *ANET,* op. cit., p. 613. I prefer to render 'harrow' as 'weapon'.

38 A. Heidel, *The Babylonian Genesis,* op. cit., p. 70. On this general theme, see A.F. Alford, *When The Gods Came Down,* op. cit., pp. 194-96.

39 An example is J. Brook, *Our Rock Who Art in Heaven,* Sinclair Press, 2000. Brook covers much of the same ground as I covered in *When The Gods Came Down,* but concludes that God was a comet. Close, but no cigar.

40 V. Clube & B. Napier, *The Cosmic Winter,* Basil Blackwell, 1990.

41 Ibid., p. 165.

42 R. Temple, *The Crystal Sun,* op. cit., p. 288.

43 *Collins English Dictionary,* Collins, 1979, p. 363.

44 For example, the Egyptian Coffin Texts, Spell 1080. Note that the Sumerians called meteoritic iron 'KU.AN', i.e. 'heavenly metal', whilst the Hittites called it 'the black iron of the sky'.

45 A.F. Alford, *When The Gods Came Down*, op. cit., pp. 64-65, 70, 80, 122-23, 125-26.

46 See discussion in ibid., pp. 86-92.

47 Hence the agricultural facets of the rising-and-dying gods Osiris and Tammuz.

48 M. Eliade, *A History of Religious Ideas*, Volume 1, op. cit., p. 60. A useful source on the Akitu festival is H. Frankfort, *Kingship and the Gods*, op. cit., chapter 22.

49 In *The Myth of the Eternal Return*, op. cit., p. 35, Eliade writes: 'A sacrifice not only exactly reproduces the initial sacrifice revealed by a god at the beginning of time, it also takes place at that same primordial mythical moment; in other words every sacrifice repeats the initial sacrifice and coincides with it. All sacrifices are performed at the same mythical instant of the beginning...'. The sacrifice of all sacrifices is, of course, the physical planet of God.

50 A.F. Alford, *When The Gods Came Down*, op. cit., chapter four.

51 Plutarch, *De Iside et Osiride*, cited in E. A. Wallis Budge, *Legends of the Egyptian Gods*, op. cit., p. 218.

52 A.F. Alford, *When The Gods Came Down*, op. cit., pp. 145-49.

53 On Eridu and the AB.ZU, see comments in C. Penglase, *Greek Myths and Mesopotamia*, op. cit., pp. 22, 43-44, 108.

54 Useful sources on this subject include D. Meeks & C. Favard-Meeks, *Daily Life of the Egyptian Gods*, op. cit., and C. Penglase, *Greek Myths and Mesopotamia*, op. cit., which focuses particularly on 'the journey of the gods'. See also note 152 to chapter thirteen, below.

55 On the significance of the creation of man in the image of the gods, see A.F. Alford, *When The Gods Came Down*, op. cit., chapter eight.

56 Ibid., pp. 207-8.

57 Plato, *Republic III*, 414d-e (trans. G.M.A. Grube/C.D.C. Reeve). Cf Plato, *Statesman*, 274, and Plato, *Menexenus*, 237-38.

58 Per Socrates in Plato, *Republic III*, 414c.

CHAPTER ELEVEN: SECRET COSMOS

1 The myth of Oceanus and Tethys. See Homer, *Iliad*, 196 ff.

2 See W. Burkert, *Greek Religion*, op. cit., p. 196.

3 See note 10 to chapter eight, above.

4 Plato, *Statesman*, 268-69. The myth is linked to 'the sign of the golden lamb'.

5 On 'broad Earth', see Homer, *Iliad*, 8.150, 21.387. On 'broad-breasted Earth', 'broad-pathed Earth' etc, see for example Homer, *Iliad*, 16.635, and Hesiod, *Theogony*, 116-119, 499, 531, 619, 719. On 'broad Heaven', see for example Homer, *Iliad*, 5.866, 7.176, 8.74, 20.302, 21.267; Homer, *Odyssey*, 1.68, 4.379, 4.478, 5.184, 6.151, 12.344, 16.183, 19.40; and Hesiod, *Theogony*, 47, 375, 703, 747, 840. On 'broad Tartarus', see for example Hesiod, *Theogony*, 867, and Aristophanes, *The Birds*, 693 ff. Similar adjectives were applied to Heaven and Earth in the Near East; see M.L. West, *The East Face of Helicon*, op. cit., pp. 143, 169, 220-21.

6 On the 'broad sea', see M.L. West, *The East Face of Helicon*, op. cit., p. 221. On the 'broad *aither*', see W.K.C. Guthrie, *Orpheus and Greek Religion*, op. cit., p. 140 fragment 167. The great oath of the gods was personified by Styx, the river of Heaven and Earth (see Hesiod, *Theogony*, 397-401, 774-806).

7 Hesiod, *Theogony*, 125-28 (trans. M.L. West).

8 See, for example, Plato, *Epinomis*, 977b. The idea is discussed in C. Penglase, *Greek Myths and Mesopotamia*, op. cit., p. 132.

9 Homer, *Iliad*, 8.1-34. The translation is a composite of M. Hammond, *Homer The Iliad*, op. cit., p. 118, and R. Lattimore, *The Iliad of Homer*, Chicago, 1951. The golden rope motif may have its origins in the Mesopotamian idea of the lead-rope that was the mainstay (*marsaku*) of Heaven and Earth; see M.L. West, *The East Face of Helicon*, op. cit., p. 371, where he discusses the lead-ropes of Marduk, Gula, Erra, and Shamash.

10 Homer, *Iliad*, 8.413, 18.185, 20.4. Cf Hesiod, *Theogony*, 113.

11 Homer, *Odyssey*, 11.571-93.

12 W.K.C. Guthrie, *Orpheus and Greek Religion*, op. cit., pp. 141 (fragment 222), 173 (gold plate from Thurii).

13 On the Elysian Plain, see Homer, *Odyssey*, 4.562-68. On the garden of the Hesperides, see R.
    Graves, *The Greek Myths,* op. cit., pp. 507-8. On the island of Thrinacie, see Homer, *Odyssey*,
    12.127-42, 12.260-402. On the island of Erytheia, see R. Graves, *The Greek Myths,* op. cit.,
    pp. 494-96. On the idea of a 'fair meadow' in the Underworld, see W.K.C. Guthrie, *Orpheus
    and Greek Religion*, op. cit., p. 141. On the principle of regions being relocated from the
    subterranean Underworld to the West for poetic effect, see chapter eighteen of this book. On
    the significance of cattle in the Underworld, see notes 88 and 89 to chapter thirteen, below.

14 Plato, *Phaedo*, 109a-111c, 114c (trans. G.M.A. Grube). Cf Plato, *Phaedrus*, 250-51.

15 Plato, *Republic VII*, 529b.

16 On the return to unity, see Plato, *Epinomis*, 992b.

17 Plato, *Republic VII*, 523-33.

18 Plato, *Republic VII*, 525a-527c ('geometry *is* knowledge of what always is'); Plato, *Timaeus*,
    47a-b.

19 Plato, *Republic VII*, 527d-530d; Plato, *Timaeus*, 47a-b; Plato, *Epinomis*.

20 Plato, *Epinomis*, 991e-992a; W.K.C. Guthrie, *Orpheus and Greek Religion*, op. cit., p. 220.

21 Plato, *Republic VII*, 531d, 532d-e; Plato, *Timaeus*, 90d.

22 Timon the Pyrrhonist (3rd century BC) accused Plato of plagiarising Philolaos in *Timaeus*. See
    G. de Santillana & H. von Dechend, *Hamlet's Mill*, op. cit., p. 231.

23 See E.C. Krupp, *Echoes of the Ancient Skies*, op. cit., pp. 329-30. The surviving fragments of
    Philolaos are recorded in K. Freeman, *Ancilla to the Pre-Socratic Philosophers: A Complete
    Translation of the Fragments in Diels, Fragmente der Vorsokratiker*, Basil Blackwell, Oxford,
    1966, pp. 73-77. For further information on Philolaon cosmology, see the sources cited in R.
    Temple, *The Crystal Sun*, op. cit., chapter seven.

24 An excellent review of this subject appears in R. Temple, *The Crystal Sun,* op. cit., chapter
    seven, although the author has an axe to grind in favour of refraction rather than reflection
    (despite his cited authorities insisting, for the most part, on reflection). See also F.M. Cornford,
    From Religion to Philosophy, op. cit., p. 232.

25 On the Island of Fire, see A.F. Alford, *When The Gods Came Down*, op. cit., and A.F. Alford,
    The Phoenix Solution, op. cit., indexed references. It is also relevant to note the epithets which
    the Pythagoreans used for the Central Fire: 'Guard-house of Zeus', 'Hearth of the World',
    'Mother of the Gods', 'Altar', 'Meeting-Place', and 'Goal of Nature'; see R. Temple, *The
    Crystal Sun,* op. cit., pp. 271, 276. Finally, we should recall the fire that was buried in the
    Underworld in the theories of Anaximander and the Orphics.

26 Hesiod, *Theogony*, 721-27 (trans. M.L. West). Cf Homer, *Iliad*, 8.1-34.

27 It is thus established conclusively that the Central Fire was not the Sun, as some authorities
    maintain, but an Inner Earth. Accordingly, it is not the case that the Pythagoreans knew a
    heliocentric Universe, nor that they were moving away from a geocentric Universe.

28 F.M. Cornford, *From Religion to Philosophy*, op. cit., pp. 218-19.

29 Ibid.

30 Plato, *Phaedo*, 109e-110a (trans. G.M.A. Grube).

31 Plato, *Phaedrus,* 247c-d (trans. A. Nehamas & P. Woodruff; I have paraphrased slightly). This
    was the place where our souls had been born per *Phaedrus,* 249-52.

32 Plato, *Epinomis*, 990a. There appears to be a contradiction in *Epinomis*, 986a-b, 987b, and
    Timaeus, 38b-d, where the eighth orbit is identified as the sphere of stars; and yet the stars were
    visible. The key to the code is that the sphere of stars was a visible cipher for the orb of the
    invisible exploded planet.

33 Plato, *Timaeus*, 39d. Here, eight orbits are said to come into line with the sphere of stars ('the
    circle of the Same'), implying the existence of a significant, eighth visible body. It is probable
    that this eighth orb was Sirius, which moves differently from the other stars, and which was
    regarded in ancient times as a cipher for the exploded planet.

34 See Plato, *Timaeus*, 42b. The idea may have been drawn from the Orphic belief that the sphere
    of stars had been spun off from the fire of Heaven that fell into the Underworld.

35 Plato, *Republic VII,* 540a. Cf the 'true Light' in Plato, *Phaedo*, 110a, the Light in the pillar of
    light in Plato, *Republic X*, 616b ('the Vision of Er'), and cf the idea, discussed earlier, that the
    Sun merely reflected or refracted light and heat towards the Earth. This is the same Light
    described by Philo: 'This Light is the star, beyond the heavens, the Source of the Stars that are
    visible to the senses... and from which the Sun and the Moon and the rest of the stars, both

errant and fixed, draw their light...' (G.R.S. Mead, *Thrice Great Hermes*, Vol I, p. 161).
36 Plato, *Phaedrus*, 249c.
37 Plato, *Republic VII*, 530b-c. In harmonics, too, a focus on the audible caused scientists to miss the higher picture (*Republic VII*, 530e-531a).
38 F.M. Cornford, *From Religion to Philosophy*, op. cit., p. 187.
39 Plato, *Phaedo*, 59c. Simmias and Cebes were Pythagoreans from the city of Thebes. Philolaos is named as their leader in *Phaedo*, 61d. Whether this is an authentic account is a moot point. It is also notoriously difficult so separate the ideas of Socrates from those of Plato. F.M. Cornford, for one, believes that Socrates may have been more familiar with Pythagorean ideas than has commonly been supposed (*From Religion to Philosophy*, op. cit., pp. 247-48).
40 See note 51 to chapter six and note 33 to chapter nine, above. *Aither* was the binding agent of the Universe; hence in the Orphic creation myth, Zeus asks Night: "How can I have all things one and each one separate?", and Night replies: "Surround all things with the ineffable *aither*, and in the midst of that set the heavens, and in the midst the boundless Earth, in the midst the sea, and in the midst all the constellations with which the heavens are crowned."; see W.K.C. Guthrie, *Orpheus and Greek Religion*, op. cit., pp. 81, 139.
41 Hence the idea in Euripides that Zeus *was* the *aither*. See W.K.C. Guthrie, *Orpheus and Greek Religion*, op. cit., p. 185.
42 M.L. West, *Hesiod, Theogony & Works and Days*, op. cit., p. 64.
43 M.L. West, *The East Face of Helicon*, op. cit., p. 288.
44 F.M. Cornford, *From Religion to Philosophy*, op. cit., p. 66; G.S. Kirk, *The Nature of Greek Myths*, op. cit., p. 46; W.K.C. Guthrie, *Orpheus and Greek Religion*, op. cit., p. 80.
45 G.S. Kirk, *The Nature of Greek Myths*, op. cit., p. 46.
46 R. Caldwell in L. Edmunds ed., *Approaches to Greek Myth*, op. cit., p. 359.
47 M.L. West, *The East Face of Helicon*, op. cit., p. 288 (cf p. 367).
48 W.K.C. Guthrie, *Orpheus and Greek Religion*, op. cit., pp. 81, 140 (fragment 167). Another Orphic hymn cites the body of Zeus as containing fire, water and earth, *aither*, night and day, Metis and Eros (ibid., p. 97). Hence Zeus was 'the foundation of Earth and the starry heavens' (ibid., pp. 82, 140).
49 Hesiod, *Theogony*, 886-98 (trans. M.L. West).
50 Hesiod, *Theogony*, 923-24.
51 C. Penglase, *Greek Myths and Mesopotamia*, op. cit., p. 232; W. Burkert, *Greek Religion*, op. cit., p. 142. 'Heads' and 'mountains' were popular metaphors in the ancient exploded planet cults; see A.F. Alford, *When The Gods Came Down*, op. cit., and A.F. Alford, *The Phoenix Solution*, op. cit., indexed references.
52 A further example can be cited. In the Orphic Derveni text, Zeus swallows the phallus of the first cosmic king. See W. Burkert, *The Orientalising Revolution*, op. cit., p. 217.
53 Hesiod, *Theogony*, 453-62 (trans. M.L. West, though I have paraphrased slightly).
54 Hesiod, *Theogony*, 497-501 (trans. M.L. West; 'Pytho' signifies Delphi).
55 An remark in Plato, *Euthyphro*, 6a, suggests that Ouranos indeed swallowed his own sons.
56 M.L. West, *The East Face of Helicon*, op. cit., p. 285; R. Temple, *The Crystal Sun*, op. cit., pp. 321-24.
57 I. Donnelly, *Atlantis: The Antediluvian World*, op. cit., p. 445; R. Temple, *The Crystal Sun*, op. cit., p. 321. Hence *baetuli* were regarded as 'moving stones' and 'stones of self motion', and were chained or tied down in temples accordingly; see ibid., and also I.S. Serra, 'Gods Who Fell From the Sky' in *Meteorite*, 6:2 (May 2000), p. 27.
58 Hesiod, *Theogony*, 813-15 (cf 741); M.L. West, *The East Face of Helicon*, op. cit., p. 288.
59 Hesiod, *Theogony*, 694-704 (trans. M.L. West).
60 Hesiod, *Theogony*, 116-19, 123-26 (trans. M.L. West, though I have amended 'bright air' to *Aither*', and to avoid confusion I have followed the lead of other scholars in rendering Tartara, plural, as Tartarus, singular).

CHAPTER TWELVE: GENESIS OF THE GODS

1 Plato, *Cratylus*, 397c-d, but cf Herodotus, *Histories*, 2.52. For an orthodox academic approach to the meaning of *theoi*, see the references in notes 75 and 76 to chapter four, above.
2 Plato, *Timaeus*, 40d-41a. See discussion in chapter four of this book.

3   Plato, *Timaeus*, 41a (trans. D.J. Zeyl).

4   Plato, *Epinomis*, 984d-e. See quotation in chapter four of this book.

5   Hesiod, *Works and Days*, 120 ff (trans. M.L. West, though I have paraphrased slightly). Cf Plato, *Republic V*, 469a.

6   Cf Plato, *Republic VII*, 540b-c: the true philosopher, after death, would be worshipped as a *daimon*. See also W. Burkert, *Greek Religion*, op. cit., p. 181.

7   Book of the Dead, trans. Normandi Ellis, in R. Bauval & G. Hancock, *Keeper of Genesis*, William Heinemann, 1996, p. 283. Compare Pyramid Texts, Utterance 332, para 541, where Osiris the king stated: "I have ascended in a blast of fire, having turned myself about."

8   On the legend of the Phoenix, see Herodotus, *Histories*, 2.73. The model for the Phoenix was the ancient Egyptian Bennu-bird, alias Re/Osiris.

9   See note 44 to chapter seven, above.

10 Hence W. Burkert writes in *Greek Religion*, op. cit., pp. 202-3: 'In myth, the gods often have a mortal double who could almost be mistaken for the god except for the fact that he is subject to death, and indeed is killed by the god himself... Myth has separated into two figures what in the sacrificial ritual is present as a tension.'

11 Plato, *Timaeus*, 22b-23c.

12 Hence the genre of myths involving the planets Saturn and Jupiter. All can be explained by the exploded planet hypothesis, the idea of the world ages, and the succession myth.

13 M. Griffith ed., *Aeschylus:Prometheus Bound*, op. cit., p. 150: the overthrow of Typhoeus 'symbolises the final overthrow of chthonian savagery by Olympian civilisation'. The idea is inspired by the description of the Titans, e.g. 'they thought, in their obstinate self-confidence, that they would be the masters effortlessly through crude violence.' (Aeschylus, *Prometheus Bound*, 207-8). See also W. Burkert, *Greek Religion*, op. cit., p. 247; Burkert refers to 'an unstable aristocratic rule at the end of the dark age', but states that there is unquestionably more to the gods than this.

14 R. Graves, *The Greek Myths*, op. cit., pp. 38, 42.

15 V. Clube & B. Napier, *The Cosmic Winter*, op. cit., pp. 166, 192.

16 W. Burkert, *Greek Religion*, op. cit., p. 128.

CHAPTER THIRTEEN: THE OLYMPIANS UNVEILED

1   W. Burkert, *Greek Religion*, op. cit., pp. 127, 262, 280; R. Graves, *The Greek Myths,* op. cit., pp. 41, 165; C. Penglase, *Greek Myths and Mesopotamia*, op. cit., p. 84.

2   Hesiod, *Theogony*, 690-705 (trans. M.L. West, though I have rendered 'sky' as 'heavens').

3   R. Graves, *The Greek Myths,* op. cit., Index. Cf W. Burkert, *Greek Religion*, op. cit., pp. 125-26; Burkert notes the origin of the name Zeus from the Indo-European name *Dyaus pitar*, 'Father of the Day', and thus concludes naively that Zeus was simply 'the luminous day sky'.

4   W.K.C. Guthrie, *Orpheus and Greek Religion*, op. cit., pp. 82, 140 (fragment 168).

5   For example, Homer, *Iliad*, 9.457. See W. Burkert, *Greek Religion*, op. cit., pp. 196, 200-1; M.L. West, *The East Face of Helicon*, op. cit., pp. 373, 537, 562-63.

6   W. Burkert, *Greek Religion*, op. cit., p. 200.

7   See note 1 above.

8   W. Burkert, *Greek Religion*, op. cit., p. 280. These initiation rites may be traced to an older Mount Ida in Phrygia (in western central Asia Minor), where the Dactyls ('Fingers') were acolytes of the great mother-goddess Cybele. Here, the Dactyls were called Kelmis, Damnameneus and Akmon. The latter name, meaning 'Thunderbolt/Anvil', underlines the meteoritic aspect of this cult (P. Green trans., *Argonautika*, op. cit., p. 224).

9   C. Penglase, *Greek Myths and Mesopotamia*, op. cit., p. 84.

10 On Zeus *Baetylus*, see R. Bauval & A. Gilbert, *The Orion Mystery*, op. cit., pp. 201-2. A similar stone, shown to the historian Pausanias at Gythium, was known as Zeus-Kappotas, i.e. 'Zeus fallen down' (ibid.).

11 P.K. Hitti, *History of Syria*, London, 1951, p. 312.

12 G.A. Wainwright, 'Letopolis' in *JEA* 18 (1932), p. 161.

13 It is characteristic of the meteorite in myth that it enters the Underworld. Cf Hesiod, *Theogony*, 139-46, 502-7: the Cyclopes 'who gave Zeus his thunder and forged his thunderbolt... they returned thanks for his goodness by giving him thunder and lightning and the smoking bolt,

which mighty Earth had hitherto kept hidden.'

14 Hesiod, *Theogony*, 453 ff.

15 Homer, *Iliad*, 14.339 ff, 18.365. Mount Ida symbolised the Mountain of Heaven and Earth. Strictly speaking, the sacred marriage took place in the Earth rather than in Heaven (which the clouds signify here). Homer has adapted the scheme for poetic effect.

16 Ap. Rhodios, *Argonautika*, 4.96. Zeus and Hera were the archetype of the married couple, with Hera being the archetype of consummated marriage (see W. Burkert in *Greek Religion*, op. cit., pp. 132, 219). R. Graves in *The Greek Myths*, op. cit., pp. 50, 53, notes the tradition that Hera's wedding night with Zeus lasted three hundred years.

17 W. Burkert, *Greek Religion*, op. cit., p. 131.

18 Ibid., pp. 17, 135.

19 Ibid., p. 132.

20 C. Boer trans., *The Homeric Hymns*, op. cit., pp. 168-71 (*Hymn to Pythian Apollo*). On Typhaon, see note 27 to chapter two, above.

21 C. Boer trans., *The Homeric Hymns*, op. cit., pp. 168-69 (*Hymn to Pythian Apollo*). Cf Homer, *Iliad*, 1.585 ff, 18.395-99, and Hesiod, *Theogony*, 927-30.

22 The heavenly birth from the goddess motif is found in two important Near Eastern myths: the Egyptian myth of Nut giving birth to her five Children of Chaos, and the Mesopotamian myth of Mami/Ishtar giving birth to mankind.

23 Homer, *Iliad*, 5.720-72; Ap. Rhodios, *Argonautika*, 4.642-43 (trans. P. Green).

24 Homer, *Iliad*, 15.17-24 (trans. M. Hammond). The fate of Hera is to be compared to that of Zeus on Olympus during the rebellion of the gods, *Iliad*, 1.399 ff. On the binding with the golden rope motif, see note 9 to chapter eleven, above. The treatment echoes what Marduk did to Tiamat in *Enuma Elish*.

25 W. Burkert, *Greek Religion*, op. cit., p. 134.

26 Similarly, the myths of Egypt allude to the goddess Hathor/Isis descending from Heaven and taking over the Earth.

27 Hesiod, *Theogony*, 886-923.

28 W.K.C. Guthrie, *Orpheus and Greek Religion*, op. cit., pp. 82, 139 (fragment 145): 'Aforetime was she Rhea, but when she came to be called mother of Zeus she became Demeter.' See also Hesiod, *Theogony*, 453 ff, and Homer, *Iliad*, 14.196 ff. It is as if Rhea becomes Demeter alias Hera.

29 Hesiod, *Theogony*, 177-79 (trans. M.L. West). This would make Ouranos a cognate of *Khaos*.

30 S.N. Kramer, *The Sumerians*, op. cit., pp. 200-1.

31 W. Burkert, *Greek Religion*, op. cit., p. 159: "her name betrays a mother, but exactly what kind of mother remains a mystery. The interpretation as Earth Mother which was current in antiquity ... is unsatisfactory both linguistically and materially...'. Ibid., p. 175: 'Neither Demeter nor the Great Goddess of Asia Minor is to be identified with Earth.'

32 C. Boer trans., *The Homeric Hymns*, op. cit., p. 97 (*Hymn to Demeter*).

33 Ibid., pp. 93-94; W. Burkert, *Greek Religion*, op. cit., p. 160. On the significance of the fiery torches, see note 12 to chapter ten, above.

34 C. Boer trans., *The Homeric Hymns*, op. cit., pp. 106, 114. Cf W. Burkert, *Greek Religion*, op. cit., p. 187, and M.L. West, *The East Face of Helicon*, op. cit., p. 113. Scholars fail to understand that Demeter has entered the Underworld in the Homeric hymn. Fortunately, there is a version of this myth in which Demeter explicitly enters the Underworld of Hades in order to recover her daughter; see C. Penglase, *Greek Myths and Mesopotamia*, op. cit., p. 133.

35 C. Boer trans., *The Homeric Hymns*, op. cit., pp. 119-20; W. Burkert, *Greek Religion*, op. cit., p. 160. Cf the Hera festivals (note 25 above). Cf also the Mesopotamian myth of *Ishtar's Descent to the Underworld*.

36 C. Boer trans., *The Homeric Hymns*, op. cit., pp. 125-26, 130, 132-33 (*Hymn to Demeter*).

37 On *Dia* 'of the sky', see R. Graves, *The Greek Myths*, op. cit., p. 209. Alternatively, the name can be read as *De-meter*, meaning 'from, or out of, the sky'. The modern word 'dematerialise' sums up exactly what happened to Demeter, Hera and all the other sky-goddesses.

38 R. Graves, *The Greek Myths*, op. cit., pp. 93, Index. Cf Plato, *Cratylus*, 404c, and W. Burkert, *Greek Religion*, op. cit., p. 159.

39 Homer, *Odyssey*, 11.214, trans. Fitzgerald, cited in R. Temple, *The Crystal Sun*, op. cit., p. 253.

40 C. Boer trans., *The Homeric Hymns*, op. cit., p. 133. We should reconsider also the cries of the

Eleusinian initiands: "Rain", and "Conceive", to Heaven and Earth respectively.
41 Hesiod, *Theogony*, 133-35, 405-9.
42 Hesiod, *Theogony*, 409-11.
43 Hesiod, *Theogony*, 919-21.
44 R. Stoneman ed., *Pindar The Odes and Selected Fragments*, op. cit., pp. 330, 338.
45 Pindar, *Paean 7b*, 50-52 (trans. G.S. Conway & R. Stoneman).
46 C. Boer trans., *The Homeric Hymns*, op. cit., pp. 152-55. In the course of the negotiation, Delos expresses her fear that new-born Apollo will scoff at her rocky landscape 'and then he'll turn me upside down and push me into the depths of the sea with his feet, and then the great waves of the ocean will wash over my head for ever.' (ibid., p. 153; cf Herodotus, *Histories*, 7.6, 7.235). This is worth noting in view of the fate of Atlantis.
47 C. Boer trans., *The Homeric Hymns*, op. cit., pp. 150-51. Cf the 'mountain-high' dark wave that features in the myth of Poseidon and Tyro (Homer, *Odyssey*, 11.240 ff).
48 The translation is a composite of C. Boer trans., *The Homeric Hymns*, op. cit., p. 156, and G.S. Kirk, *The Nature of Greek Myths*, op. cit., p. 124.
49 An interesting parallel to this is the myth of Rhea, pregnant with Zeus, crossing over to Crete so that Gaia might nurse and rear her son (Hesiod, *Theogony*, 476 ff).
50 R. Stoneman ed., *Pindar The Odes and Selected Fragments*, op. cit., p. 372.
51 R. Graves, *The Greek Myths*, op. cit., Index; G.A. Wainwright, 'Iron in Egypt' in *JEA* 18 (1933), pp. 3-15. On the importance of Letopolis in Egypt, see R. Bauval & A. Gilbert, *The Orion Mystery*, op. cit., pp. 210-11, 216-17.
52 W. Burkert, *Greek Religion*, op. cit., p. 144.
53 Ibid., p. 219.
54 G.S. Kirk, *The Nature of Greek Myths*, op. cit., p. 58; Plato, *Cratylus*, 404e. On other ideas, see Plato, *Cratylus*, 405-406, R. Graves, *The Greek Myths*, op. cit., p. 57, M.L. West, *The East Face of Helicon*, op. cit., p. 55, and W. Burkert, *The Orientalising Revolution*, op. cit., p. 197.
55 Plato, *Republic IV*, 427c. Cf Pindar, *Pythian 8*, 58-61. The idea of *arche polou* is suggested by an Orphic text which applies this epithet to the god Oceanus; see G. de Santillana & H. von Dechend, *Hamlet's Mill*, op. cit., p. 191.
56 C. Boer trans., *The Homeric Hymns*, op. cit., pp. 168-72 (*Hymn to Pythian Apollo*); J.G. Frazer, *The Golden Bough*, op. cit., p. 224.
57 C. Boer trans., *The Homeric Hymns*, op. cit., p. 175; I have paraphrased the translation slightly. The ship motif is often used in ancient myths to denote a journey from Heaven to Earth.
58 On Phoibos, see Homer, *Iliad*. On Aiglatas, see W. Burkert, *The Orientalising Revolution*, op. cit., p. 78. On Lykeios, see W. Burkert, *Greek Religion*, op. cit., p. 144. On the flowing hair, see Pindar, *Pythian 9*, 5. On the golden sword, see Hesiod, *Works and Days*, 771.
59 See Homer, *Iliad*, and *Homeric Hymn to Pythian Apollo*; also Pindar, *Pythian 8*, 61. On the remoteness of Apollo in the heavenly north, see *Homeric Hymn to Pythian Apollo* and W. Burkert, *Greek Religion*, op. cit., pp. 146, 148.
60 G.A. Wainwright, 'Letopolis' in *JEA* 18 (1932), p. 161.
61 Ibid.
62 Ibid. On the image of Diana at Ephesus, see Acts 19:35.
63 On *Dia* 'of the sky', see R. Graves, *The Greek Myths*, op. cit., p. 209. The term *na* was used in Western Asia and Mesopotamia to denote a stone from Heaven (i.e. a meteorite).
64 C. Boer trans., *The Homeric Hymns*, op. cit., pp. 609-70 (*Hymn to Aphrodite*). Artemis was renowned as a goddess of animals, hunting and sacrifice. Her name possibly derives from *artemes* 'strong limbed'.
65 R. Graves, *The Greek Myths*, op. cit., p. 75.
66 I.S. Serra, 'Gods Who Fell From the Sky' in *Meteorite*, 6:2 (May 2000), pp. 25-28. Serra notes that Cybele was worshipped in the form of a statue of the seated goddess with an iron meteorite forming her head! On the connections between Cybele and meteoritic metalworking, see note 8, above. Cybele was called 'Mother of the Mountain'. Her priests, representing the god Attis, the lover of the Mother, practised self-castration, symbolising the separation of Heaven from Earth. See W. Burkert, *Ancient Mystery Cults*, Harvard Univ. Press, 1987, p. 6, and W. Burkert, *Greek Religion*, op. cit., p. 179.
67 Velikovsky, *Worlds in Collision*, op. cit., p. 294.
68 That Apollo brought floodwaters to the Earth is evident from Herodotus, *Histories*, 4.158,

where the sky is said to leak at a fountain of Apollo in Irasa.

69 In addition to this, it would seem that Apollo and Artemis were associated, from an early date, with the visible symbols of the Sun and the Moon, thus sowing further seeds of confusion.

70 Homer, *Iliad*, 5.887; W. Burkert, *Greek Religion*, op. cit., p. 169.

71 W. Burkert, *Greek Religion*, op. cit., p. 169. See also Hesiod, *Theogony*, 934-36.

72 C. Boer trans., *The Homeric Hymns*, op. cit., p. 60 (*Hymn to Ares*). Similarly, in Babylonia, the war-god Nergal was associated with the red planet Mars.

73 Homer, *Iliad*, 5.352 ff.

74 Homer, *Iliad*, 5.384 ff; M.L. West, *The East Face of Helicon*, op. cit., pp. 297-98, 362-63.

75 Homer, *Odyssey*, 8.267-367.

76 It should be noted, however, that Hephaestus also had a palace on heavenly Olympus.

77 Scholars do not understand that the Argo sailed from Heaven into the Underworld, for the original myth has been obscured by geographical embellishments. This is a new interpretation, inspired by the exploded planet hypothesis, and I will justify it in a future publication.

78 Ap. Rhodios, *Argonautika*, 2.404-7; Apollodorus, *Library*, 1.9.16; Euripides, *The Phoenician Women*, 638-73 (cited in G.S. Kirk, *The Nature of Greek Myths*, op. cit., p. 157).

79 Ap. Rhodios, *Argonautika*, 2.1172-76. Herodotus, *Histories*, 4.59, 62, reports that the Scythians worshipped Ares in the form of ancient iron swords placed atop large mounds.

80 It was a dark, misty, high-roofed cave; see C. Boer trans., *The Homeric Hymns*, op. cit., pp. 18-19, 34 (*Hymn to Hermes*). Cf Hesiod, *Theogony*, 938-40.

81 R. Graves, *The Greek Myths,* op. cit., Index; W. Burkert, *Greek Religion*, op. cit., p. 156; M.L. West, *The East Face of Helicon*, op. cit., p. 34. Hermes was also linked with the invention of speech; the word *hermeneus* 'interpreter' may have been derived from the use of *omphali* as oracle stones.

82 W. Burkert, *Greek Religion*, op. cit., p. 156, writes: 'That a monument of this kind could be transformed into an Olympian god is astounding.'

83 On the link between the herm and the phallus, see W. Burkert, *Greek Religion*, op. cit., p. 90.

84 Homer, *Odyssey*, 1.39; Homer, *Iliad*, 2.103; W. Burkert, *Greek Religion*, op. cit., p. 157.

85 J.B. Pritchard ed., *ANET*, op. cit., p. 112: 'The exercise of the Enlilship his eyes view. The crown of his sovereignty, the robe of his godhead, his divine Tablet of Destinies Zu views constantly. As he views constantly the father of the gods... As Zu views constantly...'.

86 W. Burkert, *Greek Religion*, op. cit., pp. 157-58, 196.

87 M.L. West, *The East Face of Helicon*, op. cit., pp. 550, 573; W. Burkert, *Greek Religion*, op. cit., p. 158.

88 The theft of the god's cattle was a popular theme in the Greek myths. On the theft of Apollo's cattle by Hermes, see C. Boer trans., *The Homeric Hymns*, op. cit., pp. 18-58 (*Hymn to Hermes*); significantly, the cattle disappeared just as the Sun went down, and the theft coincided with the invention of fire and the beginning of sacrifice.

89 On the use of 'cattle' and 'sheep' as metaphors for meteoritic storms in Mesopotamian myths, see A.F. Alford, *When The Gods Came Down*, op. cit., indexed references. In the Greek myths, Atlas had a thousand herds of cattle and sheep, which were seemingly metamorphosed into the golden apples of immortality (the word for sheep and apples was the same, *melon*).

90 Hesiod, *Theogony*, 941-43; W.K.C. Guthrie, *Orpheus and Greek Religion*, op. cit., p. 82. On the true identity of Semele, see note 102 below.

91 Dionysus was born at Mount Nysa; see C. Boer trans., *The Homeric Hymns*, op. cit., p. 14, 16 (*Third Hymn to Dionysus*). Homer, *Iliad*, 6.130 ff, describes how Dionysus was driven down from Mt Nysa and dived into the deep sea, to be protected by Thetis. Euripides, in *Bacchae*, 83 ff, describes how Dionysus 'the roaring one', was brought down from the mountains. In view of the connection to Osiris and the burning of Dionysus' mother, the name Nysa may derive from the Egyptian *Nsrsr*, 'the Island of Fire'; see A.F. Alford, *When The Gods Came Down*, op. cit., p. 398, and cf the myth of Poseidon hurling Nisyros island against the giant Polybotes.

92 R. Graves, *The Greek Myths,* op. cit., p. 108 (it could also mean 'tree', ibid., p. 107). On the hobbling god or king ritual and motif, see ibid., pp. 108, 315-16.

93 J.G. Frazer, *The Golden Bough*, op. cit., p. 224; W. Burkert, *Greek Religion*, op. cit., p. 224; R. Graves, *The Greek Myths,* op. cit., pp. 118-19.

94 W. Burkert, *Greek Religion*, op. cit., pp. 90-91, 167; R. Stoneman ed., *Pindar The Odes and Selected Fragments*, op. cit., p. 150.

95 On *mesu*-wood, see A.F. Alford, *When The Gods Came Down*, op. cit., pp. 125, 315, 425.
96 R. Graves, *The Greek Myths*, op. cit., pp. 118-20; M. Eliade, *A History of Religious Ideas*, Volume 1, op. cit., pp. 369-72.
97 Herodotus, *Histories*, 2.42, 2.123, 2.144-45, 2.156.
98 Plutarch, *De Iside et Osiride*, 35, 364e-365a. Modern scholars accept this identification.
99 W. Burkert, *Ancient Mystery Cults*, op. cit., p. 160 (note 119). In a similar vein, the Orphics stated that the dismembered Bakchos symbolised the soul of the world; see W.K.C. Guthrie, *Orpheus and Greek Religion*, op. cit., pp. 127-28. Modern scholars seem content to understand Bakchos as signifying the preparation of wine or the passion of the harvest. And yet they recognise that the Greeks regarded the dismemberment myth as an unspeakable mystery (see, for example, W. Burkert, *Greek Religion*, op. cit., p. 298).
100 See W. Burkert, *Greek Religion*, op. cit., pp. 161-67, 280; M. Eliade, *A History of Religious Ideas*, Volume 1, op. cit., pp. 357-73; C. Boer trans., *The Homeric Hymns*, op. cit., pp. 9-17 (*Hymns to Dionysus*); Euripides, *Bacchae*, 83 ff.
101 Euripides, *Bacchae*, 83 ff. See G.S. Kirk, *The Nature of Greek Myths*, op. cit., p. 130.
102 The 'mortal woman' Semele personified the Earth, as some scholars have indeed suggested on etymological grounds; see M. Eliade, *A History of Religious Ideas*, Volume 1, op. cit., p. 357.
103 Euripides, *Bacchae*, 83 ff. See G.S. Kirk, *The Nature of Greek Myths*, op. cit., p. 130. The same myth was told of Asklepius; see W. Burkert, *Greek Religion*, op. cit., p. 120.
104 Homer, *Iliad*, 13.11-38. Cf W. Burkert, *Greek Religion*, op. cit., pp. 136-37.
105 M.L. West, *The East Face of Helicon*, op. cit., pp. 381-82; W. Burkert, *Greek Religion*, op. cit., p. 139.
106 *Encyclopaedia Britannica*, 1999 std edition. Cf W. Burkert, *Greek Religion*, op. cit., p. 136.
107 In Aeschylus, *Seven against Thebes*, 308, for example, all springs are said to be sent by Poseidon; see W. Burkert, *Greek Religion*, op. cit., p. 139.
108 Homer, *Iliad*, 15.172. See discussion in chapter eighteen of this book.
109 Homer, *Iliad*, 15.193-94.
110 Homer, *Iliad*, 15.154 ff.
111 R. Graves, *The Greek Myths*, op. cit., pp. 60-61; W. Burkert, *Greek Religion*, op. cit., p. 138; M. Eliade, *A History of Religious Ideas*, Volume 1, op. cit., pp. 264-65. Both Poseidon and Demeter were worshipped in the form of horses in Arcadia; see G.S. Kirk, *The Nature of Greek Myths*, op. cit., p. 225.
112 Despoena was an *alter ego* of Demeter per R. Graves, *The Greek Myths*, op. cit., p. 62.
113 W. Burkert, *Greek Religion*, op. cit., p. 138.
114 Hesiod, *Theogony*, 280-85.
115 Poseidon is perhaps to be envisaged as a horse descending from Heaven (comet imagery once again?). Hence the rituals of drowning horses in honour of Poseidon; see W. Burkert, *Greek Religion*, op. cit., p. 138.
116 R. Graves, *The Greek Myths*, op. cit., pp. 508-9.
117 *Encyclopaedia Britannica*, 1999 standard edition (one of two possibilities listed). Cf M. Eliade, *A History of Religious Ideas*, Volume 1, op. cit., p. 265.
118 Exploded planet symbolism may also be detected in the cult of Taureos-Poseidon, which involved great bull sacrifices (see W. Burkert, *Greek Religion*, op. cit., p. 138), and in the ritual at Onchestos of crashing a riderless chariot in Poseidon's honour (ibid.). Another giveaway clue is that Poseidon helped to build the wall around Troy (Homer, *Iliad*, 7.454, 21.445).
119 Homer, *Odyssey*, 3.406-11. See W. Burkert, *Greek Religion*, op. cit., pp. 39, 44.
120 G.S. Kirk, *The Nature of Greek Myths*, op. cit., p. 191. On Pylos, see W. Burkert, *Greek Religion*, op. cit., p. 44.
121 W. Burkert, *Greek Religion*, op. cit., p. 139.
122 Ibid., p. 137.
123 R. Graves, *The Greek Myths*, op. cit., p. 59.
124 Plato, *Critias*, 116d-e.
125 C. Boer trans., *The Homeric Hymns*, op. cit., pp. 173-80 (*Hymn to Pythian Apollo*). The Cretan ship was indeed on its way to Pylos, the city of Poseidon, when it was intercepted by Apollo in the form of the dolphin.
126 Hesiod, *Theogony*, 886-99, 923-28.
127 Ap. Rhodios, *Argonautika*, 4.1310-11.

128 C. Penglase, *Greek Myths and Mesopotamia*, op. cit., p. 236.

129 Hesiod, *Works and Days*, 63 ff. Hyginus in *Fabulae*, 144, states that Athene gave Pandora *anima*, i.e. the breath of life (C. Penglase, *Greek Myths and Mesopotamia*, op. cit., p. 202).

130 W. Burkert, *Greek Religion*, op. cit., p. 141.

131 Ibid., and *Encyclopaedia Britannica*, 1999 standard edition.

132 W.K.C. Guthrie, *Orpheus and Greek Religion*, op. cit., p. 140 (note 177); Hesiod, *Theogony*, 924-26 (trans. M.L. West).

133 Homer, *Iliad*, 4.75-78.

134 Homer, *Iliad*, 5.738-51 (trans. M. Hammond).

135 Homer, *Iliad*, 2.446-49 (trans. M. Hammond).

136 Homer, *Iliad*, 21.399-400 (trans. M. Hammond).

137 Homer, *Iliad*, 15.306-10 (trans. M. Hammond).

138 Homer, *Iliad*, 18.203-6.

139 Comet imagery is also seen in another form of the aegis – the Gorgon's head, surrounded by snakes. See W. Burkert, *Greek Religion*, op. cit., p. 140. On the thunderbolt/meteorite equation, see note 12, above.

140 W.K.C. Guthrie, *Orpheus and Greek Religion*, op. cit., p. 140 (fragment 179). The Cyclopes bore the intriguing surname 'Circle-eyes' (Hesiod, *Theogony*, 144).

141 R. Graves, *The Greek Myths,* op. cit., p. 45; W. Burkert, *Greek Religion*, op. cit., p. 140.

142 R. Graves, *The Greek Myths,* op. cit., p. 44, Index. One Pallas was a Titan; another was the father of the Moon; another begot the fifty Pallantids (ibid., p. 45). The most popular story, in Apollodorus, *Library*, 3.12.3, had it that Pallas had been the playmate and foster-sister of Athene, whom Athene had slain in a tragic accident.

143 W. Burkert, *Greek Religion*, op. cit., pp. 139-40. Cf Plato, *Cratylus*, 406d-407a.

144 W. Burkert, *Greek Religion*, op. cit., p. 140.

145 Ibid.

146 R. Graves, *The Greek Myths,* op. cit., pp. 623-24, drawing on Apollodorus, *Library*, 3.12.3. On p. 628, Graves points out that the term Palladium referred to 'a stone or other cult-object around which the girls of a particular clan danced... or young men leaped.'

147 Ibid., p. 623.

148 Ibid., p. 628.

149 Ibid. Graves goes on to explain how the shield became a metaphor for meteorite; hence Ovid's report of the shield of Mars that fell from Heaven. Cf W. Burkert, *Greek Religion*, op. cit., p. 140, where the Palladion is paired in ritual with the shield of Diomedes.

150 W. Burkert, *Greek Religion*, op. cit., p. 140.

151 Ibid., p. 232.

152 C. Penglase, *Greek Myths and Mesopotamia*, op. cit., p. 94; W. Burkert, *Greek Religion*, op. cit., p. 79.

153 W. Burkert, *Greek Religion*, op. cit., pp. 98, 100, 120, 141, 232. On weaving the dress of Hathor/Isis, see Coffin Texts, Spells 483-486, in R.O. Faulkner, *The Ancient Egyptian Coffin Texts*, Volume II, Aris & Phillips, 1977, pp. 128-31.

154 Citation from W. Burkert, *Greek Religion*, op. cit., p. 140.

155 Ibid., and R. Graves, *The Greek Myths,* op. cit., p. 45.

156 At the initial, physical fall of the god, his aethereal double is raised to Heaven; this double is then able to descend and ravage Earth again and again until he is deposed by a son (see the myths of Ouranos, Kronos and Zeus respectively).

157 W. Burkert, *Greek Religion*, op. cit., p. 140.

158 I.S. Serra, 'Gods Who Fell From the Sky' in *Meteorite*, 6:2 (May 2000), p. 26.

159 Note also the idea that the aegis was the Gorgon Medusa's flayed skin, flayed from her by Athene (R. Graves, *The Greek Myths,* op. cit., p. 127), and cf the myth of Apollo flaying Marsyas and nailing his skin to a pine-tree (ibid., p. 77).

160 C. Boer trans., *The Homeric Hymns*, op. cit., pp. 137-38 (*Hymn to Athene*). See note 74 to chapter one, above.

161 Ibid., pp. 168-69 (*Hymn to Pythian Apollo*); Homer, *Iliad*, 18.393 ff.

162 Homer, *Iliad*, 1.585 ff.

163 Homer, *Iliad*, 18.369 ff; 21.325 ff; W. Burkert, *Greek Religion*, op. cit., pp. 167-68. The idea that Hera threw Hephaestus out of Heaven because of his lameness is an anachronism. His

lameness surely resulted from his fall.

164 Homer, *Iliad*, 1.594; Ap. Rhodios, *Argonautika*, op. cit., 3.40-43, 4.760-64, 4.925-29; R. Graves, *The Greek Myths*, op. cit., p. 88; W. Burkert, *Greek Religion*, op. cit., p. 168; M. Griffith ed., *Aeschylus:Prometheus Bound*, op. cit., p. 153.

165 Homer, *Iliad*, 18.116-155, 18.356-617.

166 It is pertinent to note the fiery torch race which the Greeks held in honour of Hephaestus; see Herodotus, *Histories*, 8.98.

167 W. Burkert, *Greek Religion*, op. cit., pp. 167, 267, 281-85; W. Burkert, *The Orientalising Revolution*, op. cit., p. 153; W.K.C. Guthrie, *Orpheus and Greek Religion*, op. cit., pp. 123 ff.; R.H. Brown, *Stellar Theology and Masonic Astronomy*, op. cit., pp. 16-18; Herodotus, *Histories*, 2.51, 3.37.

168 W. Burkert, *Greek Religion*, op. cit., pp. 167-68. Cf Plato, *Critias*, 109c.

169 Pindar, *Olympian 7*, 33-38 (cf fragment 34). The translation is a composite of G.S. Conway & R. Stoneman, and C. Penglase (*Greek Myths and Mesopotamia*, op. cit., p. 231).

170 Apollodorus, *Library*, 1.3.6. Apollodorus also recognised the tradition, cited in Euripides, *Ion*, 452-57, that the axe had been wielded by Prometheus. This famous deed was commemorated on the east pediment of the Parthenon and depicted on vase paintings from the 7th century BC, some of which showed Hephaestus fleeing the scene with his sacred axe.

171 Hesiod, *Theogony,* 927-28 (trans. M.L. West).

172 R. Graves, *The Greek Myths,* op. cit., Index. Cf the Sumerian myth of *Inanna's Descent to the Underworld*; after three days and three nights, Inanna was resurrected. The idea was probably inspired by the three days of invisibility in the cycle of the Moon.

173 Apollodorus, *Library*, 3.14.6; R. Graves, *The Greek Myths,* op. cit., pp. 96-97; W. Burkert, *Greek Religion*, op. cit., pp. 143, 229.

174 Plato, *Critias*, 110a-b.

175 Homer, *Iliad*, 18.477 ff.

176 Egypt and Mesopotamia, too, were lands of numerous, competing exploded planet cults.

CHAPTER FOURTEEN: THE ATLANTIS STORY

1 On the corrupting effect of wealth, see Plato, *Republic IV*, 421d ff, *Republic VIII*, 550 ff, and *Laws IV*, 705b; in the latter, Plato writes that an excess of economic wealth is 'pretty nearly the worst thing that could happen' to an evolving state.

2 Plato, *Republic V*, 473c-e (trans. G.M.A. Clube/C.D.C. Reeve; I have paraphrased slightly). Cf *Republic VI*, 501e.

3 Plato, *Letter VII (To the Friends and Followers of Dion)*, 326a-b (trans. G.R. Morrow; I have paraphrased slightly).

4 Plato, *Republic VII*, 540a-b (trans. G.M.A. Clube/C.D.C. Reeve).

5 Plato, *Republic V*, 473a.

6 Plato, *Republic VI*, 499b, 502a-b; *Republic VII*, 540d-541b. Cf Plato, *Laws III*, 677-80 (a possible hint that a further cataclysm was required?).

7 Timaeus was a Pythagorean from the city of Locri in southern Italy; he was probably a fictional character. Hermocrates was a military general and statesman from the Greek colony of Syracuse in Sicily. Critias was an Athenian, who became one of the city's thirty tyrants after the Peloponnesian War; he was Plato's great-grandfather on his mother's side.

8 Plato, *Timaeus*, 17c (trans. D.J. Zeyl). The subject had been raised by Socrates' guests (see *Timaeus* 20b). An unnamed fourth guest had been present then, but he missed the follow-on meeting due to illness. Perhaps this was Pericles (see C. Gill, *Plato The Atlantis Story,* Bristol Classical Press, 1980, p. 32). Or perhaps it was Plato himself (cf. Plato, *Phaedo*, 59b).

9 Plato, *Timaeus*, 19b-c, 20b (trans. D.J. Zeyl).

10 Plato, *Timaeus*, 20a (trans. D.J. Zeyl).

11 Plato, *Timaeus*, 20d.

12 Plato, *Timaeus*, 20d-21a (trans. D.J. Zeyl). Cf *Timaeus*, 21d.

13 Plato, *Timaeus*, 20e. There is some confusion as to whether this ought to be six generations; see C. Gill, *Plato The Atlantis Story*, op. cit., p. 39. It should be noted that Plato belonged to this family tree, Critias being his uncle or great-grandfather on his mother's side.

14 Plato, *Timaeus*, 21b. The name Apaturia sounds like the Greek word which meant 'deceptive/

illusory'; see C. Gill, *Plato The Atlantis Story,* op. cit., pp. 40, 75.
15 Plato, *Timaeus,* 22b (trans. D.J. Zeyl).
16 Plato, *Timaeus,* 22c (trans. D.J. Zeyl).
17 Plato, *Timaeus,* 23b-c.
18 Plato, *Timaeus,* 23e-24a (trans. D.J. Zeyl; I have paraphrased slightly). The connection between Athene and the city of Sais is attested in Herodotus, *Histories,* 2.28, 2.59, 2.170, 2.175.
19 Plato, *Timaeus,* 24d-25a (trans. D.J. Zeyl).
20 The name 'Pillars of Heracles' was used both for the straits of Gibraltar and the straits of the Dardanelles (which marked the entrance to the Black Sea). But there is no doubting which straits are intended here, for only the former lie opposite the Atlantic Ocean.
21 Plato, *Timaeus,* 25a-c (trans. D.J. Zeyl).
22 Plato, *Timaeus,* 25d (trans. D.J. Zeyl, but I have amended the first lines from 'Afterwards' to 'Further back; see discussion in chapter twenty of this book).
23 Plato, *Timaeus,* 25e.
24 Plato, *Timaeus,* 26c-d (trans. D.J. Zeyl).
25 Plato, *Critias,* 108e (trans. D. Clay).
26 C. Gill in *Plato The Atlantis Story,* op. cit., pp. 43, 53, refers to this as a 'casual error', a 'slip'.
27 In view of the discussion to come in ensuing chapters, the omission of both the Athenians' fate and the floods might be a hint that the Athenians actually personified the floods.
28 Plato, *Critias,* 109a. The word 'emerge' alludes to the idea that races were born from the earth.
29 Plato, *Critias,* 109d (trans. D. Clay).
30 Plato, *Critias,* 110a-b. Two of these names incorporate the idea of 'birth from the earth' .
31 Plato, *Critias,* 110b-d, 112b-c.
32 On the connections between the warrior class and the ideal state in *Republic,* see C. Gill, *Plato The Atlantis Story,* op. cit., pp. xiv-xv, 31.
33 Plato, *Critias,* 110e-111c (trans. D. Clay).
34 Plato, *Critias,* 111a-b (trans. D. Clay).
35 Plato, *Critias,* 112a (trans. D. Clay).
36 C. Gill, *Plato The Atlantis Story,* op. cit., p. 57, noting the similarity to *Timaeus* 25d.
37 Plato, *Critias,* 113c-d. The name Leucippe meant 'white mare', whilst the name Evenor meant 'good or brave man' or perhaps 'controlling the reins'. The pairing evokes the myth of Evenus and Alcippe, in which Evenus, a famous chariot racer, killed his own horses and drowned himself in a river; see Apollodorus, *Library,* 1.7.8; C. Gill, *Plato The Atlantis Story,* op. cit., p. 60; R. Graves, *The Greek Myths,* op. cit., pp. 246-47, Index.
38 Plato, *Critias,* 113d. There are echoes here of the divine succession myth, which would imply that Clito personified the Earth. The name Clito meant 'famous' or 'splendid'; see C. Gill, *Plato The Atlantis Story,* op. cit., p. 60.
39 Plato, *Critias,* 113d (trans. D. Clay).
40 Plato, *Critias,* 113e, 117a. The twin springs (warm and cold) motif is found in the legendary river Skamandros at Troy; see Homer, *Iliad,* 22.148 ff.
41 The twins theme was popular in ancient myths. In the Greek myths, one thinks of Apollo and Artemis, Otus and Ephialtes, Castor and Polydeuces, Heracles and Iphicles, Zethus and Amphion, Aegyptus and Danaus, and Neleus and Pelias, whilst in the Roman myths, one thinks of Romulus and Remus. The most obvious explanation for the twins motif is the Sun and Moon, although we should not discount a transient phenomenon such as a splitting comet.
42 Plato, *Critias,* 114a-b (trans. D. Clay).
43 Presumably centuries or millennia, though the time scale is not actually stated.
44 Plato, *Critias,* 114e, 116b-d. The account is vague, and it may be possible that some of these metals were imported (see *Critias,* 114d-e). On *oreichalkos,* see discussion in later chapters.
45 Plato, *Critias,* 116a.
46 Plato, *Critias,* 114e, 115a-b.
47 Plato, *Critias,* 115a-b (trans. D. Clay).
48 Plato, *Critias,* 114e, 116d.
49 Plato, *Critias,* 115c-d (trans. D. Clay).
50 Plato, *Critias,* 116c.
51 Plato, *Critias,* 116c-e. Note the winged horses; in the myths of Poseidon and his brothers Zeus and Hades, horses were normally of the winged and flying variety.

52 Plato, *Critias*, 116e-117a.
53 Plato, *Critias*, 115c-e.
54 Plato, *Critias*, 115d-e. The Grand Canal was 50 stades long, i.e. approximately 9.1 kilometres.
55 Plato, *Critias*, 117c.
56 Plato, *Critias*, 116a, 116b-c.
57 Plato, *Critias*, 116a.
58 Plato, *Critias*, 116b, 117e. The circumference of the island can be calculated at nearly 400 stades, i.e. approximately 73 kilometres. This was the length of the sea wall. In ancient myths, walls often symbolised layers of planetary crust; see A.F. Alford, *When The Gods Came Down*, op. cit., indexed references.
59 Plato, *Critias*, 117e.
60 Plato, *Critias*, 117e (trans. D. Clay).
61 Plato, *Critias*, 117c-d.
62 Plato, *Critias*, 118a-b (trans. D. Clay).
63 Plato, *Critias*, 118a (trans. D. Clay).
64 Plato, *Critias*, 118a, 118c-d. The plain is said to be oriented 'towards the sea, in the middle of the whole island'. Ten thousand stades represents an unbelievable 1,829 kilometres.
65 Plato, *Critias*, 113c, 116a, 115e. The island diameter of 127 stades is calculated as follows: the central island, 5 stades, the rings of sea and land, 3, 3, 2, 2 and 1 stades in width (each to be doubled to get a diameter for the city), and the distance from the city to the true sea, 50 stades (to be doubled to get a diameter for the island). Hence $5 + 22 + 100 = 127$.
66 See C. Gill, *Plato The Atlantis Story,* op. cit., figure 4 and p. 67 (scheme based on Friedlander, 1958).
67 Plato, *Critias*, 119c-120c.
68 Plato, *Critias*, 120d (trans. D. Clay).
69 Plato, *Critias*, 121b-c. The idea is probably metaphorical; see chapter twenty of this book.
70 This is the reason scholars generally give for the unfinished story; see, for example, C. Gill, *Plato The Atlantis Story,* op. cit., p. 72. For my own ideas, see chapter twenty of this book.
71 Plato, *Timaeus*, 20c, 26c-d, 27a-b; Plato, *Critias*, 108a-c.
72 Plato, *Critias*, 114d-e.
73 Plato, *Timaeus*, 25a-b, Plato, *Critias*, 114c. On the significance of these incursions, see chapter twenty of this book.
74 Plato, *Timaeus*, 25b (trans. D.J. Zeyl).
75 Plato, *Critias*, 120e-121c (trans. D. Clay). In this passage, one catches a glimpse of marvellous subtleties in Plato's story. The name Atlantis, 'daughter of Atlas', derived from Atlas which in turn derived from *A-tlao*. Here, the prefix *A-* could mean either 'without' or 'together', and hence *A-tlao* could mean either 'without bearing/suffering' or 'bearing/suffering together'. Sure enough, the Atlantians began by bearing their wealth without difficulty (just as Atlas supported the Heaven with 'untiring hands'), but ended up by suffering together when their island sank beneath the sea.
76 On the parallels between ancient Atlantis and 4th century Athens, and the moral of the story, see C. Gill, *Plato The Atlantis Story,* op. cit., Introduction, pp. xvii-xx.
77 A good summary of Athens' decline, paralleling many aspects of the Atlantis story, may be found in V. Ehrenberg, *From Solon to Socrates*, op. cit., Parts VI, VII.
78 C. Freeman, in *The Greek Achievement*, op. cit., p. 268, speaks of 'a civilisation that seemed on the verge of dissolution' – this in Plato's day.
79 C. Gill, *Plato The Atlantis Story,* op. cit., pp. xviii, 62, 66. Cf Plato, *Gorgias*, 519a.
80 C. Gill, *Plato The Atlantis Story,* op. cit., p. 64. The statue of Zeus, made by Pheidias, is ranked among the Seven Wonders of the World.
81 C. Gill, *Plato The Atlantis Story,* op. cit., pp. 68, 71, highlighting the parallel to the moral decline of Persia discussed in *Laws*.
82 Plato was very active politically. See Plato, *Letters,* especially *Letter VII*. It should be noted that the city of Sais fulfilled many if not all of the requirements of Socrates' ideal state (Plato, *Timaeus*, 24a-c). Was Plato hinting at the need for an Egyptian model?

CHAPTER FIFTEEN: ONCE UPON ATLANTIS

1 Crantor, *c.* 300 BC, wrote a commentary on *Timaeus*, calling it 'pure history'; later, *c.* 1st century BC, the geographers Posidonius and Strabo both treated it as a factually true story. See C. Gill, *Plato The Atlantis Story,* op. cit., Introduction, p. vii.

2 Per Strabo, *The Geography*, 2.3.6. See C. Gill, *Plato The Atlantis Story,* op. cit., p. vii.

3 C. Gill, *Plato The Atlantis Story,* op. cit., p. vii; J. Ferguson, *Utopias of the Classical World*, London, 1975, chapters 12 and 14.

4 I. Donnelly, *Atlantis: The Antediluvian World*, Dover Publications edition, 1976.

5 D.S. Allan & J.B. Delair, *When the Earth Nearly Died* (American edition entitled *Cataclysm!*), Gateway Books, 1995; A. Collins, *Gateway to Atlantis*, op. cit., chapter 22; R. Flem-Ath & C. Wilson, *The Atlantis Blueprint*, Little Brown, 2000. These latter two works cite the research of Edith and Alexander Tollman of Vienna University's Geological Institute.

6 I am not the first to raise this point. See, for example, J. Westwood, 'Lost Atlantis' in J. Flanders ed., *Mysteries of the Ancient World*, Weidenfeld & Nicolson, 1998, p. 136.

7 Herodotus, *Histories*, 9.27.

8 Herodotus, *Histories*, 6.109, citing Miltiades. This was before the Peloponnesian War, which Thucydides said was the greatest war ever fought by Greeks or non-Greeks.

9 Herodotus, *Histories*, 7.20-21.

10 Herodotus, *Histories*, 1.170, 6.2.

11 Herodotus, *Histories*, 3.122. Herodotus states that Minos was of a pre-human race and that the first human to master the Aegean was Polycrates of Samos.

12 Plato, *Timaeus*, 21a.

13 For the most part, the Egyptians were happy to know that it was year x of the reign of pharaoh y. There is evidence for a long-term calendar based on the 1,460-year cycle of Sirius, but this is nothing like the Saite calendar that we are looking for.

14 The actions of the Egyptian gods are mostly ascribed to *Zep Tepi*, 'the First Time'.

15 A.F. Alford, *The Phoenix Solution*, op. cit., pp. 115, 122-23, 344-49, 361, 367-68.

16 See R. Kunzig, *Mapping the Deep*, Sort of Books, London, 2000, pp. 36-37, 41-42, 64-75. Cf G. Hancock, *Fingerprints of the Gods*, Mandarin edition, 1996, chapter 50, p. 488; A. Collins, *Gateway to Atlantis*, op. cit., pp. 45, 49-50; R. Schoch, *Voices of the Rocks*, op. cit., p. 88; J. Westwood, 'Lost Atlantis' in J. Flanders ed., *Mysteries of the Ancient World*, op. cit., p. 130.

17 See note 53 to chapter seven, above.

18 Crete and Thera are old favourites; more recently, popular writers have suggested Antarctica, the Americas, and Cuba.

19 G. Ashe, *Atlantis: Lost Lands, Ancient Wisdom*, Thames and Hudson, 1992, p. 30. Remarkably, the description of Atlantis is more than twice as long as that of ancient Athens.

20 Plato, *Timaeus*, 20d.

21 Plato, *Timaeus*, 21d.

22 Plato, *Timaeus*, 26e.

23 Plato, *Critias*, 110d; Plato, *Timaeus*, 26d.

24 Blind faith in the truth of myths remains a widespread phenomenon today.

25 Plato, *Timaeus*, 21c-d (trans. D.J. Zeyl).

26 Plato, *Critias*, 113a (trans. D. Clay, but I have rendered 'legend' as 'tale').

27 Plato, *Critias*, 112a-b, 112d.

28 Plato, *Critias*, 110d-111e.

29 Plato, *Critias*, 110e.

30 Plato, *Critias*, 111e (trans. C. Gill, *Plato The Atlantis Story,* op. cit., p. 57).

31 Plato, *Critias*, 112d (trans. D. Clay).

32 C. Gill in *Plato The Atlantis Story,* op. cit., p. 57, comments: 'Profusion of water, as well as of crops, is common in idealised pictures of the past.' See also note 39 below.

33 Plato, *Critias*, 114e-115b, 117a-b, 118b-e.

34 Plato, *Critias*, 115a-b, 117b (trans. D. Clay).

35 See note 44 to chapter fourteen, above, and Plato, *Critias*, 114d.

36 Plato, *Critias*, 114e (trans. D. Clay).

37 Plato, *Critias*, 114e. On the meaning 'mountain bronze', see C. Gill, *Plato The Atlantis Story,* op. cit., pp. 61-62.

38 Plato, *Critias*, 113c, 118b (trans. D. Clay).

39 C. Gill, *Plato The Atlantis Story*, op. cit., pp. xiii, 57, 62. Several other mythical utopias could be mentioned. Diodorus Siculus wrote of an enormous island Hespera that possessed an abundance of sheep and goats, and 'fruit-bearing trees of every kind' (*Library*, III). Aeschylus wrote of the land of the Gabioi 'where neither plough nor earth-breaking hoe cuts the land, but the fields, sowing themselves, bear abundant livelihood to mortals.' (*Prometheus Unbound*, XII). Other examples, from Homer's *Odyssey*, are cited in note 43 below.

40 Hesiod, *Works and Days*, 111-19 (trans. M.L. West). Cf Atlantis in Plato, *Critias*, 114e-115b, 'the island provided... the island produced... the island bore... they took all these products from the earth...'

41 Homer, *Odyssey*, 7.82 ff, 7.112-32 (trans. E.V. Rieu/D.C.H. Rieu). The garden of Phaeacia had two springs, as did Clito's hill in the centre of Atlantis. The city boasted high walls, a temple of Poseidon (the father of the people), harbours and ships, just like Atlantis (although the ships were not used for commerce). The island also boasted high mountains.

42 Homer, *Odyssey*, 6.204.

43 Homer, *Odyssey*, 5.30 ff, 7.315 ff, 8.445, 13.75 ff. Odysseus slept while the Phaeacians rowed him home in less than a day, their ship hidden in mist and cloud. The other fairy tale lands comprised Aeolia, Aeaea, Thrinacie, Ogygia, the island of the Sirens, the country of the Lotus-eaters, the land of the Cyclopes (where 'all the crops spring up unsown and untilled'), the fertile land of goats, the land of the Laestrygonians, and the cliff of Scylla; on these, see chapter eighteen of this book. Homer also tells of a mythical island named Syrie 'out beyond Ortygie, where the Sun turns in his course... famine is unknown there and no dreadful diseases plague the people... the men and women of each generation die peacefully in their homes'.

44 Homer, *Odyssey*, 8.369, 6.265 ff, 7.30 ff, 7.315 ff, 8.30 ff, 8.563 ff.

45 Homer, *Odyssey*, 7.35-36, 8.557 ff (trans. E.V. Rieu/D.C.H. Rieu).

46 Homer, *Odyssey*, 7.56-62.

47 Homer, *Odyssey*, 5.35-36, 6.3-12, 6.200-5, 6.279, 7.201-6.

48 Homer, *Odyssey*, 8.563-70. On the wall of mountains, see note 3 to chapter nineteen, below.

49 Homer, *Odyssey*, 4.561-68 (trans. E.V. Rieu/D.C.H. Rieu, although I have amended 'world's end' to 'ends of the Earth'). The idyllic scene reflects that on Olympus as described at *Odyssey*, 6.41-47 (see note 52 to chapter six, above, and cf Plato, *Axiochus*, 371c-d).

50 Hesiod, *Works and Days*, 167-73 (trans. M.L. West; I have paraphrased slightly). The Islands of the Blessed also feature in Pindar, *Olympian 2*, 68-72 (see citation in chapter eighteen of this book), and in Plato, *Republic VII*, 540b. The name Elysium possibly meant 'field of El' (El was the fallen god in Ugaritic myth).

51 Plato, *Critias*, 113d. The central island of Clito counts as one of the six rings.

52 The Greek myths feature many examples of sex between god and mortal woman. In the case of Poseidon, he slept also with Tyro, who bore the twins Pelias and Neleus; with Aithra who bore Theseus; with Libya, who bore Agenor and Belos, and with Europa who bore Euphemos. In the case of Zeus, his sexual exploits are too numerous to mention, but his fathering of Dionysus upon the mortal woman Semele provides an excellent example of Heaven and Earth imagery (see chapter thirteen of this book).

53 Plato, *Timaeus*, 20d.

54 Plato, *Timaeus*, 22a-b.

55 Plato, *Timaeus*, 22e, 23b-c.

56 Plato, *Timaeus*, 23d.

57 Plato, *Timaeus*, 23e-24a (trans. D.J. Zeyl).

58 See, for example, Plato, *Laws IV*, 713b: 'countless ages before the formation of the states... in the age of Kronos...' (the full citation appears later in this chapter).

59 Hesiod, *Works and Days*, 109 ff. See also note 85 below.

60 See note 23 to chapter twenty, below.

61 Plato, *Laws III*, 677d (trans. T.J. Saunders).

62 F.M. Cornford, *From Religion to Philosophy*, op. cit., pp. 210, 228, 238 ('thirty thousand seasons' equals ten thousand years).

63 Plato, *Phaedrus*, 248e-249a (trans. A. Nehamas/P. Woodruff; I have paraphrased slightly). This is an Orphic idea; see F.M. Cornford, *From Religion to Philosophy*, op. cit., p. 178.

64 Plato, *Phaedrus*, 257a. Cf Plato, *Phaedrus*, 249b; Plato, *Republic X*, 615a.

65 M. Griffith ed., *Aeschylus:Prometheus Bound*, op. cit., pp. 103, 225, 283-84; R. Graves, *The Greek Myths,* op. cit., p. 510.
66 Homer, *Odyssey,* 11.633.
67 Homer, *Iliad*, 5.854-61 (trans. M. Hammond; emphasis added).
68 Homer, *Iliad*, 14.148-49 (trans. M. Hammond).
69 Plato, *Republic VII,* 527e.
70 Plato, *Statesman*, 270a (trans. C.J. Rowe).
71 M. Griffith ed., *Aeschylus:Prometheus Bound*, op. cit., p. 103.
72 Ibid., pp. 283-84.
73 Plato, *Laws III,* 676a-c.
74 On Egypt being ten thousand years old, see Plato, *Laws II*, 656e-657a. Here, Plato emphasises that ten thousand years is to be taken literally; but far from implying a historical period, the idea is that Egypt *really is* older than other states, and that its age *really is* a perfect (symbolic) ten thousand years.
75 Plato, *Epinomis*, 987a (trans. R.D. McKirahan Jr.; emphasis added).
76 The number '9' occurs repeatedly in Greek writings, often in conjunction with the number '10'. Take Zeus, king of the gods. He lay with Mnemosyne for *nine* nights so that she might become pregnant with the Muses (*Theogony*, 56). In due course, Mnemosyne then gave birth to the *nine* Muses (*Theogony*, 60).
Take the goddess Leto. She suffered in labour for *nine* days and *nine* nights, before giving birth to Apollo. In order to fetch the birth-goddess down from Olympus, Iris was sent up to Heaven bearing as a gift a necklace that was *nine* cubits in length. (*Homeric Hymn to Delian Apollo*).
Take Kore (Persephone). She went up to the bed of Apollo and bore *nine* daughters with faces of flaming fire (Orphic fragment 197).
Take Artemis. For her attendants, she chose a myriad of *nine* year-old nymphs (Callimachos, *Hymn to Artemis*).
Take the god Hephaestus. He was said to have fallen from Heaven into the sea, whereupon he was rescued by Thetis and Eurynome, and worked as a craftsman in their hollow cave for *nine* years (*Iliad*, 18.400).
Take the giants Otus and Ephialtes. They declared war on Olympus in their *ninth* year, when they were *nine* cubits across the shoulders and *nine* fathoms tall (*Odyssey*, 11.311-12).
Take the Hydra of Lerna. This monster had *nine* heads, eight of which were mortal and the *ninth* immortal (Apollodorus, *Library*, 2.5.2).
Take the hero Patroclus. When he charged at the Trojans, he killed 'thrice *nine* men' (*Iliad*, 16.784.
Take the Greek wall in the Trojan War. Apollo and Poseidon destroyed it in a flood lasting *nine* days (*Iliad*, 12.28)
Take the island of Crete. It supposedly had *ninety* towns; its ruler, king Minos, would enter the mysterious cave of Zeus every *nine* years; and every *nine* years he would exact a tribute from the Athenians of seven maidens and seven men (*Odyssey*, 19.175-80).
Take the ark of Deucalion. It floated for *nine* days and *nine* nights before coming to rest on the peaks of Mount Parnassus (Apollodorus, *Library,* 1.7.2).
Take the western Ocean. It was composed of *nine* swirling rivers which surrounded the Earth, with a *tenth* river that belonged to the subterranean house of Styx (*Theogony*, 788-92).
This idea of nine followed by a tenth was a common formulaic motif in Greece.
In *Theogony*, if any god broke a sacred oath (made on the waters of Styx) he had to descend to Tartarus and be cut off from his fellow Olympians for *nine* whole years; but he could rejoin them on Mount Olympus in the *tenth* year (*Theogony*, 800-4).
In the *Iliad*, the story begins with *nine* days of plague and ends with *nine* days of funeral preparations for Hector (who will be buried on the *tenth* day). The Trojan War then lasts for *nine* years and ends in the *tenth* year.
In the *Iliad* and the *Odyssey*, the formulaic expression 'for *nine* days... then on the *tenth* day' crops up repeatedly. Odysseus, for example, spends *nine* days drifting at sea before reaching the country of the Lotus-eaters on the tenth day; later, he spends another *nine* days adrift before being washed ashore at Ogygia on the *tenth* night (*Odyssey*, 7.252-54, 9.83-85, 12.447-48).
Similarly, Niobe's children are said to lie in their blood for *nine* days before being buried by the gods on the *tenth* day (*Iliad*, 24.609-12).

In *Theogony*, similarly, it is stated that: 'for *nine* nights and days a bronze anvil might fall from Heaven, and on the *tenth* reach the Earth; and for *nine* nights and days a bronze anvil might fall from Earth, and on the *tenth* reach Tartarus.' (*Theogony*, 723-26.)

In ancient Greek ritual, the same pattern is found. On the island of Lemnos, for example, all fires would be extinguished for *nine* days once a year, until new fire, fetched from the sacred isle of Delos, would be brought ashore on the *tenth* day.

Why were the numbers '9' and '10' so important to the Greeks? What did they signify? The probable explanation, in brief, is as follows.

In the case of '9', the significance of the number lies firstly in the nine months of human pregnancy which reflected exactly nine cycles of the Moon, i.e. nine lunar months. The act of childbirth, repeated by generation upon generation of women, enabled mankind to cultivate the Earth and worship the gods into eternity. Pregnancy and childbirth thus established, in effect, the immortality of the human race.

In addition, it must have struck the ancients as amazing that this property of immortality, attaching to the number '9' through childbirth, was mirrored by a remarkable and unchanging property of the number '9' in mathematics. For it is a curious fact that when the number '9' is multiplied by any other number, the product is always a number where the digits add up to '9' (this property can clearly be seen, for example, in the series 9, 18, 27, 36, 45, 54...).

These factors together would almost certainly explain the significance of the number '9' in ancient times.

As for '10', this number, too, has an interesting mathematical property, deriving from the fact that when it is multiplied by any other number, that other number never loses its original form. Thus, for example, the number '8' becomes '80', and the number '80' in turn becomes '800', '8,000' and so on. The form of the number ('8' in this case) is thus preserved and not corrupted – a feature in keeping with the aims of Pythagorean and Platonic philosophy.

To the Pythagorean brotherhood, of whom Plato evidently was a member, the perfect heavenly number was '10', supposedly because 'all men, whether Greeks or not, count up to ten, and, when they reach it, revert again to unity'. The Pythagoreans thus studied nature in the form of numbers, using as a basic model the so-called '*tetractys* of the decad', based upon the simple addition of $1 + 2 + 3 + 4 = 10$. The Pythagoreans believed that this *tetractys* of the decad contained the nature of the whole Universe and they would swear an oath by it: 'By him who gave to our soul the *tetractys*, which hath the fountain and root of ever-springing nature'.

Plato – as a Pythagorean initiate and avid reader of Greek poetry and literature – would have been well aware of the significance of '9' and '10' as outlined above, and this was no doubt a factor in his decision to make Egypt 10,000 years old and Athens 9,000 years old. (Cf *Timaeus*, 21a-b, in which he notes that Critias was 'around ten years old' when he heard the Athens and Atlantis story from Elder Critias who was 'pretty close to ninety years old'.)

77 M. Eliade, *The Myth of the Eternal Return*, op. cit., p. 125. Incidentally, the related Zarvanite system predicted that the current Universe would end in the twelve thousandth year.

78 J. Verne, *Twenty Thousand Leagues under the Sea*, trans. M.T. Brunetti, Penguin Books, 1994, p. 266 (original edition in French, 1869).

79 Plato, *Laws IV*, 713b-e (trans. T.J. Saunders).

80 Hesiod, *Works and Days*, 109-21 (trans. M.L. West). As West notes in his commentary: 'Every reference to a golden age in Western literature and speech derives directly or indirectly from this passage.' For a different perspective of the golden age. See Plato, *Statesman*, 269-72.

81 Hesiod, *Works and Days*, 126-33 (trans. M.L. West; I have paraphrased the first line slightly). A precedent for the hundred-year childhood is found in the Sumerian King List of Lagash, in the era that followed the Flood; see M.L. West, *The East Face of Helicon*, op. cit., p. 316.

82 Hesiod, *Works and Days*, 138-42 (trans. M.L. West). The motif of men ceasing to make offerings to the gods is found also in Hurro-Hittite myths of the end of the golden age; see M.L. West, *The East Face of Helicon*, op. cit., pp. 103-4, 315.

83 Hesiod, *Works and Days*, 143-56 (trans. M.L. West, though I have paraphrased slightly).

84 The heroes were god-like but half-gods in the sense that they had mortal bodies wrapped in immortal armour of bronze. Significantly, perhaps, the armour of Odysseus was fabricated in Heaven by Hephaestus, and it shone like the light of a blazing fire (Homer, *Iliad*, 18.134-47, 18.369 ff, 19.1-28, 22.129-34).

85 The age of heroes is generally considered to be a separate tradition and an interpolation in the

scheme. See M.L. West, *Hesiod, Theogony & Works and Days*, op. cit., Introduction, p. xvi; M.L. West, *The East Face of Helicon*, op. cit., pp. 312-13, 318-19.

86 Plato, *Protagoras*, 320-22. See citation in chapter one of this book.

87 The name Prometheus meant 'forethought', the name Epimetheus 'afterthought'.

88 See note 82 to chapter one, above.

89 See note 66 to chapter one, above. An interesting reference to Prometheus appear in Ap. Rhodios, *Argonautika*, 3.842 ff. In order to protect Jason against the bronze bull and the sown men, Medea applies a potion which is called 'the Promethean charm'. Apollonios explains that the charm was made from the root of a plant which originated when the blood of Prometheus rained down from Heaven onto the Caucasus Mountain. Cf Aeschylus, *Prometheus Unbound*, VIII, 26-28: 'this body of mine, from which the drops, melted by the heat of the Sun, constantly bespatter the rocks of the Caucasus.'

90 Hesiod, *Works and Days*, 70-97 (trans. M.L. West). The jar (*pithos*) signifies the Underworld, as it does in other myths involving Ares and Eurystheus respectively. Pottery scenes show Pandora rising up out of the earth. It should be noted that Pandora is not a human woman per se. Rather, she is an *alter ego* of Gaia, who will produce human women in her own likeness (after her marriage to Epimetheus). See *Theogony*, 570-82 and C. Penglase, *Greek Myths and Mesopotamia*, op. cit., p. 209. Hence Hesiod says 'from her [Pandora] is descended the female sex' (*Theogony*, 591).

91 Hesiod, *Works and Days*, 174-78.

92 Apollodorus, *Library*, 1.7.2 (trans. R. Hard; I have paraphrased slightly; emphasis added).

93 See C. Penglase, *Greek Myths and Mesopotamia*, op. cit., p. 227. The traditions are confused and overlapping. Some believed that Prometheus had married Pyrrha; others that Prometheus had married Pandora and fathered Deucalion; others that Epimetheus had married Pandora and fathered Deucalion and Pyrrha; others that Deucalion had fathered Pandora; others that Prometheus, or Deucalion, with Pyrrha, had fathered Hellen, the ancestor of all the Hellenes.

94 W.K.C. Guthrie, *Orpheus and Greek Religion*, op. cit., p. 80.

95 L. Edmunds ed., *Approaches to Greek Myth*, op. cit., p. 15.

96 C. Gill, *Plato The Atlantis Story*, op. cit., Introduction, p. xii.

97 Plato, *Critias*, 110a-b (trans. D. Clay; I have paraphrased slightly).

98 Apollodorus, *Library*, 3.14.1 (trans. R. Hard). According to Apollodorus, Cecrops renamed the land of Athens (formerly Acte) as Cecropia, and it was during his days that the gods took possession of Athens and other cities. On the serpent or half-serpent form of Erichthonios, see Apollodorus, *Library*, 3.14.6 and Hyginus, *PA*, 13, 166.

99 C. Gill, *Plato The Atlantis Story*, op. cit., Introduction, pp. xiv, xxiii (cf p. 40).

100 L. Edmunds ed., *Approaches to Greek Myth*, op. cit., p. 15.

101 I have more to say in future books and articles on both Greece and other ancient cultures.

CHAPTER SIXTEEN: THE FALL OF ATHENS

1 I. Donnelly, *Atlantis: The Antediluvian World*, Dover Publications edition, 1976.

2 See, for example, C. Gill, *Plato The Atlantis Story*, op. cit., Introduction, p. xv.

3 Plato, *Timaeus*, 17c, 19b-c (trans. D.J. Zeyl).

4 Plato, *Timaeus*, 126c-d (trans. D.J. Zeyl).

5 Plato, *Republic IX*, 592a-b (trans. G.M.A. Grube/C.D.C. Reeve; I have paraphrased slightly). Cf Plato, *Republic VI*, 497b-c: 'the best constitution... is really divine', and *Republic VI*, 500e: 'the divine model'.

6 Plato, *Republic V*, 472-73: 'Didn't we say that we were making a theoretical model of a good city?', 'don't compel me to show that what we've described in theory can come into being exactly as we've described it. Rather... a city could come to be governed in a way that most closely approximates our description'. It is, as F.M. Cornford, puts it in *Before and After Socrates*, op. cit., p. 61, 'a pattern in the heavens that has seldom been realised on Earth'.

7 Plato, *Timaeus*, 23d-e (trans. D.J. Zeyl).

8 Plato, *Critias*, 108e (trans. D. Clay).

9 C. Gill, *Plato The Atlantis Story*, op. cit., p. 53 (cf p. 43).

10 Plato, *Timaeus*, 23c. As C. Gill notes in *The Atlantis Story*, op. cit., p. 40: 'Divine foundation of

human cities is an important theme in the story.' Cf the founding of Sais by Athene (*Timaeus*, 21e) and the founding of Atlantis by Poseidon.

11 Plato, *Timaeus*, 21d (cf. 20e, 24a).

12 Plato, *Timaeus*, 23d (trans. D.J. Zeyl); Plato, *Protagoras*, 320-22; Plato, *Statesman*, 274c-d; Plato, *Menexenus*, 237e-238c; *Homeric Hymn to Hephaestus*, 20.3 ff.

13 Plato, *Timaeus*, 23e (trans. D.J. Zeyl).

14 Plato, *Timaeus*, 21a, 26e (trans. D.J. Zeyl).

15 Plato, *Critias*, 110c-d, 112b-c. The acropolis is the high place of Athens and was therefore associated with Heaven and the abode of the immortals. Since the word *Ath-* meant 'high', it seems likely that the acropolis inspired both the name of the city, '(the city) of the Athenians', and the name of the goddess Athene, 'the high lady'.

16 Revelations, 21:2 (trans. NIV). See M. Eliade, *The Myth of the Eternal Return*, op. cit., pp. 8-9.

17 A.F. Alford, *When The Gods Came Down*, op. cit., pp. 145-49, 161-62.

18 Ibid., p. 166.

19 Ibid.

20 Ibid., pp. 144-45; J.B. Pritchard ed., *ANET,* op. cit., p. 122.

21 A.F. Alford, *When The Gods Came Down*, op. cit., pp. 154-59.

22 S.N. Kramer, *History Begins at Sumer*, op. cit., pp. 24-25; S.N. Kramer, *The Sumerians*, op. cit., pp. 269-73.

23 Ibid.

24 It is my interpretation that the seven 'mountains of Anshan' signify the mountains of the Underworld. Scholars do not understand the nature of this journey 'from the shoulder of Anshan to the head of Anshan'. A major clue is that, in a related myth, the traveller must cross both the mountains and 'the dreaded river of Kur' – the river of the Underworld (see S.N. Kramer, *The Sumerians*, op. cit., p. 258).

25 S.N. Kramer, *History Begins at Sumer*, op. cit., p. 27 (trans. S.N. Kramer; I have paraphrased slightly).

26 A.F. Alford, *When The Gods Came Down*, op. cit., pp. 119, 160-61.

27 M.L. West, *The East Face of Helicon*, op. cit., p. 249.

28 S.N. Kramer, *History Begins at Sumer*, op. cit., p. 24; S.N. Kramer, *The Sumerians*, op. cit., pp. 271-72.

29 T. Jacobsen, *The Treasures of Darkness*, op. cit., p. 253 footnote 227. Inside the tree, 'the eagle's talon of the Imdugud-bird... makes blood run down the mountain, down Kurmush.'

30 J.B. Pritchard ed., *ANET,* op. cit., p. 45. See also S. N. Kramer, *The Sumerians*, op. cit., p. 187.

31 J.B. Pritchard ed., *ANET,* op. cit., p. 46 (I have paraphrased slightly).

32 The translation is a composite of J.B. Pritchard ed., *ANET,* op. cit., p. 47, and S. N. Kramer, *The Sumerians*, op. cit., p. 189. The heaped-up dust motif is paralleled in the story of the fall of Aratta; see S.N. Kramer, *History Begins at Sumer*, op. cit., pp. 25-28.

33 A. Heidel, *The Gilgamesh Epic and Old Testament Parallels*, op. cit., pp. 171, 172.

34 T. Jacobsen, *The Sumerian King List,* University of Chicago Press, 1939, pp. 77, 85, 93, 95 (emphasis added). The incredible time scales suggest that these were mythical, pre-human kings. The destruction of Kish and Uruk is paralleled in *The Curse of Agade* (J.B. Pritchard, ed., *ANET,* op. cit., p. 647); here, Enlil frowns his forehead and, like the Bull of Heaven, destroys Kish and grinds Uruk into dust, this as a prelude to Agade carrying off the kingship.

35 T. Jacobsen, *The Treasures of Darkness*, op. cit., p. 78; S. N. Kramer, *The Sumerians*, op. cit., p. 188. Uruk, similarly, is said to be 'the handiwork of the gods'.

36 T. Jacobsen, *The Sumerian King List,* op. cit., pp. 71-77 (emphasis added).

37 See M. Eliade, *The Myth of the Eternal Return*, op. cit., chapter one.

38 The anomalies include Anu being present in Shuruppak, Utnapishtim being told to sail down to the Apsu (the Underworld), the Anunnaki lighting up the skies, and the ship being roofed like the Apsu. In addition, there is an emphasis on the term 'ancient Shuruppak', as if to suggest that the city no longer existed. See A.F. Alford, *When The Gods Came Down*, op. cit., pp. 142-43, 168-89.

39 The translation is a composite of J.B. Pritchard ed., *ANET,* op. cit., p. 94, and A. Heidel, *The Gilgamesh Epic and Old Testament Parallels*, op. cit., p. 85, but I have amended 'horizon (of Heaven)' to read 'foundation of Heaven'.

40 A.F. Alford, *When The Gods Came Down*, op. cit., pp. 175, 181-82, 186-87.

CHAPTER SEVENTEEN: THE FALL OF MAN

1 R. Graves, *The Greek Myths,* op. cit., pp. 99, 169, 381, Index. Eris, strife personified, was a goddess, the sister of Ares, who 'sets her head in Heaven while walking on the Earth' (Homer, *Iliad,* 4.443).

2 Homer, *Iliad,* 2.547-48 (trans. M. Hammond). Hence the names Erichthonios and Erysichthon both contained *chthon* ('land'), commemorating the land from which they had been born.

3 Plato, *Critias,* 109d.

4 Apollodorus, *Library,* 2.1.1, 3.8.1; R. Graves, *The Greek Myths,* op. cit., pp. 27-28, 51, 773.

5 Euripides, *The Phoenician Women,* 638-73; Ap. Rhod., *Argonautika,* 3.1179-87; Apollodorus, *Library,* 3.4.1; R. Graves, *The Greek Myths,* op. cit., pp. 195-98; M.L. West, *The East Face of Helicon,* op. cit., pp. 448-49; W. Burkert, *The Orientalising Revolution,* op. cit., p. 153.

6 C. Calame, 'Narrating the Foundation of a City' in L. Edmunds ed., *Approaches to Greek Myth,* op. cit., pp. 292-93.

7 The Achaeans claimed Pelops, the son of Tantalus, as their ancestor; his dismemberment and rebirth from the cauldron probably signified his birth from the earth. The Argives claimed that the first man had been Danaus or Phoroneus (on the latter, see note 29 below). On Lemnos, the first man was said to have been Kabeiros. In the cult of the Kabeiroi, the first man was also called Pratolaos.

8 G.S. Kirk, *The Nature of Greek Myths,* op. cit., p. 273.

9 Hesiod, *Theogony,* 572; *Works and Days,* 61-62.

10 For example, Xenophanes (6th-5th centuries BC) stated: 'We are all born from earth and water.' See M.L. West, *The East Face of Helicon,* op. cit., p. 237.

11 Plato, *Protagoras,* 320d (trans. S. Lombardo/K. Bell). Cf *Protagoras,* 321c-d. In *Timaeus,* Plato added the all-important soul-substance to this mixture.

12 Plato, *Menexenus,* 237c-d (trans. P. Ryan).

13 C. Calame, 'Narrating the Foundation of a City' in L. Edmunds ed., *Approaches to Greek Myth,* op. cit., p. 293.

14 On Delos, see Pindar, *Paean 7b,* 42-49, and fragment 33d. On Kalliste, see Ap. Rhodios, *Argonautika,* 4.1741 ff. On the Symplegades, see Herodotus, *Histories,* 4.85. On Rhodes, see Pindar, *Olympian 7,* 54 ff. On Cyprus, cf the myth of Aphrodite being born from the sea. On Sicily, see R. Graves, *The Greek Myths,* op. cit., p. 156 (it was supposedly a missile that had been flung during the battle of the Titans). In addition, there were mythical floating islands such as Aeolia (Homer, *Odyssey,* 10.1 ff), and the far-distant Floating Islands (alias 'the Turning Islands') where the sons of Boreas caught and overcame the Harpies (Ap. Rhodios, *Argonautika,* 2.285 ff). Herodotus also speaks of a floating island called Khemmis at Buto in Egypt, which was first made to float when Leto concealed Apollo inside it (*Histories,* 2.156).

15 C. Boer trans., *The Homeric Hymns,* op. cit., pp. 1, 8.

16 Plato, *Timaeus,* 23d-e (trans. D.J. Zeyl).

17 Apollodorus, *Library,* 3.14.6 (trans. R. Hard). Cf Euripides, *Ion,* 267 ff. The myth alludes to the idea of Athene as Mother Earth, but is carefully contrived to maintain her reputation as a virgin goddess. The wool (*erion*) is a pun on the name of Erichthonios.

18 The parallel to the Mesopotamian myth is plausible, for scholars are certain that the Greeks adapted a Mesopotamian flood myth during the 6th century BC. See G.S. Kirk, *The Nature of Greek Myths,* op. cit., pp. 261-63, 269-71; M.L. West, *The East Face of Helicon,* op. cit., pp. 480-82, 489-94, 581; C. Penglase, *Greek Myths and Mesopotamia,* op. cit., pp. 3, 218-29. The creation of men from stones, however, is thought to be a much older Greek myth (M.L. West, *The East Face of Helicon,* op. cit., p. 493, note 167).

19 R. Graves, *The Greek Myths,* op. cit., pp. 141, Index. Cf Pyrrha to *pyra* 'fire-place' and to *pyrrhiche,* the fiery war-dance of Pallas Athene. In addition, it is interesting to note that the pre-human king of Athens at the time of Deucalion's flood was called Cranaus, meaning 'rocky or stony' (R. Graves, *The Greek Myths,* op. cit., pp. 322-23, Index).

20 A.F. Alford, *When The Gods Came Down,* op. cit., pp. 243-44. On the celestial significance of the term 'river bank', see note 80 below.

21 R. Graves, *The Greek Myths,* op. cit., pp. 27-28.

22 Ibid.

23 Europa had been carried off by Zeus in the form of a bull (R. Graves, *The Greek Myths,* op.

cit., pp. 194-98). On the meanings 'east' and 'west', see M.L. West, *The East Face of Helicon*, op. cit., pp. 448-49, 451; W. Burkert, *The Orientalising Revolution*, op. cit., p. 153. Scholars do not understand the nature of this journey, since they do not appreciate that the spring of Ares was in the Underworld.

24 See, for example, G.S. Kirk, *The Nature of Greek Myths*, op. cit., p. 157, citing Euripides, *The Phoenician Women*, 638-73. Afterwards, Kadmos had married Harmonia and both had been transformed into serpents and translated to the Islands of the Blessed; see Euripides, *Bacchae*, 1330 ff, cited in G.S. Kirk, *The Nature of Greek Myths*, op. cit., p. 158, and R. Graves, *The Greek Myths,* op. cit., pp. 198-200.

25 Ap. Rhodios, *Argonautika*, 3.404-21, 495-500, 1028-62, 1176-87, 1275 ff. See also the summary in Apollodorus, *Library*, 1.9.23.

26 Heraclides, fragments (4th century BC); Apollodorus, *Library*, 1.7.1; Ovid, *Metamorphoses*, i-ii. On the source of Prometheus' fire, see note 82 to chapter one, above.

27 O. Kern, *Orphicorum Fragmenta*, Berlin, 1922, 60-235 (Olympiodor). See W. Burkert, *Greek Religion*, op. cit., pp. 188, 297-98, and W.K.C. Guthrie, *Orpheus and Greek Religion*, op. cit., pp. xxi, 174-75, 194.

28 Hesiod, *Works and Days*, 143-45 (see citation in chapter fifteen of this book). Cf *Theogony*, 187, 562-64, and see also M.L. West, *Hesiod, Theogony & Works and Days*, op. cit., p. 65, R. Graves, *The Greek Myths,* op. cit., p. 194, and C. Penglase, *Greek Myths and Mesopotamia*, op. cit., p. 206.

29 R. Graves, *The Greek Myths,* op. cit., pp. 193-94. Cf Plato, *Timaeus*, 22a (it was said that Phoroneus had engendered Sparton, 'the sown one', and Niobe, 'snowy').

30 W. Burkert, *Greek Religion*, op. cit., pp. 281-82. Kabeiroi meant 'great/powerful'.

31 Plato, *Protagoras*, 320d (trans. S. Lombardo/K. Bell).

32 Hesiod does not make a big thing about cataclysms marking the changes in the world ages, but the idea is fundamentally implicit. Cf Plato, *Statesman*, 268-73, *Timaeus* 22-23, and *Laws III*.

33 Pindar, *Paean 9,* 20-21 (trans. G.S. Conway/R. Stoneman). Cf Virgil, Fourth Eclogue, 'now a new race descends from the celestial realms'.

34 Hesiod, *Theogony*, 207-10. Hesiod suggests that the Titans were named on account of their straining (*titaino*) inside the womb of the Earth (*Theogony*, 161, 209). This is plausible, but is only one half of the story. In Near Eastern myths, an important motif is the straining of gods inside the womb of *the sky-goddess*, (e.g. Tiamat or Mami/Ishtar) who was about to explode. The original Titans surely came down thus from the Mountain of Heaven.

35 W.K.C. Guthrie, *Orpheus and Greek Religion*, op. cit., pp. 173, 174. Cf the strange saying reported by Philo: 'Behold Man, whose name is East'.

36 See M.L. West, *The East Face of Helicon*, op. cit., pp. 116, 314-15.

37 Hesiod, *Works and Days*, 109-24 (trans. M.L. West).

38 Cf the myth of Ea slaying Apsu in *Enuma Elish*; see A.F. Alford, *When The Gods Came Down*, op. cit., pp. 100, 201.

39 In support of this, none of Hesiod's other races was accorded the special honours paid to the golden race.

40 Hesiod, *Works and Days*, 126-33. See the citation in chapter fifteen of this book.

41 On the heavenly symbolism of gold, see the discussion in chapter nineteen of this book.

42 Pindar, *Pythian 10*, 35-43 (trans. G.S. Conway/R. Stoneman). See comment in G.S. Kirk, *The Nature of Greek Myths*, op. cit., pp. 132-33.

43 See, for example, R. Graves, *The Greek Myths,* op. cit., p. 513.

44 Hecataeus, in Diodorus Siculus, *Library*, II.47 (see R. Graves, *The Greek Myths,* op. cit., p. 80); R. Temple, *The Crystal Sun,* op. cit., pp. 171-85.

45 Pindar, *Pythian 10*, 28-30 (trans. G.S. Conway/R. Stoneman). See comment in M. Eliade, *A History of Religious Ideas*, Volume 1, op. cit., p. 269: 'the country and its inhabitants belong to mythical geography.' See also V. Ehrenberg, *From Solon to Socrates*, op. cit., p. 182 'fairy tale people almost beyond the frontiers of the world', and H. Bowden ed., *Herodotus The Histories,* Everyman, 1992, p. 308: 'the Hyperboreans... are not an historical, but an ideal nation.'

46 Herodotus, *Histories*, 4.13 (cf 3.116 and Pausanias, 1.24.6).

47 Herodotus, *Histories*, 4.36 (trans. G. Rawlinson). Notus was a personification of the south or southwest wind. In *Histories*, 4.16, 4.25, 4.32, Herodotus opines that no-one has any exact knowledge of Hyperborea; even the poet Aristeas of Proconessus reported tales of Hyperborea

only from hearsay (Aristeas was a 7th century BC poet who claimed to have been transported by Apollo to see northern lands, but only as far as Issedonia).

48 Herodotus, *Histories*, 4.33-34. The maidens were accompanied by five male guards called the Perpherees, 'bringers of plenty'.

49 Herodotus, *Histories*, 4.35. After recounting this tale, Herodotus makes a curious remark: 'As for the tale of Abaris, who is said to have been a Hyperborean, and to have gone with his arrow all round the world without once eating, I shall pass it by in silence.' An interesting reference to the Hyperborean maidens is found in Plato, *Axiochus*, 371a; here, it is said that they brought to Delos inscribed bronze tablets which told of the fate of the soul in the 'other world'.

50 Hyper meant 'above' or 'beyond'. Boreas personified the North Wind which was said to fertilise women, animals and plants.

51 R. Graves, *The Greek Myths,* op. cit., p. 28. See earlier discussion of Ophion and Eurynome.

52 Diodorus Siculus, *Library*, II.47 (see R. Temple, *The Crystal Sun,* op. cit., pp. 172-73). The temple is placed on an island, but both appear to be metaphors for the same thing. Tradition had it that Apollo's mother, Leto, had been born on this Hyperborean island; that Apollo had been taken to Hyperborea on a swan or in a chariot drawn by swans (symbolic of a spiritual journey); and that Apollo used to visit Hyperborea every 19 years.

53 R. Temple, *The Crystal Sun,* op. cit., pp. 173-85.

54 R. Graves, *The Greek Myths,* op. cit., pp. 239, 281, 507, 513. In *Argonautika*, 4.611-18, Apollonios Rhodios reports the tradition that when Apollo was exiled from Heaven, by command of Zeus, he journeyed thence to 'the holy clan of the Hyperboreans'.

55 The reader may note the mixed metaphor. In ancient myth, Heaven could be *either* in the north *or* in the east; the Underworld could be *either* in the south *or* in the west (but usually the latter). Another example of this confusion occurs with the Ethiopians; on the one hand, they were held to be a people of the remote south (e.g. Strabo, 1.2.27), and yet on the other hand they were held to be a mythical people of the remote west (see Homer, *Iliad*, 1.422-24, 23.205-6; *Odyssey*, 1.22-24, 5.282-87).

56 Fallen races included the Phaeacians (literally 'the shining ones'), who had migrated to the west from Hypereie, 'heavenly place', and the Cyclopes who had once been their neighbours there (see chapter fifteen of this book). For a parallel example of a resurrected race, see Plato, *Phaedo*, 111a-c.

57 W. Burkert, *The Orientalising Revolution*, op. cit., pp. 125-26.

58 C. Penglase, *Greek Myths and Mesopotamia*, op. cit., p. 228 (see also pp. 3, 197-229).

59 The Greeks did have a myth of subterranean men. In the *Homeric Hymn to Hephaestus*, it is stated that men once 'lived in mountain caves like wild beasts', whilst in Aeschylus, *Prometheus Bound*, Prometheus states that men formerly lived 'underground, deep in caverns closed to the Sun', where they lived like worker ants, not knowing the seasons, nor agriculture, nor the domestication of animals. The focus of the Greek myths, however, is the emergence of man from the soil; here, the Greeks may have been confused by an ambiguity in the Mesopotamian myths (see note 63 below); alternatively, G.S. Kirk may be right when he suggests that the Greeks found the 'slave of the (subterranean) gods' idea repugnant (*The Nature of Greek Myths*, op. cit., pp. 65, 274).

60 J.B. Pritchard ed., *ANET,* op. cit., p. 68. Kingu's status is clear when one appreciates that *Enuma Elish* begins with Apsu-Tiamat *in the sky*.

61 A.F. Alford, *When The Gods Came Down*, op. cit., pp. 198, 203-4.

62 Ibid., pp. 2-3, 196, 202-4.

63 A.F. Alford, *When The Gods Came Down*, op. cit., p. 199. Cf the lines in the myth of *Enki's Journey to Nippur*: 'In those remote days, when destiny was determined, in a year (full of abundance), which Anu created, when people sprang up from the earth like herbs and plants, then Lord Enki, lord of the AB.ZU . . . built his temple in Eridu.' The people are probably to be imagined springing up inside the Earth rather than from the Earth, but there is an ambiguity here which may have influenced the Greek myths.

64 Cited in C. Penglase, *Greek Myths and Mesopotamia*, op. cit., p. 205. Cf the lines in the Ziusudra myth cited in A.F. Alford, *When The Gods Came Down*, op. cit., p. 191.

65 S.N. Kramer, *The Sumerians*, op. cit., pp. 285-86.

66 See, for example, *Lamentation over the Destruction of Ur*, in J.B. Pritchard ed., *ANET,* op. cit., pp. 462-63 (cited in A.F. Alford, *When The Gods Came Down*, op. cit., p. 191). Might this

myth lie behind Plato's myth of spherical pre-human beings in *Symposium*, 189-93?
67 The Ziusudra myth. See J.B. Pritchard ed., *ANET*, op. cit., p. 44.
68 J.B. Pritchard ed., *ANET*, op. cit., p. 514. I prefer to render the last line '. . . destruction approaches mankind' slightly differently. Cf the Old Babylonian version in S. Dalley, *Myths from Mesopotamia*, op. cit., pp. 31-34; one very evocative line reads 'the bright faces [of Mami's people] are dark for ever.'
69 The translation is a composite of J.B. Pritchard ed., *ANET*, op. cit., p. 94, A. Heidel, *The Gilgamesh Epic and Old Testament Parallels*, op. cit., p. 85, and J. Gardner & J. Maier, *Gilgamesh*, Vintage Books, 1985, p. 235. Cf the *Atra-Hasis Epic*, cited in S. Dalley, *Myths from Mesopotamia*, op. cit., pp. 32-33.
70 S. Dalley, *Myths from Mesopotamia*, op. cit., p. 31; J.B. Pritchard ed., *ANET*, op. cit., p. 94.
71 S. Dalley, *Myths from Mesopotamia*, op. cit., pp. 31-33, 94.
72 Ibid., pp. 31, 94.
73 J.B. Pritchard ed., *ANET*, op. cit., p. 94.
74 J.B. Pritchard ed., *ANET*, op. cit., p. 43 (cf p. 459: 'the black-headed ones were carried off into their family places.'). See also A. Heidel, *The Babylonian Genesis*, op. cit., p. 72.
75 See, for example, *Epic of Etana* in J.B. Pritchard ed., *ANET*, op. cit., p. 114.
76 A.F. Alford, *When The Gods Came Down*, op. cit., pp. 207, 194-96.
77 Ibid., pp. 207-8.
78 Ibid., pp. 206-8.
79 The same myth was told in more straightforward versions. In one Sumerian myth, cattle and grain were created first in Heaven in the 'creation chamber of the gods', and were lowered to the Earth subsequently by the gods Lahar and Ashnan. In another myth, two brother-gods brought down barley to the land of Sumer ('which knew no barley') from the heavenly 'mountain' where it had been stored by Enlil. See A.F. Alford, *When The Gods Came Down*, op. cit., pp. 187, 194-96. Cf the Greek myth of Triptolemus (Apollodorus, *Library*, 1.5.2).
80 On the 'river bank' metaphor and the celestial river, see A.F. Alford, *When The Gods Came Down*, op. cit., indexed references. The prime example of the celestial river in Greece is the River Eridanus which features in the myth of the fiery fall of Phaethon from Heaven; see Ap. Rhodios, *Argonautika*, 4.595 ff, and G. de Santillana & H. von Dechend, *Hamlet's Mill*, op. cit., pp. 193, 250-62.
81 Homer, *Iliad*, 24.609-11 (trans. M. Hammond).
82 Homer, *Iliad*, 24.612-16. In Plato, *Timaeus*, 22a-b, Niobe seems to be connected to the myth of Deucalion's flood.
83 *The Epic of Gilgamesh*. See J.B. Pritchard ed., *ANET*, op. cit., p. 94 (emphasis added).
84 Ibid.
85 *Atra-Hasis Epic*. See S. Dalley, *Myths from Mesopotamia*, op. cit., p. 31 (emphasis added).
86 *The Epic of Gilgamesh*. See J.B. Pritchard ed., *ANET*, op. cit., p. 94 (emphasis added).
87 J.B. Pritchard ed., *ANET*, op. cit., p. 93.
88 S.N. Kramer, *History Begins at Sumer*, op. cit., pp. 20-29; S.N. Kramer, *The Sumerians*, op. cit., pp. 269-73.
89 See note 32 to chapter sixteen, above.
90 J.B. Pritchard ed., *ANET*, op. cit., p. 613. In the same vein, the god Ninurta was nicknamed 'the flood-wave of battles'. It is worth noting that the poets of Mesopotamia and Greece routinely used the language of cosmogony to describe the battles of men. One army of men would 'fall' upon another like a raging storm, and its weapons would 'rain down'. The king would attack his adversary 'like a blazing flame'. Fear would 'fall' upon the enemy. The men would 'mix' in battle, unable to see one another in the chaos.
91 The Guti were a real people, the dreaded enemy of Sumer, but as such they were the perfect metaphor for cosmic disaster. Cf *The Curse of Agade* in J.B. Pritchard ed., *ANET*, op. cit., p. 649: 'Enlil lifted his eyes to the mountain, mustered the wide mountain as one, the Guti, the unsubmissive people, the countless men of the land... Enlil brought them down from the mountain; they covered the earth in vast numbers, like locusts...'.
92 Isaiah 13:4-5. Cf Joel 1:15, 2:1-5, 2:10-11. El Shaddai was the original name of Yahweh-Elohim; significantly, it meant 'God of the Mountain' or 'God of the Mountain Peaks'.
93 The key piece of evidence seems to be the scene depicted in Figure 10, which dates to the mid-5th century BC (later myths stated that Erichthonios was the son of Hephaestus and Atthis, or

of Hephaestus and Athene). The Erichthonios child was half-serpent like Cecrops. Athene reared it in secret, concealing it in a chest, which she entrusted to the daughters of Cecrops. The sisters had been forbidden to look inside but did so, discovering a coiled serpent beside the child (although some said that Erichthonios *was* the serpent). For their sins, the daughters were destroyed by the serpent, although some said that they went mad and threw themselves off the acropolis. Cecrops is perhaps to be equated to the Elder Erichthonios; see note 98 below.

94 W. Burkert, *Greek Religion*, op. cit., pp. 136, 230. Cf p. 138: 'A sinking into the depths so that only a pool of sea remains... defines the Erechtheus myth.' Scholars have noted intimate links between the cults of Erechtheus and Poseidon, and have suggested that the latter took over the former; see W. Burkert, *Greek Religion*, op. cit., pp. 96, 136, 221. (Note that in Greek myth, Poseidon was reputed to have competed with Athene for possession of Athens and Attica.)

95 According to myth, Theseus had been fathered by Poseidon when he ravished Aithra on the Sacred Island (almost certainly a code for the Earth). See W. Burkert, *Greek Religion*, op. cit., pp. 98, 136. Greek art shows Theseus rising up out of the earth (ibid., p. 207).

96 Both motifs clearly signify a descent into the Underworld (cf M. Eliade, *A History of Religious Ideas*, Volume 1, op. cit., p. 286). On the dive into the sea, see R. Graves, *The Greek Myths*, op. cit., pp. 338-39, and cf the myths of Hephaestus, Asteria, and the combat between Kronos and Ophion). On the adventure in the labyrinth, see R. Graves, *The Greek Myths*, op. cit., pp. 336-41, and W. Burkert, *Greek Religion*, op. cit., p. 102.

97 See C. Sourvinou-Inwood, 'Myths in Images: Theseus and Medusa as a Case Study' in L. Edmunds ed., *Approaches to Greek Myth*, op. cit., pp. 393-45. Theseus was famed for his various exploits with females who by and large personified Mother Earth (in my opinion).

98 Curiously, there was an adult Erichthonios, who was said to be the inventor of charioteering in battle attire. At the Panathenaia festival, the ancient deed of Erichthonios was re-enacted by the king, who would leap from a hurtling chariot, race on foot and seize the land; see W. Burkert, *Greek Religion*, op. cit., pp. 232-33.

99 Plato, *Critias*, 110b, 112a-b.

CHAPTER EIGHTEEN: MYSTERIES OF THE DEEP

1 Plato, *Critias*, 114a-b (trans. D. Clay).

2 See note 49 to chapter fifteen, above.

3 Pindar, *Olympian 2*, 68-72 (trans. G.S. Conway & R. Stoneman).

4 On this idiom, see, for example, Homer, *Iliad*, 3.322, 6.19, 7.131, and *Odyssey*, 10.175.

5 As Plutarch would later put it: 'many people believe that, once purified [initiated], they will go on playing and dancing in Hades in places full of brightness, pure air and light' (Plutarch, *Non posse*, 1105b). On Heaven being off-limits to man, see note 3 to chapter four, above.

6 This idea is noted in M.L. West, *The East Face of Helicon*, op. cit., pp. 153, 156. In Egypt, the idea was popular owing to the strength of the solar cult. As regards Mesopotamia, see S.N. Kramer, *The Sumerians*, op. cit., pp. 132-35, and G. Roux, *Ancient Iraq*, op. cit., pp. 100-1.

7 Homer, *Odyssey*, 10.189-91 (trans. E.V. Rieu/D.C.H. Rieu). On Aeaea, the island of Circe, see the interesting notes in M.L. West, *The East Face of Helicon*, op. cit., pp. 407-8.

8 Homer, *Odyssey*, 10.490-91. Cf *Odyssey*, 24.204, where the Halls of Hades are said to be 'under the secret places of the Earth'.

9 Homer, *Odyssey*, 11.13-22 (trans. E.V. Rieu/D.C.H. Rieu; I have paraphrased slightly). The Cimmerians were a real people, but we are dealing here with a mythical race whose name signified gloom and darkness; see M.L. West, *The East Face of Helicon*, op. cit., pp. 425-26.

10 Homer, *Odyssey*, 10.507-15 (trans. E.V. Rieu/D.C.H. Rieu; I have paraphrased slightly).

11 Hesiod, *Theogony*, 509-11. Very little is known about Iapetos; his name sounds non-Greek (could it mean 'falling sky'?).

12 Pindar, *Pythian 4*, 289-92 (trans. G.S. Conway & R. Stoneman). Atlas' father was Iapetos.

13 Hesiod, *Theogony*, 519-20; Homer, *Odyssey*, 1.53-54; Herodotus, *Histories*, 4.184; Aeschylus, *Prometheus Bound*, 347-50; Plato, *Phaedo*, 99c. Today, a surprising number of people labour under the misapprehension that Atlas supported *the Earth* upon his head and shoulders (a mistake perpetuated by Donnelly, op. cit., p. 105, and *ANET*, op. cit., p. 122). This is true only in the esoteric sense of Heaven being 'the true Earth'!

14 Herodotus, *Histories*, 4.184: 'a mountain called Atlas, very taper and round; so lofty, moreover,

that the top (it is said) cannot be seen... The natives call it the Pillar of Heaven.' Cf Pomponius Mela's description: 'its summit is higher than the eye can reach; it loses itself in the clouds; also it is fabled not only to touch with its top the sky and the stars, but also to support them.'

15 On the Pillars of Heracles symbolising the limits of the known world, see Pindar, *Olympian 3*, 44; Pindar, *Isthmian 3/4*, 30; Pindar, *Nemean 3*, 22; Pindar, *Nemean 4*, 69. See also comments in M.L. West, *The East Face of Helicon*, op. cit., p. 464, and R. Stoneman ed., *Pindar The Odes and Selected Fragments*, op. cit., pp. 28, 219.

16 Homer, *Odyssey*, 1.52 (trans. E.V. Rieu/D.C.H. Rieu). Hence Phoenician sailors would seek the blessings of Atlas before venturing beyond the Pillars of Heracles.

17 Hesiod, *Theogony*, 519-22 (trans. M.L. West).

18 Hesiod, *Theogony*, 215-17; R. Graves, *The Greek Myths*, op. cit., pp. 50, 507. The Hesperides were sometimes said to be the daughters of Atlas. On the golden apples, see note 33 below.

19 This would explain a strange remark by Pliny that voyagers would pass Mount Atlas en route between the islands of the Gorgons and the islands of the Hesperides; see A. Collins, *Gateway to Atlantis*, op. cit., pp. 94-98.

20 Hespere meant 'evening' or 'setting Sun', and Erytheis meant 'crimson', i.e. the colour of the setting Sun; see R. Graves, *The Greek Myths*, op. cit., pp. 127, 129, Index; G.S. Kirk, *The Nature of Greek Myths*, op. cit., p. 192. On the Erythraean sea, see Herodotus, *Histories*, 1.203, 4.42, 7.89.

21 Hesiod, *Theogony*, 731-51 (trans. M.L. West). Cf *Theogony*, 808-20, 850-52: 'the Titans down in Tartarus with Kronos in their midst'.

22 This fact is noted by C. Gill in *Plato The Atlantis Story*, op. cit., Introduction, p. xiii.

23 Hesiod, *Theogony*, 616-24 (trans. M.L. West). Cf *Theogony*, 154 ff.

24 Herodotus seems to make a pun on this deeper meaning in *Histories*, 3.115.

25 Hesiod, *Theogony*, 820, is explicit on this point of ejection of Heaven. It was later suggested that Atlas had been one of the leaders of the Titans, although nowhere was he accused of any specific acts of violence or cruelty.

26 Hesiod, *Theogony*, 515-17 (trans. M.L. West). 'Lawless' Menoitios is accused of 'wickedness and overbearing strength'.

27 Hesiod, *Theogony*, 522-23 (trans. M.L. West). 'Crafty' Prometheus is accused of taking sides with mankind by giving them fire and attempting to deceive Zeus in the deal between men and gods at Mekone. On the Aeschylus version of his punishment, see chapter four of this book.

28 Hesiod, *Works and Days*, 85-91; Plato, *Protagoras*, 320-22. Whilst the name Prometheus meant 'forethought', the name Epimetheus meant 'afterthought'.

29 Hesiod, *Theogony*, 719-820, 850-52, 867; Homer, *Iliad*, 8.477 ff: 'the uttermost limits beneath earth and sea, where Iapetos and Kronos sit without enjoyment of the beams of the Sun... but all round them is the abyss of Tartarus'; *Iliad*, 14.201-2: 'wide-seeing Zeus banished Kronos under the earth and the harvestless sea.'; *Iliad*, 14.274, 15.226: 'the gods below with Kronos'; *Iliad*, 14.278-79: 'all the gods under Tartarus, who are called Titans'. A later tradition imagined that Kronos had been released from Tartarus to rule the paradisiacal Islands of the Blessed in the West.

30 Pindar, *Nemean 3*, 21-26 (trans. G.S. Conway & R. Stoneman).

31 Diodorus Siculus, *Library*, IV.18.5; R. Graves, *The Greek Myths*, op. cit., p. 495. The Pillars comprised Mount Atlas and the Rock of Gibraltar.

32 Hesiod, *Theogony*, 289-95, 979-83; R. Graves, *The Greek Myths*, op. cit., pp. 494-506. The name Erytheia meant 'Red Island' (it lay in the Atlantic which was formerly called the Erythraean sea). Geryon had a dog, Orthos, just as Hades had a dog, Cerberus. A significant detail in the myth, per Apollodorus 2.5.10, is that Geryon's cattle were close to the cattle of Hades, which would suggest that Erytheia of the western Ocean belonged truly underground. On the significance of 'cattle' in the myths, see notes 88 and 89 to chapter thirteen, above.

33 Apollodorus, *Library*, 2.5.11; R. Graves, *The Greek Myths*, op. cit., pp. 507-14. According to Hesiod, *Theogony*, 333 ff, the golden apples were guarded by a fearful serpent, Ladon, 'in a hidden region of the dark Earth, at its vasty limits', i.e. on the slopes of the subterranean Mt Atlas. The golden apples were said to be the fruit of immortality.

34 Apollodorus, *Library*, 2.5.12; R. Graves, *The Greek Myths*, op. cit., pp. 514-20.

35 See, for example, G.S. Kirk, *The Nature of Greek Myths*, op. cit., pp. 184, 188.

36 Hesiod, *Theogony*, 326-32; Apollodorus, *Library*, 2.5.1; R. Graves, *The Greek Myths*, op. cit.,

pp. 465-69; R. Temple, *The Crystal Sun,* op. cit., p. 288.

37 Hesiod, *Theogony,* 314-20; Apollodorus, *Library,* 2.5.2; R. Graves, *The Greek Myths,* op. cit., pp. 469-72. It is surely no coincidence that Lerna was known as a gateway to the Underworld.

38 Apollodorus, *Library,* 2.5.3; R. Graves, *The Greek Myths,* op. cit., pp. 472-74. Ladon was also the name of the serpent who guarded the golden apples in the Underworld.

39 Apollodorus, *Library,* 2.5.5; R. Graves, *The Greek Myths,* op. cit., pp. 478-81. On the significance of 'cattle' in the myths, see notes 88 and 89 to chapter thirteen, above.

40 Apollodorus, *Library,* 2.5.6; R. Graves, *The Greek Myths,* op. cit., pp. 481-83, and see chapter twenty of this book.

41 Apollodorus, *Library,* 2.5.7, 3.1.3-4; R. Graves, *The Greek Myths,* op. cit., pp. 483-84. In Greek myths, labyrinths always symbolised the Underworld.

42 Apollodorus, *Library,* 2.5.9; R. Graves, *The Greek Myths,* op. cit., pp. 486-94. The girdle of Hippolyte was allegedly an ancient piece of bronze armour, which was displayed either in Mycenae or in the Argive sanctuary of Hera (perhaps it was the kind of metaphorical 'mountain-bronze' that fell from Heaven). In truth, the Amazonians of the remote west were a mythical subterranean race; see note 40 to chapter twenty, below.

43 Apollodorus, *Library,* 2.5.4, 2.5.8; R. Graves, *The Greek Myths,* op. cit., pp. 475-78, 484-86. As regards these labours and others in the first nine, scholars generally visualise the action taking place in the real world. They have little appreciation of the celestial basis of the myths, and little concept of how these myths were transferred from celestial to geographical settings.

44 A prime example of this idea may be found in *The Epic of Gilgamesh,* despite the fact that the hero failed in his attempt to remain permanently in the abode of the immortals.

45 M.L. West, *The East Face of Helicon,* op. cit., p. 144. The equation is not exact (ibid., p. 145), but it is extremely important in so far as it goes.

46 This idea is noted in J. Westwood, 'Lost Atlantis' in J. Flanders ed., *Mysteries of the Ancient World,* op. cit., p. 130: 'The ancient Greeks envisaged the Atlantic as part of the Ocean which encircled the world... the Greeks knew little of it, believing it unnavigable. To the Roman historian Tacitus, writing in AD 98, the Atlantic was still 'the unknown sea'. This reputation is precisely why many other mysterious, paradisal islands were located in it...'.

47 R. Graves, *The Greek Myths,* op. cit., p. 497; L. Edmunds ed., *Approaches to Greek Myth,* op. cit., p. 193; I. Donnelly, *Atlantis: The Antediluvian World,* op. cit., pp. 82, 301; A. Collins, *Gateway to Atlantis,* op. cit., p. 105. The Pillars were also named after Briareos, the guard over Kronos.

48 Homer, *Iliad,* 14.201-2. See also note 29, above.

49 Homer, *Odyssey,* 10.1-79. See also R. Graves, *The Greek Myths,* op. cit., p. 160.

50 Homer, *Odyssey,* 10.135 ff.

51 Homer, *Odyssey,* 12.39-55, 12.158-201.

52 Homer, *Odyssey,* 1.5-10, 11.107-18, 12.127-42, 12.297-399, 19.275-76.

53 Homer, *Odyssey,* 1.13-16, 1.48-60, 1.85-89, 4.555-61, 5.14, 5.55 ff, 6.170-72, 7.243-59, 9.28-29, 12.447-50, 23.333-37. On Ogygia, see discussion in chapter nineteen of this book.

54 Homer, *Odyssey,* 5.33-43, 6, 7, 8, 13.1-186. The island was said to resemble a shield (5.281).

55 On the Lotus-eaters, see *Odyssey,* 9.84-104. On the Cyclopes, see *Odyssey,* 9.106-31, 9.167 ff. On the Laestrygonians, see *Odyssey,* 10.80-133.

56 Homer, *Odyssey,* 12.

57 See comments in M.L. West, *The East Face of Helicon,* op. cit., chapter 8.

58 Plato, *Timaeus,* 24e-25a (trans. D.J. Zeyl/I. Donnelly). Cf C. Gill, *Plato The Atlantis Story,* op. cit., p. 44: 'the continent in a true sense, "the true continent"...'

59 J. Allen, *Atlantis:The Andes Solution,* The Windrush Press, 1998; I. Zapp & G. Erikson, *Atlantis in America: Navigators of the Ancient World,* Adventures Unlimited Press, 1998. The idea dates back to the 16th century at least.

60 The idea was later picked up by Plutarch (1st century) who wrote of 'the great continent by which the Ocean is encircled' (Plutarch, *The Face of the Moon,* 26.941a-c, cited in A. Collins, *Gateway to Atlantis,* op. cit., p. 104). The idea is also found in the writings of Aelian (2nd century), who cited Theopompus (a younger contemporary of Plato). Theopompus had the satyr Silenus speak of a continent that was 'infinitely big' and which 'surrounds the outside of this world' (A. Collins, *Gateway to Atlantis,* op. cit., p. 30).

61 Herodotus, *Histories,* 4.36. Cf *Histories,* 2.21, 2.23, 4.8; Homer, *Iliad,* 18.400; Homer,

Odyssey, 23.243. See also C. Gill, *Plato The Atlantis Story,* op. cit., Figure 2, and M. Griffith ed., *Aeschylus:Prometheus Bound,* op. cit., p. 115. The same idea is evident in Poseidon's epithet 'Encircler of the Earth'. *Apsorrhoos* possibly meant 'of Apsu, the stream of the cosmic basin'; see M.L. West, *The East Face of Helicon,* op. cit., p. 148.

62   Homer, *Iliad,* 18.400; Homer, *Odyssey,* 20.65.

63   C. Gill, *Plato The Atlantis Story,* op. cit., p. 44. As Gill notes, Plato is also upgrading Oceanus from the status of an encircling river to a 'true sea'.

64   See, for example, C. Gill, *Plato The Atlantis Story,* op. cit., Figure 1.

65   Homer, *Iliad,* 14.199, 14.244. Figures 11 and 12 also make sense of Hesiod's description of Oceanus as a ten-streamed river; whilst nine of its streams encircled the Earth, the tenth, the Styx, was located in the Underworld and connected to Heaven (*Theogony,* 774-806).

66   Homer had visualised the shores of a continent on the far side of the western Ocean, namely 'the banks of Ocean'. See *Odyssey,* 10.509 ff, 11.21, 11.157-60 (perhaps the Cyclopes, too, dwelt on this distant continent, *Odyssey,* 9). Both Homer and Hecataeus had envisioned the Ocean-stream as encircling the world.

67   In Mesopotamia, this arrangement comprised the Apsu inside the Kur. Of course, the whole Earth orbited, as did the other planets, in a much greater cosmic ocean – a thought that may have occurred to Pseudo-Aristotle who wrote in *De Mundo*: that: 'as our islands are in relation to our seas [the Mediterranean] so is the inhabited world in relation to the Atlantic, and so are many other continents in relation to the whole sea; for they [the continents] are as it were immense islands surrounded by immense seas.'

68   The earliest records of islands and a continent in the West appear in Homer's *Odyssey* and in Hesiod's reference to the Islands of the Blessed. Similar ideas were present in the earliest versions of the *Argonautika*. Plato drew on Homer in particular to generate his idea of Atlantis and the true continent beyond (see also Plato, *Epinomis,* 992b). Around the same time, Scylax wrote of a mysterious Phoenician island, Cerne, which was twelve days' sail from the Pillars of Heracles, and a mysterious continent, beyond Cerne, which was inhabited by the Ethiopians (it was said that the Phoenicians had originated from the Atlantic, and that mythical Ethiopians dwelt at the westernmost limits of the Earth). Around the same time, too, Theopompus spoke of a continent that was 'infinitely big' and which 'surrounded the outside of this world'; on this continent there had lived giants including a race known as the Meropes; one day, these peoples (ten million of them) had set sail across the Ocean towards the Greek islands, but had turned back in dismay upon reaching the island of Hyperborea. Later, *c.* 300 BC, Pseudo-Aristotle speculated in *De Mundo* about unknown continents lying beyond the Ocean, and wrote in *On Marvellous Things Heard* of a secret 'desert island' of the Carthaginians which was situated in the Atlantic. Around 100 BC, Marcellus wrote of seven islands in the Atlantic which had been sacred to Persephone and three other huge islands there which had been sacred to Hades, Zeus and Poseidon respectively; the inhabitants of the latter had preserved the tale of an even greater Atlantic island, sacred to Poseidon, which had once existed. In the 1st century BC, Diodorus Siculus wrote in *Library,* Book III, of a mysterious island in the West, Hespera, which was home to the Amazonians, and he described how this tribe had fought against the Atlantioi and the Gorgons, the former originating from the far distant shores of Ocean; and in *Library,* Book V, Diodorus Siculus described a magnificent island in the Atlantic, reminiscent of Atlantis, which had been discovered by the Phoenicians. In the 1st century AD, Plutarch wrote in *The Face of the Moon* of the island Ogygia and three other islands in the West, in one of which Kronos had been confined; five thousand stades from Ogygia, he said, and not so far from the other islands, there lay 'the great continent by which the Ocean is encircled'; and in *Lives,* Plutarch wrote of a pair of Atlantic islands, the Fortunate Islands, which had been discovered accidentally by Phoenician sailors. Also in the 1st century AD, Pliny the Elder echoed all of these various ideas in speaking of 'six islands of the gods' ('the Fortunate Islands'), the Isle of Atlantis, the Cassiterides ('Tin Islands'), the Gorgades islands, and two islands of the Hesperides, all of these lying in the Atlantic. It can be seen, from all of these references, how the idea of a lost island of the West has thrived and flourished over the millennia. A good source on all of these legends is A. Collins, *Gateway to Atlantis,* op. cit, chapters 1, 5, 7.

CHAPTER NINETEEN: ATLANTIS DECODED

1 Plato, *Critias,* 113d (trans. D. Clay).
2 See notes 37 and 38 to chapter fourteen and note 52 to chapter fifteen, above. The death of Clito's parents Evenor and Leucippe is evocative of the exploded planet succession myth in which both the Heaven-god and the Earth-goddess were supplanted by a new divine couple.
3 The tradition of a city or island of the Underworld being enclosed by a wall or a ring of mountains is found also in the myth of Atlas surrounding the garden of the Hesperides with high mountains (R. Graves, *The Greek Myths,* op. cit., p. 507), in the myth of Poseidon threatening to surround Phaeacia with a ring of high mountains (Homer, *Odyssey,* 13.148-58), and in the myth of Poseidon and Apollo building a wall around Troy (Homer, *Iliad,* 7.454, 21.445). Cf also Ap. Rhodios, *Argonautika,* 3.1085 ff. All of these myths recall the Near Eastern myths in which gods descended from Heaven to Earth with a 'wall' of mountainous debris (see chapter eight of this book); hence the popular myth of a deity being buried beneath a mountain (e.g. Tiamat, Typhoeus, Telphusa).
4 T. Jacobsen, *The Treasures of Darkness,* op. cit., p. 228. See also note 7 to chapter seven, above. The idea of a seven-ringed Atlantis appears in the writings of Proclus, citing the third century Neoplatonist Amelius; see A. Collins, *Gateway to Atlantis,* op. cit., pp. 100-1 (I do not share Collins' surprise at this claim; it *is* consistent with *Critias*).
5 C. Gill, *Plato The Atlantis Story,* op. cit., p. 63.
6 Plato, *Critias,* 118a.
7 A.F. Alford, *The Phoenix Solution,* op. cit., pp. 216-22.
8 Plato, *Timaeus,* 24e (trans. D.J. Zeyl).
9 Plato, *Critias,* 108e (trans. D. Clay).
10 Plato, *Critias,* 113c, 116a, 115e. On the calculation of the island's diameter, see note 65 to chapter fourteen, above.
11 Plato, *Critias,* 113e. The lines are evocative of Homer, *Odyssey,* 11.157-60, where the river of Oceanus can only be crossed 'in a well-found ship'.
12 Plato, *Critias,* 115e.
13 A. Collins, *Gateway to Atlantis,* op. cit, p. 54.
14 Homer, *Odyssey,* 1.51-52. Another daughter of Atlas was the mountain-nymph Maia, who was the mother of Hermes (Hesiod, *Theogony,* 938).
15 Homer, *Odyssey,* 5.54 ff, 7.244-59. Calypso belonged to the race of Nymphs. Her name meant 'hidden' or 'the veiled one' (from the root *kalypt-,* meaning 'to conceal/veil'); see R. Graves, *The Greek Myths,* op. cit., p. 730, and M.L. West, *The East Face of Helicon,* op. cit., p. 410.
16 Homer, *Odyssey,* 1.50: 'a lonely island far away in the navel of the sea'.
17 Ibid., and see G. de Santillana & H. von Dechend, *Hamlet's Mill,* op. cit., p. 295.
18 R. Graves, *The Greek Myths,* op. cit., pp. 138, 147.
19 G.S. Kirk, *The Nature of Greek Myths,* op. cit., pp. 135, 261, 269; I. Donnelly, *Atlantis: The Antediluvian World,* op. cit., p. 89.
20 I. Donnelly, *Atlantis: The Antediluvian World,* op. cit., p. 89.
21 In support of this idea, it has been noted that the name Ogygia shares the same root as Oceanus (the intermediate form being *Ogen-*). There is a sense here of something huge, primeval and watery. See R. Graves, *The Greek Myths,* op. cit., p. 730, and G. de Santillana & H. von Dechend, *Hamlet's Mill,* op. cit., pp. 199-200. Cf the giant Og in Hebrew folklore.
22 The connection is noted by C. Gill in *Plato The Atlantis Story,* op. cit., pp. x, xiii.
23 R. Graves, *The Greek Myths,* op. cit., pp. 127, 507; A. Collins, *Gateway to Atlantis,* op. cit, p. 55.
24 Pindar, *Nemean* 2, 11; Apollodorus, *Library,* 3.10.1; R. Graves, *The Greek Myths,* op. cit., pp. 144, 152, 154, 165; A. Collins, *Gateway to Atlantis,* op. cit, pp. 55, 82-83. The name Pleione meant 'sailing queen' (from *plei* 'to sail'). A few decades before Plato, a historian named Hellicanus of Lesbos composed a work entitled *Atlantis* in which he referred to the seven Pleiades nymphs as the Atlantides, literally 'the daughters of Atlas'. Later, in the 1st century BC, Diodorus Siculus described how these Atlantides had lain with the gods and heroes to become the mothers of much of the human race; afterwards, they had been immortalised in the Pleiades constellation. One of the Pleiades nymphs, Elektra ('the radiant one'), was the mistress of the Samothracian mystery cult and was associated with a chain of holy islands in

the remote north, at the mouth of the mythical River Eridanus; see W. Burkert, *Greek Religion*, op. cit., p. 284, and Ap. Rhodios, *Argonautika*, 1.915-21, 4.505-6.

25 Hesiod, *Theogony,* 215-16.

26 Hesiod, *Works and Days*, 384-85 (trans. M.L. West; I have paraphrased slightly).

27 This ties in neatly with the tradition of the Atlantides/Pleiades cited in note 24, above.

28 Diodorus Siculus, *Library*, III; also in Philo's adaptation of Sanchuniathon's *Phoenician History* (2nd century AD). See A. Collins, *Gateway to Atlantis*, op. cit, p. 82, and R. Temple, *The Crystal Sun,* op. cit., p. 321. Atlas was one of four sons of Ouranos and Ge (Gaia), the others being El, Baityl and Dagon.

29 A. Collins, *Gateway to Atlantis*, op. cit, p. 55.

30 This theory fits extremely well with Diodorus Siculus' presentation of Atlas as the first astronomer who had taught man 'the doctrine of the sphere'. Admittedly, Diodorus' remarks might have been aimed at the depictions of Atlas supporting the heavens in the form of a sphere, decorated with the visible stars. But nevertheless, there is a hint here of the Pythagorean and Platonic mysteries, in which the sphere of the visible Universe was regarded as a cipher for the 'true' sphere of the invisible God. Thus the sphere borne by Atlas would have encapsulated the very essence of the mysteries; to the uninitiated, it would simply have represented the visible heavens, but to the initiated it would have signified the invisible sphere of God, who had created the visible Universe in his own mysterious image.

31 Cf the wall and falling mountain motif in note 3, above.

32 Plato, *Critias,* 114e (trans. D. Clay).

33 Plato, *Critias,* 116b-c (trans. D. Clay).

34 Plato, *Critias,* 119c-d (trans. D. Clay).

35 Homer, *Iliad*, 14.289-91 (trans. M. Hammond; I have paraphrased slightly).

36 Homer, *Iliad*, 14.254-56 (trans. M. Hammond). Cf *Iliad*, 15.18-24.

37 Homer, *Iliad*, 1.589-94, 18.394-405. Cf also the old myth in which Kronos and his followers fought Ophion and his followers, with each attempting to push the other out of Heaven and into the depths of Ocean; see Ap. Rhodios, *Argonautika*, 1.503-6, and G.S. Kirk, *The Nature of Greek Myths*, op. cit., p. 238.

38 Hence the idea of the Olympian gods living in golden palaces, wearing golden clothes, sitting on golden thrones and drinking from golden goblets. And hence, too, the idea of the golden age, during which the golden race of men had lived on the planet of Heaven.

39 The idea of 'fallen gold' is fundamental to the Greek myths. It appears, for example, in 'the golden rope' which connected Heaven and Earth, and in 'the sign of the golden lamb' which marked the cataclysmic reversal of the Sun's motion. The most telling examples are those that place the fallen gold in the Underworld. Such is the case with 'the golden tree' and 'the golden apples' that grew in the garden of Atlas and the Hesperides. Such is the case, too, with the Golden Fleece which Jason and the Argonauts sought in the Underworld. And such is the case with 'the golden bough', whose light Aeneas used to navigate his way through the Underworld. In each of these examples, the fallen gold stood for the cataclysmic fall of Heaven. Hence, in the *Argonautika*, the Golden Fleece emitted a bright glow 'like a flame' and 'like the lightning of Zeus'. Hence the golden bough lit up the Underworld like a fiery torch. And hence the gold cloak (*peplos*) of Aphrodite had an appearance 'brighter than blazing fire'.

40 Meteoritic iron is surely also the explanation of the mysterious 'adamant' (the 'unconquerable' metal) that crops up sporadically in the Greek myths.

41 Herodotus, *Histories*, 4.5-7.

42 Herodotus, *Histories*, 4.5 (trans. G. Rawlinson).

43 Herodotus, *Histories*, 4.7.

44 Hence, too, Atlantis' abundance of all other minerals. The point should not be missed that the wealth of Atlantis corresponded to the wealth of the Underworld itself; hence the Roman name for the Underworld was Pluto, deriving from the Greek *ploutos*, meaning 'wealth'.

45 Democles, cited in Strabo, 1.3.17. During the reign of Tantalus, violent earthquakes caused entire villages to disappear, Mount Sipylus to be overturned, marshes to be turned into lakes, and Troy to become submerged; see R. Graves, *The Greek Myths*, op. cit., p. 391.

46 Ibid., Pausanias, 7.24.7, and Pliny, *Natural History*, 2.93. According to Pausanias, 'it [the city of Mt Sipylus] disappeared into a chasm, and from the fissure in the mountain water gushed forth, and the chasm became named Lake Saloe. The ruins of the city could still be seen in the

lake until the water of the torrent covered them up.' See R. Graves, *The Greek Myths,* op. cit., p. 391, and J. Westwood, 'Lost Atlantis' in J. Flanders ed., *Mysteries of the Ancient World,* pp. 135-36.

47 Pausanias, 7.24.7. See note 46, above.

48 R. Graves, *The Greek Myths,* op. cit., p. 391. For a historicist approach to the legend of Atlantis and Mt Sipylus (modern Manisa Dagi in Turkey), see P. James, *The Sunken Kingdom: The Atlantis Mystery Solved,* Pimlico, 1995.

49 R. Graves, *The Greek Myths,* op. cit., pp. 387-93.

50 Ibid. Tantalus was hung from the bough of a fruit-tree which overhung a marshy subterranean lake; the water lapped against his waist and sometimes reached his chin, but when he tried to drink it, it would slip out of reach; similarly every time a piece of fruit dangled near his lips, a gust of wind would blow it just out of reach. The name Tantalus seems to reflect this balancing act as well as the balancing of the meteoritic stone over his head.

51 Pindar, *Paean 7b,* 43-49 (trans. G.S. Conway & R. Stoneman). Cf Pindar, fragment 33d (ibid., p. 372).

52 Pindar, *Paean 5,* 40-42; Pindar, *Olympian 6,* 59.

53 R. Graves, *The Greek Myths,* op. cit., p. 753.

54 This myth of Delos sheds a great deal of light on the birth myths of Greek islands, both in this world and in the subterranean sea. Cf note 14 to chapter seventeen, above.

55 On the strange union of Tartarus and Gaia, see Hesiod, *Theogony,* 820-23. The myth would make sense if Tartarus was a fallen Heaven.

56 On the acts of swallowing by Ouranos, Kronos and Zeus, see chapter eleven of this book.

57 Anaxagoras, cited in R. Temple, *The Crystal Sun,* op. cit., p. 288.

CHAPTER TWENTY: THE WORLD VOLCANO

1 Plato, *Timaeus,* 24e (trans. D.J. Zeyl).

2 Plato, *Timaeus,* 25b (trans. D.J. Zeyl).

3 One of the greatest volcanic explosions of human history occurred in Greek territories, namely at Thera/Santorini during the 17th century BC. The Greeks were surely aware that Thera was the remnants of such an explosion. In addition, the Greeks were familiar with volcanic activity at Lemnos and Sicily (Mount Etna); see note 15 below.

4 W. Burkert, *Greek Religion,* op. cit., pp. 137-38. Poseidon was known as 'the Earth-shaker'.

5 On Ereshkigal, see *Nergal and Ereshkigal* in J.B. Pritchard ed., *ANET,* op. cit., p. 511. On Inanna, see *The Epic of Gilgamesh* in J.B. Pritchard ed., *ANET,* op. cit., p. 84.

6 E.A. Wallis Budge, *From Fetish to God in Ancient Egypt,* op. cit., pp. 455-56.

7 In Mesopotamia, temples were built upon sacred stones that contained the powers of the world below, and the god or king was imbued with the power to keep the forces of chaos at bay. If the temple was desecrated, the god removed, or the king dethroned, the forces of evil would be released. Thus in the *Erra Epic,* Marduk states that: "I shall rise up from my dwelling and the control of Heaven and Earth will be undone. The waters will rise and go over the land. Bright day will turn into darkness. A storm will rise up and cover the stars of the heavens. An evil wind will blow and the vision of people and living things will be obscured. *Gallu*-demons will come up and seize . . . The Anunnaki will come up and trample on living things." (see S. Dalley, *Myths from Mesopotamia,* op. cit., p. 292). In effect, the unleashing of the forces of the Underworld amounted to a reversal of the creation. In Egypt, this was known idiomatically as 'the world turning upside down'.

8 D. Meeks & C. Favard-Meeks, *Daily Life of the Egyptian Gods,* op. cit., pp. 103-4.

9 S. Dalley, *Myths from Mesopotamia,* op. cit., p. 286 (trans. S. Dalley).

10 Ibid., p. 309 (trans. S. Dalley; I have paraphrased slightly). The Mesopotamian poets often referred to mankind as 'the cattle of Shakkan' or 'the cattle of Sumuqan' (ibid., p. 295).

11 Ibid., pp. 308-11.

12 J.B. Pritchard ed., *ANET,* op. cit., pp. 103-4, 507-12 (cf p. 110).

13 I. Velikovsky, *Worlds in Collision,* op. cit., pp. 249-50, 279. Erra/Nergal was also a god of plagues and was thus associated with the effects of comets (ibid., pp. 266-68).

14 One possibility, noted by Ernst Howald in 1939, is the myth of *The Seven against Thebes.* See W. Burkert, *The Orientalising Revolution,* op. cit., pp. 108-14. I have considerable doubts,

however, over the proposed interpretation.

15 On Lemnos, see R. Graves, *The Greek Myths,* op. cit., p. 88. On Etna, see Hesiod, *Theogony*, 859-72; Pindar, *Pythian 1*, 15-29; Apollodorus, *Library*, 1.6.3; M. Griffith ed., *Aeschylus: Prometheus Bound*, op. cit., p. 153.

16 Plato, *Timaeus*, 25c.

17 Plato, *Laws II*, 656e-57a. Cf *Timaeus*, 22e, where the myths of Egypt are said to be the most ancient in the world. Cf Herodotus, *Histories*, 2.2, where only the Phrygians are more ancient.

18 Ap. Rhodios, *Argonautika*, 4.261 ff. The Arcadians, also known as Pelasgians, became confused with the Danaans after Danaus and his fifty daughters came to Argos, possibly from Egypt (Strabo, 5.2.4, Herodotus, *Histories*, 2.171). The Arcadian city of Lykosoura was said to be the oldest city in the world (W. Burkert, *Greek Religion*, op. cit., p. 279). But some said that the Athenians were the most ancient of the Greek races (Herodotus, *Histories*, 6.106, 7.161).

19 Plato, *Timaeus*, 25b-c (trans. D.J. Zeyl).

20 Cf A.F. Alford, *When The Gods Came Down*, op. cit., pp. 289-94, 299-301.

21 J.B. Pritchard ed., *ANET*, op. cit., p. 63.

22 Hesiod, *Theogony*, 688-712. Scholars think that the expression 'chthonic Titans' may be anticipatory (see note 55 to chapter one), but I would argue that it should be taken literally.

23 Several supposedly human wars may in fact have been based on the Heaven vs Underworld archetype, e.g. the Amazonians vs the Atlantioi, the Athenians vs the Amazonians, the Gorgons vs the Amazonians, the Centaurs vs the Lapiths, the Greeks vs the Trojans, and the Seven vs Thebes. In addition, the Underworld would sometimes instigate the war against Heaven, e.g. Kronos vs Ouranos, Zeus vs Kronos, Typhoeus vs Zeus, and the Giants against the Olympians.

24 On *herma*, and Hermes vs Argos, see notes 81 and 84 to chapter thirteen, above.

25 Plato, *Timaeus*, 25d (trans. D.J. Zeyl/A.F. Alford).

26 Such is the translation in all the versions that I have seen.

27 C. Gill, *Plato The Atlantis Story,* op. cit., Vocabulary, p. 94.

28 It makes no sense because Plato describes ancient Athens as a land-based civilisation, without maritime capability. The Athenians cannot therefore be envisaged as sailing from Greece into the Ocean beyond the Pillars of Heracles. Such logic is sidestepped neatly if we envisage the Athenians as descending from Heaven.

29 Plato, *Timaeus,* 24e, 25b-c; Plato, *Critias,* 108e.

30 Plato, *Timaeus,* 25d (trans. D.J. Zeyl/A.F. Alford).

31 Plato, *Critias*, 108e-109a (trans. D. Clay).

32 A. Collins, *Gateway to Atlantis*, op. cit, pp. 14, 43-47, 79, 91, 104-5, 142, 164, 172, 188, 196.

33 To cite but two examples from Greece: Aristophanes, in *Frogs*, states that travellers to the Underworld will come to 'a mass of mud and ever-flowing filth', whilst Plato, in *Phaedo*, 69c, has Socrates state that: "whoever arrives in Hades uninitiated and unsanctified will wallow in the mud." In addition, man was, of course, created from the mud/clay of the Underworld (which had fallen from Heaven); hence the use of mud/clay in rituals (see W. Burkert, *Greek Religion*, op. cit., p. 78, and M.L. West, *The East Face of Helicon*, op. cit., p. 51).

34 R. Graves, *The Greek Myths,* op. cit., pp. 481-82.

35 Ibid., p. 779.

36 Cf the dreaded Harpies and 'birds of Ares' in the *Argonautika*, which would likewise have allegorised the fall of the sky.

37 Herodotus, *Histories*, 4.178-91; R. Graves, *The Greek Myths,* op. cit., pp. 147, 611. P. Green in *Argonautika*, op. cit., p. 274, comments that Lake Tritonis may be mythical, and he refers to 'geographical problems' in identifying it.

38 Ap. Rhodios, *Argonautika*, 4.1309-11; R. Graves, *The Greek Myths,* op. cit., pp. 44, 46. According to one account, Lake Tritonis was Athene's mother.

39 Herodotus, *Histories*, 4.179; Ap. Rhodios, *Argonautika*, 4.1223-1622.

40 In *Bibliotheca Historica*, Diodorus Siculus (1st century BC) tells a fascinating story of a war between two neighbouring peoples, the Amazonians and the Atlantioi. The Amazonians, he says, were a group of savage, war-loving women, who lived on the island Hespera in the midst of Lake Tritonis (they were renowned as 'the equals of men', 'man-haters' and 'children of Ares'). The island Hespera, he says, was of 'great size' and had abundant sheep and goats, as well as 'fruit-bearing trees of every kind'. The Atlantioi, for their part, were 'the most civilised men' of the remote west, who had built 'great cities' which were reputedly the birthplaces of

the gods. Diodorus placed them 'westward' of Lake Tritonis 'in the regions which lie along the shore of Ocean'. Turning to the account of the war, Diodorus describes how the Amazonians began their conquests by crushing the tribes in the region of Marsh Tritonis. Afterwards, their queen Myrine ('Sea-goddess') led them into battle against neighbouring peoples, of whom the Atlantioi were the first. With three thousand cavalry and thirty thousand infantry, Myrine stormed the Atlantioi's capital city of Cerne and captured it, putting the men to the sword and enslaving the women and children. In due course, she rebuilt the city, renaming it Myrine, and made peace with the surviving Atlantioi, whom she protected against the attacks of the hostile race of Gorgons. According to the theory advocated in this book, the Amazonians and Atlantioi were mythical subterranean races, and their war took place in the Underworld.

The Amazonians ('moon-women') were famed for their acts of war, including an attack on Attica and Athens. This ancient war had been instigated by Theseus who visited the Amazonian land and seduced their queen Antiope, whom he carried off by ship. The Amazonians, outraged by this act, then 'poured their hosts into Attica'. But Theseus repelled this invasion, thereby achieving great fame. (His victory was regarded as one of the most magnificent deeds in the history of Athens, and was commemorated accordingly in the city's great funerary orations and in its most famous works of art.) It is possible that this two-stage war involved the descent of the Athenians into the Underworld, followed by an invasion of the world above by the subterranean Amazonians (Theseus having founded Athens there). Unfortunately, the myth is too faded to recover the full meaning with any degree of certainty.

For further information on the affairs of the Amazonians, see Herodotus, *Histories*, 9.27, R. Graves, *The Greek Myths,* op. cit., indexed references, and A. Collins, *Gateway to Atlantis*, op. cit, pp. 80-81.

41 Diodorus Siculus, *Library*, III.55. See R. Graves, *The Greek Myths,* op. cit., p. 148, and A. Collins, *Gateway to Atlantis*, op. cit, p. 81 (the translation in the latter seems to lose the point).

42 Ap. Rhodios, *Argonautika*, 4.1223-76. The name Libya was often used metaphorically by the Greeks to refer to the Underworld.

43 C. Gill, *Plato The Atlantis Story,* op. cit., p. xviii, compares the city of Atlantis not only to Athens but also to Babylon and Ecbatana (descriptions thereof appear in Herodotus, *Histories*). In addition, Atlantis may have been modelled on mythical cities, e.g. Phaeacia (ibid., p. 64).

44 See note 3 to chapter nineteen, above.

45 See note 24 to chapter nineteen, above. Whilst Plato did not specify an exact number, later writers spoke of six or seven islands lying in the Atlantic (because some saw only six stars in the 'seven-star' Pleiades constellation).

46 Plato, *Timaeus*, 25a-b.

47 If the reader can spot any problems, he should let me know. I will publish valid criticisms on the Eridu website http://www.eridu.co.uk.

48 On the Dodds quote, see L. Edmunds ed., *Approaches to Greek Myth*, op. cit., p. 55. On the Rice quote, see A.F. Alford, *The Phoenix Solution*, op. cit., Foreword.

CHAPTER TWENTY-ONE: THE TRUE ATLANTIS

1 For an overview of Van Flandern's scientific evidence for the exploded planets hypothesis, see the detailed summary on my website (www.eridu.co.uk).

2 Plato, *Phaedo*, 110a.

3 Plato, *Republic VII,* 521d, 529b; Plato, *Timaeus*, 29a-b, 31a, 39e.

4 W. Burkert, in *Greek Religion*, op. cit., p. 322, writes: 'Through Plato reality is made unreal in favour of an incorporeal, unchangeable other world which is to be regarded as primary.' Similarly, F. Cornford, in *Before and After Socrates*, op. cit., p. 64, writes: 'the world of perfect Forms contains all that is truly real.'

5 See A.F. Alford, *When The Gods Came Down*, op. cit., pp. 98-101, 318-19.

6 R.T. Rundle Clark, *Myth and Symbol in Ancient Egypt*, op. cit., p. 247 (cf. pp. 77, 244-49).

7 Osiris personified Heaven and Isis personified the Earth; hence the miraculous birth of their son Horus symbolised the creation of life in the Earth. The Egyptian pharaohs, as incarnations of Horus, were living incarnations of the principle of life on Earth.

8 On *ki-sir*, see A.F. Alford, *When The Gods Came Down*, op. cit., pp. 122-23.

9   See, for example, S. Dalley, *Myths from Mesopotamia*, op. cit., pp. 15, 36.
10 Genesis 1:1-2. On the occulted aspects of the Genesis creation, see A.F. Alford, *When The Gods Came Down*, op. cit., chapter 9.
11 Genesis 7:22. See R. Alter, *Genesis*, W.W. Norton & Co., 1996, p. 33.
12 Genesis 2:7. The term used for 'breath' is not *ru'ach* but *neshamah*. The term *nephesh chaiyah*, here translated 'living being', may also be rendered as 'living soul'.
13 Hence the famous line "Let there be Light", followed by the separation of the Light from the Darkness (the Underworld). See A.F. Alford, *When The Gods Came Down*, op. cit., chapter 9.
14 Hesiod, *Works and Days*, 120-25.
15 F.M. Cornford, *From Religion to Philosophy*, op. cit., pp. 6, 128-29.
16 Ibid., p. 234 (fragment 28).
17 Ibid., pp. 230-31. Cornford observes that Love is the same as the soul or *physis*.
18 See the citations in this book, pp. 8, 176, 181, and note 33 to chapter nine, above.
19 W.K.C. Guthrie, *Orpheus and Greek Religion*, op. cit., pp. 81, 139.
20 Ibid., pp. 94, 142. See also W. Burkert, *Greek Religion*, op. cit., pp. 319-20.
21 F.M. Cornford, *From Religion to Philosophy*, op. cit., pp. 218-19.
22 Plato, *Phaedo*, 110a; Plato, *Phaedrus*, 247c-d.
23 W. Burkert, *Greek Religion*, op. cit., p. 131.
24 See note 1 to chapter four, above.
25 J.M. Cooper ed., *Plato: Complete Works*, op. cit., p. 557.
26 Plato, *Timaeus*, 29b-c.
27 W.K.C. Guthrie, *Orpheus and Greek Religion*, op. cit., p. 239.
28 Plato, *Letter VII (To the Friends and Followers of Dion)*, 344c (trans. G.R. Morrow).
29 Plato, *Republic III*, 382c-d, 414b-c, 459c-d.

APPENDIX A: THE DEMIOURGOS DECODED

1   Plato, *Timaeus*, 29b.
2   Plato, *Timaeus*, 29e.
3   Plato, *Timaeus*, 30b-31b, 37d.
4   Plato, *Timaeus*, 32a-c; see also *Timaeus*, 35-36, 43, 47d.
5   Plato, *Timaeus*, 41d-e.
6   Plato, *Timaeus*, 42d. Curiously, the souls were planted in other celestial bodies too.
7   Plato, *Epinomis*, 992a.
8   Plato, *Timaeus*, 27d-29a; Plato, *Republic VII*, 529b.
9   Plato, *Timaeus*, 41a, 41c, 42e.
10 Plato, *Timaeus*, 40c.
11 Plato, *Timaeus*, 39e (trans. D.J. Zeyl). Cf *Timaeus*, 39d.
12 Plato, *Timaeus*, 30a (trans. D.J. Zeyl).
13 Plato, *Timaeus*, 34a (trans. D.J. Zeyl). Cf *Timaeus*, 34b, 36e.
14 Plato, *Timaeus*, 48a (trans. D.J. Zeyl).
15 Plato, *Timaeus*, 49a, 50d, 53a-b.
16 Plato, *Timaeus*, 37c; Hesiod, *Theogony*, 116-17: 'broad-breasted Earth, secure seat for ever of all the immortals who occupy the peak of snowy Olympus'.
17 Plato, *Timaeus*, 28b. Cf Plato, *Gorgias*, 508a; Plato, *Epinomis*, 977b.
18 F.M. Cornford, *Before and After Socrates*, op. cit., p. 67.
19 Plato, *Timaeus*, 41d-e, 42b (trans. D.J. Zeyl). Cf Aristophanes, *Peace*, 832 ff.
20 See Plato, *Timaeus*, 90a: "The soul raises us up away from the Earth and toward what is akin to us in *Ouranos*, as though we are plants grown not from the Earth but from *Ouranos*... " (trans. D.J. Zeyl).
21 Plato, *Phaedrus*, 247b-e (trans. A. Nehamas/P. Woodruff; I have paraphrased slightly).

APPENDIX B: CLARIFICATIONS

1   Plato, *Phaedrus*, 275e.
2   Personal email correspondence 30/5/2000.

INDEX